VERGING ON EXTRA-VAGANCE

Fig. 1. Tom Elliott, a bicyclist of extra-Vagance (Portuguese), marketed by
P. T. Barnum in 1883. Not directly addressed in this book, his image
nevertheless evokes its "homegrown Dada spirit"—in this case American (see
"Rehearsals" and Chap. 6). Photograph from Princeton University Library.

VERGING ON EXTRA-VAGANCE

ANTHROPOLOGY, HISTORY,
RELIGION, LITERATURE,
ARTS . . . SHOWBIZ

James A. Boon

PRINCETON UNIVERSITY PRESS   PRINCETON, NEW JERSEY

Published by Princeton University Press, 41 William Street,
Princeton, New Jersey 08540
In the United Kingdom: Princeton University Press,
Chichester, West Sussex

Library of Congress Cataloging-in-Publication Data

Boone, James A.
Verging on extra-vagance : anthropology, history, religion,
literature, arts . . . showbiz / James A. Boon.
p. cm.
Includes bibliographical references and index.
ISBN 0-691-01632-1 (CL : alk. paper)
ISBN 0-691-01631-3 (PB : alk. paper)
1. Anthropology—Philosophy. 2. Culture—Philosophy. I. Title.
GN33.B63 1999
301′.01—dc21   98-35712

This book has been composed in Times Roman

The paper used in this publication meets the minimum requirements
of ANSI/NISO Z39.48-1992 (R 1997) (*Permanence of Paper*)

http://pup.princeton.edu

Printed in the United States of America

1 3 5 7 9 10 8 6 4 2

1 3 5 7 9 10 8 6 4 2
(Pbk.)

For Jim and Florence Peacock

By the "principle of courtship" in rhetoric we mean the use of suasive
devices for the transcending of social estrangement. There is the
"mystery" of courtship when "different kinds of beings" communicate
with each other.
(Kenneth Burke, 1950)

I fear chiefly lest my expression may not be *extra-vagant* enough, may not wander far enough beyond the narrow limits of my daily experience, so as to be adequate to the truth of which I have been convinced.

Extra vagance! It depends on how you are yarded. . . .

. . . I am convinced that I cannot exaggerate enough even to lay the foundation of a true expression.

Who that has heard a strain of music feared then lest he should speak extravagantly any more forever?

(Henry David Thoreau, circa 1850)

You can expect "pure persuasion" always to be on the verge of being lost, even as it is on the verge of being found.

(Kenneth Burke, circa 1950)

Contents

_____ *Illustrations* _____

> J'essayais maintenant de tirer de ma mémoire d'autres "instantanés,"
> notamment des instantanés qu'elle avait pris à Venise, mais rien que ce
> mot me la rendait ennuyeuse comme une exposition de photographies,
> et je ne me sentais pas plus de goût, plus de talent, pour décrire maintenant
> ce que j'avais vu autrefois, qu'hier ce que j'observais d'un oeil minutieux
> et morne, au moment même.
> (*Proust,* A la recherche du temps perdu; see Chap. 5.)

> I tried next to draw from my memory other "snapshots," those in
> particular which it had taken in [Bali], but the mere word "snapshot" made
> [Bali] seem to me as *ennuyeuse* as an exhibition of photographs, and . . .
> I had no more taste, no more talent for describing now what I had seen in
> the past, than I had had yesterday for describing what . . . I was, with a
> meticulous and melancholy eye, actually observing *au moment même*.
> (*Proust,* Remembrance of Things Past; I have substituted another *nom de
> lieu* and restored a few terms from Proust's original.)

Preface

AnThoreaupology: An Invitation

IN *A Week on the Concord and Merrimack Rivers*, Henry David Thoreau, professing that "the wisest man preaches no doctrines, he has no scheme," declared his love for reading scriptures of Hindus, Chinese, and Persians even more than their Christian and Hebrew equivalents (1985: 57). Later on, in 1852 or so, winding down *Walden*, Thoreau denounced imperialist expansion, plus "the maggot in their heads" of that Patriotism driving the parade and expense of Exploring Expeditions. He even questioned the worth of rounding "the world to count the cats in Zanzibar" for some presumed instrumental end of quantification. (This famous admonition was echoed generations later by Clifford Geertz, whose interpretive turns across anthropology and sister pursuits inform one aspect of the present book.)[1]

Retrenched on his since-celebrated shore, Thoreau paradoxically sought to "travel farther than all travellers" by embracing manifold tongues and customs; he paused sagely to voice an apprehension that provides my title's keyword:

> I fear chiefly lest my expression may not be *extra-vagant* enough, may not wander far enough beyond the narrow limits of my daily experience, so as to be adequate to the truth of which I have been convinced.
>
> *Extra vagance*! It depends on how you are yarded.
>
> The migrating buffalo, which seeks new pasture in another latitude is not extravagant like the cow which kicks over the pail, leaps the cow-yard fence, and runs after her calf, in milking time.
>
> I desire to speak somewhere *without* bounds; like a man in a waking moment, to men in their waking moments; for I am convinced that I cannot exaggerate enough even to lay the foundation of a true expression.
>
> Who that has heard a strain of music feared then lest he should speak extravagantly any more forever? (1985: 580–81)

Now, I too, Thoreau's reader, am convinced—this point cannot be sufficiently exaggerated—that Thoreau truly meant these words. Are present readers willing to be convinced in turn?

Even when asking his question, Thoreau presumably was not able to exaggerate enough even to lay the foundation of a true expression. From that fact readers may infer that the true, so far as it can be expressed, is no less so for being foundationless: *extra-Vagant*.[2]

This book shares Thoreau's apprehensiveness about expression adequate to experience. Opposing schematic dogmas and narrow patriotisms, Thoreau embraced the world of narratives available to him. His manifold wanderings welcomed paradoxes of exaggeration: truth's condition. Desirous of farthest travelling—actual or imagined—he sustained ironies of inescapable domesticity. Thoreau rummaged amongst tongues and customs, hoping to perform translated-truth *convincingly*. His prose oscillated between rhetorics of authority: first-person ("I fear"), third-person ("lest he should speak"). Yet, Thoreau repeatedly inscribed scenes of speaking as if his text could draw readers near. Anxieties of not conveying extra-Vagance *enough* to wakeful listeners (readers, really) led him to music, allusively.[3]

Yes, all that Thoreau never forgot. This book follows suit, along disputatious paths of interpretive theory, semiotics, area research, fieldwork, media studies, and cultural critique—ever since Thoreau, and before. Even in our "postmodern" day of disciplinary diversity, aspects of ethnography, travel tales, hybrid *histoires*, novelistic discourse, and composite arts still resonate with Thoreau's perplexities and enthusiasms. Remembering the chances Thoreau took, I have cultivated a hyphenated genre of essay-*étude*—fluid, concrete, and deviating. Essay-*études* offer nondogmatic ruminations that twist, dart, and swerve with the subject studied; their boundaries remain porous, syntax shifting, pedagogy nondidactic (mostly). Analogies could be drawn with musical *études* that fluctuate among keys—those of Scriabin, say. Such writing hopes to be met halfway by equivalent acts of reading; it dreams that reading-writing might become, intermittently at least, *ensembled*.

Thoreau's words are one primary inspiration, or pretext, for this book's asymptotic approaches to rites and texts, genders and genres, languages and literatures, politics and poetics, and merchandised commodities. (I encapsulate a vacillating tradition of such "essayistics" at the close of Chap. 3.) Another luminary in related endeavors was Kenneth Burke, whose tactics of *verging* in and on circumstantial rhetoric provide this book's other title-term.[4]

In truth, though, my essays' "origins and methods" verge farther, and nearer, than even the names of Thoreau and Burke imply. I like to fear that Thoreau might have approved such "flungedness." To his democratized doubts about expressing a true *foundation*, American Thoreau added the following clarification:

> The volatile truth of our words should continually betray the inadequacy of the residual statement. Their truth is instantly *translated*; its literal monument alone remains. (1985: 580–81)

May the words of Thoreau cited (a literal monument alone remaining on the page) sustain readers through these acts of translating his extra-Vagance into alternative fence-leapings, crossings, crossovers, and possible betrayals . . . all of them *volatilely* true, or desiring to be.

Acts of extra-Vagance abound in human rituals and interpreting them, ludic languages and translating them, and multimedia and transposing them; engaging such acts can help unsettle cozy dogmas, complicate critical clichés, and reshuffle scholarly and popular prejudices. Toward those ends Part One of this book addresses "diacritical" rites and texts—performances and discourses that seem made for contrast (they are a mainstay of evidence in anthropology, religion, history, and area studies). Part Two accentuates reflexive intricacies of inscribing cross-cultural encounters. Part Three displays—seriocomically when feasible—intractible disciplinary disputes about cultures and eras, diversely theorized.

More comparative motives and motifs interlace these pages than ordinarily adorn standard social science, technical semiotics, or contemporary Cultural Studies stressing issues of "race," class, gender, or sexual preference. While profoundly sympathetic with the latter's inclusiveness, I am anxious also not to slight different differences: religions, vernacular languages, alternative styles of critical tastes. This book foregrounds specific representations for the "polyphony, polytheatricality, polymorphics, and polygraphics" they convey.[5] Its essays verge extra-Vagantly on hybrid cultures and times, where diversities both bold and delicate intersect, collide, or pass each other by.

Following the Preface reader-browsers next encounter three "Rehearsals." One salutes a polymath clown-savant; the second invokes opera as a plural art, likened in turn to aspects of ethnographic, historical, and literary genres (all of which become convincing by exaggerating—I am still echoing Thoreau's paradoxes of plausibility). A third "Rehearsal" nods toward other scholars who have now and then wandered into "show business."

Reader-adventurers enter Part One through a neologism: "ultraobjectivity"—a synonym for *relative* relativism. I coin this lexical monster—derived literally from innocent-looking dictionary definitions—to help dispel specters of *absolute* relativism. (Many folks, among them "ethicists," who hanker after one firm foundation still find plural possibilities threatening). Parts One and Two together interrelate ethnography, comparative intellectual history, and experiential synaesthesia. Chapters revolve around odd incidents and "accidence"—fleet meetings, funny footnotes, half-forgotten melodies—that punctuate researches about Bali, Indonesia, and comparable places.

Specifically, Chapter 1 revisits Ruth Benedict's neglected theme of menstrual seclusion in Native American ritual: Kwakiutl especially, Zuni excepted. I liken Benedict's process of reading rites (and our process of reading her) to the rites themselves. Something is made of Benedict's citing early

Nietzsche, to whatever extent she misread him (as anyone might!). More is made of Benedict's *textual* relations with Jane Belo and Margaret Mead, both of whom analyzed women's trances in Bali. I aggravate dilemmas of appreciative versus polemical reading by parrying yet another tardy attack on Mead—this one by a journalist. Caustic rebuttal has become the ritual mode characteristic of an agonistic scene known as academia.

Chapter 2 switches from one gendered topic (menstrual seclusion) to a contrasting one: foreskin removal or retention in many religions and times (Islamic/Hindu, Jewish/Christian, medicalized/anti-). The essay's point of departure is my unplanned ethnography of Buginese circumcision (Islamic, male) during long-term research among uncircumcising Hindu-Balinese. I survey sundry accounts of relevant *rites de passage*, but linger over two striking narratives: (1) Montaigne's Early Modern masterpiece of travel writing; (2) an 1890s medical history inclined to universality yet provocatively allegorical. My commentary declines to "enlighten" away true dilemmas of *contrastive empathy*. Interpreting either own or others' presence or absence of circumcision cannot be easy—a fact often ducked in politics for liberation. Today's knowledge brokers—like certain *philosophes* before them—tend to forget that ritual-understanding is often volatile, always difficult.

Chapter 3 pursues kindred difficulties and aporias in the uneasy history of Balinese studies, entangled in various colonialist and presumably postcolonial enterprises. Jane Belo's remarkable ethnography (already tapped in Chap. 1) reenters the picture. Now, however, reading between Belo's lines casts dappled light not on observed trances among Balinese but on possible "transferences" among Balinists—including one artistic virtuoso (Walter Spies) and one anthropologist-plus (Gregory Bateson). Bateson's unforgettable paragraph about commemoration orchestrates the entire chapter, much as Thoreau's passage on extra-Vagance spirits forth the whole book. Indeed, many authors, texts, terms, and fieldsites (Bali, Manhattan . . .) reappear throughout these chapters in various guises and under diverse auspices. That is part of the book's motivic arrangement, its *techniques d'essai*.

Part One's broader claims are anything but new: Because cross-cultural evidence is already interpretive, anthropology requires nonstop rereading rather than one-shot diagnosis. Methodical analysis, even when dutifully double-checked later on, squeezes inquiry into strangleholds that choke off the ironies of comparative translation. Each chapter links reading itself to a mode of ritual: (1) cyclic rereading freshly analogized with stylized menstruation; (2) Midrashic commentary anciently analogized with male circumcision; (3) a deviating "area studies" obliquely analogized with rubrics and relics of *mémoire-oubli*. Rites of forgetful-remembrance, of course, proliferate not just in Balinese studies (and in Bali) but in any historical pursuit or cultural formation. At every level or scale—local, imperial, national, disciplinary, personal, familial—ritual concocts ambivalent recall of bygone times (all of them are).[6]

Plucky reader-rememberers brush with further extra-Vagances in Part Two: fragmentary travel; narrative sighs; fretful translation of sense and nonsense, both spoken and written. Chapters 4–6 play on, with, and against "first person" ethnography—whether thine or mine. I retail several ethnographic encounters multi-mediated by pulp novels, old movies, broadcast TV, and boom-box tapes inadvertently overheard. The confessional mode of Chapter 4 is comic; the recollective mode of Chapter 5 is melancholic; Chapter 6 is a medley of both modes, and then some.

Chapter 4 conjures up "cosmopolitan moments" as a mock commodity form that "keeps happening" to this anthropologist-consumer. My winking and blinking (back tears) souvenirs may resonate with blushing moments in the lives of readers. But if they do not, it could be because for tastes there is no accounting—despite the best efforts of Bourdieu and company, intent on diagnosing distinctions.[7]

Chapter 5 commemorates museum going in ethnological museums, art museums, *Wunderkammern*, museums-in-a-book. My prose of as-if museums keeps registering something Leon Edel isolated in the work of Henry James: *tristimania* (depression that drives creation).[8] This reader's preferred exponents of *tristimania*—James, Proust, Ruskin (and I include Twain)—call to mind sad places "like Venice" (e.g., Bali, Tahiti, Manhattan). Chapter 5 slides rhetorical melancholia (*not* nostalgia) alongside other exhilarations and dejections evoked by diverse voyagers, ethnographers, and shamans—all of whom, I assume, both seek and mourn translated truth of sorts.

Chapters 4 and 5 together imply several critical challenges. To voices parading their escape from longing, I virtually riposte: Into what? Against magic's many detractors—who back one or another logic of causality or *cogito*—I nearly query: Do not intricate arts of coincidence deserve seriocomic scrutiny? Coincidence, after all, does happen—and across cultures too. It need not be aloofly relegated to exotic irrationality, condescended to as literary preciosity, or dismissed as starry-eyed "synchronicity."[9]

Chapter 6 delves into magical words, vernacular lingo, inevitably uncanny dictionaries, tragic loss, sacrifice, humor, and comedy-theory. My essay couples Mark Twain's ultralocal verbiage (or aping thereof) with the eloquent ethnology of Marcel Mauss. This tactic may seem strange; it is. Twain, twinned, stands for a gamut of vernacular modes in his novels of speaking and speechifying. Mauss, compared and comparing, conveys a gamut of ritual genres in his essays on exchange, magic at the margins, sacrifice, prayer, and body techniques. Each author, extra-Vagant in his own right, is extra-Vagantly pastiched in my pretended "posting the banns" of a shotgun alternative wedding between Twaintalkin' and Mauss*écrits*.

Chapter 6 does not aim to establish revised norms for academic inquiry. Rather, mingling Mauss's and Twain's disparate positions may "exaggerate enough" (still Thoreau) to begin expressing the trickiness that is guaranteed whenever one translates among ritual vernaculars, transgressive styles, and ways of interpreting them. Trickiness impresses me as the very stuff (foundation?) of anthropology, both interdisciplinarily and solo. But is this stuff serious or comic? An interlingual answer dawns: *Mais* yep.

Francophones could call this book's implementations of comedy-theory *expériences* in point of view, register of voice, genders (*genres*), genres (*genres*), and levels: highbrow/low and in between; arcane/pop and in betwixt; *sublimitas/humilitas/et cetera*; longhair/short or (summoning Twain again) shaggy, bald, toupéed, ironed, beehived, cornrowed, pompadoured, *usw*. Like my earlier works, this one commits *satire*—in Lyotard's sense of "saturated with genres." I remain inspired by such rhetorical worlds as Balinese *topeng*; *Märchen*-buffs may notice throwbacks to Early Romantic thwartings of singular propriety by Novalis, Jean Paul, Hoffmann. (Lyotard, by the way, pinches many moves from Friedrich Schlegel.)[10]

Part Three is a little different; reader-critics may want to nibble here and there rather than wolf it down whole. Each seriocomic essay participant-observes occasions of university or everyday life or reviews works that are ambiguously scholarly and/or commercial. I try to cut theory close to the bone of circumstance: bodies, beliefs, rights, jokes, suffering, violence, laughter, tears, commemorations, commodity fetishes. I eschew subjugating comparative reading to partisan agendas, however worthy a given *cause* may be; politics of any slant should not repress true obliquities and real difficulty.

Part Three hops from vividly various islands (Bali, Manhattan), to ones variant-still (Kalimantan, Sri Lanka). Readers visit "Borneo" via memoirs of colonial careerist Charles Hose. We glimpse "Ceylon" through old imperialist invective that defamed not just "native" subjects (multiply construed) but European rivals as well; one butt of colonialist vituperation (in this case British) was the nearly-same (in this case Dutch)—a complication in earlier discourses often underestimated in postcolonial studies. My essays oppose old and recent officialdoms, to be sure; but I also doubt avant-garde incursions and question prepackaged psychotherapies possibly more arrogant than self-advertised. Colonialist accounts and contemporary positionings are both revisited to flag a recurrent irony: Strange bedfellows connect "here" with "there" and "now" with "then." Can a postmodern tomorrow be any different?

Part Three extends credit for risky extra-Vagance from Thoreau back to Chaucer and forward to scholars as wildly diverse as Gita Mehta on ashram groupies, Louis Dumont on hierarchy (this time Occidental-style), and Jonathan Goldberg on sexualities ("sodometries," to be precise). I question efforts to hoist medieval and Renaissance tomes into present-day identity politics. I also mull Jacques Derrida's wilfully maddening take on Marcel Mauss's ethnology of gifts. And I redirect, with winks and winces, Mariana Torgovnick's attack on *Tarzan*—an easy target in our antimodernist age. All the scholars just mentioned—whether postmodernist, not-that, always-already, precocious, or belated—are complicated; and those they critique may be equally so.

Part Three itself critiques wholesale postmodernism; yet I endeavor to make my critique other than wholesale. Polemic that unduly generalizes just may be half the problem. Nevertheless, it is important *generally* to undo pat sequences of "isms," which do not happen the same way the world over. Postmodernism, too, like positivism long before it, deserves disaggregating and inflecting; doing so requires rereading that acknowledges its own cultural and historical contingencies. That isn't easy. Paradoxically, this book's relatively relativist vergings stick to one path: I continually doubt agendas that envision a uniformist politics or ethics of progress toward the global Good (including goodly *différance*). I also try to deflect any standardized "manifesto"—even one gone progressively pro-cyborg.

To Part Two's composite scenes of world expositions, circus humbugs, opera shops, old Smithsonian and older Louvre, Part Three adds newer venues: the Whitney, media spectacle, and mega-themeparks (Disney enclaves, Singapore, etc.) To savants who still react huffily when disciplines factor in popular rites and carnivalized commodities, I can only say that we should by now have learned to know better. It seems conspicuously ill advised at our millennium's end to segregate the supposedly serious (political, economic, religious) from the patently showy. Showbiz, for better or worse, seems here and elsewhere to stay; it may always have been, really.

Part Three concludes with a rebuttal to portions of Mary Douglas's lively anthropology of grids, groups, and "goods." Douglas's declared antipathy to Thoreau(!) triggers my final leap to the "World of Coca-Cola" (which museum opened in Atlanta shortly before Coke's "marketeers" prepared to invade Indonesia). In this state-of-the-art scene, capitalism's keynote commodity stages self-celebrations of and for consumer-habitus. Coke's promotional simulacra could, I suppose, afford postmodernist theorists and shoppers their ideal spree (the kind illustrated in Umberto Eco's *Travels in Hyperreality* [1986]). However, my personal experience (when encountering these exhibitions just before returning to Bali) felt extra-Vagantly Thoreauvian—*without* bounds, wakingly. Efforts to be adequate to that foundationless truth round off Part Three. Several *Encores* and an *Envoi* wrap everything up.

———————

The book thus explores extra-Vagance in disparate scenes—multiritual Bali, overbuilt Manhattan, ever-vanishing Venice—and at unexpected moments: ones that may have leaped for Kierkegaard or jolted Benjamin.[11] The topic of "moments" alludes as well to "the Romantic moment" (*chronos* suddenly becoming *kairos*) and to "the Modern moment" (discovering charismatic virtue in trivial objects or events) of Pater, Proust, James, Woolf, Joyce, and perhaps too Ginsberg's "strident parody of . . . the transforming vision" (M. Abrams 1971: 418–19, 423).

Echoes within these echoes include Early Romanticism's own revisitings of Renaissance hermeticism, to question the mechanistic worldview and analytic divisiveness of Enlightenment schemes:

> The esoteric view of the universe as a plenum of opposed yet mutually attractive, quasi-sexual forces—which was discredited and displaced by Cartesian and Newtonian mechanism, but was revived in a refined form, in the *Naturphilosophie* of Schelling in Germany and of Coleridge in England—proceeded, by a peripety of intellectual history, to feed back into scientific thought. (M. Abrams 1971: 170–71)

My cross-cultural essays oscillate between "histories of ideas" advanced by such scholars as Abrams, A. Lovejoy, and particularly Frances Yates; and alternative "archaeologies" associated with Foucault, who staged other ways to question mechanistic analysis and diagnosis.[12] I keep wondering where comparative writing and reading could lead if theorists stopped normalizing method (or antimethod) as an aftermath to an "enlightenment" that purged hermetics and hermeneutics alike. A possibly parallel project is Michel Serres's "attempt to re-enchant the world":

> Serres is a fundamentally pre- or non-modern thinker, and is therefore somehow more post-modern than any alleged postmodernist, because he does not give credence to the Enlightenment rationalism that, according to postmodernists, has failed. (S. Critchley 1996)[13]

Diverse esoteric traditions—Gnostic, Neoplatonist, Kabbalist, alchemical, liturgical, theatrical (and one could add, ironically, "Foucauldian")—weave in and out of Western institutions of religion and transgression: our theories of political power, ideals of marriage and renunciation, and callings of abstinence and/or expenditure. Affinities do exist between such European formations and non-Western heterodoxies—for example, Tantric codes of Hindu-Buddhist Bali.[14]

Personally no esoterist, I nevertheless confess a certain "musicalism."[15] Although issues of music are largely set aside in this study, several specific suggestions play a key role.[16] One is a rumination by George Steiner:

> No epistemology, no philosophy of art can lay claim to inclusiveness if it has nothing to teach us about the nature and meanings of music. Claude Lévi-Strauss's affirmation that "the invention of melody is the supreme mystery of man" seems to me of sober evidence. The truths, the necessities of ordered feeling in the musical experience are not irrational; but they are irreducible to reason or pragmatic reckoning. This irreducibility is the spring of my argument.

> When it speaks of music, language is lame. Customarily, it takes refuge in the
> pathos of simile. (1989: 19)

Works by Steiner (and Lévi-Strauss) adumbrate music, languages, cultures,
politics, literatures, histories, silences, and translation. Steiner rejects deconstruction's nonstop war of *différance* waged against logocentric presence; he
disputatiously reinstates a bond between presence and absence. (Whether, say,
Steiner or Derrida remains more "faithful" to Nietzsche, Benjamin, etc. deeply
concerns many critical thinkers these days.)[17]

Save one sally through opera, this book engages music only tangentially:
background, underscore, overheard—refuged (in Steiner's terms) "in the pathos of simile," or a promise of simile-to-come. Chapter 3 alone pushes music
front and center. There I parallel phenomena of chromatic (versus diatonic)
scales with augmented modes of gender difference. My elbow of analogy
pokes between music and sociopolitical theory in a way that harks back to a
different angle in Kenneth Burke, who compared arpeggios (versus chords) to
Hegel's dialectical device of transcendence:

> The point is this: If you strike *do-mi-sol* simultaneously, you get a perfect con-
> cord. If you add *fa*, thus playing *do-mi-fa-sol*, you get a discord. But if you draw
> this discord out into an arpeggio, by playing the four notes not simultaneously but
> in succession, they are not felt as a discord. Rather, they are transformed into a
> melody, since the dissonant *fa* acts merely as a passing note. . . .
>
> Thus Hegel's "dialectic of history" attempted the union of contradictory aims,
> in trying to make the passing note of an arpeggio fit as concord in a simultaneity.
> A logic being ideally all done before you begin, anti-Hegelians get their opportu-
> nity to object that his logic of development, if true, would make development
> impossible. Thesis, antithesis, and synthesis would all exist simultaneously and in
> equal force. But by stretching them out into a temporal arpeggio, he can depict the
> thesis as prevailing in greater percentage at one time, the antithesis at another, and
> the synthesis as an act of transcendence at still another. [18]

Foregoing Hegelian "arpeggios," I propose instead a metaphor of "chromatics," in hopes of modulating reductive dichotomies—modernist/post-, cir-
cumcised/un-, high/low, old/neo-, androgynous/straight—into interpretive
equivalents of half-tones. Chromatic nuance requires all the black keys with all
the white; it significantly augments possible scales without excluding conventional diatonic propriety. Chromatic genders, genres, rites, sites, and scholars
seem immanently worth rereading—chromatically. "Ultraobjectivity" (Chap.
1) is one awkward name for what may result when this (Thoreauvian?) effort
is made.

VERGING ON EXTRA-VAGANCE

Rehearsals

To BEGIN exercising extra-Vagance in many modes and keys, I sample a few saturated authors and topics: (1) a spirited corpus by Kenneth Burke; (2) the hybrid genre of opera, always difficult to know how to take; and (3) two masters of transgression, Herman Melville and Stanley Cavell (a strenuously Thoreauvian philosopher attentive to critical theory, Hollywood comedies, television's facticity, and more).[1] Readers may want to skip any or all of these multidisciplinary warm-ups; the choice is yours.

AN ENDLESSLY EXTRA-VAGANT SCHOLAR:
KENNETH BURKE

The reading of Freud I find suggestive almost to the point of
bewilderment. Accordingly, what I should like most to do would be
simply to take representative excerpts from his work, copy them out, and
write glosses upon them. Very often these glosses would be straight
extensions of his own thinking. . . . Such a desire to write an article
on Freud in the margin of his books must for practical reasons here
remain a frustrated desire. . . .
Freud's terminology is a dictionary, a lexicon for charting a vastly
complex and hitherto largely uncharted field. You can't refute a
dictionary. The only profitable answer to a dictionary
is another one.
(K. Burke, 1957)[2]

As the "later" Freud to the late Burke, so Burke (and Freud) to this always-belated author, intent on reading Burke as he read others. Saluting I. M. Richards, Burke derived an "ironic attitude" from diverse historic configurations: Socratic, Austenian (Jane), Romantic, Modernist (postmodernist name-brands had not yet materialized). Burke's irony—irremediably hard to pin down—is neither holier-than-thou nor self-sure; and he is never, never glib. Or so Burke, about to footnote Falstaff as well, implies in *A Grammar of Motives* (1945):

True irony, however, irony that really does justify the attribute of "humility," is
not "superior" to the enemy. True irony, humble irony, is based upon a sense of
fundamental kinship with the enemy, as one . . . is *indebted* to him. . . . This is the

irony of Flaubert, when he recognizes that Madame Bovary is himself. . . . Folly and villainy are integral motives, necessary to wisdom or virtue. (1962: 514–15)

Burke appreciated Thomas Mann's irony too, a variety clarified by Erich Heller: "Mann's highly ironical traditionalism . . . modeled itself on the classical products of literary history but at the same time could not help 'parodying' them."[3] (I cite Heller from his afterword to a slightly stilted translation of *Der Tod in Venedig* by none other than Kenneth Burke.) Elsewhere Burke addressed "Greek love" (relevant to the novella he translated) and Socratic ironies—a classic pedagogical topic recently revitalized in the work and life of Michel Foucault and his diverse disciples and detractors.[4] Here's how Burke began:

> Biologically, Greek love was an offence, since its fruitfulness would not be that of tribal progeny. It was thus the "representative crime" of the Athenian enlightenment, the practice that corresponded in the realm of transgression to the pedagogy of Socratic intercourse in the realm of the transcendent and ideal.
>
> Socrates was thus accused of the "representative" transgression. And whatever may have been the realities of the case in the literal sense, the structure of the *Phaedrus* shows that he was a "corruptor of youth" in the transcendental sense. He was thus resigned to the hemlock. . . .
>
> Ironically, then, this theorist of transcendence was the victim of a transcendence transcended. (1962: 426–28)

"The victim of a transcendence transcended!" Similar twists in dialectics (subsequent to those scapegoating Socrates) advanced rhetoric through history to the stage of Burke's own "counterstatements" marshalled against many foes: Hitler, Fascism, the Cold War, and triumphal dichotomies of any stripe. These were the critical battles Burke relentlessly waged.[5]

My initial "Rehearsal," barely underway, already suggests that Burkian irony was and remains nonstop. Current readers may find their every experience pre-Post-It-ed "in the margins of his books." (Again, this notion of margins—but not of postmodern Post-Its—is dutifully drawn from Burke himself, embroiled, as stipulated above, in Freud.)

In 1965, thanks to extra-Vagant assignments by James Peacock (an interdisciplinarian destined to become President of the American Anthropological Association thirty years later), this student suffered a "first contact" with Burke, who has since received spotty canonization in extraliterary circles: symbolic anthropology (e.g., Peacock 1975); critical philosophy (e.g., Sills and Jensen 1992); and so forth.[6] My little corpus, too, stands (dwarfishly) on the shoulders of Burke-as-giant. (For a perfectly devious guide to misreadings of the "dwarves on shoulders of giants" *topos*, see the vintage Menippean satire by Robert Merton, a giant among ironic sociologists.)[7] In *From Symbolism to Structuralism* (1972), I poached Burke's pastiches of Marxian slogans against "critiques of critical criticism" to help explicate a circumstantial poetics in Lévi-Strauss's artful ethnology. In *The Anthropological Romance of Bali* (1977), I framed a history of Balinese research with Burke's metaphors about perspectives through incongruity; my fieldwork covered Balinese ancestral ideology and dynamics of leadership—Burke's "socio-anagogic" dimensions of culture.[8]

In *Other Tribes, Other Scribes* (1982) I synoptically matched Burke's dramatism with the interpretive anthropology of Clifford Geertz; later Geertz's *Works and Lives* (1987) saluted Burke as its "governing inspiration at almost every point."[9] In 1984, rumor came back to me that *Other Tribes* had annoyed Marxists—possibly because it opened a commentary on Marx and Mauss (plus Durkheim) with cloth coats. Had Marxists forgotten what Burke remembered: "Marx says that the modern division of labor began in earnest with the manufacture of Cloth"?[10] Or did they disapprove juxtaposing scholars whom they needed to believe diametrically sundered? Again, my inspiration was Burke, who tactically conjoined Marx on cloth with an apparent antithesis, Thomas Carlyle; in *Sartor Resartus* Carlyle "is not writing a book on the clothing industry":

> He is writing a book about symbols, which demand reverence because, in the last analysis, the images of nature are the Symbols of God. He uses Clothes as a surrogate for the symbolic in general. Examining his book to see what they are symbolic of, you find how Carlyle resembles Marx: Both are talking about the kind of hierarchy that arose in the world with the division of labor. (1962: 642–43)

Burke's *Grammar of Motives* seems almost to coin a contrary-trio of Marx, Carlyle, and Lévi-Strauss's *Tristes tropiques* (as yet, when Burke wrote, unwritten):

> Reading *The German Ideology* and *Sartor Resartus* together, with the perhaps somewhat perverse pleasure of seeing how they can be brought to share the light that each throws upon the other, we might begin with the proposition that mystery arises at that point where different *kinds* of beings are in communication. In mystery there must be *strangeness*; but the estranged must also be thought of as in some way capable of communion. There is mystery in an animal's eyes at those moments when a man feels that he and the animal understand each other in some inexpressible fashion. (1962: 639)

Such a-chronism (as-if reading the concluding cat-winks of *Tristes tropiques* before the fact) can occur because the world's shifting genres and rhetorical transformations form a closed book, seemingly.[11]

In *Affinities and Extremes* (1990), I adapted Burke's foxy way (called "logology") of countering dichotomies to investigate Dutch and British colonialist representations, Bali's ritual-rhetorics, and Margaret Mead's *Lebenswerk*. Panoramic discourses entangle Bali, the East Indies, Europe, India, and the world in each other's flows; to explore them I even heeded Burke's advice to apply Alexander Pope to devious interpretive aims, "if one were feeling ironical."[12]

Devotedly revisiting Burke, I find him nevertheless forever elusive. His readers can only go on beginning again—replicating the experience that Burke designated "the ambiguity of starting points . . . either as the inaugurating moment . . . or as the point abandoned" (1962: 406). Still, my hunch persists that Burke's "attitude toward history" suits cultural anthropology *cum* critical theory, and cultural studies too. "Humble irony" may offer few answers; but without it, the palpable doubt that admits recognition of plural cultures, histories, *and critiques* would be difficult to imagine, impossible to enact.

Burke's *Grammar of Motives* plots "antinomies of definition" of any term, including "motive." "As soon as we encounter, verbally or thematically, a motivational simplicity," he advises, "we must assume as a matter of course that it contains a diversity" (1962: 101). Motives of "motive" lead Burke to oscillate with Wagnerian *Leitmotive*—by way of eros/thanatos in the "Liebestod" in *Tristan*, which Burke accurately declares already "implicit Tannhäuser." (More precisely, *Tannhäuser* became explicitly Tristanian when Wagner reworked it into his ripened style of endless transitioning.) Burke calls *Tristan*'s plot a "'perfect paradigm' for a 'myth' so equating Eros and Thanatos that any 'combat' between them becomes transformed into a species of 'concerted action'. . .(in the idea of a musical *concerto* . . .)" (1966: 390). Burke considers mythic "language" harmonic rather than melodic, counter-*chronologique* (my term), and subversive of manifest plot; these insights recall and/or anticipate another (imperfect) Wagnerite: Lévi-Strauss.[13]

Burke, then, broached highest art (if *höchste* is the word for Wagnerian music drama). But Burke was no Mandarin; an earthy chap, he viewed popular amusement as "basic" to capitalism—rather like production. Recalling another ironist of sorts, Marcel Mauss, Burke cross-read motives of "the gift," "magic," and "money." Burke pegs money as a "capitalist psychosis"—a gloss reminiscent of Ruth Benedict's manner of labeling configurations (this time pinned on the right donkey).[14] Like Simmel (and Weber reading him), Burke lodges money's "profit motive" in renunciatory reinvestment.[15] He thus took seriocomically something that Marx (as Frankfurt School theorists have indicated) mysteriously neglected; but Burke's assertively casual style of talking out his argument was all his own:

> In sum, if you have an unpleasant piece of work to be done, and don't want to do it yourself, in a slave culture you may get this done by force . . . or in a pious culture you may get it done "religiously". . . . But in a capitalist labor market, all that is necessary is for you to say, "Who'll do this for five dollars?"—and men press forward "independently," of their "own free will," under orders from no one, to "voluntarily" enlist for the work. . . . And though the work might "in itself" be

drudgery, in time this shortcoming was rectified by the growth of the "amusement industry" to the point where it formed one of the biggest investments in our entire culture. And by going where one chose to be amused, one could enjoy for almost nothing such a wealth of performers, avid to entertain, as was never available to the most jaded of Oriental potentates, however vast his revenues. Under . . . "market law," . . . men could be "substantially" free in willing to obey the necessities of monetary wage and monetary tax (or "price"), *wanting* to do what they *had* to do, uniting "I must," "I ought," and "I will." The noun for this union of necessity, duty, and volition was "ambition." Another such was "enterprise." (1962: 93)[16]

To underscore phantasmagoric consumption, Burke invoked none other than Henry Adams, who showed that ritual extravaganzas are key to the "education" of *homo capitalismus*:

Henry Adams' pairing of Virgin and Dynamo clearly suggests two contrasting orders of power. . . . his *Education* seems to be a rebirth ritual whereby the author would finally bring himself to see himself in terms of impersonal "force," while renouncing the strongly *familial* sense of his identity (the "eighteenth-century" self) with which his life began. His book traces a kind of attenuated self-immolation. . . . It is at the successive world's fairs and international expositions that Adams gets his "education." Of the Chicago Exposition in 1893, we are told that "education ran riot" there. . . . And it is in the "great gallery of machines" at the Paris Exposition of 1900, that he found "his historical neck broken by the sudden irruption of forces totally new," forces which he compares and contrasts with the forces of the Christian Cross, on the grounds that both kinds, in their way, have been revolutionary. (1962: 120–21)

As I noted in a "Prelude" to *Affinities and Extremes* (1990), America's own Henry Adams carefully crossed such cultures as Ceylon and Tahiti; he also factored in world exhibitions, as Walter Benjamin did later.[17]

Adams, in short, was an historian of extra-Vagance—in the Thoreauvian sense this book commends. Adams proved a fitting contemporary of William James, who also felt "called" to witness excess ironically. As Stephen Webb has summarized:

James is attracted to religious excess precisely because it is difficult to concretize or define, and his blend of fascination and frustration is a key element of his success in crafting [*The Varieties of Religious Experience*]. . . . a treatise about excess, that is, about the trope of hyperbole. . . . James's own rhetorical style articulates the excessive religious experiences that he recounts and . . . his book tells us about excess itself and magic and the danger of this troubling but much neglected figure of speech. . . .

Exaggeration, or hyperbole, is a species . . . of both praxis and language; in either arena, excess is that which goes too far for a reason . . . ; it is held in suspicion. Indeed, the rhetorical tradition, following Aristotle's connection of exaggeration with adolescence . . . frequently maligned hyperbole as the trope that lies. . . .

. . . James was drawn toward the full range and drama of religious excess. . . . James's own rhetoric both responds to and helps delimit the trope of extravagance.[18]

It is hardly surprising that William James's attraction to exaggeration attracted Burke *ensuite*. Burke cited James's insights about Dionysius extra-Vagantly (I'd say): "It is super-lucent, super-splendent, super-essential, super-sublime, super everything that can be named". (1962: 854) Via William James (and Henry), Burke elaborated both revolutionary moments and the "mystic moment" (one might also call it "magical"): "the stage of revelation after which all is felt to be different". (1962: 305) Again, Burke omits from such *sacra* neither politics, literature, nor popular culture. For example, his anecdote about elevator riding and Jimmy Durante movies "preludes" a commentary on Proust:

> In *The Past Recovered*, where Proust is writing of the various moments in his life that all had the same quality (being all in effect *one* moment, in deriving from the same principle) he says that these many occasions in essence one were like a peacock's tail spread out. (1962: 307)

Burke thus transgressed back toward his theoretical goal: motives of ironic-dialectic. Such was *his* "enterprise."

Oh, there is so much in Burke! Perhaps enough has been adduced to convince readers that everywhere in this book, too, Burke lurks (including its *Encores and Envoi*, where alternative quotations orchestrate retrospectively what is now being rehearsed). Not that any reader could perfectly concur with Burke; such accord may be quite impossible, dialectically and ironically. Still, anything this reader writes feels *like* footnotes and marginalia (compare this simile to music's pathos)—lagging behind Burke's serious sport.

Kenneth Burke is one reason why I cannot buy into promotions that advertise today's critical theory as more ironic than yesterday's. (Other reasons are Franz Boas, James Frazer, F. Schlegel, Menippean satire, and cultures' and history's carnivalizings.)[19] Indeed, to congratulate oneself—or those -isms one favors—for exceeding another's irony seems a singularly unironic thing to do. That flaw afflicts some postmodern "irony," I suspect . . . (Oops!). Irony doesn't exactly grow, does it? Nor can discourse quite "progress" into irony—and out of belief, credulity, sincerity, naïveté, or even positivism. Irony is routinely repressed in "official" formats, to be sure; yet even there it may be intrinsically implicit, obtaining from human negativities and multiplicities. In short, any assumed absence of irony is (was) also ironic.[20] So there . . . paradoxically.

A SIMILAR GENRE: OPERA

Opera, The Extravagant Art (1984), a book by Herbert Lindenberger, stresses multiperspectival planes within opera tied to society, politics, and history. European opera embeds narratives in plural tongues and registers—a dimension Lindenberger associates with Bakhtin's theories of generic interchange and the dialogism of the ever novel "novel." He also factors in Menippean satire—a polylogue "tradition" that has been blurring the West's mobile genres (including travel-writing and ethnography) since the second century of the common era; or so I have argued.[21]

"Last remaining refuge of the high style," opera sustains an aesthetics and politics of carnivalized questioning through hyperbole, excess, and overt artifice. Opera harnesses irreducible disparities between music/text (or music/drama) in performances that entail a "self-conscious, often parodistic reworking of the past."[22] And opera evolves and advances by continually shifting its conventions.

The hybridity of opera pertains to institutions and praxis as much as texts and tunes. Derived from ecclesiastic music and secular masques, operatic techniques have kept merging and detaching song and speech, score and libretto, singers and orchestra, narrative and tableau, recitative and aria, plus orchestral equivalents for solo/ensemble/chorus/etc. "Opera" both arranges and dialectically overthrows its featured incongruities by advancing monumental productions. Their costs and scale of resources expended seem almost to rival the most expansive activities of courts and states, such as military technology and regimental show. (I have interjected a slight note of hyperbole.)

Varieties of opera transform as theatricality pushes through current limits of know-how. Elaborate results ensue: eye-popping mechanics of Jacobean masques; diverting machineries of eighteenth-century opera houses; Italian castrati (mandated in Rome; produced in Berlin); ticket distributions during Paris's "Age of Offenbach"; Bayreuth's electricity; *Heldentenor*; derivative genres (e.g., underscored movies).[23] Such wizardry extends to broadcast opera that relies on cameras developed for fast-tracking sports events and expertise in concealing technical paraphernalia (like that devised to disguise the game of golf as a pristine pastorale; televised golf has become an exponential extravaganza of helicopter and blimp shots, camouflaged panopticon-towers, and chemical "base"—synthetic fertilizer). The stakes of delivering *gesamt* goods to *gesamt* audiences keep escalating. Perhaps an anthropologist can be forgiven for designating this inflation a "potlatch potential" that links modernity and postmodernity (so-called).[24]

Over time, opera augments musical theatrics: orchestra size, instrument varieties, vocal styles, laser lights, divas' circuits. Simultaneously opera heightens archaisms: revitalized formats, resurgent modes, and (happily) museumized war-horses. Opera's on-going self-upping (symmetrical schismo-genesis?) ensures episodic crises in patronage, if "crisis" is a suitable term for so regular an event. The worldly "story of opera" consists of tales of anxiety over infrastructure: (1) attracting bourgeois ticket buyers when aristocratic resources dry up (Mozart); (2) inventing national loyalties where no "nation" quite exists (Verdi); (3) courting anachronistic kings when Prussian bureaucrats turn deaf ears (Wagner); (4) securing state backers when economies, whether fettered or free, expand (Strauss, Boulez); (5) luring mass audiences to sway corporate sponsors who underwrite "public" betterment (PBS, gratefully); (6) matching superstar tenors to World Cup competitions, and repeating the performance, incrementally.[25]

Thus, a perpetual dilemma of securing backers and gratifying buffs propels opera—an intrinsically exaggerated performance mode, one that harnesses the felt contradiction between speaking and singing. That sing/speak predicament could be called *motivic* in Kenneth Burke's sense; it threads dialectically from low *Singspiel*, through the presumed heights of epic opera, into doubly ironic returns upon either (Richard Strauss, say, coupled with Hoffmansthal).[26] By adding to Burke a bit of Bakhtin plus a dash of Geertz, I could designate opera a chronotope in motion—sounding and displaying motives *of* and *for* the fact that "these jokers are singing/speaking." Hence opera's extra-Vagance: its outsized settings, often "exotic"; its routinely excessive plots—about incest, fratricide-parricide-soricide-matricide-suicide-deicide . . . , mistaken identities, comic overdrive, love won or lost through marriage and/or/as death. Hence too the abundant fringes said to bubble beneath opera's masks and song: Masonic orders, Neoplatonist subversion, Bohemian subcultures, upscale aestheticisms, gay vocalities, afficionado queens, mathematicians, Parisian theory wars, and further persuasions, transgressions, and status symbols likely to be continued.[27]

Opera's diverse formats (*seria, buffa*, grand, *-etta* . . .) for straddling song and speech variegate its dominant (tonic?) rhetorical inclination: to foreground both ceremoniousness and buffoonery—the very features suppressed when other genres go "realist." Lindenberger likens all of opera to baroque drama. He poses an incisive thought experiment: ". . . Imagine an encyclopedic rhetoric of standard operatic situations, with the proper distinctions articulated as to which musical style fits which situation at any particular moment in history" (1984: 32). Such a catalogue of rhetorical situations, I think, might amalgamate Walter Benjamin's allegorizings of history's *Trauerspiele* with Northrop Frye's "comic" anatomizings of the world's literary modes—in a kind of tragicomic array (see Chap. 6).

Opera's on-stage extra-Vagance is complemented by elaborate systems of patronage and their politics. Mozart's *Magic Flute*, for example, crossed over not just oratorio, folktale, and Freemasonry, but court versus bourgeois audiences and *Singspiel* financiers. Wagner too merged the leading edge of musical practice with his regrettable ideology for *aufhebung*-ing future sponsorship. This pragmatic dialectic joined innumerable realities and fictions suffusing Wagner's *Ring*—that *summa* of "invented tradition." Nor did Wagnerian practicality stop there. *Parsifal*'s ethos of festive consecration folded mere Christian world-renunciation into a higher pessimism gleaned from Schopenhauer-on-Buddhism. (That theme had been scheduled by Wagner for a "negative" music drama all its own—*Die Sieger*.)[28] *Parsifal*'s earliest hearers—including its most celebrated anti-enthusiast, Nietzsche—may have overlooked or repressed something crucial. Unlike Wagner's *Lohengrin* (less contradiction-laden), *Parsifal* "restored" a simulated liturgical setting by compositing "heresies" and orthodoxies. Its radical hybridity topped off the catalogue of real and legendary theatrics mounted by Wagner's works in endless recapitulation. The continuing power of *Parsifal*'s multiforms may be tokened, ironically, by its eventual broadcast from New York's Metropolitan as a kind of Holy Week opera, conducted nowadays by James Levine. There may be only one word for it all—Extra-Vagant.[29]

Opera's "translatability" across political circumstances is matched by an intense "interoperality." Early operas transformed and transgressed liturgical oratorios (hybrids in their own right); later operas reincorporated predecessors, both musically and dramatically. Wagner too embraced favored forerunners—Mozart, Weber, Beethoven, perhaps Berlioz; just as he purged detested rivals—Meyerbeer, Meyerbeer, and Meyerbeer. After *Rienzi* Wagner's listeners were obliged to continue to hear his works differently: "progressing" toward *Parsifal*, it retro-auditively turned out. Wagner's compositions rewrote the way his previous achievements could be received. I have elsewhere traced this dynamic process of corpus formation on Wagner's part to willful echoes of it by Lévi-Strauss, who adapted Wagner's principles of *musical* composition (plus Debussy's appreciative parodies) in his anthropological readings of transitions throughout Amerindian myths. Lévi-Strauss's *oeuvre* shows that opera—polylingual, intertextual, multi-media—may even inundate certain styles of *sciences humaines*.[30]

Rich precedents for mixing opera with *Geisteswissenschaften* ring out from the history of critical theory; as Gloria Flaherty demonstrates for Germany:

> [Gottsched's] disciples, like Scheibe, might have thought that contemporary opera was a far cry from Greek tragedy, but they would not accept his complete denial of its artistic potential. . . . Their opposition to the concept of generic purity supported the tendency to reexamine and reconsider the role of music and spectacle in ancient theater.
>
> That tendency became stronger in the 1750s. . . . Their search was not purely antiquarian. They wanted to discover meaningful ways to reform indigenous thea-

ter and to stimulate feelings of cultural unity among their countrymen. This seemed especially urgent to writers in Berlin where royal patronage supported French neoclassical drama and Italianate grand opera. The austerity of the one seemed as bad to them as the complexity of the other, so they strove to find a middle course [!] that would be compatible with the German spirit. Their desire to understand that spirit resulted in reevaluations of the middle ages and the six-teenth century as well as of classical antiquity. They developed a strong affinity for Shakespeare . . . his ability to unify great diversity. . . . They devoted as much effort to the performing arts of antiquity as Winckelmann did to the plastic arts. And opera, both in practice and in theory, became one of their more important considerations. . . . Lessing investigated . . . their declamation, pantomime, chi-ronomy, saltation, and other nonverbal means of communication. . . . (Flaherty 1978: 284–87)[31]

These earlier investigations grew increasingly elaborate, not just historically but cross-culturally. Lessing was joined by no less a theorist than Herder, whose local "worlds" anticipated both cultural anthropology and operatic arts:

> The more they studied, the more they compared the territorial particularism of the German lands with the city-states of ancient Greece. . . . The chorus presented as many problems for them as it had for their long line of predecessors. Some writ-ers thought Klopstock had successfully resolved those problems with his bardic songs. Others pursued Lessing's suggestion about substituting the modern orchestra.
>
> Among them was Herder, who tried his own hand at quasi-operatic, melodra-matic texts in the early 1770s. . . . Elements of the *Melodrama, Monodrama, Duo-drama, Singspiel,* and *Lyrisches Drama* became all-pervasive in German thea-ter. . . . In 1798 . . . by constructing a dialogue that . . . was able to lead his readers though a maze of aesthetic ideas . . . , he used opera to exemplify the work of art as a carefully circumscribed, artificial little world (*eine kleine Kunstwelt*). (Flaherty 1978: 287, 296)

Opera, like "culture" in certain theories, implies *eine kleine Kunstwelt* (call it local).[32] One wellspring of opera's hybridity is its basic doubleness of score-libretto—a non-redundancy that nevertheless plays at reinforcing meanings. This fundamental ambiguity may underpin opera's penchant for paraphrasing earlier instances of itself, its habit of pastiche. Pastiche is more than "mere" in any extravagant art (in Lindenberger's sense), because multiplicities of form mean that no "quotation" altogether lacks "difference." In worlds of extra-Vagance (in my adaptation of Thoreau's sense), each repetition implies trans-formation; every copy *slides*.

A few treasured classics help clarify my argument here. Richard Strauss's *Rosenkavalier* deliberately evoked and echoed Mozart's *Le Nozze di Figaro*, just as *Die Frau ohne Schatten* did *Die Zauberflöte*.[33] Yet, as Lindenberger notes, Hoffsmanthal (Strauss's librettist) "rejected the term *imitation* and insisted instead on the word *analogy*" (1984: 104). Strauss's pastiches brought out palimpsestic qualities of any musical-textual composition: a work's future of being heard back into the compositions it has written itself over. This may have been the face of opera that Theodor Adorno meant to signal in *Versuch über Wagner* when he chided: "The closer opera gets to a parody of itself, the closer it is to the principle most inherent to it."[34] Alas, and characteristically, Adorno anticipated an escape from self-parodying, if *bürgerliche Oper* could one day emerge emancipated from its bourgeois-dom. It is not as an apologist for *la condition bourgeoise* that I doubt Adorno's utopian prospectus in such matters. Rather, I doubt Adorno because it seems clear to me that inherent self-parody extends far beyond a provincial historical phase of Western city-life and its customary alienations.

Conspicuously diverse cultures and eras produce palimpsestic and parodic forms tantamount to "operatic." Indeed "culture" in certain disciplinary senses implies just such "doubtability" of originality; doubt in turn implies reflexivity, or something like it: the shamanic perhaps?[35] Be that as it may, I only wish to resonate operatic extra-Vagance with aspects of plural cultures that ethnography inscribes and different eras that history portrays—formations festooned with ritual and political institutions subject to comparison.

Opera—both extravagant art and commodified extravaganza—is much more besides. Styles of Western opera consolidated by the nineteenth century continue at the close of the twentieth, with setbacks and resurgences. Parallels may perhaps be drawn with pursuits of ethnography, history writing, and the novel—both before and after being transformed into postmodern experiments that critical critics today love or hate to hate or love. For all that, the Romantic-Modernist era in certain respects beats on, or repeats (Rabelaisian undertones acknowledged). As the millennium looms, varied enterprises keep devising ways to displace here-and-nows into theres and thens, persuasively evoked. The arts I call extra-Vagant—opera, ethnography, history, novel—convey circumstantial senses of dramatic differences. They mingle high-lifes and vernaculars, the epochal and everyday; they enact tensions of translating languages, dialects, cultures, texts, and times of diverse proclivities. They are irreducibly poly-.[36]

But my optional rehearsal in Lindenberger's extravagant art of arts perchance grows o'er expansive. Enough said, then, about opera. As in Hölderlin's *Hyperion*,

> the shape of the novel [plus ethnography? history?] . . . like that of the human life
> it represents, is circuitous yet open-ended; and its coda terminates appropriately
> on an unresolved chord: "So dacht' ich. Nächstens mehr." "So did I think. More
> in my next." (Abrams 1971: 244)

PLUS MELVILLE, CAVELL, COMMODITY-LIFE; SHOWBIZ

Thoreau's mid-nineteenth century was an operatic era long before Kenneth Burke's and longer still before now. America *then* could conceivably have pursued policies less Jacksonian than those actually implemented. After finally sloughing off slavery, the government of our re-United States nevertheless perpetuated its Indian-hating, Pacific-vanquishing ways. One near-contemporary of Thoreau who fervently decried U.S. expansionism was Herman Melville. Indefatigable browser among world scriptures, plus ethnographies then available, Melville also voyaged to and fro, authoring exotic travel tales (*Typee, Omoo, Mardi, Moby Dick*) and no less extra-Vagant homey narratives brushed by Susquehannah winds (*Pierre, The Confidence Man*).[37]

I have twice keyed empirical studies to Melville's figural ones; in these pages, too, "something further" follows Melville's many masquerades—both his sketches and his finished compositions.[38] For example, on Sunday, April 5, 1857, Melville visited Venice. "For a long time I used to" be ignorant that my discursive turns in Chapter 5 were prefigured in Melville's casual *Journal* (1989: 118–20). (May that fact of counterchronology enhance the salience of coincident travels divided by a century and more—Melville's and mine.) Melville's rascally passage could have served as "overture" or scattered epigraphs to this book; his jottings deserve comparison with alternative "gondalizings" from Mark Twain's *Innocents Abroad* (1979: 896–911; see concluding note to Chap. 5).

When description turns disturbingly intertextual, something "Melvillian" may occur. My cross-cultural essays nominate further candidates for adjectival apotheosis as well: Benedictine (Chap. 1); Montaignesque (Chap. 2); Batesonian and Debussian (Chap. 3); Nabokov-Geertz-Benjamin-Stendahlian (Chap. 4); Henry Jamesish (Chap. 5); Maussian (Chap. 6). Proceedings become a bit Proustian (*partout*), Freudian (*hier und da*), and de-Derridean (Chap. 10). This book's *author*—a Melville addict and Balinist—feels more Twainian (and William Jamesian) than otherwise; yet the way he remembers among cultures gets crowded—like cultures "themselves"—with ventriloquisms.

Sticking for the moment with Melville, it behooves me to stress a radical potential in that scrivener's inducements to be read. Michael Rogin contends that *Pierre* (Melville's countertranscendentalist "romance") represents America's *Eighteenth Brumaire*, making Melville himself something *like* "America's Marx." I find Rogin's claim persuasive.[39] Melville, I would add, was a "Marx" versed in considerably more cultures than his simile (whose works I nevertheless prize). Why, then, have critical critics been more enthralled by Marx than by Melville? I find their response mystifying.

Things may now be a-changing.[40] Regardless, the long-term neglect of Melville in political theory and the relative triumph of Marx possibly stems from a feature of American intellectual life (such that it is) cogently earmarked by Stanley Cavell. Responding to a complaint by global critic Gayitri Chakravorty Spivak—that the American "style of thought" (including Cavell's) lacks the concept of ideology—Cavell voiced his vintage reply in a quixotic "conversation" with an absent opponent:

> I think a related cultural difference between American and European intellectual life is that the American (with isolated exceptions) has no sacred intellectual texts, none whose authority the intellectual community at large is anxious to preserve at all costs—no Marxian texts, no Freudian, no Hegelian, no Deweyan, and so forth. Every text stands at the level of professional journal articles, open for disposal. (I am not considering the Declaration of Independence as a candidate for such a text.) If the concept of ideology depends for its usefulness on its functioning with such favored texts, then its absence in American intellectual life would be explained by the absence of such texts, I mean texts so conceived. Since my paper rather deplores the absence of Emersonian and Thoreauvian texts as something like sacred common possessions, I should add here that this absence is not wholly, or just, deplorable. But it surely makes for drastic barriers to communication, both within American intellectual life and between American and European thinkers. (Cavell 1984: 59)[41]

Regrettably, in this provocative exchange neither Spivak nor Cavell remembered to mention, say, India's intellectual life, among other worlds.[42] Still, I could not agree more with Cavell about difficulties of correlating various continental or hemispheric brands.

Cavell's canny, funny *faux*-chat back at Spivak reminds me of an equally appealing comment by Paul Auster about national characters of consciousness-raising. Here it is:

> It would be wrong . . . to set up a simple dichotomy between radicalism and conservatism, and to put all things French in the first category and all things English and American in the second. The most subversive and innovative elements of our [English language] literature have frequently surfaced in the unlikeliest places and have then been absorbed into the culture at large. Nursery rhymes . . . do not exist as such in France. Nor do the great works of Victorian children's literature (Lewis Carroll, George Macdonald) have any equivalent in French. As for America, it has always had its own homegrown Dada spirit, which has continued to exist as a natural force, without any need of manifestoes or theoretical foundations. The films of Buster Keaton and W.C. Fields, the skits of Ring Lardner, the drawings of Rube Goldberg surely match the corrosive exuberance of anything done in France during the same period. As Man Ray (a native American) wrote to Tristan Tzara from New York in 1921 about spreading the Dada move-

ment to America: "Cher Tzara—Dada cannot live in New York. All New York is Dada, and will not tolerate a rival . . . ." (Auster 1984: xxxiii)

Chapter 6 will requote this incisive remark about customary *loci* separating national styles of subversiveness. By that time this book's own (American) "homegrown Dada spirit"—evoked in its frontispiece illustration—will have circulated interculturally, counternationally, and transtextually, blurring *genres* all the while.[43]

Auster's insight pertains to French, British, and American oppositions. Were it extended to German canons of innovation, *Märchen* might loom large; again, Abrams's synopsis is handy:

> Into these meditations [*Die Lehrlinge*] Novalis inserts a light-hearted *Märchen* which serves as the type for the romance as a whole. The story tells how Hyazinth, enticed by the tales of a strange man "from foreign lands," abandons his home and Rosenblüte. . . .
>
> At the center of [*Heinrich von Ofterdingen*, 1799–1800], too, is a *Märchen*, told by the master poet Klingsohr . . . which assimilates the imagery of Revelation, Canticles, contemporary metallurgy and galvanism, and the Hermetic quest for the Philosopher's Stone . . . ; the result transforms the familiar fairy tale into a cosmic myth. In the notes he wrote for an intended poetics, Novalis indicated . . . "The *Märchen* is as it were the canon of poetry—everything poetic must be *märchenhaft*." And the writer of the *Märchen* is the bard who present, past, and future sees, and who sees the future as a return to a bettered past: . . . "With the passage of time, history must become a *Märchen*—it becomes again what it was in the beginning." (Abrams 1971: 248–49)[44]

I accumulate these mentions of Novalis's *Märchen*, W. C. Fields's films, and Rube Goldberg's *bricolages* to ratify play across media, generations, politics, and comedy—including a "madcap" genre (a.k.a. screwball) dear to Stanley Cavell—one that might have pleased Melville as well, had he lived to witness movies like they, alas, used to be.[45]

Where's the Showbiz?

> Hollywood is a mythical locale, part of whose function is to cause
> people to imagine they know it without having taken its works
> seriously, like America.
> (*Stanley Cavell,* Themes Out of School)

Inspirited by both Dada and Cavell—who recounts "rehearsing" his appreciation of Beethoven by learning first to love Jerome Kern's *Swing Time* (RKO, 1936)—I should also disclose less elevated muses.[46] Once upon a time it was academically unseemly to admit popular tastes. Then came media analysis and

Cultural Studies hard upon it—developments open to all manner of transgression. Scholars now can even confess familiarity with "show business"—comparative "show business yesterday" in my case. (I shy away from buzz; my responses are dulled by the sameness of contemporary cutting edges.) Between, for example, Nietzsche's *The Birth of Tragedy* (1872) and Paramount's *The Birth of the Blues* (1941; screenplay by Harry Tugend and Walter DeLeon), I would be sore pressed to choose the more momentous, if invidiously obliged so to do. Nietzsche *invented* an interpretive crossover between Greek drama and Wagner's *Tristan*; perhaps ill-founded, it nevertheless shone. Tugend and DeLeon crossover-interpreted African-American vocalizings and mainstream crooning—in "an easy-going Bing Crosby vehicle roughly based on the formation of Nick LaRocca's Original Dixieland Jazz Band, supposedly the first white group to play black music."[47] Both "births" were and are stupendously controversial appropriations; each merits seriocomic scrutiny of its transfiguring ironies, dilemmas, injustices, sadness, and exuberance. But that's another book, doubtless by another author.[48]

"Where, then, *is* the showbiz in these heteroclite chapters?"—media moguls, postmodern consumers, and all who like their commodity-fetishes full strength might jointly complain. My answer is less evasive than it seems. Showbiz remains just where the anthropology, history, religion, literature, and arts are: dispersed. I concoct no concentrated Showbiz-studies curtained off from other concerns. I hope to avoid both: (1) haughty dismissal of the "culture industry"; (2) in-the-know braggadocio unoutraged by any fashion, however cheeky. Neither a Madonna-watcher nor beset (consciously) with Paglia-envy, this author makes no case for or against triumphal hedonistics.[49]

Instead, readers bump up against showbiz just like anything else in cultural life: Where you find it. "The show business" (a coinage of P. T. Barnum) includes Barnum's own American Museum and comparable displays (Part Two).[50] Showbiz is that "Perry Mason" series that dogged this ethnographer back and forth between Java/Bali and home (Chap. 4). Lévi-Strauss once compared showbiz celebrities—"stars"—to shamans; he threw in psychoanalysts for good measure (Lévi-Strauss 1963: Chap. X). Similarly, a striking Shasta shaman co-stars with Ruth Benedict in this book's Chapter 1; and showbiz became the livelihood of those U-twins clinically diagnosed as "homosexual," whose fate haunts a footnote from Belo's work on Bali (Chap. 3).

More grandly, "show business"—like its companion phenomenon, tourism—riddles the world with commodified practices that are no more extravagant (really) than politics, economics, or religion.[51] Varied show businesses—from *Singspiele*, operetta, and Tin Pan Alley (my personal ticket-selling passions), through MTV, CD-ROM, and the Internet (others' hidden fee-laden bailiwicks)—may be (post)modernity's "rehearsal hall" of and for simulacra. But what does this commonplace—one reaching from, say, Baudrillard back to Baudelaire (and further)—teach us, theoretically?[52] And how do we go about learning it, ethnographically? Time may or may not tell. Meanwhile, show business—like no business I know (or on second thought, like several)—overlaps with what one might call "know business." Indeed, know business ("the knowledge industry"?) may be more like show business ("the culture industry") than many scholars in the know business, long inclined to dismiss show business (Adorno, for example), could bring themselves to acknowledge.[53]

My own fetal exposure to showbiz probably began with the movies Mom and Dad were seeing in 1945–46 (one possibility: *Spellbound*; I never dared ask). My aesthetic preferences barely ripened before movie-land's fall into CinemaScope (1953). (Fans who found this dimensionality depraved even then are bracing themselves as digital TV verges on relapsing, virtually, into elongated screen size.)[54]

No expert in amusement industries—just another consumer of images and sounds—I have nevertheless occasionally commented on cross-cultural representations and various video technologies. Despite my "minimalist" media-savvy, three prior observations of anthropology meeting showbiz may be worth summarizing here.

A book about Lévi-Strauss and French Symbolist poetics paused to salute the then-furthest *Fernsehen*:

> Apollo 11 was sitting on the moon; mankind had made its giant leap. Therefore, a television news reporter was interviewing some Atlanta, Georgia, high school students to gauge their reactions. Of one bright-eyed girl he soberly demanded: "What is this going to do to your religion?" To which she sincerely replied, "Well, I don't know; I suppose if God wants us to go to the moon and back, He'll let us, and if He doesn't, He won't." Then the newsman slyly queried, "What, then, if the men *don't* make it back from the moon?" And the girl pertly concluded, "Well, I don't know; if you don't make it the first time, try, try again!" She smiled sweetly. (Boon 1972: 101–102)

I thought that moment nicely elucidated Lévi-Strauss's notion of "social discourse"—*bricolage* that displaces stultifying impasses. Social discourse converts cumbersome contradictions into alternative bric-a-brac. It may be composed of mythic and totemic fragments or of anthropomorphic cosmologies pieced together with this-worldly clichés. "[It] can even maintain pious moon-shots in the face of divine wrath. . . . Ask *any* native; and, up pops *la pensée sauvage*" (1972: 101–102).

A later book about Bali commented on cinematic devices common to old flicks and newer ethnographic films, or really movies (made for TV, eventually):

> Such "Demillean" restaging of initial contacts is [a] tenacious rhetorical device in the romantic imagery of ethnological literature. Anthropology's counterpart to rhetorical commonplaces (*topoi*, such as "the world upside down" or "boy as old man" [*puer senelis*]) is "captain greets king" or, more recently, "collectivity wel-

comes fieldworker." This latter *topos* remains very much alive [in] a recent television broadcast of a film made of Margaret Mead's return to one of her Pacific
islands for a generation-later restudy. Ms. Mead is rowed up in a boat and the
jubilant natives run out *en masse* to welcome her (evidently, collectively awaited)
return. We are not told how she was concealed while the *other* crew got the beach
camera into position. (Boon 1977: 226; slightly edited)

Showbiz techniques of illusioning "first contact" kept progressing on
through Carl Sagan's wildly popular *Dragons of Eden* (1977). In 1982, I
stooped to tweak the legendary astronomer's bestseller for its pipedream of
interplanetary "easy understanding"—a vision if anything more prevalent today. Sagan's *Dragons* began by citing Darwin's portrayal of Fuegians but
remained oblivious to its ideological distortions. He (Sagan) concluded by
promoting the famous visual icon of the human species, commissioned by
NASA to inform aliens-anonymous about ourselves. My reservations were
expressed this way:

> ... the unacknowledged complexities behind the cross-cultural stereotypes that
> begin [*Dragons of Eden*] might even cast an anthropological shadow over extra-
> terrestrial stereotypes concluding it ... : the highly publicized illustration of a
> man and a woman *au naturel*, duly measured, his hand raised in greeting to some
> unknown recipient of their intended message.... (Boon 1982a: 42)

Sagan dramatized his marvelous mission with a universalizing "humanistic"
question: "Could [the icon's] significance ... be deduced by beings with very
different biologies?" Having confirmed that the waving hand can be decoded
by a token terrestrial "other" (today's Sioux), Sagan never slowed down
enough to wonder truly whether the *whole image*—touted as the "first artifact
of mankind to leave the solar system"—would necessarily communicate as
intended even to earthily different eras and uncoached cultures. My critique
reasoned as follows:

> The picture of earthlings transmitted by the *Pioneer 10 and 11* spacecraft was
> fabricated with Enlightenment-like simplicity, "in what is hoped is easily under-
> stood scientific language," to convey "some information on the locale, epoch, and
> nature of the builders of the spacecraft." Let us imagine, however, that the mes-
> sage is received according to conventions that have in fact divided earthlings
> (with the same biology). Merely imagine that, unlike the native of NASA, ex-
> traterrestrials employ interpretive codes no more alien or exotic than those found
> in extra-Enlightenment hermeneutics. If so, NASA's message would "communi-
> cate" that earthlings (evidently childless and naked) are, of all things, innocent
> prelapsarians. Imagine now *their* surprise, if ever they should land! (Boon 1982a:
> 42; slightly edited)

I reiterate a dated commentary for its possibly renewed relevance, now tha
hopes of interspace communication intersect with "hypes" of cyberspace com-

munication. On the information highway too, I see no "easy understanding" in the offing; an old adage in Boasian irony may still obtain:

> Earth's own diversity of cultures (and eras) is as mind-bending as a speculative diversity of natures. . . . Contemporary *philosophes* [like to imagine] that communication across galaxies [and Internet*s*] might be simpler, more direct, less symbolically contorted than communication across cultures. "Shades," snorts the anthropologist, "of science fiction." (Boon 1982a: 43)

Shades as well, I would add today, of show business-then, Sagan-style.[55]

My earlier attention to TV broadcasts (of moon shots), movie-illusions (of Mead), and commercialized sciences of communication intensifies in this book's leaps and jolts among popular culture, ethnography, history, religion, etc. With theorists who demur at this *mélange*, I partly sympathize: Showbiz should give pause. But with scholars who, loftily *sérieux*, persist in eschewing evidence of commodity-life, I grow impatient. Everyday tastes and commercial expenditures clearly matter on the global scene. On the other hand, I too question media analysts (and ethnographers aping them) who assume that consumption and its promotions matter *most*. The composite difficulty is that popular marketing and media matter *too*—along with longed-for revolution, varieties of religious conversion, psychologies of abjection, relentless bureaucratization, the handover of Hong Kong, a little *höchste Lust*, and bio-power— to list just a few of history's dynamic openings and constrictions.[56] Yes indeed, showbiz matters too.

Part One

RITUALS, REREADING, RHETORICAL TURNS

Some old Elizabethan play or poem contains the lines:

> . . . Who reads me, when I am ashes,
> Is my son in wishes . . . .

The relationship, between reader and writer, of son and father, may have
existed in Queen Elizabeth's time, but is much too close to be true for
ours. The utmost that any writer could hope of his readers now is that they
should consent to regard themselves as nephews, and even then he would
expect only a more or less civil refusal from most of them. Indeed, if he
had reached a certain age, he would have observed that nephews, as a
social class, no longer read at all. . . . Finally, the metre does not
permit it. One may not say: 'Who reads me, when I am ashes,
is my nephew in wishes.'
The same objections do not apply to the word 'niece.' The change restores
the verse, and, to a very great degree, the fact. Nieces have been known to
read in early youth, and in some cases may have read their uncles. The
relationship, too, is convenient and easy, capable of being anything or
nothing, at the will of either party, like a Mohammedan or Polynesian or
American marriage. No valid objection can be offered to this change in
the verse. Niece let it be! . . . . The uncle talks: . . . .
(*Henry Adams,* Mont Saint Michel and Chartres, *1904*)

Fig. 2. An 18-year-old Balinese (in this case male) inclined to trance, visited by a deceased uncle who designated him as ritual officiant for his metal-smith kingroup (*pande besi*); here the youth presides at his first ceremony. (Author's photo, 1972)

Fig. 3 An elderly Brahmana woman, also a ritual specialist, by virtue of her celibacy and reputedly minimal menstrual pollution. (Author's photo, 1972)

CHAPTER ONE

Re Menses: Rereading
Ruth Benedict, Ultraobjectively

Objective . . . existing only in relation to a knowing subject or willing
    agent . . . belonging to the sensible world and being intersubjectively
    observable.

Ultra- . . . going beyond others, or beyond due limit: extreme; beyond
    what is ordinary, proper, or moderate: excessively.

Read . . . to discover by interpreting outward expression or signs . . . to
    attribute a meaning.

Re- . . . again, anew, back, backward. . . .
                         (*Webster's New Collegiate*)

Règles . . . Syn. de menstrues
                    (*Petit Larousse*)

Menstrues . . . Menstrua, periods, menses, catamenia; (*fam.*) monthlies
                 (*Cassell's French Dictionary*)

INTERPRETIVE ARTS in cultural anthropology have conventionally been declared too "subjective" by champions of experimental methods that isolate
proper "objects" for disinterested observation and controlled verification. A
standard countercharge by "hermeneutic types" is that positivistic dismissal of
interpretation fails its own tests: Models of objectivity distinguished from "the
subjective" are reductionist; methodological abstraction suppresses evidence
of concrete ambiguities from diagnoses that fantasize tidy hypotheses and rigorous results.[1]

    I side with interpretive skepticism regarding objectivity in cultural matters.
However, far from simply disavowing "objectivity," I object to narrow positivism in hopes of a fuller objectivity (perhaps I do so subjectively). One could
call the beast "ultraobjectivity"—which *Webster's* helps me (ambiguously)
define as that which is "intersubjectively observable" in the "extreme . . . beyond what is ordinary, proper." Other names for the beast exist, including
"radical empiricism" in William James's sense.[2] Regardless, any reader may
press toward ultraobjectivity (variably denominated) by revisiting intensive
representations of cross-cultural comparison.

    Whatever one's science, craft, or art, strenuous rereading may augment
doubt rather than achieve any certainty. Salutary doubt springs from empirical

and textual details of intricate social, political, and linguistic configurations. Doubt flourishes in circumstances of conflictual *translation*—the very circumstances where anthropology transpires. That is a fancy, rather than plain, "objective fact"; one might even call it extra-Vagant. This fancy-fact consigns fieldworkers (plus those they read and those who read them) to a fate of continual interpretation. Why, then, should scientists, or humanists, or those opposing either, regret this fate or wish life's perplexing rituals (including rereading) to be otherwise?[3]

To advance anthropological tasks of ritual rereading, this essay explores neglected twists in a canonical text, Ruth Benedict's *Patterns of Culture*. Benedict herself sometimes approached rituals as "readings" of experience by practitioners of distinctive cultures. She also read other challenging thinkers: Nietzsche for one, Jane Belo for another (who herself interpreted that much-studied place, Bali, Indonesia). Benedict, moreover, cited Margaret Mead's findings from Samoa early on in a guarded, yet generous way; they helped fill out her comparative patterns of duress in rites of passage. We shall see that Belo flatly challenged Mead's claims about Balinese mothers, when Mead was still very much around to respond; yet the living Mead continued to "nurture" Belo professionally.

Ruth Benedict, Jane Belo, and Margaret Mead—following Franz Boas— considered themselves scientists of sorts, as do I. Benedict and Belo's ideas about cultural research may be more adequate than those of Mead's tardy adversaries—Derek Freeman, most tenaciously. Her detractors tend to imply that findings from a given culture—Samoa, and so on—can be restudied and definitively disproved or verified (an assumption to which Mead herself was not immune). The livid literature still swirling around Freeman's "desecration" of the dead Mead can be surveyed in H. Caton's *The Samoa Reader: Anthropologists Take Stock*. I find this collection loaded (rather than objective), because it assumes the central issue to be "cultural determinism," which the editor reifies into something that theory is either for or against. Subtler standards of evidentiary parodox—pertaining to "Samoa," "science," "description," etc.—are available in studies by I. Brady, B. Shore, and other work underrepresented in the Caton volume.[4]

If the opinion I have just tendered makes readers suspect this author of pro-Mead/anti-Freeman sentiments, that very response reveals how reductive polarizations thrive on polemics waged in the name of "objectivity." Ultra-objective reading tries to weather these storms, occasionally parodies its own complicity in them, and trusts that they will blow themselves out . . . eventually.

Unlike Freeman (or Tessel Pollmann, whose attack on Mead's work in Bali I counterattack below), both Benedict and Belo found Mead's analyses susceptible of different construals, even without contrary evidence. That profound inkling of multiplicity also reverberates in Benedict's hints that her own arts of interpretation resembled those of cultures that she "intersubjectively observed." Or so I construe her.

ÜBER BENEDICT

In *Other Tribes, Other Scribes* (1982)—an off-beat book modeled in part on Ruth Benedict's syncopations—I suggested that *Patterns of Culture*, never pat, quivers between diversity and integration to the end. In *Affinities and Extremes* (1990), I emphasized ironies of Benedict's influence on Gregory Bateson's *Naven* and Mead's *Sex and Temperament*. Sensitive studies by R. Handler (1986, 1990), B. Babcock (1986), and others have accentuated different complexities of Benedict; C. Geertz (1987) has elaborated her Swiftian sense of "own culture" contrasted among other "others." Benedict's ever-shifting effects on her readers may spring from our tendencies to misremember how her writing "configures" its own reception. That is the hunch developed here.

I began repeatedly teaching *Patterns of Culture* (1934), *The Chrysanthemum and the Sword* (1948), and Benedict's letters and poems twenty-four long years ago (Oh, Lord). A persistent response, by lay students and professional scholars alike, never ceases to arouse my curiosity. Readers in the midst of *Patterns of Culture*—proceeding phrase to phrase and page by page—may savor the quivering style and substance. Yet, once emerged from our experience, we cannot re-cognize that quality after the fact. *Remembering having read* Benedict, we make her arguments and writing more centered, measured, balanced—yea, more "Apollonian"—than would have been observed in the actual reading thereof. What might "explain" this counterempirical fact of forgetful-remembering?

One likely culprit is those dichotomous frameworks borrowed by Benedict from other authors, whose slogans govern all too well how readers assimilate her shifting cross-cultural judgments. An example is Nietzsche's famous formulation of Apollonian/Dionysian (balanced/intoxicated) that Benedict culls from his *Birth of Tragedy*, which dates from the time he still championed Richard Wagner.[5] Benedict stipulates that Nietzsche helps her foreground "major qualities that differentiate Pueblo culture [Zuni] from those of other American Indians" (1934: 79). Phrased this way, her demonstration implies differential emphases across cultures, not essential identities.

Benedict eases Nietzsche's diametric contrast onstage in a gradual and qualified way. Apollonian versus Dionysian joins her other framing devices for contrastive configurations: *Gestalt*, *Struktur*, Dilthey's idealist *Weltanschauungen*, Spengler's Apollonian and Faustian extremes (designated by

Benedict "opposed interpretations of existence"); and most lyrically, Edward Carpenter's tag for a hopelessly extroverted West "endlessly catching its trains" (55). Benedict thus catalogues, as I see it, an "arc of configurations" *of* concepts of configuration. Among such possibilities, she accents Nietzsche's "eternal contradiction," employing it heuristically to highlight dramatic contrasts in cultures and their rituals.[6]

Benedict's emphasis on "selection" stems from the linguistics of Edward Sapir, a key ingredient of her work and life:

> It is in cultural life as it is in speech: selection is the prime necessity. (23)
> The great arc along which all the possible human behaviors are distributed is far too immense and too full of contradictions for any one culture to utilize even any considerable portion of it. Selection is the first requirement. Without selection no culture could even achieve intelligibility. . . . (237)[7]

Benedict too interpretively *selects* Nietzsche's notion from a fuller array of philosophical and literary visions. She need not delve deeply into Nietzsche's work (much less into Wagner's work, into which Nietzsche had deeply delved). Rather, Apollonian/Dionysian serves as a "positional" dichotomy; its sides are never dialectically resolved by Benedict, as they were in Nietzsche's *Birth of Tragedy* on its way to Wagner:

> The effects wrought by the *Dionysian* also seemed "titanic" and "barbaric" to the Apollinian Greek; while at the same time he could not conceal from himself that he, too, was inwardly related to these overthrown Titans and heroes. Indeed, he had to recognize even more than this: despite all its beauty and moderation, his entire existence rested on a hidden substratum of suffering and of knowledge, revealed to him by the Dionysian. And behold: Apollo could not live without Dionysus! The "titanic" and the "barbaric" were in the last analysis as necessary as the Apollinian. . . .
>
>   Contradiction, the bliss born of pain, spoke out from the very heart of nature. . . . (1977 [1872, 1886]: 46)

Also sprach Nietzsche, or early Nietzsche engulfed by Wagner's music-drama, a fulsome dialectic that Benedict never quotes thusly.

Again, Benedict restricted her use of Nietzsche in ethnographic matters, although he conceivably may have meant more to her personally ("subjectively").[8] Yet, despite the fact that Nietzsche's duality is presented as just one among many possible themes, we readers retrospectively fixate on the diametrics, rather than the multiple field that spirits them forth, so to speak. Benedict's study tends to be remembered as the Apollonian/Dionysian ("Let's see, was that Zuni/Kwakiutl?") book. This is a fact of readers' response that I have observed objectively—and a contradiction ("bliss born of pain?") that I, a re-reader, am longing to understand ultraobjectively.

Another aspect of *Patterns of Culture* may aggravate matters: the text's eloquence—an uncustomary attribute of anthropological prose, certainly now and even then, when Benedict wrote.[9] Her sentences, paragraphs, and chapters configure movements to closure that end by transfiguring the very contents conveyed. Conclusions to the controversial Zuni chapter, for example, round off as follows:

> Like their version of man's relation to other men, their version of man's relation to the cosmos gives no place to heroism and man's will to overcome obstacles. It has not sainthood for those who,
>
> > Fighting, fighting, fighting,
> > Die driven against the wall.
>
> It has its own virtues, and they are singularly consistent. The ones that are out of place they have outlawed from their universe. They have made, in one small but long-established cultural island in North America, a civilization whose forms are dictated by the typical choices of the Apollonian, all of whose delight is in formality and whose way of life is the way of measure and of sobriety. (129)

By "eloquence" I intend Benedict's own "way of measured" prose, her careful cadences of rhythmic repetitions: "of life . . . of measure . . . and of sobriety."

A seemingly opposite but somehow similar closure occurs at the other, Dionysian extreme of Benedict's focal cases.[10] Despite her insistence on ambivalences of Dionysian "double aspects" ("at once death-bringers and saviors from disease," she declares them), readers tend rather to recall startling negatives of her textual curtain ringing down the Kwakiutl chapter proper:

> The megalomaniac paranoid trend is a definite danger in our society. It faces us with a choice of possible attitudes. One is to brand it as abnormal and reprehensible, and is the attitude we have chosen in our civilization. The other extreme is to make it the essential attribute of ideal man, and this is the solution in the culture of the Northwest Coast. (222)

My long years of striving to teach Benedict reveal that her arresting comparison and compound declarative sentence inhibit students from attending to matters covered in six subsequent pages, still describing Kwakiutl, but slipped into the next chapter, "The Nature of Society."

There Benedict resorts again to Boasian issues of variability rather than integral wholes (even *comparatively* constituted ones). Her crisp discussion and its notes emphasize historical dislocations of Kwakiutl from Salish lands to Vancouver Island. She outlines apparent shifts in patterns of residence and inheritance and discusses possible conflicts between earlier conditions and later matrilineal adjustments. Such dimensions are the very ones that Benedict's critics often have accused her of neglecting. She even warns against mistaking her Zuni/Kwakiutl contrast as the "Procrustean bed of some catch-word characterization" (228), but to little avail. What readers process—or rather, what processes readings—is that overdrawn duality that reinforces an unshakeable impression of closure projected onto chapters that are actually no more "integral" than the cultures they represent.

At the risk of sounding suspiciously insistent, let me belabor my interpretive crux. Readers of Benedict "really" encounter a manifold, dislocated text about manifold, dislocated cultural processes. But our recall of that experience selectively reduces the devices her discourse unleashes; we retrospectively tidy up topics that actually spill over boundaries of chapters less rounded-off than her style of prose leads us to remember. Readers thus commit a perhaps inevitable "misreading" (a term I borrow with trepidation from Harold Bloom and those anxiously influenced by him).[11] "Misreading" should not be misread as simply an inaccurate reading. Rather, misreading, as it pertains to Benedict, implies ex post facto "correction" of heterogeneous, irregular experience into exaggerated pattern—a process reminiscent of the process Benedict reveals in extreme rituals.

The way a reader's memory bestows form on Benedict's presentations thus resembles those heightened performances—Zuni prayers, Dobu sorcery, Kwakiutl Cannibal dancing—that afford her interpretive entrees into cross-cultural configurations. After all, if reading—or (mis)remembering-having-read—is not a ritual, what is it? Our misreading Benedict inadvertently adds another case in point to her demonstration that rites convert subtly shifting multiplicities into bolder contrasts. How fitting, then, that readers cannot quite deflect Apollonian/Dionysian dualities from memories of Benedict's descriptive accounts that were—ultraobjectively—not so confined by them as we seem to recall.

One aspect of Benedict's study that explicitly "decentered" her Nietzschean dichotomy derived from the way she stitched together contrastive cases. Benedict literally displaced any Apollonian-Zuni/Dionysian-Kwakiutl diametrics by inserting *Patterns of Cultures'* critical Dobu chapter, summarized from Reo Fortune's book. Let me try to recollect how her triangulated ethnographies worked.

The Dobu of Melanesia represent a third typological extreme, figured against Zuni on the one hand and Kwakiutl on the other. Dobu sorcery and alternating matrilocality contrast with: 1) Zuni priesthood and strong matrilineality; and 2) Kwakiutl shamanism and a transitional stage of transmitting privileges via the maternal uncle (short of outright corporate matrilineages). A further, finer weave of contrasts tightens her Native American and Melanesian comparisons as well, which accentuate variations among Zuni/Hopi/Navaho/Apache and Kwakiutl/Salish/Haida, respectively. Even in her more concentrated Dobu chapter, that culture's extreme configuration of "limited good"—whereby "any man's gain is another's loss" (146)—is juxtaposed with the different ethos of Trobrianders, trading partners with Dobu in the famous *kula* ring documented by Malinowski.[12]

I call these finer gradations "chromatic"; they are little noticed in readers' "diatonic" recall (see Chap. 3). Nor in my teaching experience does Benedict's axis of comparison between Kwakiutl and Dobu register resoundingly, despite her occasional judgments borrowed from lexicons of psychopathology: Kwakiutl "paranoia" and Dobuan "jealousy" (the latter term evokes an ethos of marriage bonds organized as competitive relationships). Neither Benedict's schemes of multiple variations nor her unfortunate diagnostic labels for Dobu and Kwakiutl dispel readers' fantasies that her shifting text—actually covering many sides of social organization and ritual practice—simply fleshes out a singular dualism, filched from a mad philosopher. Even when readers do manage to remember past an Apollonian/Dionysian (Zuni/Kwakiutl) dichotomy to the Dobu and Kwakiutl axis, we fixate on the sensational (doubtless ethnocentric) psychologistic emblems rather than the quiddities in Benedict's account. Again, I base these observations on my teaching experience.

Fleetingly, then, a rereading may help remind us that Benedict does not fundamentally brand cultures as psychotic or even neurotic. Rather, she unfolds demonstrations of rituals effecting a relative semblance of coherence. She argues that cultural "integration" is ordered LIKE a psychosis is ordered (275). The force of the simile is paramount (and musical, I find): any culture's "normality" is configured as a field of contradictions held together by reinforced replications of pattern, but also by bold opposition to alternatives implicitly resisted: Zuni/not-Apache, nor even Hopi; Dobu/not-Trobriand; Kwakiutl/not Salish nor Haidalike (although becoming more "matrilineal"). Rereading Benedict may help us remember—momentarily, at least, before repression sets in—that her text compares any culture's patterning to "complexes" conceivably deemed deviant in another culture.

The term "complex" nowadays tends to carry technical undertones associated with Jungian analytical psychology.[13] But I am using it more generally, as Jane Belo did when she described the "puppet complex" in Balinese aesthetics, sensibilities, and shadow-selves:

> The puppet complex, then, could be summed up thus: A puppet is that which represents a spirit. Plays are originally representations of nonhuman spirits. By dramatic connotation, actors and dancers are like puppets, for they behave in accordance with a spirit which is not their own. By connotation of the mystery of life and death, a baby is like a puppet, for it is mysteriously imbued with a spirit. Conversely, a puppet is like a baby, for it is small and lovable, its ways are unaccountable. Little children make the best, the most puppetlike dancers.
>
> When people went in trance, they would behave like children. They would cry, call out to father and mother, express urgent and unpredictable desires, and would not be quieted until these desires were satisfied. Being like gods, they would

behave like children. In some way the gods themselves are children. (Belo 1960: 11–13)

Belo's superb summary strikes me as an exemplarily ultraobjective moment in Balinese ethnography—which topic will enter this essay on Benedict directly.

Meanwhile, I fear that my rereading of Benedict may by now impress readers as wanting to propose a correct interpretation, rather than to imagine ways of displacing inevitable misreadings. Paradoxically, however, I can only offer evanescent rereadings remembering Benedict's text—ones striving, but likely failing, to grow less governed by the centering effects of her eloquence or by that Apollonian/Dionysian dichotomy. Attuned to that ultrobjective motive, I turn now to manifest strategies behind *Patterns of Culture* and to fragmentary ritual practices featured in Benedict's semi-thick descriptions.

ENDLESSLY CATCHING HER DRIFTS

Patterns of Culture grew out of Benedict's review of American Indian vision quests, which were largely but not exclusively male. She drew on several approaches: diffusionist studies, pioneering Boasian surveys by Robert Lowie, and related work by Alfred Kroeber. But unlike those efforts, Benedict extended her comparisons even to the marked *absence* of individualized ritual ordeals and ecstatic suffering. To include Zuni—significant for lacking vision quests—creates a kind of survey-plus: configurations with a difference, pursued across negative ethnographic examples and contrary cases. Benedict liked things multiple, as well as "wildly irregular."[14]

Apparently forgotten, or at best passingly observed, by critics of *Patterns* are hints of a parallel survey of another ritual topos—menstruation (26).[15] Benedict announces the topic of girls' puberty by sketching various rites of passage that display dramatic practices of purity/pollution: first, Carrier Indians who figuratively bury alive novice menstruaters, isolating them for three years; second, Apache attitudes about first menses as occasions for supernatural sources of beneficial cure. Benedict at once complicates comparisons with a paragraph on Australian boys, subjected to ordeals of subincision, one of the most elaborate genital operations documented in ethnography. She rounds off her minisurvey with Mead's then-recent news from Samoa that "natural turbulence" need not accompany female adolescence, that institutionalized stress during sexual maturation is not universal.

I can confirm that wildly diverse readers—advocating everything from cultural interpretation to sociobiology—tend to retain from Benedict's intricate paragraphs only their "relativism," thus obscuring her precise mode of comparative composition. Her text multiplies empirical cases, including apparently polar ones; after plotting the striking three-way opposition of menstruation practices that set off Carrier/Apache/Samoa, she fairly inserts evidence about male ordeals. Her approach entails not a washed-out relativism but intensified, manifold extremes. (I have tried to emulate Benedict's interpretive devices, only to be dis(re)membered in turn by preferentially "objective" readers and misremembered by more ultraobjective ones, myself included.)[16]

Benedict drew on the strongest part of Mead's Samoan study to illustrate cultures where menstruation is not endowed with ritual significance. However, she need not have mentioned Mead or Samoa at all, because the most pertinent example of a decided absence of public trauma around menses is Zuni. Although the contrast among Carrier, Apache, and Zuni is never stipulated explicitly by Benedict, its implications are dispersed throughout her book. Zuni is key comparatively for lacking ritual ordeals of *both* vision quests and menstrual pollution-seclusion. This distinctive Pueblo configuration thus stands out thematically ("Apollonian") and ethnographically in a double respect. Benedict eventually drives the point home 100 pages after saluting Samoa, a bare 17 shapely paragraphs from the end of her Zuni chapter:

> Their handling of menstruation is especially striking because all about them are tribes who have at every encampment small houses for the menstruating woman. . . . The Pueblos not only have no menstrual huts, but they do not surround women with precautions at this time. The catamenial periods make no difference in a woman's life. (120)

It is against this dramatic dearth among Zuni (and Samoans too) that the Kwakiutl appear in strongest contrast. To my mind the contrast is more than diametric; it is downright dialectical. Unlike Zuni, Kwakiutl accentuate Dionysian excess; they also accentuate menstruation, but for male as well as female protagonists. (That particular switch I call the dialectical part.)[17]

Benedict gathers evidence of ritual reversals in a section on Kwakiutl "Cannibal dancing"—developed from Boas's and George Hunt's materials—which documents vivid ideas of pollution under the sign of menstruation. Following an adroit allusion to the contrasting ethos of "Oceanic epicurean cannibalism," Benedict portrays Kwakiutl practices without explicitly designating menstrual rites an underlying issue. But she should not really need to; objectively (or really, ultraobjectively), the relevant details are there for the reading. Not only are first menses of daughters occasions for potlatch redistribution (244), but initiates into the Cannibal society were exorcized of their frenzy with smoke from cedar bark stained with the "menstrual blood of four women of the highest rank." A four-month tabu imposed on the male Cannibal dancer isolated him in a polluted state, complete with techniques of mediation:

> He used special utensils for eating and they were destroyed at the end of the period. He drank always ceremonially, never taking but four mouthfuls at a time, and never touching his lips to the cup. He had to use a drinking-tube and a head-

scratcher. For a shorter period he was forbidden all warm food. When the period of his seclusion was over . . . he feigned to have forgotten all the ordinary ways of life. He had to be taught to walk, to speak, to eat. . . . he was still sacrosanct. He might not approach his wife for a year, nor gamble, nor do any work. Traditionally he remained aloof for four years. (179)

Benedict neglects to indicate that these very utensils were specifically required in menstrual huts throughout Native American cultures—again, Zuni excepted.

Variable practices ranging across New World menstrual codes have since been traced in Lévi-Strauss's *Origin of Table Manners*, where he compares European ideologies of education to Native American ethics for governing the proprieties of daughters. Here is just one summary from Lévi-Strauss's empirical demonstration throughout 2200 pages of *Mythologiques*:

. . . the veil lifts to reveal a vast mythological system common to both South and North America, and in which the subjection of women is the basis of the social order. We can now understand the reason for this. The human wife's parents-in-law are not content just to present her with domestic utensils and to teach her the correct way to use them. The old man also proceeds to carry out a veritable physiological shaping of his daughter-in-law. In her pristine innocence, she did not have monthly periods and gave birth suddenly and without warning. [According to the myths] the transition from nature to culture demands that the feminine organism should become periodic, since the social as well as the cosmic order would be endangered by a state of anarchy in which regular alternation of day and night, the phases of the moon, feminine menstruation, the fixed period for pregnancy and the course of the seasons did not mutually support each other.

So it is as periodic creatures that [according to the myths] women are in danger of disrupting the orderly working of the universe. Their social insubordination, often referred to in the myths, is an anticipation in the form of the 'reign of women' of the infinitely more serious danger of their physiological insubordination. Therefore, women have to be subjected to *règles*. (Lévi-Strauss 1978: 221–22)

Although Lévi-Strauss proved a devoted rereader of Boas's (and Benedict's) work, he made no mention in this regard of Kwakiutl variations and inversions.[18]

Benedict's chapter shows that Kwakiutl, whether regularly or in historical crisis, ritually phased their practices into an extreme dialectical form. I interpret that form as the equivalent of hyperperiodicity, ultramenstrual cycles. (Hyper- and ultra- both translate *über*.) The striking Cannibal dancer himself is ritually treated as superfemale—overly secluded, too much mediated, extra-regulated—but with the gender sign reversed. Perhaps one could designate this exaggeratedly Dionysian role an *Überfrau*—Ultrawoman? Still nervously re-

membering that Benedict read Nietzsche, I also recall that topsy-turvy ritual
configurations—or their extra-Vagant fragments—have time and again been
shown by ethnographers and historians to link cultural continuity with historical conflict and extreme duress. It is just such conflict and duress that the
Kwakiutl themselves were likely living out—long before Franz Boas and
George Hunt wrote—and Ruth Benedict after them, and I (among so many
others) after her.

Again, turning Benedict's book page by page and case by case, we readers
encounter dispersed defamiliarizations of menstruation; but we tend then to
erase them. To my knowledge *Patterns of Culture* has seldom been commemorated for its insights into distinctions of gender, figured across diverse ritual
extremes, including the Kwakiutl. Readers' blindness to such available insights may stem in part from the book's paucity of information on Northwest
Coast womens' lives—apart from techniques of salmon pressing (a detail that
I sheepishly retain from my first skimming of *Patterns* during early adolescence—wasn't it?).[19]

Our reading-recall perhaps "screens," as some psychoanalysts might say,
ultraobjective images of male Cannibal menstruators; Benedict's contents are
processed, or mangled, into the equivalent of an "objective" index—a technique of labeling that irons out the outlandish. To understand better what I
mean, consider this actual fragment from the real index of *Patterns of Culture*:

MAGIC Dobu . . . Zuni
MAIDU California
MALINOWSKI, B.
MANUS
MARRIAGE (nine subentries)
MEAD, Margaret
MEDICINE Charms (Dobu) . . . Societies (Zuni)
MENSTRUATION Zuni [*Punkt* . . . the sole subentry!]
MENTAL HYGIENE, Western
MEXICO, Northern, religious alcohol, whirling dance
   (See also Aztecs)
MIDDLETOWN . . . (289)

This apparently innocent index omits (of all entries) reference to Kwakiutl
under "menstruation." Deceptive index-makers (like us misremembering readers) have virtually censored emphasis on menstrual seclusion that Benedict's
text disperses in evidence of Northwest Coast ritual inversions. (Recall as well
that the Kwakiutl chapter, once juxtaposed with the Zuni, was displaced to
third position by the inserted Dobu chapter.) Readers and index-makers alike
inadvertently expurgate—indeed, "Apollonianize"—even Benedict's description of Kwakiutl Cannibal dancing—one of the more palpable evocations of
Dionysian transgressive intoxication available from the literature called an-

thropology. I am trying to reread this outlandishly factual literature ultraobjectively (and extra-Vagantly), rather than indexing it toward any particular *cause*, agenda, or alternative ecstasy.

I ask again: Does Benedict's eloquence—even when presenting hypermenstruating men—cancel our capacity to retain what our acts of reading "experience"? Does her prose effectively configure our recollection into Apollonian forms? And does the same phenomenon occur with the Shasta shaman in the final chapter—a no less Dionysian figure (female this time), also reconfigured into Apollonian form, if remembered at all?

The Shasta woman takes center stage just after Benedict's famous section on homosexuality, *berdache* transvestism, and male/female role reversals—something of a relativist brief for impassioned tolerance. The Shasta, although alluded to earlier in *Patterns*, serves finally to close the elaborate parentheses opened by Benedict with the Digger Indian chief (a Christian, by the way), whose haunting proverb (reproduced in her Chapter 2) also provides the book's initial epigraph and sustained feeling-tone: "Our cup is broken now." In a rare, quasi-dialogic moment, Benedict portrays the Digger chief speaking directly to the author:

> A Chief of the Digger Indians, as the Californians call them, talked to me a great deal about the ways of his people in the old days. . . . When he talked of the shamans who had transformed themselves into bears . . . , his hands trembled and his voice broke with excitement." (21)[20]

That quavering tone recurs and intensifies with the Shasta shaman who—although known to Benedict only through Roland Dixon's 1907 study—is made to sound immediate, full-voiced, and utterly personal. Neither trance nor catalepsis is ever pretty, even if "honored in the extreme," as among women in Shasta culture. Benedict, having only encountered this speaker in print and translation, nevertheless inscribes her possession possessingly; I can only paraphrase fragments of her moving passages:

> The imagined voices commanding she sing or be shot.
> The dreams of grizzly bears, free falls, and swarming yellow jackets.
> The violent moaning transposed to spirit's songs, until blood oozed from her mouth.
> Seizure at the threshold of death.

Following what I hope readers will forgive my calling Benedict's ultraobjective evocation of yet another *Überfrau*, she intones a blessing-like rounding-off:

> From this time on she had in her body a visible materialization of her spirit's power, an icycle-like object which in her dances thereafter she would exhibit, producing it from one part of her body and returning it to another part. From this time on she continued to validate her supernatural power by further cataleptic

demonstrations and she was called upon in great emergencies of life and death for curing and for divination and for counsel. She became, in other words, by this procedure a woman of great power and importance. (267)

This charismatic Shasta—truly extra-Vagant—may receive preferred treatment from Benedict, if any voice did; but the point would be hard to prove. Nor did Benedict flatly favor Zuni culture over others, as many readers like to imagine or would prefer. I quote her:

> Certainly, it is said, exploitation of others in personal relations and overweening claims of the ego are bad whereas absorption in group activities is good; a temper is good that seeks satisfaction neither in sadism nor in masochism and is willing to live and let live. A social order, however, which like Zuni standardizes this "good" is far from Utopian. It manifests likewise the defects of its virtues. It has no place, for instance, for dispositions we are accustomed to value highly, such as force of will or personal initiative or the disposition to take up arms against a sea of troubles. It is incorrigibly mild. (246)

Benedict's judgments—even, I suspect, of her preferred Shasta—keep quivering as her prose keeps reverberating. Objective readers may dream of knowing exactly what Benedict (and Shasta shaman) meant; ultraobjective readers more realistically rest content to dwell precisely on textual and contextual particulars revealing, and palpably, how difficult such knowledge is to gain.

I have been asking whether we can read Benedict's readings (of other's readings, including Roland Dixon's) in a way that remembers both the eloquence of her prose and the descriptions of distress that her style ends (as received) by smoothing over. I desire to keep reading Benedict as she apparently read Zuni (from speaking with them), Shasta (from reading of them), and others, too—including Nietzsche, Virginia Woolf, and Japanese culture. How Benedict doubtless misread the 1924 mistranslation of Nietzsche's *Birth of Tragedy* at her disposal, would open into dialectics too contorted for an essay-*étude*, or perhaps even for a gargantuan tome. How Benedict read Virginia Woolf would swamp us in *The Waves*, which Benedict happened to be perusing when writing *Patterns*.[21] How Benedict read Japanese culture she generously discloses when setting forth interpretive tactics in *The Chrysanthemum and the Sword*, a work initiated in wartime and profoundly mindful of political realities:

> The study of comparative religions has flourished only when men were secure enough in their own conviction to be unusually generous. They might be Jesuits or Arabic savants or unbelievers, but they could not be zealots. The study of comparative cultures too cannot flourish when men are so defensive about their own way of life that it appears to them to be by definition the sole solution in the world. . . .
>
>   In studying Japan, I was the heir of many students. Descriptions of small details of life were tucked away in antiquarian papers. Unlike many Oriental people they

have a great impulse to write themselves out. They wrote about the trivia of their lives as well as about their programs of world expansion. They were amazingly frank. Of course they did not present the whole picture. No people does. . . .

I read this literature as Darwin says he read when he was working out his theories on the origin of species, noting what I had not the means to understand. What would I need to know to understand the juxtaposition of ideas in a speech in the Diet? What could lie back of their violent condemnation of some act that seemed venial and their easy acceptance of one that seemed outrageous? I read, asking the ever-present question: What is "wrong with this picture?" What would I need to know to understand it?

I went to movies, too. . . . (1948: 5, 7)[22]

But can Benedict's successors ever manage to read Benedict this way too, along with such cultures as she inscribed (including her own)—resisting zealotry (and reductive objectivity), even while adverse political circumstances keep engulfing the present (as they did the past)? Can we interpret Benedict, and can "other" cultures interpret each "other," generously yet critically, seeking what is wrong with the picture? What does a reader need to know—and I don't mean just "biographically"—to understand Benedict's text resulting from her readings? To do unto Benedict and each other what she does unto Kwakiutl/Zuni/Dobu/Digger/Shasta/US—that would be my ultraobjective motive of and for periodic cycles of *règles de relire*.

AND BELO

Obliquely implementing the "rubric" just coined, this essay now verges on Jane Belo, as promised, if only to recover from manifest overinvolvement with Benedict. Belo may have matched Benedict in personal complexities and possibly surpassed her in psychological frailty. Moreover, Belo related to Benedict, and Benedict to her, as each other's—hold onto your hats—reader. Belo was an ethnographer *extraordinaire* of Balinese culture; in 1949 she published intricate work on Bali's celebrated witch dance (*Rangda and Barong*), which Benedict had read the year of her death. In fact, Belo's book thanks Professor Ruth Benedict "who patiently went over the original material and whose deep understanding of culture was an inspiration to all who knew her" (Belo 1949: v).[23]

Belo's later *Trance in Bali* (1960) refers to Benedict's demonstrations that "personality trends considered abnormal in our culture may be highly valued in another culture and therefore are considered *no longer abnormal*;" and Belo adds:

Ruth Benedict, who made the classical distinction between Apollonian and Dionysian configurations of culture, went over our material with great care and came to the conclusion that the distinction could not be applied to Balinese culture. Their customary poise and moderation resembles the Apollonian, while the outbreak into trance, approved and recognized in the culture, is nearer to the Dionysian." (Belo 1960: 6, 1)

Trance in Bali also credits Margaret Mead (and Gregory Bateson) with showing Belo the light of culture and personality theory; they inspired her to convert to "proper" fieldwork methods, even to techniques of clocked documentation. Belo thus appreciated Mead from the start; and Mead was her benefactor during tragically crazy political circumstances in wartime Bali (discussed in Chap. 3).

But Belo's 1949 study—the very one that Benedict patiently went over—had taken exception to Margaret Mead's views on Balinese women, mothers in particular. There Belo rather sharply rejects Mead's view of Rangda as the Balinese "Mother Figure representative of the total feeling toward the mother," extended in a substitution "carried over into adulthood until the young man looks forward to marrying a girl who will turn into a witch;" Belo argues instead:

> Rangda serves only as a representation of the fear aspect of the Mother Figure. There is a split in the feeling toward the mother, the destructive, witchlike, devouring, and deathly side of her represented in the Rangda, which Mead and Bateson have stressed, and the loving, beautiful, food-giving aspect of the living woman. (Belo 1949: 38)

Let *me* go on citing, ultraobjectively and selectively, a convoluted episode later in Belo's fine ethnography. *She* has been citing (likewise) her own sequential notes from 1937—which were stopwatch-timed to the week, day, hour, and minute, in the fashion of Mead and Bateson. They run as follows:

Sindoe, April 26, 1937

It is 1:50 A.M. The girls take down the little gods from the shrine, hold them in the right hand, by the waist. They form two lines, facing the Durga shrine, and libations are poured before them. The *gamelan* is playing a delicate tinkling tune. The two lines face each other, cross and recross.... The *gamelan* plays the climactic music (called *batel*) as if this were the moment to go in trance, but it does not happen....

The men continue with the order of the ritual, the ceremonial "crossing of spears" (*maloeang toembak*). Ketjig (who is possessed by a tiger) and I Poetoe go into trance and do the self stabbing before the Durga shrine. The small boys shout.... It is nine minutes past two. The girls take the little gods again. Moenet (one of the young married women, an excellent dancer) leads with the brazier.... begins a wild dance, her eyes staring. This starts them all off. Simultaneously, Ketjig begins to do *ngoerek* (self stabbing) in the center. A little plump girl, Ngales, about fourteen, falls down on her knees, her legs one to each side, crying loudly and hysterically. The girls go on dancing; one by one they give a shout and fall down crying. Ketjig falls flat on the offerings on the sand, but just lies there stiff, does not devour any of them. (1949: 48)

Could an empirical record appear more objective? Hardly, I think. Yet Belo interrupts her self-citing description by abruptly inserting other notes taken eight months later in the same temple by Margaret Mead. Indeed, Belo cites Mead's description—whose claims she is rejecting—verbatim, from 9:00, 9:38, 10:10, 10:11, 10:19, and further o'clocks. I here cite Belo interrupting herself by citing Mead (also interrupting herself):

> Dajoe [of Brahmana caste] goes down on her knees, digging the *boeng boeng* (little god) into the ground, head down. The old priest comes and takes the *boeng boeng*. Dajoe holds her hands clasped between her knees, continues to sway . . . Dajoe is getting more excited. . . . Ketjig gives a yell, faces each and glares into her face. . . . Second girl goes down, knees pointing out, wide apart, also digs the doll into the sand, screaming and crying. Moenet dances over her. Moenet gives the impression of being a sort of presiding genius, infinitely more advanced in the mysteries which are under foot [afoot?]. . . . Ngales goes down, digs her doll *into her lap* and into the sand. Priest drags Dajoe forward, in tears. . . .
>
>   10:10 P.M.   . . . Moenet . . . weaves in and out, touches the ones on the edge, gathers them into the group. (Comment) This is the most witchlike thing I have seen in Bali, the lightness, the sense of weaving a spell, catching the neophytes in a net with cool, light, impersonal Evil, is very strong. (1949: 50)

Again, it is critical to note that Belo cites Mead's "objective" description interrupted by Mead's own "subjective" comment on Balinese women's witchlikeness. But before Belo returns to the next day of her own description of eight months beforehand (Sindoe, April 27, 1937), she interjects a dissenting commentary on Mead's description plus comment. I reiterate: Belo interrupts Mead's own self-interrupting notes—notes that Belo had used to interrupt her own "own" notes that form the bulk of her study's evidence. And Belo's sudden insight—possibly pertinent to certain theories that became prevalent in psychological anthropology—is arresting:

> It is also quite clear that [Margaret Mead] sees in the little god figures something equivalent for the female to the kris (ceremonial dagger) of the male, something between a phallus and a baby. In her view, as in mine, there is an underlying principle of female fertility symbolically expressed in the little puppet-like figures. But the witchery, the threat, and the evil quality she sees surrounding this aspect of the ceremonial I tend to see rather in the Rangda manifestations and in the undifferentiated aspects of the Durga theme. (1949: 51)

"Something between a phallus and a baby." This phrase sounds to this rereader something like a *Leitmotiv*.

"SOMETHING BETWEEN A PHALLUS AND
A BABY" (COUNTERPOINTS)

I know no more powerful insight into a "subjectivity" possibly guiding Mead's endeavors overall—in Samoa, Manus, Omaha, New Guinea, Bali— than Belo's critical insight. Her extreme "take" on Mead could even be called *ultra*-; and it apparently passed the muster of Ruth Benedict's perusal of the manuscript of Belo's 1949 book. That receptive reading by Benedict of Belo (and of Mead) is one reason for my continued praise of Benedict and Belo alike.

But might Belo's memorable image—"something between a phallus and a baby"—also illuminate why Mead's lifetime of cross-cultural research and her outsized professional example keep provoking reactionary responses from successors of diverse persuasions driven to refute her? To ponder that matter requires veering into works less worthy of rereading than Benedict, Belo, *or* Mead—works dismissive of fuller contradictions and obliquities. Into that "explanatory" task I now lapse for a spell.

Attentive readers of Mead's *Blackberry Winter* may recall that occasional insinuations at others' expense laced her memoirs. Mead's writings nevertheless transcend self-serving strategizing, or so I have argued (Boon 1990a: Postlude). One recent effort again to reduce Mead's work to transparent careerism is T. Pollmann's "Margaret Mead's Balinese: The Fitting Symbols of the American Dream" (1990). Although published in an academic journal, this article relies on journalistic clichés too simplistic to capture intricate episodes in Balinese studies, including Mead's.[24]

A former reporter with *Vrij Nederland* (later Head of Public Relations at the Netherlands' Rijksdienst Monumentenzorg), Pollmann offers second-string investigative reporting of nonnews. Her piece "deploys" to the past familiar ploys from up-to-date tabloid techniques: (1) ready-and-willing references to sexual preferences (e.g., Mead and her "guru" Benedict as lovers; Walter Spies's penchant for males); (2) easy assumptions that "informants" duped the likes of Mead (in colonialist contexts) but that "sources" today give the straight dope to investigators like herself or her collaborators; (3) instant conversion of difficult dilemmas into packaged epithets, to prove the reporter is in the know. Pollmann thus turns real predicaments into sarcastic-sounding copy; for example, she tags Mead's immensely complex part-mentor thusly: "Franz Boas, the godfather of modern American anthropology, is a German Jew who left his fatherland and came to America. In Germany he experienced the rise of anti-semitism. It marked him" (1990: 7). After a passing reference to nature/nurture, eugenics, and all that, Pollmann puts Boas "on the nurture side" and drops the matter. (Less snappy stories on Boas are readily available.)[25]

Pollmann aims to expose the naïveté of interwar connoisseurs of Balinese culture, including certain anthropologists then and later:

> In a way the Boasian anthropologists are the opposite of those anthropologists today who go to the Third World to change the fates of the natives. And yet they are alike: both reckon that they will have political influence at home. Both suffer from wishful thinking. Both sympathize too easily with political ideologies which change countries in [sic] police-states. (1990: 9)

Pollmann's own wishful thoughts and sympathies go largely unexpressed. She seems convinced that she has scooped the "inside" Balinese story (with acknowledged help from a Dutch historian here, an American political scientist there). Interviews "fifty years later" with I Madé Kaler (Mead and Bateson's assistant) are introduced as though his memory simply deposited accurate records from half a century ago. I Madé Kaler now reveals that he "was never open with them"; Pollmann seems to think that Mead, or Bateson (of all epistemologists!), would have assumed the contrary.[26] Intent on ancient tales, Pollmann fails to headline that "the Balinese" might still be unopen with the interviewers she credits, and they with them.

Pollmann thus provides contemporarily testy critique about Mead and her calling but not about herself and her own; she even presumes to speak *for* I Madé Kaler (of all "natives"!). Left aside are how "intersubjectivities" become translated and paraphrased (by her)—an issue as central to journalism as it is to ethnography.[27] A similarly slick countercritique might ask whether the patronizing style Pollmann exposes in colonialist-era descriptions is an object of "denial" in her own. Her slurs bypass tangled motives and evidence, projecting instead quick tidbits of sexual preferences, political bents, and perhaps national zeitgeist as well—all so many symptoms of this or that.

Such "objectivity"—whether directed at "natives" observed or "observers" observed—underestimates contradictions of Balinese and Balinists alike. (Ultraobjectivity invites attending to both—in this case to Mead.) Richly riddled Mead certainly was, in her guises of Balinist, Samoist, and what I once called Ms. American *Anthropologiste*. Her *Lebenswerk* unsettled diverse dichotomies, thereby transgressing some identities that may be sacred to Pollmann, Freeman, and other ardent detractors or backers. Among them are male/female, humanist/scientist, journalist/scholar, single issueist/ multiperspectivalist, gay/straight, curator/professor, homespun/globetrotter, therapist/relativist, matriarch/feminist, spouse/divorcee, Episcopalian/free-thinker, and various opposings of daughter/mother/grandmother/granddaughter. In such respects Mead's life and work indeed managed "something between a phallus and a baby"—due cause continually to reread her.

Alas and paradoxically, my digression against Pollmann abruptly left off rereading Benedict and Belo-on-Mead. At this juncture whose puppet (or in Balinese terms, puppet-child-god) was I? What forces governed my lapse into an analysis that risks dismissing Pollmann as she dismissed Mead (and as Mead *sometimes* dismissed others)? Why not leave that objectionable task to other "objectivities?" How can these polemical paragraphs and the essay-*étude* they counterpoint manifestly contradict each other's stated desires and fervent resolve? For an answer to this (rhetorical) question, do not ask me (a hermeneutic type); rather ask someone like Pollmann herself (as I have here imagined her), or someone like Pollmann's imagined Balinese. Yes, ask "them," if such consistent, unambiguous, nondialectical, unironic "informants" exist—whose reportage is there for the diagnosing. That fact I salutarily, and at risk of self-contradiction, doubt . . . ultraobjectively.

REOPENINGS

Recall again, readers, my avowed motive for interjecting Jane Belo's constructive dissent from Margaret Mead's analysis of Balinese women. I wanted to savor the thought of Ruth Benedict happening upon an extra-Vagant aphorism—"something between a phallus and a baby"—during her encounter with Belo's text acknowledged in its introduction. My half-winking notion of ultraobjectivity pertains to spiraling arts of rereading "toward the panoply"—arts common to cultural acts and interpreting them. Against ideas of objectivity that imply singular strategies of proof and refutation, "ultraobjectivity" participates in ambiguities of cultural practices that multiply translate diverse differences. Any translator of cultures is personally and historically enmeshed.

Certainly Ruth Benedict was, whose nonfiction *Patterns* I have revisited as written-read, emphasizing "the workings of the style"—a phrase P. Mahoney uses to signal Freud's place in a tradition of *pensée pensante*:

> Typically, Freud's composition is processive, not uniformly unidirectional but still progressive amid its ebbs and floods. Its essence can be to an extent appreciated by a glance at the change from the Ciceronian to the Baroque style in the 16th century." (Mahoney 1987: 163)

"Processive writing" engages readers (including Freud as his own reader and, I think, Benedict as hers) in experiences of and as *reading* that parallel what Burke called "symbolic action."[28] Ritual equivalents of "processives" grace and embroil cultures through times. Whatever we call this phenomenon—"processive riting"?—it seems worth emulating on the page.

Accordingly, my repetitious essay in reading Benedict-reading-cultures culminates by recalling facts of Benedict's reading Belo's reading of Margaret Mead's reading of Balinese ritual extremes, including mothers. I do so in order better to imagine a glint in Benedict's readerly eye that may have matched the quiver/quaver in her masterly prose. Cross-cultural evidence exhibits vergings, overlappings, and intertextualities so heady that scientists (facticity types), humanists (interpretive types), or antihumanists (deconstructive types)—among other diatribing tribes dispersed among and against disciplines—can only keep reopening evidence of their endless enigmas.

Ultraobjectively, "processive reading" seems *not unlike* (to soften with litote my musical-pathos simile) an *über*menstrual cycle. And we have seen that, judging from comparative rituals, *Übermenses* entail—cross-culturally, historically, and even *entre-genres*—periodic seclusion (selectively negate-able) and eternally extra-Vagant return.

Of Foreskins: (Un)Circumcision, Religious Histories, Difficult Description (Montaigne/Remondino)

... What is this prepuce? Whence, why, where, and whither?
(*P.C. Remondino*, History of Circumcision, *1891*)

FORESKINS are facts—cultural facts—whether removed or retained. Absent versus present prepuces have divided many religions, politics, and ritual persuasions. Plentiful too are styles of describing—often more thinly than thickly—practices of circumcision: travelogues, sermons, universal histories, doctrinal exegeses, encyclopedias, ethnographies, medical treatises, etc. (Un)circumcision involves signs separating an "us" from a "them" entangled in various discourses of identity and distancing. In the world's extra-Vagant history of ritual practices, foreskins have been no less diversely read than menses.

This essay engages a shifting semiotics of un(circumcision) in culture-crossings from the sixteenth century, and before, through the Enlightenment, and since. I eventually dwell on two manifestly extravagant texts: an Early Modern reading of circumcision among other ritual varieties and rarities (Montaigne's 1580s travel narrative); an encyclopedic diagnosis judging circumcision by presumably absolute standards (P.C. Remondino's 1891 *History*). Despite my dramatic leap from Montaigne to Remondino (whose narrative, by the way, converts Montaigne's account to its own scheme), I do not seek simply to reiterate a now-comfortable dichotomy between Medieval-Renaissance hermeneutics versus Enlightenment analysis that extends to modernist practices of knowledge. Rather, I refer interpretations of "epistemologies" to disquieting evidence of ambiguous ritual differences inscribed in contrasting genres—travelogues, ethnographies, and universal histories, among others. I stress Muslim/Hindu, Judeo/Christian, and surgical/antisurgical positions in discourses of circumcision/uncircumcision, in order to *refract* any easy periodization of times present or past. A fuller project could add, say, a fragmentary fourteenth-century "Stanzaic Life of Christ," whose typological format foregrounds the circumcision; or the astounding ethnography of "circum-incision" inscribed in John Layard's monumental yet fragmentary *Stone Men of Malekula* (1942). (Any such fragment of description, a beginning, may

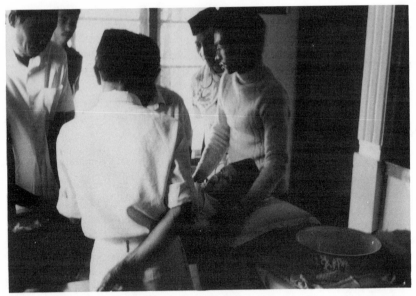

Fig. 4. A Buginese (age: seven years) being circumcised (and photographed by kinsmen with better cameras than mine). This son becomes, bodily, a complete member of the mosque community, eventually to be buried.
(Author's invited photo, 1972)

Fig. 5. Next door, a Balinese (age: three permutational months), being ceremonialized differently. This son becomes, nomenclaturally, a complete microcosm, eventually to be cremated after exhumation. (Author's photo, 1972)

resemble a lexical prefix [*Vorsilbe*], if Freud and this essay pertain to each other.)[1]

My connected fragments from ethnography, histories of ideas, intertextual travel, and panoramic ethnology afford neither sequential story, proper argument, nor symptomatic analysis. Rather, juxtaposing them yields insights analogous to those offered me one day when I, an ethnographer, was led unwittingly from the scene of Hindu-Balinese uncircumcision to a contrary place.

THIS ESSAY'S ETHNOGRAPHIC BEGINNINGS

Here we may call again on the custom of circumcision which—a kind of
"Leitfossil"—has repeatedly rendered us important services.
(*Freud,* Moses and Monotheism)

It was a dank and sultry afternoon (Indonesian, *sore*) in 1972. Obliviously engaged in fieldwork on Balinese ancestral practices, caste distinctions, marriage and politics, I was accosted by a Buginese acquaintance who affably urged me to witness a circumcision ceremony (*sunat*) the next day in his Islamic compound. This unanticipated byway was described in a short digression to my ethnography of Hindu-Balinese rites; here are some extracts about the Buginese:

At 6:15 a.m. the surgeon arrived, and the initiates were ushered into a room lighted by the dawning sun, with a plastic-covered operating table, a shelf of instruments, medicine and cleansing agents, a tape recorder playing Arabic songs, and a lone calendar on the otherwise blank whitewashed walls. . . .

Each boy was held down by three or four men, including the conspicuously proud father. From eight to ten men mulled about, plus one vagrant tot in an orange dress who kept running up to inspect the initiates. The other women and girls watched from behind a partition. The first boy suffered most acutely; although the foreskin was stretched and clamped and partly anesthetized, the cuts provoked uncontrolled screams. "Too much blood with this one," the operator murmured in Indonesian. With much comforting, laughter, and prattle by all around, he quickly finished cutting, applied an antiseptic and bandage, and attached a protective brace to keep the boy's formal *sarong* from irritating the wound. The second initiate fared better, the last was exemplary. The latter's father, swelling with pride, related his son's stoic endurance and unflinching control even during the anaesthesia injection to the boy's similar courage at the dentist's office. Finally, all three were perched in their mosque attire on linen-covered pillows to await the communal feast later in the day. (Boon 1977: 210ff)

My entire evocation stressed festive tonalities; it was singled out for praise in a professional review.[2] This unexpectedly favorable reception led me to wonder how my few pages compared to the history of describing such rites in Indonesia—and everywhere else through all recorded time. (In those days we anthropologists were a bit overreaching.)

My vignette of Buginese *sunat* in otherwise uncircumcizing Hindu-Bali differed from several precedents in Indonesian studies. Clifford Geertz's remarkable *Religion of Java* (1960) depicted Javanese circumcision as if shared across contrasting cultural identities: syncretist-peasant (*abangan*), reformist-Muslim (*santri*), and courtly-bureaucratic-propped-up-by-colonialist-regime (*prijaji*).[3] Because my principal topic was rites outside Islam, I presented foreskin removal as a diacritical dividing Buginese and Balinese, despite their frequent cooperation and even intermarriage. Earlier, Dutch scholars had surveyed circumcision practices (*besnijdenis*) to gauge intensity of Islamic identity (of Buginese, for example, dispersed from their home territory of Sulawesi.)[4] Nothing so *diagnostic*—or "symptomatological," in Foucault's terms—entered my portrait of a rite so "right" in Buginese sensibilities yet so antipathetic next door:

> There simply could be nothing less Balinese: a painful initiation rite in an image-less, flowerless, smokeless, holy-waterless cell. . . . Balinese informants could not even bring themselves to discuss circumcision per se; at the thought of it they were disgusted to the same degree Buginese are disdainful of Balinese for not practicing it.
>
> Conversely, in death rites it is Muslims who abhor Balinese corpse preparation and later cremation and Balinese who disdain the Muslim community for refusing such responsibilities. (Boon 1977: 212)[5]

One anthropological task required my siding with neither, even sympathizing with both. That at least is how I saw things then, still do in the age of cultural critique, and still may thereafter.

Since fieldwork in 1972 (and subsequently), it has proved increasingly difficult to convey the convivial ambiance—especially when showing slides—of four Buginese boys (average age, seven years) being de-foreskinned. Students and colleagues in today's moralistic climate dispute any "well-wishingness" of such fêtes. Assumptions of coercive dimensions prevail among listeners—whether, I assume, circumcised or uncircumcised, feminist or masculinist, Marxist or not, hermeneuts or positivists, politically correct or less-than. Across such differences that divide my audience (and often divide me), a shared reaction sets in: Suspicions of trauma are voiced; charges of damage levied; the plight of victims identified with. *They* (my listeners) choose to be no less judgmental about *another's circumcision* than did my uncircumcising and flamboyantly cremating Balinese friends. I, on the other hand, having "been there"—*chez* gregarious Buginese—accepted a diacritical rite offensive to many "Westerners" (again, whether circumcised or not) and, if the subject comes up, to many Balinese.[6]

My subsequent exploration of circumcision in comparative discourse between Indonesia (both Islamic and "Indianized") and Europe (both Judeo- and Christian-) started with the sixteenth century. For example, in Europe I tracked Huguenot notions of circumcision as a similitude of sodomy associated with the Papacy and whatever people it "contaminated." I also broached images of "anticircumcision" (Hindu-Tantric icons of bedizened foreskins) from Pigafetta's 1520s account of East Indies rituals. In that study I tried to convey why such elusive evidence thwarted historicist evaluation in its own day and still should in ours.[7] This essay continues those efforts.

ALTERNATIVE BEGINNINGS FOR HISTORIES OF DIFFICULT DESCRIPTION

Intellectual historians might want to begin with Foucault's controversial notions of a "classical episteme" that led to diagnostic explanation (supplanting hermeneutics of similitudes) promoted as the Enlightenment. Foucault contests styles of power-knowledge consolidated during the seventeenth and eighteenth centuries; he associates them with institutions of control characterized by the impersonal gaze: sanitized inspection of distanced, de-voiced, dissectible "objects" made visible. Panoptic prison technologies presumably became underpinnings to a "discourse of modernism," implemented by clinical-minded regimes whose business was to colonize bodies, extract labor, and suppress resistance.[8]

Alternatively, historians of ideas might want to start with the temporal eclipse of Renaissance heterodoxy by the combined forces of the Reformation and Ramism. Such scholars as Frances Yates have shown that early modern Neoplatonists cultivated arts of permissive "Phantasy" devoted to eros and pneumatic magical sciences. Eventually their devices were purged by "rational" censoring procedures that rewrote history accordingly. In his synoptic study of *Eros and Magic in the Renaissance*, I. P. Couliano reviews a "Reformation" (common to Protestantism and Catholicism) that was hostile to Neoplatonist resemblances and analogies of microcosm and macrocosm (what Foucault designated the "preclassical episteme"):

> If the Catholic Church did not abandon its cult of images and the celibacy of its priests, there are other fields in which the Reformation, both Protestant and Catholic, arrived at the same results. We have only to think of the persecution of witches or the fight against astrology and magic. . . .
>
> The idea of the infinitude of the universe is not the only one which, extolled in the Renaissance, strikes terror in succeeding eras. . . . As soon as God withdraws into his complete transcendence, every human attempt to examine his design runs into a ghastly silence. . . .

To read in the "book of Nature" had been the fundamental experience in the Renaissance. The Reformation was tireless in seeking ways to close that book. Why? Because the Reformation thought of Nature not as a factor for rapprochement but as the *main thing responsible for the alienation of God from mankind.*

By dint of searching, the Reformation at last found the great culprit guilty of all the evils of individual and social existence: sinning Nature. (Couliano 1987: 202, 208; emphasis in original)

Either style (Foucault's or Couliano's) of representing past ideas or epistemes itself relies on diverse styles and genres of "document."[9] One such genre is the travelogue: a kind of writing-as-if one had "been there," but briefly, *en passant.* Another is ethnography, or its equivalent: a kind of writing-as-if one had "been there" longer, dwellingly. Both these genres contrast in turn to universal history, a kind of writing-as-if one had been everywhere, anonymously and omnisciently. A given genre's rhetoric is written to be *read* accordingly: travelogue as if the reading-voyage could be fleet; ethnography as if the reading-stay could be participant; universal history as if reading could occur neutrally, a-positionally. Each rhetoric, then, indeed implies distinct paces of negotiating distance or intimacy when "voyeuring," observing, translating, understanding, knowing . . . ; pick your betrayal.

Some critical thinkers today promote travel-tropes as a superior brand of *theoria.* Scholars as disparate as Edward Said and James Clifford aspire to motility; they decry general "presenting" of a *them*; they challenge disciplines to evade stable categories, overturn positivist documentation, rattle "ethnographic authority."[10] My responses to radical declarations "against fixity" are mixed, in part because of peculiar histories of describing certain rituals.

Circumcision, for example, has been travel-told since the sixteenth-century, and before. Accounts often transgress distinctions between "travelogue" and "ethnography;" indeed, upon encountering circumcision, the latter genre may prefer to resemble the former: to hurry on past, to avoid dwelling, to resist even as-if participation and/or collaboration in another's rite. This sudden haste can *look* like high critical motility or resistance to participant authority; but it may *be* just the opposite: reactionary. I am reminded of certain sixteenth-century European discoverers—Tomé Pires, for example—who narrated commonplace fears that they would wind up involuntary "Muslims" (read: circumcised) even in the East Indies.[11]

Although wary of recent "anti-authoritativeness"—now often authorized as "postmodernist"—I do appreciate continuities between current critical fashion and centuries-long blurrings of travel-writing, ethnography, history, and literature. Thomas More's *Utopia,* for example—handed down since 1518 through tricky translations of its punning Latin—was an Early Modern exercise in verisimilitudinous travel-telling; More framed his imagined "no-place" in a purposefully excessive present tense. Along with Lucian's *True Story* (Thomas More translated Lucian), *Utopia* was a prominent forerunner of the now-defamed "ethnographic present." The captivating format, decidedly ahistorical, spans nearly two millennia (Lucian, to More's Hythloday, to Malinowski); it could be paraphrased something like this: "I voyaged there, and am here to tell you that in Utopia (or some other no-place or someplace) *they* do thus and so."[12]

Another example of pre-postmodern travel-troping was Lévi-Strauss's *Tristes tropiques* (1955), which critiqued a wide range of discovery accounts and narrated voyages—including his own—that converted the New World into "evidence for" the Old. Substituting figural regret for the ineffable, plenitudinous tropics, his prose recaptured a spectrum of the politics of description: tribalisms, caste, colonialisms, democracy, even reformist Islam likened to France. Differences thus engaged by Lévi-Strauss became mutually "chromatic," along with the "self" engaging them.[13]

TOWARDS A CHROMATICISM OF UN/CIRCUMCISIONS

Ambiguous difficulties reverberate in rhetorics and rituals of circumcision/uncircumcision—practiced, reported, inscribed, interpreted, advocated, condemned, tolerated, puzzled over. Over time our ritual *topos* has been "diacritical" to diverse peoples and personages. It marks off Muslim Indonesian from Hindu-Balinese Indonesian, but not from so-called Hindu Javanese (or Tengger) Indonesian (see R. Hefner 1987). *Sunat* can differentiate any Muslim from any Hindu man, and some Muslim from non-Muslim women (if the term "circumcision" be admitted for infibulation, excision, or other female alteraton.) Because my ethnography, as noted above, began with Muslim (versus Bali-Hindu) experience, I might cite *The Encyclopedia of Islam* (1957), which designates male circumcision and female excision (*khafd*) by the term *khitan*. This entry also mentions practices of *ghusl*, necessary if "the two circumcised parts have been in touch with one another". Clearly, any description of anyone's ritual practices relies on controversial categories subject to contestation.

Un/Circumcision has divided Pauline precepts from Christ, Christian from Jew, unmedicalized laggard from medicalized modern; and demedicalized postmodern from still-surgicalized establishmentarians (to echo slogans of recent disputes). This category of "controls" may be stretched to include women's labia or clitoris along with men's foreskin or *plus-que*-foreskin—among other bits of bodies. Contrasts separate neighboring groups who "circumcise" neither women nor men or just men. Ethnographic surveys often combined "Circumcision, Incision and Subincision" (W.H.R. Rivers, 1926), from European, Mid-Eastern, Indonesian, Australian, Melanesian, Mesoamerican, and Native American spheres.[14] The topic has been elided with castration, eunuchism and "infibulation, muzzling, and other curious customs" (Remondino 1891). The modern tendency is to lump together practices that target body parts analytically categorized as "genital."

It may be unnecessary to add that any constant content across cases—e.g., blood—remains disputed. For example, Eilberg-Schwartz ties together "blood," descent, pruning or "the fruitful cut," seeking to make Israelite circumcision (male, infant) thematically coherent. I personally doubt a given complex of usages can "add up," given anomalies implicit in diacritical rites. This difficulty makes it all the more pressing to profess empathy towards alter (*autre*), rather than *own*, circumcisions or uncircumcisions.[15]

Desires to inscribe experience from the vantage of "own circumcision" trigger paradoxes of memory and forgetting which depend on relative age, but only in part. The movie *Europa Europa*, based on a novel-memoir by S. Perel, dramatizes as-if unforgettability of "own" circumcision (as an infant) in the most tragic times of National Socialist anti-Semitism.[16] On the other hand, a striking memoir of "own" will-to-be-circumcised from childhood-into-manhood graces P. A. Toer's Indonesian story *"Sunat"*; (which I cite here in D. Lombard's fine translation):

> Comme tous mes autres camarades, je n'avais qu'un désir, celui d'être un bon musulman.... "Ne bouge surtout pas!" me conseilla l'un des assistants.... Je regardais mon sang épais et noirâtre qui coulait comme un filet et se mêlait lentement au cendres de l'assiette.... Tous mes espoirs de devenir un vrai musulman s'évanouirent..., car je me rendais bien compte que mes parents étaient pauvres et que nous ne possédions pas ce qu'il fallait pour faire un pèlerinage.[17]

Beyond, or short of, such imaginatively personal accounts, circumcision and presumably related rites have been associated with an unwieldy array of functions, features, causes, and effects. These include: Bonding age grades and dividing generations; implementing social exchange and rivalry; spilling blood, inflicting ordeals, remaindering prepuces, occasioning stoicism, ... ; making boys into men, ordinary men into prophets, a people into chosen or condemned, men into women ("symbolic wounds"); turning phalluses into vaginas, human penises into marsupial-like ones (Australia) or rhinocerous-like ones (Borneo). Diverse diagnostic explanations claim such rites enhance or diminish virility, fertility, sacrality, holiness, or other kind of potency, either to augment or to limit population growth, and thereby cure or cause disease.

A scholar of varied (un)circumcisions soon becomes resigned to cover at best eclectically either cryptic or tortuous sources explaining, cataloging, justifying, condemning, or otherwise representing types of circumcision, or activities categorized with "it." My own eclectic reading list begins as follows: Maurice Bloch's *From Blessing to Violence* could token studies of circumcision and statecraft (in this case Madagascar); Suzette Heald's "The Making of Men [in] Gisu Ritual" can stand for sensitive accounts in the fashion of V. Turner; Karen Paige's "The Ritual of Circumcision" could illustrate simplistic "medicalized" arguments against circumcision.... (I continue this start in the notes.)[18] Utterly too abundant (and wildly opinionated) even to begin listing are exposés against clitoridectomy in African and Islamic areas and elsewhere, often lumped with circumcision as "mutilations." Also, a discourse of sexual preference (in and out of the gay community) for foreskins or their absence exists; it can become intolerant of ethnography's differences.[19]

This may be the place to mention Derrida. During my explorations of un/circumcision's particulars, a relevant book suddenly appeared (*Derrida* [1993], by Bennington and Derrida)—first in French and quickly in English. Derrida's book entwines *sur*-Augustinian "circumfessional" footnotes around an as-if subtext: his present-absence of prepuce. Is it just "me," or does his *écriture* seem rather obsessive? Here's a dose:

> Bennington: ". . . Let me say that J.D. surprises me less than he thinks or pretends to think when he exhibits his circumcision here, for a long time now he has been talking of nothing else. . . ." (327)
>
> Derrida: ". . . For years I have been going round in circles, trying to take as a witness not to see myself being seen but to re-member myself around a single event, I have been accumulating in the attic my 'sublime,' documents, iconography, notes, learned ones and native ones, dream narratives or philosophical dissertations, applied transcription of encyclopedic, sociological, historical, psychoanalytical treatises that I'll never do anything with, about circumcision in the world, the Jewish and the Arab and the others, and excision, with a view to my circumcision alone, the circumcision of me, the unique one, that I know perfectly well took place, one time, they told me and I see it but I always suspect myself of having cultivated, because I am circumcised, *ergo*, cultivated, a fantastical affabulation." (59)

What can I add to Derrida's circumcision that he has not? In my essay's comparative sense of *autre* un/circumcisions (e.g., Buginese), Derrida represents something of an antithesis: "own circumcision" inscribed and translated as a new center of *marges*. Considerable commentary and secondary second-guessing is bound to ensue from these positions assumed by Derrida, who inimitably deconstructs his auto/biographical traces.

Even with Derrida, my fragment of a token survey has barely scratched the iceberg tip of variable indicators and claimed consequences of un/circumcision "itself." Associated practices and ideas may be no less paradoxical to particular (un)circumcisees or (un)circumcisors (I include infant circumcision, without suction, to be discussed below). In short, *the copiousness of significations still devolving on circumcision and uncircumcision is the beginning and end of this essay.*

Historically, (un)circumcision enters sectarian discourses in multifarious guises. Again, examples include: (1) Java's fourteenth century, when Indicized courtly rites (cremating, not circumcising) eventually became Islamized (circumcising, not cremating); (2) Abrahamic versus Pauline Judeo-Christian liturgies as practiced or described on through Renaissance-Reformation ritual and iconography. In Judeo-Christian-Islamic worlds distinctions have revolved around options of infant/child/adolescent/adult circumcision—plus, again, some noncircumcision for Christians and some female "circumcision" for Muslims. To my knowledge, neither regularized circumcision of corpses nor prenatal circumcision—now perfectly conceivable—is practiced, although it is hard to keep abreast of developments. Believe it or not, the new U.S. technologies of laboratory-grown skin (hairless so far, but already capable of healing) seeds its cultures with infant foreskins.[20]

A key Scriptural tradition pertaining to relative age of circumcision inhabits Genesis 17:24–27 (New English Bible):

> Abraham was ninety-nine years old when he circumcised the flesh of his foreskin. Ishmael was thirteen years old when he was circumcised in the flesh of his foreskin. Both Abraham and Ishmael were circumcised on the same day, and all the men of his household, born in the house or bought with money from foreigners, were circumcised with him.

All of Genesis 15–26 deserves continual rereading, through "Isaac [a prototype first infant circumcisee] and his wife Rebecca laughing together" (Gen. 26:8).

It remains impossibly urgent to become versed in relevant Biblical, Midrashic, Patristic, Kabbalistic, Gnostic, Talmudic, and Islamic commentaries and traditions, particularly where one renders the other extra-Vagant. For example, as Hammoudi points out: "La tradition musulmane rapporte que Ibrahim mène Ismail et non pas Isaac au sacrifice; il y a cependant des divergences entre auteurs musulmans à ce sujet" (95).[21] It is still worth verging through the "world history" of ritual differences—what are designated diverse "sacraments" by A. M. Hocart, who emphasized Oceanic Fiji, Buddhist Ceylon, and Vedic-Moghul-Hindu India.[22] Regarding contrasts that became Catholic versus Protestant in the sixteenth century, I recall (with Eugene Vance) Augustine's lingering trope of his pen's phallic tongue and its chaste, circumcised lips, plus exegetical sublimations of Saints' lives. One could contrast Luther, if only to remain ecumenical, who construes Genesis (and circumcision) very much otherwise in his *Works*, eventually anti-Jewish.[23]

Judeo-Christian themes of sacrifice, including circumcision, occupied Hubert and Mauss's fundamental essay on the ethnography and history of covenants, *Sacrifice: Its Nature and Function*:

> The victim takes his place. It alone penetrates into the perilous domain of sacrifice, it dies there, and indeed it is there in order to die. The *sacrifier* remains protected; the gods take the victim instead of him. *The victim redeems him.* Moses

had not circumcised his son, and Yahweh came to 'wrestle' with him in a hostelry. Moses was on the point of death when his wife savagely cut off the child's foreskin and, casting it at Yahweh's feet, said to him : "Thou art for me a husband of blood." The destruction of the foreskin satisfied the god; he did not destroy Moses, who was redeemed. There is no sacrifice into which some idea of redemption does not enter." (1964: 98–99)

I consider this Durkheimian study paramount. Eilberg-Schwartz argues, correctly I think, that "circumcision and sacrifice have overlapping functions"; but his study overlooks Hubert and Mauss, plus key works by Hocart and Max Weber that foreground sacrifice, covenant, and sacrament. Their approaches erode (as even Herbert Spencer's did, whether or not intentionally) any boundary presumed to separate "world religions" from "primitive" ones. Insights into what Eilberg-Schwartz renders thematically as "the savage" *in* Judaism are available in comparative studies of sacrifice (Judeo-Christian, Islam, Hindu, etc.). His challenge to interpret Israelite religion less exclusivistically sometimes seems to imply that "the savage" has been a constant idea of "other," against which the "chosen," "civilized," or "rational" congratulates itself. Were the history of "othering" so stably polarized, it would have proved far easier to ameliorate.[24]

In sum, history's worlds, too, have yielded nonstop commentary about (un)circumcision plus arguable "substitutes" ("sacraments" in the semiotic sense) in rites of atonement, forgiveness, manna, and sacrifice. To recall such difficulties that have long pervaded the European scene, I might cite Peter Brown's *The Body and Society*:

Paul's apostolic mission had left the Christian communities with one decisive *lacuna*. He had imposed strict moral codes on all pagan converts; but he had bitterly resisted any attempt to encourage pagans to adopt the clear badges of a separate identity provided to those who converted to Judaism. They were to bear no physical mark on their bodies—no circumcision. They were to engage in no careful discrimination of clean and unclean foods—that would have involved a clear choice of dining companions and even separate marketing facilities (no *kashrut*). They were to observe no clear distinctions between profane and holy days—no Sabbaths and new moons. Many other Christians felt that they could not afford to be so off-hand with the venerable Law of Moses. In the cities of the Diaspora, Judaism continued to appeal to pagans precisely because it was an ancient religion as punctilious as their own. Jews observed the solemn rhythms of high festival. They held to codes of purity. They gave men and women an opportunity to approach, in a disciplined and thoughtful manner, the "things that lie between nature and culture, half-wild, half-civilised.". . . (1988: 59)

Coincidentally Brown's splendid summary, covering dire conflicts over the entire course of Judeo-Christian experience, ends by applying to "us" a phrase from Greg Dening's *Islands and Beaches* (1980).[25] That book happens to meditate upon the remotest "othered" left in the wake of Europe's global expansion: the Marquesas, which Herman Melville also visited. On that extra-Vagant note, I close this section that has resonated diversities of sacrifices past and present.

I remind readers that my panoramic glimpses of histories' rites began with an ethnographically inspired quest for precedents—anywhere, anytime, regardless of the commentator's own condition—for nonjudgmental depiction of diacritic un/circumcision. It is now time to reveal that my *recherche* has led back to Montaigne. It feels, I confess, like coming home—whether "home" to Montaigne or to subjects he describes, I cannot tell; some form of recognition, perhaps uncanny, occurs. Regardless, when this anthropologist reads toward the sixteenth century, he begins to suspect "it might as well be Bali." (How, I wonder, might Montaigne have inscribed East Indies' practices—including Hindu-Balinese contraries, among Muslims—had he voyaged, painfully, thither to witness chords of differences? Read on.)

MONTAIGNE'S PRE-ENLIGHTENMENT EMPATHIES FOR MANY AN "US"

> It is the undiligent reader who loses my subject, not I.
> (*Montaigne,* Essays)

Among the texts circumscribing circumcisions and/or uncircumcisions that this "I" has discovered from sundry centuries, none is steadier than sections of Montaigne's *Travel Journal*. This long-lost, indirectly transmitted narrative exemplifies dimensions of Montaigne's writing stressed by D. L. Schaefer: double-voiced, heterodox, and ironic—penned with various audiences in mind by an author ostensibly of orthodox persuasion.[26] Schaefer adds that Montaigne dissimulated in his private family records too. His travelogue (also not intended for publication) was only discovered in the eighteenth century; evidence of it keeps emerging. In the case of Montaigne, then, rereading is undoubtedly appropriate; that much *je sais*.

The travels Montaigne described—co-authored by a secretary it seems—cannot *necessarily* be taken as true; nor are they certainly false. Related problems and opportunities characterize any effort to pull Montaigne into anyone's present—whether D. Frame's 1983 translation (foreword by Guy Davenport) employed here, or W. Waters's 1903 translation that deleted descriptions of Montaigne's bodily suffering, thus expurgating a vital early-modern travel-motive.[27] Constant censorings are the condition in which we read Montaigne, and any other extra-Vagant text, then or now.[28] But what about foreskins?

Passing mention of circumcision-as-diacritical is made by Montaigne, writing in the first person in French. (Switching later to Italian, he tries "to speak this other language a little, especially since I am in this region where I seem to hear the most perfect Tuscan speech, particularly among those natives who have not corrupted and altered it with that of their neighbors" [126].) "Montaigne" reports a "memorable incident" involving one Giuseppe—forced to be circumcised and become a Turk, then ostensibly redeemed to Christianity through sacraments; he remained, however, "implicitly" Islamic, winding up a strategic go-between, a kind of jack-of-all-sects.

That much, at least, one gathers from Montaigne's text—compiled of hearsay from Giuseppe's relatives, just across the street—all about disguises among foes, friends, neighbors, and even mothers and sons (in Italy!); I abbreviate:

> An inhabitant of this place, a soldier named Giuseppe, who is still alive and commands one of the galleys of the Genoese as a convict, and several of whose near relations I saw, was captured by the Turks in a battle at sea. To regain his liberty he became a Turk (and there are many of this condition, and especially in the mountains near this place, still alive) was circumcised, and married in their territory. Coming to pillage this coast, he . . . [was] caught by the people, who had risen up. He had the presence of mind to say that he had come to surrender deliberately, that he was a Christian. He was set at liberty a few days later, came . . . to the house opposite the one I am lodging in; he entered and encountered his mother. She asked him roughly who he was and what he wanted; for he still had on his sailor's clothes, and it was strange to see him there. (124)

A recognition scene ensues, followed by maternal embrace after a decade's separation. The mother dies soon after; the shock had proved unbearable, as her doctors foretold. Then:

> Our Giuseppe was feted by one and all, was received into the Church to abjure his error, and received the Sacrament from the bishop of Lucca, with several other ceremonies. It was just humbug: he was a Turk at heart.

Montaigne's own re-narration of this tale of deceit then enters Giuseppe's relatives' narrative present-tense:

> To return to the Turks he steals away from here, goes to Venice, and mixes with them again. Resuming his travels, here he falls into our hands again; and because he is a man of unusual strength and a soldier well versed in naval matters, the Genoese still keep him and use him, well bound and fettered. (124)

So that's how Giuseppe became an Italian Turk, an unreconverted slave in Genoa's employ.

This picaresque story reads like circumcision's anticipation of *Candide*: our hero/culprit negotiates a borderland ("Venice") between Catholicism and Islam. Might Montaigne's *Travel*-text—as discourse—be experienced by readers as something *like* a sublimated equivalent to such cross-cultural, multilanguage, intersectarian carryings-on?

Be that as it may, Giuseppe's roving tale of present/absent foreskin stands in sharp contrast to the *Journal's* ultralocated account of "the most ancient religious ceremony there is among men." Montaigne refers here to the circumcision of the Jews, witnessed in the early 1580s on January 30, in Rome, as detailed by his secretary, on a page of manuscript authenticated by its proximity to a parenthetical passage inserted in the margins in Montaigne's own hand.[29] Before carefully observing this ethnographic episode, let me underscore the copiousness of religions, landscapes, cuisines, and bodies that Montaigne registers as he sallies away from his since-celebrated home base, his tower. Even Rome's Jews—deemed timeless in their circumcising—contribute evidence of festive contrasts—including that "renegade rabbi who preaches to the Jews on Saturday after dinner in the Church of the Trinity," with sixty other Jews in compulsory attendance (92).

If Rome's Hebrew enclave harbors variety, how much more mottled is Switzerland's landscape of Reformations:

> We saw a great many men of learning. . . . Monsieur de Montaigne judged that they were not in agreement over their religion, from the answers he received: some calling themselves Zwinglians, others Calvinists, others Martinists; and indeed he was informed that many still fostered the Roman religion in their heart. The form of giving the sacrament is generally into the mouth; however, anyone who wants may put out his hand for it, and the ministers do not dare to touch this *chord* in these *differences* in religion. (14; emphases added)

Comparable chords of differences form, along with Montaigne's physical ills and profound misery, the very fabric of his travel-text. In Germany, for example (one I shall recall later):

> We went to see the Church of the Holy Cross. . . . They make a great celebration there about a miracle that occurred nearly a hundred years ago. A woman would not swallow the body of Our Lord. Having taken it out of her mouth and put it, wrapped in wax, into a box, she confessed; and they found the whole thing changed into flesh. For this they cite plenty of attestations, and this miracle is written down in many places in Latin and in German. They show under crystal that wax, and then a little morsel having the redness of flesh. This church is roofed with copper, like the house of the Fuggers. . . . (38–9)

Montaigne's account seems everywhere evenhanded and open-minded, despite its proximity in time to the Saint Bartholomew's Day tragedy:

> The town was originally entirely Zwinglian. Later, when the Catholics were recalled, the Lutherans took the place of the Zwinglians; at present there are more

Catholics in positions of authority, although they are greatly outnumbered. Monsieur de Montaigne also visited the Jesuits here and found some very learned ones. (39)

Catholics too display pungent contrasts: "Whereas we join our hands in prayer to God at the elevation of the host, [in Switzerland] they stretch them apart wide open, and hold them thus raised until the priest exhibits the pax" (17). Such chords of difference even harmonize poultry: "[In Germany] there is also an aviary twenty paces square . . . all full of birds. Here we saw some Polish pigeons, which they call Indian . . . ; they are large, and have a beak like a partridge" (37).

Could an author more conscientiously inscribe cultures as intersections of sectarian/cultural/linguistic/avian contrasts, collisions, and accommodations? (Wily Montaigne compared differences of words to differences of birds.)[30] To commemorate the 1530 embrace between Charles V and Ferdinand of Hungary and Bohemia, his travelogue notes the Italian/German polyglossia of language and liturgy around Trent (44). Always ecumenical himself, Montaigne even applauds the far-from-ecumenical Pope Gregory XIII for endowing colleges for Greeks, English, Scots, French, Germans, and Poles. Montaigne's extra-Catholic, indeed extra-Christian, catholicity extends to his most "personal" topic: those killingly painful kidney stones. He gladly contacts diverse experts and amateurs of bodily ailments—among them, "an old patriarch of Antioch, an Arab, very well versed in five or six languages of that part of the world, and having no knowledge of Greek or any other of our tongues, with whom I had become quite intimate, [who] made me a present of a certain mixture to help my stone, and prescribed the use of it for me in writing" (87). His text includes the prescription "in order that, if I should lose his writing, I may find it here" (87). The Arab's remedy (doubtless devised through "interpretation" more than "diagnosis") required a drug to be taken "in a dose the size of two peas," five times, "leaving out every other day."

Montaigne's entire *Journal*—including that most pragmatic note of a recipe for health, recorded against loss—just keeps sounding the chords of religious, sectarian, and liturgical *differences*. A travelogue of our own reading-voyage through Montaigne's text might circumscribe *his* descriptions as implicit emulations of myriad, musical fountains at the Villa d'Este:

> Here I examined everything most particularly. . . . The gushing of an infinity of jets of water checked and launched by a single spring that can be worked from far off. . . . The music of the organ . . . effected by means of the water, which falls with great violence into a round arched cave and agitates the air that is there and forces it, in order to get out, to go through the pipes of the organ and supply it with wind. . . . Other springs they set in motion an owl, which, appearing at the top of the rock, makes this harmony cease instantly, for the birds are frightened by his presence . . . elsewhere noise as of cannon shots. . . .

There are ponds or reservoirs. . . . The mouths, being thus turned inward and facing one another, cast and scatter the water . . . produce a continual rain falling into the pond. The sun . . . engenders a rainbow so natural and vivid that it lacks nothing of the one we see in the sky. This I had not seen elsewhere. (99)

If there is a discourse resembling this aqueous prism—one that effects across cultures an agitated similitude of scintillating variations—Montaigne's *Journal* may embody it. His ebullient evocations emerge, despite unspeakable spasms of agony produced by urinary malfunctions in an age of horseback travel. And midway through the travel-text occurs that sustained narrative of circumcision.

Montaigne's ethnography of Rome's Jews commences thusly:

He had already seen their synagogue at another time, one Saturday morning, and their prayers, in which they sing without order, as in the Calvinist churches, certain lessons from the Bible in Hebrew. . . . their doctors each in turn give a lesson on the Bible passage for that day, doing it in Italian. . . . (80)

Parallels offered and the scene set, the rite begins (N.B.: I here truncate Montaigne's account, just as I did my own, of Buginese, above. When obliged to excise description, ethnographers inevitably exaggerate a sense of climax or catharsis):

It is done in . . . the lightest room of the boy's house. They give the boys a godfather and a godmother, as we do; the father names the child. They circumcise them on the eighth day from their birth. The child is wrapped in our style; the godfather unwraps him below, and then those present and the man who is to do the operation all begin to sing. . . . they hold that he who has circumcised up to a certain number . . . when he is dead has this privilege, that the parts of his mouth are never eaten by worms.

After details about the instruments, he describes the operation:

He takes his member and with one hand pulls back toward himself the skin that is over it . . . keeps the cutting edge from injuring the glans and the flesh . . . with a knife he cuts off this skin, which they immediately bury in some earth . . . there in a basin . . . for this mystery. After that the minister with his bare nails plucks up also some other particle of skin . . . and tears it off. . . .

Montaigne's description culminates:

It seems there is much effort and pain in this; however, they find no danger in it and the wound is always cured in four or five days. The boy's outcry is like that of ours when they are baptized. . . . They hastily offer some wine to the minister, who puts a little in his mouth and then goes and sucks the glans of this child, all bloody, and spits out the blood he has drawn from it, and immediately takes as much wine again, up to three times. . . . red powder, which they say is dragon's blood, with which he salts and covers the whole wound. . . . A glass full of wine . . . which he blesses by some prayers. . . . takes a drop of it with his finger to the boy's mouth to be sucked; . . . this glass . . . to the mother and the women . . . to drink what wine is left. . . . Another person takes a silver instrument, round as a tennis ball . . . (pierced with little holes, like our cassolettes), and carries it to the nose, first of the minister, and then of the child, and then of the godfather: they suppose that these are odors to confirm and enlighten minds for devotion. He meanwhile still has his mouth all bloody. (Montaigne 1983: 80–83)

Montaigne's intricately observed passage—here telegraphed—deserves revisiting by readers. His paragraphs evenly convey not just foreskin removal but the later-notorious scene of "suction." The enacted image of a mouth placed round a wounded glans penis enters this travel-text's company of other sacramental extremes—such as that waxy bit of Christ's flesh, uningested, glimpsed in the reliquary mentioned earlier. Subsequent centuries' diverse officialdoms and the states pressuring them would prove unwilling to accommodate this "theatricality" of circumcision rites. In France, for example, suction was ultimately forbidden by the Hebrew Consistory and then by national law in 1854, as we shall see.

But that was a long, long time—and an Enlightenment—away from Montaigne's mode of displaying circumcision in a world of dramatic ritual usages.[31] We must beware, I think, of post-Renaissance notions of proper orality versus genitality that ratified "rational" repressions of olfactory and tactile meanings. Interpreters who aspire to become unanachronistic ought not project later assumptions back to the bodies (and souls) surrounding that "mouth all bloody" of 1580. Yes, unethnocentric readers must question subsequent "diagnostics" if only because "enlightened" investigators—whether against circumcision or for it—have clinically promoted them. Never was this more the case than in the late nineteenth century, part of the "post-pre-classical episteme" still prevalent today—in some intellectual historians' constructions.

SYMPTOMATOLOGICAL CONTRAST:
DR. REMONDINO'S DIAGNOSTICS

The fate of foreskins is vividly analyzed according to assumptions of so-called modernity—an era envisioning absolute fixity—in P. C. Remondino's *History of Circumcision* (1891), No. 11 in the Physician's and Students'

Ready Reference Series. Absolutely *not* a travelogue, this captivating work by a doctor and health officer from San Diego County consolidates conjectural prehistory, would-be universal history, Lamarckian and/or Darwinian evolution, and several theologies in a declared, general "war against prepuces." (It would, of course, be just as "modern" to be universally, diagnostically *for* foreskins).

Remondino—rigorous laboratory worker, autodidact, humane professional, popularizer, and enthusiastic dabbler in world history—clinches his case against the outlaw prepuce with a pitch to the financial industry:

> . . . a prepuce was a dangerous appendage at any time, and life-insurance companies should class the wearer of a prepuce under the head of hazardous risks, for a circumcised laborer in a powder-mill or a circumcised brakemen [sic] or locomotive engineer runs actually less risk than an uncircumcised tailor or watchmaker. . . . It would be interesting to know, from the statistics of some of these companies, how much more the Hebrew is, as a premium-payer, of value to the company than his uncircumcised brother. Were they to offer some inducement, in the shape of lower rates, to the circumcised, as they should do, they would not only benefit the companies by insuring a longer number of years, on which the insured would pay premiums, but they would be instrumental in decreasing the death-rate and extending longevity. (290)

The book graphically depicts ill effects of prepuces sure to make all but the most medical-minded reader wince: syphilis, phthisis, phimosis, cancer, gangrene of the penis, sysuria, enuresis, and retention of urine. Those are just a few of the maladies visited upon retainers of foreskins, whose presence/absence is made symptomatic of virtually every clinical effect. One could call Remondino's "episteme" ultradiagnostic.[32]

With Remondino, as with Montaigne (plus other authors in this essay), I scrupulously avoid explaining away attitudes toward un/circumcisions by the author's own "identity," or the mother's. (That question is conceivably as complex for Remondino as for Montaigne!) Despite its professed "enlightenment," Remondino's account demonstrates thoroughgoing hyperbole. If I were not already profoundly sympathetic to certain own and others' circumcisions—as well as uncircumcisions among, say, Hindu-Balinese—I might well have become so upon reading Remondino, whether in 1891 or 1991 (time of writing).[33]

Remondino blends his persuasive etiologies with compelling metaphorical flights of fancy:

> There is a weird and ghostly but interesting tale connected with the Moslem conquest of Spain, of how Roderick, the last of the Gothic kings, when in trouble and worry, repaired to an old castle, in the secret recesses of which was a magic

table whereon would pass in grim procession the different events of the future of Spain; as he gazed on the enchanted table he there saw his own ruin and his country's and nation's subjugation. (7)

Having implied that circumcised Moslems surpassed Gothic rivals, Remondino's argument turns allegorical, practically Frazerian:

> Anatomy is generally called a dry study, but, like the enchanted brazen table in the ancient Gothic castle, it tells a no less weird or interesting tale of the past. Its revelations lighten up a long vista, through the thousands of years through which the human species has evolved from its earliest appearance on earth, gradually working up through the different evolutionary processes to what is today supposed to be the acme of perfection as seen in the Indo-European and Semitic races of man. Anatomy points to the rudiment—still lingering, now and then . . . in some one man . . . —of that climbing muscle which shows man in the past . . . nervously escaping up the trunk of a tree in his flight from . . . carnivorous animals. . . . The now useless ear-muscles . . . also tell us of a movable, flapping ear capable of being turned in any direction to catch the sound of approaching danger, . . . the ear being then used for some more useful purpose than having its tympanum tortured by Wagnerian discordant sounds. (8)

Remondino's evocations of pre-Wagnerian pragmatic ears (along with pre-bourgeois survivals of olfactory skills that I here delete) preface a panoramic vision of human progress which seems simultaneously Hegelian, Darwinian, and Lamarckian. History surges from the circumcised priesthood of ancient Egypt to eventual eradication of our species' vestigial flaw:

> Nature—always careful that nothing should interfere with the procreative functions—had provided him with a sheath or prepuce, wherein he carried his procreative organ safely out of harm's way, in wild steeple-chases through thorny briars and bramble-brakes. . . . This leathery pouch also protected him from the many leeches, small aquatic lizards . . . from the bites of ants or other vermin when, tired, he rested on his haunches on some mossy bank or sand-hill. (9)

Disputing Renan, Remondino hails forerunners of practices that accelerate Nature's own advancement toward a heartier humanity:

> Man has now no use for any of these necessaries of a long-past age, —an age so remote that the speculations of Ernest Renan regarding the differences between the Semitic race of Shem and the idolatrous descendants of Ham . . . seem more as if he were discussing an event of yesterday . . .—and we find them disappearing, disuse gradually producing an obliteration of this tissue. . . . The other conditions have nothing that interferes with their disappearance; whereas the prepuce, by its mechanical construction and the expanding portions which it in-

closes, tends at times rather to its exaggerated development than to its disap-
pearance. (10)

Remondino's introduction advises that medical history confirms the budge
evolution required from Civilization to advance beyond the rudiment foreskin.
His anachronistic similes conclude by revisiting the primitive phallus gone
unprotected: "In those days, but for the . . . preputial envelope . . . , the glans
penis of primitive man would have often looked *like* the head of the proverbi-
ally duel-disfigured German university student, or the Bacchus-worshiping
nose of a jolly British Boniface" (206; emphasis added).

———————

Remondino's style of treatise is "enlightened" in a profounder sense than "sec-
ularized"; it demonstrates a thorough faith in progress: the amelioration of
humankind in part through human agency. Medical analysis is easily recon-
ciled with select Scriptures; for example, the Old Testament readily accommo-
dates scientific evolutionism and etiologies of social diseases:

> We may well exclaim, as we behold this appendage to man, —now of no use in
> health and of the most doubtful assistance to the very organ it was intended to
> protect, when that organ, through its iniquitous tastes, has got itself into trouble,
> and, Job-like, is lying repentant and sick in its many wrappings of lint, with
> perhaps its companions in crime imprisoned in a suspensory bandage,—what is
> this prepuce? Whence, why, where, and whither? At times, Nature, as if impatient
> of the slow march of gradual evolution, and exasperated at this persistent and
> useless as well as dangerous relic of a far-distant prehistoric age, takes things in
> her own hands and induces a sloughing to take place, which rids it of its annoy-
> ance. In the far-off land of Ur, among the mountainous regions of Kurdistan,
> something over six thousand years ago, the fathers of the Hebrew race, inspired by
> a wisdom that could be nothing less than of divine origin, forestalled the process
> of evolution by establishing the rite of circumcision. (10)

This theme leads on to a powerful chronology of the persecution of Jews, with
annotations:

> I. 167 B.C. Antiochus forbids Hebrew mothers to circumcise sons, under penalty
>   of death. . . .
> II. 218 A.D. Heliogabalus is himself circumcised. . . .
> IV. Constantine: death for Hebrews who circumcise slaves.
> V. Justinian: Hebrews may not raise children as same.
> VI. 7th cent. Unbaptised banished; renunciation of circumcision and Sabbath re-
>   quired.

His list ends with persecutions by Saracens and finally the fifteenth-century
Spanish Inquisition. The legacy of repression points up a phenomenal vitality

of circumcision: "Its resistance and apparent indestructibility would seem to stamp it as of divine origin" (67).

Remondino's suggestions of supernatural teleology behind circumcision's history season his mottled scheme of secular-scriptural medical progress. Indeed, vestiges of "pre-enlightenment" ideas may linger in his notions of a divine plan (the sloughing off of foreskins)—a process susceptible of acceleration by human arts in tune with world destiny. Such notions vaguely resemble Neoplatonist alchemical ideas about accelerating the globe's growth into perfect elements, to hasten the Book of Nature's too gradual transformation of substances back into gold's equivalent, thus redeeming all matter: subterranean, aqueous, and hypereal.[34] But Neoplatonist cure (part of Foucault's "pre-classical episteme") was thoroughly organic; it still considered matter later deemed "inorganic" (e.g., metals) to be living—perhaps "ert" (rather than inert).

Recalling those "beginnings" (Foucault or Couliano) invoked at the present essay's outset, I might generalize as follows: Only after concern for microcosmic-macrocosmic affinities yielded to convictions of a "dead" nature—advanced as a "reform" against magical-erotic arts (and concepts of "sinning Nature")—did the "discourse of modernism" consolidate around universalized diagnosis and analytic knowledge.[35] Or, to recast matters in the ideological idiom of some contemporary partisans (e.g., J. Lewis, 1967): Remondino's 1891 treatise promoted among surgeons and their clients what became the most common operation routinized in the era of triumphant medicalized technologies. (My personal view would be radically—and relativistically—more Montaignesque.)

Remondino draws his specific cases principally from encyclopedic "histories" (themselves an Enlightenment discourse) and from general accounts derived from them over the seventeenth to nineteenth centuries. Still, Remondino's 1891 *History*, which I am using to illustrate one style of universalizing prescribed circumcision, tries to incorporate a little sixteenth century evidence—including Montaigne. How?

To begin at the beginning, consider the decorative frontispiece of Remondino's book ("From an old sixteenth century Italian print in the author's collection, representing the scene of the Holy Circumcision"). One could contrast other iconographic traditions, which he neglects, that also emphasized Christ's circumcision, such as Hendrik Goltzius's "Life of the Virgin" series (1593–94; it includes the circumcision, the visitation, Holy Family, and Adoration.) Sixteenth-century artists experimented with diverse solutions to dilemmas of representing Biblical narrative through historicism or typification. Goltzius's devices displayed not just anachronistic garb and setting common in Renaissance illustrations of such scenes, but eyeglasses on Christ's circumcisor. On the other hand, Remondino's frontispiece composites furnishings and architecture of early modern Europe with apparently historicized costume. Remondino's *History*, of course, does not comment on such dilemmas of illusioning or emblematizing the past. The frontispiece is a visible sign to label the book's object of analysis *circumcision*—captioned as "Hebraic Circumcision," although the source-reference declares the illustration "Holy Circumcision." So tagged, the visual device levels distinctions between Hebrew and Catholic and reduces contradictory rites represented to decorative diagnosis. I read Remondino's frontispiece as an inadvertent emblem of what makes his study "Enlightened," even when depicting sixteenth-century depictions.

I am unqualified to pursue further (or indeed this far!) lively art historical debates about emblems, illusions, typifications, and descriptions—such as those waged against iconology in Svetlana Alper's *The Art of Describing*.[36] To compensate for my inadequacy in this regard, let me mention a persuasive icon of circumcision that once fell beneath my touristic gaze, or perusal. Dating from 1505–10, it can be visited in Brussels (just where, I forget): the "Retable dit de 'Saluces'," showing "La Vie de la Vierge et l'enfance du Christ." The moment of cutting is carved in high relief, a spatter of red pigment applied to the wood. The circumcision scene in an adjoining "retable domestique," dating from 1480, does not depict the act of cutting. My ethnographic curiosity wanders toward possible responses of devotees confronting these respective icons (see below, "Boutade I").

Similar extra-Vagances come to mind when encountering Remondino's material on "Miracles and the Holy Prepuce," a survey of eighth to eighteenth-century sanctuaries reputed to house bits of Christ's foreskin, of curative power to devotees. "In the internecine wars of the sixteenth century," he writes, "the abbey [of Charroux, founded by Charlemagne in 783] fell into the hands of the godless and heretical Huguenots and the holy relic disappeared" (72). But again, Remondino makes little "history" of disputes between Catholics and Protestants, of the Reformation's rejection of thaumaturgical ideals, or of germane sectarian positions. His universalizing style skips from the Huguenots to the abbey's demolishment in 1856, when an unearthed piece of desiccated flesh was declared Christ's lost prepuce. Remondino's discourse converts events themselves into visual-decorative diagnostics. The implied "authority" of his description doubts the magical efficacy of relics from any century, while professing faith in the health efficacy of circumcision of every century. What *is* Enlightenment?[37]

———————

This brings us again to Montaigne, or to his travelogue's fate in *The History of Circumcision*, which summarizes in a "reasonable" fashion the focal scene revisited at length above. Remondino (or perhaps versions he employed) deletes much that seems specific to Montaigne's comparative narrative through "chords of difference." Remondino transmogrifies resonant details into a standardized sequence of averaged examples. As a consequence, Montaigne's account of odors that induce devotional attitudes (in Rabbi, godfather, and circumcisee alike) and his repeated references to the mouthful of preputial blood are sloughed off. Remondino cuts instead to an 1886 account (taken from the *Cyclopedia of Biblical, Theological, and Ecclesiastical Literature*) of "circumcision in our modern synagogues." He thus elides Montaigne's *Journal* entry with ritual usages whose primary oral dimension is verbal-aural rather than tactile-olfactory. After briefly alluding to knife, wound, and bandages, the *Cyclopedia* cites sublimated responses of congregation, circumciser, and father. Regretfully, I here abbreviate words that are sensorily concrete and surely moving in their own way—albeit different from the rites that Montaigne wrote about having witnessed:

> "Blessed is he that cometh to be circumcised and enter into the covenant. . . ." "Thy father and mother shall rejoice. . . ." "Blessed art Thou, O Lord our God, King of the Universe! . . . As he hath entered into the law, the canopy, and the good and virtuous deeds. . . ." (149)

Remondino next reviews later prohibitions of "Mezizah, the fourth or Objectionable Act of Suction," and approves history's progress toward proper measures of beneficial prepuce eradication:

> By virtue of this decree a regulation was passed by the Consistories on the 12th of July 1854, ordering that thereafter circumcision should only be performed in a rational manner, and by a properly qualified person. Suction was likewise abolished, and the wound directed to be sponged with wine and water. This decree and the resulting regulations have been of the greatest benefit to the French Israelites, and some attention to the matter would not be amiss in the United States. (157)

In Remondino all circumcision that can be surveyed—anywhere, anytime—is enlisted in the ranks of a unified species of practice—reduced to medical benefits and ratified by rationality. And he extends this diagnosis to Montaigne's travel-telling of a dramatically different ritual from a possibly different episteme across significantly different times.

CONCLUSION: ETHNOGRAPHIES ENTRE-EPISTEMES, OR, GNOSIS/DIAGNOSIS

In Foucauldian schemes of critique (here "deployed" relatively ironically), rationalized approaches to normalized knowledge gathered force through the seventeenth century, became standard during the eighteenth century, lingered (culminated?) in late nineteenth-century clinical-mindedness, and endure to-day in the "analytic gaze." With respect to the topic (un)circumcision, such Enlightenment views may be phrased as follows: "Modern" circumcision is seen not as something one does (or has done), or does not do, to be like oneself and different from another—relationally, diacritically, significantly; rather circumcision of any variety is seen as something one does, or does not do, to be better, or worse, on a presumably absolute, knowable, measurable, and diagnosible scale.

Such an attitude establishes the possibility of a pro-circumcision vision of the prepuce as something that Reason (deified?) may help Nature (personified?) outgrow, relegate to a past, leave behind, slough off. This was Remondino's position. But the opposite vision is simultaneously facilitated, whereby totalizing "rationalizers" could declare the prepuce universally justified, of absolute advantage intact. The imagined outcome in either diagnostic is neutralized sanitation: undialectical health "itself," overall. The discourse associated with this future processes universality from the findings of incidental travel-writing or locally specific ethnographies. Ritual accidentals of dramatic, liturgical, and sectarian difference wind up synthesized in a conformist progress—whether toward proper circumcision (as in Remondino) or, tragically, toward intolerant uncircumcision in a history of totalitarian prejudices too notorious to need reviewing here.[38]

This brings me back to hermeneutics—whether in Early Modern discourse or in subsequent murmurs dispersed beneath those Enlightenment analytics that supplanted interpretation. I here intend "early modern" less as an historicist construction than as a figural "non-now" posed as an *altérité* to modernity or its postmodern extension. The sixteenth century has become a time (or chronotope) scholars consider to be prior to universalist codes of diagnostic othering. Moreover, the 1500s (including Montaigne's 1580s) partly consolidated "travel writing" as a mode of description—when reading-the-world promised to reveal copious rarities and varieties and, through them, verities. Travel writing, and perhaps ethnography, ever since can only wish it were so, or recognize ironically that it cannot be so, or, more radically, could not have been so, even then. (That insight, possibly, was one profundity of Lévi-Strauss's *Tristes tropiques*.)

Regardless, counterdiagnostic description recalls aspects of Montaigne's "episteme," wherein circumcision, to keep to our example, is something one does (or has done), or does not do, to be like oneself and different from another—relationally, sectarianly, culturally. In such formations (un)circumcision *means* variably, intricately, and ambivalently; none of its realizations *ameliorates* analytically, symptomatically, or uniformly. Un(circumcision), moreover, has been and remains a topos of exaggerated contrasts—there and here, then and now. Such rituals-*cum*-rhetoric effect chords of differences across a medley of senses—not just visual and verbal, but tactile, sartorial-material, aural, and olfactory too. Here is one textual example:

> Then Noah built an altar to the Lord. He took ritually clean beasts and birds of every kind, and offered whole-offerings on the altar. When the Lord smelt the soothing odor, he said within himself, "Never again will I curse the ground because of man, however evil his inclinations may be from his youth upwards. (Gen. 8: 20–21)

Smelling too enters covenants—whether signified by rainbows, foreskins, or other "sacrifices" that oscillate among and as hybrid sectarian contrasts. Such semiotics call into question the predominance of any single sensory channel (e.g., the visual) and set in doubt the isolability of "genitality," among other categories progressively fixed ever since the Enlightenment.[39]

Speaking of which, should not theories of Enlightenment be self-doubting rather than credulously self-congratulating? Following Kant's question as to the nature of *Erklärung*, ought not any such critical spirit turn critique on itself as well? Ritual may help in this regard. For example, many critical theorists today still universalistically equate sexuality with genitality; they thus reduce historical and cultural bodies (and souls) to these dimensions, despite their oft-professed goals of transcending bourgeois constriction, discontent, and symptomatic repression.[40] But has not ethnography taught attentive readers that supposedly "genital" rites are as polysensory as any others?

———————

For all that, a persistent characteristic recurs in varied circumscriptions of circumcision/uncircumcision, including the present one: an unsettled tonality marked by either reticence or overkill. (The latter rhetoric proliferates in current sexual politics against ritual "mutilation"—the general category universally applied.) In recent and venerable sources alike—whether pro-, con-, analytically "neutral," or interpretively empathetic—words about (un)circumcision tend to be hypertrophied: either oddly laconic and allusive or overwrought and effusive. This ritual *topos* keeps calling forth the textual marks and prose registers of obsession.

Even in acknowledging this trait, ever so measuredly, my essay (joining many studies it cites) runs the risk of appearing obsessive—likely guilty of saying too little or too much. (I have tried here to be true to these ambiguities, so prevalent across different genres describing circumcision-or-not.) The peril of seeming obsessed seems to me worthy, because diacritical rites—once begun in and over times and cultures—can never be escaped or erased. Finally, to utopian critics (including some "postmodern" ones), who foresee a lasting solution regarding whether to circumcise or uncircumcise, I can only conclude with a celebrated reminder from Freud:

> In this case, too, the *unheimlich* is what was once *heimisch,* home-like, familiar; the prefix "un" is the token of repression. (1955)[41]

BOUTADE I. EAVESDROPPING ON EXPERT ICONOGRAPHERS

The effusive/laconic tonality my essay has signalled can be further illustrated from anecdotes of discussions I once overheard. Un/circumcision crops up in strange scholarly places, including a conference on "Iconography at the Crossroads" in central New Jersey. The papers roamed widely: rethinking Warburg and Panofsky's art history; decoding cryptic meanings of crucifixes in light of gender and class; addressing the accent on "body" that befell Christian art in Leo Steinberg's *The Sexuality of Christ in Renaissance Art and in Modern Oblivion*.[42] One paper on Florence—by a gifted social historian of Renaissance ceremonies and ideologies—explored possible affects among devotees when beholding painted and sculpted icons. He considered naked infants versus bedraped Christs; the cross-dressing of crucifixes by female worshippers; male ambivalence vis-à-vis Christ's genitalia; the Church's anxieties that monks or laymen would suffer erections when viewing naked figures; the somatic-interpretive theme of Christ's unavoidable erection during crucifixion (like male martyrs at the moment of hanging—I recalled from *Billy Budd*); the vogue for idealized and/or pruriant crucifixion scenes of sensualized suffering.[43]

During the session's lively question period, an inordinately prominent scholar of art history in the audience stood to make the following declaration, more or less: Of three known icons (two crucifixions and one deposition) where—exceptionally—Christ's genitals were visible (in the deposition, through a veil gauzily), none demonstrated an erection and none, he added almost as an afterthought, was circumcised. Customarily this critically astute art historian is wary of claiming definitive visual evidence even for highly conspicuous motifs. But, before anyone could query how positive he could be that the foreskin depicted was altogether intact, the coffee break intervened. Was his bold comment intended to demonstrate bravado in addressing any iconographic details whatsoever? (Any ethnographer present would have noted folks growing all abuzz and atitter.) There's that telltale, obsessive-seeming ambivalence wherever un/circumcision looms.[44]

His observation about uncircumcised crucifix genitals calls to mind S. Gilman's *Sexuality: An Illustrated History*, which suggests that Christian icons showing Christ uncut may serve to deny his Jewish identity (1989a: 41). (Gilman's vast work explores how representations and discourses sustain underlying prejudices, such as anti-Semitism, homophobia, etc.) Any iconography's implications, however, are convoluted. We saw above that attributes other than the foreskin may be "archaeologically" inaccurate in early modern representations (e.g., Goltzius's). Moreover, Christ's circumcision became featured in some Church-sponsored devices, as Steinberg, Simon Schama, and other scholars have stressed.[45] Even the *denial* of circumcision, then, is no constant "symptom;" significance varies across schemes that make differences particular.

Back to the conference. The moment just described of titter-producing, iconographic audience response was not the end of my eavesdropping. During the break I approached the podium to greet the principal speaker (and a friend)—that social historian of Florence. But I was forestalled by a conferee in process of summarily upbraiding him for having alluded to castration as making victims "woman-like," for having associated male homosexual receiver-roles with feminine "passivity"; and worse. She actually proclaimed his paper to his face misogynist. I next heard my friend—whose feminist credentials are actually impeccable—reply that he had only been paraphrasing Renaissance Florentine views. Whereupon she decried *him* for not decrying *them* every step of the way. He kept the "conversation" going—doubtless to get both himself and his Florentines relatively off the hook—by adducing a case of "even worse mysogyny": Islam. During Islamic circumcision rites, he assured his accuser, dominant male Muslims reduce passive males to utter subjugation. This assertion—well beyond either interlocutor's realm of expertise— received for him her first nod of approbation. *Pace.*

What has transpired during this revealing exchange? At a moment of internecine hostility among Europeanists (feminist attacking misogynist), an "even worse" *other* is suddenly invoked, against which both sides can join forces. Islam—as usual poorly covered (perhaps especially when circumcising)—had leapt to his mind as a transparent case of politics pure and simple: the unfettered dominance, he assumed, of senior males over novice boys or youths and women alike.[46] Customarily, this historian's work stresses subtexts, nuances of ceremony, role reversals, and switched signs and circuits. He tends to evoke every imaginable veil between practices interpreted and dead certainty; in the realm of Renaissance pageantry, he finds subtleties where others wrongly infer patent chauvinism. Yet, having read a recent fieldwork account of circumcision in Morocco (as he later told me, although unfamiliar with work on female "circumcision" elsewhere), he managed to conclude that Islam entailed unproblematic patriarchy (of male over male).

Again, this wonderful historian deals imaginatively and sympathetically with issues of both worship and repressions (e.g., homoerotics/homophobia) in Christianity.[47] Yet under attack by a feminist assailant, he tried to parry a tired critique by abruptly invoking "Islamic circumcision." At that fleeting moment, my friend seemed to be implying that matters of ritual and power *elsewhere* might be explained by "symptomatological" analysis. I might have done likewise, although with different examples, in similar circumstances.

Will we never finally outgrow (or regress from) Enlightenment diagnostics? Is there no Montaignesque "space" left for real ambiguities of what historian-anthropologist Greg Dening has called theatricality—a "space" (Foucault might have discoursed, *and* Frances Yates might have *memoried*) ungoverned by anyone's uniform gaze, whether uncircumcising *and* not?[48]

To beckon once again more nuanced descriptions of Islamic variations on (male) circumcision (including the role of women), let me cite Jaffur Shurreef's pungent account of "Moosulmans" in India in 1832:

> It is customary with some women (for others have no faith in it) never to have a child circumcised *alone*, but always along with another to make an even number; ... they get some poor woman's son to be circumcised with theirs. [Or] they substitute an earthen *budhna* (or pot having a spout); in the mouth of which, they insert a *pan ka beera* (or betel-parcel)... and, after circumcising the boy, they cut off the *pan ka beera* (or betel-parcel); which is to represent a second circumcision. ... They guard the boy against the contact of dogs, cats, and other defilements—such as women who are *unwell*; for it is supposed, that to see them or receive their shadow is unlucky. ..." (1832: 43–46)

This scene of intricate, sensory circumcision in Islamic India helps me remember what I glimpsed in Indonesia in 1972: a chromatic possibility along the scale (*gamme*) of differences separating circumcising Muslim Buginese (who bury) from uncircumcising Hindu-Balinese (who cremate). Universal standards and reductive analytics promoted by conformist states and schools of diagnosis suppress such chromaticisms of ritual practices (see Chap. 3). Montaigne, as I reread him, proceeded otherwise.[49]

BOUTADE II. EVADING/EXHIBITING FREUD

"Symptomatological" *analyses* of circumcision—whether pro or con—continue today even after Freud's *Moses and Monotheism* (1938). That endlessly controversial work may have cancelled Jewish(-Egyptian) circumcision as a basic ingredient in Europe's tragic history of "othering." Or did *Moses and Monotheism* attempt the end of (or the last) patricide? (Alternative questions exist).[50]

Brooding on these possibilities, among copious other ones, I seek ways to inscribe (un)circumcision comparatively, ways that resonate with another Freudian project: celebrating the *unheimlich*. Anyone confronting Freud's possible cancellation of circumcision could keep interpretations ecumenical by simultaneously reinstating it. I think here of Henry Adams, who (nearly) begins his 1918 *Education* (an autobiography eerily in the "third person") with a paragraph that imagines himself having been Jerusalem-born and circumcised under the name "Israel Cohen" (3). It strikes me that Adams could well have begun: "Adams Jewish? . . . Were Adams Jewish . . . ," if only to anticipate Freud's 1938 "beginnings" *re* Moses, as Egyptian. Little seems to have been beyond Henry Adam's imagination—including Tahiti, although he had truly "been there."[51] Henry Adams may well have anticipated Freud.

The few puffs of Freud in my pages suggest either an inability or a reluctance to address his work squarely or to second-guess the master. Other scholars have shown more daring; I might mention works by S. Gilman, E. Santner, D. Boyarin, and particularly J. Geller, whose complex writing project may go Freud one better. I would also salute sly studies by J. Malcolm; comparative psychoanalytics in G. Obeyesekere (1990); and earlier efforts by such scholars as P. Rieff (1954, 1979), among others.[52] These approaches raise my hopes of one day commemorating Freud's aftermath in suitably *comparative* writing— as K. Burke and P. Mahoney possibly encouraged.[53]

In the matter of Freud's intertextual life, difficult ambiguities continue augmenting, as Freud doubtless foretold, the more successors presume to know. To appreciate this fact—which I call "ultraobjective"—I sometimes tap peculiarly revisionist readings of Freud—such as P. Vitz's investigations of his Catholic nanny.[54] Odd slants provide tactical antidotes against standardized scholarship—Peter Gay's, for example—that unduly "ameliorates" Freud, heroically.[55] Ever-spiraling intricacies of interpreting Freud interpreting (Freud interpreting) have come a long way—progressed? regressed?—since Ernest Jones's biography (1953–57) attributed filial piety to the very subject who made patricide a household word!

Disarmingly, Freud's lifeway—despite its mists and contradictions—keeps winding up monumentalized, ennobled, indeed "enlightened." (Will a similar fate befall Derrida? Jones, by the way, made nothing much of Freud's "own circumcision.")[56]

To counter such reductive promotion of Freud into normalized exemplarity, this reader still oscillates Freud's own sense of "uncanny" with his controversial as-if histories—including *Moses and Monotheism*, a book about foreskins, in fact.

What does an interdisciplinary ethnographer *want*?

Fig. 6. A Balinese temple *candi*, silhouetted; this particular split gate frames a memorial to wartime (World War II; Japanese occupation; brief Dutch resumption; Indonesian *merdeka*) that also rearranges the past. (Author's photo, 1972)

Fig. 7. An inner gate (*padu raksa*) in North Bali. Rites and tales associated with the temple's founder were researched by the Dutch before World War I and reworked by Balinese between-the-wars. (Author's photo, 1982; on the persons seated, see Chap. 13)

CHAPTER THREE

About a Footnote: Between-the-Wars Bali;
Its Relics Regained

BEFORE PROCEEDING, consider scrupulously these scrupulous words of anthropologist Gregory Bateson:

> An event occurs, for example, a battle is fought, or a man is born or dies, or writes a book. Then memory of this event centers later around some relic or, lacking a relic, we set up a tablet or memorial to the past event, and either the relic or the memorial becomes an influence which pushes those who come after to perpetuate the sociological effects of the original event. Thus we invest the past with real authority and set it, like a policeman, to the business of governing the present. Sometimes the precepts of the past do not quite suit us or the past event is not dramatic enough for our taste, then we are compelled to emend or to embellish the story woven around the relic. (1937:133)

Bateson's words—ultraobjective and worth intoning—grace "An Old Temple and a New Myth," an article about rearranging contemporary concerns to render plausible, and alluring, the past. That piece was occasioned by Balinese culture, ritual practice, and speech, meticulously recorded and translated. Identical words could be applied also to the book compiled by Jane Belo, in which Bateson's essay was republished over thirty years later. Belo's *Traditional Balinese Culture* (1970) purported to represent an event: "Balinese studies in the 1930s." And Belo's book evokes the past by embellishing the story woven round the relic, occasionally investing it with authority, like a policeman. For readers today Bateson's words become a gift from interwar Bali that illuminates how that very subject (including Bateson's words themselves) would subsequently be commemorated. In the following pages I accept Bateson's gift and recirculate the above-cited passage as epigraphs, or perhaps rubrics.[1]

This chapter's fragments are scored with phrases from Bateson. My compositional technique is inspired perhaps by surrealism, perhaps by musical examples that figure in our story. Readers can entertain such possibilities behind this composite text of disparate data, strange interludes, unexpected connections, and undecidable questions interlacing fieldworks and remembering them.

Like Proust's, our subject is memory, or the writing-construction (the commemoration) of memories—partly shared ones: semi-social-facts from a charmed circle's sense of *entre-deux-guerres*.[2] Margaret Mead enters often, but tangentially, into this tale of interwar Bali, as do Jane Belo and Walter

Spies. Bateson, although a key protagonist, has been converted to a source of "leading motives." I hope thereby to surmount artificially "centered" histories of disciplines, verging instead on extra-Vagant alternatives to heroic or even antiheroic histories of encounter.

As we proceed, I allude to psychoanalytic views of repression and displacement, and I consider in passing one case (Culture and Personality) of many disciplinary movements made to appear inevitable through acts of retrospection. Yet my subject is *texts* of commemoration, not *lives* presumably "behind" those texts—lives that others may subject to psychologistic investigation. The present study strives *not* to become certain familiar things: *not* an exposé of prominent figures; *not* a cynical revelation that Balinese studies are about Balinists as well as Bali (this kind of point should no longer be "news," if it ever was); and *not* an ode to the good old *d'antan* days of those oh-so-yester years.

To resist the above-mentioned plots, without suppressing evidence of their appeal to others, I pursue ambiguities that are fluid, resonant, charged with specificity. My prose commemorates prose commemorations; its proper signature may be the "key" of Debussy—misty fragments neither obscurist nor subjective, heightened with half-tones of precision and reflexivity.

Fragment 1: "We invest the past with real authority"

War is—besides hell, sorrow, and suffering—a "space" (Michel Foucault might have said) around which gathers a *vor dem*, a *nach dem*, and, alas, an "inter." Like revolution, "war" betokens the essence of "eventness": the headline, the declared, the won/lost. "War" represents FACT *en majuscules*; then come the wrenching details. Upon the hinge of "wartime," near-forgottens turn into ordered recollection; the ensuing mode is often commemorative, sometimes elegiac.[3]

Theories of knowing and knowledge occasionally contest whether war-events or revolution-events exactly happen as constructed. A postwar classic in doubting the priority of anything originary was Lévi-Strauss's famous dissolution of "1789":

> Both history and ethnography are concerned with societies other than the one in which we live. Whether this otherness is due to remoteness in time (however slight), or to remoteness in space, or even to cultural heterogeneity, is of secondary importance. . . . What constitutes the goal of the two disciplines? Is it the exact reconstruction of what has happened, or is happening, in the society under study? To assert this would be to forget that in both cases we are dealing with systems of representations which differ for each member of the group and which, on the whole, differ from the representations of the investigator. The best ethnographic

study will never make the reader a native. The French Revolution of 1789 lived through by an aristocrat is not the same phenomenon as the Revolution of 1789 lived through by a *sans-culotte*, and neither would correspond to the Revolution of 1789 as conceived by Michelet or Taine. (1963:17)

In order to reconcile history and ethnography-ethnology (and "hot" and "cold" societies), Lévi-Strauss questioned the underpinnings of chrono-logics. He displaced sequences that some ideologies misconstrue as time's own story of itself. Such challenges to the authority and priority of events have burgeoned in both modernist literature and postwar *sciences humaines*.[4] Foucault too, in his mid-career classic (*Les Mots et les choses*) resisted "symptomatological history"—plumping instead for contrastive histories of possibilities, of imagined "otherwises."

In systems of representation called "history," war epitomizes those events presumed to have a before and an after. "War," moreover, coaxes other experiences and reminiscences into a centralized format of upheaval. Some might call war, so imagined, intellectually hegemonic. Even a critical movement that doubts historical causality and determinant contexts—surrealism, for example—is made to bow to "war," even by scholars sympathetic to that movement. Hence, Walter Benjamin on "Surrealism": "What sprang up in 1919 . . . fed on the damp boredom of postwar Europe."[5] Hence too, Lévi-Strauss's suggestion that surrealism—ostensibly the least legacy-laden of -isms—was less ahistorical than sometimes portrayed: "Le surréalisme aussi savait à l'occasion s'inspirer du passé" (1983a: 342).[6]

James Clifford's seminal essay "On Ethnographic Surrealism" (1981) explored rich associations between desired incongruity and anthropology's attraction (often denied officially) to "the exotic, the paradoxical, the *insolite*."[7] Clifford accentuates such scholars as G. Bataille and M. Leiris; but other, less subversive-looking scholars—Burke and Lévi-Strauss, for example—have also championed incongruity and at least occasional surrealism. Clifford starkly poses "the surrealist moment" in ethnography as "that moment in which the possibility of comparison exists in unmediated tension with sheer incongruity" (1981: 563). My sense of surrealism (ethnographic and otherwise) is less absolute: more a mediated tension with incongruity than an unmediated one; more a fragmentariness still somewhat discomforted by not being "whole," or proper—but not nostalgic for that condition, and dubious of its plausibility. Regardless, as Clifford argues, the result of writing toward incongruity—even, I think, when mediated—is "collage," or something like it.

Thus, through processes of *various* surrealist constructions, "après la guerre" becomes the pretext for revisiting a period only eventually construable as interwar. One's sense of that time becomes recontextualized in light of a subsequent fact: a war-fact. "Interwar" becomes construed as a time of difference, of otherwise, in any "history." Histories by anthropologists complicate matters by locating the interwar and otherwise in another place, an ordinarily uneventful place: a fieldwork place. In this event betweenness intensifies; the condition of *entre-deux-guerres* grows exponential.

Fragment 2: "An event occurs, a battle is fought, or a [wo]man . . . writes a book"

To help set in motion arts of commemoration, I linger over an arresting example of recontextualization. My material is ethnographic; the era is, again, interwar (the "age of," among other things, surrealism); the scene is Bali; the subject is Belo. With reference to all this, after World War II—during the continued routinization of psychotherapeutic styles of analysis—"something happened." It is time to speak of Jane.[8]

In 1968, Jane Belo composed her introduction to *Traditional Balinese Culture* (1970), which saluted a company of scholars, performers, and enthusiasts (foreigner and Balinese alike) resident during the 1930s, outside the Dutch colonial administrative establishment. Upon Belo's death, Margaret Mead added a capstone epitaph in *her* customary manner: "She has been a lovely part of all of our lives for the thirty years we have studied Balinese culture together. She brought delight to all she touched" (Mead 1970b). Belo's book's gnomic binding displays luminous, spidery blotches of figures-against-field—a cover "derived from a Batik tapestry in the Margaret Mead collection." The striking design encourages Rorschach responses, or so it strikes me. Regardless, the tome so shrouded became (doubly) a *tombeau*: of and to Bali-then and Belo.

Students of Hollywood's history may recognize the following facts: post-1929 movie studios benefited from an onrush of talented technicians and performers, refugees from the breadlines, willing to work cheap.[9] There resulted labor-intensive, highly wrought productions: Warner Brothers and MGM musicals, Disney animation. . . . Bali too—deprived of tourist guilders, pounds, and dollars during the world's long aftermath of Black Tuesday—harbored gifted stayers-on. Some were adrift; others waited, belts tightened, for the economic and political tides to turn. Connoisseurs of otherness, of indisputably "star quality," parked in Bali; and many Balinese, not uncagily perhaps, intensified their ceremonial displays accordingly:

> And, in fact, in the 1930s, when they were told that the reason fewer tourists were coming to Bali than in previous years was that there was a world depression, the Balinese responded by celebrating an elaborate purification and propitiation ceremony in Besakih, the head temple on the slopes of the Great Mountain, in order to bring the world depression to an end. (Belo 1970: xi)

Belo's early work included her vanguard account of Balinese kinship and endogamy, and a compelling study of ideas and practices surrounding twin births. These pieces alone place Belo in the first rank of Balinese ethnographers; with her entries on "temperament" and on conventionalized children's drawings, they form the core of *Traditional Balinese Culture*. Except for Colin McPhee's piece on Balinese music and two typically unclassifiable articles by Gregory Bateson, the remaining articles are incidental, popular items: brief reconnaissance reports; summaries of "Balinese character" and practices of socialization, etc.

The collection's striking features include its array of foreign contributors, whose sobriquets festoon Belo's introduction: Walter Spies—artist-writer, musician, *bon vivant*, polyglot (Russian, German, French, English, Javanese, Balinese, Indonesian); Colin McPhee—(ethno)musicologist, and Belo's middle husband; Claire Holt—scholar of dance, sculpture, archeology, and art history, and all-round Indonesianist; Arthur Waley, Orientalist—together with his companion, Beryl de Zoete, renowned choreographer; Katharane Mershon from California—professional dancer, past director of the Pasadena Playhouse, amateur nurse, autodidact in Balinese Brahmana high rituals, and wife of her dancing partner, Mack Mershon, brilliant photographer; Margaret Mead and Gregory Bateson—anthropologists and married to each other. Those *were* the days.

Now for a key sequence of contacts. Although Belo and Mead had met at Barnard when both studied under Boas, Belo's earliest materials from Bali (on twins) were collected independently of Mead and before Belo first encountered Bateson in 1934. Belo, however, had read Mead's works on Samoa and Manus before completing her research on Balinese families and temperament. In New York in 1934, Belo helped kindle Mead's interest in Bali; then in 1936, upon Belo's return to Bali, strong ties developed. Belo was converted to topics in Culture and Personality promoted by Mead, and to intensive fieldwork techniques favored by Mead and Bateson. These extravagant methods involved photographing, filming, and multiply recording and inscribing ritual events by employing several Balinese and non-Balinese as multisensory "stenographers" (you might say). Mead and Bateson's intricate semiotics—combining their brand of "writing lesson," "viewing lesson," "hearing lesson," etc.—form part of a distinctive history of description and captioning in Balinese studies.[10]

Although Belo's important work on Bali's temple festivals (1953) remained closer in spirit to standard ethnographic documentation, her influential account of exorcist rites surrounding witch Rangda (1949) stressed themes and frameworks from Culture and Personality. The full flowering of Belo's conversion to Mead and Bateson's program of research was Belo's *Trance in Bali* (1960; discussed above in Chap. 1).

These points bring me to an entry in *Traditional Balinese Culture* that I have delayed mentioning—one inserted before the book's concluding item (Bateson's "The Value System of a Steady State"). Its author, T. M. Abel (not a Balinist) remains uncommemorated in Belo's introduction. Instead, the article just lies there, juxtaposed; its title: "Free Designs as a Personality Index: A Comparison of Schizophrenics with Normal, Subnormal, and Primitive Culture Groups." I quote some characteristic snippets:

> The other primitive group, the Balinese (Group VI), has had much less cultural contact with white people [than has the Navaho]. . . . [The Balinese] hate tests and are suspicious of their purpose.
>   . . . Dr. Mead [in her letter of February 12, 1938] described the personality structure of the Balinese as follows: "The whole emphasis of the education is to scatter, disintegrate, separate one response from another, and to make only very superficial verbalistic associations. It's not so much that the Balinese can't take in a new idea, as that they can't take in anything *whole*; their own receptivity is a honeycomb. Every new idea has to be chopped into little bits." (Abel 1938: 380)

Mead's casual remarks do look unfortunate when isolated in this way by Abel. This kind of comment animated Mead's copious correspondences to non-professional readers, her grandmother in particular.[11] But in her protracted work on Balinese behaviors (particularly in Bateson & Mead 1942), Mead modifies such hunches by adducing fuller contexts of communication and styles of interaction. Abel on the other hand immediately imposes a prepackaged symptomatics:

> This factor probably accounts for the making of the discrete ununified lines in the designs. This same factor may be the one dominant in the behavior of schizophrenics. Certainly one of their marked characteristics is disorganization of the total personality, and inability to integrate different aspects of their world of new experiences. They failed to build up a constructive plan for a design, but were successful in drawing the correct number of lines. (1938: 381)

By this point in Abel's diagnosis, the antecedent of "they" is unclear: Balinese or schizophrenics? (Should this disorganization in Abel's own account lead readers to diagnose its author as schizophrenic—or "like a schizophrenic"—too?)

Abel's instant short circuits across culture and psychoses should not be confused with subtler works in Culture and Personality, including some of Mead's books and particularly Benedict's *Patterns of Culture* (1934), which compared *styles* of cultural integration with *styles* of integration of neuroses or psychoses (see Chap. 1). In contrast, Abel's essay compared not styles (of problem personalities) with styles (of cultures) but decontextualized symptom with symptom; it appears to label Balinese as schizophrenic: "Their performance was like that of the paranoid schizophrenics [in her samples], and we have suggested that their attitude and modes of thinking were the same" (1938: 383).

I raise this question not to challenge anew faulty models of psychological parallels long discarded by subtler theorists of Culture and Personality, but to illustrate arguments from an atypical article that was deemed appropriate—at least obliquely—for the tome *Traditional Balinese Culture*.[12] Belo joined Abel's piece to the other studies, including her own, as if they could be assimilated to its terms. Her 1970 volume attached simplified psychologistic reductions to descriptions of culture which, when first published, were relatively innocent of "symptomatological" analysis. This kind of revisionism characterizes many styles of retrospection, including some of Mead's own popular and journalistic work (and that of Pollmann discussed in Chap. 1).[13]

Belo may have inclined toward these reassessments in 1968 for reasons of personal stress. I leave such private matters aside, to explore ironic ramifications ("rhizomes" perhaps) possibly animating her juxtapositions. "Like a policeman," then, Belo's memorial of 1968 managed retrospectively to make certain interwar accounts of Bali appear to say something different from what they would have been saying before. Bearing this paramount point in mind, I turn, hesitantly, to a mysterious footnote.

Fragment 3: "Sometimes . . . the past event is not dramatic enough for our taste"

It is a venerable custom among anthropologists to present *humble* facts of ethnography in a *sublime* style. Practitioners of this rhetorical strategy range from James Frazer (unsurprisingly) and early Malinowski to Robert Lowie.[14] Jane Belo followed suit. The opening of her initial study of Bali seems redolent of epics past, a near pastiche of grandiloquent narrative:

> On the night of September 18, 1933, twins were born to a woman of Sukawana. When the family saw that the twins were a boy and a girl, they knew that this was a great wrong, that disaster had come upon their village. A brother of the father ran to the open place before the *bale agung*, the village temple. There he beat upon the *kul-kul*, the hollow wooden alarm, so that all the men of the village would come together to hear the direful news. And the sleeping villagers awoke in their tiny houses, still warm with the dying coals of the evening fire, and came forth wrapped in their blankets, for at night it is bitter cold on the slopes of the Gunung Penulisan. (1935: 5)

In the year 1968, further sentences occurred to a woman of New York. When she saw that her original study was inadequately prefaced, she wrote a new analysis obscurely related to the original's evidence that opposite-sex twins signify incest in Bali—an event regularly deemed auspicious for high-born houses and catastrophic for commoners. Belo's new note of 1968 refers to Balinese indifference to monozygotic/dizygotic distinctions, to Balinese obliviousness to ideas of exceptional ties between twins, and to Balinese casualness about homosexual play (*main-main*). These features she abruptly contrasts to "Western culture," interjected via footnotes to two postwar psychoanalytical articles: Jules Glenn's "Opposite Sex Twins" (1966) and F.J.A. Kallmann's comparative study of homosexual male twin "index cases" (1952). Belo then concludes:

> There is also to be found in the psychoanalytic literature evidence of strong sexually based attraction between boy and girl twins which comes to light in analysis, as of the adolescent boy-twin who would only find satisfaction by masturbating before a three-way mirror, looking at his own anus and thinking of his sister. Likewise [?] to studies of homosexuality to be found in both of a pair of monozygotic twins. I have nothing to add. (Belo 1970:4–5; question mark mine)

I, on the contrary, have much to add. What might this masturbating boy twin, fixated on his reflected sister-anus, be doing here in 1968? (At this juncture my reading verges on "surrealism" in Clifford's more extreme sense, in the vein of Bataille and Leiris: a surrealism conjoining the sublime and the vulgar, and "licensed to shock.")[15]

Whence Belo's allusions? Whither do they point (besides Trickster)? What is the nature of the psychoanalytic texts that Belo insinuates alongside her data from 1935? How should my study of Belo's peculiar book proceed? What opportunities does her "scandalous" recontextualization (re-textualization?) afford a history of comparative disciplines, or a history of the histories of such disciplines? How manifold may the resonances of stories about culture crossing become and yet remain receivable? To prolong these questions, I turn to Belo's new references—standard fare in some psychoanalysis, but certainly bizarre from the vantage of Bali.

MR. C'S SISTER-ANUS (PSYCHOANALYSIS)

Fragment 4: **"Then we are compelled to emend"**

Belo's first reference relates not just the dreams but the fancies of one Mr. C.:

> He and his sister were brought up close together. Mr. C. recalled their being bathed together and sleeping in the same room. Even at nineteen he shared a room with his sister. The twins shared the responsibility of cleaning the house since both parents were at work. When they were alone they fought, duplicating their parents' relationship to each other. . . . The parents and relatives . . . glowed at seeing them together as if they were a unit.
>
> During latency he knew one twin stuck the other with a fork, but he did not know who did it. . . .
>
> Although he shared a room with his sister, who looked like a movie star, he first thought himself not attracted to her. Later he recalled sexual excitement in her presence. He recalled that masturbation started at thirteen. At times he would look in the mirror while masturbating so as to be able to see his own anus. Analysis

revealed this looking at his mirror image to be a reflection of his wish to see his sister. (Glenn 1966: 740)

Because Belo had nothing to add in 1968, her readers were left to wonder what she read into this risqué representation from a psychoanalytic scene of multiple transgression. Anyone compiling a list of conceivable sexual repressions "imaged" by Mr. C. would hardly know where to begin, or stop: (1) Homosexuality with a *différance*? (2) Autoeroticism through doubling and repetition? (3) Incestuous bisexuality *à un*? (4) A degraded platonic androgyny: the pursuit of the (w)hole called love? (5) Hermaphroditism in the age of mechanical reproduction (mass-produced mirrors)? (6) Imaginary heterosexuality via reversals, condensation, and self/other substitutions? (7) A carnivalized image (through parodic inversion) of Ovidian dual-sexuals: male bodies with female "soul" entrapped? The longer any list of bottom-line irregularities grows, the more persuasive, or entrapping, its alternatives may become: *all* of them. These symbols of trangression begin—mysteriously, outrageously—to reinforce each other; such is the power of such imagery and myth. But by the same token, the longer the list grows, the less relevant *any* of its items, or Mr. C., appears to anything specific—e.g., Balinese culture.

Jane Belo's article of 1935 documented the place of incest in Balinese values of aristocracy and divinity. However important the topics of homosexuality and masturbation may be, they were not the subject of evidence she collected in the early 1930s. Moreover, unhappy Mr. C. before his mirror seems hardly—how should one put it?—"Balinese." To repeat, Belo elects to add nothing to her unexplained invocation of Mr. C. And drawing up a list of sexual possibilities yields results that seem almost to parody sorts of hidden themes in many styles of psychosexual investigation, including psychoanalysis.[16]

"Originally," Belo's study of twins detailed specific social circumstances of symbolic ambiguities of gender, status, and birth order. Her important insights into cosmology, routine practices, and folklore helped stimulate studies of Balinese performing arts and daily life, where dramatic depolarizations of gender punctuate dance, drama, refined comportment, and ritual. It was only in her later note that Belo juxtaposed a plot radically psycho-something-or-other with an earlier, "innocent" ethnography.

As late as 1949, Belo was content to interpret Bali's "arts and crafts" ethos (including graceful males and occasional transvestism) in images of cyclic differentiation/undifferentiation in a "self-perpetuating personality system" (1949: 59). Developing Bateson's notions of "steady state" values and perhaps Mead's (1935) important schemes of gender and temperament, Belo crowned her study of Rangda (1949) with Bali-Hindu iconography of boy-and-girl twins, figures of the "original couple." She mapped circuit switching among male/female, males in female roles, and females in male roles; she showed how male/female distinctions shift, permute, intensify, and lapse across phases of rites. Here nothing was reduced to psychologistic symptoms; nothing even allusively suggested intermingled indices of homosexuality, androgyny, bisexuality, hermaphroditism, and so forth. The sensationally blurred image of Mr. C. became attached to publications of Balinese evidence only after a longer lapse of time.

(I should reiterate that I make these points neither to challenge the anthropological school of Culture and Personality, nor to assess merits or drawbacks of psychoanalysis. Rather, I am rereading commemorations of an episode in a discipline's past—one subsequently seasoned with allusions to bits of psychosexual themes and pieces of diagnosis. An inspiration for my proceeding in this manner of essay—which obviously runs a risk of rekindling the very kinds of plot it wishes to distance—was J. Malcolm's tale of Freudian archivists, breathtakingly published in serial form, "originally" in the old *New Yorker*.)[17]

Fragment 5: "or to embellish"

The second reference in Belo's new footnote—Kallmann's 1952 profile of U.S. homosexual twins—contains a psychoanalytic tale sadder still than Mr. C.'s. The following extract may demonstrate what Belo left vague and illustrate the particular variety of narrative involved. To help readers "hear" Kallmann's clinical account more as a stylized mythic rendering redolent of tragic form, I italicize paired contrasts and constructions about similarity/difference and first/second; I also print the selection's thematic heart in "warlike" *majuscules*. I do not consider this intrusion into Kallmann's diagnosis of index cases cheating. Devices that underscore possible slants and angles of any conventionalized analysis are fair play, provided one owns up to them. While italics may distort readings, the greatest distortion of all would be to make the following report sound neutral or "objective"; my aim is to read it ultraobjectively:

> Because of the general significance of this monozygotic pair of schizophrenic twin brothers concordant as to homosexuality and death by self-destruction, it may be mentioned that the U. twins were of English-German descent, from a thrifty middleclass family, and the only sons of their parents (they had an older sister). Their early lives were uneventful, except for the fact that one of them (the *second* with respect to delivery and suicide) required plastic surgery on account of a disfiguring facial birth injury (*left lower* jaw) which seemed to have been responsible for a certain retardation in physical and mental development. In 1942, the twins entered *different* branches of the Armed Services from *different* universities, in spite of their histories of overt homosexual behavior and although the disfigured twin had been a conscientious objector. Within less than a year, they developed *similar* schizophrenic symptoms in *different* theaters of war, but at practically the *same* time. Following shock treatment in *different* hospitals, they were unable to readjust themselves to civilian life, apparently because they were

equally defective as to personalities and equally unmanageable in their tendencies to PERIODIC VAGABONDISM. The suicides were committed *before* and *after* the death of the mother (one *at home*, the other *away from home*) and were ascribed to fear of readmission to a mental hospital. (Kallmann 1952: 291–92)

This passage in my copy of the 1952 *Journal of Nervous and Mental Disease* is tearstained. May none of us, readers, identify with this devastating tale, yet may all of us sympathize. Ensuing irritation dries my eyes as Kallmann discloses his clinical conclusions, as if to explain "how the leopard got its spots":

In this tragic manner, the U. twins served to confirm our recently expressed opinion that "the suicides of two twin partners are apt to occur but will only be observed by chance (not directly related to one another even under similar conditions of unfavorable family background, social frustration, or emotional maladjustment), and therefore will be extremely rare." The photographs of the pair are withheld upon the request of the twins' father. (1952: 292–93)

On that last note, the tears resume.

Kallmann does manage to include portraits of "three concordant one-egg pairs," eyes masked: the J. twins, the O. twins, and the K. twins (lanky entertainers posed at age twenty-two, like a visually stuttered Fred Astaire). Kallmann regrets that "further clinical or photographic data cannot be revealed since most of the twin index cases of this survey are still subject to the laws of the State of New York" (1952: 294).

I pass over Kallmann's dated diagnosis of "fixation or regression to immature levels of sexuality" and his craft's ungainly analytic views (even the more liberal ones) of homosexuality as "an alternative minus variant in the integrative process of pyschosexual maturation rather than . . . a pathognomonically determinative expression of a codifiable entity of behavioral immaturity" (1952: 294). My concerns lie elsewhere. What could have prompted Belo to append a reference on one-egg pairs to her classic study of opposite-sex Balinese twins—a study utterly unconnected to Kallmann's index cases? What, moreover, are we to make of this tragedy of periodic vagabondage, homosexuality, Armed Forces, hospitals, and theaters of war? The story, or one of its possibilities, continues.

Fragment 6: "The story woven around the relic"

Were this chapter employing subheadings rather than extracts of Bateson atop its fragments, readers would now be beginning "Censored Postcards." If the full rays of Walter Spies's renown could be projected back on interwar Bali, Jane Belo's lunar glow might be outshone. There is insufficient room—even in a textual strategy of fragments—to telegraph vital facts of Spies's life and art between his birth in Moscow in 1895, where (like Vladimir Nabokov born four years later in St. Petersburg) he absorbed the twilight of Czarist culture in privileged diplomatic circles, and his death in 1942, drowned off Sumatra by a Japanese bomber. Suffice it to say that this painter-polyglot-musician-musicologist-dancer-photographer-archeologist-ethnographer-botanist-entomologist—raised in the worlds of Rachmaninoff, Scriabin, and Richard Strauss, steeped in Cubism and educated in Expressionist Dresden, displaced via Holland to the traditionalist courts of Java where he became Master of the Sultan's Music—found fulfillment in Bali after 1927.

There can be few rivals to Spies in the history of crossing cultures. His was a kindly charisma, his open-door residences a blend of the *salon*, the *café*, and the academic *équipe*. If ever an individual dandy reoriented an era's sense of an entire people, it was interwar Spies-in-Bali. Spies opened Balinese studies beyond the narrower spectrum of official Dutch ethnography (interesting enough in its own right), devoted to encyclopedic documentation of temple types, customary law, land rights, and "archeologizable" art. Spies helped direct an entire generation, some of it "lost," to issues of performance and the interrelation of the arts. He never challenged Dutch ethnographic and administrative authority; rather he provided a richly peripheral alternative vantage point.[18]

To sustain my (sincere) vein of accolade would advance the cult of Spies that has intensified since 1964, when Hans Rhodius prepared *Schönheit und Reichtum des Lebens: Walter Spies (Maler und Musiker auf Bali, 1895–1942)*. This spendid tome stands to Spies's work in Bali much as de Zoete and Spies's own *Dance and Drama in Bali* (1939) stood to Balinese performing arts. Rhodius's *Walter Spies*, moreover, helped hitch the name of Spies to new agencies for the revitalization of Balinese arts and Balinese studies, one in Bali and one in the Netherlands. Conventional tributes to Spies (including some from the 1930s) identify his sensibility with the essence of "Balineseness"— always a dubious kind of claim. Spies himself, then, has been commemorated along with Balinese culture. Indeed, the construct "interwar Bali" has come to coincide with the impact and influence of Walter Spies.

A major exhibition of works by Spies and Balinese artists he influenced was held in 1980 at Amsterdam's Tropenmuseum; its lavish catalogue and introduction (Rhodius & Darling 1980) condense discussions from Rhodius's still more elaborate volume (1965). In Bali in 1981, I happened upon a review of this English-language account in a tourist newsletter distributed at the Bali Beach Hotel, the aging flagship of government-backed tourism flowering during President Suharto's era. The Spies phenomenon thus enters the convoluted history of patronage and commercialization of Balinese arts, performance, and—one might say—life.[19]

It is time, again, to speak of Jane. *Walter Spies* (1965) may have helped determine Belo to edit *Traditional Balinese Culture*; her 1968 introduction mentions Rhodius's tome (to which she contributed); there Spies's writings and pictures were interleaved with homages by artists, scholars, and celebrities whom Spies hosted in Bali—among them Charlie Chaplin, Leopold Stokowski, and Margaret Mead. Art historian Claire Holt's contribution is especially telling. She evokes Spies's mystery and paradoxical personality in images she also applied to Bali:

> Walter's radiant presence could shrink into . . . almost literal effacement. . . . He . . . never asserted himself aggressively, whether in delight or disgust—the two poles in his scale of moods. Was there something in this non-concentrated ego that was not only peculiar to Spies but also to the people among whom he lived? And did he efface himself in the presence of authority or officialdom or strangers just as any Balinese would unless born to rule and exercise his prerogatives? Did Spies bring to the island within him that sense of just *being* and not of either becoming or achieving, which are the mainsprings of Western man? Just to be, like a lake that mirrors the skies . . . ? (Holt 1965: 312–13)

Claire Holt and Jane Belo had shared adventures with Spies in the early 1930s, when the striking trio explored the islands off Bali's southeast coast. Holt's spirited reconnaissance report of that mission prefigured her later testimonial. Belo remained unnamed, tagged as the "family expert" and ethnographer of twinship on the team. Holt's prose style altered when presenting Spies—the protagonist in a prototypical exotic escapade, presumably constructed by Holt out of his reported evidence. This patch of indirect discourse and suspenseful climax stands out in sharp relief from the surrounding, rather routine narrative, based exclusively on Holt's own observations:

> About one kilometer north of Swana pass, there lies a tremendous cave, the Goa Karangsari. Walter Spies descended into it through a small traplike opening and found himself in complete darkness. Walking downward through a narrow passage, he suddenly came into a larger cave and from there into still another one, till, finally, there were large vaulted halls with stalactites hanging down and all the hollow uncanniness of deep caves. This seemed to be a whole hollow mountain. After a fair amount of wandering about, the man accompanying Spies told him to stop. He was to go no further. Before them lay a small pool of brilliantly transparent water. "This is the bath of the *dedari* (heavenly nymphs)," declared the guide. (His name, by the way, was Kichig, and a preciously helpful soul Kichig proved afterward!) So beyond the bath of the heavenly nymphs no one should pass. (Holt 1936: 75)

This obscured epiphany may strike readers of E. M. Forster as a displaced "Marabar Caves," that haunting heart of the ambiguities comprising *A Passage to India* (1924).[20] Evidently, Spies's charisma was manifest early on. As is proper in "relic-ing", recent commentators have sought to restore and rekindle that charisma, harnessed to fresh projects.

Belo's own "Appreciation of the Artist Walter Spies" in Rhodius's volume recalls how she and her husband (Colin McPhee) first met Spies in 1931. She depicts years of friendship in their houses in Bali, just six miles apart; she evokes Spies's profound emotions, boyish buoyancy, and ethereal good looks "with blue eyes, a longish aquiline nose, beautifully cut and very mobile lips," athletic build, restless gestures, and delicate brushwork (Belo in Rhodius 1965: 317–18). Others waxed equally eloquent about the person and the painting of Walter Spies, and all, including Margaret Mead, affirmed his generosity: "It was Walter who found us a house, it was Walter who found us our first servants, it was Walter who found the carpenter to build our house in the high mountains, and most of all it was Walter who gave us our first sense of the Balinese scene" (Mead cited in Rhodius 1965: 359). To judge by Spies's letter of 1938 to Lady Mary Delamere, whom Rhodius identifies as the "Schwester der Countess Mountbatten of Burma und Enkelin von Sir Ernst Cassel," Belo's esteem was reciprocated; Spies numbered Belo among Bali's primary attractions.

Belo's memories of Spies may have been more intricate than anything she states openly in 1968. Mead, as was her wont, divulged evidence that Belo left veiled. Mead's "Memories of Walter Spies" end with an abrupt exposure, plus a somewhat pat diagnosis to round things off:

> Walter Spies's choice of Bali and of a continuing light involvement with Balinese male youth, seemed part of his repudiation of the kind of dominance and submission, authority and dependence, which he associated with European cultures, and which could be revived in him when he encountered officialdom or rank. . . . The very disassociated impersonality of Bali gave him the kind of freedom that he sought. (Mead in Rhodius 1965: 359)

Mead laced retrospectives on her life and work with suggestive insights, but so fleetingly conveyed that they can take on an air of insinuation rather than argument. Some might find it less than fitting that such allusions conclude paragraphs that opened by declaring utter indebtedness to Spies for much that Mead and Bateson were to learn of Bali. But twists of this kind often lent a provocative edge to Mead's modes of commemoration.[21]

Complicated facts surrounding Walter Spies's death were outlined in Rhodius's *Schönheit und Reichtum* in 1965; they have since been condensed in a translation by John Stowell (Rhodius & Darling 1980). Although none of this information was new, it had not been summarized so clearly or publicly. Those were, to be sure, the worst of times: Nazi-occupied Holland was insecurely ruling its East Indies; newly promoted officials were seeking clout and scapegoats; policies were shifting toward right-wing conformities of law and order. Specifically, the last viceroy of the Netherlands Indies, a war hero, resuscitated long-lapsed restrictions on suspect behavior, including homosexuality. Officials well disposed toward Spies were replaced; he was caught in a dragnet and confined on December 31, 1938. After three years of artistically productive imprisonment, he was shipped toward Ceylon with other German internees; on January 19, 1942, near Nias, the *Van Imhoff* was sunk by a Japanese bomb. The last relic of Walter Spies is a *Briefkaart* marked "*gecensureerd*." In *both* Rhodius's commemorative volume and that of Rhodius and Darling, *both* sides of the fateful postcard are illustrated; the images serve literally as a *momento mori*.

Rhodius discovered a "blessing in disguise" in Spies's disgrace: the famous prison paintings, which include magical-realist Balinese landscapes drawn from Spies's memory-imagination alone. Appropriately, and perhaps accurately, Rhodius's idealized portrayal of creativity transcending the enemy casts a mantle of innocence back upon details that had been "grossly exaggerated" by "petty-minded" vengeful officials beset by "neurotic hysteria":

> In Bali, friendships between members of the same sex have always been allowed more open and intense expression than is the case in most Western societies, caught in the maze of their own taboos. This attitude was clearly shown by the father of Spies's young friend. When the lawyer asked if he was angry at Mr. Spies's conduct, he replied: "*Kenapa*? (But why?) He is after all our best friend, and it was an honour for my son to be in his company, and if both are in agreement, why fuss?" (Rhodius & Darling 1980: 45)

Neither Rhodius's lilting version nor a more caustic retrospect on Spies's fate was offered by Belo in her 1968 commemoration—at least not explicitly. But biographers of some of our protagonists have shown that Belo had already known the facts that Rhodius revisited in 1964. Indeed Belo herself had possibly been a potential victim of the same wartime forces; her correspondence reveals that she may have hinged memories of Bali on the trauma of Spies's last years. Relevant material later appeared in Jane Howard's study of Mead's life, colleagues, and times. Howard cites Mead's well-known mention of "a witchhunt against homosexuals" that "broke out in the Pacific [and] echoed from Los Angeles to Singapore" (1984: 209). Mead wrote that she and Bateson returned with Belo to Bali, because the situation seemed unsafe for her to go back alone. Howard cites Belo's letter of February 10, 1939, describing a South Bali official's effort to oust foreigners who could not be kept under surveillance. Another of Belo's letters mentions the government's "clean-up of certain misdemeanors to which residents of these parts were prone. . . . Walter and four others have been in prison in Den Pasar since the first of January" (Howard 1984: 209–10). Other fragments from Belo suggest the tenor of those days:

> All of us who lived in a pleasant way have been investigated—police in and out of our houses, all our servants arrested and questioned. Of the 34 dancing girls in my village, all were questioned on my habits, down to a 3-year old. . . . Colin had

kept it a secret that we were divorced last July. . . . At least half the [European] people living in Bali have been asked to leave, or have left of their own accord, one dares not wonder why . . . the Balinese think the whole white caste has gone mad. . . . Thank heaven for the Batesons and their firm scientific reputations to back us up. (Howard 1984: 210)

We have come to another awkward moment in this story. Having cited this much from Howard, I decline to interrogate Belo's private side, or Mead's. The present commemoration leaves such plots to their biographers (e.g., M. C. Bateson 1984), given my conviction that "biography" does not *explain* the texts of those whose lives it presumes to reconstruct.[22] Were I to pursue "the Belo story" or "the Mead story" insofar as each pertains to Balinese studies and anthropology's history, I would strive not to reduce their arts and works to symptoms (of politics, sexuality or anything else), but to weave resonances of their writing—including ethnography, memoirs, and commemorative tomes— into selections of shifting tonalities: a music not necessarily in a singular key. It is this interpretive possibility that the next fragment opens *via* Walter Spies.

Fragment 7: "The relic or the memorial becomes an influence which pushes those who come after to perpetuate the sociological effects of the original event"

I have isolated Belo's odd footnote and hesitantly surmised parallels between its references' psychoanalytic narratives and the way Belo possibly repressed remembering Walter Spies and company. This reading may seem to brush that "symptomatological" diagnosis I seek to avoid. My goal, however, is not to disentangle but to dissolve any "original event" suspected of lying behind the chains of commemoration whereby Bali, Spies, between-the-wars, Belo, and Bateson's words became "relic-ed." Yet even with original events and psychosexual symptoms unfixed, flickering solidarities perpetuate themselves through a transtemporal chain of successive memorialists—yet another "charmed circle." In this historical process, moreover, mists seldom evaporate; they rather thicken, along with specificities: *obscurum per obscurius*. And if mists thicken, so might description, ultraobjectively.

Spies's disgrace—and Belo's relative reluctance (versus Mead's readiness—less preferable, I feel) to mention it—reminds us that any commemoration selects strands from a fuller panoply. Accentuation produces distortions: recognizable kinds of story. In the extreme, tabloids (e.g., Pollmann 1990) sniff out salacious subcurrents papered over in rosier remembrances. My fragmentary aim is otherwise: to rekindle concern for the panoply and to resist opting for a particular plot line, without, however, repressing the fact that psychoanalytic readings have beckoned several commentators, understandably.

Walter Spies's public glory was this: he embodied the interrelation of the arts that came to betoken "Balinese culture." Spies's public disgrace arose from his playing into the hands of reactionary forces. The larger-than-life polarities of Spies in Bali (glorious/disgraced) and of Belo and Mead commemorating him may inhibit interpreting indeterminables or reading toward the panoply. If a memorialist—Holt or Mead, for example—even allusively passes the wand of "deviance" over Spies's rich dimensions, those dimensions are magically reduced to compensatory displacement. Similarly, if a memorialist passes the wand of "interwar" over Bali's swirling cycles of influences, they are reduced, as if by sorcery, to indices of "aftermath" and "foreshadowing." Both magical techniques may yield engrossing stories; that much is clear from Mead's enthralling *Blackberry Winter*. But to construe such a "history" as the true story is to misrepresent how the past happens, how it becomes constructed—whether in histories of cultures, of cultural studies, or of such disciplinary movements as "Culture and Personality" and its many contemporaries and successors: functionalism, structuralism, hermeneutics, deconstruction, *dan lain lain*.[23]

Sensational polarities materialize in diverse theories of cultures, personalities, and historical periods. Critics (including this author) cannot rest content simply to deny the adequacy of polarities, because polarities (exaggerated, reduced contrasts) themselves become social and ideological facts: motives of and for action. Therefore, polarities must be countered: stereotypes must be doubted, questioned, reopened, and turned against each other, particularly when diagnostics start aligning comfortably across "types" of culture, personality, or era. Zeitgeist-y notions that "likes attract" are no less objectionable when casually implied. For example, Mead's occasional style of alluding to "sexual preferences" and Abel's set style of comparing a culture's standard behavior to "that of the paranoid schizophrenics" can latch onto each other. Further supposed symptoms then coagulate, perhaps under a tacit rubric of "decadence." Thus, when commemorating interwar Bali, Belo's footnote seems to elide differences among depolarized gender, male grace, androgyny, homosexuality, hermaphroditism, and other antitheses of twofold male/female distinctions, as if such "symptoms" by nature slosh together. Unquestioned assumptions about normality/breakdown endure in such allusions and arguments, even when tolerance is recommended, sometimes patronizingly.

To counteract, or at least displace, these familiar and recurrent analytic proclivities, I initiate an alternative reading of Spies vis-à-vis interwar Bali. The following exercise is ironic and tentative: on the surface it reroutes or deflects previous hints of affinity; in its depth it tries to dis-*spell* this very style of analysis, itself included. In the ensuing paragraphs, both Spies and Bali are my relics.

Even if Walter Spies's work—his painting, writing, music, life—stood *for* anything (a dubious proposition), it would not likely have been a simple assault on "proper polarity," such as separate male/female sexual identity. Everything in his canvasses projects sensuality, idealized Balinese youths included. Their pervasive erotics stem from interplays of elements—hillscape/ waterscape/skyscape, dream/actuality, observation/recollection, and legend/ genre painting. He produces near-continuous modulations among different senses, perspectives, media, and ways of knowing/imagining. Spies's art is fundamentally chromatic: not diatonic. That may be critical to what Holt called Spies's "just *being*" (versus achieving).

Similar qualities animate Spies's ethnography of performances and his musical interests—particularly a lifelong devotion to several works by Debussy. Spies's first contact with Javanese music in the Yogya court was filtered through previous exposure to Debussy, whose own chance hearings of Javanese gamelans in fin-de-siècle Paris is a celebrated episode in the annals of "exotic" influence on European ears.[24] There occurred a spiral of cross-cultural listening—gamelan heard by Debussy, Debussy heard by Spies, preparing the way Spies would later hear gamelan scales, cycles, and notes. Spies's own creations also incorporate Debussian transitions and transpositions: chromatic steps across visual, aural, and tactile codes, or programmatic evocations of their correspondences. Appropriately, "Debussy" entered Spies's last recorded words, commemorated forty years later by G. J. Resink:

> The last mention of Debussy's name occurs in a postcard that Spies mailed in 1942 from his prison camp of Kotatjane, in Aceh . . . : "I sent you today a little painting. . . . It's a fantasy inspired by the viewpoint we have mornings in the mountains (*brouillard* [mist]). It should be considered only a little prelude, in the fashion of Debussy." . . . Here Spies expresses himself through his fourth "avatar," that of painter. And the word "brouillard" evokes at once the title of Debussy's prelude, "Brouillards," of the *Douze Préludes II* (No. 1). Here Spies, the master of the plastic arts [*plasticien*], comes very close to the composer of the *Images* for orchestra [and] of the two *Images* suites for piano . . . , the instrument of preference for both of them. (Resink 1984: 47; my translation)

I return, figuratively now, from musicality to sexuality, or rather gender. Here, readers, is an analogy—musical chromaticism (smallest intervals) : gender ambiguity (sometimes called androgyny). Here is the flip side—diatonic scales : patent polarization of male/female. To schematize—polarized gender : androgyny :: diatonic : chromatic. Androgyny, then, suggests chromaticism on the keyboard of gender.

My analytic metaphor of "chromaticism" stems not just from Debussy and Proust, among other literary modernists, but from Lévi-Strauss, too. A drift toward chromaticism of ever finer distinctions, ultimately "exhausting" sharp mythic polarities, is a major vector of his *Mythologiques* and subsequent studies. Lévi-Strauss's enduring attention to chromatic variations was neglected by critics who reduced his texts, or their reading of them, to fixed binarisms. (I have traced chromatic connections among Lévi-Strauss, Proust, Debussy/ Wagner and related topics elsewhere. Regarding the crucial cross-cultural issue of musical preferences: for now, "I have nothing to add.")[25]

Let me amplify my analogy. Conventionally polarized gender suggests diatonics: more whole steps, restricted clear-cut tonalities. In the interpretive scheme I propose here, androgyny is no periodic or peripheral breakdown from normal, healthy, polarity. Rather, chromatic androgyny contains all the tone differences of the diatonic plus the positions (notes' intervals) that the diatonic suppresses or makes "accidental." In this dainty dialectic, this music-inspired metaphorical mix, the chromatic (androgyny) contains the diatonic (polarized), even though the diatonic defines the standard against which chromaticism can be heard as subversive to tonal propriety. Androgyny, then, tends toward chromatics; it provides smaller intervals between the diatonic ones, but also includes them. In Western music the history of a diatonic/chromatic distinction entails a play of suppression and emergence: even when diatonics prevail, the chromatic remains tacit and encompassing. Chromaticism implies ambiguity in matters of tonality (and key) *from the perspective of diatonic expectations and norms*. I am only suggesting that androgyny be similarly construed in matters of gender.

If one must isolate "complexes" of personalities, cultures, and eras (N.B.: one mustn't), then aspects of a culture's, a person's, or an era's musicalities are conceivably as apposite as their sexualities and/or schizophrenias. These *genres* too blur. Alerted to Spies's manifest and public "musical preferences," I diagnose—or rather "gnose"—transpositions among small intervals and different sensory arenas. Affinities between Spies and Bali would hinge not simply on his (code word) "androgyny," but on his Debussian arts, or on a theory of chromaticism that could harmonize them with androgyny in the fuller sense suggested above. Recall, then, Debussy:

> By thus drowning or blurring the sense of tonality (*en noyant le ton*) a wider field of expression is ensured and seemingly unrelated harmonies can be approached without awkward detours. . . . Tonality was to be submerged; it was not to disappear. And the purpose of this was to secure expression for a richer, not a shrunken field of associations, transcending the limitations of the mechanical piano like the "immeasurable" keyboard which Marcel Proust was later to describe, the keys of which were to touch upon myriad sensations and which Proust believed was still, even then, almost unknown. (Lockspeiser 1962: 61)

Bali, then, *entre-deux-guerres*, becomes a land-time of chromatic play and intermingling close intervals, "objectively" recalled, alas, as a culture period blighted by the breakdown of large-intervalled normality, such as male/female. Such recall is "war"; war is hell (not heaven): sensational, reactionary, unnuanced, unambiguous (and therefore untrue) overpolarity. This sounds like the cadence to my constructed, fragmentary story; but it isn't.

P.S.: BLACKBERRY TROPICS

This prolonged, "censored postcard" of a chapter concludes rather by acknowledging two towering commemorations of interwar ethnology, *Triste tropiques* (1955) and *Blackberry Winter* (1972), in reverse order. Admittedly, they have been with us from the start.

Mead's redoubtable autobio-ethnography (an irresistible genre—compare *Variety*'s category of "Bio-pic") flirts with catchword diagnoses of cultures, personalities, and epochs without itself ever committing the most excessive ones.[26] *Blackberry Winter* shapes a story by converting anything it remembers into personal advantage: a vector of a successful career. This style of memoir also characterizes certain kinds of psychotherapy and certain schools of historical narrative (of selves, of times, of cultures). Mead's selective reminiscences aggrandized her profession (and mine), glorified her circle, and justified her research decisions. One extreme example of this tendency was her justification for a fieldwork locale in highland Bali. Here Mead's hindsight turned native hardship and medical distress to methodological advantage:

> It was a village in which most courtyard walls consisted of bamboo fencing, instead of the clay walls which, in other villages, shut each courtyard off from sight. I had already learned how much time was consumed in courtesies and gifts of refreshment on every occasion when one entered a courtyard, and I realized that in Bajoeng Gede one could catch a glimpse of what was going on in a courtyard as one walked along a street without actually entering the house. . . . The entire population suffered from hypothyroidism, and about 15 percent of the people had a conspicuous goiter. This deficiency of thyroid had the effect of slowing things down so that there was simplification of action, but without a loss of pattern. (Mead 1972: 232–33)

It is not that Mead's works were insensitive to misery or suffering. But to construe crumbled house walls and hypothyroidism as a means instantly to acquire slow-motion scenes of private life bespeaks an imagination (and haste) of a distinctive sort. Mead willingly bypassed all that folderol of indigenous courtesies that would have slowed her down. *Blackberry Winter* betrays a similar rush past colleagues and associates, many evoked in quick snatches of stereotype. When Mead's pungently canny remarks start to crowd in on each other, there is no time to opt for a given set of symptoms as determinant, no time for a final cross-cultural or interpersonal diagnosis. Had Mead in fact plumped for a final, general theory, all possibilities of "thick description"—not to mention "reading toward the panoply"—would have been thwarted. To her lasting credit, she did not (strategically, I surmise); her

Fig. 8. A view outside unimproved, yet uncrumbled, houseyard walls behind which everyday activities remain concealed from passers-by, including fieldworkers. (Author's photo, 1972)

Fig. 9. Puppet theater, too, weaves commemorative narratives. Here a shadowless *wayang lemah* is set to show a story "fitting" the ritual ripening of the same first-born Brahmana seen in Fig. 5.

pace—past broken walls, hypothyroidism, and colleagues—never slackened. Especially in her popular studies, Mead happily managed to outrun certain evident deficiencies. This fact helps explain their value and appeal: their adaptability to current issues and their continuing capacity to arouse readers (see Chaps. 1, 7).

How different was the retrospective of *Tristes tropiques* (1955/1972) on the paradoxical possibilities of constructing an anthropological tale of anthropology's past. Yet it too gained deserved popularity and renown. Lévi-Strauss's rhythm of recall is unremitting: nonstop transpositions across all codes, which correspond, shift, change places, and ultimately dissolve. The third chapter is characteristic: a comedy of travel experience "relived," but backwards (as conceived). Proustlike, the text begins in/as memory:

> . . . I was rediscovering with delight a host of vegetable species that were familiar to me since my stay in Amazonia. . . . I reflected on the painful scenes . . . and tried to link them with other experiences of a similar kind . . . (17)

Step by serial step, readers continue reversing:

> Only a little while previously, a few months before the outbreak of war, in the course of my return journey to France, I had visited Bahia . . . a few days earlier I had met with a similar experience . . . (18)

Still more distant pasts cycle through this spiraling return:

> Fortunately, at that time, every Brazilian official still had inside him a concealed anarchist, who was kept alive by the shreds of Voltaire and Anatole France which impregnated the national culture even in the depths of the bush. (19)

Memories of experience in reverse lead on to memory of memories in this dispersal toward a different "*entre-deux-guerres*" from the one my essay has been considering:

> But perhaps I would not have behaved so brazenly had I not still been influenced by the memory of an incident which had shown South American policemen in a very comic light. Two months previously . . . (19–20)

Increasingly Proustian, the writing of the account enters the time portrayed, as various memories compound:

> Although up till then I had fared better than my companions, I was none the less preoccupied by a problem to which I must now refer, since the writing of this book depended on its being solved . . . (22)

Sifting his recall of Puerto Rico and Martinique through stereotypes of exiles that antagonists had projected onto himself—Vichy emissary, Jewish Freemason, etc.—the narrator ends his chapter, "The West Indies," with a parody of Proustian sensibilities that rivals Proust's own parodies:

And so, it was at Puerto Rico that I first made contact with the United States; for the first time I breathed in the smell of warm car paint and wintergreen (which, in French used to be called *thé du Canada*, those two olfactory poles between which stretches the whole range of American comfort, from cars to lavatories, by way of radio sets, sweets, and toothpaste. . . .

The accidents of travel often produce ambiguities such as these. Because I spent my first weeks on United States soil in Puerto Rico, I was in future to find America in Spain. Just as, several years later, through visiting my first English university with a campus surrounded by Neo-Gothic buildings at Dacca in Western Bengal, I now look upon Oxford as a kind of India that has succeeded in controlling the mud, the mildew and the ever-encroaching vegetation. (24–25)

Everything becomes displaced, "West Indianized," including Europe and the U.S. The irony, perhaps even the self-directed sarcasm, of Lévi-Strauss's superb punch line is devastating:

O.K.: I could enter American territory; I was free.[27]

Tristes tropiques "tropes" the flotsam of interwar history, cultures, and states into different chapters, a number of them comic. (Still today, many readers want *Tristes tropiques* to be a *Blackberry Winter*; it isn't.) Everything is fractured, ruined, and reversible; its mode of rescuing order from *oubli* may be likened to "myth." When *Tristes tropiques* was first published in 1955, its plot was the discovery of a metaphorical resemblance between the ways narrated memory and New World mythology arrange metonymies (fragments recollected). The plot remains the same today. In a pivotal episode, "Crossing the Tropics" (or "crisscrossing the tropes"), different sensory orders, introspection/description, memory/experience, New World and Old, and East and West are all transposed: not confused, but transposed. The prose of concocted metaphors across world-historical metonymies fabricates correspondences. It readies readers to enter the book's tribal evidence through the gate of its chapter on "Saõ Paulo," between-the-wars.

At one level Lévi-Strauss's method of multiple analogies across disparate codes avoids nothing. Yet certain costs accrue. The prose—at least if hastily perused—slips too evenly past effects of fixations, repressions, and reductionist symptoms—just the kinds of things Mead's insinuations accentuated. Such blind spots and coagulations do *happen*—however untenable this may be for an epistemology of ever-transposing "conditions of possibility." And fixations, reductionisms, and blind spots that do happen can hurt. *Tristes tropiques* and the concept of myth that it foreshadows seem to smooth what is rough, level what is bumpy, or render "spirited" what may feel to practitioners desperate, or perhaps ridiculous. *Tristes tropiques* was an initial entry in Lévi-Strauss's sustained comparison of conceptualized (*conçu*) experience (*vécu*) to a music (a harmonics?) of meanings (*sens*) rather than sounds (*sons*). Like the *Mythologiques* that succeeded it, his text pushes to the brink of complete chromaticism, where one is apt to forget (to renounce?) the power and effects of chunky polarities and political interests. They seem almost emulsified. Nevertheless, to its lasting political credit, the book's tones of conventionalized regret remained nonpatronizing and unmawkish, while many of its critics did not.[28]

One obvious and available antidote to *Tristes tropiques* is *Blackberry Winter* (there are others, perhaps preferable, but less obvious). The two make an odd combination: Lévi-Strauss's transforming as-if lamentations and Mead's mead, her gusto, her semidiagnosis of everything encountered. One might try interweaving these two modalities, provided the former, the "tropics," remain encompassing. Indeed that temporary reconciliation has been one tonality of the present essay-*étude*, though not, I hope, the dominant one.

CONCLUDING COMMEMORATION

What does the feeling for closure fostered by print have to do with the
plotting of historical writing, the selection of the kinds of themes that
historians use to break into the seamless web of events around them
so that a story can be told?
(Walter Ong [1982: 172])

Historian of anthropology George Stocking once suggested the relevance of "unilineal descent group" models of intellectual movements to anthropology's history; yet he cautioned not to overextend them (1984: 134).[29] I second that caution, extra-Vagantly. "Proper" histories of disciplines tend to imply that issues and -isms develop unilineally and from within. An alternative notion of movements and receptions highlights "charmed circles"—constellations of expatriates, émigrés, amateurs and professionals ("Native" and "Stranger" alike) engaged in dislocated writings and performance.[30] Such assortments of conventional and unconventional scholars and artists are a recurrent context of and for cross-cultural critical studies (anthropology included), as well as cults of the arts. To dwell upon so strikingly nonunilineal (bilateral?) a context of comparative research as interwar Bali helps further unsettle professional convictions of direct influences through the generations of a closed discipline.

Both the "charm" of Balinese studies and a sense of the foreordainedness of the approach consolidated as "Culture and Personality" intensified after the facts, if they were facts. *This* fact underscores the importance of commemoration in anthropology's tales of its past; such narratives can be fruitfully compared to other varieties of cultural construction. The intricate arts of selective recall help shape both ethnographies and histories thereof. "Fieldwork," too, is as much memory as event.[31]

These inescapable issues deserve repeated consideration. They need not be relegated to brief allusions, pseudoprefaces, apologetic digressions, self-congratulatory subjective asides, or avant-garde treatises too quick to declare themselves "reinvented" (or, by now, rereinvented) and sometimes disdainful of straight, academic ethnography. The straight, I submit, is crooked too; and so is the crooked. What an opportunity for rereading!

Paradoxically, certain historical moments, including some fieldwork contexts, seem almost to happen as memory the moment that they are happening, or so we remember. One general phenomenon that can happen nearly *as memory* (or seem to) the moment that it happens is music.[32] And musical analogies may help rescue resonant episodes in intricate crossings of cultures, particularly where others have inclined to "blackberry" them. (Recall that in Chap. 1, I critiqued V. Pollmann for blackberrying the blackberrier! Bateson might have called Pollmann's move, and perhaps mine as well, "schizmogenesis.")[33] As implied above, even "*tristes-tropiques*-ing" past encounters is not altogether adequate either, although Lévi-Strauss's "processive" writing strikes me as much the preferred tonality of the two. Hence the present essay's provisional hybrid: Blackberry tropics.

Jane Belo, "my heroine" in the present commemoration, stopped short of "blackberrying" Bali and Balinists; she had nothing to add to the outré footnote that I have extra-Vagantly amplified. Respecting her right to fall silent, I nevertheless "opened" (Michel Foucault might have said) second guesses of Belo's tome-tomb of "traditional Balinese culture." I did so in order to intensify readers' awareness of panoplies at play whenever, in Bateson's giftlike words, "events become reiics." Such surrealistic possibilities include when "a man is born or dies, or writes a book." Or, I would add, when a woman is born, or dies, or writes a book . . . or gives birth. The son can never repay her.

INTERLUDE:
Essay-*études* and *Tristimania*

If this chapter's rereadings seem hesitant, an entry in cinematographer Robert Bresson's notebook may clarify why:

> Precision of aim lays one open to hesitations. Debussy: "I've spent a week deciding on one chord rather than another."[34]

I may be charged with relativism for chromatically engaging differences, unduly dichotomized in other diagnoses. My *relative* relativisms echo earlier anthropologists—Ruth Benedict (as seen in Part One); Marcel Mauss (to be seen in Part Two); and more. In these essay-*études* their works become *evidence* added to the evidence they engaged. And, as Chapter 2 suggested, nonabsolutist description recalls Montaigne's travels throughout chords of difference.

Coincidentally, philosopher Stephen Toulmin has called Clifford Geertz's "thick description" a reintroduction of Montaigne's "omnivorous ethnography" in our current age. In *Cosmopolis* Toulmin reminds the "modernity" sponsored by universalist philosophers and scientists of its "other origin":

> Whatever was gained by Galileo, Descartes, and Newton's excursions into natural philosophy, something was also lost through the abandonment of Erasmus and Rabelais, Shakespeare and Montaigne. . . . The humane attitudes of openness, re-laxation, and bawdiness . . . were driven underground not long after 1600. (1990: 43–44)

Toulmin reconsiders the rise of seventeenth-century dogmatism, when logicians' "myth of a clean slate" came to dominate "the modern world view." Questioning Cartesianism's drive for rational certainty, Toulmin helps reinstate styles of doubting-knowing, mindful of translations' contingencies. This realm of knowledge(s) exhibits "legitimate uncertainty, ambiguity, and disagreement"; its demonstrations are more "reasonable" than rational; their significance is timely, not timeless; their dimensions are Lilliputian, not Leviathan—particular and informal, rather than diagrammatic or mathematical. (To Toulmin's culprit of official Cartesianism, one might add dogmatic Ramism as well.)[35] Toulmin's recipes for revitalized concrete *expériences* in *"Que sais-je?"* are in a word "ethnographic"; and their mode of implementation is essayistic.

Cross-cultural essay writing (along with essay riting and essay recollecting) questions predetermined boundaries. Openly manifold, it is not an easy genre to read. "What," one reviewer demanded of an earlier version of Chapter 3 (published in a volume on the history of anthropology) "is all this *doing* here?" "Who," he added, "could know these things?"[36] This critic, who sounded even more biting in French, seemed to imply that Debussy has no bearing on cultural comparison. (But Walter Spies assumed otherwise; and he composed his life's work accordingly, with profound impact on Balinese ethnography, for better or worse; remember, too, that Debussy did indeed hear gamelan orchestras.) Or perhaps my disgruntled reviewer—whose response I can certainly understand—wished "repressed" psychoanalysis would obligingly remain one thing and anthropological interpretation another. (But Jane Belo's footnote suggests quite the contrary; it was Belo's mysterious "lead" that I partially followed.)

Belo's footnote may verge on a melancholy topic that Leon Edel terms *tristimania*—when discussing Henry James's staggering "Notebooks":

> Criticism has failed to recognize that depression itself can be a driving force to powerful creation. I think of T.S. Eliot writing *The Waste Land* when he felt his

own life to be a waste; the depression may have caused some of his misjudgments which Pound corrected, but the creative power was generated by despair. Another modern instance is Virginia Woolf, who created her novels as a defence against melancholy and relapsed into her manic state when they were done. This is the *tristimania* described by the first great American psychiatrist, Benjamin Rush, and we see its presence in Proust, in Joyce, in Gide—whose long narcissistic journals he himself published frequently; or in the endless journalizing of Anaïs Nin who began her notebooks as a long letter to an absent father. Notebooks, diaries, journals [Edel omits ethnographies] are often repositories of grief and despair—Kafka told us that writing was for him a form of prayer. Even the more camera-like journals of Edmund Wilson, or earlier the nature-mirror journals of Thoreau, reflect existential struggles, an overpowering need to write the book of the Self in order to find peace of the soul.

James's colloquies reveal distinct fantasies of ritual. (Edel 1987: xii–xiii)

Many critics today split such company as Edel salutes into female/male, or American/European, or gay/straight, or Gentile/Jew, or loser/winner, or nostalgist/ironist, or diarist/fictionalist, or liberal/radical, or cutting edge/ square, or borderland/mainstream, or worse. I prefer to keep such "bifurcates" merging, and I question efforts that would diagnose away *tristimania*— whether sincere, staged, or undecidably either or both.

Those same critics might conceivably fault Edel's company—Eliot, Woolf, Gide, Kafka, Wilson, . . .—for being too Occidental; or inattentive to issues of class and race; or aestheticist, or otherwise defective. Perhaps; the company nevertheless merits revisiting as unreductively as contemporary consciousness allows. (Chapter 3 has thus skirted possible *tristimania*; Chapter 5 will try again.)

Essay readers, essay writers, and essay reviewers may be doomed (but privileged too, I find) to navigate perilous waters between unsure shores—unloosed from customary moorings, as C. Geertz once put it.[37] To mix still further metaphors of and for interpretation, I note that Greg Dening (1980) calls cross-cultural "horizons" "beaches"—shifting zones of contrary forces, frequented by "native" and "stranger" bedfellows.[38] Part Two of this book keeps combing such zones—littered with "defamiliarizations" beyond the familiar ones. Not just "Bali" but other ambiguous place-names will wind up in synesthetic recall of essay-*études*. I do not assert this hybrid genre's folksy tropes and tearful jokes dogmatically. It would be idle to claim for these anecdotal episodes any rigor beyond what ultraobjective readers may be generous enough to credit in uneasy vergings on extra-Vagance.

Part Two

MULTIMEDIATIONS: COINCIDENCE, MEMORY, MAGICS

Virtual life, as literature presents it, is always a self-contained form, a
unit of experience, in which every element is organically related to
every other, no matter how capricious or fragmentary the items are
made to appear. That very caprice or fragmentation is a *total effect*,
which requires a perception of the whole history as a fabric
of contributive events.

Actual experience has no such closed form. It is usually ragged,
unaccentuated, so that irritations cut the same figure as sacrifices,
amusements rank with high fulfillments, and casual human contacts seem
more important than the beings behind them. But there is a normal and
familiar condition which shapes experience into a distinct mode, under
which it can be apprehended and valued: that is memory.
(*Susanne Langer, "Virtual Memory,"* Feeling and Form, *1953*)

It reminds me of a movie I saw last month out by Lake Pontchartrain.
(*Walker Percy*, The Moviegoer, *1960*)

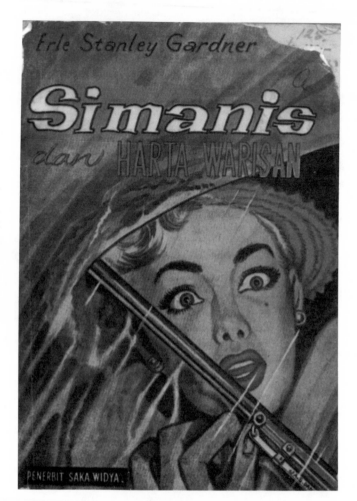

Fig. 10. A copy of the initial Indonesian book jacket that greeted this reader in 1971; the shop also sold regional printed fare.

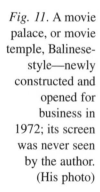

Fig. 11. A movie palace, or movie temple, Balinese-style—newly constructed and opened for business in 1972; its screen was never seen by the author. (His photo)

CHAPTER FOUR

Cosmopolitan Moments:
As-if Confessions of an Ethnographer-Tourist
(Echoey "Cosmomes")

Either to execute or to ironize first-person discourse is, as we all know,
risky business.
(*J. Boon,* Affinities and Extremes)

CULTURES cannot be crossed, nor can their crossing be captured, *simply.* Any ethnography refracts. No comparative representation, old or new, develops straightforwardly, however political or apolitical its enabling enterprises profess to be. For example, complexity and contradiction have prevailed at intersections of East Indies realms, European colonialisms, and Indonesian societies since the sixteenth century. These discursive encounters span: Early modern mercantilism and warfare; subsequent "high colonialism," with its labor-intensive plantations for export crops; late nineteenth-century ethical policies and expanded philological enterprises; ensuing nationalist movements, postcolonial nationalism, and commercial "internationalism"—each with distinctive varieties of tourism.[1]

This essay adds to that history by narrating—through a pastiche of self-promoting styles of travel-telling—a true encounter with a Javanese mystic who construed the narrator coincidentally. I then multiply fragments that multiply this motive, intertextually. Although my study derives from post-1968 (U.S.) and post-1965 (Indonesia) transnational circumstances, its ironies pertain to the *longue durée* of languages and cultures in tragicomic collision. But to insist on this fact may place too much weight on a jocose effort.

Elsewhere I have addressed medleys of Balinese, Indonesian, Indicized, and Europeanized institutions laden with contradictory voices, rhetorics, dilemmas, promises, setbacks, victims, virtuosi, and reversals in the play of power, status, and gender.[2] This essay tries to keep magical-coincidence (Indonesian, *kecocokan*) returning to and from the margins of cultures in translation.

FIRST ATTEMPT AT PRELIMINARIES

Our principal scene, Bali, harbors a minority Hindu polity in a nation whose Islamic majority is diverse and distinctive in its own right. Indonesia was assembled from the remains of the Dutch East Indies, after a brief and devastating Japanese occupation during World War II. Balinese society, inclined to hierarchy, has assumed varied shapes over a long-literate, multilingual, and mottled history on the outskirts of several so-called world systems—including Hinduization and modern tourism. Bali has been and remains something of a cornucopian "chronotope": places-in-times.[3]

Consider a few characteristic twists in events from colonial Bali. The Dutch territorially subjugated the north in the 1840s, the south only after 1906–08, with some complicity by rivalrous royal houses.[4] Declared by and large off-limits to Christian missionary efforts in the late nineteenth century, Hindu-Bali was promoted in part as a kind of religious preserve exemplary of the Netherlands' new "ethical policy" for fostering "self-rule." After the 1880s, Bali became an ideal haven for Dutch steamship tours for the same reasons it had been strategically important to Britain during the heyday of Anglo-Dutch rivalry: it lay just off Java. We saw in Chapter 3 that Bali's renown during the 1920s and 1930s was cultivated by Walter Spies, hired away from a Javanese sultan by a Balinese raja, who possibly hoped this virtuoso could attract foreign interest and help insulate Balinese arts and customs from "Javanization." Such colonial convolutions foreshadowed pragmatics of packaging Bali for tourist markets still accelerating today. I note these hybridities from Bali's past to help readers recognize particular *rencontres* inscribed in this essay as something other than postmodernist.[5]

Dominant schools in current postmodern critique challenge pat claims of "knowing" the Other (or for that matter the Self); they question the politics or even the possibility of authoritative description. In these projects I too participate. However, ironies in dated discourse are richer than today's warriors against essentialism and Orientalism tend to acknowledge. Part One of this book illustrated some elements of epistemological and ethical self-doubt from earlier arts of ethnography. This essay adds to that effort in a different fashion.

I here take for granted now-commonplace misgivings about that zenith of anthropological authenticity: an ethnography "gone native"—perfectly congruent with another's culture. (That, at least, is what anthropology's detractors like to assume the discipline's aim was, essentially; see Chap. 11). This essay addresses a flip side of that critical coin: the nadir (many assume) of inauthenticity—superficial touristic experience. I reason this way: Challenging anthropology's legendary zenith necessitates revisiting its legendary nadir as well; the two critical moves are inseparable. This exercise therefore pursues ironic possibilities of ephemeral encounters taking on fresh authority. (Secretly, however, its author remains among those who prize sustained episodes of ethnographic exchange—call him a double agent.)

It may help to reiterate. Today's critical thinkers routinely dispute claims of ethnographic "authority"—said to disguise, inevitably, a cooptation of power.

Although I do not fully buy into this cozy proposition (it just seems too easy), I grant it here to explore an inviting corollary: the elevation of apparently inauthentic encounter into a disguised brand of profound understanding. This chapter opens ludic prospects of coincidental, touristic knowledge gaining comparative ascendancy.

By professional standards I commit a regression, moving backwards in memory from careerist expertise. I nurse suspicions that the process of repressing first impressions may distort how cultures truly get crossed. I bother old-fashioned certitudes that something like ethnography is altogether distinct from superficial travel; yet I also question new-fangled dogma that everything is a phantasmagoria of Baudrillardian simulacra. By parodying recourses to rhetorics of self-therapy, including collaborative ones, I encourage readers to peer into the abyss of superficial subjectivities, hoping thereby to rekindle desires for ethnography deflected from patently ideological agendas in this imperfect, political world.

Even to parody earnest, first-person reportage runs the risk of sounding self-indulgent, and unserious too. Stendhal, at least, advised as much in *De l'amour*—written of and through his displacement from France to Italy and Germany for fifteen years, after the break-up of the Napoleonic empire in 1815.[6] (Coincidentally, while Stendahl was in Italy, half a world away Britain gained control of Java from the Dutch, and for the same reason: Napoleon.) Anyway, Stendahl explained himself as follows:

> I may be charged with egotism for the form I have adopted. But a traveller is allowed to say: "*I* embarked at New York for South America. *I* went up to Santa Fe de Bogota. Midges and mosquitoes bothered *me* on the journey, and for three days *I* could not open *my* right eye."
>
> The traveller is not accused of being too fond of the first person singular; all these *I*'s and *me*'s are forgiven him because to use them is the clearest and most interesting way of relating what he has seen.
>
> It is to be clear and graphic, if he can, that the author of this journey into the little-known regions of the human heart says: "I went with Mme Gherardi to the salt mines of Hallein. . . ." All these little things have really happened to the author. . . . (Stendahl 1975: 25)

It is Stendahl's tardily recognized classic in philosophical travel-telling that provides my "preliminaries" now under way with their "first attempt/second attempt" formulation.

SECOND ATTEMPT AT PRELIMINARIES

Professional anthropologists engage in a specialist activity called "fieldwork," designed to usher intensely observed elsewheres into ethnography—a kind of writing-to-be-read. Even fieldworkers of domestic situations—the late Erving Goffman was one superb example—may frame evidence as if it were witnessed cross-culturally and inter-lingually.[7] These are familiar facts—ever since Clifford and Marcus's *Writing Culture*; or since Lévi-Strauss's *Tristes tropiques*; or since Bateson's *Naven*; or since. . . . [8]

Less familiar, perhaps, is the fact that the strategic isolation built into fieldwork occasionally folds over on itself, yielding sudden distance from distance. Whether flushes of doubled alienation return full circle to the too-ordinary or spiral to higher planes of remove is exquisitely difficult to decide. To sustain, prolongingly, such difficulty is to cultivate what I shall be calling the cosmopolitan moment. To inscribe, paradoxically, such difficulty is to engage palpable ironies of representation. When glimmers of second-order alienation punctuate the course of crossing cultures, ethnographers may neglect to document them, so enchanted are we with having gained, ostensibly, the first-order alienation of fieldwork proper. My as-if confessions—proceeding from self-satire to other-parody and (I hope) beyond—aim to fill this regrettable gap in the anthropological record.

The pages that follow (and by now precede) gather many motives from the history of travel tales, including fragments of Vladimir Nabokov's *Lolita*, like the following one (here Humbert Humbert is writing; Alfred Appel, mercifully, has annotated; the passage should be read in a Russo-Cambridge-Berliner-Parisian-Upstate-New-York accent, but not necessarily in that order):

> I remember as a child in Europe gloating over a map of North America that had "Appalachian Mountains" boldly running from Alabama up to New Brunswick, so that the whole region they spanned—Tennessee, the Virginias, Pennsylvania, New York, Vermont, New Hampshire and Maine, appeared to my imagination as a gigantic Switzerland or even Tibet, all mountain, glorious diamond peak upon peak, giant conifers, *le montagnard émigré* in his bear skin glory, and *Felis tigris goldsmithi*, and Red Indians under the catalpas. That it all boiled down to a measly suburban lawn and a smoking garbage incinerator, was appalling. Farewell, Appalachia! Leaving it, we crossed Ohio, the three states beginning with "I," and Nebraska. . . . (Nabokov 1970: 211–12)

My post-1968 crossings of cultures commemorate equivalent ambiguities: Appalachia, Switzerland, Bali, or Tibet? As Humbert Humbert implies, not even Dolores ("Dolly")—alias Lolita—knows.

(Phonetic and etymological resonances among "Lolita, Dolores, Dolly," and related names help orchestrate the hyperorchestrated *Lolita*.[9] My inchings toward a burlesque of ethnographic confession—i.e., both a parody of confessions and a confession—is prompted in part by Nabokov's "number" [called *Lolita*] on literary-psychotherapeutic confessions. This genre requires "winks" about "works" mentioned—books, cultures, filmstars. For example, any resemblance between a few formulations that follow and Geertz's intricate sentences about cockfights or religion is purely coincidental. Coincidence-writing, like the magics it echoes, is inescapably overlapping, layered, parentheses-laden, and both explicit and allusive. [Still in parentheses] let me add that performance versions of this essay interspersed canned musical extracts it mentions. This patently outlandish tactic struck some listeners as unscholarly; others found it true to neglected aspects of culture-crossing, or so they reassured me. Similar diversity of response may persist among readers, even those willing to imagine hearing tuneful interludes.)

One last warning. My exercises in Nabokovian coincidence—which we shall see might equally be called "Javanese"—also covet affinities with the Marxist-mystic snapshots and illuminated aphorisms of Walter Benjamin and, if that isn't cosmopolitan enough, with contradictions dotting the novels and essays of Walker Percy. First, Benjamin (to be read scrupulously with a worldly accent, one tragically so):

> We penetrate the mystery only to the degree that we recognize it in the everyday world, by virtue of a dialectical optic that perceives the everyday as impenetrable, the impenetrable as everyday. . . . The reader, the thinker, the loiterer, the *flâneur* are types of illuminati just as much as the opium eater, the dreamer, the ecstatic. And more profane. (1978: 190)[10]

And now, less profanely, Percy (to be read precisely with any regional accent, one comically so):

> After a lifetime of avoiding the beaten track and guided tours, a man may deliberately seek out the most beaten track of all. . . . (Such dialectical savorings of the familiar as the familiar are, of course, a favorite stratagem of the *New Yorker Magazine*.) The thing is recovered from familiarity by means of an exercise in familiarity. . . . Such a man is far more advanced in the dialectic than the sightseer who is trying to get off the beaten track. . . . This stratagem is in fact, for our complex man, the weariest, most beaten track of all. (1975: 48–49)[11]

The ensuing cosmopolitan moments inscribed from Indonesia and elsewhere oscillate among motives of Nabokov's redoublings, Benjamin's Baudelairian loitering, and Percy's profound movie-going plus passionate post-sightseeing—not to mention Proust.

These notes of an ethnographer-rebecoming-a-tourist (or a mystic) encourage readers to heed Percy's advice, regress, and proceed dialectically further than simply leaving the beaten track. So, *allons-y*; rather, *marilah kita* (*Nota Bene*: All Indonesian terms in this interlingual essay are pronounced approximately as in operatic Italian).

PART THE FIRST: EXOTIC MOMENTS

We interrupt these preliminary intertextualities to narrate a dramatic entry into Indonesia's most storied isle:

> My wife, daughter, and I arrived, malaised and different, in Bali, which, being Bali. . . .

Not bad, I guess, but better try again.

> Oh, I had struggled all right during those dark and stormy days. Drilling Indonesian and Dutch; beginning Balinese; mastering kinship theory, conquering comparative social structure; advancing through Vietnam protests and grant competitions; doubting throughout 1968–71, along with everyone else, anthropology's and everything else's relevance. When suddenly, through the kind offices of several professors, a well-intentioned foundation, and an eminent Indonesianist, I found myself assigned to help survey local social science researches, such that they were, in Java and Bali (ostensibly to help; I was far too green to matter). Nothing, however, in my struggles, training, or doubts prepared me for those initial encounters.

First Specimen: Native to Native, or, Me-me-me.

> The long and narrow peninsula of Malacca, extending South-eastward
> from the territories of Birmah, forms the most southerly point of all Asia.
> In a continuous line from that peninsula stretch the long islands of
> Sumatra, Java, Bali, and Timor; which, with many others, form a
> vast mole, or rampart, lengthwise connecting Asia with Australia,
> and dividing the long unbroken Indian ocean from the
> thickly shaded Oriental archipelagoes. . . .
> Those narrow straits of Sunda divide Sumatra from Java . . . [and those
> straits of Gilimanuk, Java from Bali. . .].
> (*Melville*, Moby Dick *[emended, or extended]*)[12]

Ironic inklings (foretastes) of first meetings in Bali began in central Java. I was assisting at (in the French sense) interviews of representatives from a range of social classes—from peasant to general—active in so-called *kebatinan*. This vigorous "mystical" movement had important implications for Indonesia's political and religious future, especially since the collapse of Communism (and Sukarno) in 1965. At one session that I recall only too well, a kindly charismatic greeted me with proclamations of precognition as to my face and name.

The latter recognition was familiar enough in 1971, even when encountering nonmystics. Those were the (original) 007 days, when all languages—or so it seemed—shared a universal feature. "James Boon" reminded the world's ears of "James Bond." (Not, alas, its eyes: foreviews of my visage, therefore, were more mysterious.) It didn't take our *kebatinan* friend long to spin an explanatory spiel so ingratiating that even my fledgling Indonesian could master his meaning. We had met during his sleep last night in a dreamscape ("Tadi malam saya bermimpi tentang Tuan James Boon") that included, among other compatriots, Doris Day (in Indonesian, "Doris Day"). Again alas, on that occasion I failed to record the specific film fodder interlacing that magnetic seer's celluloid-informed visions. I only knew I had seen it all.

In Java, my still-quaint standards of authenticity precluded absorbing lessons from what I would later realize was a not-untypical mode of accessing exotica. An essay like this couldn't be written then (perhaps unregrettably); but nowadays, during "high postcolonialism's transnational flows," do we have any choice?

Putting *kebatinan* out of mind, I readied to cross the straits, to proceed "east of Java." A brief flight Bali-ward from Surabaya sustained that initial welcome's portent. On a prop-job small during politics nervous, passengers were triple checked against an official list, each of us summoned individually to his seat. The Third World loudspeaker blared "James Boon," whereupon an assembled crowd burst into the Indonesian equivalent of uncontrollable titter, then a show of real disappointment upon espying a *personnage* decidedly not Sean Connery file humbly on. Airborne, the flamboyant pilot (brandname: *Garuda*) dared a breathtaking pirouette round East Java's foremost volcano, before landing in equally theatrical Bali.[13] Here airport taxis still wound through bustling lanes—past ricelands, ritual shrines, and masses whose constant toil marks life 'neath the swaying palms of this strangely Hindu land. Again, that was long-gone 1971, first year of Pan-Am's Pacific jumbo jets.

Whenever and wherever political conditions prevail that make research less than "free," an ethnographer upon arrival must quickly assure that he or she can exit too. During 1971, exit/reentry permits were particularly iffy in Indonesia, a nation then engaged in its first general elections since the 1965 massacres that preceded Sukarno's fall. These circumstances, plus a planned rendezvous with my wife and infant elsewhere in Asia before resuming work in Bali, led me forthwith to the only place authorized to book flights and confirm requisite papers, or try to: the infamous, the international, the inauthentic Hotel Bali Beach. Tickets approved, exit/reentry argued into legitimacy, those other ubiquitous palms greased, I resolved at once to disassociate my anthropological self from this ultramediated zone offensive to all ideals of fieldwork experience, or even to serious travel. (It has since been outdone.) Object: a "real"

Balinese (or bust), i.e., one behind neither a ticket counter nor a steering wheel. Relevant entries of my journal—labeled "First in-formant"—read something like this:

> Exhausted, overstimulated, I slouch past sea-taxis hawking passage to Turtle Island, toward a barricade dividing me off from Bali's uncapitalized "beach" and, I assumed, from Bali. And it came to pass: at the border's edge, up popped a native, mine to befriend.

Our conversation began—as they do in Indonesia—with conventions of itinerary-checking: Where are you going? (*Mau ke mana?*) Where have you been? Where were you a little while ago? Where are you from (*Dari mana?*) We eventually arrived at the customary next plateau of interaction: "How many children do you have?"

He was pleasant enough, eventually successful, I suppose, although I never saw him again. I seasoned our Indonesian exchanges with Balinese terms and titles, to show that I was by no means just a tourist; he seasoned our Indonesian exchanges with a stab at English ("daughter, er, ah, sister") to show, possibly, that he was by no means just an informant. I learned some things about Dewa Made Rai (I still think of him as "Dari Mana"): he had approached, actually, to peddle a younger brother's ("*kakak*, er, ah, *adik*") "genuine" Balinese paintings—a steal at 700 rupiah. I "promised" in Indonesian "to buy one next week when I returned from Hong Kong." He said I could find him in Gianyar or Den Pasar between which he motorbiked *banyak* kilometers through-scorching-heat-to-school; he had been writing his *skripsi* for three years while earning extra cash. I still have the calling card he proffered: its first line gives his high-caste title (*Dewa*); its fourth his university; its third his "faculty" (in the continental sense); and its second his graduate division major: *Antropologi*.

I bypass the too painful and obvious ironies of this climax in a distant voyage round half the world to discover t'other. I sidestep implications pursued since: that Balinese anthropologists are "native" too, like British, French, Dutch, and American ones, among others. That in a seemingly shrinking world of folk less "indigenous" than "anthropologist," one does well to inquire how cultures became perceived as "native"—not to mention "cultures"—in the first place. Instead, I here celebrate that moment in 1971, whereupon—oh, miracle of translation—Indonesian *antropologi* was transfigured into American "anthropology" during an incipient fieldwork encounter that strikes me now—many more than fifteen years later, forgetfulness having much more than accomplished its task—as momentously cosmopolitan and appropriately coincidental.

(At this juncture in this essay's performance versions, select extracts of the song discussed below were played as a prelude; a still scratchier version was repeated later as a postlude.)

Second Specimen: Our Song

Mysteries more embarrassing still link three separate fieldwork stints and, I begin to suspect, all future stints as well. The self-contrived connection is TV's ultimate classic—need I name it?—*Perry Mason*, the original, of course.[14] In eventful 1968, the wife, who calls me "the husband," and I—first year graduate students, newlywed and dirtpoor—economized by cultivating therapeutic connoisseurship in late-night reruns, cheaper by far than psychiatrists, particularly in Chicago. Some are born predisposed to overtures and what were once happily (before Derrida) called "prefaces": devices that allusively and/or flamboyantly establish powerful, pervasive, and short-lasting moods and mediations, thus modulating passage between business as usual (life) and the world of the book, the screen, the performance.[15] *Perry Mason*'s immortality had been assured by its opening titles, whose intricacies rival many a "cultural system." Initial shots for each morality play—revised just twice (wasn't it?) during the series' nine year history—disassembled the courtroom into a composition sweeping from balcony past judge's bench, prosecution table, and defender's amanuensis (friends call her Della), round the pivotal, inward gaze of ever-present Perry. This miniaturized music drama was paced by that unforgettable fifties themesong, the only thing preservable in remakes. I can't describe it; you have to know it. A little like *Breakfast at Tiffany*'s "Hubcaps and Taillights," and mercifully free (originally) of the droning beat of deconstructive disco, its sliding syncopations captured much that is worthy in the rhythms of this world.[16] In solemn '68, "the wife and the husband" would end each day of historical defeat in mock-upbeat enthusiasm, converting the show's final strains of recapitulation to a private choreography we called the "Perry shuffle." (You see, children, those years were pre-VCR; we had to watch what was on when it was, and walked *many* miles-through-freezing-snow-to-school.)

Our desperate silliness persisted as long as local programming allowed. That bit of home-therapy must have been important: for, in 1971, when asked abruptly by a distinguished scholar, mentor, and patron what kind of study I hoped to write about Indonesia, I could only think to respond, without (believe it or not) elaboration, "Something like the *Perry Mason* credits." That he kindly disregarded the slip and took me half-seriously anyway sealed my eternal blushing gratitude. What, then, could be more beside any point whatsoever than this: ever since, for this fieldworker the two bilabial-liquids of "Bali" and "Perry" have remained seriocomically intertwined. And yet . . . and yet . . . Itemized evidence of selective affinities follows. Sure, its circumstantial; but don't forget, I've got Perry on *my* side.

Defense Exhibit A. Still sheepish over my amateurishly dropped-guard and "off-the-wall-ism" before a thoroughgoing professional, I put it out of mind en route to Indonesia in May 1971. Whereupon, entering my initial *toko buku* in steaming Jakarta, the first thing I spied was *Simanis dan Harta Warison* (loosely: "Sweetie-pie's Inherited Wealth") translated from the American original, "The Case of the Sulky Girl."[17] Out of all the books, the billions and billions of books, in earth's uncounted bookstores, Erle Stanley, it had to be you. I bought just one copy and commenced memorization. (Language drill wasn't finicky, as long as it was Indonesian.)

Defense Exhibit B. Back again in 1972, my project in bilingual Bali (Indonesian and many-leveled Balinese) altered through the year. Most projects do; all fieldworkers have their explanations and rationalizations, their "Because, whys." Because of unforeseen developments in the dynamics of Balinese status, I focused increasingly on ancestor group activities. Because of a debilitating disease, my wife, daughter, and I remained in one location rather than sampling three. Because my wife taught deaf Balinese children nearby, we minded less. Because our illness periodically sapped most energy and all strength, I worked more in Indonesian and less in Balinese. Because our hospitable hosts were opponents of the local leadership, I traced interregional networks and marriages, including ties with Javanese, Buginese (markedly Islamic), and Chinese, plus ancestor group endogamous unions (weddings between patriparallel cousins: i.e., children of brothers or children of children of brothers) favored in certain circumstances. Because past Socialist Party affiliations alienated many of my friends and subjects from the Nationalist Party powers that were (including segments of the academic establishment), I felt obliged to offer requisite scholarly reciprocities not to social scientists in Bali's university but to its law school. Here is the drift of this expandable list: While my fieldwork ordeals, local Balinese politics, and some deep concerns of informants (e.g., ancestral legacies) and of intelligentsia (e.g., property law) seemed disparate indeed, in a funny way they converged. I had hundreds of books with me in Bali: in Balinese, Indonesian, Dutch, and so forth. But one and only one of them turned out to be a concentrated word-list of research opportunities at hand: good old, translatable Erle.

Defense Exhibit C. I wrote a dense dissertation and then a complicated book about contradictory values in contemporary Balinese hierarchies and the corrosive history of "evidencing" them. Gardner's *Simanis* was playfully acknowledged in a dedication to my co-victim, who alone knew that, somehow, just as Perry had gotten us through epochal 1968, he helped us survive near-fatal 1972. Then in 1981, coincidence (Indonesian *cokcok*)—and even, as it were, description—thickened; things got serious.

I had set up ethnographic shop in a tourist area which facilitated quick access to parts of Bali where commercial pressures were altering cremation ceremonies and, to a lesser extent, marriage rites. Bearing gifts, I wished to visit

Fig. 12. A segment of the state temple (*Besakih*) coordinated with a political movement (*gerakan Pasek*) that intensified in Bali during 1972, and after. (Author's photo)

Fig. 13. An extra-Vagant vehicle (Studebaker '51) hired to help friends from Tabanan visit kinfolk in Karangasem; left, that "extraordinary elder" emotionally recalled by his son in 1982; right, "the wife" whose husband snapped this shot (1972).

but not to disrupt our hosts from before. Revised fieldnotes from June 10, 1981, convey (to me) a poignant and information-laden return:

> a.m. Feel good; still drilling Indonesian and reviewing a bit of Balinese. Toast, jam, and coffee. Unruly bladder, perhaps because of crab asparagus soup last night (*sup asperg kepeting tadi malam*). . . . 7:00. *Naik bemo* (board a jitney) to Den Pasar. Slightly fatigued, I slip into a "cafe" to order unsweetened coffee, request access to a urinoir (*boleh ke belakang?*), and pick up clove cigarettes before the long bus ride. All three tiny goals achieved (rare in fieldwork, comprised almost exclusively of little defeats); thus, elation. . . . I learn, alas, that the antique vehicles once plying the route to Tabanan have been replaced with streamlined models: faster, dangerous, diminishing the views over housewalls provided by highslung bus rides of yore. I successfully jockey for a window seat on the landscape side; could be worse; *relative* elation. *News on view*: The roadside is littered with portable Bali-Hindu shrines for sale as garden decorations to motorists (many of them Muslim) en route to Java. The school called Saraswati (Hindu goddess of learning) has been expanded. Untouristic Tabanan sports a new arts pavilion named for its celebrated interwar dancer (Mario), complete with gigantic, post–social realism statue of a peasant woman bearing burdens on her head (*memikul*). Other political rumblings are evident in the new district office, now headed by a Javanese, hand picked by Jakarta over Balinese rivals, including one from that once-Socialist faction mentioned above. And so forth, darkeningly. *Felt emotions*: I de-bus on a crossroads next to the shop owned by a fond father (*Bapak*) from before. During our un-Balinese bear hug he informs me, chokingly, that *his* father had indeed been exhumed and cremated (*diaben*; i.e., the corpse had received the ritual respects required of dutiful descendants). His greeting reacknowledged me as a friend and admirer of that extraordinary elder who had spent his final months wanting to recollect his own life and Bali's recent history with a devoted outsider, and doing so (he died several days after our departure at the end of 1972). That was then. Now his son and I talk family affairs and *plus ça change*. He managed his many children's schooling with profits from the shop's photocopy machine—long the only one in the district. The old neighborhood has really developed: full-time electricity, piped water, phones, and just recently, TV broadcast from ever-watchful Jakarta. Worries include his wife's ongoing complaints, an un-Balinese dearth of grandchildren, and a son who had married out to Australia, now back temporarily.That son, intricate in his own right, I later discover had learned to apply words like "workaholic" to his father: not disrespectful, perhaps, but different from the lapsing honorifics indigenous to Bali. Whether this son will permanently return home is a pressing concern.

My original notes—with their considerable evidence of post-1965 Balinese unrest and dire dilemmas—continue, halting and goosefleshed. The present narrative's climax, however, is not the jottings themselves (no poststructuralist, I) but their backdrop. Returned to my wee bungalow that evening, sworn forever off asparagus soup, I settled on the veranda to recall-record *minutiae* of observation and conversation. (Never turn in before completing your day's fieldnotes, that aforementioned mentor wisely advised, as he himself had been counseled and I counsel today; some things continue.)

I checked a few key references in my own book on Bali, per chance brushing past its dedication page and, pen poised, readied to write the account extracted above. I must now confess that I had not failed earlier to glimpse a peculiar foursome in the adjoining cabin: two California lads plus "consorts" ("pick-ups?"—their native term I overheard was less delicate) from downunder. And it was from their direction that, suddenly, those old sweet sounds, or nearly so, wafted through the frangipani. God's truth: Un-believe-able. Granted, this later version *was* disco. (What would you expect from the ghetto blaster, or should I say boombox—1981 was pre-Walkman, remember—of two surfing studs and their Aussi chicks [birds?] cruising-carousing through what they wished were Tiajuana?) But heard at that precise moment on that day of days, "our song," even degraded, might as well have been Perry himself shuffling to a Balinese *gamelan*. *This* was authentic. I'll never get over it. And yet . . . and yet . . .

Ordinarily, what should we—Nabokov's children—make of ultraoutlandish coincidence—e.g., Bali-Perry (bilabial-liquid)? Ordinarily, not much, I profess; and please, nothing at all, if prefabricated "fate" deflects one from fieldwork proper.[18] Coincidences confessed—even when phonetically reinforced—are no substitute for ethnography. Yet they do happen. And every now and again, just to set the record straight (or crooked), one feels inclined to commend coincidence much as Della Street in *Simanis*, echoing the jury, commends Perry:

Anda menang.

You win.

Karma, or showbiz? Not even Della, delightful Della, knows.

COMMENTARY: *QU'EST-CE QUE C'EST QU'UN* COSMOPOLITAN MOMENT?

> An infinity of error makes its way into our Philosophy, through Man's
> habit of considering himself a citizen of a world solely—of an individual
> planet—instead of at least occasionally contemplating his position as
> a cosmopolite proper—as a denizen of the universe.
> (*E. A. Poe*, Marginalia)[19]

Weary of mythemes, gustemes, epistemes, and the like, I shall designate my topic not the high analytic "cosmomeme" but the low comic "Cosmome": rhymes not with "phoneme" but with "tome," "foam," "Om," "Rome," and, in my native dialect, "poem."[20] The COSMOME (alternate spelling KOZMOM): irreverent rejoinder to brand-name methodologies—a comedically concrete, sheepishly particular spurt of intersensory (mystical?) fluttering.

Difficult to define, impossible to predict, the beast is unmistakable when it strikes. Ingredients of a vintage Cosmome are multilingual, ambiguous, cross-temporal, a little learned (a dangerous thing), supercilious, and winking, with so many elbows poking out in convergence that its foreordainedness seems karmic, or is it Calvinist? (Compare Gita Mehta's *Karma Cola*: "That's either Karma. Or it's showbiz.")[21] Either way Cosmomes bring factors distant into propinquity teasing. The fleet leaps effected are lower than Kierkegaardian, but no less exhilarating for being so. Simultaneously self-dissolving and self-indulgent, Cosmomes achieve both perspectives through incongruity (per Kenneth Burke) and incongruities through perspective, or contradictory perspectives, yet ones less comfortable, cozy, and clichéed than your average Escher etching.

Circumstances conducive to Cosmomes include: (1) When random broadcasts are within overhearing distance; (2) when music, text, conversations, scene, and temporal flux half-mockingly correspond; (3) when disparate channels of sight, sound, taste, and touch stretch across languages; (4) when the grand and the frivolous do a do-si-do. There would, in dialectical brief, be no Cosmomes were languages not diverse; cultures not plural; time not ongoing; the present not displaced; intentions not subvertible; the senses not transposable; form not fragmentary; media not multi-; the arts not, *de temps en temps*, *gesamt-*; disciplines not many; understandings not partial; interpretations not. . . inter-; experience not ironic; messages not clumsily communicated; life not written; the universe not, conceivably, a closed book; and subjunctive conditions not liable negatively to be itemized. Because all these nots *are*, the Cosmome IS!

During a cosmopolitan moment, the trivia maddeningly, perversely, and involuntarily retained in everyday life effect unspeakable synapses between the ordinary and far-flung, producing an echo of concerted performance or, failing that, a concoction of pseudo-punchline. "Cosmopolitan" in this case implies no pat universal order achieved by some citizen of a post-Revolutionary world, although this possibility, too, remains in play. Rather, Cosmomes enact collisions of provincialisms, tribal enthusiasms, narrow views, and "local knowledge" so intense and multiply allusive that they cancel each other out, empty one into the other, launch equivalent stereotypes, as if all parties in history's carnival of cultures might be ready mutually to celebrate the outlandishness of each in quasi-apocalyptic parodies of redoubled dialectics, of too radical remove. *Voilà: c'est ce que c'est qu'un* Cosmome.

Even at home, the crazy currents of a Cosmome strike only an aficionado or two amidst others who do not get it. ("Others who do not get it" are guaranteed

COSMOPOLITAN MOMENTS **117**

during fieldwork.) Your ideal-type Cosmome is thus both social (involving others) and nonsocial (unshared to the hilt). *Un*promising contexts for Cosmomes include pushy happenings that jab captive audiences to the brink of outrage: P. T. Barnum, *Monty Python*, the stridently experimental, the contentedly Pop (although these shows too have their appeal). Likewise ill-suited are in-the-know groups relishing innuendos at the expense of a hypothetically insensitive outgroup, as in campy film-buff audiences, angry protests, and movements countercultural (although these demonstrations, too, have their importance). Cosmomes, in contrast, incline the one in-the-know to feel not so much superior as kind of silly in "getting it," yet gradually to give way.

Additional attributes of a Cosmomer caught in the act: (1) You don't know whether to laugh or cry, and do. Reading, for example, "Mahasiswa Antropologi" on my first Balinese interlocutor's calling card, I knew not whether to laugh or cry, and did. Or did I giggle, tearingly? I can't remember, I can't remember (check the notes). (2) Intersensory rhythms become duple and then some; the pace is multiply quick, very quick. It may feel like Wagner's conclusion to Act I of *Siegfried*, like some of Strauss (Richard), and maybe all of Mahler, his *First*, at least. Here ostensible ditties recur, becoming leitmotivic to wind up quasi-archetypal. Their final thunder reveals that they (the ditties) are all there is, and all there need be. This essay's confessions are accordingly offered in the paradoxical hope of promoting Cosmome-musicality even among the Cosmome-deaf.

Lower-brow analogies derive from filmdom, or rather movieland. Cosmomes evoke motile cameras, booms and zooms, revolving stages, invisible treadmills, with overlaid narrative and undercurrent score. Their coordination is nearer Busby Berkeley than his pale revival in video. (Between MGM-then and MTV-now there is, I churlishly declare, a loss, dammit, a loss).[22] Devoid of the total control and technological rush now standard in slick *Star Wars*-style spectaculars, Cosmomes remain reminiscent of musicals gone by, raggedy extravaganzas and rather intimate: mine, all mine (to each his own).[23] I once met a mystic and movie buff who seemed to share this view, and I dedicate these notes to that empathetic encounter between Doris Day familiars: one Javanese, the other not.

(Happily, Doris Day's unhappy life has been illuminated by John Updike—ultimate *New Yorker* litterateur—who boldly confesses past and present seduction by productions from America's hegemonic culture industry. Updike's "Suzie Creamcheese Speaks" assesses Day's autobiography movingly; the piece coincides in *Hugging the Shore* with Updike's essay on "Pinter's Unproduced Proust Printed," in turn juxtaposed with his salute to Borges:

> Whereas the polylingual erudition of Eliot and Pound was part of a worldwide search for an authenticity that would help make the native language and tradition

new, Borges's erudition, with its quizzical touchstones of quotation and its recondite medieval and Oriental references, is a parody of erudition wherein the researched and the fabricated lie side by side ironically—a vast but claustrophobi-
cally closed system that implies there is no newness under the sun. The must of
alchemists' libraries pervades his learning; his chaos of texts. . . . [708])

Equally parenthetically, friend Freud called certain Cosmome-potential the
uncanny—plus, perhaps, a dash of oceanic; he seems to have neglected the
zany, or did he? Freud's "aftermathers" trap matters between on the one hand
the whole, the true, and the proper, versus on the other hand (the left one) the
damaged, the false, and the deviant. I question such crisp distinction. Cosmomes prove corrosive of models of "other" today prevailing: poststructuralist, Heideggerian, deconstructionist, dialogicist, Marxo-feminist, hermeneu-
tico-phenomenological, lit-crit Lacanian, whatnot. Cosmomes offer time-outs,
brief respites—or the illusion thereof—from such threadbare dilemmas as "Je
est un autre," or "L'autre est un je (un jeu?),", or "L'autre est un autre autre,
oder noch ein anderer." Any such othering is itself othered when Cosmomes
effect bursts of *ostrenanie* in overdrive or *Verfremdung* all over again. You
make contact with the *données immédiates de la connaissance* of distanced
distance, thus raveling too-determinant polarities of unremitting consciousness-raising frequent among solemn theorists of Otherdom. Altogether to ignore the occasional, ultralocal Cosmome is to diminish the human salience of
our high-critical manifestoes. End of prolegomena.

Cosmomes twinklingly imbue the detritus of living, reading, thinking, traveling, viewing, listening, and remembering with, if not purpose or form, at
least point, edge, lilt, contour, effervescence, fizz. Sounds a bit like pop-
Proust *nicht wahr*?—Americanized, consumerized, minus that ultimate
heightening onto the stilts of cumulative retrospect wherefrom Proust salutes
ART in capital letters as redemptive, albeit ironically so. Although Proust's
madeleine moments (of synesthesia that recapture times lapsed) are not cosmopolitan moments, the two may sometimes start to taste the same. Moreover, writing Cosmomes, like Marcel writing *madeleines* or Martinvilles,
may actually induce concrete circumstances to allemand with words. Proust
went on to recommend that we write as we read (especially as we read
Ruskin): *in situ*, between the page and the landscape, eyes/fingertips tacking
between page and topography: sentences read or written interpenetrated by
ones overheard.[24]

The Proustian thrill's spectrum of senses sustains an encyclopedic "fiction-
ing" of the whole *Belle Époque* and its wartime postlude. Less epiphanal than
Proust's ex post facto advance into as-if coherence, Cosmomes rather retract
into overlapping disconnectedness. Still, without Proust (a personal favorite),
just as without fieldwork, this travel-reader could never have recognized a

Cosmome and certainly would never have tried writing one. And it took a Javanese mystic movie-goer—content in his counterorthodoxy—to bring it all home.

PART THE LAST: AT HOME WITH COSMOMES

My final confessions illustrate a not-Bali-but-New-York-New-York state of mind—or is it Switzerland, Nabokov's Nebraska, or Tibet? Regardless, the Big Apple remains a locus classicus of Walker Percy's "dialectical savorings of the familiar as the familiar," or contacting the alien known. (I apologize, of course, to Californians, Balinese, and other Pacific-rimmers, for the provincialism of the following example. Any resemblance between this representation, styled to suggest that Cosmomes can be quiescent even when they happen in New York, and the old *New Yorker*'s format is purely coincidental.)

Third Specimen: Rockefeller Plaza, NYC, USA, New World, Earth, Universe, Cos. . . .

There now is your insular city of the Manhattoes, belted round by wharves as Indian isles by coral reefs—commerce surrounds it with her surf. Right and left, the streets take you waterward. Its extreme down-town is the battery [even before the "people rode in a hole in the ground" and "the Bronx was up" . . .], where the noble mole is washed by waves. . . . Look at the crowds of water-gazers there.
(*Melville,* Moby Dick: *Chap. 1; update inserted*)

Manhattan's own Rockefeller Plaza, off-season, is a virtual Automat of Cosmomes, a precast scene from which "A Friend Writes." Those pages, and the plaza they taste like, package alternative zones of high urbanity, confident enough in its privilege to sympathize with the off-beat, down-to-earth, and everyday. While both pages and plaza sometimes seem smug, their sage councils and arch devices include quick-witted debunkings of their own pretentiousness as well. And neither, readers may have noticed, eschews ads, provided the salespitch is upscale. A final parallel is happily conspicuous: Rockefeller's bronzes and *The New Yorker*'s cartoons.

September 10, 1983. "A Friend of Ours Writes from Rockefeller Plaza." Awash in bromeliades and epigrams. Like Bali's riceland, the promenade's pavement slopes; the fountain's water can't. Slope-sided, flat-watered fountains sport flexible floral borders and would-be permanent sculptures, vandal-thwarted. "Wisdom and Knowledge shall be the stability of thy times." Similar-but-different denizens of the deep astride variant sea-creatures, poised opposite cute critters, also marine. My on-the-scene ethnographic catalogue of these oozie metamorphoses:

1. Crab; *en face*: merman, prick-finned on a buck-lipped carp.
2. Turtle; *en face*: mermaid on a dolphin, sidesaddle.
3. Starfish; *en face*: mermaid again, this mount long-snouted.
4. Starfish again; *en face*: finless female astride a shark.
5. (Missing [vandals?]); *en face*: mermaid unsidesaddling less baroque carp.
6. (Missing [intake valve?]); *en face*: horned trumpeter on carp.

The garden surrounds are four-square, punctuated by palmettos: hence Palm-square, so near and yet so far from Times Square.

Although, as Umberto Eco reminds us, "there is nothing more wonderful than a list, instrument of wondrous hypotyposis," that last bit strikes even *me* as too contrived; familiarly familiar estrangement may be hardest to enlist at home, particularly in the first person.[25] May I, then, offer fragmentary ingredients for some other "friend to write": Soaring Gothic mullions and integrated pigeon-stops; promenade's slopes; Prometheus's pit.[26] The sound of water's reflection in Singer shop windows (since then, there's been a change in brand). Multilingual bookstores. Polyglot guests. Travel bureaus. The gilt; the banners, the *grande place* Brussels-likeness of it all.

Another visit, less inviting but profounder, found Prometheus's restaurant a rink whose music is concentrated and canned: Canned concentrate. In Manhattan's March 1984, doubly off-seasoned because February and it had do-si-doed, a narrow ray of sun glinted off Prometheus *et moi*, we alone spotlighted, loitering. Fountains frozen, Christmas lights retained, intermission declared, the ice-machine cometh to smooth the ice. Avoiding cheap coincidence (e.g., on this trip my funding was also by Rockefeller), I only recall the piped-in music, not quite muzak: "Fly me to the Moon," and "My kind of town, Chicago is . . .". Oh, fond dislocation. Skaters, resume.

During Rockefeller's less untropical, friendlier-for-writing off-season, background songs remain dispersed, along with background speech and signs.

September 10, 1983, again. Winds polydirectional. Diverse *flâneurs* converge on Prometheus's pit, less abyss than eddy. Aeschylus's words—toward which bromeliades slope, o'er which Radio City towers—in truth divert through multiple currents and many wavelengths a plural flow. The inscription: "Prometheus teacher in every art brought the fire that hath proved to metals a means to mighty ends." The separate-but-equal other words: "Nikon Takes New York," "Newsweek 11:07," "Chase Manhattan bank." The passers-by (I level languages): "Gorgeous. . . . Look at the turtle. . . . Well, I like that. . . ." The wooden benches. *My* friends, the bromeliades. Foodstands. A woman dabs / a tissue in / the shark pool / wipes / the edges of / her lips. John D.'s creed: " . . . Only in the purifying fire of sacrifice is the dross of selfishness consumed and the greatness of the human soul set free." What a friendly place for friends to write! Yet flaws in the multinational flagstaffs are strengthened by makeshift braces that conceal from view meant-to-be-seen snatches of what Prometheus bears—his message—whose circle is the zodiac, names written *inside the ring.*

Some spaces are, as space, as eccentric (and extra-Vagant) as those *Eccentric Spaces* that Robert Harbison has revealed in prose, guidebooks, catalogues, and subway maps.[27] All Cosmomes are. Rockefeller Plaza is one of them. (SO TOO MAY ETHNOGRAPHY BE DEEMED THE SPACE— PLACE, *TOPOS*—OF CROSS-CULTURAL INSCRIPTION.) This plaza-place, I now realize, is no barrier (cabbies to the contrary notwithstanding) to the never sleeping city's gridded streetscape. It is more a ha-ha, a sunken separater—*not* a fence. Yes *I*, illuminated loiterer, find echoes of ha-has here (and in Cosmomes else- and everywhere), much as Gary Schmidgall's *Literature as Opera* finds ha-has prefigured in Handel:

> The position of the English garden in the history of landscaping bears some interesting parallels to the place Handel occupies along the continuum between the older Italian Baroque opera and the Classical opera of Mozart. . . . The new emphasis in landscaping was upon the picturesque. Walpole praised the invention of the ha-ha (a sunken, concealed fence) [one blocking cows from the lawn, thus letting vistas of pasture appear continuous] for making the walk through a fine garden like the experience of a "succession of pictures." . . .
>
> The "sunk fence" brought the art of man and the art of nature closer together, made the distinguished line more subtle. . . . In opera, Handel was having the same effect. In his operas we see the struggle between traditional formulas and the urgency of natural, truly dramatic expression—in other words, the struggle between artificial "neatness" and incisive, direct "rudeness." We see the relinquishment of the da capo aria where it would be painfully redundant, the development of differing emotions in duets and trios, a new simplicity of utterance (which looked forward to the artistic Rococo). . . . We frequently see Handel abandon what Walpole called the "prim regularity" of tradition." (Schmidgall 1977: 45)

Rockefeller Plaza: Manhattan's ha-ha; Cosmomes: life's; (cultural anthropology: disciplines'). Thank you, John D. R.: The money may be dirty, but the Cosmomes are pure. Ha-ha. Sunk fence. Which brings us to the punchline.

(At this juncture in performance versions of this paper, moments were played from the title song of the musical comedy discussed in the concluding example. [Uncoincidentally, a derivative of this same number, with other lyrics, became Ferdinand Marcos's last campaign song.] The original song ended with a female solo backed by a male chorus; the lyrics go "Dolly will never go away again"; the last word is sustained and the chorus repeated, as is customary in popular finales, even when not written by Jerry Herman.)

Fourth and Final Specimen: An Afternoon at the Opera-Shop

Fieldworkers to Manhattan (perhaps many a native as well) often seek spots to escape the sensory assault, to render it background, to displace the place (or bracket it). In inclement weather, Rockefeller Plaza precluded, my outs include the Grand Central balcony bar and the nearby waters of the equally Grand Hyatt: post-ostentatious lobbydom, plus free jazz ensemble. To this list of briar patches, I add a place called "Metropolitan," particularly its Opera Shop. Cynical query: Is the shop here for the opera or the opera for the shop? Which "motivates" which? Parallel question: Do products promote movies or movies products? Such unanswerably circular needs/desires drive the history of hybrid arts, commercial reproduction, and the culture industry.[28]

So reflecting, innocently, I entered in 1984 (wasn't it?) the Metropolitan Popera Shop. I exited guilty, a fully aware consumer: VCR-victorious, desiring to xerox life itself in reprints now moving, already technicolor, soon CinemaScope (registered trademark). Indeed it was this field experience—along with Doris in Java, Perry in Bali, and reading Proust and Nabokov, among others—that fixed for all time Cosmomes in my once unrisen consciousness. Here are my notes:

> *I* have capitulated, purchasing Puccini placemats, *Ring Cycle* glossies, a cut-rate *Rosenkavalier,* and other high culture gift suggestions. Appropriately, a Pioneer Laser Video Disc Player punctuates this Lincoln Center scene with strains of— guess who?—"Hello Dolly!" (exclamation point theirs). "Hello Dolly: the Movie!," that is, not the authentic original. A strikingly *artistique* duo of Asian mien wanders up; one nudges his friend, gestures screenward, uttering "Herro Dorry, Calor Channing." I barefly stifled a blurted correction: "No, no; Balbla Stleisand!"

(Forgive my notes; twice forgive me. How superior is his near-expertise in U.S. stardom to all my gaffes in Balinese cosmology. Would that my manglings of Indonesian pronunciations were as subtle as his lilting Japanese reversals of liquid consonants. I not only prefer his charming English to my ghastly Balinese; I favor his accent in American over my own.)

> As Louis Armstrong trumpets onto center-screen for his famed cameo, the twosome approvingly approaches an *Aida* poster, deep in discussion of their favorite *corolatula lore*: "Rucia de Ramamool."
>
> Meanwhile, sixteen folks or so (I'm jotting quickly) gather gazing at the celebrated production number. An errant flash, the screen goes blank. Hushed pause. Stylish cashier abandons post to fumble with the apparatus, to flip (switch?) the disc. Between the title-song's conclusion and its recap (da capo?) that makes literal that incomparably final "Aaaggaaaainn!"—she must switch (flip?) the disk.

Can you follow me, readers? Altogether now, repeat: Between the Metropolitan Opera Shop's Laser "Hello Dolly!" 's climax and renowned reprise, the *disck* gets flitched. (Oh, for an instant replay/reprise of prose!)

Enough. I apologize to non-Operashop-goers for the eccentricity of this example. I apologize to all Occidentals and Orientals for alluding to (y)our accents (this letter-play marks one poignant point of this essay-*étude*). I—an eastern (U.S.) Westerner (world) displaced—apologize to universal readers for attempting a representation that may require being read repeatedly and in intertextual relation even to itself, where ironies abound. I apologize for everything, which is purely coincidental. "I may be charged with egotism for the form I have adopted"—Stendahl sighed.

Is enough. Amidst these cross-cultural, multimedia comminglings: pop/serious, Orient/Occident, stage/screen, screen/screen, absent/present, viewing/writing, hearing/reading, Opera/shop; during this *gesamt*-like instant of anti*gesamt*, I seek beseechingly among the assembled eyes awaiting the blank screen's "Aaaggaaaainn" again for mutual recognition. Nothing. *I* soar into disparity; they stay. I prance; *they* price the Pioneer. The inescapable pathos: I alone get/got it. I only am escaped alone to tell thee, to commemorate the Cosmome! Call me Satchmo.[29]

Last Confessional Note: I, an opera-going Appalachian anthropologist, once a *Mahasiswa*, in the field wherever, am sporadically drowning, drowning in the variations, the coincidence, the mad, mad, mad, movie-mad rush of inauthentic affinities, whose magical concoctions may yield, winkingly, intersensory pleasure, not bliss . . . or *is* it? Am *I*? *Where* am I? In the field? Not? Where *am* I? Bali? Busby? Baudelaire? Benjamin? Broadway? Hello? Hollywood? Herro? Anybody there? *Dari mana*? Rockeferra Praza? Perry? Percy? Della? Dolly? Dorry? Doris . . . Day? Dolores? Lolita? Dolly? Dolly, Doris will never go away *again* . . . Wonderful woman.

CHAPTER FIVE

Why Museums Make Me Sad (Eccentric Musings)

> The museum, twentieth-century parody of a temple, is all that we have,
> physically, of the past; and Joyce begins *Finnegans Wake* in a museum.
> *(Guy Davenport, 1981)*

> . . . The essential present character of the most melancholy of cities
> resides simply in [Venice's] being the most beautiful of tombs. Nowhere
> else has the past been laid to rest with such tenderness, such a sadness of
> resignation and remembrance. Nowhere else is the present so alien, so
> discontinuous, so like a crowd in a cemetery without garlands for the
> graves. . . . The shopkeepers and gondoliers, the beggars and the
> models . . . are the custodians and the ushers of the great museum—they
> are even themselves to a certain extent the objects of exhibition. It is in the
> wide vestibule of the square that the polyglot pilgrims gather most
> densely; Piazza San Marco is the lobby of the opera in the intervals of the
> performance. The present fortune of Venice, the lamentable difference, is
> most easily measured there, and that is why, in the effort to resist our
> pessimism, we must turn away both from the purchasers
> and from the vendors of *ricordi*.
> *(Henry James, 1892)*

ANY MUSEUM, any museum at all, makes me sad.[1] Ethnological museums, art museums, ethnic museums, museums of these museums. Permanent museums, traveling museums, museums as travel; museums in the rough or on the mall. Literal museums, and figurative: without walls (ambiguous and permeable, anyway), or with. Williamsburg. Books read as a museum (some of them designed to be, some not); rituals enacted as a museum. Cities. Experience "itself" as museum: a play of context-begging specimens, oddly captioned, regarded *de loin* or *à proche* even by the one doing the experiencing. "Cultures." Museums are a locus of dislocated fragments, displayed in-coincidently with the motives of their production, revalued along other lines of exchange or schemes of competition, and not necessarily secondarily.

Now, the phantasmagoria I call "museum-making" is not exclusively the activity of history's Winners—whether Rome, Napoleon, Britannia, Fascists, America over-*alles*, or multinational expansionists-exhibiters-exhibitionists—all those political forces rightly critiqued in contemporary Cultural Studies.

Rather, in the wake and eddies of official, established "museum" swirls more museum, not just *salons des refusés* but collections that decontextualize, and differently, the vanquishers, made-seen from the vantage of those vanquished. Here is one striking, sad example, from the pen of Pacificist Greg Dening:

> If young George III of England needed a crown to be king in 1760 and to sit on the Coronation Stone of Scotland and Ireland, then a twelve-year-old Pomare of Tahiti needed the *maro ura* to be *ariii nui*, chief, in 1791, and to stand on the robing stone of his *marae*, that sacred preserve of his titles.... His *maro ura* was a feather wrap ... parakeet ... dove ... man-of-war bird.... In the feathers was a history of sovereignty, more mnemonic than hieroglyphic, capable of being read by priests who had the custody of the past.... In 1792 William Bligh saw Pomare's *maro* at Tarahoi near Matavai. When he saw it, he drew it, and in that drawing we have our only relic of it.... Bligh saw something else in the *maro ura* besides Skinner's auburn hair. It was the most famous thing of all. He saw a British red pennant sewn into the body of the girdle, as a lappet or fold of its own. Tarahoi was a Tahitian museum of their contact with the European Stranger. The hair, the skulls, Cook's portrait, the red bunting were cargo. They were Strangers' things remade to Tahitian meanings and kept, as in some archive, as documents of past experiences that were repeatedly read for the history they displayed. They were products of the ethnographic moments between Native and Stranger, interpretations transformed into things and read for their meaning in ritual actions that displayed them and preserved them. (Dening 1986: 104–05)

The "othered," then, make museums, too. As Dening's account reveals, however, Pomare enjoyed power; in Tahiti's home factions one could even say he dominated.

Every culture—or more precisely any history of encounters between self-styled Native and self-styled Stranger—yields products equivalent to the Tahitian relics of skirmishes with the British "them." Since fieldwork in Bali in 1971–72 and subsequently, I have mulled evidence from Hindu-Bali's representations (deposited in "relics") over a history and actuality of dislocations, borrowings, countertypings and ethnologizings by non-native and native forces too, each with its politics and poetics. It is not just that all ranks of Hindu-Balinese have made museumy emblems of "others"—Dutch and British colonials, Muslims, Japanese occupiers, anthropologists, tourists, all manner of non-Hindu-Balinese—but that they inscribe differences "within" as well. What we now call Balinese culture entailed processes of tradition-inventing and explicit "museumification." Around 1817, Bali was famously declared a living archaeological remain of pre-Islamic Java by Stamford Raffles and documented accordingly by the British during their brief period of control in the Dutch East Indies. A century later Balinese agents, who wished to preserve autonomy from both the Dutch and the Javanese, enlisted Walter Spies to enhance the international renown of Bali's arts. As we saw in Chapter 3, this move—probably both cagey and sincere on all sides—helped launch the consolidation of Balinese studies still prevalent: a virtual cult by diverse outsiders and insiders of select lifeways and artforms of three or four million souls whose "basic virtuosity" remains wet-rice cultivation.

Balinese texts and practices, then, have been dramatically archaeologized, curated, archivized, ethnographed, philologized, touristized, and performance-studified. The long history of demarcating Hindu-Balinese culture took a European turn after 1597; since that time various world forces have spawned constructions of certain places to make them appear "living museums": not just Bali, but Venice, Switzerland, Bayreuth, Nepal, Vienna, certain royal courts, select rural enclaves, distinct ethnic neighborhoods, and so forth. Any notion of "living museum" deserved and deserves contestation and ironic response. For anything construed as "museum" may convey—like a Tahitian feather-cape—sadness and melancholy, but sometimes gladness too.

MELANCHOLY-MIRTH

Museums perhaps make me sad because of what they reveal about representation; sadness savors of resignation to the museum-likeness (perhaps even museuminess) of what the museum would on first thought appear to be a museum of. If there is no *of* to museums—only more museum (representations without immediate reference, makings for-the-removal)—then that must be what makes me sad . . . or melancholy.

Yes, melancholy, like the perpetrator of that ultimate museum-book, so resembling and reassembling of the world, the museum-world of fragments: fragments wrested from their pasts and elsewheres to be exhibited and categorized, yielding in their juxtaposition aphorisms of coincidence:

> The *Anatomy* looks like a crude assembly of quotations and it is indeed a vast mobilization of the notions and expressions of others, yet it is not they but the rifler who is revealed. Books are his raw material. . . . Burton makes a cosmos [really, a museum] out of quotations. He raids the writings of the past, which he often finds neglected or in ruins, and reassembles them in a structure of his own, much as the ruins of Rome were pillaged by the builders of the Renaissance and worked into the temples and palaces of a new civilization. (Jackson 1977: ix)

The same quality of pillage attaches to the new d'Orsay, the renewed MOMA, and the old and new and in-between Smithsonian; but also to any old cabinet of curiosities and the meanest matchbox-collection hoarded by would-be Joseph Cornells, or just hoarded. The quality extends even to analyses and meditations—whether academic, professional, or casual—of and on these crude assemblies.

Burton's prose, so like a museum, was produced when cabinets of curiosities were coming into fashion (like libraries before them) in the country houses of readers for whom Burton—that "squirrel-like collector of innumerable good things to learn" and "English importer of the world's wisdom"—wrote (Merton 1985: 3, 280). His collected quotations and commentaries both mimicked such cabinets and catalogued their rarities and varieties: exquisite pieces of men and women, birds, and beasts. Burton rifled to a degree that smacks of parody, anticipating those satires of maniacal collecting by his successors. By 1676, for example, Thomas Shadwell's play, *The Virtuoso*,

> centers round the ridiculous exploits of the virtuoso himself, Sir Nicholas Gim-crack. . . . In 1710 Addison amused himself and his readers by making up Gim-crack's will, and publishing it in the *Tatler*. It was full of absurd legacies: one box of butterflies, a female skeleton and a dried cocatrice to his wife; "my receipt for preserving dead caterpillars" and "three crocodile's eggs" to his daughters; "my rat's testicles" to his "learned and worthy friend Dr. Johannes Elscirckius." . . .
> (Girouard 1978: 175)

No curator—indeed, no enthusiast of museum going—could help blushing when confronting such merry lists of outright obsessions. Another side of sadness is satiety, of melancholy mirth.

MISAPPREHENSION AND PILLAGE: A BRIEF HISTORY

Those ruins of Rome likened above (in my collected quotation about Robert Burton) to *The Anatomy of Melancholy*'s raw materials (really oft-cooked quotations) were also pillaged by creators of the "first public museum." Or so I heard it explained in a wonderful lecture in 1974, aimed at rekindling the spirit of Erwin Panofsky at Princeton. I keep forgetting the distinguished art historian's name, emeritus even then, and have never traced the published version. But his hearty quest of iconographic evidence remains—many years later, forgetfulness having indeed accomplished its task—lodged in my museum-mind of fragmentary recall or invention. That lecture possibly altered my view of the very nature of art history, ethnographic activity, other cultures, and motives of museum going.

History's "first public museum," it turns out, was the brain-child of agents of an early-Renaissance pope, who assembled in one place various chunks of classical statues removed from their previous medieval reinstallations. The lecture's punchline of convergent detective work speculated on pitmarks marring the renowned "boy pulling the thorn from his foot." Might these scars result from the fact that the figure, which earlier adorned (Middle Ages-fashion) a column at a pilgrimage site, had been stoned and pelted by the faithful whose lower vantage made him appear a representation of onanism. (You have to picture it.) Did, then, a Medieval reinstallation of Roman ruins, sub-sequently reinstalled otherwise in a Renaissance collection, inadvertently display traces of prior use, trails of earlier activities of misapprehending museum-goers?

Rome pillaged pillagers and was pillaged in turn, and not only by the Re-naissance. My own fate of sadness, or museumy melancholy-mirth, seems now sealed by that lecture long ago and keeps being reconfirmed in museums, in lectures about museums, in collections about museum collections, and in books about these. (Where feasible, this essay's references acknowledge my indebtedness to museum catalogues, or *are* museum catalogues—e.g., Hew-ison 1978; there is no question here of primary, much less original, sources.) Yes: pillage pillaged, and sure to be pillaged again. That may be what muse-ums, museum-going, remembering museum-going, and writing of all three (afterward, in process, and in anticipation) are all about. These experiences help us ponder whether pillage is and was our irreducible condition, whether human production possibly occurs in anticipation of inevitable plunder as much as hoped-for retention.

Such brooding is heightened in ethnographic museums, colonialist muse-ums, and imperialist museums—indeed in any collection that arranges booty of conquest and expansion (see Stocking 1983). Many are the varieties of such spoils—"mobilizing the notions and expressions of others"—since the Age of Discovery. Sixteenth-century "fardles of fashion" arranged monstrosities and curiosities along neoplatonist lines of affinities and antipathies—rhetorics shared with apothecaries, *anatomies moralisées*, and alchemical worlds.[2] With the triumph of Linnaean principles, classification ramified into Natural Theol-ogy and radiated through Victorian piety and bourgeois ethics of leisure—culminating in the "heyday of natural history" (Barber 1980). Our own muse-ums descend from both the post-Napoleonic impulse of "omnium gatherum" resulting in world expositions and its more ludic counterpart: Barnumesque humbug and ballyhoo (see below).

The same quality of pillaging marks, contrapuntally, displays of ethnic, re-gional, or otherwise antinationalist museums whose declared aim is to resist centrist appropriation. In either case, I think, museums remain places to con-vene with an historical and cultural muse of exponential plunder with its dis-tanced codifying, exaggerations, captionings, fractured commentary, and exer-cises of making-visible (Boon 1982a: Part 1). Through such devices and spoils viewers progress, and visualize.

We all of us have our favorite instances of "bearded-lady" catalogues from odd museums past, often in striking continuity with odd museums present. One long-ago, nowaday-seeming museum that makes me mirthful and mourn-ful was the Brighton aquarium, which extravagantly overspilled its professed *raison d'être*—the then-new fashion and technology of displaying marine life.

Indeed, Brighton mounted an ethnological extravaganza that rehearsed the Crystal Palace's unintentional representation of British colonial transgressions (as recently construed in George Stocking's allegorical reading).[3] As Barber describes:

> By the 1850s the attractions advertised at Brighton Aquarium consisted of giants, midgets, Zulu chieftains, Javanese temple dancers, and Dame Adelina Patti. No hint of "Piscatorial Science." Westminster was given over to Laplanders, human cannonballs, and Benedetti the sword-swallower, and every other aquarium had made similar adjustments or else closed down. (Barber 1980: 123)

Yes, Brighton too anticipated many midways of strange-but-true cultures later dispersed—from Peale's Philadelphia to all-America's Washington, D.C.

Although Peale's Museum had first brought the spectacular and misnomered Mammoth to America's city of brotherly love, it failed to make sufficient commercial adjustments (of the kind devised at Brighton) to stave off competition from P. T. Barnum's "Grand Colossal Museum and Greatest Show on Earth." Intent on outdoing Peale's Mammoth Mastodon, Barnum brought to the West from Siam a "sacred white elephant, no such animal ever having been permitted to leave the land of the Buddhists"; (that display, which Barnum later considered a crowning achievement, links him, sadly, to Southeast Asia's artifacts and relics.)[4] On the other hand, Peale's closed by 1845, leaving the field of exhibiting extravaganzas open for the Smithsonian's future eminence. And who could deny that the Smithsonian has also survived by juggling science and entertainment—both of them so-called?

SMALL BOYS RECOLLECT

I draw here on childhood memories of stories about notorious Smithsonian exhibits, retailed among prepubescent youths biking innocently along woodland trails maintained by the Mariners Museum, before that wondrous institution levied a twenty-five cent price-of-admission charge or replaced its (to us) legendary, malfunctioning Coke machine that often coughed back more change than it accepted. Such features meant much to boys then. (Today, I'm told, the Mariners Museum in Newport News, Virginia, costs abundantly more and sports a postmodern entrance pavilion.)

I also draw on two years' employment with the Smithsonian's Center for the Study of Man in the Natural History Museum, 1969–71. Those unforgettable years contained some mirth produced by the early folklife performance festivals, plus much melancholy from protests then pitting against each other unlikely antagonists, willing and unwilling. Painful dilemmas surfaced in the interstices of public purposes, when history was trying to become young again. One that sticks in my museum-memory involved a lone guard in the then-Museum of Science and History (wasn't it?). True to his charge, this modest and congenial individual—a worker who, unlike curators, could not easily be confused with a "power establishment"—tried to preserve order during an assault on the men's room by a band of females who from his vantage must have appeared marauding (they looked like flower children). The band, apparently, had been galvanized by Disneyland-length lines blockading access to their "normal" facilities. Their sole intent—so far as I could discern, observing from the near distance—was to liberate alternative plumbing for their biological relief. In every respect of rights for the dispossessed, his political interests lay with theirs. But he could countenance neither contradictions of gender distinctions in certain unmentionable areas nor transgressions of his sanctum's regulations. The horde turned on him; it was not a pretty sight or sound. And in that telling instant, along with several more consequential updatings in 1969–71, the Smithsonian ceased cataloguing history and entered it. But to remark as much is to commit a distinction this essay is trying to beg.

BRIDGE TO JAMES . . .

I offer this digression into tangled issues—of different parties' convictions as to what is proper to museums, if they are to be *relevant*—not to decide them. I am neither praising nor blaming either: (1) anticurators for staging carnivals, when their sacred task should be to advance rigorous ordering of specimens; or (2) curators for remaining mindlessly scientistic, when their sacred task should be to satisfy popular enthusiasm, mass demands, or aficionados' peccadilloes. I am not here seconding conventional critiques of museums either for living off the backs of taxpayers or for catering to the fancies of elite patrons, or both.

Instead, I want to make several interrelated suggestions tangential to such critiques: (1) That museums necessarily conjoin contradictory desires, including the mature (propertied) and the youthful (less so), and perhaps even the reactionary and the subversive; (2) that classification and captioning have something potentially both ennobling and prurient about them; (3) that museum-going by nature enmeshes the seemingly serious and the apparently voyeuresque. Can anyone, moreover, think longitudinally back along a lifetime of personal museum experience or motives for frequenting places museum-like without recognizing the child-man or child-woman or child-something in each of us?[5] This compositeness of motives, then, is another reason why museums—places like P. T. Barnum's, the Louvre, and everything in between or on either side—make me sad, or melancholy. As they did, but differently, Henry James.

... STILL MODULATING

Accordingly, let me add to this essay's collection of quotations (including quotations about Burton's collection of quotations) several specimens from James's autobiographical *A Small Boy and Others*. From this treasure trove I select not the celebrated climax of visual-sensual-nightmare-ecstasy in the Galérie d'Apollon ("the Louvre being, under a general description, the most peopled of all scenes not less than the most hushed of all temples"), when James, although still "uncorrectedly juvenile," "happily cross[ed] that bridge over to Style by suddenly envisioning a just dimly-descried figure that retreated in terror before my rush and dash ... my visitant was already but a diminished spot in the long perspective, the tremendous, glorious hall, as I say, over the far-gleaming floor of which, cleared for the occasion of its great line of priceless vitrines down the middle, he sped for *his* life, while a great storm of thunder and lightning played through the deep embrasures of high windows at the right" (197). No, I set off (indent) not that mock (or not) climax; I choose instead fragments from the astonishing section 12, ten extraordinary pages of print (stretched from P. T. Barnum's Manhattan to echoes of London's Crystal Palace) where James collapses into *figures* of and for reminiscence the entire range of exhibits, exhibitions, and exhibitionism that history has slipped into human experience under the rubric "museum."

JAMES DISPLAYED

Here then, selectively edited and boiled down (i.e., curated) are some not-to-be-missed extracts of Henry James that I have assembled for readers' viewing; please linger:

> I turn round again to where I last left myself gaping at the old ricketty bill-board in Fifth Avenue; and am almost as sharply aware as ever of the main source of its spell, the fact that it most often blazed with the rich appeal of Mr. Barnum, whose "lecture-room," attached to the Great American Museum, overflowed into posters of all the theatrical bravery disavowed by its title. It was my rueful theory of those days—though tasteful I may call it too as well as rueful—that on all the holidays on which we weren't dragged to the dentist's we attended as a matter of course at Barnum's, that is when we were so happy as to be able to; which, to my own particular consciousness, wasn't every time the case. The case was too often, to my melancholy view, that W[illiam]. J[ames]., quite regularly, on the non-dental Saturdays, repaired to this seat of joy with the easy Albert—*he* at home there and master of the scene to a degree at which neither of us could at the best arrive; he quite moulded truly, in those years of plasticity, as to the aesthetic bent and the

determination of curiosity, I seem to make out, by the general Barnum association and revelation. It was not, I hasten to add, that I too didn't, to the extent of my minor chance, drink at the spring; for how else should I have come by the whole undimmed sense of the connection?—the weary waiting, in the dusty halls of humbug, amid bottled mermaids, "bearded ladies" and chill dioramas, for the lecture-room, the true centre of the seat of joy, to open: vivid in especial to me is my almost sick wondering of whether I mightn't be rapt away before it did open. . . . (1983: 89–90)

In such scenes and through such devices, H. Dupee argues, Henry James "refined his gaping habit into a form of creative vision, thus liberating himself from the more paralyzing effects of his estrangement, his 'otherness'" (Dupee: xii).

Observe again the intricate passage exhibited. There James credits to Barnum's publicity announcements—"in their way marvels of attractive composition . . . bristling from top to toe" with an analytic "synopsis of scenery and incidents" casting its "net of fine meshes"—his "present inability to be superficial about which has given in fact the measure of my contemporary care" (90). That confessed, in a prose that had learned to echo these very effects, James goes on to "question memory as to the living hours themselves" in that "stuffed and dim little hall of audience, smelling of peppermint and orange-peel"; he treats ironically his own involvement in these invocations and recollections, and doubtless the reader's involvements too:

> The principle of this prolonged arrest, which I insist on prolonging a little further, is doubtless in my instinct to grope for our earliest aesthetic seeds. . . . Is it *that* air of romance that gilds for me then the Barnum background—taking it as a symbol; that makes me resist, to this effect of a passionate adverse loyalty, any impulse to translate into harsh terms any old sordidities and poverties? The Great American Museum, the down-town scenery and aspects at large, and even the up-town improvements on them, as then flourishing?—why, they must have been for the most part of the last meanness: the Barnum picture above all ignoble and awful, its blatant face or frame stuck about with innumerable flags that waved, poor vulgar-sized ensigns, over spurious relics and catchpenny monsters in effigy, to say nothing of the promise within of the still more monstrous and abnormal living—from the total impression of which things we plucked somehow the flower of the ideal. (95–6)

James's museum-memory runs from such tacky beginnings—certain to be transcended (or not)—to subsequent outings at Niblo's and then Franconi's. Their harlequins and orthodox circuses (under tents with Roman chariot-races) later struck him as rather like:

> the vaster desolations that gave scope to the Crystal Palace, second of its name since, following—not *passibus aequis*, alas—the London structure of 1851, this

enterprise forestalled by a year or two the Paris Palais de l'Industrie of 1855. (98)

James even offers a cure for museum-goers' fatigue: when dragging after his cousins through these courts of edification:

> I remember being very tired and cold and hungry there . . . ; though concomitantly conscious that I was somehow in Europe, since everything about me had been "brought over." . . . headaches quite fade in that recovered presence of big European Art embodied in Thorwaldsen's enormous Christ and the Disciples, a shining marble company arranged in a semicircle of dark maroon walls. (98)

This already-extraordinary material I have just quoted becomes even more so when James fosters suspicions that he could have produced his body of writing without ever going to Europe (even Venice), just from "experiencing" by way of Barnum's *affiches* or this pseudo-Crystal Palace (the pseudo-squared!) that "vast and various and dense" something or other that "Europe was going to be."

> If this was Europe then Europe was beautiful indeed, and we rose to it on the wings of wonder; never were we afterwards to see great showy sculpture, in whatever profuse exhibition or of whatever period or school, without some renewal of that charmed Thorwaldsen hour, some taste again of the almost sugary or confectionery sweetness with which the great white images had affected us under their supper-table gaslight. The Crystal Palace was vast and various and dense, which was what Europe was going to be; it was a deep-down jungle of impressions that were somehow challenges. . . . (98)

But to experience how truly subversive James's *Small Boy* becomes, visitors to my essay should travel to the book itself, which ultimately traces the origins, or at least the motive power of James's representations of Europe to an experience in a museum, and a tawdry one at that. Yes, visit the book itself; although its author is no longer available, he has left a legacy of writing for us to despoil. James, I assume, would be the last to claim or wish to escape museumy appropriation or the cycle of relics.[6]

"SPECTACULARITY" MERCHANDIZED, AND LIVED

In certain of their aspects—ones savored by James with that characteristic hypersensitivity of self-consciousness that he mastered or suffered—museums seem virtually designed to jumble, even to reverse, signs of mature reflection versus more juvenile longing—particularly the "juvenile" longings (in Susan Stewart's sense) that adults characteristically confess.[7] What viewers do (even straighter ones than James) amid the exhibitions, captions, and other viewers of museums is view, and perhaps eavesdrop. I am uncertain that this "way of seeing" can ever be simply ameliorative. No more so than, say, opera, ethnography, theater, politics, ritual, philosophy, technology, or education—extra-Vagant all. Yet, the inevitably tawdry "spectacularity" of museums may after its fashion be no *less* wholesome than other sorts.

Regardless, things and processes museumlike may be said to loom wherever viewers (or their *semblables*) are guided, willingly or not, among artifacts, samples, labels, light, stereotypes, categories, drawings, feathers, skulls, visual murmurs, and other goers. Nowadays, goers (to museums, zoos, theaters, operas, and the like) engage in *viewing* and *scoping*, much as Michael Baxandall shows Renaissance artisans exercised their eyes in *voluming* and *evaluating*. Modernist and/or postmodernist occularity ("just looking") may indeed be a way of eyeballing worlds of as-if merchandise—not-for-purchase except in samples, quotations, and reprints offered at journey's end—"in the shop" (see Chap. 4).

Thus, museums on the one hand remove sacra from normal commodification; on the other hand they fuel the circulation of simulations in the age(s) of mechanical (and manual, and electronic) reproduction. Walter Benjamin's celebrated insights into auras and copies, and into world exhibitions, have become canonical in critical theory addressing activities of demarcating visible goods into detachability, movability (and movies).[8] Museuming, we all become—yes, each of us, regardless of party, preference, or *Zeitgeist*—little Grandvilles:

> The enthronement of merchandise, with the aura of amusement surrounding it, is the secret theme of Grandville's art. . . . This is clearly distilled in the term *spécialité*—a commodity description coming into use about this time [1798, 1855, 1867] in the luxury industry; under Grandville's pencil the whole of nature is transformed into *spécialités*. He presents them in the same spirit in which advertising—a word that is also coined at this time—begins to present its articles. He ends in madness. (Benjamin 1978: 152)

To preserve a resistant stance toward any powers that would constrict my personal viewing habits (and perhaps to postpone madness), whenever the present author museum-goes, he takes along a book other than the exhibition catalogue, ready to intervene vagrant reading into scenes of *spécialités*. (I employ the same extra-Vagant tactic during fieldwork: learned it from a native.) Since 1992, that book could well be the very volume about museums and museum books, in which an earlier version of this essay first appeared (see Karp and Lavine 1991). Moreover, I customarily do ethnography of museum-going even when participant-observing the strange haunts of museum-goers—not without what Stephen Greenblatt (1991a) calls "resonance and wonder," and not without irony as well. Perhaps these devices and tactics only make me sadder. Nevertheless, I here offer some notes from my eclectic archive of museum-remembering and museum-reading. Recalling Greg Dening on Tahiti's possession, any such notes resemble a personal *maro ura* from a museumed past. In no particular arrangement, they may be either curated or disposed; or selectively sketched or redrawn, by some other Bligh: the reader.

GALLERY-GONDOLA I: PROUST-RUSKIN

You can visit Den Haag (*deux étoiles*), enter the Mauritshuis Museum (*trois étoiles*), sit devotionally before Vermeer's *View of Delft*, and hear French passers-by reciting, as if by memory, not Proust on Vermeer but the *Guide Miche*'s quotation of Proust's narrator on Vermeer, which may be precisely what is proper to recite in this kind of going-viewing. That fitting caption from a not-so-prosy guidebook was repeatedly intoned by travelers, as I overheard them: "le plus beau tableau du monde."[9] This pillaging of Proust by *Miche* was thus pillaged in turn by guidees, who murmured aloud the accolade, despite the propinquity of a silence-seeking reader of Vermeer's *View*, or rather viewer of Vermeer's visual reading of Delft's "horizonal" curvature and (according to Svetlana Alpers) "diffused circles of light, that form around unfocused specular highlights in the camera obscura image."[10] So far as I, eavesdropping, could discern, this activity did not make the French passers-by themselves melancholy, or for that matter mirthful. But who knows? *Ces français, enfin!* However, such rhythms of reappropriation did make Proust (or his narrator) sad, or melancholy, or musical. That narrator, moreover, remained mindful of memory's art of refiguring into palimpsests lost layers of captioned fragments—themselves residues from pasts and places already fragmented and captioned, *like* museums.

Pillage upon pillage upon pillage was the prose of Proust, and his predecessors. Indeed, Proust pillaged and "pastiched" a *mélange* of prosers, including Ruskin; he even translated Ruskin's *Sesame and Lillies*, there discovering a calling to write cumulative remembering that superceded mere re-collection. Among the works of Ruskin despoiled by Proust under his mother's persuasion were celebrated verbalizings and visualizings that advocated a fresh sense of place and past for perhaps the most pillaged place of all: Venice.[11]

We should recall that Ruskin's *Stones of Venice* followed not just Byron's forebodings of Britain's parallel fate ("Albion! . . . in the fall of Venice think of thine . . . "), but a hundred years and more of Grand Touring:

Venice had known a century and a half of tourism when Mr and Mrs John James Ruskin first brought their son to the city in 1835. Venice was not what it once had been—but then that was part of the romance of the place [only then?]. The eighteenth-century English visitor had come, ostensibly for educational reasons, as part of the Grand Tour, and the pleasures taken there had been set against the backdrop of a decadent but still lively and independent city state. Napoleon ended all that. In 1797 his army demanded the surrender of the city and the resignation of the Doge, thus bringing to an end the history of an aristocratic republic that once had ruled a Mediterranean empire. When in turn the Napoleonic empire was dissolved in 1815, Venice settled down to being a colony of the Austrians. The great days were over.

Tourism on the other hand, revived.[12]

Ruskin's museumizing of Venice both saved it from a certain kind of touristic packaging (that had earlier saved it) and launched a new wave and style of Venice-savoring that would save it again, and again. And Venice has remained never as it was.

Nor can Venice herself (spouse of the sea) be absolved from guilt in plundering and profiteering. Venice began making herself a museum, or more precisely a reliquary, many centuries before Ruskin-reading voyagers and voyeurs joined in converting Venice into a composite emblem of politico-aesthetics, hoping to redeem industrial Europe. Nine centuries, at least:

> Soon after the fall of Haifa [the Venetians] set sail for home bearing with them, apart from the trophies and merchandise from the Holy Land, the saintly relics they had brought from Myra. On their arrival, which was neatly timed for St Nicholas's Day, they received heroes' welcomes from Doge, clergy and people, and the reputed body of the saint was reverently interred in Domenico Contarini's church on the Lido.
>
> Did the ceremony have a slightly hollow ring? It should have done, because the luckless churchwardens of Myra had told the truth. Thirteen years before the Venetians arrived there, a group of Apulian merchants had indeed removed St Nicholas's body and had carried it back in triumph to Bari, where work had immediately begun on the basilica bearing his name. . . . Since the crypt of this glorious building had been consecrated as early as 1089 by Pope Urban himself, and . . . in the intervening years . . . must have been seen by countless Venetian sailors . . . , it seems scarcely conceivable that the Doge and his advisers were unaware of the Bariot claims. . . . We can only conclude that . . . the Venetians, normally so level-headed, were yet perfectly capable of persuading themselves that black was white when the honor and glory and profit—for the financial advantages from the pilgrim traffic were not to be despised—of the Republic demanded that they should.
>
> So far as they were concerned, the true corpse of St Nicholas lay in his tomb on the Lido. Several centuries were to pass before the claim was discreetly withdrawn. (Norwich 1982: 80–81)

If ever a city were destined to wind up museumed, and they all in a sense may be, it is/was Venice. (And if ever an island were destined to wind up museumed, and they all in a sense may be, it is/was Bali.)[13]

When Proust's narrator inscribed Venice, he was writing in the wake of a seemingly exhaustive cataloguing by Ruskin, called by Proust's character Bloch (not by Proust) "one of the most tedious old prosers you could find" (Proust 1981, I: 795). Yet, it was precisely reading Ruskins and seeing Titians that enabled Proust's narrator (in the retrospect of his writing) to have anticipated a Venice. These preconceptions, however faulty, figured in his "knowing Venice" ever after, including after "being there" in earnest, with his Mamma— paying visits "upon the crest of a blue wave, by the wash of the glittering, swirling water, which took alarm on finding itself pent between the dancing gondola and the resounding marble. And thus any outing, even when it was only to pay calls or to leave visiting-cards, was threefold and unique in this Venice where the simplest social coming and going assumed at the same time the form and the charm of a visit to a museum and a trip on the sea" (Proust 1981, III: 644).

At a later point in *À la recherche du temps perdu* ("Here's to Researching Lost Tense," I sometimes translate it), recall is depicted as impoverished into mere voluntary memory, even of Venice:

> I tried next to draw from my memory other "snapshots," those in particular which it had taken in Venice, but the mere word "snapshot" made Venice seem to me as boring as an exhibition of photographs, and I felt that I had no more taste, no more talent for describing now what I had seen in the past, than I had had yesterday for describing what at that very moment I was, with a meticulous and melancholy eye, actually observing. (Proust 1981, III: 898)

Later still, through a celebrated awakening of involuntary memory that linked uneven paving-stones in the Guermantes' courtyard to a similar stumble in St. Mark's Baptistry, the narrator learns to credit both his anticipations and his recollections as mediators of any "experience itself." More accurately, any experience itself is stretched between the irreducible poles of anticipation/ recollection; it is this stretch that the narrator can finally write. He thus recounts how he became emboldened to compose the very prose we have already read and how he ultimately managed not to discount his naive dreams of the Venice-museum that cannot be reached; such expectations form part of any place-name's reality (Boon 1972: 144). Accordingly, Proust's narrator (call him Marcel) earlier in the volumes had observed (ultraobjectively, I think):

> Similarly, in later years, in Venice, long after the sun had set, when it seemed to be quite dark, I have seen, thanks to the echo, itself imperceptible, of a last note of light held indefinitely on the surface of the canals as though by the effect of some optical pedal, the reflexions of the palaces displayed as though for all time in a darker velvet on the crepuscular greyness of the water. One of my dreams was the synthesis of what my imagination had often sought to depict, in my waking

hours, of a certain seagirt place and its mediaeval past. In my sleep I saw a gothic city rising from a sea whose waves were stilled as in a stained-glass window. An arm of the sea divided the town in two; the green water stretched to my feet; on the opposite shore it washed around the base of an oriental church, and beyond it houses which existed already in the fourteenth century, so that to go across to them would have been to ascend the stream of time. (Proust 1981, II: 147–48)

But please don't mistake Proust to be yearning for the past; his resignation to prosing the synesthetic effects of an "optical pedal" is the opposite of romantic. He continues:

This dream [Which? His? the dream that is Venice?] in which nature had learned from art, in which the sea had turned Gothic, this dream in which I longed to attain, in which I believed that I was attaining to the impossible, was one that I felt I had often dreamed before. But as it is the nature of what we imagine in sleep to multiply itself in the past, and to appear, even when new, to be familiar, I supposed that I was mistaken. I notice, however, that I did indeed frequently have this dream. (Proust 1981, II: 148)

GALLERY-GONDOLA II: JAMES, STILL SMALL

There was another writer between Ruskin and Proust who declared not only Venice a museum of pillaging but himself a pillager of his own past and his predecessors, including his near-contemporary Ruskin. This particular tedious old proser, reporting from Italy in 1873, 1877, 1882, 1892, 1900–09—a generation, more and less, before Proust (1871–1922)—was Henry James (1843–1916). James just kept writing and writing of Venice and Venice that there is no more to be written, rather like Cicero saying that nothing needs to be said. Perhaps this resolve led James's descriptions to verge on comparisons, similes even. *The Aspern Papers*, for example, likens Venice's relative quiet to an apartment's or a theater's:

Without streets and vehicles, the uproar of wheels, the brutality of horses, and with its little winding ways where people crowd together, where voices sound as in the corridors of a house, where the human step circulates as if it skirted the angles of furniture and shoes never wear out, the place has the character of an immense collective apartment, in which Piazza San Marco is the most ornamented corner and palaces and churches, for the rest, play the part of great divans of repose, tables of entertainment, expanses of decoration. And somehow the splendid common domicile, familiar, domestic and resonant, also resembles a theatre, with actors clicking over bridges and, in straggling processions, tripping along fondamentas. As you sit in your gondola the footways that in certain parts edge the canals assume to the eye the importance of a stage, meeting it at the same angle, and the Venetian figures, moving to and fro against the battered scenery of their little houses of comedy, strike you as members of an endless dramatic troupe. (1976: 103–4)

Now, museums lack brutal uproar and contain clicking heels too; and James's travel-writing—in certain respects as rich as his fiction—availed itself of another parallel which portended all future complaints by a century of tourists decrying the proliferation of their own kind:

> The Venice of to-day [1882] is a vast museum where the little wicket that admits you is perpetually turning and creaking, and you march through the institution with a herd of fellow-gazers. There is nothing left to discover or describe, and originality of attitude is completely impossible. (James 1988: 10)

But please don't mistake James to be sharing this craving to discover and describe. His previous remarks have just assigned so humdrum an urge to the creature against which he aims his every sentence: "The sentimental tourist's sole quarrel with his Venice is that he has too many competitors there. He likes to be alone; to be original; to have (to himself, at least) the air of making discoveries" (10). James's own originality of attitude absolves both himself of making discoveries and Venice of providing secrets to disclose. He is willing repeatedly to reread and rewrite over and under, after and before, all the reading and writing that provides evidence of the palimpsest that is Venice, even in the being there. Or, as James put it: "Reading Ruskin is good; reading the old records is perhaps better; but the best thing of all is simply staying on . . . to linger and remain and return. . . . The danger is that you will not linger enough" (10).

James's fiction sometimes countered the conventionality of familiar descriptions from the catalogue of Venetian local color by imagining twinkling reversals, as when *The Aspern Papers* turn into Amsterdam:

> The gondola stopped, the old palace was there; it was a house of the class which in Venice carries even in extreme dilapidation the dignified name. "How charming! It's grey and pink!" my companion exclaimed; and that is the most comprehensive description of it. It was not particularly old, only two or three centuries; and it had an air not so much of decay as of quiet discouragement, as if it had rather missed its career. But its wide front, with a stone balcony from end to end of the *piano nobile* or most important floor, was architectural enough, with the aid of various pilasters and arches; and the stucco with which in the intervals it had long ago been endued was rosy in the April afternoon. It overlooked a clean, melancholy, unfrequented canal, which had a narrow *riva* or convenient footway on either side. "I don't know why—there are no brick gables," said Mrs Prest, "but this corner has seemed to me before more Dutch than Italian, more like Amsterdam than like Venice. It's perversely clean, for reasons of its own; and though you

can pass on foot scarcely anyone ever thinks of doing so. It has the air of a
Protestant Sunday. . . ." (1976: 15)

But when travel-writing, James becomes like a museum-goer who lingers long
enough to become jaded, yet then lingers longer to become something more,
something resonant and plangent, although not merely that. His missives
hang out the conventional dirty laundry of poverty, filth, scuffling peddlers:
"There is a great deal of dishonour about St. Mark's altogether, and if Venice,
as I say, has become a great bazaar, this exquisite edifice is now the biggest
booth" (1988: 14). No one could take a more jaundiced view than James of the
merchandizing of Venice, of the rifling of a past that history left behind:

> The antiquity-mongers in Venice have all the courage of their opinion, and it is
> easy to see how well they know they can confound you with an unanswerable
> question. What is the whole place but a curiosity-shop, and what are you here for
> yourself but to pick up odds and ends? "We pick them up *for* you," say these
> honest Jews, whose prices are marked in dollars, "and who shall blame us if, the
> flowers being pretty well plucked, we add an artificial rose or two to the composi-
> tion of the bouquet?" They take care in a word that there be plenty of relics, and
> their establishments are huge and active. They administer the antidote to pedantry,
> and you can complain of them only if you never cross their thresholds. If you take
> this [inevitable?] step you are lost, for you have parted with the correctness of
> your attitude. Venice becomes frankly from such a moment the big depressing
> dazzling joke in which after all our sense of her contradictions sinks to rest—the
> grimace of an over-strained philosophy. (43)

Yet even here James keeps viewing, lingering, remaining, and returning. He
layers glimpses of these very "halls of humbug" with their "intervals of hag-
gling" into the "soft plash of sea on the old water-steps" heard through the high
windows of the homes laid waste, pillaged, to the profit of curiosity-shops
whose huge advertisements, nevertheless, offer "some of the most striking
objects in the finest vistas at present" (variously, 43). James's sentences, moreover, push beyond the parody they offer of hackneyed comparatives and super-
latives from guidebook opinionating: "If it's very well meanwhile to come to
Turin first it's better still to go to Genoa afterwards. Genoa is the tightest
topographic tangle in the world, which even a second visit helps you little to
straighten out" (65). Indeed James, or his sentences, linger(s) so long that
he/they become resigned to flirt with an incorrectness of attitude and perhaps
more than willing to be ravished by the sight of Grand Canal and gondoliers.
Gondoliers, certainly:

> From my windows on the Riva there was always the same silhouette—the long,
> black, slender skiff, lifting its head and throwing it back a little, moving yet

seeming not to move, with the grotesquely-graceful figure on the poop. This figure inclines, as may be, more to the graceful or to the grotesque—standing in the "second position" of the dancing-master, but indulging from the waist upward in a freedom of movement which that functionary would deprecate.... nothing can be finer than the large, firm way in which, from their point of vantage, they throw themselves over their tremendous oar. It has the boldness of a plunging bird and the regularity of a pendulum. Sometimes, as you see this movement in profile, in a gondola that passes you—see, as you recline on your own low cushions, the arching body of the gondolier lifted up against the sky—it has a kind of nobleness which suggests an image on a Greek frieze. (20)

This particular grotesque-graceful prose agglomeration of voyeurings and visionings by James of his museum-city's most conspicuous custodians was published in 1882; replete with both unexpected twists and not-a-little hackneyed copy even then, it proceeded to apotheosize these "children of Venice ... associated with its idiosyncrasy, with its essence, with its silence, with its melancholy" (22). Ten years later James was still wearing out through overuse (and therefore pushing beyond) conventional views—still returning to and repeating, with choicest variations, the same kind of seeing garnished with old obsessions never out-grown and never left behind. His developing prose, its freshness of Style, remains ever an attic of many pasts, a museum of museums of museums ... plundering everything that transpires there. Thus, in 1892:

Of the beautiful free stroke with which the gondola, especially when there are two oars, is impelled, you never, in the Venetian scene, grow weary; it is always in the picture, and the large profiled action that lets the standing rowers throw themselves forward to a constant recovery has the double value of being, at the fag-end of greatness, the only energetic note. The ... solitary gondolier ... is, I confess, a somewhat melancholy figure. Perched on his poop without a mate, he re-enacts perpetually, in high relief, with his toes turned out, the comedy of his odd and charming movement. He always has a little the look of an absent-minded nursery-maid pushing her small charges in a perambulator. (44–45)

Henry James, although of the view that "a rhapsody on Venice is always in order" knew full well that "the catalogues are finished" (38). His writing offers nothing complete, only accidence.[14] And his description delivers no references (even though filled with familiar labels of places, paintings, standard sites, and architectural wonders), if only to counter what automatically accumulates in any visitor's gondola:

"The [museumy] Grand Canal may be practically, as an impression, the cushioned balcony of a high and well-loved palace—the memory of irresistible evenings, of the sociable elbow, of endless lingering and looking; or it may evoke the restlessness of a fresh curiosity, of methodical inquiry, in a gondola piled with references. There are no references, I ought to mention, in the present remarks. . . . (38)

That remark will be the last reference in the present essay's catalogue of rifled quotations, vantages, and points of view. Yes, that remark will be the last reference in this gondola of a chapter, wishing that it, too, had none. But please don't mistake me. I am not saying that museums make me sad (or melancholy-mirthful) for the same reasons that the museum-city of Venice (and suchlike) made James or Proust—or Mann allegorizing "Death" there, or Wagner dying there—sad or melancholy. This luxury of self-identifying remains unopen to yours truly, if only because the works of James and Proust are among worthy relics now to be borne to "museums," so that reading them may be intervened among scenes of spectacularity. My power to curate James and Proust—cataloguing them amongst other fragments and captions—only keeps the museum-likeness, the museuminess, going. And this power over *them*—distanced into memory's purview—makes "me" sadder still.

————————

There is a Leviathanic Museum, they tell me. . . .
(Herman Melville, 1852)

The Venetian gondola is as free and graceful, in its gliding movement,
as a serpent. . . .
(Mark Twain, "gondolizing," 1869)[15]

Litterytoor 'n' Anthropolygee: An Experimental Wedding of Incongruous Styles from Mark Twain and Marcel Mauss

(OR, WHY "VERNACULARITY" IS TRICKY TO TRANSLATE;

PLUS SEVEN THEORIES ABOUT MAGIC, THE TRAGIC, HUMOR,

SACRIFICE, AND SO FORTH)

THIS CHAPTER engages several ways of enacting vernaculars in tension with officialized languages. Edges between colloquial dialects and dressed-up linguistic usage are a key locus of anthropology, sociolinguistics, folklore, literary studies, some philosophy, and critical theory attentive to the politics of translation. Genres of ethnographic description and novelistic narrative open toward "magical words" and related heteroglossias: subversive slang, resistant humor, the animated speech of marginalized voices.

Aspects of magicality and "the comic" figured importantly in the work of Marcel Mauss, France's premier ethnologist between the World Wars. (By "comic" I intend "the fullest human extent of forensic complexity.")[1] My essay winds up with Mauss's variegated studies comparing social rites and techniques; but it begins conspicuously elsewhere—with Mark Twain's variegated novels mimicking humorous speech. I stage a crossover between eccentric formats: Twaintalk AND Mauss*écrits*; that grammatical copula betokens an "improper scene" of segues between as-if highs and ludic lows—the lettered and the less so.

My coupling of Twain and Mauss—or heteroclite disciplines each represents—draws inspiration from "the Author, Explanatory" that prefaces *Huckleberry Finn*:

> In this book a number of dialects [and disciplines] are used . . . pains-takingly, and with the trustworthy guidance and support of personal familiarity with these several forms of speech [and discourse].
>
> I make this explanation for the reason that without it many readers would suppose that all these characters [and texts] were trying to talk [and write] alike and not succeeding. [My inserts][2]

TWAIN-TALKING (POSED AS A SPEECH DELIVERED TO AN AUDIENCE OF NON-AMERICAN ACADEMICS, VERSED IN ENGLISH AS A BOOKISH SECOND LANGUAGE; THE ERRATIC LECTURER IS TRYING TO TRANSLATE)

Folks, this here speech is about literature and anthropology—or perhaps literariness (*ostrenanie-ski*) and "culturality" (*Kulturellheit*)—plus some smidgins of linguistics, a science more up my alley than I aim to advertise.[3] I pinched that bit from *Huckleberry Finn* to conjure up contexts of tricky verbiage, intertextuality, and vernacular life. You know the hybridities I mean: where all sorts of blokes speak and listen, and sometimes even write and read. I'm talkin' multilingual, composite-coded circumstances of folks interpreting and getting interpreted back. Why writers may even try writin' like speech, and speakers speaking like writing. Yessir, in this crazy locus— this tipsy topos—print can ape talk. And *vice versa* [v-eye-see-verse-uh]— i.e., talk may try passing for a text that is palimpsestic from a long way back.

Now, such strange goings-on happen just where us anthropologists, *littérateurs*, and linguists like to hang around (Indonesian, *bergaul*). One sucha place I've been to is quatrilingual *Suisse*, fairly "federalized" in offical language policies (polyglossia), yet simultaneously riddled with many-cantoned diversity of idiom (heteroglossia?).[4] Another one I know 'bout is Hindu-Bali. Balinists tend to describe copiously that land's polyglot performances, festooned with hierarchy, exchange, inequalities, and reversals. For example:

> Balinese rituals in practice are as hybrid as the historical evidence "entexting" their past. They are intermedia, multilingual, and polyscriptive: high/low Balinese, Kawi, Sanskrit mantras, Indonesian, pastiches and parodies of foreign tongues, including touristspeak, Arabic, etc. Ritual cyclically accelerates the circulation of production in every sensory realm and material medium [including spoken and written literary production]. *Pedanda*-backed Siwaic ceremonies are in the business of cremating corpses [not circumcising sons, as ceremonies are in the business of doing next door in Islamic Lombok and Java]. . . . Local rites adjust attributes of social life to presumably ancestor-pleasing dimensions and malady-preventing ones. An on-going process across time and languages, rituals assert, sometimes obliquely, contrastive identities in a field of meanings always political, of course, but not only that. I call these properties "ritual-cum-rhetoric," a kind of pastiche mantra to evoke a history (provided it be multiplied) of "complex polyglossia" underscored in the works of Mikhail Bakhtin. . . . Bakhtin [however], credits a deliberate hybridized resistance only to that genre he calls the

"novel" (1981: 358–66). Yet, it is to this reflexive, "intentional double-voiced and internally dialogized" discourse that [I have compared] Balinese ritual with its rhetorics, plus any "history" that manages to leave traces thereof. (Boon 1990a, 66–67)

Just how effectively so-called carnivalization can resist oppressive regimes is a matter hotly disputed these days in "Bakhtin studies" and rival critical circles.[5] Regardless, without "dialogized discourse," it is hard to imagine how any subversiveness could happen at all, efficacious or otherwise.

Lotsa tongues, uttered and inscribed, get mixed up between *langue* (so to speak) and *parole* (so to write).[6] Some folks write and/or speak, say, *Hochdeutsch* and low, or suave French and less; or High Balinese and un-Sanskritized Austronesian *Sprache*, among innumerable refined standards and counterofficial usages. Theories of poly-heteroglossia help semiotic-sorts rethink any static oral/literate dichotomy; so do phenomena of "drift" (in Edward Sapir's sense), pidginizing, creolizing, standardizing, "speechifying," national language "building" (*Bildung*), "literary language" efflorescence, ethnic language resurgences, and always-sticky politics of (counter)canonicity.[7] Languages' pulsings and thrustings mark contradictory dynamics of edification and subversion that constitute actual discourses over time—the literary and spoken sequiturs to an imagined Babel's collapse.

Mentioning Babel, it seems *à propos* to acknowledge George Steiner. I'm talkin' 'bout his panoramic celebration *cum* lamentation of everything one guy's polylingual European learnedness could grasp of the world's hermeneutic destiny: never-ending translation. Steiner's philosophy and fiction commiserate with humanity's history of and as interpretation; he underscores not just the hideousness of the Holocaust but the arch-hilarity of *Private Lives*, among abundant other *altérités* (which Steiner translates as "alternities").[8] Part-way along his lifeway of corpus-building—which in 1989 resulted in *Real Presences* (a title designed to infuriate deconstructionists)—Steiner concluded *After Babel*'s "Topologies of Culture," with a wondrously apposite conditional (and a rare short sentence in that magisterial tome): "It would be ironic if the answer to Babel were pidgin and not Pentecost" (1975: 470).

Having just saluted (and implicity praise-parodied) Steiner's *After Babel* and its aftermath, I wouldn't want to forget Derrida's "Des Tours de Babel," revolving in part around Walter Benjamin's calling (*Beruf*) to that task called translation (*Übersetzung*).[9] Derrida's rather effervescent evasiveness affords a counterbalance to Steiner's weightiness. (One thrill of Benjamin's writing to my way of thinkin' is that it is neither, or both.) Some folks—ethnographers for instance—may have reservations about vintage (or stock) Derrida that friends in other critical rackets would find pedestrian: Derrida's phrase-making seems more interested in itself-as-text than in *others*. That said, I can still cite Derrida-on-translation, translated, hoping to sound a quasi-comic tone:

> The "tower of Babel" does not merely figure the irreducible multiplicity of tongues; it exhibits an incompletion, the impossibility of finishing, of totalizing, of saturating, of completing something on the order of edification, architectural construction, system and architectonics. . . . First: in what tongue was the tower of Babel constructed and deconstructed: In a tongue within which the proper name of Babel could also, by confusion, be translated by "confusion." The proper name Babel, as a proper name, should remain untranslatable, but. . . .
>
> . . . Let us start again [*Repartons*] from the "symbolic." Let us remember the metaphor, or the ammetaphor: a translation espouses the original when the two adjoined fragments, as different as they can be complete each other so as to form a larger tongue in the course of a sur-vival that changes them both. For the native tongue of the translator, as we have noted, is altered as well. Such at least is my interpretation—my translation, my "task of the translator." It is what I have called the translation contract: hymen or marriage contract with the promise to produce a child whose seed will give rise to history and growth. (Derrida 1985: 165–66, 191–92)

I person'ly always-already emphasize—as Derrida (here at least) does not—that marriage-exchange is an inherently *comique* institutional genre. I also note, before continuing to cite Derrida, that his allusion to reproduction and growth might have invoked a *femme enceinte*, in the manner of Julia Kristeva, when proceeding:

> A marriage contract in the form of a seminar. Benjamin says as much, in the translation the original becomes larger; it grows rather than reproduces itself—and I will add: like a child, its own, no doubt, but with the power to speak on its own which makes of a child something other than a product subjected to the law of reproduction. This promise signals a kingdom which is at once "promised and forbidden where the languages will be reconciled and fulfilled."
> This is the most Babelian note. . . . (Derrida 1985: 191)[10]

Well, that's about all the Derrida I have time for, folks. I just wanted to catch a bit of his drift (a tad Twainian to my ultraobjective ear). Later this essay will speculate 'bout some comedic incongruities in a long-term, worldwide "politics of translation" oscillating betwixt and between pidgins and Pentecosts. I thought I'd better warn you.

One more comment beforehand. It may be that Derrida sounds Twainian to yours truly because, like Gertrude Stein (whose writing effects a humorous "there" that *is* there), "I am an American."[11] In this regard, let me swipe a nifty theoretical point from a neighbor fellow I've never met named Paul Auster. His smart, bilingual edition of *Twentieth–Century French Poetry* reviews some issues in French-versus-British-versus-American critique; he points out different textual "scenes" where national styles of subversiveness well up:

> It would be wrong . . . to set up a simple dichotomy between radicalism and conservatism, and to put all things French in the first category and all things English and American in the second. The most subversive and innovative elements of our [English-language] literature have frequently surfaced in the unlikeliest places and have then been absorbed into the culture at large. Nursery rhymes . . . do not exist as such in France.Nor do the great works of Victorian children's literature (Lewis Carroll, George Macdonald) have any equivalent in French. As for America, it has always had its own, homegrown Dada spirit, which has continued to exist as a natural force, without any need of manifestoes or theoretical foundations. The films of Buster Keaton and W.C. Fields, the skits of Ring Lardner, the drawings of Rube Goldberg surely match the CORROSIVE EXUBERANCE of anything done in France during the same period. As Man Ray (a native American) wrote to Tristan Tzara from New York in 1921 about spreading the Dada movement to America: "Cher Tzara—Dada cannot live in New York. All New York is Dada, and will not tolerate a rival. . . ." (1984, xxxiii; capitals added)[12]

As I was saying awhile back, if you folks can still tolerate my national brand of "corrosive exuberance": so ludic are languages' multiplicities that some damn fool may even attempt to deliver orally (as I am now) from a typed page (as I have here) writing studded with colloquialisms. (This brand of foolishness was brilliantly smuggled into anthropological linguistics in Dennis Tedlock's nervy book, *The Spoken Word and the Work of Interpretation*, that tackled all sorts of difficulties in translating and printing Mayan narrative and Zuni storytelling.)[13] Anyway, here I am, delivering a script in a composite ideolect of academese and U.S.-yokel. (Or does my idiom emulate, or simulate, dialect-writers like William Faulkner?) Regardless, what I am *énoncé*-ing is not the *chez vous* speech of most, if any, of my "readers."

Now, I need to open apologetic parentheses, with ulterior motives. I reason that a non-native speaker's expertise cannot realistically be expected to extend to panoplies of colloquial usages. "Foreigners," for example, owe an American dialect nothing more than attempted fluency in such standards as have arisen in the history and politics of making English "proper" *for* translation. Nevertheless, this here essay-*étude* (in the guise of a talk) must transgress conventional international proprieties, given its topic. For this I sincerely beg pardon; I truly wish my talk could deploy, say, Richter's (Jean Paul's) speech-parodying German, or Rabelais's effusively improper French, rather than Twain's latter-day equivalent American.[14] But it just can't. I only practice proper French (pretty good), and proper German (too little, alas), and the limited Dutch inscribed in East-Indies colonialist ethnography (a highly restricted officialese!), among European tongues; plus some Indonesian and a smidgen of Balinese elsewhere. We are all, then, deficient in each others' colloquialisms . . . and magics.[15]

Here is the motive for (and moral of) both my *apologia* and the possibly annoying devices of this essay's delivery. It is because human languages exist dynamically as vernaculars—as deficiencies (and opportunities) vis-à-vis each other—that anthropology and literature happen. Many tasks in both pursuits broach "vernacularity" (which I rhyme with hilarity, which alliterates with hysteria). Both Litterytoor and Anthropolygee poke around in locales and metropoles where proprieties—themselves multiple and shifting—compete with carnivalizings that keep outrunning stricter controls, or some of them at least. A passion for vernacular experience makes strange companions out of paradoxical disciplinary pursuits. Litterytoor, cultural anthropolygee, and sister *sciences des langues* gloss and inhabit texts and contexts of slippery *Sprache*. Acts of translation thereabouts (or anywhere, really) are inherently provisional—never definitive. Anyway, no translation is justified in aspiring to permanence. Nothing can *actually* coincide with that "virtual translation" that, for Benjamin, could only belong to the "original" between its lines.[16]

But hold on, now; don't get all riled up. Translation's provisional nature doesn't preclude striving for *relative* adequacy. (This point is so vital, I oughtta italicize it). That may be why Litterytoor (novels, at least) smuggles vernacular speakings into its elevated writing. And Anthropolygee searches out volatile truths by inscribing each-*other*'s "magical words." At their best, I opine, these pursuits counter two prevalent forces: (1) official regimes demanding that cultures be converted into standardized frameworks; (2) marketplace pressures requiring that comparisons be commoditized for quick and easy consumption. (That point I oughtta italicize twice.) Yessum, together Litterytoor and Anthropolygee resist conformist description and evocation; they actively question sanitized norms or slick packagings that routinely separate "literate" from "oral" or an "us" from a "them." No wonder practitioners of Litterytoor and/or Anthropolygee feel plum tuckered.

BEGIN AGAIN

My essay's title-terms (in Burke's sense) are misspellings; always tempting to spell "missspellings." This brand of joking coinage, too, I snitched from a literary-journalistic genius. Now, friend Twain did some traveling across cultures; I like to imagine that, born later, he might have become an anthropologist-*auteur* as versed in cross-cultural as he was in intertemporal travel:

> When I came to again . . . there was a fellow on a horse looking down at me.
> "Fair sir will ye just?" said this fellow.

"Will I which?"

... I judged it best to humor him ... to go with him ... we did not come to any circus or sign of a circus. So I gave up the idea of a circus and concluded he was from an asylum. But we never came to any asylum—so I was up a stump, as you may say. I asked him how far we were from Hartford. He said he had never heard of the place. . . . At the end of an hour we saw a far-away town. . . .

"Bridgeport?" said I, pointing. "Camelot," said he.[17]

Twain never stops playing with learnedly unlearned language; his "litterytoor" has become a canonical entry in the dictionary of Huckspeak (I mean Huck-speech, not *Hochsprache*). Too bashful to tackle *Huckleberry Finn, per se,* I shall steal from Neil Schmitz's brilliant book on humorous writing in American literature, *Of Huck and Alice.* (*His* title, alluding to Ms. Toklas, is devised to enunciate colloquially—*'F 'uck 'n' Alice*—signifyin' the difference that speaking makes.) I don't know a finer reading of Twain or of Gertrude Stein's gaiety and genius. Again, Schmitz's book, and my title, depend on literary theories of misspelling, a relatively docile form of linguistic resistance:

> ... the first misspelled word in *Huckleberry Finn,* and the last, is *sivilize.* [N.B.: not *sivilise*] ... Misspelling releases the word from its imprisonment in the Dictionary. . . . and therein lies the metaphor. *Sivilize.* It is a written word that has gone over to the side of speech. . . . In this specific mode, humor necessarily alienates the "civilized" writer, who is bound to the Dictionary. . . . Humor has its theses, and the first is that writing wrongs speech. Civilize me, the style sez, and I cease to speak. . . . The humorist debases the privilege of writing. And readers who see it . . . are themselves abruptly liberated from the rectitude of writing, paroled. What thing in the nature of things can seriously withstand the confound-ment of misspelling? The lesson Huck's line breaks, "sivilize me," is the lesson we all learn when we learn for better or worse, how to spell *civilize.* (Schmitz 1983: 33)

I have inserted "[N.B., Not *sivilise*]" into Schmitz's passage about Twain seri-ously—i.e., playfully. Mark Twain's colloquial humor was also international, alert to Britishisms, along with America's "Missouri negro dialect; the extre-mest form of the backwoods South-Western dialect; the ordinary 'Pike-County' dialect; and four modified varieties of this last" (Twain 1977: 2). One wink from American to British may be the spelling of a name Twain's "Bur-lesque Autobiography" bestows on an eleventh-century ancestor: Arth*our* Twain (1979: 874). To the present lowbrow (American) *authour,* spelling could hardly get funnier.[18] Perennial paradoxes cluster around Schmitz's pas-sage on "mispellings;" I'll emphasize one of them. In order for humor to write (spell) wrong (rong), standardized conventions must prevail against which to misspell. An oft-noted development in the politics of printing, lexicography, and philological production has been earmarked by Hugh Kenner (saluting

Walter Ong) thusly: "Uniformity of spelling ... gave each separate word a stable identity to the eye, whatever its equivocal status for the ear."[19] (In publications on the history of colonialist and post-colonialist ethnological accounts, I have occasionally preserved evidence of nonstandardized spelling; my resistance to anachronistic enforcement of a uniform orthography has not endeared these studies to certain philologists or even historians. Imagine!)[20]

To recognize any *miss*-spelling as such requires familiarity with constructions of correctness; innocence of the invented standard would preclude writing or reading a given misspelling "right." Misspelling—a rhetoric of humor—retains a *Geschmack* of that propriety that it renders contingent. It may be true, as Neil Schmitz argues, that humor "is skeptical of any discourse based on authority—misspeaks it, miswrites it, misrepresents it" (1983: 11). But that skepticism requires authorities-for-the-countering; it cannot imagine them altogether absent. In short: Anarchistic, humor is not, whatever else it may be (e.g., anachronistic). Schmitz's terrific take on funny writing, despite lapses, almost "always already" recognizes the fact that humor cannot do without policings to upend. Schmitz, moreover, adds salient insights about phoneticized printing:

> In effect, humorists must wrest their writing from proper writing, and this they do in a style that enhances speech values and sets these values against the prescriptive values of writing. ... this is at first a small stratagem for the humorist, an obvious device—phoneticized writing—but in this simple device lies the potent metaphor Speech, and here, in Huckspeech, the significant history of American humor begins. In *Huckleberry Finn* style is theme. How, then, does Huckspeech shape its beautiful wrong in the formality of the text, the text that demands the alienation of the letter-perfect? (1983: 27)

At risk of offending linguists, I personally (and ultraobjectively) designate phoneticized writing of any kind a comic technique, just as misspelling is a device for contrarying Dictionary-writ.[21] Techniques of phoneticized printing have flourished in research on unfamiliar sound-systems (e.g., ethnographies of speaking) and in writing "dialect" literally. Descriptive linguistics, then, relies on a generically humorous mode of comparative inscription in striving (scientifically) to delineate all human "speeches." This copious process and possibly impossible dream is a globe-girdling comic endeavor, one the late Northrop Frye might have deemed "apocalyptic" (on which, more anon). Pidgins or Pentecosts? And will we ever know?

BEGIN AGAIN AGAIN (LEXICAL INTERLUDE)

Some of the doubts that have thus arisen are removed if we consult Grimm's dictionary.

We read: . . . [pages ensue].

Thus *heimlich* is a word the meaning of which develops towards an
ambivalence, until it finally coincides with its opposite, *unheimlich*.
Unheimlich is in some way or other a subspecies of *heimlich*. Let us
retain this discovery. . . .

(Freud, "The 'Uncanny' "—which essay becomes even eerier in
translation, as page after page of bilingual dictionary entries are
"translated back," thus heightening the effect of *heimlich* and *unheimlich*
coinciding or reconverging.)

Enter Freud.[22] Having borrowed one old misspelling (Litterytoor) and "ne-
ologized" another (Anthropolygee; true enthusiasts might prefer An-
Thoreaupolygee), I want to pull in two more "words about words" (that's
Burke's designation, so much nicer than "meta-words")—in this case,
words about official language versus carnivalized usage. In other words, instead of beginning against the dictionary (or its official spellings), let's begin with it. Let's let Ole Man Dictionary subvert itself, semantically, without lowbrow devices of misspelling. Ever comparative, I shall employ my
abashed American *Webster's* instead of my unabashed (microscopic) *OED*.
As I think I just said, on deck are two quasi-erudite words in English that
harbor contradictory meanings, including meanings of unerudite. The words
of which I speak are both examples of polysyllabic, professorial verbiage
that refer to a kind of language contrary to the one they themselves represent. (But they imply its opposite as well—fancy that!) These odd words,
over which I have already spilled so many words, are "vernacular" and
"colloquial."

(Grist for psychoanalysis: Some nights I dream that anthropological and
literary disciplines have always been pursuing translations of every people's
enactments of "vernacular" and "colloquial." What if Malinowski had
searched out Trobriand usages glossable as "colloquial," rather than, say,
"magic." What if Mauss had read through Oceanic evidence for equivalents
of "vernacular," rather than "*mana*." Or did they, effectively?)[23]

But I was about to cite dictionary definitions not for "slang" (is "slang"
vernacular for vernacular?) but for "vernacular;" or perhaps I'd better begin
with "colloquial," because it's a bit easier.

COLLOQUIAL:

Pertaining to common and familiar conversation; unstudied, informal . . . as in
intimate speech among cultivated people, in familiar letters, in informal speeches
or writing, but not in formal written discourse (*flabbergast*; *go slow*; *harum-
scarum*) . . .

Colloquial speech may be as correct as formal speech

See Colloquy. . . .

COLLOQUY:
Mutual discourse, esp. a somewhat formal conference; as a *colloquy* about religion. (*Webster's*)[24]

Now, let's see if I've got this straight. A colloquy's mutual discourse is formal—uncolloquial—although colloquial speech may be as correct as formal
speech, only correct otherwise. I'm beginning to feel flabbergasted, however
slow I *go* in reading this dictionary-definition, as harum-scarum as Freud's
"*unheimlich*" (canny?). ("Harum-scarum," by the way, means reckless, wild,
rash, according to my microscopic *OED*.) Now for our highbrow term for
"slang."

VERNACULAR:
Belonging to, developed in, and spoken or used by, the people of a particular place,
region, or country; native, indigenous—now almost solely used of language. . . .

I wonder if I oughtta translate "native, indigenous" as *heimlich*—homelike?

VERNACULAR (continued):
Pertaining to the native or indigenous speech of a place, written in the native, as
opposed to the literary language. Characteristic of a locality; local, as a house of
vernacular construction. "A *vernacular* disease." (Harvey)

Must one—I presume to muse—translate "local" as *heimlich*, or *unheimlich*:
homelike-but-not?

VERNACULAR (continued again):
Of persons, that use the native, as contrasted with the literary, language of a place;
as *vernacular* poets, *vernacular* interpreters. (*Webster's*)

Hmmmmmmm. "Vernacular construction; vernacular disease, vernacular poets, vernacular interpreters."

"*Vernacular* interpreters!" What are European *littérateurs*—ever since
chansons de geste, at least—if not "vernacular interpreters," or rather vernacular interpreters of vernacular interpreters? I cite R. Howard Bloch's thrilling
Etymologies and Genealogies of medieval French literature, or what he astutely calls "literary anthropology":

This is not to suggest that the improper use of linguistic signs is not an important
characteristic of the Old French *chanson de geste*. On the contrary, verbal impro-
priety abounds and seems often to spark dramatic interest. Sacrilegious oaths . . . ,
exaggeration . . . , blasphemy . . . , broken promises, impossible situations . . . ,
lies . . . , and jokes . . . all serve as catalysts to thematic development. The
"straight" narratives generated by such dislocations of the proper constitute, in
fact, potent dramas of language. (1983: 102)[25]

Bloch, however, makes one troubling move; he tends to credit a "true" epistemological shift exclusively to a recent turn in the history of critical discourse:

"Yet despite the detachment of words from meaning through blasphemy, boasts, lies, and jokes, the inherent contradiction of representing such linguistic transgression is never really explored [in *chansons de geste*]" (1983: 102). Whether or not different literary historians credit such *doubt* (versus credulity) to Old French *écriture*, I have my doubts about Bloch's tendency to congratulate the "present" Derridean moment as a "crisis of representation" come of age. Bloch vaguely evokes a *passé* "then," a time "where language seems to break down [and] we find instead a strong desire for recuperation . . . ," (1983: 103), as if that strong desire can now be escaped (or evaded), thanks to the advent of deconstructive reading. To congratulate a *now* over a *then* is as suspect (by anthropological standards) as congratulating a *here* over a *there*, or an *us* over a *them*.[26] That latter gesture no genuINE anthropolygeest can afford. Back to the dictionary.

"*Vernacular* interpreters." I ask you: What are cultural anthropologists if not "vernacular interpreters" dependent on those "vernacular poets" (themselves "vernacular interpreters") called shamans and curers and indigenous exegetes, among other "natives" (*heimlich*?) willing or obliged to speak/write in and as scenes of translation.

And what was Mark Twain if not a "vernacular interpreter," indeed a "vernacularizing" vernacular interpreter, anticipating folks like Faulkner: "I don't see how a city no bigger than New York can hold enough people to take the money away from us country suckers." (That's *The Sound and the Fury*, published in 1946, when Faulkner was continuing nineteenth-century humorous modes in his "stylistic approaches to the raft and the Mississippi.")[27]

And what, I hasten to add, was ethnologist-Sanskritist Marcel Mauss, if not a "vernacular interpreter" of rituals and words, and words about words—including magical words, and exchange-words, and sacrificial-cycles of words. Mauss translated worldwide "colloquial" words, so far and indefatigably as to insist, in 1902–03:

> There is no such thing as a wordless ritual; an apparent silence does not mean that inaudible incantations expressing the magician's will are not being made. From this point of view, the mechanical rite is but a translation of the unspoken incantation: a gesture is a sign, and also a language. Words and actions become absolutely equivalent and that is why we find descriptions of the non-verbal rites presented to us as spells. Without any formal physical movement a magician can create, annihilate, direct, hunt, do anything he wishes with the aid of his voice, his breath, or merely through his will. . . . (Mauss 1972: 57)

Momentarily my essay-*étude* will modulate from Twain's *ear* for the vernacular over to Mauss's *ink* for the comparative-colloquy. Marcel Mauss penned masterpieces of eloquent inquiry attuned to magic's "terrific confusion of images, without which, to our way of thinking, the rite itself would be inconceivable" (1972: 62).[28] But first let me enter one last note about "VER-NACULAR," a subversive dictionary note no less contradictory than *un-heimlich* becoming *heimlich*, that so caught Freud's fancy.

"Vernacular," it seems, stems etymologically from Latin *vernaculus*, meaning "born in one's house, native." "Vernaculus" stems in turn from *verna*, meaning a slave born in his master's house, a native, of uncertain origin. Now if that ain't a hoot: history's tragic and true hoot. Here indeed lies a volatile translation and an extra-Vagant one: The very root of vernacular's "native" is a slave born in his master's house . . . of uncertain origin.

MAUSS'S ESSAYS: MAGICAL GIFTS

> There are magical systems which are perfectly conscious of their diversity
> and refer to it with special words and metaphors.
> *(Mauss)*

Marcel Mauss's career spanned the *fin de siècle* through World War II; he was France's leading ethnologist between the death of Emile Durkheim, his uncle, and the ascendency of Lévi-Strauss. With other Jewish scholars associated with *L'Année sociologique* (among many colleagues in other academic outfits), Mauss found himself turned by History back into a *verna*, into a slave born in his master's house, . . . into an embodiment of "uncertain origin" purged by totalitarian nations. During his final years in the aftermath of the Vichy regime, Mauss lapsed into morose incapacity. We may never know whether his condition should be characterized as a vacated depression in the clinical sense or a more baroque madness, endowed with both fullness and emptiness—the malady of prophets.[29]

Discussing Mauss's classic "Essai sur le don," James Clifford's *Predicament of Culture* reminds readers:

> *The Gift* is an allegory of reconciliation and reciprocity in the wake of the First World War. As is well known, the war had a devastating impact on Mauss; its sequel in 1940 would deprive him of the will to work and think. With the breakdown of evolutionist master narratives. . . . (1988: 65)

Earlier, in *Writing Culture*, Clifford recommended rescuing "history" back into *The Gift*, which he deemed "an admirable example of science deploying itself in history":

> The book was written in response to the breakdown of European reciprocity in World War I. The troubling proximity it shows between exchange and warfare, the image of the round table evoked at the end, these and other urgent resonances

mark the work as a socialist-humanist allegory addressed to the political world of the twenties. This is not the work's only "content." (1986: 160)

Scholars should certainly situate Mauss's unsettling, politically *engagé* essay in the historical circumstances that occasioned it. Yet we must not reduce the work to a "window on," or reflex of, its immediate context. "Essai sur le don" (1925) warrants reading both contextually, as it "deploy[ed] itself *in* history," and textually as it countered the very history it was (and is) in. The same point applies to those rites and institutions Mauss explored: they are not simply ingredients *in* a container called history (or even *in* containers called histories, pluralized against the fallacy of universal History).

The Gift's possibly paradoxical suggestions about a general development from rituals of exchange to monetized markets—what Clifford calls its "evolutionist master narrative"—has been repeatedly debated. Before broaching seriously "comic" components of Mauss's earlier and later essays, I can illustrate two important schools of response with works by Marshall Sahlins and Michèle Richman.

In *Stoneage Economics* (an artfully pseudo-historical title) Sahlins finds *The Gift*'s "historic merit" to be correcting precisely "this simplified progression from chaos to commonwealth, savagery to civilization" associated with Hobbes (1972: 179). Sahlins rightly, I profess, absolves Mauss of idealizing consensual societies; rather Mauss "transposes the classic alternatives of war and trade [taken for granted in formalist-economic assumptions] from the periphery to the very center of social life, and from the occasional episode to the continuous presence" (Sahlins 1972: 179, 182). Mauss's interpretation, I would add, foregrounds the affective charge of social and countersocial rituals, including magic, sacrifice, symbolic classifications, economy and exchange, marriage and trade, "techniques of bodies," and concepts of the person. His intertwined topics included "money," an institutionalized delay of return-in-kind that he compared to magic. Money bridges, as magic cancels, the gap between a wish and its fulfillment.

One constructively dissenting response to Mauss's *don* was M. Richman's *Reading Bataille*, which attempted to move beyond "the weak point in Mauss's reading of archaic exchange" toward Bataille's notion of *dépense*: profuse expenditure, exhibitionism, effusive output, radical profanity, irrespective of anticipated return. Engrossingly, Richman sets Bataille in conversation with Nietzsche, Derrida, and others—all in contrast to Mauss. But to do so, she effectively detaches Mauss's "gift" from "sacrifice," arguing that he "optimistically" pursued a past "irretrievably lost," given modern society's "sharp distinction between the economic and the social" (Richman 1982: 15). But could Mauss really be guilty of dreaming up a restored "meeting of morality and economics" or even a hoped-for "symbolic" reconstruction, as Richman implies? Surely not; for, in the sketch on *Sacrifice*, he had written, with Hubert, this passage (already cited in Chap. 2 and worth repeating):

> The victim takes his place. It alone penetrates into the perilous domain of sac-
> rifice, it dies there, and indeed it is there in order to die. The *sacrifier* [my italics]
> remains protected; the gods take the victim instead of him. *The victim redeems*
> *him.* Moses had not circumcised his son, and Yahweh came to "wrestle" with him
> in a hostelry. Moses was on the point of death when his wife savagely cut off the
> child's foreskin and, casting it at Yahweh's feet, said to him: "Thou art for me a
> husband of blood." The destruction of the foreskin satisfied the god; he did not
> destroy Moses, who was redeemed. There is no sacrifice into which some idea of
> redemption does not enter." (1964: 98–99)

Such commentary may suggest less dream of final redemption than resignation to on-going dearth, whether in Vedic or Pentateuchal constructions—
both of which Mauss intensively investigated. Sacrifice for Mauss, like
money (and credit), implies constitutive debt or dearth (compare "doubt").
And dearth—a culturally-construed, not natural, "scarcity"—coestablishes
"economy" and "society," two aspects of the desire to give and be given debt
(*Schuld*).[30]

Mauss's sense of "loss," then, may be unending. Figuratively, loss pertains
to what can neither be repaired nor redeemed by receiving-from-elsewhere.
Loss in this sense implies "desire" (and the erotic), much as Georg Simmel
envisioned it in 1900:

> The necessity of proceeding in a roundabout way in order to acquire certain things
> is often the occasion, and often also the reason, for considering them valuable. In
> human relations, and most frequently and clearly in erotic relations, it is apparent
> that reserve, indifference or rejection incite the most passionate desire to over-
> come these barriers, and are the cause of efforts and sacrifices that, in many cases,
> the goal would not have seemed to deserve were it not for such opposition. (1978:
> 87)

Mauss's writings interrelate principles of social exchange, economic conversion, sacrifice, and magic. Magic, for Mauss, encompasses techniques of
subverting regular controls that many critics now equate with Bataille's
dépense. As Mauss argued:

> Taking everything into consideration, we find the same idea in magic which we
> found in sacrifice. Magic involves a terrific confusion of images, without which,
> to our way of thinking, the rite itself would be inconceivable. . . . Between a wish
> and its fulfillment there is, in magic, no gap. (1972: 62)

Mauss's interpretations covered premonetized, premodern and inframodern
enactments of indebtededness; he referred modern economy to magic's an-
economic "plenty," abundance, and copiousness. Magic is something like the

counter-propriety inherently figured within and against social and economic orthodoxy: the other side of *le propre*.

I am mindful of Mauss's unhappy person, his work's historical contexts, and critical readings of his critical readings of various rites. Nevertheless (or therefore), I consider themes of resilience uppermost in his essays. It is doubtful that Mauss naively lamented the loss of archaic usages; more likely, his expositions were meant to be *mimetic* of rituals upon which they reflected.[31] Mauss's writings inscribe the very rhythms of delay, exchange, and return evident in comparative cultural practices of magical resistance, ascetic dearth, and cyclic "redemption," a metaphor that is not necessarily nostalgic, optimistic, or *religiosus*.

In a way Mauss's essays reveal history deployed, so to speak, "exchangingly, sacrificially, and magically." *The Gift*, of course, emphasizes both trade and marriage (*commercium et connubium*) in systems of reproduction; much like Weber, elsewhere.[32] For Mauss, ritual sacrifice entails death and victimage in full cycles—what Lewis Hyde, in his Maussian book also called *The Gift*, designates evergreen compost: birth from rot, repeatedly:

> [Osiris's dismembered body] is not just reassembled, it comes back green. With him we return to . . . the Tsimshian coppers cut apart at a chief's funeral, the Kwakiutl coppers dismembered and riveted back together with increased value. . . . And the gift . . . : a property that both perishes and increases. Osiris is the mystery of compost: "It grows such sweet things out of such corruptions." (1982: 182–83)[33]

This brings us back to comedy. Institutions of marriage, remarriage, or ongoing reproducibility (including a sacrificial attitude toward renewal) are generically "comic"—one of the shapes that histories take. Among hosts of literary historians who affirm that the comic and tragic conspire, I might cite Harry Levin's *Playboys and Killjoys*:

> Comedy and tragedy both sprang from parallel, if not identical, origins—insofar as classicists have been able to explore them, from sacrificial feasts and other religious ceremonies. . . . Comedy has been traced back to the revel, or *komos*, which in turn looks ahead to the Aristophanic finale, the wedding or *gamos*. Phallephoric processions, orgiastic dances featuring satyrs rather than heroes, were a comic counterpart to the stately tragic dithyrambs, which had fostered panegyric rather than invective. (1987: 16)

It is *The Gift*'s complex invocation of "the comic" that I wish now to consider.

A principal concern of Mauss was Brahmanical rites of sublimated sacrifice. Pivotal in "Essai sur le don" are Sanskritic "theories of the gift" with Mauss's extensive commentary, punctuated with his striking claim: "*Toute cette*

théorie est même assez comique." (Cunnison's influential translation misconstrued this remark as "This is a quaint theory.")[34] Following Brahmanic ideology, priests officiate at ritual sacrifice; like cows, priests are for giving (or
being given to), not for spending (*dépense*) or consuming. To fully appreciate
what may be "comic" in this Indological topic, I shall cite Mauss's passage at
length, restoring key words deleted in Cunnison's translation and still under-
played, I think, in a newer one (Mauss 1990):

> Other principles of Brahminic law awaken reminiscences [*étrangement*] of certain
> Polynesian, Melanesian and American customs we have described. The manner of
> receiving the gift is curiously similar. The Brahmin has invincible pride (*orgueil*).
> He refuses to have anything to do with markets (*le marché*) [*même il ne doit
> accepter rien qui en vienne*]. In a national economy with towns, markets and
> money, the Brahmin remains faithful to the economy and morality of the old Indo-
> Iranian shepherds (*pasteurs*) and other aboriginal peasants of the great plains. He
> maintains the dignity of a nobleman in taking offence at favours towards him.
>
> *Toute cette théorie est même assez comique.* A whole caste which lives by gifts
> pretends to refuse them, then compromises and accepts only those which are of-
> fered spontaneously . . . on condition, to be sure, of some slight purification (*expi-
> ations*). The bond that the gift creates between the donor and the recipient is too
> strong for them (*les deux*). The recipient is in a state of dependence upon the donor.
> It is for this reason that the Brahmin may not accept and still less solicit from the
> king. . . .
>
> The gift is thus something that must be given, that must be received and that is,
> at the same time, dangerous to accept [*prendre*]. The gift itself constitutes an irrev-
> ocable link especially when it is a gift of food. The recipient depends upon the
> temper of the donor, in fact each depends upon the other. Thus a man does not eat
> with his enemy. All kinds of precautions are taken . . . [the sources expatiate] . . .
> as only Hindu authors can . . . gifts, donors and things given are to be considered
> in their context [*relativement*], precisely and scrupulously. . . . There is etiquette at
> every step. It is not the same as a market where a man takes a thing objectively for
> a price. Nothing is casual [*indifférent*] here. (Mauss 1967: 57–58)

Indeed, nothing is indifferent in this comedy of "contracts, alliances, transmission of goods, bonds created by these transfers." Everything palpitates in this
"classical" Hindu scene where purified Brahmins and sublimated sacrifice oppose market transactions. A Sanskritic "theory of the gift" is "comic" in its
techniques and etiquette of pretended refusal coupled with charged values that
join donor and recipient (Brahmin) in obverse dependence. This case serves
Mauss as a touchstone example from history's long-term "transitional phase"
of what he calls

> the spirit (*ce principe*) of gift-exchange . . . characteristic of societies which have
> passed the phase of "total prestation" (between clan and clan, family and family)

but have not yet reached the stage of pure individual contract, the money market (*marché ou roule l'argent*), sale proper, fixed price, and weighed and coined money. (1967: 45)

(I am quoting Mauss's *conclusion première*; his tripartite concluding conclusions "really" conclude the essay. Mauss's readers have often neglected his multiple endings, so suited to the essay form's customary ironies.)[35]

The Gift's ethnological evidence stems largely from this so-called "transitional phase"—one that seems to expand into everything we know of cultures and histories: a *longue durée* indeed! Careful reading of Mauss suggests that virtually any exchange system is somehow "transitional," even those extremes of (1) "total prestation" (such as reciprocation between two parties contrasted as "other" to each other through mutual indebtedness); and (2) monetized markets and hypermediated "contracts." Neither a total prestation nor a market can be perfectly "at home" to its pure principles; to quote again Lewis Hyde:

> Put generally, within certain limits what has been given us as a gift may be sold in the marketplace and what has been earned in the marketplace may be given as gift. Within certain limits, gift wealth may be rationalized and market wealth may be eroticized. (1982: 274)

I would state just as generally one further elaboration from Mauss: that "*assez comique*" Sanskritic theory of gifts—as necessarily offered (*rendre*) but dangerously taken (*prendre*)—might be said to form the heart of *comédie* called *humaine*.

The passage from Mauss revisited above displays paradoxes and deceptive valences of reciprocities and hierarchies whose nuances he carefully compared. Mauss's own nuances of tone were appreciated by Michel de Certeau, who also noted his relevance to social resistance as well as perpetuation. De Certeau detects both explicitly in *The Gift* and between its lines insights into practices marginalized by forces of economic or political domination. In *Arts de faire* (*The Practice of Everyday Life*), de Certeau observes:

> The actual order of things is precisely what "popular" tactics turn to their own ends, without any illusion that it will change any time soon. Though elsewhere it is exploited by a dominant power or simply denied by an ideological discourse, here order is *tricked* by an art. Into the institution to be served are thus insinuated styles of social exchange, technical invention, and moral resistance, that is, an economy of the "*gift*" (generosities for which one expects a return), an esthetics of "*tricks*" (artists' operations) and an ethics of *tenacity* (countless ways of refusing to accord the established order the status of a law, a meaning, or a fatality). "Popular" culture is precisely that. . . .
>
> This practice of economic *diversion* is in reality the return of a sociopolitical ethics into an economic system. It is no doubt related to the *potlatch* de-

scribed by Mauss, an interplay of voluntary allowances that counts on reciprocity and organizes a social network articulated by the "obligation to give." (1984: 26)

Like Mauss, de Certeau opposes *potlatch* to monetized market transactions; diversionary counterprestations by the disempowered are aimed against central institutions of alienation but also against rival counterprestations of other underlings. De Certeau also seconds suggestions in Mauss that *potlatch* cannot be totally absent; nor can an abstract-individualized market quite become absolute:

> In our societies, the market economy is no longer determined by such an "emulation": taking the abstract individual as a basic unit, it regulates all exchanges among these units according to the code of generalized equivalence constituted by money. . . . However that may be, the *potlatch* seems to persist within it as the mark of another type of economy. It survives in our economy, though on its margins or in its interstices. It is even developing, although held to be illegitimate, within modern market economy. Because of this, the politics of the "gift" *also* becomes a diversionary tactic. In the same way, the loss that was voluntary in a gift economy is transformed into a transgression in a profit economy: it appears as an excess (a waste), a challenge (a rejection of profit), or a crime (an attack on property). (1984: 27)

The "economic crime" of waste has affinities with magic's copiousness as Mauss evoked it: that excess of ludic expenditure, the cancellation of desire's gap. De Certeau too finds *dépense* implicit within *don*; he grasps dimensions of gift-giving that evade economic propriety-*cum*-property—much as humor might.

De Certeau's own essays in *Arts de faire* seem to me akin more to Mauss's aphoristic writing about "magic" than to *The Gift*'s measured exposition, whose style of presentation mimics institutions of regularized exchange described.[36] Indeed, I suspect that Mauss's *oeuvre* overall embodies diverse figural devices, a self-conscious array of *techniques* of exposition.

Shifting styles of commentary certainly characterize the co-authored essays. For example, Mauss's study of sacrifice (with Hubert) reads like echoes of oscillations between sacred (i.e., set-apart) passages and exegesis, lending it a rather Pentateuch-like, or Upanashad-like, quality (see the quotation cited above). Markedly different is Mauss's "sketch" on magic: it is littered with pungent formulations, chock-a-block with bursts of lexical energy, harum-scarum with fragmentary, definitional swerves.[37] I consider memorable epigraphs to be rhetoric's equivalent to magic—separable, isolated, metonymic, condensed. Myth-like (in Lévi-Strauss's precise sense), aphorisms may hold up in translation or at least remain recognizable *as translated*.[38]

With that possibility in mind, I here cite seven bursts from Mauss's translated *esquisse*, arranged in reverse order:

1. Magic is the domain of pure production, *ex nihilo*. With words and gestures it does what techniques achieve by labour. (1972: 141)

2. Magic has a veritable predilection for forbidden things. (129)

3. Magic, like sacrifice, requires and produces an alteration, a modification in one's state of mind. This is expressed by the gravity of the actions, the changed nature of the voice and even by the use of a special language, the language of spirits and gods. (128)

4. Thanks to the idea of *mana*, magic—the domain of wish-fulfilment—is shown to have plenty of rationalism. (127)

5. It is even possible that inductive reasoning was first learnt in the school of magic. (126)

6. The idea of magical efficacy is ever present and plays far from an accessory part, since it enjoys the same role which the copula plays in a grammatical clause. It is this which presents the magical idea, gives it being, reality, truth, makes it so powerful. (122)

7. . . . magic, like religion, is a game, involving "value judgments," expressive aphorisms which attribute different qualities to different objects entering the system. (121)[39]

In a nutshell, then, the essay on magic, which likens magic to aphorisms, is itself replete with aphorisms. Mauss's writing here may be as rhetorically self-aware as Twain's "talking." Apt aphorisms, after all, often have a humorous ring because of their very aptness. For example, what wakeful reader could stumble upon #2 above—"Magic has a veritable predilection for forbidden things. . . ."—without laughing aloud in some kind of recognition? Again, I contrast the prose of *The Gift*—no less mindful of its rhetorical devices, I'd wager—which avoids epigraphic insight, preferring systematic exposition. Similarly, exchange rites themselves relegate magical practices to the margins and interstices of mutual obligation, marriage, trade partners, and associated regularities.

Let me underscore again my analogy between institutional configuration (think of Benedict) and figural mode (think of Burke): If *magical* utterances imply the aphoristic, *gifting* utterances imply the conversational (the latter insight actually belongs to Lévi-Strauss).[40] Regardless, different modes of ritual language in Mauss (including formats of prayer) are articulated relationally, with respect both to the communication implied and to the locus of its occurrence. Thus, Mauss evokes the typical "scene" of magic—which is at the same time the locus (topos?) of aphorism—as follows:

Magical rites are commonly performed in woods, far away from dwelling places, at night or in shadowy corners, in the secret recesses of a house or at any rate in some out-of-the-way place. Where religious rites are performed openly, in full public view, magical rites are carried out in secret. Even when magic is licit, it is done in secret, as if performing some maleficent deed. . . . Thus, as far as society is concerned, the magician is a being set apart and he prefers even more to retire to the depths of the forest. Among colleagues too he nearly always tries to keep himself to himself . . . working in a private capacity; both the act and the actor are shrouded in mystery. (1972: 23)

I read Mauss's shifting vantages of comparison as something like a genre-theory (or a theory of modes) of ritual institutions. In his relational scheme, everything that occasional magic is *not* routine debt-giving *is*: reciprocal, public, open, social, manifest, cyclic. Yet magic joins sacrifice at the opposite end of the same axis:

> two extremes which form the differing poles of magic religion: the pole of sacrifice and the pole of evil spells. Religion has always created a kind of ideal towards which people direct their hymns, vows, sacrifices, an ideal which is bolstered by prescriptions. These are areas which are avoided by magic. . . . (1972: 24)

Note that Mauss includes both "system" and its counterings (*dépense?*). Posed from the vantage of religion, "gifting" (social and public) contrasts on the one hand with personal, asocial, incidental magic; and on the other hand with sacrifice—the "social pole" of magical incantation. Phrasing these relationships more generally: *le don* is socially reciprocated desire; magic is personal desire: gapless wish liable to go unreciprocated. But this risky, asocial "magical" business is itself socially valued. By the same token magic bends to religious ends in sacrifice. (Also germane are asocial ascetics who are socially valued—a key theme in such scholars as Hocart, Dumont, and perhaps even Deleuze.)[41]

In matters of performative genres and their associated institutions, Mauss's own rhetoric covers the gamut: (1) exchange, which implies marriage, trade, and comedy; (2) sacrifice, which implies priestly liturgy, redemptive death, and commentary; (3) magic, which implies prophecy, social negation, and aphorism. Like history "herselves," Mauss's essays pulse to ritual rhythms of relay, delay, and return. *Toute cette théorie est*, truly, *assez comique*. Indeed, it was already comic (i.e., tragicomic) in Sanskrit; and it is doubly (reflexively?) so in Mauss's reading. Thus, the theory may never have been exactly "logocentric" before Derrida presumed to deconstruct it (see Chap. 10).

Mauss's work could be interpreted as a partial "anatomy" of worldwide rites, just as famous "essays" by Northrop Frye would later offer an "anatomy" of worldwide texts. As Frye's *Anatomy of Criticism* stipulated, the genre "anatomy" (from which Frye pinched his title) implies parodic, possibly apocalyptic visions of historical cyclicity and tragicomic circularity: "The theme of encyclopaedic parody is endemic in satire and in prose fiction is chiefly to be found in the anatomy. . . . " (1957: 322).[42]

Finally, for the sake of abrupt circularity, folks, I might just mention that Northrop Frye too had read Mark Twain (but evidently not, alas, Marcel Mauss); and Frye (whom I also read) went so far as to claim in his own encyclopedic parody:

> In *Huckleberry Finn* the main theme is one of the oldest in comedy, the freeing of a slave, and the *cognitio* tells us that Jim had already been set free before his escape was bungled by Tom Sawyer's pedantries. (Frye 1957: 180)

THE END: TWAIN AND MAUSS, TWINS—ALTERNATIVELY MARRIED

> This party was one of those persons whom they call Philosophers. He was twins, being born simultaneously in two different houses in the city of Boston.
> *(Mark Twain, "The Late Benjamin Franklin" [1979: 89])*

Well folks, my essay-*étude*'s in a pickle: up a stump; it's too long already but has a lot more to say. So, I'd better wind up or down with a list of conclusions: "seven," a magic number.

1. Marcel Mauss addressed history's cross-cultural gamut of ritual practices and exchange systems, from structures of nervous reciprocity among clans, to monetary markets of centralized states. He contrasted magical techniques to regularized rites of "giving" indebtedness. His distinctions between magic/gift and personal/social overlap with other formulations: heterodox/orthodox and vernacular/official. We natives experience "magical" utterances and scripts as the equivalent of foreign-words-at-home. Magic implies alien speech or writ within the segmented community responsive to the words' power and allure. One might call magic something like "heteroglossia" (Bakhtin's usage), isolable in its own right and peppering rituals of sacrifice, exchange, and "comic" hierarchy, among other topics visited in Mauss's *oeuvre*. "Magic," then, is alien heteroglossia even at home; Mauss wrote about it (and wrote it) in an erudite style. "Dialect" is at-home heteroglossia even elsewhere; Twain wrote about it (and wrote it) in a colloquial style. Hence the affinity, across a difference, between the likes of Twain and the likes of Mauss. Hence, too, the marriage of their discourses attempted in this chapter's ritual rereading thereof.

2. Mauss's essays help readers recognize rites as rhetorical practice: powers in and of persuasion. Ritual activities (including words) partake of multilayeredness, inter(con)textuality, and evasiveness—the very properties associated by some anthropologists with "cultures" and by many literary theorists, rather exclusively, with "texts." What I have called ritual-*cum*-rhetorical aspects of social life include a subversiveness akin to humorous writing and speaking, or a writing-speaking hybrid. One tried and true stylistic recourse in both fiction (the novel) and description (ethnography) is to coagulate the *hoity-toity* (overbaked?) and the *cru*.[43] Equivalent recourses exist, I s'pose, in all times and cultures, including nonliterate ones for sure. As so many (anti)disciplines together have shown: different worlds of difference foster varied ways of displaying and debunking knowledges, erudition included. Litterytoor and Anthropolygee keep engaging and enacting parodic practices that transgress proprieties—some gleefully glad, some sad (*tristes rites, tristes textes, tristes . . .*), many both.

3. One current of contemporary critical opinion—too familiar to need documentin'—considers parody (or any attitude tinged with it) "postmodern." This assumption, I fear, forgets shifting ironies of literary modernism, on back to early Romantics, Renaissance description and censorship, medieval semiotics, and Lucianic genres—just on the "Western" front. "Parody," moreover, pervades the vastness of non-European practices of "indigenous" heterodoxies. To name two from a perfectly copious list: so-called Tantric tactics of Hindu and Buddhist domains; gender-inflected travesties performed along the edges and in the interstices of New Guinea social cycles.[44]

I salute worlds of comparative parody not to imply that self-conscious vernaculars of ritual-*cum*-rhetoric are necessarily "always already," but just to signal how un-new and recurrent they remain, cross-culturally and historically. Why, one multivocal, polylingual classic called *Max Havelaar* (Multatuli 1860)—an ethnography-laden satire and *the* canonical novel consolidating Netherlandish "literature"—even helped (when partially translated into Javanese, Malay, etc.) topple Dutch colonialism in proto-Indonesia. Maybe.[45]

4. Humorous modes of practice counter an orthodoxy without which they would have nothing to resist. "Comic" forms may prove resilient among forces of violence, pain, inequalities, and suffering inflicted by powers intent on oppression. "Motives" of "comic" intertwine tears, death, repressions, and harm—along with laughs, life, assertions, and hope. "Victimage," too, became a key rubric of Burke's adventurous dramatism addressing the fullness of humanity's forensic play.[46]

5. Ethnography credits virtuo-agency in styles of persuasion not just to critical theorists but to "plain folks" despite their (our) subjugations. Deep duplicities and arcane multiplicities obviously characterize high-flying deconstruction as well as those logocentrisms it pretends to contest. But similar qualities obtain in low-down jokes, earthy laments, everyday resistance, commodity consumption, and rituals of just gettin' by. "Weapons of the weak," then, cannot be isolated from their (our) other regalia—less reactive than assertive and reflexive.[47]

For me, Anthropolygee remains an art of reading diverse blokes and *folks* in our plights and enthusiasms. Now, "folks" include intelligentsia, with our (anti)metaphysics, theories, and manifestoes. And Anthropolygeests must read them (us) too—like Litterytoorists . And v-eye-see-vers-uh. Really, though, neither Anthropolygee nor Litterytoor should elevate fancy-folks-writin' *over and against* plain-folks-talking (or vice versa). No siree, folks. Whatsmore, plain-folks ain't plain atall; they just *know* how to talk that way; tricky devils.

6. For all these reasons a transgressive partnership of anthropological and literary-historical study seems peculiarly suitable. I even advocate a multidisciplinary *ménage à trois, quatre, cinque ou six* of anthropology, history, and literature, plus religion, arts, and showbiz—each significant-other inflected by (infected with?) a linguistic turn. This ensemble keeps interpretation open to many *genres* of marriages (both literal and figurative)—bilateral cross-cousin, polygamous, same-sex, bourgeois, Heaven-and-Hell—and their copious contraries—asceticism, licentiousness, divorce, celibacy, autoeroticism, and so forth.

Inspired in part by Balinese Tantric tropes, I see Litterytoor 'n' Anthropolygee as unidentical-twin disciplines. This incestuous union represented by Twain *and* Mauss embraces the most vernacular and colloquial tensions, contradictions, and conflicts that comparative evidence (as-written and misspelled, as-read and "misprisioned") illuminates or clouds. To engage in extra-Vagant (anti)weddings among anthropology, literature, and suchlike still risks ruffling the feathers of both these strange birds in the aviary of *sciences des langues*. Why?

7. Mauss and Twain's "disciplines," I feel, should keep exploring old anthropological topics (kinship, say) and classic literary figures ("like" similes), which, after all, keep getting invented. I fret about litero-ethnographics that rub out difficulties on one side or the other—social structures or textual tropes—to advance a pat disquisition against power. Ironically, a familiar "sameness" results when critical voices and choices are consolidated into political "correctitude." Surely pursuits forged in part from comparative discursive humor—e.g., Litterytoor *and* Anthropolygee—must question *nouveau* antidisciplinarianism along with all the other standard academic brands.

You know, folks, it ain't easy bein' twins, 'specially when they're married . . . I mean domestic partners. Why things just may be gettin' trickier still, 'stead of plainer—what with clones and all.[48]

Part Three

CROSS-OVER STUDIES, SERIOCOMIC CRITIQUE

Looking over [African] Augustine's long series of quests, questions,
and "inquisitions," we see the self-portrait of an inquirer who, though
he did not say so in so many words, had experimented tirelessly.
Infant spontaneity; childish play; adolescent perversity; imaginative
engrossment in the poetry of Rome and Greece; aesthetic liberalism;
amours both rowdy and conscience-laden; metropolitan careerism as
a rhetorician (a mixture of teaching and salesmanship); astrology;
skepticism or systematic doubt (in the style of the Academics);
Stoicism . . . ; "colony-thinking" (if we may so designate the kind of
intellectual association that nearly led to the outright setting up of a
communal establishment); Manichaeanism; the Platonists; and even
a touch of Aristotelianism . . .
(*K. Burke,* Rhetoric of Religion, *1970*)

I am attracted to movie stars, but not for the usual reasons.
(*Walker Percy,* The Moviegoer, *1960*)

A Little Polemic, Quizzically

> Marxism has many faults, the most obvious being that it is a poor critique
> of Marxism. But, like the German philosophy, English economics, and
> French politics from which it sprang, it also has many virtues. And it can
> be wholly rejected only at a great sacrifice of intelligence.
> (*K. Burke,* Language as Symbolic Action)

OVER long ages of crossover endeavor—ever since Augustine and before, in
North Africa and elsewhere—callings to *translate* (*übersetzen, menter-
jehmahkan*, . . .) have energized imposing cavalcades of eccentric scholars.
One marquee of stellar names (limited arbitrarily to twenty, dropped
unchronologically, with seriocomic epithets to convey their diversity) might
conceivably read:

Bronislau Malinowski (quintessential "fieldworker"; Polish émigré; died at
Yale)

Benjamin Whorf (quintessential anthropological linguist; fire insurance agent)

Panini (founding Sanskritic-grammarian)

Augustine, again (Derrida's original?)

Edward Sapir (émigré-poet-linguist; died at Yale)

Anne Freemantle (socialist; linguistic historian)

Ludwig Wittgenstein (erratic philosopher; matched lifestyle)

Claude Lévi-Strauss (de L'Académie française; memorized Offenbach)

Lewis Carroll (antilogician with rough edges)

Ferdinand de Saussure (Swiss local; *sémioticien*)

Charles Sanders Peirce (American local; semioticist)

Roman Jakobson (polymath; died at Harvard)

Henry Louis Gates (alternative canon-builder; new *New Yorker* writer; alive at
Harvard)

Julia Kristeva (post-*Tel Quel*euse)

Michel de Certeau (ex-Jesuit, historical *flâneur*)

E. Valentine Daniel (Sri Lankan Tamil; Chicago-educated; mother Anglican; a
friend of mine)

Wilhelm van Humboldt (enthusiast of Old Javanese, or Kawi)

Vladimir Nabokov (a.k.a. Vivian Darkbloom, Sirin, etc; old *New Yorker* writer;
lingered at Cornell; died in *Suisse*, deeply regretted)

Homi Bhabha (Professor of Hybridity; wonderfully gregarious)

Johanna Schopenhauer (long outshone her son)
. . . .[1]

Abundant alternative marquees are no less salient; any I devised would feature both important celebrities crowding today's academic marketplace and older figures often now accused—sometimes unfairly—of avoiding ramifications when politics turned ugly, angry, or violent.[2] I favor approaches to slippery *significance* that link power, struggle, and conflict to co-realities: laughter, suffering, grief, occasional regrets, brassy tricks, *jouissance* (write it in Latin if you prefer), death, and desire of one sort or another. Desire is not always, or perhaps ever, pretty. Indeed, desire can be dire. Desires include ascesis, "sublimated" delay, sadomasochism (if we must), and orgasm—in the plural, to be sure, *soit* wet *soit* dry.

One recent scholar who understands "desire" in ways that parallel "culture" (as some anthropologists have construed it) is Gilles Deleuze. Deleuze deems "desire" (or I could substitute "culture"; indeed I desire to) more than compensation for a deprivation (a *want*).[3] Doses of Deleuze's "desire," now available in a *Reader*, are possibly mellower in the *assemblage* than they appeared as his corpus emerged (but maybe I'm wrong). Regardless, marvelously inflected are desire's "nomadic" percolations:

> Do you realize how simple a desire is? Sleeping is a desire. Walking is a desire. Listening to music, or making music, or writing, are desires. A spring, a winter, are desires. Old age also is a desire. Even death. Desire never *needs* interpreting, it is it which experiments [emphasis added]. Then we run up against very exasperating objections. They say to us that we are returning to an old cult of pleasure, to a pleasure principle, or to a notion of the festival (the revolution will be a festival . . .). By way of objection they hold up those who are stopped from sleeping . . . and who have neither the means nor the time for a festival; or who . . . are suddenly struck by a horrible old age or death, in short all those who suffer: don't they "lack" something? And above all, it is objected that by releasing desire from lack and law, the only thing we have left to refer to is a state of nature, a desire that would be natural and spontaneous reality. We say quite the opposite: *desire only exists when assembled or machined.* You cannot grasp or conceive of a desire outside a determinate assemblage, on a plane which is not preexistent but which must itself be constructed. All that is important is that each group or individual should construct the plane of immanence on which they lead their life and carry on their business [again, "compare *culture*"].

A little later Deleuze keeps "rhizoming" along:

> The only spontaneity in desire is doubtless of that kind: to not want to be oppressed, exploited, enslaved, subjugated. But no desire has ever been created with nonwishes [again again, "compare *culture*"]. Not to want to be enslaved is a

nonproposition. In retrospect every assemblage expresses and creates a desire by constructing the plane which makes it possible and, by making it possible, brings it about. Desire is not restricted to the privileged; neither is it restricted to the success of a revolution once it has occurred. It is in itself an immanent revolutionary process. It is constructivist, not at all spontaneist.

. . . Never will we point to drives which would refer to structural invariants, or to genetic variables. Oral, anal, genital, etc.: We ask each time into which assemblages these components enter, not to which drives they correspond, nor to which memories or fixations they owe their importance, nor to which incidents they refer, but with which extrinsic elements they combine to create a desire, to create desire [again again again, compare *culture*].

Eventually, very eventually, Deleuze provides examples; these include Clara Schumann and the following palpitations:

Pleasures, even the most artificial, or the dizziest, can only be reterritorialization. Desire does not have pleasure as its norm, but this is not in the name of an internal lack which could not be filled, but on the contrary by virtue of its positivity; that is, of the plane of consistence that it traces in the course of its process. It is the same error which relates desire to the law of the lack and to the norm of pleasure. It is when you keep relating desire to pleasure, to the attainment of pleasure, that you also notice that something fundamental is missing. To the point where, to break these preformed alliances between desire-pleasure-lack, we are obliged to make detours through bizarre fabrications, with much ambiguity. Take, as an example, courtly love, which is an assemblage of desire connected to feudalism as end. Dating an assemblage is not doing history, it is giving the assemblage its coordinates of expression and content, proper names, infinitive-becomings, articles, haecceities. (So that's what doing history is ?) [The wink is Deleuze's.] Now, it is well known that courtly love implies tests which postpone pleasure, or at least postpone the ending of coitus. This is certainly not a method of deprivation. It is the constitution of a field of immanence, where desire constructs its own plane and lacks nothing, any more than it allows itself to be interrupted by a discharge which would indicate that it is too heavy for it to bear. Courtly love has two enemies which merge into one: a religious transcendence of lack and a hedonistic interruption which introduces pleasure as discharge. It is the immanent process of desire which fills itself up, the continuum of intensities, the combination of fluxes, which replace both the law-authority and the pleasure-interruption. The process of desire is called "joy," not lack or demand. Everything is permitted, except what would come and break up the integral process of desire, the assemblage. This is not something to do with nature: on the contrary, it requires a great deal of artifice to exorcise the internal lack, the higher transcendent element and the apparent exterior. Ascesis, why not? Ascesis has always been the condition of desire, not its disciplining or prohibition. You will always find an ascesis if you think of desire. (Deleuze 1993: 136–40)

To this difficult proposition, the present book subscribes. Readers who prefer philosophic aphorisms to aesthetic seaflows of such prose as Deleuze's might desire an alternative way he expressed kindred ideas: "One ventures from home on the thread of a tune" (1993: 202).

Seriocomic critique discerns seriocomic desire even among dour scholars inclined to manifestoes. Young Karl Marx, for example—judging from Edmund Wilson's always-refreshing portrait in *To the Finland Station* (1972)—penned poetry to his beloved Jenny; Marx's life remained entangled in heroic imagery that Adorno would likely have declared *bourgeois*.[4] (Only a purist would object to Marx's "Promethean" hybridities.) Or consider Edward Said, whose once vanguard, now touchstone, exposé of Europe's intolerant Orientalism has not precluded his engagement with canonical Western musical works that he is guilty of performing, and publicly.[5] (Said is objectionably accomplished; color me green.) Parts of Said's own complicated "positionality"—his enviable combination of talents and backgrounds—get rather erased by those outsized polemical constructions (e.g., "Orientalism") with which he assails the past and the present alike. To better appreciate true multiplicities in the crossover existence of critical critics—Marx the poetaster, Said the piano *Meister*—I personally revert to Said's *Beginnings* (1975). Other folk—local blokes, colonial officials, and even "Imperialists"—may have an *Anfang* as mixed as Said's and a sequel as contradictory.[6]

Unfortunately, Said's admirably mottled and modulated *Beginnings* has been overshadowed by his more monolithic *Orientalism* (1978). That work's headline-theory of duplicitous complicity reigns rather supreme in certain critical industries, whose contemporary moguls regard any claim of authenticity as an ideological mystification and every *auctores* as expropriative. Filmmakers, too (including the superb Trinh Minh-ha) join the polemical fray. They often confuse high-handed styles of patronizing narration in old fieldwork documentaries (a fit subject for derision) with the general *essence*(!) of "ethnographic authority"; whose multiple enigmas they consider fleetingly, if at all.[7]

But there are paradoxes in the war against master-narratives; and they pertain even to critics who acknowledge said paradoxes. James Clifford, for example, cannot avoid reinscribing pretensions of expert superiority over works he finds naive—including (partially) Said.[8] Recent efforts to reassert epistemological skepticism couched in travel-tropes still imply that the new *voyageur* manages better than previous ones to draw nearer "elsewhere"—China, say, as visited by Stephen Greenblatt.[9] (One novel whose ironies incorporate *aporia* of authoritative reading and describing is Julian Barnes's *Flaubert's Parrot* [1984], a winning fiction of travel-scholarship.)

An "attitude" (in Burke's sense) called "seriocomic" embraces such paradoxes of critical mastery/submission. That attitude's seriocomic scruples cloud sunny agendas for securing the moral high ground, whether idealistically once-upon-a-time or uncompromisingly *now*! Its seriocomic wariness modulates *any* uniform voice—oppressive, appeasing, or radical. Its seriocomic skepticism extends even to prophecies of a triumphal coming-of-age in Cyborgia.

Fearing to sound the killjoy in 1991 (see H. Levin 1987), I left unfinished a book review that began as follows:

> Invited by *Discourse* to assess Donna Haraway's *Primate Visions*, I can only view her work through the same critical lens it uses to inspect scientific primatology plus popular enchantment with monkeys, apes, and kindred critters. Despite my nagging doubts as to whether Haraway escapes certain pitfalls of discourses she contests, I second those who affirm that her critical intelligence is inordinantly keen (e.g., Joan Scott, Barbara Johnson, and others far from the history of science, as well as some scientists, even some primatologists).
>
> *Primate Visions* mounts a devastating attack on sexist, racist, and classist forces lurking beneath hankerings of scientists and consumers alike to know "other primates." Haraway exposes political inequalities embedded in any enterprise that researches, collects, displays, documents, promotes, hunts, rescues, preserves, conserves, explains, diagnoses, interprets, converses with, emulates, interrogates, or otherwise analyzes, compares, and differentiates apes-imagined and apes-in-fact—enterprises "authored" by their evolutionary next-of-kin. This is powerful, upsetting stuff. Nevertheless, the book's blockbuster style may give certain reading-primates some pause, just as gender-coded representations (e.g., *National Geographic* White-women scientists voyeuring Third-World fauna) give Haraway pause. Consider, for example, the book's culminating diagnosis-prognosis about "all participants" in some kind of "postmodern world":
>
>> My argument is that all the participants in the boundary-eroding discourses of body, jungle, and space in nuclear, late-capitalist culture are part of a postmodern cyborg world of communication, technology, war, and reproduction. (1989: 401)
>
> Haraway's penchant for overweening proclamation actually gives *this* reading-primate more than pause; it stops him dead in his reading-tracks, much as that old "patriarchical" scientific hubris did. *Both* styles of generalization drive me ba-

nanas. Do you suppose that my body is reacting against a resemblance where it hoped to experience a difference?

That's as far as I got. It may have been the exclusivistic *look* of Haraway's ambitious program for a liberated "world"—so SINGULARLY cyborg—that struck me dumb; I'm not sure.[10]

Drumbeats of liberation, legion in brand, tend to drown out earthy ambiguities—the very stuff of cultures. Humankind's profuse foibles are worth attending to seriocomically: terror *and* jubilation; bodies not just glamorized but grungy (and all-too-soon deteriorating); diseases both epochal and pedestrian; variegated preferences, inflected and blurred. Everyday imperfections slip through dichotomies of pro/con, phobia/philia, yesterday/tomorrow, integral/fragmentary, or organic/cyborg. (Nor does that old stand-by, normal/deviant, often or perhaps ever apply.) Differences, moreover, "that make a difference" (*per* Gregory Bateson) in desire (*per* Gilles Deleuze) extend beyond the highly salient triumvirate of gender-class-race. Desires and, alas, prejudices are just more diverse. I'm sorry, but they are.

These observations bring me to current trends in theoretical issues which, while important, already seem slightly hackneyed. Some time ago, programmatic treatises in anthropology and cultural studies began to sound rather like this:

> The world is a space of locals (*alias* "natives") gone global and globals (*alias* "citizens of the world") gone local. GLOBALOCALS *now* body forth hybridities: *différances* made to be deconstructed (*alias* disaggregated). Every-body's subject positions are aflow (*alias* crossing) throughout borderlands and ethnoscapes (*alias* "cultures") intent on evading the cyber-scopic, hegemonic gaze (*alias* politics as usual).

My quick pastiche is not meant to ridicule such formulations, often enough forceful.[11] Indeed, I wish only more power to folk who think, disport, and protest according to notions just simulated. But it is important to remember as well that "identities"—contested, contesting, collaborating, and combatting in this way—*still* become mediated in "boundaried" formations: official languages, religious persuasions, national citizenships, nasty regimes, benevolent dreams, convictions of choice, varied vernaculars, subversive dodges, disciplinary counteralignments, books dedicated to loved ones—even Doris Day movies, and transnational *Antropologi* calling cards (see Chap. 4). How possibly to make something of such venerably dynamic curiosities is a "day" that Part Three encourages readers again and again to seize.

Readers, to be sure, can only do so "reflexively." I thus conclude these quizzical polemics by affirming that seriocomic reflexivity characterizes "native" practices too. Theorists err, I declare, when we deem reflexivity (or theory) solely "ours" (Indonesian *kami*). Reflexivity is not the exclusive property of therapeutic hawkers of cures for damaged "selves." Nor is it limited to "new ages" or cutting edges—whether postmodernist, or before that, modernist, Romanticist, Enlightenment, or Renaissance (in reverse order). Reflexivity has never, I tell myself, been the patented commodity, even figuratively, of an "emergent" theoretical trademark—Marxist, functionalist, structuralist, hermeneutic, deconstructionist, dialogical, postcolonialist, cyborgian, hybrid . . . Rather, reflexivity and irony and exponential winks (and such) characterize anyone's vernacular language, routine rituals and consumptions, and mundane (nomadic) desires. To assume differently—to believe that reflexivity is confined to grandly embattled segments of intelligentsia—would: (1) enthrone CULTURAL CRITIQUE as a confidently elite consciousness; (2) hitch subversiveness's star to abstract forces; and (3) deny seriocomic crossover and extra-Vagant ethnography their more-than-alternative due.

Here ends Part Three's prolegomenon; now for some uncanny, subheroic specifics.

CHAPTER SEVEN

Against Coping Across Cultures:
Self-help Semiotics Rebuffed

This piece originated in the mid-1980s. Since then, U.S. history has modulated from Donahue on through Oprah, Sally, Geraldo, and dozens more. The cable era of "talk shows" thus dawned, eclipsing those "broadcast" voices evoked at my essay's conclusion. Self-help semiotics have expanded accordingly, crushing many styles of interpretation and critique under their juggernaut. Some relevance may remain in my contestation.

Since a first version was published, we have lost Milton Singer, but not his work or his example.

IN *Man's Glassy Essence* (1984), anthropologist Milton Singer posed the self as object and subject of semiotic systems; this study formed a vital part of his life's project to compare diverse value complexes—from entrepreneurship to constructions of personal identity—in India and the West (or more precisely, greater Madras and greater "Yankee City").[1] With his distinctive combination of erudition and wit, Milton Singer turned Americanized semiotics (from Peirce to Sebeok) and Indianized structures (from traditional to modern) towards each other, illuminating their respective civilizations.

Having once played jester to Singer's philosopher-king, I here resume the role of antic sidekick to profound learning.[2] Milton Singer clarified the high semiotics of "cultural performance" implemented in comparing India and Euro-America. This essay sizes up the low therapeutic side of some "semi-semiotics" of self-help popularized in promotional encounters between Anglo-American culture and India, plus a range of other "others."

As antithetical entries in the global sweepstakes of self-help publications, I nominate anthropologist Colin Turnbull's epic *The Human Cycle* (1983), and cultural critic Gita Mehta's scalding *Karma Cola: Marketing the Mystic East* (1981). After cross-reading these two extremes, this essay considers an earlier work with surprising similarities, a quaint confessional by the long late Charles Hose, *Fifty Years of Romance and Research, or a Jungle Wallah at*

Large (1927). My critical tactics are these: countering subjectivity with subjectivity, fighting froth with froth, undercutting current clichés with *platitudes passées*, and comparing psychobabble of now with colonialist pomposities of yore. I try to strike sparks first between Turnbull's first-person avowals and Mehta's hip slogans, and then between both of them and Hose's earlier pieties, plus my own dated doggerel. Toward raising trendy self-help into self-questioning consciousness, my cheeky readings adopt the rhetorics they doubt in order to wear them out—with apologies to all.

TURNBULL'S TURN

Now-a-*Donahue*-days in U.S. medialand and "public culture," spokespersons for many academic disciplines popularize findings by converting intricate motives of research into psychotherapeutic objectives and a journalistic moral or "message." Self-help anthropologists often suggest that Providence scattered diverse languages and customs over an otherwise whole Mother Earth to provide lessons in tolerance—to teach all people mutually, cross-culturally, to cope. A vivid instance is Colin Turnbull's *Human Cycle*, a book apparently made (to order) to give its readers—and viewers of shows talking it up—solace.

Positively no footnotes and a single reference intrude upon Turnbull's two hundred and eighty-three (283) pages of resolve squarely and forthrightly to parallel his tribulations with the hardships and triumphs of other souls and selves, be they Pygmy novice, Buddhist abbot, or Hindu *sannyasi*. Although *The Human Cycle* is dedicated to Arnold van Gennep's classic *Rites of Passage* ("*Rites de passage*," the aforementioned reference) alert readers may find more echoes of Gail Sheehy's *Passages* ("*Paaeehsages*") fleshed out with Turnbull's very-own-true-life-crises and fieldwork experience, and marketed accordingly.[3]

Basically, Turnbull's book converts human (includes women and children) existence—the bad times and the good, the thin with the thick—into a tidy succession of arts: becoming, transformation, reason, doing, and being. These stages represent what many would call childhood, adolescence, youth, adulthood, and old age. Born British, now "being" in America, Turnbull feels free to disclose his personal preference for any puberty other than the one he suffered:

> I cannot think of a single culture I know that handles this crucial stage of life more abysmally than we do [an ethnologist as wily as Gita Mehta (see below) might immediately wonder whether he has considered subincisionists]. . . . It should be a criminal offense that this natural, wholesome, and utterly wonderful signal of

the transformation of a young body into something else should be . . . associated
with dirt and impurity, if not with sin. (81)

The crux of his book is a just-so tale of awakening into liberation from society's reactionary taboos that alienated erstwhile youths from Nature's innocent
pleasures.

"Supportiveness" spills over every page. "Saints are few and far between,"
observes Turnbull, "but we do not have to be Tibetans or abbots to give something of ourselves—and we all have something worthwhile to give. . . ." (246).
That's a relief: Even without renunciation (not much fun) or going Tibetan, we
can all get into sharing, giving, learning, being, being in touch with ourselves
individually, and helping others be in touch with themselves individually too.
Confronted by nonstop conspicuous kindheartedness, even readers who are
fairly "nice guys" may fail to suppress retorts of the kind perfected in *Karma
Cola*'s style of sarcasm (to be sampled momentarily). Fortunately for Turnbull, his book was published after Mehta's; unfortunately for us, it was published before Walker Percy's knowingly unprophetic *Lost in the Cosmos: The
Last Self-help Book*.[4] Turnbull's text brings out the "Mehta" in me. It's *Mister
Rogers* across cultures; *Sesame Street* gone native; global "free to be," total
"you and me."[5] The sweetest part of Turnbull's scheme is that everything
winds up not with death but "The Art of Living." A not-so-tiny hint of immortality is tucked in as the last word, the benediction:

> We are like the piglets who like it that way, and have quite forgotten the ecstasy
> of divinity. Like them, for us the human cycle has become so bogged down in the
> muddy business of survival rather than being a soaring flight of rich fulfillment.
> (283)

Really, the book ends right there, soaringly.

Turnbull's earlier works include the much-taught *Forest People* (1961) on
the affable Mbuti, hunter-gatherers of northeastern Zaire (still affable in *The
Human Cycle*) and the much-condemned *Mountain People* (1972) on the tragically unaffable Ik, whose historical and environmental woes are omitted from
The Human Cycle. Some readers now find *The Forest People* more sanctimo-
nious than they once realized. Some observers doubt whether an earlier,
clearer alarm sounded about the plight underlying *The Mountain People*
would have helped victims of starvation anyway, given Uganda's political
circumstances. In 1984 *The Human Cycle* might have renewed such controversies; however, a brief correspondence in the *New York Times Book Review*
was bumped by bigger news: Derek Freeman's attack on Margaret Mead.
Even posthumously, Mead alone seems able to garner sustained media coverage for anthropological issues, always difficult to convert to headlines or even
special features.[6]

In the *London Review of Books* Edmund Leach entered the non-fray about Turnbull by declaring his utter exasperation with *The Human Cycle*: "That a professor of anthropology should cast himself in the role of Old Testament prophet calling his fellow sinners to repentance is more than I can take" (Leach 1984: 22). Quick on the draw as always, but careless of aim as usual, Leach attempted to implicate longtime rival Lévi-Strauss in Turnbull's preacherly ploys. Leach mistakenly declared Turnbull's rhapsodies about spirit "a mode of expression . . . very Lévi-Straussian" and confused Turnbull's first person reminiscences with the prose devices of *Tristes tropiques*. Lévi-Strauss's subjective narrative constructs a sampler of confessionals, travelogues, philosophies, and ethnographies; his is a formulaic quest that "crosses over" into both the world of the tropics and, as important, the world of tropes. The patent irony of the "je" in *Tristes tropiques* is reiterated by Lévi-Strauss in *Mythologiques* (and by his English translators John and Doreen Weightman). A pastiche of styles of discovery, *Tristes tropiques*' contrastive comparisons seek "to find a language" for depicting the limits of cross-cultural discourse. Whatever one may think of Lévi-Strauss, a project could hardly be more remote from Turnbull's.[7]

Leach possibly found Turnbull's casual, colloquial, self-invoking exposition a bit close for comfort. Leach's *A Runaway World* (1968), based on his Reith lectures, brimmed with personal and professional counsel for a troubled globe. Rather than revisiting (or rethinking) his own confessions of being trained as an engineer, Leach simply brands *The Human Cycle* "reflexive anthropology" (*sniff*), a presumably passing genre that he deems "highly fashionable in the United States." Leach might more accurately have tagged Turnbull "confessional anthropology of self-help." As persons experienced in American schools of semiotics know (*counter-sniff*), "reflexive anthropology" betokens intensifying recognitions by ethnographers that their descriptive and comparative devices are themselves culturally and historically contingent interpretations. Leach's major works helped advance this development, but his testy reviews sometimes lost sight of this fact.[8]

Whether or not Turnbull's style of self-help is one's cup of tea (and in this instance I obviously share Leach's distaste), its distinguishing features repay careful scrutiny. The book's hyperbole illustrates recent sales pitches for popularizing ethnography. A comical disparity separates the book's contents from its jacket cant: "Astonishing, extraordinary, passionate and illuminating, inspiring . . . destined to become a classic . . . one of the world's major contemporary social scientists." A string of suggestive but modest memoirs covering a career as bumpy as most thus enters what Cannel and Macklin have called *The Human Nature Industry* (1973). The inflated packaging of Turnbull's loosely woven, highly selective ethnography and autobiography seems designed to fill a genuine void left by the loss of Margaret Mead. Mead's accomplished arts of they/me cross-illumination seldom even heuristically separated the strands of other- and self-investigation. But her descriptions and confessions were geared to popular issues that she helped formulate: from generation gaps to various modes of liberation. Mead, then, helped *make* the times. She wrote a cross-cultural *Passages* before Gail Sheehy, not after her. Mead earned the vast audience she attracted.[9]

Not so Turnbull. Long after *The Forest People*, *The Human Cycle* discloses his gradual awakening to playful Mbuti eroticism and metaphors of copulating with the forest. He can now digress into Mbuti sex, and into unexpurgated Westminster schoolboy sex as well. (Possible movie material?) It is predictably revealed that Turnbull, no stranger to *Weltschmerz*, has brushed with evil: his Nazi nanny Irene was succeeded by Roman Catholic nanny Felman, "a lovely German woman from Wipperfurth," who introduced him "by mail to her younger brother, Hans, who was an active member of the Hitler Youth" (62). (Definitely, movie material.)

Turnbull laces the melodrama with repeated avowals of a comparative "I'm O.K. You're O.K.," uptight repressives excepted. Here is an example from "Childhood: The Art of Becoming":

Earth, water, air, and fire: the forest itself. Through these symbols the Mbuti are constantly reminded of Spirit, for wherever they are, whatever they are doing, those symbols surround them and even permeate their whole being. In the more artificial world we have built for ourselves we are not so fortunate; such effective symbols are harder to come by, particularly if we have never learned to employ our whole being as a tool of awareness. But that does not mean that Spirit is inaccessible to us. I am sure that many like myself groped their way through childhood aware that there was something lacking and found their own Great-uncle Willie, their own Rule Water, their own Arthur Poyser, and their own counterpart of what music was for me. All I am saying is that our form of social organization merely allows it to happen as an accident, if at all, whereas that of the Mbuti writes it into the charter from the outset, at conception. (77)

There now, doesn't that make us feel better? We too can learn from Uncle Willie to hush, grope, listen to running water, and see our own reflection in a Rule Valley stream, or anywhere else for that matter. Primed early on for sentimentalized responses to "natural symbols," Turnbull had a ready-made empathy for forest people, or so he tells us. The rest, according to his book, is history.

It would be child's play, but clearly "unbecoming," to go on caustically exposing, as Gita Mehta might, the transparent semiotics of *The Human Cycle*; its too-conversational style and format; its too-casual first person and pretentious colloquialisms; its studied elimination of any and all scholarly apparatus, irksome jargon, or cumbersome kinship diagrams deemed to alienate readers from books anthropological. To counteract likely suspicions that I am misrepresenting Turnbull's text or exaggerating the degree it condescends to a readership imagined by those marketing it, I can only cite the climax in this cross-cultural therapy without barricades:

> I used to love it when two trees were close enough near the top for me to jump from one to the other in the bland rather than blind conviction that the lower branches would break my fall. *I really should have been born an Mbuti* [italics added]. Rooftops were irresistible, only dangerous when you got too close to the edge and could see down. . . . There were only two friends with whom I could share my play life, and they were both what were called "tomgirls." They shrank from nothing until one of them asked me if I knew what boys did to girls in deserted homes, and all I could think of was urinating. I was then made aware that urinating, or whatever boys *did* to girls, was improper [italics in original]. (68–69)

Do readers want or need to know this? Must Turnbull, too, tell it like it is and was? Dreaming that incomparably impossible dream of being *born Mbuti*—of what cut is left conveniently unspecified—he beseeches us to resist artifice, to get into nature and supernature, and to be ourselves being with others being themselves too. This kind of *passage* is all that this book is.

FIRST COMPARISON (DYADIC): MEHTA

Gita Mehta's *Karma Cola* (1979) allows me to frame Turnbull's excesses against ones diametrically opposed. Again, it is Mehta's voice, a polar extreme, that my quickie put-downs of *The Human Cycle* have thus far been mimicking. Mehta sounds bitter-bitter to Turnbull's saccharine-sweet, spleen to his *idéal*. The author—an Indian educated in the West, her bookjacket announces—strips all the goody-goodyness off going Hindu.[10] She compares such spiritual quests to an alternatively extremist passage well beyond the pale of Turnbull's gingerly metaphors: "To go from the monomania of the West to the multimania of the East is a painful business. Like a sex change" (36). Ugly, funny, unfair, insightful chapters portray Mehta's encounters in decadent ashrams (compare Boccaccio on monasteries), besieged by guru-groupies who merely add touches of tackiness to her homeland's "implacable Eastern cruelty that lays the blame on the doer" (39). Mehta is often facile, but it still hurts. No question of or room for benevolence here. Any advocate of "Eastward Ho!" is fair game—Huxley, Yeats, the Beatles, and Ginsberg—during, after, and before, the Hippie era:

> Those were the days when everything was in flux. There were rumors about Tab Hunter. Elvis Presley had just made a movie with a scene set in a whorehouse. Now a famous, published, avant-garde American poet had looked upon India and

pronounced it free. Naturally Calcutta thought his reference was to the carnal. Before you could say snap, the Beat prophet was encircled by *vers libres* satyrs. (70)

The book's barbs include preposterous slogans of East/West transgressions, including Joycean hybrids of Sanskrit/Cockney: "Om is where the art is" (197). Relentlessly skewering the half-bakedness of West/East encounters, Mehta's diatribe cuts both ways: "Hindu thought is without dogma and dogged by Dharma"; "no one *teems* like we do" (192, 86).

Readers may end convinced, as I was beforehand, that hyperbole and hard-sell can be important factors when cultures contact. Indeed, such rhetorical forces may be as vital as, say, religious rationalization in the history of cross-cultural discourse.[11] The figurative style includes both ultradenigration and ultraprettification of others; it stretches from missionary propaganda to touristic come-ons, both designed in part to convince the gullible to book passage—either to save *them* or to join them. Simply to denounce the exaggerated style is to capitulate to it; nor can ethnographers completely avoid commercializing "the other;" we may as well factor that fact into our interpretations.

Mehta deigns to explain her *super* title:

> It would appear that when East meets West all you get is the neo-Sanyasi, the instant Nirvana. Coming at the problem from separate directions, both parties have chanced upon the same conclusion, namely, that the most effective weapon against irony is to reduce everything to the banal. You have the Karma, we'll take the Coca-Cola, a metaphysical soft drink for a physical one. (107)

She provocatively lists linguistic influences at work in Indian English today, including her own parodic prose. The postwar availability of Dell Comics (here Mehta and I converge) is credited with moving Anglo-Indian rhythms from orotund elocutions of colonial days to the "fractured prose of America." Turnabout, as usual, becomes fair play:

> By the Sixties, modulation had given way to acceleration. The explosive shorthand of America seemed infinitely preferable to the dilatory obliqueness of England. . . . On the other side of the planet the world's fastest speech looked for new words for slowing down. For twenty years we had burrowed in their vocabulary, now they scavenged in ours. Together with their own "laid backs" and "mellowed outs" went our Karmas, Sadhanas, Nirvanas, Tantras, and Sanyas. With language as with goods you take what you need. The British took from us jodhpurs and bungalows, riding breeches and colonial cottages, words for a more settled times. We had taken the idiom of modern America because it seemed to have no discernible provenance, a spontaneous verbalism that embraced the immediate as well as the immediate future. But now that America has taken our most complicated

philosophical concepts as part of its everyday slang, things are getting sticky. (103)

As we have seen, British Turnbull, gone American, compounds certain offenses that Mehta exposes. Even when criticizing Westerners who consider India essentially "spiritual," Turnbull avows that his own experience in Banares taught him how to have everything all ways:

> At the university I practiced the art of learning; at the *ashram*, where I lived, I learned the art of being ecstatic, and at the age of twenty-six went through my second adolescence, properly this time. Between the two of them I began to learn the art of reason, the proper application of knowledge. (147)

Again, Turnbull's probably well-intentioned pages idolize his personal quest in the *gurukula*. Mehta travesties any such devotion to renouncers' "first miraculous micturition" (83). Countering "religious Esperanto" (54) with traditionally caustic free thinking (Western style), Mehta signals the paradox of visitors who discover rebirth and learning-to-live in the land of *karma*, "a bad choice for narcosis." And she wonders how travelers' self-projections can possibly find fulfillment among Indian sages, when Eastern wisdom's primary concern is "the *annihilation* of narcissism" (106; emphasis added). No visitors escape unscathed: Canadians, Australians, Germans, the British, "still conscious of the lines of Imperial Vision," and Americans, the Grand Optimists "trying for the big one—the vault from solitary into nothing. Well, they have the money and we have the time . . ." (79).

For me, Mehta is irresistible.[12] But my cross-firing her style at Turnbull has a different critical aim: to show that vivid contrasts between the hilarious *Karma Cola* and the pious *Human Cycle* are actually shallow; the two works' seeming polarity conceals a resemblance. Mehta actually plays a game similar to Turnbull's (and in mimicking her, my essay partly succumbs as well, reflexively of course). Mehta's glitzy irreverences, studded with pop-tune cliché, are as sales-conscious as the prepackaged guruspeak and exotic psychobabble she derides. She displays all those emotions common among outraged, deracinated critics: anger, anger, and anger. Mehta markets the marketing of the Mystic East. As Turnbull hitches the crossing of cultures to the star of self-help, Mehta lodges (astutely!) West-meets-East in exposés (or mock exposés) dressed out both against and as Madison Avenue hype. Turnbull and Mehta represent equivalent half-truths in opposite directions: rhapsody and bile.

My juxtaposition of *Cola* and *Cycle* is devised to suggest that their respective polemics can nicely debunk each other's pufferies. Readers might want to read both Mehta and Turnbull so that the two can cancel each other out. But if you read only one, let it be neither; let it be . . . Naipaul.

Both V. S. Naipaul and the late Shiva Naipaul (his younger, less sanguine brother) reveal disturbingly mottled qualities in cross-cultural encounters: both opportunistic and generous, both self-effacing and self-serving, on *both* sides. Turnbull soars across cultures, Mehta scathes across cultures. V. S. Naipaul—along with other informed travelers (and, I think, many hard working, language-learning, context documenting, career-making ethnographers)—limps. However, in such travelogues as *An Area of Darkness* (1964), Naipaul limps (via customs agents, visa stampers, taxi drivers, and the entire *demi-monde* of civilizations' go-betweens) across cultures exquisitely, with disturbingly surer a sense of self than most of us ever muster. Certainly Naipaul's donnish self-possession in impeccable prose disturbs critics awaiting the Trinidad-born, English-educated Indian to emerge as champion of or spokesman for the Third World, identifying exclusively with it or some narrower sector—the creole Caribbean, wounded India, etc. But Naipaul's world (and his brother's, possibly more so), consists of refugees, only refugees—himself (ironically at-home only in his utterly articulate paragraphs) included. This essay, however, is not about Naipauls.[13]

LAST COMPARISON (TRIADIC): HOSE

My second companion volume for Turnbull is another confessional penned some sixty years ago by Charles Hose, distinguished official, naturalist, and ethnographer. Hose's *Pagan Tribes of Borneo* (1910) and *Natural Man* (1926) provided an ethnological foundation for the then-exemplary Sarawak administration of the durable Charles Brooke. In 1927 Hose indulged in looking back via a self-testimonial called *Fifty Years of Romance and Research, or, A Jungle Wallah at Large.*[14]

The work's lingering Victorian confidence in civilization's superiority and steady progress leads today's readers readily and willingly to hoot at Hose (much as I indulged above in Mehtaesque potshots at Turnbull's text). Hose was perhaps asking for it, even in 1927 (an astonishingly short five years after Malinowksi's *Argonauts of the Western Pacific*). At the outset Hose stipulates that, unlike most romancers, he prefers "the solid to the sensational" (15). Yet he proceeds to detail his eerie prescience of earthquakes, to cry "Eastward Ho!," and to call his elaborate salute to Aban Jau, Chief of the Tinjar Sebops, "A Rob Roy of Sarawak" (48). "A pagan and a savage, he was one of the finest gentlemen I have ever known," Hose concludes in commemorating this late "loyal supporter of the Government":

> Relentless foe, yet firmest friend,
> When friendship we did vow,

From memory's land, I clasp thy hand
And hail thee, Aban Jau! (58–59)

Still, however florid, Hose's autobiography on the whole was nothing if not solid. Today, in fact, it appears comically solid. His reminiscence shuttles between contradictory tendencies—modesty and fanfare:

> I remember how in my time at Cambridge a saying was current concerning a distinguished Don of one of the colleges, "I am the great 'I am,' none so fine as I." The phrase became a catchword for undue self-exaltation, which I have no desire to emulate. . . .
>
> A propos of the great Frenchman [Clemenceau], I may mention that in 1898 I was honored by France in being made an Officier de l'Académie Française. From Germany in 1893 I had received the Order of the White Falcon (Saxe-Weimar), which is, I understand, bestowed on Zoologists only. I am proud of this decoration, as I obtained it on the recommendation of the great Haeckel. Another German decoration was that of the Knight of the Prussian Crown, sent to me by the ex-Kaiser through the German Consul-General at Singapore . . . [and so on]. (15, 261–62)

Hose's interim passages include (I here adopt Turnbull's scheme): "transforming" on the Cam; "reasoning" in the footsteps of his kinsmen before him; "doing" with Poppy, his lifetime better half; and living to see his offspring "becoming" and getting into "transforming" at Cambridge too.

Charles Hose thrived during those claustrophobic days when all really was "in the family," both extended and descended:

> The motto adopted by a member of the Hose Family is "Omne solum viro patria est;" and our family seems to have recognized its truth practically. . . . Thus it happened that when my uncle [father's brother], Bishop Hose [of Singapore, Labuan, and Sarawak] wrote to my family offering to get me, if possible, a Cadetship in Sarawak, of all places, and under no less a man than Rajah Sir Charles Brooke, my delighted acceptance was conveyed in the single word (since become a family joke) "Rather!" (17–18, 33)

Hose's career owed much to the Mrs. as well, whom he dutifully acknowledges: "More than a helpmate, she has been a guide and an inspiration, a companion in my voyages and a sharer in my dangers" (18). Poppy's portrait serves as frontispiece; she is saluted as his editor-secretary and commended for certain original contributions. Once, for example, during her husband's absence from the Sarawak residency at Sibu, she single-handedly pickled yet another orangutan killed by Ibans for stealing fruit; her technique faulty, the giant carcass required decapitation, so that its bloated head (a photograph is provided) could be expedited to Dr. Duckworth at Jesus College, Cambridge.

Poppy's own account of this episode is inserted into *Fifty Years* (90–92). Hose's encomium concludes: "A good all-round sportswoman, she has been worthily followed by my two children, who have already distinguished themselves, the one as a Lawn Tennis player [readers can check an action shot of Violet's backswing], the other as an Oar, who has twice gained his oars in Jesus College boats, and rowed at Henley" (18). Who could ask for anything more?

Like Turnbull sixty years later, Hose had some none-too-rosy tales to tell of Public School, including a prankish theft of eggs that, "but for the kindly discretion of the Headmaster might have involved expulsion": "A Public Schoolboy may rob nests and break bounds, but he does not lie; we owned up, received our caning, and the incident was closed" (26). (Potential *Masterpiece Theater* material?) Unlike Turnbull, Hose stayed the course, conformed: "In point of fact relations between boys and masters at Felsted were never than the best. . . . the Headmaster *is* the school; the school is what the Headmaster makes it. My gratitude I have tried to express in a practical form by sending my son there . . ." (27).

Hose's lifetime achievements included captaining Football at Felsted, playing against Oxford for the Gentlemen of Essex, leading the school bowling averages, and serving on the Cricket First XI; these experiences taught him "common sense, self-reliance, and tact" (27). His profession of faith in athleticism culminates in an anecdote on, if one may coin a British-American hybrid, "Cambridge crew":

> This year (1927) once more I was present when the Jesus first boat went Head of the River, both in the "Lents" and "Mays," and I also had the pleasure of seeing my son rowing in the Jesus second boat. Tommy Watt, as he is familiarly known to his many friends, that famous old enthusiastic Don of Jesus College, . . . said . . . as I sat next to him at the high table: "Hose, I have seen my last cricket match, and my last football and Rugger match. I have lived, thank God, to see our first boat go Head of the River once again. I can now sing *Nunc dimittis*"—then he added [coy old Don that he was]—"But I hope the boat club will not get drunk until after tomorrow night." (31)

(Definitely, *Masterpiece Theater* material.)

Contrary to any impression the passages cited may convey, Hose is not guilty simply of padding memoirs with details unrelated to his career in Sarawak. Oaring on the Cam had provided the model for annual boat races that he instituted on Borneo's Baram River, a proud accomplishment mentioned in all three major works: "When in 1900 the vice-Chancellor of Cambridge University conferred on me the honorary degree of Doctor in Science, the Public Orator, Dr. Sandys, specifically mentioned in his speech this event, which has so effectually turned the rivalry of head-hunters to peaceful competition in sport" (259). Worse policies are conceivable. Hose's engrossing chapters relate his life among sportsmen, among headhunters, then among sportsmen again, ex-headhunters now included. He recollects his life's passages as a cyclic cruise: from the river Cam to the river Baram and home again, Baram now mirroring Cam.[15]

Hose is a sitting duck for campy retorts from us postmodern readers. His work, however, may deserve better. After Sarawak Hose helped eradicate beri-beri in Malaysia and Japan; an account of this project reveals that his quaint hopes for civilization's progress (undeflected by World War I) cannot quite be reduced to outright xenophobia. In artful twists of rhetoric, Hose praises Japanese friends and colleagues; although still smugly favoring British schoolways, he concludes with a telling image of joint superiority:

> Another Japanese personal friend has been Mr. T. Kuga, formerly manager of the Mitsubishi Trading Company, and now Paris manager. His son, Taro Kuga, is shortly to enter a preparatory school in England, and on my recommendation, will, I hope, eventually proceed to Felsted and Jesus. It has been a great pleasure to me to be associated with representative men of an Island Race like our own, and a people, like us, with a World Mission. (262–63)

The usually archaic-seeming Hose (even in 1927) here sounds, unfortunately, almost ahead of his time. Any island that pulled its oar could join the team and shoulder civilization's (or rather Imperialism's) self-proclaimed burdens.

Further hints of underestimated complexities in colonialism's shadowy values glimmer through Sir Arthur Keith's preface to *Fifty Years* which commends Hose's enlightened administration based on ethnographic evidence.

> That spirit of boyish adventure and youthful outlook [Hose] carried with him to Borneo, and it abode with him there. It was because he had the power of becoming a child again that it was possible for him to enter into the native mind and see the world as Nature's savages see it—minds which swarm with spirits of all kinds— spirits which have to be obeyed or propitiated. How stupid we white men often are! We have to know each other very intimately for many years to discover the motives of conduct, and yet we can persuade ourselves that in half an hour, by a few questions, framed in imperfectly understood words, we can fathom the secrets of a native people whom we wish to rule. Charles Hose never made this mistake; he approached the tribes as one boy approaches another, and in the course of time came an exchange of secrets, and this exchange gave Dr. Hose the key to successful government. And at the same time Dr. Hose was able to enlarge the common store of that kind of knowledge which is valued and collected by anthropologists. (8–9)

Judging from Keith's preface, colonialist "paternalism" could more accurately be described as a doubled juvenilization: both They and We. Headmaster Hose, the consummate colonial official, related to his subjects less in lordly fashion than boy-to-boy. He probably truly did admire the "Rob Roy of Sarawak." Hose linked subordinate populations to the dominant power by locking both sides into displays of perpetual schoolday pleasures. Dreaming of a history that would never need transforming again, Hose governed by exchanging secrets, so to convert every headhunter to an Oar.[16]

My brief attempt here to read Hose cunningly aims not to exonerate colonialism or the anthropology sometimes in cahoots with it (and sometimes not). I aim rather to help disclose more convoluted, mythlike undercurrents in political and historical arrangements that appear straightforward. One begins to suspect significantly contradictory sides to Charles Hose (not to mention Aban Jau!). Keith's 1927 tribute can make Hose seem almost relativist, "convinced that the difference between East and West is not so great as is usually believed; under our diverse creeds, codes, customs, tongues, and skin-tint is hid the same human nature—the same reactions" (6). But exceptions doubtless marked such convictions. Keith-on-Hose even recalls moments cited above of Turnbull-by-the-Rule: "As [Hose] was learning in his boyhood the habits of plants, birds, and beasts among the marshes of the Waveney, he was equipping himself for the jungles of the East" (6). But this parallel between Hose and Turnbull is ultimately misleading. Hose imposed other-government instrumentally; Turnbull seeks self-help presumably innocently. Still, who could say whether a colonialist superiority complex à la Hose or psychologistic self-identification à la Turnbull is more imbued with so-called "cultural imperialism?" Both, as Mehta's *Karma Cola* can remind us, manage to suffocate differences. A crucial feature shared by Hose in 1927 and Turnbull in 1983 is this: Each felt compelled eventually to look back, self-regardingly, on his exotic adventures—one in a celebration of his colonialist career, the other in a searching of his personalized soul, both unremittingly, simplistically earnest.

For this reader, both Hose's anthropology in its day and Turnbull's anthropology in ours conform too closely to an era's status quo: ultra class conscious or school snobbish in Hose's case; pop democratic in our own. Still, as Hose's *Fifty Years* demonstrates, bad books can make provocative cultural and historical documents. Too near in time (and perhaps, like Leach, close for comfort) to judge Turnbull fairly or even interpret him cunningly, I daresay that sixty years hence *The Human Cycle* may reveal to future readers richer dimensions of cross-cultural self-help than I am able now to perceive. But not yet— They shall say "in their hundred voices, 'No, not yet,' and the sky said 'No, not there.'"[17]

CRITICAL CONCLUSIONS (OPPOSING ALL THREE)

Between the historical will to dominate "the other" and the personal hope to help "the self"—that is, between the extremes represented by Hose and Turnbull—there exist more subtly inflected motives of and for anthropology, area research, and cultural studies. But it is often difficult to get them across. Ardent voices of late—many of them "Mehtaesque"—have decried establishment ethnography and comparative research, charged with insufficient awareness of their collusion in colonial and postcolonial power structures. True enough, but only partly: the headline isn't that simple. Equally insistent voices have proclaimed from exotic locales their self-discovery, their breakthrough into personal coping. The present little critique has attempted to help both sorts of voices unsettle each other.

Increasingly, even professionals appear to cross cultures either unctuously to find themselves or angrily to denounce old-guard scholarship that supposedly inhibited anybody (including "the natives") from so doing. In anthropology and sister disciplines, motives beyond moralistic self-help or ideologized predecessor-denouncing have themselves become closeted. This development too should be resisted, and not just stuffily. Halting, variegated, uncocksure, responsibly and/or subversively doubting semiotics seldom make catchy headlines, book blurbs, interviews, -isms, or blueprints (agendas) for political or psychological improvement. But formats must be preserved for these less marketable narratives, too.[18] For they may be truer.

It is, indeed, this truer kind of story depicting the semiotic complexities of any and all passages between India, U.S. (us), and elsewhere—all these scratches on each other's minds and hearts—that Milton Singer persisted over many books innovatively to report. The comparative semiotics of self that he articulated transcends any and all individualistic merchandizing of self-help. Yet Singer's sense of semiotics was so full that he would doubtless require comparative theory to comprehend even the self-therapeutic motives and slogans that my essay provisionally has rebuffed. Beckoning a future scholarship that would neither simply reject self-help nor privilege it, but rather seek to understand it as one semiotics in the Peircean profusion of human signs, I conclude confessionally with a parodic moral and ironic guidelines for would-be readers of "selves"—theirs and others (including mine):

> I'm not O.K. nor, I suspect, are you O.K. Nor is my culture or any culture I know anything about O.K., particularly (*pace* Colin Turnbull) in their puberty rites. Nor will getting to know them, even getting to know all about them, help make either of us O.K. Hence, my in-depth advice to the sexually, spiritually, or otherwise hassled "Westerner," with whom I identify and sympathize, as we all should: Skip fieldwork, avoid ashrams, read pornography and/or scripture (both more therapeutic than ethnography); and hire an analyst, not an informant, a guide, or a guru.

My concluding counsel will probably sound "Charles Kuraulty," although I would prefer to echo a voice whose sparkling dignity corresponds more to the semiotic self of Milton Singer and to his teachings in the philosophy of cultural comparisons.[19] I thus profess:

> Any culture-crosser, whether personally growing, transforming, soaring, scathing, coping, or not coping at the time, should be interested not just in "himself"—this complex semiotic construction—being interested in, for example, Mbuti or Banares. He or she should be interested in Mbuti or Banares, or Britain, or U.S., or anywhere anyway. Why? Because peoples in all their peculiar social, historical, ecological, economic, political, and ritual circumstances (what Milton Singer called their "cultural performances") are *there*: becoming, transforming, reasoning, marrying and not marrying, oppressing, being oppressed, entrepreneuring, semioticizing, liberating, warring, doing, and dying—whether you or I ("me," babe) get ourselves into being there too, or not. *And that's*—critically and semiotically— *the way it is.*

CHAPTER EIGHT

Errant Anthropology, with Apologies to Chaucer

This essay is adapted from an address I was invited to deliver to the New Chaucer Society—the first, they told me, by a "non-Chaucerian," or was it "non-Medievalist?" Regardless, this fool rushed in. Surrounded by sessions touching on the most avant-garde issues—phase-four-feminism, queer theory, untold hybridities—I devised, contrarily, some throw-backs to motifs from earlier medievalisms. The last thing today's Chaucerians needed was an anthropologist telling them how to be up-to-date. The audience feigned attentiveness and, regardless of its diverse persuasions, responded politely—for which I was very grateful indeed.

CHAUCER'S Knight—whose errant style this essay will emulate—justifies his abrupt and abbreviated way to "begynne the game" of *Canterbury Tales* thusly:

> And certes, if it nere to long to here
> I wolde han told yow fully the manere
> But al that thing I moot as now forbere
> But shortly for to telle is myne entente

It is in a kindred spirit of brevity that I precipitously pronounce a transhistorical, interdisciplinary task: To disclose diverse arrays of ritual, mythic, economic, linguistic, social, artistic, and political intricacies of meanings and motives in human affairs. This endless quest keeps anthropology and kindred pursuits alert to cultures, genders, classes, ethnicities, modes of power-knowledge, religious persuasions, semiotic practices, and ambiguous texts disturbing to censorious regimes whose conformist standards suppress heterodox usage, resistance, and "literariness" or its equivalent in unwritten activity.

Anthropology's cross-cultural expansiveness has provoked accusations of complicity in Euro-America's imperialist drive. Rather than argue why such critique—often waged rather imperiously—strikes me as only half-true, it may facilitate proceedings to plead guilty as charged. Nowadays suspicions accrue not just to "monologic" ethnography but to stabs at dialogic discourse and even to simulated speech acts paraded as always-already *écriture*. Currently, all recognizable practices of knowledge or nihilism stand accused of insufficient multicultural roots, inadequate empowerment-consciousness, and bias toward one or another -ism in a suspect canon.

Chaucer-readers should thus stand forewarned: an anthropologist has infiltrated your domain; he is raring to colonize your scholarship and incorporate its findings in his disciplinary gaze and grasp. Or put positively, I profess to discover ample openness in Chaucer's manifold legacy that, I trust, can be swerved to accommodate scandalously tardy emancipations without abandoning long-term interpretive issues. May everyone remain engaged in the not-yet-dead body of Chaucer's *lettres*.

As I began by saying, one voice that Chaucer's writing ventriloquized was the Knight's. Coincidentally, my work has broached (breached?) various cultures sporting "chivalric" texts and rites of politics and desire. They include Hindu-Bali, Sanskritized in part; Brahminical India, where Ksatria sectors institutionalized their claims of Knightly prowess; and Medieval Europe, with its devious arts of ambiguous *amors*. All these cultural cases display *figures* of the "love chase" or erotic hunt, plus variously institutionalized ideals of chastity and retentive renunciation. European instances, nicely surveyed by Marcelle Thiébaux (1974), include Chaucer's exhaustive wordplay on "the pursued stag and the death-captured *heart-hart* in *The Book of the Dutchess*." Chaucer's signifiers, of course, were transformed in subsequent chivalric conceits: Tudor, Jacobean, Romantic, Victorian, modernist, etc. Histories of India and Bali, too, reveal repeated revivals and contestations of *courtoisie*; indeed, Sanskritized texts and rites are riddled with ironies resembling those found in Chaucer and his successors.[1]

When sallying comparatively among European cases, I rely on "classic" *topoi*-trackings (E. R. Curtius's *European Literature and the Latin Middle Ages*, for example) and newer tropologies, such as R. Howard Bloch's "literary anthropology" of France's Middle Ages, or Eugene Vance's readings of Chaucer's "mervelous signs."[2] Indic elaborations of intricate signs of ritual-erotics ("desire," "culture") are possibly even more panoramic and profusely varied. This matter, however, is too serpentine to pursue "shortly" (in the fashion of Chaucer's Knight). Luckily, some straighter bridges have been dropped across figurative moats separating literary studies from cultural anthropology. Multiplying my old-medievalist metaphors, I now propose to cross over a few.

STILL-PROMISING CRUSADES

Multifarious researches have converged on practices of pilgrimage, rites of passage, and ceremonies of liturgy and carnival. Vibrant work on image and pilgrimage by the late Victor Turner, together with Edie Turner, gathered the likes of Chaucer, Dante, and Ndembu culture (Turner's fieldwork *spécialité*) into a comparative *communitas* of symbolic liminality.[3] Clifford Geertz, although a profound admirer of Turner's peerless ethnography, tagged his overly general scheme of structure/antistructure "a form for all seasons" (one of Geertz's niftiest critical winks). Turner's approach, adapted from Van Gennep, struck other scholars too—from Lévi-Strauss to Carolyn Bynum—as too synthetic when implying that consensual *communitas* underlies every ritual reversal. Nevertheless, Turner compellingly dramatized dynamics of off-and-on, topsy-turvy transformation versus confirmation; these remain key concepts in studies of ritual process and political theater.[4]

Other bridges from literary history have been forged to Lévi-Strauss's *Mythologiques*, his "late structuralist" mappings of sensate categories woven through variant Native American myths. Britton Harwood (1981) reads Chaucer's "Miller's Tale" as an obbligato upon acoustical, zoological, sexual, and anatomical codes associated with charivari's ritual music and din. His approach echoes *Mythologiques*'s accent on verbal, musical, and ritual arts; encrypted synaesthetic connections across cultures and times was one "grail" Lévi-Strauss's works pursued.

Yet another bridge is the "deep play" of Balinese ritual and politics signalled, half-oxymoronically, by Clifford Geertz with a wink-and-nod to Jeremy Bentham (1973: Chap. 15). Parallel soundings of medieval literature surface in Glending Olson's (1982) notion of serious "recreation." Geertz's interpretations of theatricality in the weightiest statecraft in *Negara* (1980) proved compatible with historical investigations of *mentalités* and with New Historicist readings of representations that dissolve distinctions between literature and politics.[5] (On a subsequent wave of New Historicism, see Chap. 9.)

Other promising work highlights authoring, authority, charisma, and power transmitted in composite oral and literate practices: bookish oratory (delivered and heard); enacted manuscripts (written or dictated, and read), and disseminated print (produced and consumed). Such research crosses varied critical schools—psychoanalytic, Ong-ian, semiotic, Foucauldian, feminist, phenomenological, Marxist and its revisions, dialogist, deconstructionist, and post-those. Two appealing examples in tune with the ethnography of reading practices and power-knowledge are Ann Astell's essay on multiplicities of causes in Chaucer's books and Lynn Staley Johnson's article on "The Trope of the Scribe and the Question of Literary Authority."[6]

Mention of scribes and tropes returns me, unnostalgically, to my *Other Tribes, Other Scribes* (1982). That study's "scribal-tribal" tropes addressed European and Indic cosmologies of scrivening, plus comparative evidence of "literarity" and "rituality." From Europe's charmingly provincial textual history, I chose the Jacobean example of Samuel Purchas's "*Pilgrimes*," a globe-girdling compilation that converted to Anglican advantage rhetorics consolidated by Catholic Iberian visionaries. Because *Other Tribes, Other Scribes* was devised to echo prose-catalogues of the world's rarities, verities, and varieties (including interpretive methods), it mentioned every culture, era, performance-style, and literature I could think of. Come to think of it, however, I omitted Chaucer.

Affinities and Extremes (1990) tried to compensate; I cheated, though, by pilfering an image of pilgrimage that expanded from all of Canterbury's visitors to all of history's cultures, celebrated in the utter trickery of Melville's *Confidence Man*:

> As among Chaucer's Canterbury pilgrims, or those oriental ones crossing the Red Sea towards Mecca in the festival month, there was no lack of variety. Natives of all sorts, and foreigners.... Fine ladies in slippers, and moccasined squaws; Northern speculators and Eastern philosophers; English, Irish, German, Scotch, Danes ... Quakers in full drab, and United States soldiers in full regimentals; slaves, black, mulatto, quadroon; modish young Spanish Creoles, and old-fashioned French Jews; Mormons and Papists; ... jesters and mourners ... Sioux chiefs solemn as high priests. In short, a piebald parliament ... of that multiform pilgrim species.... [7]

Goodness, it's tough to abbreviate *The Confidence Man*, especially where it may be aping Carlyle! Even Chaucer's Knight could, I suspect, be thwarted in striving to render Melville "shortly."

Melville-on-Chaucer leads me to a transforming truth worth celebrating anew. Cultural anthropologists join Chaucer and Chaucer-readers (including Melville)—and Shakespeare and Shakespeare-readers (including Melville), and Purchas and Purchas-readers (including Melville), and Melville and Melville-readers (including Melville)—in interpreting rites of pilgrimage, divisions of labor and ceremony, covert mythological codes, "deep" as well as surface play, and gendered modes of power and inequality transmitted through oral and literate devices of authority, *auctores*, property, propriety, repression, liberation, and so forth. Like Chaucer and Chaucerians, anthropologists inscribe and translate vernacular scenes, colloquial localities, common places charged with commonplaces (topoi)—where diverse languages intersect, collide, communicate, fight, or pass each other by. The transtextual, cross-cultural adventure continues.

MULTISENSORY, MODAL COUNTERPOINT

Chaucer was an author who apparently read (orally) his written *Troilus and Criseyde* at court, or was shown doing so in a Cambridge *Corpus Christi* illustration familiar to professional literary historians.[8] Like ethnologist Marcel Mauss many centuries later, Chaucer wrote (and apparently read aloud) heteroglossia (in Bakhtin's sense)—ritual languages, languages of the marketplace, literary languages, "magical words" (see Chap. 6). Chaucer, moreover, like Bakhtin and Mauss, wrote (about) heteroglossia in many narrative modes. What else was a ventriloquist of piebald pilgrims to do?

Mention of modes carries this errant anthropologist—always striving to be both avant garde and retrograde—back to the late Northrop Frye, another canonical guy worth revisiting. Frye credited Chaucer with what I infelicitously call "meta-modality," moding on mode.[9] Critics today would add much to Frye about gender-class-race; I would toss in music, religion*s*, permeable boundaries between fiction and description, and themes of never-ending translation among humanity's polyglot realities. The latter have been dramatized in George Steiner's *After Babel*, where Chaucer, too, bows in:

> Where a passage is historically remote, say in Chaucer, the business of internal translation tends towards being a bilingual process: eye and ear are kept alert to the necessity of decipherment. (1975: 28)

Disciplinarily, I note that "keeping alert to the necessity of decipherment" is anthropology's stock in trade. Transdisciplinarily, I can add to Steiner-on-Chaucer this observation: even where a *passage is personally proximate* (as in psychoanalytic models of contradictions intimately at home in a cozy "self"), the business of translation still *resembles*, and uncannily, a bilingual (even a multilingual) process.

But I was speaking of Northrop Frye, not Steiner or Freud; so I feel obliged to cite him, "shortly," as Chaucer would say:

> Once we have learned to distinguish the modes, however, we must then learn to recombine them. For while one mode constitutes the underlying tonality of a work of fiction, any or all of the other four [you remember] may be simultaneously present. Much of our sense of the subtlety of great literature comes from this modal counterpoint. Chaucer is a medieval poet specializing mainly in romance, whether sacred or secular. Of his pilgrims, the knight and the parson clearly present the norms of the society in which he functions as a poet, and, as we have them, the *Canterbury Tales* are contained by these two figures, who open and close the series. But to overlook Chaucer's mastery of low mimetic and ironic techniques [both fonts of heteroglossia] would be as wrong as to think of him as a modern novelist who got into the Middle Ages by mistake. (Frye 1957: 51)

Cultural anthropology traditionally traffics in modal counterpoint of diverse cultures and the politics of their encounter. There are, moreover, contrapuntal modes *of* this anthropology *of* modal counterpoint. A few recent ones are Renato Rosaldo's *Culture and Truth*, Sherry Ortner's *High Religion*, Clifford and Marcus's *Writing Culture*, Dennis Tedlock's *The Spoken Word and the Work of Interpretation*, Larry Rosen's *Bargaining for Reality*, Abdellah Hammoudi's *The Victim and its Masks*, Michael Herzfelds's *Anthropology through the Looking Glass*, John Bowen's *Muslims Through Discourse*, Anna Tsing's *In the Realm of the Diamond Queen*, Talal Asad's *Genealogies of Religion*,

Richard Price's *Alabi's World*, Michael Taussig's books, and Richard Handler and Dan Segal's (both card-carrying anthropologists) *Jane Austen and the Fiction of Culture*.[10]

Anthropology's contrapuntal concern with low mimetics and "folk irony" descends in part from Chaucer, among other ancestors. Out of the throes of fieldwork emerge descriptive narratives that recall in their convoluted dubiousness—if not in their art—aspects of Chaucer's tales. All hail Chaucer then, not just as the equivalent of a prized informant whose "responses" afford evidence of medieval cultural expressions and censorings, but as a writer who anticipated textual practices eventually denominated both "literature" and "ethnography."

MENIPPEAN MODES, INCLUDING THE PARDONER

Northrop Frye is hard to shake once he's resurrected. Frye placed Chaucer in yet another tradition: Menippean satire ("Anatomies") stretching from second-century Lucian through Burton, to, as Frye stipulated, Frye.

> This creative treatment of exhaustive erudition is the organizing principle of . . . Burton's *Anatomy of Melancholy*. Here human society is studied in terms of the intellectual pattern provided by the conception of melancholy, a symposium of books replaces dialogue, and the result is the most comprehensive survey of human life in one book that English literature had seen since Chaucer, one of Burton's favorite authors. (1957: 311)

I try to extend Frye's "affinity with the Menippean tradition" into rites and texts well beyond his Biblical and Homeric bailiwick—Tantric ones, for example, contradiction-laden traditions partly suppressed by both Brahmanical and Buddhist orthodoxies and expurgated by colonialist regimes.[11] I would also note that Chaucer too, Menippean satirist that he was, suffered sanitization in reception—as early as Caxton's epochal printed edition of 1484, which promoted him as author of "good and virtuous tales" (!).

Age-old controversies of embracing and disputing such diverse voices as Chaucer's encourage me to anticipate, even today, resurgent cultural histories, and literary histories, ones attuned to gendered and politicized discourse (of course) but also mindful of multiple vernaculars, mottled literacy, and semiotic intricacy. Such work would (and does) accentuate seriocomic ambiguities of hybrid cultural texts and contexts, plus the power-plays involved in—forgive me—"de-Menippeanizing" them.[12]

Literary historians need no reminding that Chaucer's tales were hybrid with respect to genre—sonnet, sermon, *fablieau*; and to language—composite London English (East Midlands, Kentish, even South-Western dialects) infected with French and Latin. (Even my accent feels a little bit at home in Chaucer.)

Nor can readers of Chaucer forget his multiformity of represented genders, ranks, ceremony, and divisioned labor. The Chaucerian "scene of reading" bubbles with heterodox murmurs, including alchemical ones, appropriate to an inherently unsafe pilgrimage setting that defies subjugation. Indeed,

> The Pardoner is a born eunuch, whom medieval character psychology made out much worse than a man who had merely been castrated . . . evil natured, foolish, lustful, and presumptuous. . . . recognized from their lack of beard, long scrawny necks and thin bodies, high voices, and prominent, rolling . . . eyes. . . . Inclined to lechery, but unable to fulfill their desires, they are reduced . . . to boasting of them.
>
> A pardoner was officially appointed and could operate only with the permission of the bishop, who could also license him to preach—a source of much dispute with the friars, who earned part of their livelihood from the same source. In practice, [the pardoner] would often display and sell relics—bodily parts of Christ or the saints. . . .[13]

Although I cribbed this "info" from my thoroughly respectable *Oxford Anthology of* (canonical) *English Literature*, such details might appear enticingly transgressive—like exotic ethnography. To some readers, representations of the Pardoner may suggest a rather relativist position: Other cultures, other eunuchs . . . other (literary?) sublimations. To alternative readers, the "info" cited could pertain to elements of historical homophobia. All this matters (see Chap. 9).

Redonning my mask of errant anthropologist I should stress that equally intricate and conflictual rhetorical scenes and sublimations pervade rites, texts, and labors in non-Western locales—both long-literate places and ones misleadingly called "tribal." Such scenes—"the world," as it were, inscribed with other texts, and peopled with other critics—include riverine and highland New Guinea, Native American Northwest coast, and Australians ("native" ones, I mean).[14] Pilgrimes all!

FINAL FLOURISH

Thus it is that much remains to be read from the cross-cultural, historical panoply of shifting texts, rites, and rhetorics thereof. Neither the Pardoner, the Knight, nor anyone else—of any hue or *genre*—ought be forgotten. Our multiform, ambipowered, Pilgrim (anti)disciplines have hardly "begynned the [extra-Vagant] game."

CHAPTER NINE

Margins and Hierarchies and Rhetorics
That Subjugate

This essay is adapted from a plenary address to the Center for Medieval and Early Renaissance Studies (Annual Conference Theme: "On the Margins"). I was possibly invited less as an authority than as a specimen.

THE MARGINS are an unsettled place to be and an unsettling (a)position from which to speak. A marginal amongst Medievalists and Early Modern Europeanists, I also try to enact my official discipline and area—anthropology and Indonesian studies—heterodoxically. My critical stance is "carnivalized": wary of cozy metaphysics and their routinized deconstruction, alike; wearied by both nonstop disestablishmentarians and by pat credos they contest. *Ecce homo*: interpretively homeless, devoid of passport, alienated from certainties and edges as well; even the borderlands refuse me shelter.[1]

I have resolved to speak of and from such margins, rather than justify my presence as an interdisciplinary go-between—"mediation" being in bad critical aroma nowadays. Yet insecure even in this resolve, I feel a nagging urge to drum up credentials: Europeanists, your guest has published on "Jacobean Ethnology" and Renaissance discourses of diacritical rites; he has related fieldwork on Hindu-Bali's courtly peripheries to aspects of medieval European *sociétés à maisons*, drawing on Jacques Le Goff, Georges Duby, Georges Dumézil, Claude Lévi-Strauss, etc. (Boon 1990a). But to indulge this anxiety of legitimacy could cancel my "outsider" status—one presumably valued by an academic Center bent on decentering.

"Framing the margins"—to steal a title—is in full swing these days. From the upscale *marges* of deconstructive Derrida (Jacques), to the neopaganism of heretical Paglia (Camilla), the mainstream, as critics imagine it, is very much contested. Derrida converts antilogocentrism itself into something of a creed among his—how should I put it?—disciples. And Paglia outrages academic feminists—whom she declares now hegemonic—by situating their stance against pornography in the history of patriarchal prudery . . ., or something of the sort. Critical outpourings as different as Derrida and Paglia—one elite, t'other pop—frame margins diversely, in order, centrists complain, to "frame" the center.[2]

You do not need me to tell you that such goings-on may prompt reactionary responses. I might mention one Medievalist example—bull in China shop fashion, I'm afraid—whose "voice" some readers may recognize. Here's what it says:

> In an academic profession steadily infiltrated by the 1968 generation that had failed at the barricades and instead determined to take over the university, [Natalie] Davis's celebrity carried her to the presidency of the American Historical Association. What especially distinguished her work on sixteenth-century France was her admiration for all manifestations of antistatist and socially irrational behavior, including juvenile delinquency, petty crime, and familial disorder, as structurally representative of antiestablishment, protomodern revolution. The boisterous behavior of young men at Carnival (Mardi Gras) time was viewed by Davis (as by Bakhtin) as social protest.
>
> Coinciding with the teachings of neo-Marxist Frankfurt school of critical theory and also inspired by the leftist school of symbolic anthropology headed by Clifford Geertz, Davis broadened the Marxist Revolution into cultural and affective upheavals. . . . Compared with her, Marc Bloch was a moderate. (Cantor 1991: 283)

I hope that Norman Cantor's *New Criterion*esque approach to disciplinary surveillance will not provoke any boisterous protest here. I might just calmly comment that deeming Natalie Davis's history soft on anarchists seems rather farfetched; and branding Clifford Geertz's interpretive anthropology "leftist" sounds quite daft. But I bring up Cantor's book neither utterly to "other" it nor to escalate the multicultural critical wars. For, despite his peculiar polemic, Cantor earmarks a vital issue:

> The Annalist triumph was further reinforced in the 1970s with the rise of women's history and feminist doctrines. Medieval women were viewed, like the peasantry, as another alternative population contrasted with the elite male cadre of aristocratic society. Women of the medieval nobility would actually have been unhappy placed in an oppositional category, allegedly contending against their fathers and brothers. They would have resented ascription of solidarity to them against male lords and alongside peasants, Jews, heretics, and gays. But within the ideological categories of the 1970s and 1980s, this kind of polemical medieval women's history was popular and persuasive. (1991: 156)

Now, I question Cantor's invidious attribution of would-be resentments to the noble women he imagines—which attribution underpins his assumption that their sympathies could only lie with their estate, their *ligne*, or other "propriety." Nevertheless, I applaud how Cantor underscores real difficulties in the "ascription of solidarity" across times and cultures. It is good to find this complex matter signalled even by a voice that I largely disavow. We marginals, you know, must traffic with foe and friend alike.

My partly antidisciplinary inclinations would prefer that historical margins meet, unmediated by centers. I back ideas of interpretations exchanged among equals: oppressed to oppressed, abject to abject, gay to gay, vernacular to vernacular, colonized to colonized, outlaw to outlaw—on down current lists of preferred protagonists. But it remains politically and epistemologically tricky to bring margins—or their rhizomes—front and center. To illustrate why, I shall sketch four areas and examples of paradoxical concern: (1) Broodings on the imperfectibility of inclusiveness, with a few guidelines for "ethnographies of past marginality;" (2) thoughts on (Jonathan) "Goldberg variations;" (3) hunches about comparative hierarchies and heterodoxies, drawing on anthropologist Louis Dumont; (4) warnings about colonialist discourse where copious rhetoric vividly marginalizes subjugated differences *multiply*.

BROODINGS ABOUT INCLUSIVENESS

Even the fairest list *for inclusion* remains inadvertently selective—implies an "us" that "others" otherwise. From my peculiar comparative perspective—"local" in its way—I observe the following about this conference.[3]

1. Its call for papers made no mention of "Turks," "Arabs," "Moors;" indeed nothing Islamic unless it is subsumed under "heretics," "pagans," "refugees," "blacks," etc. Should Europeanists still "center" Christendom or Christians/Jews, given the many Muslims (then and now, both overt and covert) of "Europe?"[4]

2. Had "On the Margins" convened decades ago, other voices would have predominated: peasants, women, Neoplatonists; they have today gained prominence thanks to social historians, feminists, Frances Yates, etc. "Marginal identities" flagged under fresh auspices in current proceedings include "witches," classed now as "victims" rather than "superstition." Still, contemporary categories may yet offend ever-evolving politics of identity: "The disabled?"—or the medievally "under-served?" "Gypsies?"—the thorniness of this designation ramifies through academic work and popular culture as well.[5]

3. As an ethnographer of ritual practice, I note a neglect of concrete ritual marks of marginality; Christians, for example, used the category of "circumcised" to distance both Jewish and Muslim usages, whether infant, adolescent, male, or female circumcisions. Pauline Christians (as opposed to Christ) left "circumcision" of diverse stripes to "others." The politics in all this remains intricate today, along ever-changing lines. (See Chap. 2.)[6]

I offer these observations constructively. Critical scholarship can do no more than strive to reopen peripheries. "Margins," like centers, keep moving; every updated inclusivity rekindles significant anthropological questions: Was a given marginal status part of consciousness, its associated solidarity "internalized?"[7] Or has it been ascribed with hindsight, from a contemporary position that "identifies?" Were margins of yore fixed or flexible, singular or multiple, discrete or jumbled? Were trangressions of normalized propriety expected, collusions between oppressors and oppressed routine? Did heterodox fields of "marginalia" unfold along with competitive centers? Such questions invite "thick description," or the historian's equivalent—a deviated methodology, and one that is always ethically conflicted.[8]

To get more concrete, let me designate one medieval-Renaissance "scene" that seems eminently worth "fieldworking" (figuratively). It is Venice's Ghetto, replete with margins and contestations linking victims and powers-that-be (as portrayed in *The Autobiography of a Seventeenth-Century Venetian Rabbi: Leon Modena's Life of Judah*, edited by Mark Cohen [1988], with pieces by Th. Rabb, H. Adelman, N. Davis, and B. Ravid).

The term "ghetto," which originated in Venice, was first applied to Jewish quarters in the sixteenth century; I telegraph Ravid's mapping of this "process of marginality":

> Middle Ages: only individual Jews may reside in city; groups restricted to mainland across lagoon, including moneylenders—in economic "organic solidarity" with usury-phobic Christians; Jews were permitted city refuge during wars, to protect Christian loan pledges they held.

> 1509. Officials note advantage of allowing resident Jews, so to bolster treasury and provide pawnbrokers to the postwar needy. Once spatially excluded, Jews now included by temporary charter (actually renewed until Napoleonic times). Provisos that they be segregated, so not to "spread all over" Christian spaces. Micromanaged separations redifferentiate Venice's unique landscape: e.g., "New Ghetto" island with gated bridges for curfew.

> 1541. Jewish Levantine merchants request elbow-room for their merchandise from the Ottoman Balkans; accommodated with a "doubled ghetto"; the Counter-Reformation adds to the Vecchio and Nuovo, a Ghetto Nuovissimo. (Ravid 1988: 279–83)

Ravid's compressed account fast-forwards through metaphorical extensions of "Ghettos" into tragic histories of prejudice. An ethnographer of this past might explore how "on the margins" became experienced as "in the ghetto"—how those relegated there nevertheless could author their own sense of place.

This Ghetto context (like Chaucer's "Pardoner" text discussed in Chap. 8)— coagulates marginal and mainstream forces, paradoxical allegiances, contradictory solidarities, ambiguous devices, and diverse desires. Such "scenes" warrant multiple interpretations and deconstructions of their symbols, structures, ideologies, and disputed differences. They connect to venerable issues, such as Frazerian sacred-dangerous taboos and Durkheimian sacred/profane distinctions, or subsequent shifts in ideas about how these issues operate.[9] For example, in theoretical conditions that Durkheim designated "church," the center is "sacred" (set-apart), the periphery profane. In Mauss's alternative ideal-type of magic, the margins are "sacred," the center routinized (see Chap. 6). Scholars influenced by *L'Année sociologique* (e.g., Mary Douglas) have dealt with classificatory boundaries and their conscious-raising interstices—categorical "dirt" Douglas once inventively deemed it (see Chap. 12). Edmund Leach stressed ambivalances of boundaries themselves over and against what they divide:

> A boundary separates two zones of social space-time which are *normal, time-bound, clear-cut, central, secular,* but the spatial and temporal markers which actually serve as boundaries are themselves abnormal, timeless, ambiguous at the edge, sacred.[10]

Although Leach still posed binary oppositions, he argued that any organizing apparatus must be repressed if what it categorizes is to be experienced. That fact puts transgression at the heart of perception, conceptualization, and, I think, orthodoxy.

My work draws on everything just mentioned, especially Geertz's sense of systems of suasion. I accentuate dialectics implicit in *L'Année sociologique* scholarship and add dashes of deconstruction, where evidence invites. I take ritual to be constitutive, not reflective; it reduces to neither disguise nor compensation. Yes, ritual is language-like, but not just in a structuralist sense; language involves both grammar and rhetoric, and rhetoric produces both help and harm, actively. "Ritual-*cum*-rhetoric" attaches insistent distinctions and contentious differences to whatever societies circulate in and as time. These productions and reproductions—"cultures"—include differed corpses, differed babies, differed bodies, differed tears, differed laughter, differed texts, and differed negations and resistances and desires.[11]

Ritual and rhetoric enacted and interpreted in time—chronotopes, if you prefer—entail certain "politics of transgression"—to borrow a slogan from Peter Stallybrass and Allon White. "How far," they rhetorically ask, "does carnivalesque transgression remain complicit with the rules and structures which it infringes, and how far does it really subvert and radically interrogate those rules and structures?"[12] That question remains "central" to any work "on the margins."

GOLDBERG VARIATIONS

Mention of Geertz helps me segue into recent New Historicists who now "periodicize" their trade into progressive *versus* passé—the cliché of disciplinary upheaval. For example, Jonathan Goldberg's *James I and the Politics of Literature* (1983) once conveyed sympathy for un-universalist, nondeterminist, anti-antirelativist interpretation of cultures, à la Geertz. Recently, however,

Goldberg has declared a new New Historicism, said to have outgrown naive idealizations in the earlier brand—represented by Stephen Greenblatt. I have my doubts about Goldberg's narrative of progress; let me explain them.

Goldberg's latterday phase appears to be twofold: his *Writing Matter* (1990) turns further towards deconstruction, or its presentiments in Elizabethan-Jacobean practices of *écriture*; his *Sodometries: Renaissance Texts, Modern Sexualities* (1992) swerves into contemporary sexual politics, joining forces with late Foucault and Eve Sedgwick—on guard against homophobia in any history or historiography whatsoever.[13] The revised critical agenda prefers that nothing—sexuality, above all—remain "closeted," "privatized," or otherwise mired in bourgeois propensities for furtive meanings and secreted *sens*. Proponents seem ready and willing to risk overgeneralizing their particular *cause* by making the past (or its prejudices) feel very much like the present—particularly where gay issues are at stake. Indeed, dangers of "presentism" may afford *un certain frisson* to readers of *Sodometries*. Unfortunately, that response can marginalize other differences that surely "made a difference" in times gone by.

To illustrate what I mean, let me question one element of Goldberg's fascinating account of early modern tropes of "sodomy." He covers James I and rumored *semblables*, plus representations of subjugated populations branded as sodomists in European iconography of exotica. His book makes much of sexual preferences, but little of religious preferences—Catholic/Protestant, for example. Yet, it was Huguenot invective that disseminated ideas that "sodomy" resulted when specific native populations had been contaminated by contact with Papists. (I broached this material in *Other Tribes, Other Scribes*.)[14] Goldberg's index abounds in "H" entries—"Homophobia," "Homosexuality," "Homosocial Relations"—but lacks "Huguenot." On the other hand his book is garlanded (a bit too decoratively, perhaps) with that distinctly *Huguenot* iconography, all the more eye-catching for being "decontextualized"—fetchingly exposed to readers' gaze for its possible resonances with homoerotic/homophobic issues. The iconography is simultaneously sanitized of meanings that—for Protestants *then*—"othered" both Papists and peoples *they* presumably tainted.

Goldberg helps open readings of Renaissance evidence to gendered body parts and prejudicial restrictions on which may be lodged where—including a category of practice called "sodometries." Does he also mean to privilege identities forged around "sexualities" ("modern" or otherwise), to advance sexual preferences as linchpins in politics of empowerment? Goldberg's commendably artful argumentation makes it difficult to discern just how far his new New History wishes to go in this regard. But *Sodometries*—as decorated and marketed—seems to encourage inklings among implied readers that sexual politics is "determinate." The book *looks* coyly calculated to further this conviction in reception. If so, it wages its own politics of mastery and appropriation, where one school of differences effaces others.

I leave to specialists quarrels over historical relations between "modern sexualities" and sixteenth-century representations. I only recommend that the "sexual" not occlude the "religious"—such as Huguenots' hatred of "Papists" (and vice versa)—surely central in the margins of prejudice, both past and present. But I have a bolder hypothesis that brings the older history of religions and newish histories of representation closer together. Contemporary politics of such "identities" as "sexualities" may themselves be a variation on earlier politics of such "meanings" as sectarian divisions. For the sake of accord, let me designate the latter "sect-ualities." I would place Early Modern sect-ualities and modern "sexualities" in a longish *durée* of heterodox resistances to diverse regimes of normative propriety. My proposed analogy (similitude?) between solidarities of "sexualities" today and solidarities of "sect-ualities" of yore may even resonate with a Foucauldian perspective more fully than do theories attached to a contemporary *cause*. That is a big possibility of and for the ever-transforming "margins."

HIERARCHIES AND HETERODOXIES
(COMPARATIVE INSTITUTIONS)

Louis Dumont's work—as controversial in some ways as Goldberg's in others—addressed hierarchy in both Indic and Western circumstances. Dumont saw hierarchical differences as relational and reciprocal, charged with complementarity and conceivable reversibility. Hierarchy does not simply "stratify" pure over impure, but poses high priests of the impure along with high priests of the pure. Hierarchy implies a double apex (King *and* Priest) and a double nadir as well. In contrast to hierarchy stand other systems of inequality Dumont called "stratification"—with a singular apex, taxonomized rank, and a flat base; examples are regiments and bureaucracies.[15]

Dumont's anthropology ranges from Brahmanical *varna* schemes of ritual divisions of labor, to Christian schemes of liturgical specializations. Both cases integrally link hierarchal differences to their antithesis: renunciation. The dialectical conjunction of hierarchy-renunciation is opposed to the countersocial ideology Dumont calls individual*ism*. Building on Marcel Mauss, Max Weber, and others, Dumont emphasizes individualism's definitive triumph over hierarchy when Western "political economy" became consolidated as a distinct sphere of value. (Opponents of Dumont's Indian studies argue that he neglects individualist aspects of South Asian circumstances both contemporarily and historically; here I set aside these important disputes to concentrate on Europe.)[16]

In *From Mandeville to Marx* (1977) Dumont's critique of categorical "political economy" implicates Adam Smith, John Locke, and Karl Marx, among other inventors of "modernity." His work on Christian sources of individualism stretches to far earlier transformations of inworldly activity. It compares Christian premodern temporal/ecclesiastical distinctions to the double apex of Hindu hierarchy—priest-king for purity-power respectively. Because this is hardly a new idea, let me sketch a few of Dumont's angles.

Europe's "pedigree of modern individualism" stems from a "long chain of shifts" that transformed outworldly renunciation by individual ascetics into inworldly activity by ascetic individualists. A "hierarchical relativization" associated with Origen's distinction between ecclesiastical and temporal spheres became more manifest around A.D. 500:

> The reference to salvation clearly indicates that Gelasius deals here with the supreme or ultimate level of consideration. We note the hierarchical distinction between the priest's *auctoritas* and the king's *potestas*. . . . That is, the priest is subordinate to the king in mundane matters that regard the public order. . . . the level of consideration has shifted from the height of salvation to the lowliness of worldly affairs. Priests are superior, for they are inferior only on an inferior level. We are not dealing . . . with mere submission of kings to priests [i.e., with mere singular "stratification"], but with *hierarchical complementarity*. (1982: 14)[17]

Dumont here draws parallels *not* with Brahmanic India but with Vedic India, which showed "exactly the same configuration . . .: priests . . . religiously . . . superior to the king while materially subject to him" (14). The Indian case contains neither corporate unity of the faithful nor unitary organization of a priesthood; and the renouncer had yet to appear. But in both the Western and the Vedic configuration, "hierarchy is logically opposed to power"; it does not yet claim to transcribe itself in terms of power (15).

Dumont amplifies implications for the Western Church and State: "If the Church is *in* the Empire with respect to worldly matters, the Empire is *in* the Church regarding things divine" (15). Legal-minded scholastic thinkers subsequently converted hierarchical oppositions into rigid distinctions, reducing a "rich, structural, flexible use of the basic opposition . . . to unidimensional, substantial matters of either-or . . . distinctions" (15). Dumont's argument here parallels opening chapters of his *Homo hierarchicus*, which exposed colonialist theories that misconstrued caste as centralized stratification rather than multilocal hierarchies.

Dumont's coverage of European history next jumps halfway toward the modern State:

> For Gelasius's hierarchical dyarchy is substituted a monarchy of unprecedented type, a spiritual monarchy . . . the spiritual is conceived as superior to the temporal *on the temporal level itself*, as if it was a superior degree of the temporal . . . a "squared temporal." (17)

This "perversion of hierarchy" foreshadowed the emergence of an absolutist political sphere; the economic stage was thus set for calculating Capitalism and the religious stage for Calvin. Again, Dumont recalls Weber (and Troeltsch) in his boldness:

> My thesis is simple: with Calvin, the hierarchical dichotomy that characterized our field of consideration comes to an end; the antagonistic worldly element that individualism had hitherto to accommodate disappears entirely in Calvin's theocracy. The field is absolutely unified [one might better say, de-divided]. *The individual is now in the world, and the individualist value rules without restriction or limitation*. The individual is before us. . . . Hierarchical dualism is replaced by a flat continuum governed by an either/or choice. (19)

To summarize Dumont's argument: Long-term Judeo-Christian processes episodically converted holistic, social assumptions into inworldly ascetic-like practices. Diarchy and temporal/ ecclesiastical distinctions were thus ablated, and calculated gain was legitimated. Individualism became the optimal action associated with utilitarian political economy.[18]

Profound consequences for the religious sector are conveyed dramatically in Dumont's reading of Calvin:

> In the name of the self-sufficiency of the individual-in-relation-to-God, [Luther and Calvin] cancel the division of religious labor instituted by the Church. At the same time . . . Calvin most distinctly accepts . . . the unification obtained by the Church on the political side. (24)

The ultimate result for the West is institutionalization of an autonomous, "purely political" sphere; Dumont drives this theme home:

> . . . the modern State is not in continuity with other political forms; it is a transformed Church, as is readily seen in the fact of its not being made up of different functions or orders, but rather of individuals, a point which even Hegel failed to admit. (17)

Dumont's work on hierarchy-renunciation versus individualism remains sharply debatable, among Indianists and Europeanists alike. No less controversial in his anthropology of India are ideas about comparative "margins" beyond familiar institutional sectors of Varnas, sects, dominant castes, untouchability, and purity/power relations. These margins that mingle transgression with propriety include Tantric formations. (Here I draw in part from my *Affinities and Extremes*.)

Dumont's work on South Asia situates caste codes among antithetical values of renunciation, diverse developments of centralization (e.g., Mogul India, British Colonial India, nationalist India), and conventions of noncentralized exchange relations (e.g., Dravidian kinship terminologies). Sectarian movements too, enter the arena of hierarchical differences—including Buddhist and Sikh, each with its overarching vantage. Additionally, undercurrents of Tantric counterpositions "ambiguate" the history of differential identities. Dumont calls the Tantras a "truly fundamental variant of Indic histories," an antithesis to "caste" separations that is itself antithetical to caste's other antithesis: renunciation. (Weber, by the way, anticipated him here.)[19] Whether in Hindu or Buddhist variants, Tantric practices make "sacramental" what orthodoxy restricts: e.g., meat, fish, alcohol, sexual intercourse. Tantrists renounce, so to speak, renunciation, in a way that rehabilitates enjoyment (bhoga). "Tantrism," you might say, is heterodoxy "proper."

It should come as no surprise that the "ism" part of so-called Tantrism is a European coinage.[20] Regardless, Tantric practices do actually happen, sub-dogmatically. Moreover, even if the practices are only suspected—only attributed by "centrist" practitioners to their neighbors or rivals—that fact itself has real consequences, when "orthodox" persuasions frame an "other" within. There are, moreover, "extremes" of the Tantric "extreme"—left-hand as opposed to more conformist right-hand Tantrism; the former outdoes the latter in reversing standards of what is either acceptable or "sacramental."

Usages customarily designated Tantric, whether Hindu or Buddhist, do not necessarily mark off any corporate identity of "ism" (even underground). They include a gamut of transgressions—a polymorphous reservoir of ex-centric ritual possibilities. These "impurities" may be flirted with, or even adopted, by centrist sectors: Brahmanical codes, mainstream renouncers, successful sects (Lingayats, Sikhs, etc.), dynastic courts, institutions of state control, market forces of production/consumption, etc.

Again, Tantric texts and practices in Indic circumstances effectively renounce renunciation. But renouncing renunciation is a renunciation in its own right—one that echoes aspects of what it resists. (I advise against any easy comparisons with either Christian or post-Christian themes of Erlösung dem Erlöser, "redemption to the redeemer," so difficult to tag as Aufhebung, heresy, or both.)[21]

Dumont tackled Tantric dimensions on the Indic side of his comparative research only briefly. I mention them here to broach the matter of European equivalents. Possible parallels include a range of hermetic heterodoxies— Gnostic, Neoplatonist, Kabbalistic—along with institutions of carnivalized resistance that punctuate Western "history." Europe too displays episodic reverse-hierarchies opposing, in agonistic complementarity, what has been "established," "reformed," and "counterreformed" in turn.[22] Both against and through marginal murmurs of resistance (heteropraxy?), Western orthodoxy-cum-heterodoxy has been shaped, transformed, and "motived." (Again, the term "murmur" I filch from Foucault [1970]; "motive" I co-opt from Kenneth Burke [1962].)

Similarly, Tantric values and contestations are propagated through rites, texts, and tactics (in de Certeau's [1984] sense) that are not doctrinal, seldom corporate, and not necessarily cultic even subterraneanly. (I question any approach that inevitably implies cryptic hermetic creeds of Tantrism—

M. Eliade's history of religions, most prominently.)[23] Tantric tactics can run contrary to different orthodox "denominations" simultaneously (e.g., Hindu/ Buddhist in Indicized realms; compare Catholic/Protestant in Christianized Neoplatonist realms). Significant parts of history's cultures happen through and as dispersals of edgy practices like "Tantric" ones (Boon 1982a: Chap. 5; 1990a: 116–70).

Thus, to students of margins I commend an extra-Vagant interpretive "scene"—"Tantric topoi," where provocative questions intensify. Do the multiple heterodoxies of manifold hierarchy operate differently than the "excluded" ranks of simpler styles of stratification? Have marginalized voices—the Pardoner's voices, Ghetto voices—gained resonance by remaining unincorporated, disturbingly dispersed? Not quite invisible, opaque polymorphoses refract forces of regimental surveillance, evade bureaucratic stratification, and dodge centralized control. Some "Tantric practices" may be better at "deviating" from enforced conformity than are sect-ualities or sexualities when "identitied," incorporated, or made into a dogmatic *cause*. My questions and suggestions are offered as more food for critical thought "on the margins" or along what Deleuze might call their rhizomes.[24]

COPIOUS RHETORICS THAT SUBJUGATE
(COMPARATIVE DISCOURSES)

Colonialist representations marginalize intricately (see Boon 1990a: Chaps. 1–2). This fact can be illustrated by an 1803 *Edinburgh Review* that summarized Robert Percival's British survey of cultures in Ceylon, which busily denigrated every difference in sight—"wild men," Cingalese, Candians, Portuguese, Dutch. My example itself may seem marginal both to pre-Enlightenment Europe (this conference's *spécialité*) and to Bali's twists on Tantrisms in colonialist-nationalist Indonesia (mine). But history is not so neatly compartmentalized. Clusters of topoi about Ceylon actually descend from previous tropes, including medieval and Early Modern ones in Europe; and Anglo/ Dutch rivalries affected the East Indies as well.

That said, let me summarize the British colonial report in question. It portrays Candians, who had partly subjugated upland "Cingalese" and successfully resisted the Dutch. (Readers, beware: to current sensibilities the following passage seems "racist"):

> The King of Candia is of course despotic; and the history of his life and reign presents the same monotonous ostentation, and baby-like caprice, which characterises oriental governments. In public audiences, he appears like a great fool, squatting on his hams; far surpassing gingerbread in splendour; and, after asking some such idiotical question, as whether Europe is in Asia or Africa, retires with

a flourish of trumpets very much out of tune. . . . For his private amusement, he rides on the nose of an elephant . . .; if his tea is not sweet enough, he impales his footman; and smites off the heads of half a dozen of his noblemen, if he has a pain in his own. (141–42)[25]

Also skewered are Malays, transported to Ceylon by the Dutch, to serve as brokers, soldiers, and servants. (Readers, be alerted: to current sensibilities the following passage seems "racist"):

> The Malays are the most vindictive and ferocious of living beings . . . having thus broken the great tie which renders man a being capable of being governed. . . . A Malay servant, from the apprehension excited by his vindictive disposition, often becomes the master of his master. It is as dangerous to dismiss him, as to punish him; and the rightful despot, in order to avoid assassination, is almost compelled to exchange characters with his slave . . . however . . . the Malay . . . submits to the severest military discipline. . . . When assassins and bloodhounds will fall into rank, and file, and the most furious savages submit (with no diminution of their ferocity) to the science and discipline of war, they only want a Malay Bonaparte to lead them to the conquest of the world. . . . one day or another, when they are more full of opium than usual, they *will run a muck*, from Cape Comorin to the Caspian. (139–140)

Nor did the British neglect a European Other in Ceylon. (Readers, stand fore-warned: to current sensibilities the following passage seems "racist"):

> The descendants of the Portuguese differ materially from the Moors, Malabars, and other Mahometans. Their great object is to show the world they are Europeans and Christians. Unfortunately, their ideas of Christianity are so imperfect, that the only mode they can hit upon of displaying their faith, is by wearing hats and breeches, and, by these habiliments, they consider themselves as showing a proper degree of contempt, on various parts of the body, towards Mahomet and Buddha. They are lazy, treacherous, effeminate, and passionate to excess; and are, in fact, a locomotive and animated farrago of the bad qualities of all tongues, people, and nations on the face of the earth. (139)

And those Brits even targeted a Protestant "other," or perhaps "rational" other: the most threatening Other of all (actually described first). (Attention readers: to current sensibilities the following passage seems "racist"):

> Ceylon is now inhabited by the English; the remains of the Dutch, and Portuguese, the Cingalese or natives, subject to the dominion of the Europeans; the Candians subject to the king of their own name; and the Vaddahs, or wild men, subject to no power. A Ceylonese Dutchman is a coarse, grotesque species of animal, whose native apathy and phlegm is animated only by the insolence of a colonial tyrant: His principal amusement appears to consist in smoking; . . . almost as much a necessary function of animal life, as his breathing. His day is eked out with gin,

ceremonious visits, and prodigious quantities of gross food dripping with oil and butter; his mind, just able to reach from one meal to another, is incapable of farther exertion; and, after the panting and deglutition, of a long protracted dinner, reposes on the sweet expectation that, in a few hours, the carnivorous toil will be renewed. He lives only to digest. . . . (139)

Such virtuoso vituperation, then, does not simply polarize a defamed "other" against a superior "us"; rather it *multiplies* inflected images of excess, reserving special venom for the "nearly us"—portrayed familiarly as possibly the most recognizably "monstrous." For the British that uncannily similar *other* was the Dutch.

Profligate rhetorics of this sort have a long history—from Lucian's second-century *True Story* (and doubtless Hellenist narratives before), to our own day (and doubtless after). English is but one of the world's expansive languages that has catalogued excessively varieties of cultural differences. Moreover, rhetorics of vituperation (this topic too is Burke's) do not restrict themselves to remote borderlands or to "class-action" marginals divided, conquered, subjugated, stigmatized, and crowded into a bottom lump.[26] Rather, commonplaces of defamation proliferate across many statuses and peoples, including rivals and competitors far from abject. Like hierarchies, such rhetorics are neither singular nor polar; they thrive on real multiplicities of marginality. That may be one reason why vituperative rhetorics are so difficult to quash. (Think again of Venice's Ghetto and its successors; and remember that Pardoner.)

But quash them we must, perhaps by raveling the rhetorics and turning against them their own flourishes. This could become a central critical endeavor. Godspeed.

CHAPTER TEN

Evermore Derrida, Always the Same
(What Gives?)

This piece derives—Derridarives?—from a bona fide obligation that I contracted through another's initiative: to review for publication an English "translation" of Donner le temps *by one J. D. (The wages for my labor were scale). The original's tone was a bit different, but its concrete conclusion was the same. I must therefore claim-confess a laughably miniscule share of credit-blame-guilt in helping Derridaism gain further footing in the plural world of knowing-doubt and ignoring debt. For,* Given Time I: Counterfeit Money *now exists, and can be purchased. I have not pursued its equally lettristic sequel.*

One quandary is worth noting: To what "reader" would a "reviewer" have written her or his remarks? For the sake of reception, the reader might be assigned the name "Darride."[1]

> And if you look closely enough at capitalist motives, as the secularization
> of priestly symbolism, you can glimpse a similar roundabout development
> (signalized in the doctrine that profit on capital investment is justified
> as a reward for "postponed consumption").
> (*Kenneth Burke,* Rhetoric of Motives)

DEAR ME, more Derrida, always-already ever-ready, as it were, to keep going and going: Derridean. *Given Time* (a pun of Proustian resourcefulness) consists of episodic pages of lectures-inscribed. Their every line instantiates positions Derrida takes regarding duration and experiential-economic "expense"; their every line also implicates any relationship being negotiated with presumed readers. Derrida's text underwrites that relationship as part of the politics of duplicitous, counterfeiting exchange and evasion. Counterfeit exchange-evasion numbers among his works' most repeated tics (I first wrote "themes," but scratched this slip).

The reader's time of reading *Given Time* involves him or her in a discourse on madness (the madness of "pure gift"). And:

> This discourse on madness appears to go mad in its turn, *alogos or atopos . . .*
> *Atopos*, as you know, means that which is not in its place (noon at two o'clock)
> [Derrida's rather engaging, recurring device] and thus the extraordinary, the un-

usual, strange, extravagant, absurd, mad. Only an *atopic* and *utopic* madness could thus, perhaps, give rise to a gift that can only give on the condition of not taking place, taking up residence or domicile. (Chap. 2; all my essay's quotations derive from the typescript reviewed of *Given Time*, doubtless revised in print—given time.)

Evidently denying to discourses other than his own recognition of this madness-in-the-gift, Derrida credits *his* writing's traces with escaping (or evading) domiciled exchange. And he takes the reader (or "listener," in the figural vestiges of his text-as-lectures) along for the ride.

In its effort to forego "the language of restitution," Derrida's brazen book becomes either the most honest tome imaginable or the most deceitful one. (Actually this artful credit is due Melville's *Confidence Man*, a work Derrida should memorize, untranslated.) Whether or not deciding *which*—honest? deceitful?—would matter, is part of what Derrida is about. That's "deconstruction," folks, although to so name it is to rob it of half its (maddening) charm.

Given Time's lectures are de-organized into teasing delays, toying postponements, "temporizing detours" (Chap. 3), and nonstop pretexts and "excuses" (Chap. 2). They skirt margins of the history of philosophical reflections on time, memory-forgetting, antitheses of exchange, and issues of liberality. The whole book—or its denial of being able to be "whole"—exercises displacement. The author requires readers to submit themselves to being disregarded, as a psychoanalyst might require a patient—or, in Derrida's focal case, as Baudelaire's counterfeit-alms-giver might require a beggar, or a friend to whom he retails his pitiless transgression. The course of Derrida's chapters constantly reiterates this policy, replays this trick (my metaphor is drawn from "contract" bridge).

So deviated—like a septum (my simile is drawn from the nose)—are Derrida's lectures-inscribed that they even defer delay (Chap. 2). Yet readers should not confuse delay-deferred with a *present*. To do so would again be to stumble into logocentrism. One aphoristic nutshell for the study—contrasted with the possibly *faux* epigraph that actually launches it—occurs in the textual horizons of Chapter 1:

THE NECESSITY OF SUCH A DISPLACEMENT IS OF THE HIGHEST INTEREST. IT OFFERS US NEW RESOURCES OF ANALYSIS, IT ALERTS US TO THE TRAPS OF THE WOULD-BE *GIFT* WITHOUT DEBT, IT ACTIVATES OUR CRITICAL OR ETHICAL VIGILANCE. (My *majuscules*, mock-aping Mallarmé)

Is that enough for a book to do? By Derridean lights, presumably.

The as-if book seems to engage, and does, some writings of Baudelaire in a way that thrills this reader, as might an ecstatic *interpretation* unexpectedly happened upon during the ordeal/pleasure of enduring deconstruction's relentless drone. Derrida also manages to keep Mallarmé's legendary dice-throw up in the air. These contributions strike me as the book's strong suit.[2]

The as-if book also seems to engage, but does not (concertedly) the writings of Marcel Mauss and Émile Benveniste on "gifts" (*don-da-gab*), and mutual indebtedness-guilt (*Schuld*), and credit. At issue is the constitution of social life (and its resistance) through exchange transactions versus market transactions, as surveyed in comparative ethnology by Mauss or in the history of Indo-European vocabularies by Benveniste.[3] Derrida's short-changings here fill this reader with misgivings (see below).

CONTRIBUTIONS

Given Time sports exhilarating insights about Baudelaire—poet-critic of capital and of France's capitol; his *poème en prose*, "*La fausse monnaie*" intones an ultimate scene of commodity-exchange: a beggar beduped by an alms-giving fraud.[4] Baudelaire may represent for Derrida the urbane, evasive transgressive voice of "undomicilability." (Could it be that Derrida "identifies" with this position? What generous reader would deny him that right, even if he begrudges such sentimentality to others?)

The book's *écriture* unfurls around an epigraph, "The King takes all my time; I give the rest to Saint-Cyr, to whom I would like to give all." This section may be a ruse or counterfeit as well; it admits possibly hijacking the epigraph into literality. Derrida also knows how to appeal to feminist readers: "It's a woman who signs." (Is this section's appeal token?) The epigraph section disseminates a rhetoric of what I call "woodchuck chucking": "She lacks not lacking time, she lacks not giving enough. . . ." Other readers might call it casuistry (a suspicion Derrida also plays upon later).

Chapter 2 initiates a disquisition on money, nonmoney, counterfeit, minted coin, metaphors minted, titled money, and the "tricky referential structure of a title" (Chap. 3). The punning intensifies as the text approaches Baudelaire's scene of counterfeiting. Derrida's writing here, as usual, is too brilliant for words. (But why must he keep trying to "score" against Mauss-on-money—a project interrupted by Mauss's mind's tragic arrest. Why are such matters not for-given by Derrida, not *appreciated* as another's "excuse"?)

Derrida might also have cited, say, Simmel's *Philosophy of Money*. But "citing" is one gesture of acknowledgement routinely displaced by Derrida. He once mentions work on the topic of "money" (I mean the *atopical* position of money's liquidity) by Marc Shell. Shell's work, versed in philosophy-as-economics, also engages exchange's cancellations—e.g., incest. Like Derrida, Shell responds to structuralist exchange-theory with a certain edginess.[5]

Derrida's pages on Baudelaire are worth the book, or pretend to be; they advance deconstructive "critical vigilance" into fertile ground. Chapter 3 broaches Baudelaire's "dedication of the book *Le Spleen de Paris, Paris Spleen* of which 'Counterfeit Money' is but an excised morsel . . . a cash conversion of a whole." As expected, the title "Counterfeit Money" doubles back on its own counterfeit nature *as title* (Derrida on titles calls to my doubtless nostalgic *esprit* Kenneth Burke's "entitlings").[6] Derrida also addresses TOBACCO, or the *tabac*, with a nod to Native American evidence that (I bet) concerns him not one whit. (Nor may colonialist history, at whose threshhold tobacco places us, truly concern him.) Derrida next justifies indirect, impersonal *écriture*, where the issue of sincerity cannot apply. We then meet again that only apparently absent *woman*; and *presto*, the whole opening epigraph turns out to have been only ostensibly *sous rature*—a counterfeit-cancellation, you might say. The epigraph has remained something of a subtext (if such a "hidden thing" were permissible in Derridean reading). And Poe, and pipes, and purloined letters, crowd in *encore*; particularly Baudelaire's *pipe*.[7] Again, the take on "Counterfeit Money," plus allusions to moments in Baudelaire's *oeuvre*, is gripping. Chapter 3 may be (implicitly) about "greed"; it leaves readers greedy for more.

Chapter 4 meditates on possibilities of "freedom" or true-gift as embodied in counterfeit nonobligating, narrated to a friend; this is vintage Derrida (like a *controlled* wine). These pages characterize city life's positionality—all "alienatedness" and passing-acquaintances. (Baudelaire's loitering profanely sacralized such a situation, as few have—although Simmel was one of them. Thank goodness Simmel's *Philosophy of Money* was there for Max Weber to read when he desperately needed it.)[8] Sure, Derrida remains puckish: his cagey disquisitions on tobacco as *sur*-gift make fleeting mention of Lévi-Strauss's *Du Miel aux cendres* (1966), from which Derrida could be suspected (were suspicion in play) of pilfering the very equation of *cendres* with "traces". This near "lack" was all the more conspicuous (in the version I reviewed) because Derrida (nostalgically?) revisits much more elaborately all his old complaints against Lévi-Strauss.[9] (Regardless, all the *tabac* business may always-already be entangled with Richard Klein's *Cigarettes are Sublime*, anyway; who knows?)[10]

Chapter 4 also remembers to reinscribe scenes of philosophy proper: the *polis* and the metro*polis*, of both Greece and the capitalist state. Again, "Tobacco seems to open up on the scene of desire beyond need." And then the "café," locus classicus (and locus capitalistus?) of philosophizing. Derrida's moves unwind toward a discussion of *fors*. (There is no mention of Ruskin, however, although Derrida is re-covering his ground, as does Marc Shell *with acknowledgment*.)[11] Acknowledgment—thanks offered for debt-incurred—is NOT what Derrida's writing is about. This dearth could be held against it. Still, by chapter's end—or stopping—a tour de force has been turned (whether counterfeit or not) of something like a history of the Western philosophy of ethics (and economy).

If a reader were obliged in howling irony to designate a climax (not part of Derrida's antilanguage game), it may occur somewhere between these lines (or blinds) of Chapter 4:

> The all powerful cause of the cause in the pleasure I give myself by giving it to the other. An intoxicating pleasure, like tobacco or drugs [e.g., caffeine] to be as close as possible to the auto-affective *causa sui.*

And:

> That is why the friend's response is so impervious to deciphering.

And:

> The gift would be that which does not obey the principle of reason: It is, it must be, it owes itself to be without reason, without wherefore and without foundation.

Perhaps Derrida desires *Given Time*—this narrative consuming time—to be impervious to deciphering, while implying all his previous positions. Derrida can only win this game hands down, as the book's last words imply: "Would this history be, among others, all of history? In any case, and at least, a certain history of philosophy." A *certaine histoire*, I for one, gladly grant him. How such a tale became rather imperious in deconstructive circles is one of the stranger outcomes of our academic age, odd enough already.

MISGIVINGS

I find perplexing Derrida's apparent desire to restore, of all things, an aloof tradition of authorized philosophical skepticism back through a privileged set of predecessors.[12] What else *could* one call this than a "legacy?" Towards that quaint end, he "instrumentalizes" paradoxical evidence borrowed from ethnography and history. *Given Time*, for example, foregrounds "the impossibility or the double bind of the gift: for there to be gift, it is necessary that the gift not even appear, that it not be perceived or received as gift." Derrida then glosses the paradox as the necessary "forgetting of the gift," an "oblivion so radical that it exceeds even the psychoanalytic categoriality of oblivion."

All that is fine, except that Derrida thereby wrests indirect "recognition" of this paradox of gift-forgotten not just from the scholars whom he deems inadequate, nostalgic, or guilty of "exchangist rationality"; he also wrests recognition from the ritual practices of societies engaged in "categorialities" and their resistances.

Derrida is an absolute master at troping upon "absolute forgetting," (or a "forgetting that absolves," which sounds to me vaguely like Augustine).[13]

Equally endowed are Derrida's *figures* of cinder-like traces of radical forget-ting—"forgottenness" is "not nothing," although it leaves nothing behind and effaces everything. All this suggests, again, a virtual Derridian *summa*. To direct his philosophical points toward/against Heidegger's *Being and Time* may be fine; I leave that to high flyers. But to direct these points toward/against Mauss's "Essai sur le don" obligates (or so one, huffily, "would think") Derrida to *credit* paradoxical traces to comparative evidence. But that would im-ply in turn that among such evidence Derrida's *own* position can be no more than that: *a* position. Instead, Derrida hoards the very possibility of awareness of such paradox for his name-brand philosophical attitude. That strikes me as unduly stingy.

I may just be repeating what is obvious, but often forgotten and/or forgiven by (counterfeit?) friends of J.D.: Derrida is no comparativist or historian. He is also no translator of those differences (of languages, institutions, discourses) that are not lorded over by himself—the latest incarnation of anti-*philosophie*. Neither, perhaps, was Nietzsche; but Nietzsche and his readings suffered, were never blithe; for Nietzsche everything he resisted and despised counted. Nietzsche seems to me, perhaps perversely, far more giving than Derrida. Per-haps Nietzsche was just an old Romantic-modern, living down his father (a Lutheran pastor) and Wagner as well, so suspiciously a substitute father-figure (any "Oedipus" would know what to do).[14] On the other hand, perhaps not.

Derrida characteristically refuses to credit Mauss with appreciating (my metaphor is economic) the paradox that separates exchange from "pure gift." Yet Mauss did address wide-ranging ethnological evidence of—if not "pure gift" exactly (though this is debatable)—reciprocal giving-debt. Such matters are implicit in social *anticipations* of giving-debt reciprocally. Complexities of this issue are addressed in a vital literature by scholars as different as Marshall Sahlins, Michel de Certeau, Lewis Hyde, Michèle Richman, Louis Dumont, . . . [15] I do not pretend that Derrida should refer generously to this work nor that his habitual readers would expect him to. It would be futile to want the likes of Derrida, having certainly done (and *donné*) enough, to do more; credit can't be fair.

Still, the "more" (than ever-more "Derrida") I churlishly might have ex-pected from *Le Temps donné* is to credit Mauss's concern with institutions of "giving/taking" that yields a return (*donner-rendre/prendre*). Doesn't Mauss afford glimpses of zero-degree debt-giving practices? Do not the exchange systems, and economy-sacrifice cycles, and magical sprees he compared dis-play aspects of Dionysiac excess (overexpending, in Bataille's sense of *dépense*)? Surely, Mauss's overlapping studies disclosed gambling and, in-deed, counterfeiting as *sur*-economic (ultraeconomic) rather than antiecon-omic. Slighting these possibilities, Derrida contrives a way to deduct Mauss's stress on potlatch (not to mention *arts de magie*) as testimony to the "madness" inherent in presumed exchange-order. Derrida seems to imply that philosophical (or political) *naïveté* explains Mauss's "idealizing" (in Durkheim's sense) premarket prestations.[16]

Given Time's take on Mauss reminds me of what Paul de Man once showed: Derrida appropriates deconstructive moves already given by (and as) the texts of, say, Rousseau.[17] A similar foreclosing of Mauss's multiplicities is passingly executed here. Derrida is legendarily adept at such moves. What tolerant reader would want to stop him in his tracks and tricks? Any pages Derrida writes warrant reception, if only to determine if his critique will ever happen-back (specifically, I mean, and not just in the wave of blanket-books "against deconstruction," too generally diagnosed).[18] *Given Time* may or may not escape accountability (as a commodity) in the ethic of pure-gifting and alms-giving that Derrida seems desirous of offering as an advance over "exchangist" ethics.

To repeat, it is too bad that Derrida neglects many responses to Mauss and ethnographies both "behind" *Le Don* and informed by it since. Derrida picayunishly—perhaps even inaccurately—faults Mauss for failing to envision true gift. He notes that Mauss and some colleagues opposed both capitalist mercantilism and Marxist communism; but he barely appreciates how the "liberal socialism" that Mauss commended relates to ethnological evidence of noncentralized exchange-systems that preoccupied him. When Derrida says in passing that "one can only give what one has," he may have failed to "dedomicile" his own positions from "economism."[19] Has Derrida forgotten those paradoxes of alliance-exchange whereby value is bestowed only on that which, at base, cannot be retained—wherein value exists precisely as what is preinscribed to be *produced* as another's due? If *societies* are in the business of giving-indebtedness, why shouldn't Mauss (and many backers and detractors) survey and interpret variations in these arrangements without concentrating exclusively on "pure gift"—that (really not surprising) antithesis to giving-debt. (The "topic" of exchange's *atopos* is tackled in many institutionalized practices of renunciation, and studies of them—Buddhist "alms-giving," for example.)[20]

Part of *Given Time* (Chap. 2) sings Derrida's old song against "transcendental signifieds" (now "transcendental gifts") which he equates with God-terms logocentrically retained by non-deconstructive theorists. Unless, of course, Derrida's petty-sounding swipes at Mauss for "giving self-satisfied terminology lessons to the authors he has been citing" are designed to echo the very irritations to which Derrida subjects his readers (as-if listeners). Another case in point: Derrida chides Mauss for seeming to say to his readers, "Forget . . . all the foregoing pages, we'll have to begin all over again." These swipes at Mauss may also be self-mocking. Indeed, everything that Derrida says against Mauss, or any other figure in this work, can only repeat the *misgivings* his text is given to incur—can only second readers' suspicions regarding Derrida. A third case in point: Derrida charges Mauss's note on money with deception and apparent self-deception—"paying us with words while talking a lot of hot air." So, who could fault Derrida, confessedly guilty (*schuld*) of every debt he figures and annuls? (How like a savior!—minus redemption.)

Indeed, Chapter 4 seems literally to be about *parDONning Derrida*:

> As cause and condition of the thing [*chose*], it is the narrative that *gives* the possibility of the recounted thing, the possibility of the story as story of a gift or of a forgiveness . . . also impossibility. . . . So that is the kind of narrative we read.

Pardon is granted. I surrender to his confessional techniques. Readers more interested in Maori (among many other cultural practices that Mauss compared) than in Heidegger (among many other philosophers that Derrida positions) will likely leave critiquing Derrida to other philosophers and/or prose-poets. Followers who take Derrida-on-Mauss as a substitute for reading Mauss's *Gift* (about Maori, India, Trobriands, Kwakiutl, and France, among other cultures) will suffer a loss like those who took Derrida-on-Lévi-Strauss as a substitute for reading *Tristes tropiques* (see Chap. 11). But losses can be redeemed, given time.

Given Time in the meantime rests content to deconstruct an often straw-man metaphysics, thus neglecting specificities in the constituting of truly different cultural, political, and economic circumstances than the standard ones (call them logocentrism) against which Derrida directs his all-too-considerable efforts. This neglect does seem a pity (*dommage, schade*); given Derrida's gifted powers of reading (who do you suppose taught him?). But I do not want to be guilty of asking Derrida to be more than a philosopher in the old sense. For, ironically, it is a philosopher in the old sense that he has remained, or become. There may be some winking about this as well during *Given Time*, when Derrida appears to engage in what his backers have long debunked; defending (nostalgically?) his "legacy" of bringing "home" to the "present" good old antilogocentrism. But this may be wishful reading—a dream your heart makes?—on my part.

QUESTIONS PROLONGED; RESPONSE GIVEN

Derrida's antitext disarms all questions about likely payoff that publishers are wont to ask.

1. Would a teacher assign *Given Time*, given a chance (*hasard*)? *Peut-être.* One might set it beside Sartre's *Life/Situations*, illustrating philosophical aspirations to curtail ongoing indebtedness. Sartre him-*soi* carried fat wads of cash; he eschewed both disciples and investments in a future, craving that said *soi* should remain liquid—never stored, never "credited." "Like" Sartre perhaps, Derrida equates both mediating desire and measured (balancing) morality with mediocrity

(Chap. 2). This makes him a bit blind to *sociologie et ethnologie*—he is ungiven to lingering among practiced specifics of difference that anthropologists and historians (and not a few *littérateurs* and even select philosophers) tend to sweat.

It is hard to forGIVE (*parDONner*) Derrida for reestablishing conventions—perhaps despite himself—that Western (anti)metaphysics, or something resembling it, can be adequately contested from within. Cozy contentment may result from perpetually polishing Plato, continually caveating Kant, or eventually excusing Heidegger—and then appropriating the likes of Mauss (and Maori) into this familiar process.

2. What is the fate of deconstruction? I have *absolutely* no idea whether its star is still rising or finally falling. To many friends who do have some such idea, I defer. In either case *Given Time* is to be recommended, all the more if decline has set in. Derridean positions may become increasingly sympathetic as they, too, begin to suffer twilight. The late, lamented Richard Ellmann once reminded us (writing, sympathetically, of "Decadence"): "Dying cultures make the best cultures," a sentiment to which this reviewer has devoted a career to date (Ellmann 1990).

3. Should these lectures-inscribed—ready or not—be published? You bet; as a subscriber to many risky, puzzling, perhaps archaic customs, I indeed recommend continuity in the venture called "Derrida, Inc." Moreover, I mean what I just wrote. (For "I," substitute the initials "J. B." [according to guidelines provided by professional "deconstruction," an official enterprise of antiauthority in Academia Inc.]). Again I say (says I): Publish the lapidary beast. It may attract as many buyers as *Spurs* but fewer than *Writing and Difference* or *Positions*, which enjoyed the renown of revealing *différance*'s germs and most telling *marges*—pre-*Carte postale*, at least.[21]

Derrida's devotees may find *Given Time* an enchanting recapitulation (coda? reprise? sostenuto?) of his positions to date—an inviting return, a tantalizing brief, an essay deserving more welcoming reading than it, selectively, has given.

This reviewer long ago *gave* up (renounced) questioning the chutzpah-plus-effacement acted out in and as the aleatory (wheeee!) writings that Derrida decides to unleash. (Pardon any implication of intentionality on his part, unintentional on my part.) So, said reader must dodge an issue ordinarily raised: Is the book attentive to rival works relevant to its subject? Wheeling along, Derrida *d'habitude* professes being more about gaps and omissions than inclusions. His work's ruts are absence.

Put more commercially, I cannot see how a press, once started, could refuse to resume the venture of publishing-Derrida, could respond other than liberally to yet more. A publisher might want to take Derrida's writing at its *word*—i.e., logocentrically (!)—and receive it according to that ethic of postironic *écriture* it brandishes. A press inclined to poetic justice might agree to publish *Given*

Time, provided that the ROYALties (what pages of playful etymologizing the master could spin, and doubtless has spun, around that coinage: "The king takes all. . .") be DONated to the equivalent of alms-beggers extending their doleful cups in the environs where Derrida parades. (By the way, Derrida's metatroping on French *parade*, tied to parade and parry, is just plain gorgeous; how reflexive he is being here is difficult to guess—utterly reflexive, I assume.) Maybe—just maybe—Derrida has already proposed as much, so true may his practices be to the spirit of his ruminations on "pure gift"—one given without expectation of return. Well, he can afford it, even if his checks to "charity" don't bounce.

Regardless, given the etiquette of collegiality, niceties of contracts, and such, it seems unseemly for a reviewer even to imagine (seriocomically) recommending a work be published only if any ("genuine") money gained be decirculated from the cycle of mutual indebtedness that Derrida deems inadequate for framing studies of total prestations, monetized economies, or sacrifice (among other systems of "debt-given").

OH, WHAT THE HELL. Just take the thing; pay the guy; let him get away with it.

FINAL CALL AND LAST JUDGMENT

Without *Given Time*, the record of a phenomenon called deconstruction would remain incomplete.

Publish—mint (coin?)—the translation, ungrudgingly.

P.S. Suckers purchasing the book (and I will) should be sure to request a receipt.

CHAPTER ELEVEN

Taking Torgovnick as She Takes Others

Long an admirer of Marianna Torgovnick's work on novelistic closure (see Chap. 1), I was asked to review her Gone Primitive, *which crosses over from literature to ethnography. The journal was* Discourse, *edited by Kathleen Woodward, whose own incisive studies address media, society, and political responsibility. (I recently received notice that* Discourse *itself will crossover into exclusively electronic modes of distribution—"gone cyber," I suppose.) Feeling badly about having let* Discourse *down on Donna Haraway's* Primate Visions *(see above), I accepted, and this time managed to finish. Here is the review—published back in 1991, when print was still happening. A few true, seriocomic coincidences will be added directly.*

Gone Primitive: Savage Intellects, Modern Lives.
(University of Chicago Press, 1990)

Marianna Torgovnick looks to have gone postmodern—presumably to distinguish herself from modernists who, imagining they had "gone primitive," ended by expropriating voices they had "othered" and nailing difference to their regulated categories of order/disorder. So goes the familiar critique of modernity. Yet it is difficult to ascertain whether Torgovnick has gone postmodern wholeheartedly, unreluctantly, head-over-heels; and this fact is to her credit, to the extent that it is true, insofar as I can judge.

Torgovnick, professor of English at Duke, justifies her new book as "anticipated" (293) by her previous projects on narrative closure and on pictorialism and the visual arts in modernist novels (Woolf, Lawrence, etc.). *Gone Primitive* revisits these writers (Lawrence, Conrad, etc.) and editorializes on related matters with commitment and abandon. She joins forces with a rapidly expanding minidiscipline: the academic critique of history that repressed difference, objectified "them," commoditized or otherwise distanciated (either disparagingly or idealizingly) the un-us, the *non-nous*. Torgovnick aims to clarify the consolidation of modernist esthetics, politics, and prejudicial gazing that endures in the titillating merchandizing of "primitivity" in many texts and practices.

The book's array of concerns matches—margin for margin—*The Predicament of Culture* (1988) by Jim Clifford, an author Torgovnick occasionally chides for overly festive readings (40). Her own book, she explains, asks "precisely that we understand the rules governing the exchange between the modern West, the postmodern West, and the versions of the primitive they have created or endorsed." She seeks to make impossible innocent reenactments of the dramas of "us and them" that have been "staged and restaged in the modern West's encounters with primitive Others" (41). That aim is laudable (I almost said "noble") and actually venerable; but that's a long story. Nevertheless, Torgovnick's goal may be as totalizingly utopic in its own way as now-contested modernism was in its. Moreover, if Clifford seems at times a bit chipper about possibilities of polyphonic conversations in a someday-to-be de-powered world, he at least has read deeply into contexts of ethnography-making in his book (1982) on Maurice Leenhardt; and has himself hazarded a "kind-of-ethnography" about Mashpee identity—as negotiated in English, or Englishes, by adversaries in formal courtroom proceedings on Cape Cod, at which Clifford-as-ethnographer could conveniently eavesdrop (1988: Chap. 12).

Torgovnick's essays are largely, well, innocent of sensitivity to specifics of *languages* (or getting multiply different languages into some semblance of translation). Like many critics attuned to race, gender, and class, she accentuates "voice" over any particular language a voice speaks, or a writer "transcribes" for readers, like Torgovnick, to read. Invocations of "voices" may themselves become disembodied, especially when projected beyond the Francophonic, Anglophonic, Hindiphonic, Swahiliphonic, Arabophonic or otherwise phonic mainstreams—when projected, that is, into those marginalized "beyonds" where many adventurers, anthropologists, escaped artists, and those that live (and speak and write) there frequent.

Gone Primitive implements no way of surpassing today's pluralized hegemonies, each of which (like that old European colonialist hegemony) marginalizes somebody. Torgovnick's mission rather is to debunk monologic "Western" constructions, to call programmatically for depictions of non-Western realities, leaving any realization of collaborative ideals rather figurative. *Gone Primitive* talks about a lot of modernist sources. It talks about "Taking Tarzan Seriously," and fiction (pulp and high alike), and museums, and merchandizing exotica, and aestheticizing Africana, and ethnologizing persons, and curating art objects, and displaying artifacts, and travel writing, and a sometimes silly PBS adventure series on Indonesia. It talks about Lévi-Strauss's *Tristes tropiques*, which the author confesses herself now ready to read more sympathetically than earlier, when she was still under the spell of strictures imposed by Derrida (sigh). It talks about Freud, or his study, or entering it, or perusing haunting books of photographs that lead reader-viewers to imagine what it might have been like to enter it (Freud's study, that is): "Going psychoanalytic." And Torgovnick's text talks about the physicality of authors (e.g., Margaret Mead) whom she accuses of hiding the figure of their own bodies in the act of imperiously revealing "other" bodies: bodies of natives, bodies photographed voyeuristically in representations that Torgovnick is willing to reprint in her own book to raise our critical consciousness. Is that tactic OK? Readers get the picture.

Perhaps I should just admit that I cannot see this book's forest for its trees; but it might be modernist to want to anyway. So I respond and react to details. Does Torgovnick feel sheepish for having once submitted herself to deconstructive dismissals of, say, *Tristes tropiques*? Does she worry that some other monitoring device might be governing her present interpretations, unbeknownst to her or us? Or would such permanent anxiety be modernist? She commendably unpacks and destabilizes terms like "jungle" when commenting on Tarzan, possibly to show that she realizes Africa's and Southeast Asia's landscapes are varied (261–62); but that's pretty easy—classroom fare. Less critical scrutiny is directed at more harmful usages. The term "miscegenation," for example, appears rather casually whenever Torgovnick alludes to prejudices of those opposing it. In discussing *Heart of Darkness* (no surprise there), she writes: "Miscegenation challenges a boundary highly charged in the West, the boundary of race." (147) A less platitudinous, critical insight (available in Ashley Montagu's classic work against racism, *Man's Most Dangerous Myth* [1964]) is that the term "miscegenation" was likely invented as a pseudo-scientific coinage by New York journalists to lampoon not just racist fears but their pretentiousness. The sarcastic word was apparently taken "straight" by hyperserious backers of segregation and "normalized" in various state laws against certain kinds of marriage labeled so to conjure up a crime against nature. The history of intolerance is full of such cruel ironic twists: parodic gestures received hyperseriously. When resisting prejudices against "miscegenation," critics today unwittingly echo the normalized term and bogus concept.

Gone Primitive is ready and willing to fight modernism's packaging of primitivity (from Picasso's Africanisms to publishers' promotions for Malinowski's bookjackets) with a self-conscious counter-packaging whose complications could consume my entire response. The book's pictorialisms include the title-inspiring frontispiece (a Rihacek Prismacolor of a very white counter-consumer surrounded by very "native" *objets d'art*, everything thrown off by the haywire scale). Its jacket is garnished with Man Ray's gelatin-silver print *Kiki* (1926), whose juxtaposed face and mask thematize "decorative" primitivism. (So striking is this design that stacks of Torgovnick's volume could be glimpsed in a Protestant Episcopal Church Bookstore display window across from the U.N., where I happened to be strolling.) On the flap a winning snapshot of Torgovnick herself strikes this gazer thereupon as perfectly likable: just the kind of person anyone would want to share political scruples with. From the occasional mention of her daughters in the text, she sounds, like myself, a conscientious parent.

I hope that the observations just made do not sound snide; it is important to note Torgovnick's promotional photos and assertive personal digressions, because not to would deny her book the very dimensions it stresses in works by Mead and Malinowski, not to mention Henry M. Stanley (her opening case) or Conrad. She finds Conrad insufficiently critiqued by Edward Said, for which Said is critiqued in turn, alluding to Said's (and others') status as a critic "born in the third world" in a set of footnoted judgments too nuanced, and possibly even inconsistent, for me to follow (270–71). Torgovnick takes packaging very seriously; and so, I assume, must we hers.

Indeed, Torgovnick makes more of modernism's old bottles than of the various wines therein. It strikes me that Stanley, for example, put little *specifically* African in *How I Found Livingston*; while Malinowski puts much that is specifically Trobriand in *Coral Gardens and their Magic*. I consider this fact a vital difference, one that gets washed away in Torgovnick's evocation of a "male-centered, canonical line of Western primitivism" (248).

Many modernists—even colonialist officials and upscale museum directors—have professed hesitations, second thoughts and serious misgivings about representations their enterprises sponsored.[1] Yes, modernists too, occasionally, wrote/write doubtingly, and not just in private diaries. Even man Malinowski, in an intricate piece called "Baloma" (and in many asides in his "proper" ethnographies) questioned his basis of authority to represent Trobriand values—the more so the more he learned Trobriand life and language, for whatever darkling complex of motives.[2] What *they* ("modernists") consigned to alternate modes (e.g., memoirs), incidental genres, and piecemeal addenda, *we* (antimodernists?) make into whole (fragmentary) books and collections and journals. *We* today center gestures confined to *their* margins then; this is a familiar rhythm of and from history—one bound to continue, if indeed history does. That is one reason for doubting an emergent polarity between modernism and what claims to be not-it.

What is my motive in mentioning all this? Not, of course, to wage a rear-guard defense of canonical modernism. Rather I hope to wean us from the present (and presentist) inclination to congratulate "postmodernism" for at last maturing into political "correctitude," for outgrowing visualized-devoicing of "them," and for escaping the dark ages of nefarious -isms attached to race, class, and sex (rather, gender). I side with these struggles, but fear critique grows facile when it consigns every human matter of difference to those class-action categories of "Othering"—gender, class, race. Class, race, and gender have become a near litany in contesting dominant power-knowledge; the triad begins to sound virtually Hegelian. On the other hand, clarion calls to "go postmodern" may relapse into ameliorist visions of history (or the history of critique)—ones committed to optimism, just when we thought the so-called Enlightenment was "dead" in the water.

I too hope the world can become more just in areas of class (which works differently here and there), and race and gender (likewise); but I would not want to delude anyone into imagining that any improvement will be free of other otherings. Alternative inequalities continually arise among ethnicities, religious persuasions, and consumption-mediated identities: "tastes." As pertains to intelligentsia, the status group of high critiquers—versus other working-thinkers—has acquired a prestigious aura and certain material advantages as well. If going primitive became the epitome of paternalistic presumptuousness in colonialism's modernist hey-day, going multicultural has come to epitomize modernism's aftermath. And the marketability of the look of multiculturality (which aspect I distinguish from the struggling speech acts of many cultures) can produce its own puzzling conformity. While Torgovnick's book is alert to pitfalls of critical-chic, she may have authored a work too easily appropriated to such interests.

Strictly to divide critical possibilities—either a defamed modernism or a sometimes decorative postmodernism—hardly escapes the politics-as-usual that led self-styled moderns to imagine their discourse to be authentic representations of those their gazing concocted. Torgovnick's book is bound to be read; it displays all the ready signs of resistance. But her readings are best—insofar as I can judge—when they destabilize not just modernist schemes of so-called "primitives" (note that those quotation marks are modernist too!) but also the comfortable contrast between so-called modernists "gone primitive" and postmodernists gone self-reflexively *différence-différance-vive*-ing in a would-be new age of everything-as-cultural-criticism.

COINCIDENCE I. (FIT THE FIRST)

The above review's confines precluded elaborating a key "ethnographic" issue ignored in Torgovnick's critiques of such "modernist" texts as *Heart of Darkness*, *Sex and Temperament*, and *Tarzan*—namely the history of their reception *by readers* other than herself.[3] A relevant episode of *complex* reception—which is to say, reception ungoverned by the politics of a text's production—was witnessed by me on that very outing mentioned in my review (when stacks of *Gone Primitive* were displayed to window shoppers, even non-Anglican ones).

Returning home from my Saturday excursion, I took the PATH train from lower Manhattan to New Jersey. Habituees of PATH know that routine commuter-life transforms on weekend evenings, as if by magic, into scenes of family, friendship, and courtship—some scenes rough, more smooth, a few tragic, many comic. And there was I, "*flâneur*ing" (although lucky enough to have found a seat); the Torgovnick tome was tucked in my "briefcase" (a plastic bag).

Beside me stood a perfectly beautiful family (they looked like Belafontes): thirtysomething couple with son, age seven or so, intensely attentive to each other's lively words and gestures. As the train lurched along its twenty-minute run to Newark, the youngster began acting out a book he had just read. This one-boy band of interpretive virtuosity assumed the guise of all protagonists, human and animal—including the victims but the "hero" as well (after all, the kid was seven). Nor did he exclude culprits, local color, or *événements*. The performance was riveting; and his folks beamed. Although I did not quite catch the particular title, I did note the series from which it had sprung. It was *Tarzan*.

By official categories —e.g., statistics on the ethnicities of PATH riders— this family may have been "African American." And their son was taking Tarzan less seriously (à la Torgovnick) than seriocomically; he also managed to ventriloquize Jane. What is more, he made *Tarzan* matter by reauthoring it into utterances that his parents could relish and that—unbeknownst to him— one weary ethnographer had gratefully overheard.

There is a moral to this coincidence: For a critical theorist truly to interpret *Tarzan* or any other "primitivism" requires attention to how others have taken it in-the-reading. So what if this talented young minority fellow on the PATH train "identified" intermittently with Lord Greystroke. Everything in *Tarzan* may be intensively *anomalous*, at least when that extra-Vagant text is artfully received.

COINCIDENCE II. (FIT THE SECOND)

While my review was in press, Professor Torgovnick and I were both invited by John Hahnhardt to address a conference at the Whitney Museum (mid-Manhattan), all about the politics of exhibiting arts, cultures, and so forth. Other speakers included Aldona Joanaitis, Peter Wollen, Alan Feldman, and Don Preziosi—each of them versed in critiques of collecting, displaying, accessioning, and related capitalist activities (although it is worth adding that socialist regimes, too, make museums).[4] Topics included "the heritage industry"; rubbish theory; Bataille's "short circuits" between the sacred and excremental; Boas's frozen representations of Kwakiutl life; museums as social instruments for the making of modernity, disciplining of desire, and production of a past through retroaction. I believe it was Professor Preziosi who deemed museums anamorphic (or "ananamorphic?") sites ("feminized" ones) of phallocentric scopophilia; perhaps appreciating the fact that he was saying so at an event sponsored by a museum, he added that generally "the museum remains one step cleverer than its criticism."[5]

I learned much at this lively event, including the fact that my review of *Gone Primitive* had been on the mark in one respect, at least: Marianna Torgovnick is indeed likable. I even liked (with many reservations) her presentation, although people sitting next to me ardently did not. Controversial it was, and designed to be. The topic she took on was "piercing," postmodern style—nipple, eyebrow, ear, labia and clitoris, and above all penis. She may have shown snippets of a video (reputedly well known to connoisseurs) made at the Philadelphia University of the Arts, but I'm not sure. (Through the entire presentation I happened to be cleaning my eyeglasses.) A few quivering notes I managed to get down remind me that she mentioned "shafts, heads, metal bolts"; "performance face . . . he is grinning"; "genital tatooing of women"; "Hindu rituals in Sri Lanka"; "traditional societies"; "compulsive transgressions"; "modern primitives, boutiqued"; "modern piercing, privatized"; and "fringe, alternative cultural provincialism." Torgovnick's "Piercings" may have been published since; I haven't felt inclined to track it down. Her more recent work has expanded into areas of multicultural identity, such as her own Italian-American life of hyphenation.[6] This, too, I find likable.

It was a moment prefatory to Professor Torgovnick's roughly illustrated lecture that produced the coincidence at hand. From her Whitney podium she complained good-naturedly that requests to Duke colleagues in anthropology for cross-cultural evidence of so-called "piercing" had gone unanswered. Ever so hesitantly I (an ex-Duke anthropologist, perchance) raised my hand to volunteer some sources, although I didn't know quite yet what her talk would entail. Indeed, in my briefcase (again, a plastic bag) lay the draft of a review prepared for *The Journal of Asian Studies*, one its editor had solicited. Here it is, as later published (nearabouts).

The Penis Inserts of Southeast Asia:
An Annotated Bibliography with an Overview and
Comparative Perspectives.
By Donald E. Brown, James W. Edwards, and Ruth P. Moore.
Berkeley: University of California at Berkeley,
Center for South and Southeast Asian Studies,
Occasional Paper No. 15, 1988. iii, 60.

When all other "land of" labels for Southeast Asia fail, culture-trait mappers can always fall back on penis pins. The peculiar pamphlet under review finds the usages it surveys "among the more bizarre human inventions." (21) Yet, it ponders generalized correlations between "the degree of autonomy/subordination of women on the one hand, and the treatment of the penis on the other," as they pertain to "Southeast Asian thought" and "the relations between the sexes everywhere." (20–21) The authors call their hunches an "hypothesized nexus." (20)

Penis inserts—pins, bells, balls, coins, rings, wires, pig bristles, seeds, beads, broken glass, bird bones, bamboo, etc.—occur outside Southeast Asia as well. Stray references punctuate the *Kama Sutra*; small stones may be inserted in Australian subincision rites; and scattered glans "piercings" have been attested here and there (e.g., Mesoamerica) throughout world history, including a recent trend in the West's postmodern phallocentrism that impresses some observers as ultrapunk. This study mentions these examples among other genital alterations, but stresses the preponderance of penis inserts reported and rumored from Borneo, Burma, Thailand, the Philippines, and Sumatra, among other locales on the mainland and the islands.

The slim volume briefly annotates some 140 sources of dramatically variable reliability, from M. von Kuhlewein's 1930 report on his medical survey of 2500 adult male genitals in Borneo, to Pigafetta's mentions of pierced penises in his 1525 account of Magellan's voyage. Such sweeping coverage, while engrossing, retains the antiquated flavor of strange-but-true catalogues. Although many accounts are provocatively outlined, little contextual, intertextual, or even intratextual follow-through is offered. Pigafetta's text, for example, is credited with visual inspection of Cebuanos practices but just hearsay from Java. But Pigafetta never exactly reports on Java's penis inserts (bells); rather a formulaic "hearsay" about Javanese lovers is juxtaposed with extreme depictions of widow immolation and female autoprocreation; and sixteenth-century claims of "eye witnessing" are no less entangled or more objective.[7] These intricate accounts— along with arrays of ritual practices to which they allude—prove refractive to standardizing an ethnographic topic such as "penis inserts" and seeking general correlations.

The bibliography's thirteen illustrations cover disparate items. A bar, with knobs and strings attached, perforates an 1894 glans penis (uncircumcised, judging from the figure and from Islamic opposition to such [inserts] reported by scholars as historically distant as Samuel Purchas in 1617 and Anthony Reid in 1981) (52, 54). A Balinese Tintiya's lingam-blaze (one of its flaming Tantric *cakra*), which strikes the authors as "crescent-shaped barbs," is deemed pertinent to their motif (33). Two typical rhinoceris penises, naturally endowed with lateral protuberances, were reported by Tom Harrisson to be emulated in the sexual devices of certain Bornean groups. (40)

Reviewers customarily welcome any bibliography as better than none and barebones annotations as a starting point. But this study's opening essay discourages extending to it modest credit. The authors foresee researches that one day will clearly demarcate sexual augmentation from sexual restriction (as in sheaths), unambiguously differentiate female and male vantages, and ultimately answer whether penis pins are women-pleasers demanded by relatively autonomous females. These grand aims seem comically optimistic, judging from the latest "results" reported:

> Are the penis inserts actually desired by women? . . . Rodney Needham (personal communication) says that he found Bornean evidence, which he will report in the future, for women finding pleasure in the use of penis pins. . . . Derek Freeman (personal communication) reports that both he and

his wife drew the conclusion, based on inquiries with Iban men and women, that any explanation of the use of the *palang* as a woman pleaser is a male "rationalization and projection" (19–20).

What makes me think that these potential disputes will not soon be decided?

My review pertained (possibly) to Torgovnick's talk; but it bore no relation whatever to my own lecture for the Whitney conference. I have here lingered over that coincidence-laden event, because it nicely captures our crossover critical era. At a Whitney gala on "exhibitions of desire," it was the English professor who addressed conspicuously hidden evidence of ritualized *dépense*, thus polarizing her audience and even offending a sizeable segment thereof. And it was the anthropologist (I) whose lecture (perhaps as offensive, I wasn't in the audience), revolved around not penis-pins but Marcel Proust, Henry James, and James Ruskin. (That talk grew into Chap. 5 of this book; it too may provoke, though I hope not.) Torgovnick, the literary scholar, has thus gone (apparently) postmodern, "piercing"-gazing, and assertively hyphenated. The anthropologist has gone gondolizing—as Twain would say—in literary-looking descriptions, recollections, and travel-tales that may, however, be no less extra-Vagant than Torgovnick's alterations.

Let me add in my defense that, along more "traditional" disciplinary lines, I did try to provide Mariana Torgovnick relevant dope on comparative ethnography by mailing her a copy of my piece on *The Penis Inserts*. . . . She would have received it sooner, but I dared not FAX, lest anyone assigned to relay high tech communications inadvertently cast an eye on electronically transmitted words about phallic regalia of diverse strains of Southeast Asian cultures. So innocent an observer might have jumped to the conclusion (particularly at Duke) that this anthropologist is guilty of "exoticizing" *them*, of directing his disempowering gaze at *their* "primitivity." Assuming so, that observer (postmodern?) would have been wrong.

CHAPTER TWELVE

Rerun (1980s): Mary Douglas's Grid/Group Grilled

The relative datedness of this essay, first published in 1983, is part of its critical point. My light revisions leave it situated in the "Pac-Man" era, in order more vividly to contrast subsequent updating to the late 1990s, when U.S. consumer-culture seems triumphant globally: groupy grid compounded with griddy group, both simulated and dissimulating—totalized, or so it appears. But what am I afraid of?

> What are Americans afraid of? Nothing much really except the food they eat, the water they drink, the air they breathe, the land they live on, and the energy they use. In the amazingly short space of fifteen to twenty years, confidence about the physical world has turned to doubt.
> (*Mary Douglas and Aaron Wildavsky,* Risk and Culture: An Essay on the Selection of Technological and Environmental Dangers)

DATELINE, EARLY 1980s

For a month or so I'm mulling anthropologist Mary Douglas's latest effort, and along comes Extra-Strength Tylenol and then Halloween to boot—one new and one recurrent token of Americans' fear in superconcentration. The freshly perceived risks on our friendly pharmacist's shelves dovetailed with the annually perceived risk in our neighbor's treats. An image of the stricken consumer—pitifully caught in a moment of illness, seeking cure—merged with that of the innocent child, both victims of aimless evils: contaminated capsules and tainted Tootsie Pops. Like Johnson and Johnson's sales, Halloween suffered a setback. Participation dropped drastically in this ludic rite, always a threat to the property-owning classes anyway. America's "civil religion" has long felt uneasy with demonic vestiges in its counterauthority field night for the kids. Newscasters, of course, seized the coincidence, or rather the event. It wasn't the number of deaths-by-acetaminophin or trick-or-treat casualties that counted. More Chicago Tylenol-takers were probably run over that week than poisoned; and Halloween may, statistically, be safer than nearly anything else juvenile these days. No, Dan Rather doubtless noted, it's not the actual risk but the perceived risk that makes effective news copy; and abetting the perception can't hurt. Viewers never knew what real fear was until the camera slid sinisterly along the overlit drugstore aisle, an empty space where the "T" used to be; fast dissolve to lugubrious thresholds where ghostly arms extend toward us, at child's eye level, ominous candied apples. Spielberg smiles.

Whence such selective bias in our fears? Whence the reluctance accurately to measure real risk instead of taking fright over imagined danger? These are the questions Mary Douglas and Aaron Wildavsky ask; and the headline of *Risk and Culture* is: they have nailed the culprit. Douglas has long found sectarian movements reactionary, unresponsive to the serious needs of social continuity: "groupie." As for sectarian practices in other cultures—such as witchcraft accusations—she must dampen her complaints; it is anthropologically unfitting, disciplinarily "sacrilegious," to denigrate customs of another people. But when sectarian styles crop up in European history, or among contemporary American environmentalists inclined left of the political center, they are fair game.

The time seems ripe to reconsider Britisher Douglas's assessments of *nous autres Américains*. By now, of course, readers may have forgotten Tylenol and Excedrin-Plus for newer newsworthy fears. This cyclical faddism is itself significant: American apocalyptic alarms ebb and flow; but transience is no reason to dismiss the fears; indeed it underpins their cultural viability in a commercial context. I suspect, moreover, that both the political left and the political right sense as much. Douglas may be taking too literally the fear-filled utterings of informants and therefore misinterpreting them. This foible is frequent among us fieldworkers, including the best of them (e.g., Mary Douglas).

Risk and Culture advertises itself as the advance front of demystified research on cultural bias. Yet its arguments are extremely tricky, despite the authors' insistence that they are perfectly straightforward. The book recycles Douglas's grid-group formulations, which I cannot avoid reviewing (see below). Douglas officially resuscitated grid-group in a pamphlet called *Cultural Bias* (1978), which confessed her distaste for Thoreau. *Risk and Culture* draws heavily on Douglas's fieldwork among the Lele of the Congo. It revises themes from her admirable *Purity and Danger*, with its flair for social organizational aphorism: "It takes two to have sexual intercourse, but only one to cook a meal" (1966: 55).[1] And it continues the forceful critique of secularist bias in social science, advanced in *Natural Symbols* (1970). Her exposure of dismissive attitudes toward ritual, even among modern anthropologists, represents a major contribution to comparative religious studies (see Douglas 1982).

Another book, with Baron Isherwood, *The World of Goods*, approached both macro- and microeconomic practices through what I call the consumer's "potlatch potential":

> To correspond roughly with forward linkage in international trade, we would want to indicate the volume of social interaction. Consumers' social linkage could be assessed by some expenditure indicating the dependence of other homes for their consumption rituals upon the marking services produced in a given home. Relevant expenditure testifying to reciprocal sharing of consumption would be the bill for private travel, the telephone account, the amount of extra cutlery, plates, spare beds, the expenditure on entertainment, charities, clubs, church, and toys for children's friends and friend's children. A family could be heavily engaged in social linkage and poor in technological linkage—the rating would indicate different life-styles. . . . Marriage and kinship are the strongest channels for exchanged marking services and also of consumption goods.[2]

High-linkage (either social or technological) corresponds to "high grid," and low-linkage equals "high group"—bounded, undifferentiated, often egalitarian memberships. Like Marcel Mauss and some structuralists, *The World of Goods* sees consumption as an information system (rather than a needs-fulfilling system); consumers are more than mere puppets of the expropriating forces of production. Consuming is ritual activity, and commodities are values that make "visible and stable the categories of culture." This formula helps correct formalist economists' neglect of consumption values; but it needs to go further. Commodities, I would say, "make masked and dialectic the categories of culture"; moreover, what consumption-masks conceal is more complicated than opposed classes or direct exploitation per Marxism.

Much more than Douglas, Marshall Sahlins's *Culture and Practical Reason* (1976)—which sketches *pensée bourgeoise* as culturally based selections *disguised* as needs—divorces consumption from direct determinacy of the forces of nature or of society (including the dominant class). Douglas manages to sound less recondite than Sahlins because she ultimately lodges consumer strategies in social position, per utilitarian functionalism. Like certain transaction analysts, Douglas sometimes confuses motive with "interest": a singular end working to the particular party's direct advantage, as in the fiction of free market competition. (Unlike "interests," social *motives* entail contradiction, conflict, delay, trust, credit—properties of experience divided by genders, generations, ritual occupations, etc. It is hard to address overlapping, indirect motives without sounding recondite!) *The World of Goods* implies that any party—whether rich or poor, whether nation or household—simply marshals its available group or grid resources in order to "make ends meet," so to speak. I can tuck all my interpretive reservations about this model into one slightly flippant question: could it have anticipated the rise (and I pray, the fall) of

Pac-Man? "Goods," you see, can go kind of crazy; they almost seem to take on a life of their own.

Risk and Culture makes predominant a side issue from Douglas's *Natural Symbols*, which expressed regrets over aspects of 1968: "Many are struck with the parallel between student revolt and violent millennialism. Compensation theory gives as the cause insecurity or deprivation. But my own hypothesis points to a lack of adequate structuring in the university population."[3] Douglas attributed student preferences for rites of enthusiastic resistance (over ceremonies of differentiation) to millennialist thinking. She encouraged analyzing sectarian millennialism, but only to overcome it: "It behooves others to identify and resist the allurements of millennial thinking" (1970: 154). *Risk and Culture* now pins the "throwing overboard" of "differentiating doctrines and differentiating rituals" on American environmentalists who occupy an erosive borderland hospitable to her lowest-common-denominator millennialist-types. Douglas and Wildavsky forbid readers to wonder which of them is to credit or blame for what in *Risk and Culture*: Like any perfect union, "unless we had done it together, we could not have done it at all" (ix). So I shan't second-guess the partnership; but I shall second-guess simplifications it has spawned.

The book's catchy cover juxtaposes a primitive mask (with a Northwest Coast look) and a gasmask (with a deathly look). The jacket's excerpt parallels modernity's rejection of natural death (our conviction that life's end must be diagnosable) and Lévy-Bruhl's controversial portrayal of primitive mentality. "We seem to have changed places—no, we have joined the primitives. . . . ," the excerpt explains. (One can almost hear a "eureka" from that policy-minded readership the book declares it must educate.) Elsewhere Douglas (1982) suggests that our sense of bureaucratic oppression brings "modern man closer to and not further from premoderns." Cosmologically we represent another case of defensive accountability, but with blame attributed not to social agents (per witch-mongerers) but to technological forces, medical failures, and the like. Thus is *homo moderno* debunked, vividly and convincingly.

So far, so good. Douglas refurbishes an old message dear to many anthropologists: *we* are an arbitrary culture, too. Moreover, "the perception of risk is a social process"; as E. E. Evans-Pritchard devoted a distinguished career to demonstrating, "the type of society generates the type of accountability and focuses concern on particular danger" (6–7). Our fear is a social fact. (To further provoke policy-minded readers: scientists in the business of measuring natural risks themselves disagree—imagine!) Now for the twist: Douglas and Wildavsky are blowing the whistle *not* on scientistic technocrats but on nature-loving zealots. They do not ask: "Why, because scientists disagree, go on measuring?" They do not invite us to acknowledge science as arbitrary too, like cultures. They do not show that empirical demonstration may be as irrelevant to political policies or social motives as it is to religious ideals or cultural values. Rather, they expose sectarian "bias": no evidence conclusively proves that life of late has grown less safe or health worse; alarm, nevertheless, is on the rise. Witness the environmental movement, particularly its exaggerated claims. If nothing natural and nothing indisputably confirmed by science explains this augmented alarm, what does? Something social-organizational: the growth of sectarianism. The new sectarians (say, the Sierra Club and Friends of the Earth), while reminiscent of old-style sectarians (say, Hutterites and Amish), came into their own during counterculture days. They have risen from the margins to occupy the figurative border, indeed to make America a "border country."

Douglas and Wildavsky voice hope that readers now "know better than to wish to see the erosion of the center [here called a hierarchy] or the suppression of the border" (185); yet it is this very suppression that they fuel. Taking their stance in the measure of verifiable risk and—yes—cost-benefit analysis, they portray sectarian fears as inflated, unbridled, even antinomian. They are willing to grant the "border" a hearing only in "polite dialogue" (180)—admittedly a hierarchical ideal. (Did you ever try to report gently to GM that Corvairs were "unsafe, well . . . perhaps . . . at some speeds at least?")[4] The authors deny any aim to block "border" arguments by referring reductively to their social genesis: e.g., by explaining environmentalist values by the "availability of sectarian political entrepreneurs." They note that sects—expansive and schismatic over time and routinization—require enemies. But they soft-pedal the American center's needs (desires?) for sectarians. Their brief nod toward contradiction at the center is immediately qualified:

> Amid the competing claims for power, as the Progressive movement showed, are serious charges that the regime in power is corrupt, incompetent, boss-ridden, and run by secret forces. To this extent, the opposition within the establishment may sound sectarian, just because it is in opposition. But its program was really hierarchical. (157)

Although they acknowledge that opposition to American institutions historically has stemmed from two cultural sources (hierarchy and sectarianism), they charge sectarianism with irresponsibility rather than vitality, declaring it external rather than integral.

Little is made of the center's sect-like rallies round the flag when dangerous outsiders are perceived to threaten sacred borders. Douglas and Wildavsky accentuate environmentalists' apprehensions of technological disaster (which, one should say, may or may not prove true). In contrast, they portray the establishment as a judicious backer of the market and preserver of order, largely neglecting its own rhetoric of Cold War fears (which, too, may or may not prove true [or so it still appeared in 1983]). I have nothing absolute against caricatures of Friends of the Earth or Sierra Clubs, or even of Amish and Hutterites. But if these "borders" warrant caricature, so does the center. That Douglas fails to balance the account is (forgive my school-marmish tone) bad anthropology. *Risk and Culture* concludes with an amusingly superfluous confession of its own bias toward hierarchy. The policies it keeps promising are finally, I suppose, delivered: advocacy of resilience and "some degree of trust in institutions." They might as well have kissed a baby.

Respecting the book's call for reflexivity, I should say that I do not respond from their "border." I am no self-righteous, anticeremonial, nonnegotiating protestor, proclaiming doomsday unless the establishment ends its conspiracy to defile Mother Nature and destroy my eventual grandchildren by willfully extending the diabolic machine beyond the last edges of the garden. Possibly as wary of universalistic, ethical do-goodism as Douglas, I prefer—well, manners (and merit). True, I opposed Vietnam and all that; but I also decried (with Douglas) the burning of the Wisconsin card catalogues (not, however, as an equivalent crime); and I consider high church liturgy a more beautiful thing than an encounter group. I state these positions flatly here to question *Risk and Culture*'s polarization between center and border (reinforced by Douglas's grid-group scheme). In Douglas's earlier terms, I am some "dirt" in her analytic conceptualization: matter out of place, like that monstrous pangolin she once ably depicted that falls into the cracks between Lele categories of animals:

> It is scaly like a fish, but it climbs trees. It is more like an egg-laying lizard than a mammal, yet it suckles its young. And most significant of all, unlike other small mammals its young are born singly. Instead of running away or attacking, it curls in a modest ball and waits for the hunter to pass.[5]

Indeed, "pangolins" that smudge Douglas's grid-group categories of social organization do exist; nor can statistics explain us away. If, as Douglas shows, the Lele are wise enough to worship the embodiment of their own conceptualizations' exceptions, then certainly her analysis should pay us heed: "Where there is dirt, there is system" (1966: 35). This brings me to more problems with "grid-group."

Dissenters beware; grid-group analysis will trap you just when you think you've escaped. I first heard Douglas explain the system in Chicago in the winter of 1969; even in those trying times, the lecture hall was filled. We students looked, I confess, millennarian. Yet I vividly recall an extraordinarily polite professor who raised his manicured hand to express an exceedingly refined doubt about a nuance of grid-group, only to be grilled in return. Mary Douglas did not, I seem to remember, answer his question; rather she placed her interrogator in appropriate slots calculated from his upper-crust, extra-European origins, displacement to Britain for higher education, and academic career in America. Her unanswerable implication: "Now that's just the kind of question I'd expect from somebody doubly high grid, transposed to a context of radical strong group that excludes him." So, I might as well acknowledge defeat at the outset; my doubtless unfair fun-pokings are offered as further grist for grid-group.

It's like a better *Gemeinschaft/Gesellschaft*, with the hitch that both can be present or absent too.[6] It applies to any level of organization and cosmology (not just self-perpetuating societies). *Natural Symbols* (1970) listed four social types: "A relatively unbounded, unstructured system (neither grid nor group); a bounded, unstructured system (group alone); a bounded, structured system (grid and group); and structured but unbounded (grid without group)." Or, in another nutshell from *Risk and Culture*:

> *Group* means the outside boundary that people have erected between themselves and the outside world. *Grid* means all the other social distinctions and delegations of authority that they use to limit how people behave to one another. A society organized by hierarchy would have many group-encircling and group-identifying regulations plus many grid constraints on how to act. An individualist society would leave to individuals maximum freedom to negotiate with each other, so it would have no effective group boundaries and no insulating constraints on private dealings. A sectarian society would be recognizable by strong barriers identifying and separating the community from nonmembers, but it would be so egalitarian that it would have no leaders and no rules of precedence or protocol telling people how to behave. (138–39)

Douglas's most influential work correlates cosmologies and bodily symbols. My theoretical challenge concerns whether cosmological and social factors can be posed, even heuristically, as distinct components. Are not symbols of social practice and symbols of cosmological practice (i.e., ritual) both evidence of "cultures?" Douglas's vocabulary of "correlations" seems tautological, which is not to deny their utility in upsetting even more reductive schemes.

Cultural Bias calls the groupless-gridless extreme individualist: folk who "do their own thing"—like hippies and Mbuti pygmies.[7] This type pushes toward Durkheim's "anomie" (unlimited, incapacitating choice)—an area beyond the fringe to which Douglas exiles hermits like Thoreau. Perhaps this danger-zone explains Douglas's zeal for her grid-group mission:

> One of the reasons why it is important to develop a grid and group analysis is that we can identify the trends in modern industrial society which are progressively releasing the individual from the close control of strong grid and the coercion of the bounded group. But instead of being released to freedom, the individual is then drawn into a very difficult social environment, the bottom left-hand corner of the diagram. . . . That environment is a very harsh one to endure, and for that

reason, individuals either opt out of it by seeking to hedge off a commune of like-minded souls or they are forced out of it by being forced into a position of minimum choice and maximum isolation. (1979: 43)

Here all dangers converge: "The wish to escape from grid and group control throws up small groups": these are the "sectarians" that *Risk and Culture* fears. That same wish aggravates the wealth and power gap that separates off both third-world nations and low-linkage households. Finally, down in this corner strong individualism is counteregalitarian in its effects; so we lose even that. Now, I too frown upon "small group" reprogrammers; and few, save anarchists, applaud anarchy. But, has Douglas situated cultic enthusiasm or outright advocates of anomie accurately in her scheme? And can all sectarian forces, or all dissent, be equated?

VIVE THOREAU

Douglas is anxious not to be accused of social determinism, and it is a fact that her reductionism is irregular. It does, however, occur; for example, she lumps Rousseau and Thoreau as voluntary recluses off the grid-group chart, near dropouts who by some quirk needed to be heard, to write, and therefore "edged onto the social map" (1978: 44). After *Purity and Danger*, Douglas grew less able to fit articulate asociality into her scheme of social processes. She could not imagine a society that institutionalizes radical doubt among its convictions. Consider Thoreau. To Douglas, old Henry David isn't even a very good hermit:

> Not one of my favorite writers, I confess that I have met many less preaching, less egotistical characters who are more genuine hermits than he. But if we take into account that his determination to be a writer shifted his ambitions towards the more competitive end of the scale, Thoreau can hardly be set off the social map. Indeed, he is not completely honest with himself nor fair with his neighbors. (1978: 45–46)

Douglas must needs find Thoreau hypocritical. She ignores subtler modulations in his hermit-voice—those Richard Poirier calls "wary of the expansive 'I'" who performed in Thoreau's works. Where Douglas construes *doctrine* irresponsible to society, Poirier finds *pun* brimming with cultural vitality. Poirier's *The Performing Self* goes further than reprimanding Thoreau for not paying his taxes:

> The punning of Thoreau and Marvell, who are, after Shakespeare and Donne, perhaps the most seriously intentioned punsters in English before Joyce, is a way of showing that the words by which the world carries on its sensible business are

loaded with a radical content. It is within the subversive power of the poet to release that radical content. (1971: 95)

Poirier's book was a contemporary of *Natural Symbols*; its points of departure also include the dissenting sounds of 1968. But Poirier hears them as part of a "medley of voices competing for attention" long celebrated in modern literature. Poirier's strong suit—detecting rhetorical complexity and occasional irony in the voices of hermits, sectarians, the Beatles (and, I surmise, some policy-makers too)—is the weak suit of grid-group analysis.

Although Douglas salutes cultural meaning, she conventionally construes social expressions as literal rather than figurative projections of actual circumstances. She sees society and religion in both daily practice and flamboyant ideology as strategies for producing coherent, rather than agonistic, information systems.[8] She often disregards how something outside social organization can still be inside cultural values, how society can be strengthened and enriched by being denied. Has she forgotten her pangolin?

Compelling evidence of the dialectical quality of culture includes not just Lele anteaters but anyone's asceticism. While Douglas expresses admiration for enduring ascetic "corporations" (e.g., monastic orders), she slights independent ascesis and institutionalized values thereof. Although she mentions Louis Dumont's work on Indic renunciation in *Homo Hierarchicus* (1966/1980), she neglects certain ramifications. Dumont approaches renunciation as the negation of caste, which nevertheless participates in the purity/pollution values that underpin exclusivistic social distinctions (see Chap. 10). Societies do not necessarily purge but possibly perpetuate their own antitheses. In this theoretical light Thoreau too could, without inconsistency, *communicate* his hermithood as a contributing cultural value. In fact, Thoreau read literally (or "objectively"—see Chap. 1) is Thoreau read not at all; despite or because of his social position, his words must be expected to wink.

Back on Douglas's social map, strong *group* alone, when pressed, becomes the "love us or leave us" reactionary type: the xenophobic cult, its paranoid membership homogenized by invoking the enemy outsider. A milder form is the camaraderie of working-class pubmates, conformist even in their tobacco tastes, meticulously distributing the costs of every round, a gang of each other's watchdogs, where "the organization of work structures the organization of friendship" (1979: 173). Strong *grid* is represented by network pushers and shovers: your savvy operators, your New Guinea Big Men, your impression managers of any stripe. Douglas puts it this way:

Access to the Big Man is a taxing problem for everyone, but is also a problem for himself. A high value on personal privacy helps the screening process. This accords with the cardinal ethic of individual value. But the private bathroom, like the ex-directory telephone, also protects from unwanted solicitations in a society where other insulating barriers have gone down. The large-scale feast is a way of maximising the use of time in personal contacts. Ostentatious hospitality is a feature of Papuan, Kwakiutl, West African, modern industrial and any other low-grid ethnography. (1978: 12)

Such dense-pack suggestions litter Douglas's studies; she has gotten extraordinary mileage out of this vehicle. It goes everywhere: why, "Tawney's aphorism about humanity's need to pour wealth away in drink can be assimilated in grid-group analysis" (1979: 173).

Again, the scheme can admit mild-mannered conflict:

Each basic principle, the value of the group, the value of the individual, is the point of reference that justifies action of a potentially generative kind. When one wins heavily against the other, the slide starts toward strong group or towards low grid. When each pulls against the other the tension is a dialogue within society. (1978: 13)

Purity and Danger even presented a kind of society enduringly "at war with itself." But more often grid-group becomes a kind of parlor game for pigeon-holing social processes and cosmological patterns as fixed types—increasingly so, it seems, although Douglas denies this is her aim. (My own preferences in comparative typologies gravitate toward more flexible Weberian approaches.)[9]

Still, Douglas's works retain a decided strength: they obliterate smug oppositions between primitives and us or anybody else. Mbuti pygmies are as secular-minded as most anthropologists; the secular world view "appears when group boundaries are weak and ego-focused grid is strong" (1970: 139)—an interesting tautology. Or, the potlatcher is as opportunistic as any executive. Ruth Benedict had achieved as much; *Patterns of Culture* (1961) compared Dobu "paranoia" and Kwakiutl "megalomania" (both socially reinforced) to characteristics its intended readers could recognize in ourselves. Douglas, however, apparently feels that to do this much and no more is to dawdle in relativism. She warns against millennial returns to artificial strong-group. (So, by the way, did Benedict, who sounded the alarm against tribe-like xenophobia in totalitarian, centralized states.) Unlike Benedict, however, Douglas sides squarely with high grid, high group, the only conditions supporting the polite dialogue she prefers. Benedict, on the other hand, as Edward Sapir appreciated, liked cultures (and psyches) "madly irregular."[10]

Natural Symbols mapped out one representative of high grid, high group from Raymond Firth's Polynesian Tikopia.[11] Everybody likes the Tikopia; readers breathe easily in this complex cosmos with elaborately insulated, rather than crazed, responses to danger. "Like Bali," I can sigh, content also to have found a field area of high grid, high group (common in Indonesia, India, and the Pacific). But scruples cloud my satisfaction: does Bali's proclivity for trance belie Douglas's suggestion that trancelike states are "feared as dangerous where the social dimension is highly structured, but welcomed and even deliberately induced where this is not the case" (1970: 74)? Still, if Bali does both, maybe it's O.K. Besides, to raise flickering doubts would be to engage in anthropology's most tiresome game, justly tweaked by Douglas: Bongo-bongoism, or, "Not in my culture they don't." If, however, "places like Bali" can "pangolin" (i.e., ambiguate) grid/group categories, then prediction may be murkier than your standard litmus tests. Nevertheless, Tikopia, Bali, and other society-*cum*-cosmologies that Douglas's scheme makes resemble the high Middle Ages, seem to come out all right.

But Douglas has higher hopes still for high grid-high group. Over the years she tied her formulations to Basil Bernstein's controversial notions of restricted versus elaborated linguistic codes. Douglas feels that high grid, high group fosters an elaborated code, one that "challenges its users to turn round on themselves and inspect their values, to reject some of them, and to resolve to cherish positional forms of control and communication wherever these are available. This would seem to be the only way to use our knowledge to free ourselves from the power of our own cosmology" (1970: 157). Douglas implies that these circumstances help a society's hidden cultural bias become transparent and therefore governable. Extraordinary. Marxists, take careful notes: Demystification, consciousness raising, and other advantages you assume arise from exclusivistic episodes of high group (i.e., revolutionary movements that level distinctions among their enthusiasts and trumpet revelations to unmask the oppressor class) are credited by Douglas to "the elaborated code"—the communication mode of high grid, high group. (My own solution to this schism in theory: Marxists and Douglas are both wrong.) Douglas stands against any "institutional mistrust" and sides with centered networks plus flexible groupings, with social anthropology in harness. She thus opts for her cake and eating it too; such is the bullet of social responsibility that she recommends everyone (anthropologists among them) bite. I'd sooner we join Thoreau, punning hermit and winking communicator.

Risk and Culture does admit that alarmist predictions may sometimes augment welfare and sound resource management:

> . . . How is the individualist ever going to see the need for hierarchy? Never, unless the voice from the border, shocked at injustice and waste, creates a public scandal. Then the market is forced to compromise with hierarchy and the two occupy the center once more and the sectarians are pushed into the border. (181)

But Douglas and Wildavsky deny to sectarians themselves such wisdom. Like some conservatives (not, I hasten to add, all), they fear that civil righters, ban-the-bombers, anti-Vietnamers, and now environmentalists, want more, indeed that they want it all. They explain their "harsh judgment on extreme sectarian policy" as a counterweight to charges of ruthless market competition and bureaucratic inertia. *Risk and Culture* proposes a reactionary response to what it deems reactionary responses. If we follow the authors' own advice, our task becomes to determine what they themselves are afraid of. Clearly, they fear that the border will incapacitate the market and state, that passing correctives might stick. Funny: that really doesn't strike me as a verifiable risk. What do you suppose explains Douglas and Wildavsky's increasing alarm? Why are they calling for sectarians to repent, lest the center collapse?

They seem skeptical that environmentalists truly seek sources of alternative energy or policies that preclude complete capitalization of lands and waters. They suspect a universal plot behind these purportedly single interests. Douglas's and Wildavsky's fear may stem from their assumption that voluntary, end-specific organizations are on a par with born-into, end-general societies or religions, that the lobbyist and the proselytizer are equivalent. This belief in turn justifies their major scare tactic (which certainly rivals CBS on Tylenol). *Risk and Culture* conjures a total victory of single-interest sectarians who, once the day is theirs, will turn censorious, stratified, bellicose, and intolerant. (Remember now, their subject is Common Cause and the Clamshell Alliance, not Oliver Cromwell.) Those victorious sectarians will promote inequality, expropriation, and witchcraft accusations too; even their environmentalism will come to naught:

> Suppose they could dominate the political scene and still keep their guiding vision; then the whole center would be weakened by sectarian attack. . . . There would inevitably be neglect of the technical and institutional apparatus of political life, since sectarianism is set against technology and institutions. The Dutch dikes against the sea would never have been built, nor would nuclear power reactors be safely maintained. The biggest and most immediate risk, however, would be to the civic rights of the individual, not merely the risk of being born a second-class citizen in a hierarchy or of becoming one of the human derelicts which litter the marketplace but the risk of being classified as evil, as malefactor outside the protection of the law. (182)

It is hard to keep track of the issues begged in this scenario. I would gladly read Douglas and Wildavsky's imaginary fling as a parodic doomsday proclamation against the doomsday proclaimers; but they really don't seem to be winking. Their analogy with the Amish helps brand environmentalists as technophobic rather than supporters of alternative knowledges. By failing to wonder whether those scary, untended reactors (parallelled to Dutch dikes) would ever have been built under the sectarian vision, *Risk and Culture* becomes less political than partisan; and the paragraph cited represents only its milder views.

The book's historical synopsis is brief: "Once or twice in Western history sectarians have emerged from the border as a powerful force, briefly dominating the political debate in the turmoil before and after great wars." To counter this simplistic isolation of Mennonite-style ideals of self-sufficiency in the history of American religion and politics, readers might consult Sydney

Ahlstrom's *Religious History of the American People* (1972), which conveys the workings of such denominations in a "tradition" defined by the absence of a national church. An official emptiness at the center sustains plural ethical voices and lends a sectarian flavor to *any* religious or moral position—a fact liberal clergy often underscore in periods of dissent. Douglas and Wildavsky try to assess cultural selection values and verifiable risk. I doubt, however, that cost-benefit analysis can inform social motives or cultural values even at the center. (Does the Pentagon act on proof that Russia is more likely to attack than that nuclear plants are likely to melt down? These questions are not quite ones that cultures or religions ask; they traffic in ideals.) Show me an organization that ticks to the beat of cost-benefit calculations, or that assesses values in light of anything measurable at all—and I'll show you something subcultural.

Douglas and Wildavsky make bold claims in this area: Analyses of real risk *prove* that conditions *cannot be proved* to be as grim as antibureaucratic sectarians—those cosmic unity types—fear. Thus, they insist, sectarians must have "a vested interest in bad news." Let me throw in a monkey wrench: The media—a big business, for sure—employs the ideology of borderland frenzies to generate melodramas of event. Indeed, Douglas eventually hints at adjustments consistent with grid-group that account for institutionalized journalistic alarm. But to do so up front would sharply reduce the marketability of *Risk and Culture*, which melodramatically isolates *sectarian* strategies for sectarianism's survival: "disdain of the world, fear of pollution, of cancerous contamination from external intercourse." In their scheme it is impossible to be consistently both sectarian and hierarchical: the Sierra Club is a diluted compromise, and Luther, I suppose, was a poor Calvinist. Their way of describing purist sectarians recalls styles of briefs on subversives: "The *de facto* leader keeps a very low profile. He acts more as a guru or a *primus inter pares*, on the basis of perhaps a little more experience, a way with words, or a flair for tactics . . ." (148). No Friend of the Earth or Clamshell ally, they assume, acts out of larger cultural principles; he only functions to perpetuate his group by spreading superstitions of global conspiracy and the evils of technology.

I am not critiquing *Risk and Culture*'s own lapse into compensation-*cum*-conspiracy theory in order to defend sectarians (whether purist or compromised). I question this kind of analysis when directed against the Joint Chiefs of Staff as well, with their storied fears of Commies and beliefs in the benignity of military technology on the grand scale. I doubt that even the Pentagon exists only to perpetuate war in order to perpetuate itself. Similarly, I object to secularist slurs on ecclesiastics, not because I necessarily admire priests more than other workers or parasites, but because it is untenable to explain religious ideals—celibacy, for one—as simple self-interest. (In this regard it may be worth recalling that capitalism, too, as Weber taught, is a form of asceticism.)[12] No, I seek not to save sectarians alone from *Risk and Culture*; rather I seek to save comparative social analysis and cultural interpretation.

Douglas and Wildavsky pin sectarianism on some radical fringe—Hutterites and Clamshell Alliances; they then ask why "it" has grown stronger. Their final answer has something to do with civil rights and other such "causes" embraced by America's middle-class overflow from affluence. Their arguments devised to bait liberals are all too familiar: a minority's belated development of political consciousness coincided with the majority's children "elbowing each other out of the way in graduate school." Here the prose gets tacky, the imagery nasty, and the tone sarcastic:

> Black people were always a bone lodged in the throat of American individualism. They couldn't be swallowed whole and the American value system could not breathe freely with them stuck in a peculiar place. . . . Everything connected with the civil rights movement therefore, became ennobled, including its tactics. (163)

Civil rights, they suggest, was a rehearsal hall for voluntary associations that "choose to be panic-struck [*sic*] about dangers from technology rather than from threats to the economy or education because they serve their own moral purposes" (169). Grid-group analysis obliges Douglas and Wildavsky to deem alarm and responsible criticism mutually exclusive. They give no numbers on environmentalists who also organize to improve corporate investments, to refine foreign policy, or to reform education without radically deschooling society. Rather, they dream up a swarm of liberal-to-radical *Lumpen* leagues, avoiding single-interest groups elsewhere on the political spectrum: antiporno leagues, say, or pro-fallout shelter leagues (long, long ago). Restricting single-interest strategies to the left, they fail to ask whether any multiple-interest group on either the left or the right could deflect any bureaucratic structure or centrally organized set of vested interests, whether in the state, the media, or elsewhere.

The bias built into grid-group analysis inhibits perception of overlapping memberships and complex standards of value. Some of my environmentalist friends still salute the flag, act in authoritative ways to their children or students, own stock, and strive for academic promotion; one even has a maid. If this assortment of traits automatically makes them look hypocritical, that is not their fault; it is the fault of grid-group, which treats any membership, including optional and multiple ones, in analogy with exclusive memberships (one cannot be both "American" and "British," at least not *really*; one cannot be both Anglican and Baptist). The difference between a conformist sect like the Amish and a conformist interest group like Friends of the Earth is that the latter's conformism is limited and the former's is generalized. There may be turncoats in the Clamshell Alliance, but there cannot be "apostates" in the true sense of the term.

Mary Douglas has written lucidly on similar points, which fact makes her co-conspiring in *Risk and Culture* perplexing. Her anti-reductionism seems to crack when confronted by small-group egalitarian idealists; they blind her to her own previous insights. She has engaged in a book that recalls fence-builders condemning the open range; agriculturalists berating transhumants; or more exactly, generals denouncing devious guerrilla tactics, or redcoat rejoinders to militiamen who don't stand out in the open field of battle and fight like a(n) (English)man:

> These headless groups can be politically potent. They are numerous, small and unencumbered. They travel light. They are difficult to defeat because there are so many of them, and they do not stay in one place (or shape, for that matter) for too long. Beaten down here, they rise elsewhere.
>
> This combination of somewhat different groups (as well, of course, as the resonance they evoke in the general population) explains the success of their sustained assault on environmental and safety policy. (172)

Anthropologists customarily expound on such "resonance with the general population." But not *Risk and Culture*; it's after sectarians. It generalizes that extremist reformist communities proliferated with World War II's growth of service industries, galvanized as civil righters and antiwar types, and have transformed into dropouts turned political entrepreneurs with the know-how to mobilize a mail-order membership. (The Internet came later.) The sectarians, "while invoking government, are not inclined to respect it"; nowadays they feel squeezed in because the frontier has closed. It is *they* that Douglas and Wildavsky charge with undermining all responsible mediate institutions: political parties, trade unions, and churches. Expose them and things are bound to get better.

Douglas and Wildavsky paint a rosy picture of free enterprise and responsible government; they allow for sectarian criticism only if conditions grow particularly pressing. Ordinarily, market and hierarchy will produce sufficient flexibility. To marginalize sectarian voices in this way disregards conspicuous dimensions of American cultural processes—where the marketplace, the state, and sectarian values are enmeshed in a perpetual polemic that agitates the sense of dearths and desires—that spirits cycles of fashion and drives utopian urges.

———

Verging on that topic, let me reiterate the odd *trajet* of Mary Douglas's overall anthropological endeavor. She once offered cautious and refreshing caveats on our profession's pat relativism by defending victims of certain tribal modes of accountability: "The ethnography of the world seen from the eyes of the accused sorcerer has not been recorded as yet" (1970). She has lately come to defend America's political center (in the early 1980s, one could call it the right), which she *fears risks* becoming the victim of its liberal-to-left-wing single-interest groups. Douglas has long debunked everybody's pat assumptions; certainly for sheer nerve and verve few works by anthropologists rival hers. But to equate the combination of Capitol Hill, the White House, the Pentagon, Wall Street, and Madison Avenue with the loser in a witchhunt is a new milestone. Again: "Witchcraft accusations flourish in small groups in which roles are ill defined" (1970: 111). Are there such groups in the U.S.? Yes indeed: environmentalist lobbyists. And who are they accusing? The establishment. That is, as the British saying goes, strong stuff. It is the state—you remember, the agency with power, might, and legitimate means of force, free market support, etc., going for it—that is to be identified with the potential, hapless victim. Like a Tylenol-taker. Douglas has apparently decided: before the sectarians succeed in eroding authority, let's turn the tables; before they make us the scapegoat, let's make it *them*. This may be a good counterreformation ploy, but it's as risky a road to respectable cross-cultural analysis as is the millennialism it would thwart.

Enfin et encore, aimez-vous Thoreau? Siding with James Russell Lowell and Robert Louis Stevenson in a debate whose history goes unacknowledged, Douglas votes no: "Insufferably smug," she calls him. On the pro-Thoreau side, according to E. Wagenknecht's *Henry David Thoreau, What Manner of Man*, we find Bernard Baruch, Sir Thomas Beecham, Martin Buber, Charles Ives, Bette Davis, Proust, Joyce, E. B. White, André Gide, and Gypsy Rose Lee. I'd hate to have to "group" that extra-Vagant list. Moreover, Gandhi, readers may remember, claimed to have based his political philosophy on *Civil Disobedience*; "Thoreau," it has been hyped, "toppled the British Empire." Pro-Thoreau too was Robert Blatchford, who "slept with *Walden* under his pillow" and in the 1890s called local units of his Labor Party "Walden Clubs" (Wagenknecht 1981: 2–6).[13] Perhaps grid-group analysis—which I have just proved easily converts to a fancy name for guilt by association—is (retrospectively) predictive after all. Might one squeeze Douglas snugly inside, with Blatchford's successor safely outside, the high grid box? But I'll not be guilty of explaining away Douglas's vital *Lebenswerk* in this fashion. She's bound to be more than partisan; she is, after all, an anthropologist.

THE GOODS MUST INDEED BE CRAZY:
COMMODITY-FETISHISM (AND
COMMODITY-CRITIQUE) COMMODITIZED

What is the United States of America.
It is not a country surrounded by a wall or not as well by an ocean. In
short the United States of America is not surrounded.
In America they want to make everything something anybody can see
by looking. That is very interesting, that is the reason there are no fences

in between no walls to hide anything no curtains to cover anything and the
cinema that can make anything be anything anybody can see by looking.
That is the way it is.
(Gertrude Stein, Gertrude Stein's America)

A profound question concerning American commodity-life (among other national brands) is: "What do consumers desire?" Or, as Freud might have said,
"What does a capitalist system want?" Like it or not, sectarian assertions are
part of the process of renewing purpose in producing, distributing, and consuming. The center too is tinged with sectarian yearnings. Every suburban
lawn is a little Walden-dream (albeit degraded); technocrats take to wearing
beads and earrings; and ethnic dress converts to double-knit. When one frontier is closed or "border" sealed, another is opened. Alternative-seekers and
dissenters fuel the marketplace, and this fact is expected—institutionalized.
Both advertising and infrastructure confirm that odd alliances can be anticipated. As conclusive evidence against Douglas and Wildavsky's artificial separation of market, state, and utopian-flavored dissent, I offer Disney's Epcot.
Or, to get historical: Coca-Cola (registered trademark), that vanguard multinational consumer corporation that rose out of the marginalized ashes of the
South's reconstruction, merged Methodism and teetotalism against the forces
of hard liquor, capitalized on the wave of prohibition, and later formed a
league with the military to ensure that all overseas GI Joes plus the nations
they were saving for democracy got refreshed. All this emerged as an enthusiastic cult—"Coke adds life"—that could teach both nature and the world to
sing. Or, if you fear-mongers prefer: there developed a conspiracy to spread a
universal addiction to an unnutritious, caffeinated brown syrup, with fizz.
(Yet, even knowing this, for years I seldom passed a day without a "pause.")
Sure, Coke adds life! But Coke also adds "dirt"—more matter out of place;
more categories out of whack.[14] Coca-Cola: America's "pangolin" (see
Chap. 13).

American sectarians, market forces, and regulative agencies are mutually
carnivalized because American culture is commercial. Moreover, shakers and
movers may be as aware of this fact as Madison Avenue admen selling the
army that "wants you," because you've got just as much to give (and "to
live!") as a soft drink has. Everything, including sectarian fears and the Great
Society's goals, is pitched with hype, because everything is in competition
with other brands. I stress this point not because I like, or defend, American
commercial culture, but because I *live* it in possibly the only way one can—
extra-Vagantly.

Mary Douglas's admirers (who include this author) should appreciate the
case I am arguing. *The World of Goods* insists that consumers are more than
jealous strivers, herded conformists, or "prey to the advertiser's wiles" (1979:
89). It demonstrates the *sensible* thriftlessness of weak grid, low-linkage work-

ers and also the social practicality of dukes who build loyalties through "conspicuous overconsumption." One insightful page urges economists to heed evidence from ethnographies of ritual consumption. Technical studies of economies of big discrepancies and comparative advantage often ignore the significance of feasting and shopping sprees alike. In these brands of exchange, "it is a sign that we are near the hot center of a competitive system where small differences matter a lot" (1979: 145). Douglas's insight could be illustrated with rival airline styles, detergent preferences, or claims by double-decker hamburger chains, among copious commercialized connoisseurships of tiny distinctions. Associated marketing rhetoric saturates the general population and everyday life: "Which do you like *best*," countless American "kids" for several generations have ungrammatically asked, "Coke or Pepsi?" (For more comparisons of this legendary competition see *The Cola Wars*—Louis and Yazijian [1980].)

Consumption rhetorics of small-differences-that-matter-a-lot are key to America's many voices. To isolate sectarian gloom from the fuller array of political, economic, and commercial pitches (as an open-ended "cultural system") is anthropologically insufficient: foul play. Liberal and even leftist sectarians are conceivably not so naive as to hope utterly to defeat the marketplace. They possibly seek to nudge production and consumption capacities away from one hot center of slight distinctions—what kind of missile do we fund? will the Whopper outpace the Big Mac?—to another center, equally as hot, also commercial, but "just a little bit" different: what combination of hydro, wind, and solar power is suitable? Can we combine manageable transport and flood-absorbing marshlands, rather than levy the entire Mississippi? Every possibility suggest another new frontier.

By implying that sectarians are jejune and reactionary, *Risk and Culture* dismisses forces of dynamic turnover in the economy's and polity's meanings. Sectarians, I submit, do not originate in a single social sector, unless theorists construct a bland tautology between social form and ideology. Rather sectarian themes join with the market in an agonistic dialectics of commercial culture. The American world of goods—and the world of center-border disputes—is a Disneyworld of shifting *différences*. (And all this before Web sites!)

To proffer my anthropological point itself differently, I might just note that "sectarians" too participate in Horkheimer and Adorno's "culture industry."[15] I dispute aspects of their thrilling, magisterial, understandably dyspeptic analysis of 1930s-1940s U.S. marketing of arts, entertainment, and everything else. I question their Frankfurt School nostalgia for high art over and against the democratic "idolization of the cheap" (not as a basis for evaluating art but for interpreting cultural history). Adorno failed to recognize that jazz can be great, too, even if commercialized (God bless Gershwin!); and even mechanical reproduction procreates "classics."[16] I doubt, moreover, that forces monopolizing advertising represent any polarized isolate in the fashion of a proprietary class; and to Horkheimer and Adorno's insistence on similarities between the advertising slogan and the totalitarian watchword, I would add distinctions. But I still join their resounding *Dialectic of Enlightenment* (1972) in taking the excessive hype of commodity circulation very seriously, to whatever degree regretted (by modernists?) or approved (by postmodernists?).

With stunningly partial irony, Horkheimer and Adorno demonstrated the difficulty of locating any sector—whether buyers or producers, border-types or center-types—as perfectly innocent victims. True, they do say, "The culture industry perpetually cheats its consumers of what it perpetually promises" (1972: 139). But they ultimately imply that the offer is never taken literally: "The triumph of advertising in the culture industry is that consumers feel compelled to buy and use its products even though they see through them" (1972: 167). The power of the "lie" stems from the fact that no one is simply credulous, no one quite the guileless, guiltless beduped. This thoroughly Marxian view (that extends to religion as well) comes close to sophisticated anthropological theories of "belief" (which contains the kernel of its own doubt), but in a negative register.[17] Those apparently victimized by advertisers' deceptions are implicated in the forces controlling them. It is not a pretty picture of commercial culture, high culture, or culture in general; nor is it the view I espouse (especially of religion). But it does have the advantage of suggesting that all participants to an extent share the credit and, what is more important to Marxists, the blame.

Initiated natives know that exaggeration—in advertisements as elsewhere—is not to be taken literally; by the same token hackneyed clichés cannot simply be discarded. Indeed, half-believed (thus doubtable) slogans are the medium of commercial culture. Here then is my message, or lesson, for Douglas and Wildavsky: sectarian participants in America's information flow can be fully as reflexive as their opponents. Tacitly, antagonists know that this rhetorical world requires everyone to overstate any position in order to be heard, or for anything to happen. Extra-Vagant indeed is the discourse of commodity-life—both *t'huis* and globally.[18]

Update (1990s): Coca-Cola Consumes Baudrillard, and a Balinese (Putu) Consumes Coca-Cola

... Human relations tend to be consumed (*consommer*) (in the double sense of the word: to be "fulfilled" [consummated], and to be "annulled" [consumed]) in and through objects which become the necessary mediation and, rapidly, the substitutive sign, *the alibi*, of the relation.
(Jean Baudrillard)[1]

The history of Coca-Cola is a story of special moments. Moments that originated in a three-legged brass pot in Dr. Pemberton's backyard and have been multiplied billions of times around the world. Moments made familiar and universal by Mr. Candler's unique advertising and Mr. Woodruff's vision to put Coca-Cola "within an arm's reach of desire." Moments that today make Coca-Cola the most ubiquitous consumer product in the world.
(The Chronicle of Coca-Cola)[2]

NOVEMBER 21, 1991

Some years after composing the above thoughts on Mary Douglas's response to U.S. culture and human consumption practices, I was kept waiting long enough in a doctor's office to extend my peripheral reading to the *New York Times* financial pages. These words caught my eye:

When I think of Indonesia—a country on the Equator with 180 million people, a median age of 18, and a Moslem ban on alcohol—I feel I know what heaven looks like, said Mr. Keough, Coke's President. (R. Cohen 1991)

Among my academic pursuits has been exploring the history of representing Indonesian cultures over long spans of intrusion—Hindu-Buddhist, Islamic, Portuguese, Dutch, British, Japanese, C.I.A., commodity-marketing (e.g., tourism), philology, anthropology, cultural studies, alternative film and video makers, etc. And my personal history, such that it is, includes having inhabited Coke's own Atlanta at the very time a prime promoter of that fair city (Margaret Mitchell since 1936, with a little help from David Selznick since 1939) was tragically run down by a careless cabbie in 1949.[3] Despite these extra-Vagant credentials/experience in both the newest proclaimed frontier

Fig. 14. An upscale snack-booth (*warung*); its local *spécialité* ("Agung's Buddha Juice") may not have caught on; I never tried it. (Author's snapshot, 1982)

Fig. 15. A "commodity that sells commodities" now available in Bali (bottler untraced); it was but half consumed (too sweet) in Klungkung before the moment captured here. (Author's snap, 1992)

and the old home base of Keough's corporation, I was unprepared for his seemingly gleeful reduction of Indonesia (or its majority Muslims) to a dogmatic land of thirst, ripe for commercial "conversion." Reading, my eye darkened; it gazed aghast.

Keough's irreverent boast may have been overlooked by colleagues in area studies and political theory—peopled largely either by leftists who still believe in proletarian agency or economic determinists who bank (to the right) on profitable planification. I cite Keough for the benefit of either party, to suggest that it is long past high time to take "Coca-Cola marketing" seriocomically indeed. Coke's mode of multilateral merchandizing rehearses motives of and for expenditure that culminate in "Disneyfication," a process one commentator astutely calls a "comprehensive narrative of consumption."[4] To take such conspicuous forces of commodity-showbiz seriocomically requires neither simply deriding nor congratulating them; nor should they be relegated exclusively to media studies. Rather these forces too merit close rereading, now and then, here and there, to discern intricacies of reception and peculiar twists in production and distribution. Even the ballyhooing Keough is complicated; while objectionably presumptuous, his dreamed-of distribution at least was not utterly anti-Islamic—as were many views of Keough's compatriots in 1991. Motives of and for relative "tolerance" are often, perhaps always, devious.[5]

Wittingly or not, that *New York Times* piece abetted Keough's corporate interests when it editorialized: "Coke rebuts the notion that cultural differences mean there are limits on the growth potential in foreign countries" (Cohen 1991). In 1991, my critique of Keough (and the *Times*)—had it been promulgated—would have challenged their mutual assumption that Coke's global success derives from nullifying "cultural differences" through universal marketing savvy. As-if conspiratorially, both "knowledges" (Keough's and the *Times*'s) managed to obscure a cutting wedge of religious assertion basic to one legendary corporation's politics and history. The *Times* more accurately might have reported: "A beverage once underpinned by U.S. Methodism plans to capitalize on Indonesian Islam much as it earlier profiteered from prohibition back home, particularly (in both cases?) among conscripted soldiers and the families to which they return." Call it "*a* Protestant ethic and one spirit of consumerism."

Strikingly, *neither* Keough nor the strange bedfellow covering him recognized that economic strategy can be constituted by and as ritual and religious values. Abiding convictions of economism (thought to be "objective") limit those invested in them to theories that reduce cultural differences to mere obstacles to universal market access. As suggested above, such economism afflicts wildly diverse thinkers—Marxists, supply-siders, and even Mary Douglas when her work lapsed into semi-utilitarian stances. Economism blinds its believers to evidence of how extra-Vagant commodities-in-cultures can be, along with pangolin-like subjects they mediate. Yep: "Hegemonic" economism sure can befog volatile truths of consumption.[6]

A FEW MONTHS LATER, 1992

Planning a return journey to Bali, I felt increasing alarm over Keough's pronouncement—part of U.S. global dominance by means of soft drinks, movies, software, armaments, and related "exports." I resolved to drop by Atlanta's then-newest museum ("The World of Coca-Cola," opened in 1990), aiming to investigate how Coke might be plotting to target not just tropical teetotalers (*de jure*, by the way) but Indonesia's contrary Hindus—known on occasion to imbibe rice wine.[7]

As confessed above (Chap. 5), whenever museum-going, this tourist purchases the official guide to collections (here "The Chronicle of Coca-Cola") but also smuggles in contrary reading material to subvert ideologically-loaded displays pilfered and plundered from the past. For Atlanta I happened to choose *Jean Baudrillard: Selected Writings* (1988)—handy excerpts of that influential author's copious works, all of which had been dutifully digested (believe me) in the original. The present essay reports exactly what happened when Baudrillard's high critical theories of exponential simulacra and consumption's priority met more than a century's worth of hoopla billed as "the story of the most successful product in the history of commerce." To make a long story short: Either the difference was erased, or Baudrillard lost. Allow me to expatiate.

The wonders and wiles of Coca-Cola's guaranteed-refreshing marketing styles—from 1886 to the past-saturated present—include sound- and sight-bites from the "millions of advertisements and artifacts that have made and kept Coca-Cola a timeless symbol" of "unique appeal."[8] (Simulations of these simulations, often copyrighted, are available for purchase in the shop, or should one say "shop." Most reproductions bear the celebrated trademark [no inverted commas around "trademark"]—"Coca-Cola," registered in 1893, or "Coke," registered in 1945, despite the corporation's earlier admonishment to loyal customers: "Call for it by full name; nicknames encourage substitution.") Here, as I say, are some exhibited simulations that the present sight/sound/smell-seer-hearer-smeller jotted down in no particular order, while museum-going, before purchasing:

The Ideal Brain Tonic. "I just took Coca-Cola as a name, similar to other advertising names, thinking that the two "c"s would look well in advertising"—Frank Robinson. 1906, Sheet Music, "Lead Kindly Light." 1908, Vienna Art plates. 1913, Philippines. "A charming lady doesn't really need her fan/ with a glass of Coca-Cola in her hand." 1917, last calendar with old-style bottles. Drink Coca-Cola [hereafter "C-C"] from a bottle through a straw; absolutely sanitary. Contour bottle, Nov. 16, 1915 [which Japanese consider happy because pregnant-looking].[9] "C-C is always in tune with the times." Delacroix's stand at the top of the

Eiffel Tower. A Texas German-language Newspaper. "Thirst knows no time nor season; Enjoy Thirst." 1925, Arabian Nights motif: "exotic atmosphere." 1926, "THIRST IS A TOUCH OF NATURE THAT MAKES THE WHOLE WORLD KIN." "A Product that Sells Other Products." (still 1926)

When typing up these fieldnotes weeks later with a New Jersey TV running in the background, there abruptly emerged "Georgia on my Mind"—retread themesong of a "Designing Women" rerun, issuing from a channel selected earlier to tune in CBS's morning coverage of the Winter Olympics, sponsored, needless to say, by ubiquitous Coke. My typing continued:

Imitators: Koca Kola Coke-Ola. "We've Bottled up the Pirates of Business" (1916). 1939, Shanghai China trucks. 1880, carbonator. 1910, C-C in a bottle!! I touch video-screen selection for 1920s: Jazz; "Eerlijk en Verfrisschend" (Amsterdam Olympics, 1928). Market crash. 1938, 6-pack; every bottle sterilized. Cooler. Orchestra; CBS refreshes Coke Radio Time. "The Southerner exhibits an inexhaustible capacity for pausing and an inexhaustible capacity for being refreshed; to both these basic needs C-C lovingly ministers" (*Fortune Magazine*, 1931). A booklet on entertaining at home with C-C [exhibit does not mention prohibition here; later does, along with Hollywood in 1935]. 1935, Norman Rockwell. 1934, Johnny Weissmuller. 1933, Claudette Colbert. Drink C-C; it cools you. Cheesecake. THE GREATEST PAUSE ON EARTH. G-I schmaltz. 1946, reunited families; the "sprite." 1945, "Coke" equals Coca-Cola. AT THE CROSSROADS OF THE WORLD. First C-C TV program, Edgar Bergen and Charlie McCarthy.

Visitors eventually enter the exhibitions's climax—a high-tech theater whose single-channel's program I here fastforward to KEOUGH (!) on gargantuan HDTV ("the first installation in this country," his image explained, with many technical caveats that passed me by). Thus it was that I did indeed encounter Keough after all, or his simulation (cyborgs, always cyborgs); here is what it said, as far as I can remember:

This simple moment of pleasure. . . . C-C is so natural to the different cultures and lifestyles. . . . Largest product and distribution system in the world. Simple purpose . . . 80 languages. 450 million times a day [Something lost in that jingle!] Sky dive, Malibu, Osaka, Essen, Bangkok, Giza [backed up by "La Donna e mobile"], Africa, Nairobi, . . . Thai rock at Imperial Palace, Special Olympics. Singapore [I think, although too quick to call . . . maybe Hongkong . . .].

And that was it: Not a word, not one bloomin' word, about Bali. Nor did that atypical corner of Indonesia figure in the other exhibitions, a few more of which I noted:

DRIVE REFRESHED, 1950. "All the Cokes are the same and all the cokes are good" (Andy Warhol, 1975). Kit Carson [Barbara Hale's husband, but no sign of Della], 1955. "50 Million times a day. . . ." McGuire Sisters, "King Size." "Value, lift, refreshment, too," 1963, "Things go better with [Hootenanny] Coke"! [Absolutely and positively NO MENTION OF PEPSI, I mean zip]. 1931, Haddon Sundblom's STANDARD SANTA and the famous "Dear Zanta" letter [with a backward's "S": there are info-mercial limits to Word Perfect 5.1, for which I apologize to the reader].

That's all I got down, scrivening fiercely. At some point during this blitz of captions, jingles, and icons—too many of them *utterly* and unutterably familiar—I located a sheltered corner where Coke's "world" (not "community?") could be countered by opening my Baudrillard to redabble in *Le Système des objets*, *La Société de consommation*, etc., or simulacra-simulations (i.e., translations) thereof. That at least was my desire, despite certain shortcomings in his *oeuvre*'s trajectory stipulated by Mark Poster in an extremely helpful "introduction":

> In the recent essay, "The Masses: the Implosion of the Social in the Media," Baudrillard recapitulates the theme of his work in the 1980s: the media generate a world of simulations which is immune to rationalist critique, whether Marxist or liberal. The media present an excess of information and they do so in a manner that precludes response by the recipient. The simulated reality has no referent, no ground, no source. It operates outside the logic of representation. But the masses have found a way of subverting it: the strategy of silence or passivity. Baudrillard thinks that by absorbing the simulations of the media, by failing to respond, the masses undermine the code. Whatever the value of this position it represents a new way of understanding the impact of the media. Instead of complaining about the alienation of the media or the terrorism of the code, Baudrillard proposes a way out: silence. Critical theorists will certainly not remain silent about Baudrillard's paradoxical revolutionary strategy. (Poster 1988: 7)

Responseless recipients? That hardly sounds ethnographically informed (nor, I confess, does this possibly reactionary native put much stock in Baudrillard's view of America).[10]

Still, I kept reading back into Baudrillard's earlier valuable insights; for example:

> A fixed class of "normal" consumers has been created . . . according to the irreversible trend towards the American model, the ambiguity of advertising . . . *provokes us to compete*; yet, through this imaginary competition, *it already invokes a profound monotony*, a uniformula . . ., a devolution in the bliss of the consuming masses. . . . We can imagine that each individual feels unique while resembling everyone else. . . . (Baudrillard 1988: 11)

Or:

> At the heart of the project from which emerges the systematic and indefinite process of consumption is a frustrated desire for totality. (25)

And:

> In fact, we are giving too much credit to advertising by comparing it with *magic*: the nominalist lexicon of alchemy has already in itself something of an actual language, structured by a research and interpretive (*déchiffrement*) praxis. The nominalism of the "brandname," however, is purely immanent and fixated (*figé*) by an economic imperative. (27)

Plus:

> The pleasure obtained from a television or a second home is experienced as "real" freedom. No one experiences this as alienation. Only the intellectual can describe it in this way, on the basis of a moralizing idealism, one which at best reveals him as an alienated moralist. (40)

Furthermore:

> . . . this is what Galbraith does not see and along with him all of the "alienists" of consumption, who persist in their attempts to demonstrate that *people's relation to objects and their relation to themselves is falsified*, mystified, and manipulated, consuming this myth at the same time as the object. (42–43)

Finally:

> A *universal curiosity* ["universal?"] (a concept to be exploited) has as a consequence been reawakened in the areas of cuisine, culture, science, religion, sexuality, etc. "Try Jesus!" says an American slogan. *Everything* ["everything?"] must be tried: since man as consumer is haunted by the fear of "missing" something, any kind of pleasure.
>
> The themes of expenditure, pleasure, and non-calculation ("Buy now, pay later") have replaced the "puritan" themes of thrift, work, and patrimony. But this is only the appearance of a human revolution. (48, 50; my bracketed interjections)

P.S.:

> The structures of consumption are simultaneously fluid and enclosed. Can we imagine a coalition of drivers against car registration? Or a collective opposition to television? Even if every one of the million viewers is opposed to television advertising, advertisements will nevertheless be shown. That is because consumption is primarily organized as a discourse to oneself, and has a tendency to play itself out, with its gratifications and deceptions, in this minimal exchange. The object of consumption isolates. (54)

Pausing in my reading to wonder whether Baudrillard had just committed an alienist idealism of the sort critiqued ten pages earlier, I started to sense something else bothering me about his reflections. "Minimal exchange?" "The object of consumption isolates?" Does Coca-culture—by its own lights contributing the ultimate "object" (and subject) of *consommation*—really isolate?

Surrounded by Coca-Cola's "advertisements" (i.e., exhibitions *of* advertisements rather than advertisements proper), and by persons (including Americans) consuming them conspicuously *together*, I didn't quite see how.[11] I still
found worth in Baudrillard, of course, but whether his critique captured Coke
or Coke's ads captured his critique, I could not for the life of me decide.
Perhaps, it next dawned on me, it was undecidable! But then something happened that suddenly cancelled my theoretical thirst to decide even that, or to
keep assessing or cancelling Baudrillard's fast-dating critique of (and for, and
as) consumption (*consommation*). Nor was I inclined right then to pursue my
own critique of Coke and the *Times* sketched above. The task of ethnography
compels me to inscribe that something that happened (it was a local event): I
looked up . . .

. . . There above me dangled in slightly reduced scale the replica of a vintage
bottling apparatus—Coca-Cola's multiply patented answer to Rube Goldberg
(or Britain's Heath Robinson), which extra-Vagant device jostles along an
eternally returning single-file of empties—successively scrubbed, checked for
cracks, meticulously filled, capped, rechecked for flaws—in an unlikely as-
sembly line to perfection that was anything but boring to boys and girls *voy-
eur*ing the original's calibrated machinations through *vitrines* thoughtfully
provided by landlords (at the company's command) for all passers-by
(*flâneurs*). But I have slipped this essay-*étude* from a slightly aestheticized
assemblage, circa 1991, to an assembly-line itself, circa 1951, as I precipitously remembered seeing it operate on the ground floor of the building that
also housed Daddy's office, every time I got to accompany him to that (for me,
sacred, for him workaday) precinct. To glimpse again from below at age forty-
five—this was a while ago—what special occasions had let me oggle head-on
at five—such is the concocted *souvenir* quite brilliantly designed into the
entrée of Coke's museum. And I certainly drank it in.

Oh, an ardent hermeneut might try to distinguish his or her *own* experience
as more intensively "pop" than that of less authentic metaconsumers passing
through Coke's world. In my case, for example, subsequent exhibits revealed
that the plant I only half-recollected beneath the *pater*'s workplace was sited
precisely midway along the original axis of Coca-Cola's bottling enterprise (a
key strategy in its eventual global triumph): a route connecting Atlanta with
Chattanooga (Tennessee, near Rock City, which drivers should See!), bisected
by Rome (the only Georgia town mentioned, by the way, in Hitchcock's *Spellbound*). That my patriline overlay Coke's *original* distribution line almost
makes that brandname feel "proper" to yours truly (and my progenitor's middle initial was "C."). But I mention these silly coincidences not to colonize the
world's climactic commodity for my personal benefit (or identification), but to
remind readers what they (we) can only know for them(our)selves: consump-

tion too has its invented "roots"—diversely imaginative (i.e., "cultural") like other kinds.

To repeat: an ethnographic calling obliges me to report that both Baudrillard's critique of simulacra/authenticity distinctions and my critique of the *New York Times* financial pages fail to "theorize" what befell this consumer upon crossing a threshold into history according to Coca-Cola, stretched from 1883 (the year of the sacred formula's "in the beginning") through HDTV (the latest technology transmitting its commercial aura). But *franchement* and practically speaking, I never really got to intervene Baudrillard's book into this scene of Coca-Cola's self-celebrations; because right upon entering I had looked up; and Coke's initial display just blew me away.

AFTER FATHER

I do miss him; and I hope any readers lucky enough to have or have had one miss theirs. Coca-Cola loomed even larger paternally than already intimated: for the half of his life that I witnessed, Daddy snatched quick lunches of Nabs and a Coke, unwilling to steal even a noon break from his superconscientious labors in middle management; sometimes I got to check the empty bottle-bottom to calculate how far it had journeyed from its locale of manufacture (that's why you learned geography in those days). But could mourning Father—concretely, carbonatedly—explain the intensity of my submissive response (I felt virtually "Muslim") to Coke's crafty exhibits that adroitly manipulate the nostalgias of willing imbibers? No . . ., there seemed to be more along other lines: something different, otherwise ambivalent, chromatic even. But what? Maybe, just maybe it was . . . Mother?

It was only then that I remembered—possibly when choking down long-distance squirts of Coke spurted from the computerized soda fountain whose ultramodern (or is that post?) extravaganza tops off Keough's corporate show of quirky-quaint plus glitzy-tech collections—a distaff side no less *verfrisshend* with love, guilt, dreams, failures, and half-steps: the stuff of cultures (and those living them) anywhere, perhaps. Mother, like many of her gender, was a keen-witted woman who, deprived of higher education by economic circumstances and a few prejudices, became all the more grade-conscious for children she bore. Every weekday of my very scholastic early life, she prepared for her only son a tall glass (still in those days just 6 ½ oz.) of ice-filled Coca-Cola (Mother, a New Englander, never said "Coke"); it was left waiting for him (rather, me) at school's end and homework's beginning. (The familially enforced limit was one-a-day; and the regimented time to consume it after-class.) This woman (whose husband my father was) performed her gift—serving the C-C—like clockwork. Schooldays, however, were more flexible in their boundaries—not demarcated clearly but modulated into margins and borderlands of sundry clubs (an American tradition) and extracurricular activities.

That glass of "ideal brain tonic" became a barometer of ambivalence: the more condensation and the deeper the top (melted ice) floating clearly above the syrupy fluid (whose purity had remained unviolated over several generations)—and, correlatively, the flatter and more watery the hybrid liquid's taste by the time I consumed it—the profounder was an implicit accusation of diverting too many moments from study and devoting too few to home. Whether homework or home (*Heim*) in some more Freudian sense I could never discern—when Mother was alive or since.

No less than asparagus in Proust—whose readers may recall that Françoise (embodiment of *la France*) served obsessively, not as it turned out because of the rainbow hues and a distinctive odor it produced soon after ingestion in the consumer's urine (elaborately remarked by the micturating narrator); but because the under-maid (*sous-soubrette*?) subject to Françoise's authority was allergic to the polychrome phallic legume and suffered histaminic seizure when obliged to prepare it—that ritual glass of Coke *chez moi* mediated familial intricacies of kindness and resentment, generosity and jealousy, dependence and rebellion, among other everyday activities. Domestic life in cultures of consumption is no less contradictory and contestatory than that in other kinds, if other kinds there be. Anything cultural—including trademarks—deflects pat dogmas and easy diagnosis. "Fifty million times a day" (long about 1955), and my little ol' *habitus* was just one of them; each of the other 49,999,999 had its peculiar distinction.

Coke may (like Unesco) "like to teach the world to sing in perfect harmony." But culturally, Coke sustains wherewithalls of chromatic modulations among affect, coercion, loving-kindness, terror, levity, duress, and desire. Ultraobjectively, everything (or at least a lot) in anyone's life in consumer-culture ("mine," for example, any reader might say) pulses to seriocomic rhythms of merchandized meanings. The circumstances and pomp of what gets marketed—even products aspiring to universality—remain extra-Vagantly particular when we begin really rereading receptions. Thus, as Melville might have said:

> Planify away, Mr. Keough! With all your expertise, you cannot micromanage the slippery motives—among Indonesia's Muslim believers or for Atlanta's pseudo-native sons—of your product's consumption. Coca-Cola's charms were, are, and will be confidently—culturally—peculiar.

A BIT LATER, BACK IN THE FIELD: THE "ALIBI" OF BALI

In 1992, I returned to Indonesia, via Singapore, whose commercial history partly parallels Coca-Cola's (which is to say, Atlanta's). Both began in the mid 1880s—Atlanta with its trademark beverage crucial to the history of global commodity-packaging for the masses; Singapore with its trademark hotel (the celebrated Raffles), crucial to the history of global tourism-packaging for an upmarket. Coincidentally, by the 1980s Atlanta and Singapore together, I'm afraid, wound up with the world's highest concentration of postmodernity's signature-style of architecture (one synthesizing, as it were, the mass commodity with upscale hostelry): skyscraper-atriums. Indeed, Singapore imported Atlanta's foremost designer to make the old-East resemble the new-West—like twin-cities rejoined a century after birth by John Portman.[12] I paused long hours reading receptions of these postmodern spaces (by "reading receptions" I mean voyeur-ing and eavesdropping on persons trespassing there), mindful of the fact that such sites are anathema to Frederick Jameson.[13] I can only say that, ethnographically, what happens in these places/spaces/locations (*lieux*) too seems different. (But Singapore, like Atlanta, was just an interlude; on to Indonesia.)

I boarded superb Air Singapore which luckily had just initiated direct service to Bali; and silly me, I forgot to document its beverage lists. Nor have I compiled any "objective" statistics on Coke's differential impact among, say, Muslim Buginese (circumcised, buried) in Bali, as opposed to that island's majority Hindu Balinese (uncircumcised, cremated). I do not know whether Keough's strategic reliance on (supposed) Islamic abstinence implies that Bali is considered a tough market to penetrate (or figuratively, nut to crack)—much as it averted Christian missionizing for a century and more of Dutch colonialism.[14] I did, however, discover something qualitative about Coke's impact in this neck of Indonesia's multicultural woods that may please president Keough (in the unlikely event he is still in office)—despite my datum's remoteness from his product's meanings or market share in its native U.S. Southland, among other territories it has conquered.

To convey Coke's undiagnosable extra-Vagance into Indonesia requires a little backpedaling through the present consumer's earlier fieldworks, marked by ironies (Burkian ironies, I feel, more than postmodern ones) of episodic, not to say picaresque, encounter. Consider then, one Balinese life as this author's work became superficially entangled in it, and vice-versa. It is a professional anthropological custom—and a good one—to shelter "informants" (including friends) with anonymity (this is for their own protection, since no academic enterprise can control policing powers or legal accountability abroad or at home). In Balinese customs, disinclined to personal naming anyway, relative anonymity is a piece of cake. Let us call the subject of these paragraphs: I Gde.[15]

I Gde figured importantly in previous studies I devoted in whole or in part to Bali. Briefly profiled, he is an eldest son in a subline of an ancestor group of enormous consequence in the history of western Bali. He was (and is) about my age, recently married (as was I, when we first met in 1972), but not yet (then) a parent (as I already was). His wife, unlike mine, is a *mindon*—second patriparallel cousin; his favorite uncle was the charismatic force behind the fragile coherence of a fractious kingroup and marriage-alliance network. I Gde's sense of humor and mine matched (unless he fooled me into feeling so); reminiscence still finds me laughing at jokes he could crack (in Indonesian and Balinese) as we whiled away night-long vigils at temple ceremonies with undercurrent tensions of great complexity that I ethnographed. In gratitude for all I Gde had given, when preparing to depart after a year's stay, I bequeathed him a motorbike. This gesture inadvertently incurred the severe displeasure of his wife's sister-in-law (translation here is particularly difficult), who had hoped one of his cousins (her son: a fine fellow but younger, and neither as funny nor in certain respects as sharp) would be so favored. No amount of cash could compensate for her disappointment.

In 1982, I was back in Bali; I Gde helped catch me up on island-wide political-*cum*-kinship *événements* (or was that *habitus*?). Attentive to the aftermath of intricate status movements that were the subject of my research, he had become an informal observer of ethnohistory as it happened. Formally, he had secured coveted employment with a travel bureau—a fact I knew from letters, which had prompted my return-gift (*oleh*): the latest English-Indonesian dictionary in a strongly bound American edition (highly preferable to lousy local reproductions). Alas, the gift—accepted with glassy-eyed grace—flopped: because of a recent reassignment by his firm's boss, who hoped to tap a particularly animated tourist sector, I Gde was now exclusively pursuing Indonesian-Italian. Meanwhile, his family had expanded by two children (the same total as mine), beautiful as only Balinese can be (I intend no invidious comparison with my wife's and my differently attractive daughters). That cousin who once lost out on the motor bike had for unconnected reasons bailed out of Bali to Australia; indeed had married there—a fact desperately regretted by his parents, I was led to surmise.

By 1992, when I Gde and I met again, his sister-in-law (the cousin's mother) had just "left the world" (*meninggal dunia*). We remained close enough in spirit for him to counsel me not to revisit her houseyard. Her widower—a warm and compassionate man, whose nostalgia rivals my own, had a history of depression; my arrival might provoke in him despair, triggered by memories of twenty years ago when their children were young, our infant daughter was their plaything, and conditions in Bali were far happier for him than they are now. *Tempo dulu*, truly.

As for I Gde himself: risen in the ranks of his tourist business, he proudly related having been awarded by Japan Airlines a trip via Tokyo to Alaska.

"Alaska?" said I, pointing.

"Alaska," said he.

I Gde filled in my blank look by explaining that his professional *spécialité* had again switched (causing me earnestly to hope that he hadn't discarded my previous dictionary-gift). Having bid *arrivederci* to globe-trotting Romans, he was now lubricating tour groups shunting to Bali from Juneau.

I report this fact with some trepidation. Many modernist and/or postmodernist friends (with whom I sometimes sympathize) could not resist at this juncture spotlighting an ultra-transnational flow: Bali-Juneau (what a hoot). But before readers (including this reader) titter or sigh—or smirk or rue—it may be worth wondering if any prospects of and for true irony in Burke's sense—humble irony—exist here. One possibility strikes me: The incongruities of I Gde's life are really no more shrieking than my own (further details of which readers deserve to be spared), nor those of my father, who bridged cotton farm to insurance agency; nor his father before him—ex-cotton farmer (boll weevil) demoted to stockings-peddler, killed crossing a street in the town where indigence had forced him to relocate . . . and so on. All this, again, is true. And, as already confessed, my distaff side (like many another) is equally a her-story of repeated displacements.

Burkian irony could find an as-if kinship (*Wahlverwandshaft?*—Kenneth Burke, needless to say, commented, and often, on Goethe) between two unlikely "pangolins."[16] Both I Gde and I (along with so many more, too many to list) have been Balinists in a way—one "foreign" and academically, one "native" and *parawisata*ly (that's Indonesian for tourism). In stipulating this resemblance, I am promoting no edge of exponential simulatedness, inviting no titter (or tsk-tsking) about nonstop inauthenticity or antiauthority, indeed tendering no proclamation of triumph or defeat, no final critical moral of any kind. Rather, I wish to recognize interlinking, overlapping disparities—not identical, not equal, but still *comparable* (susceptible of comparison). *Lui*: A Balinese tour broker arisen from semitraditional courtliness; *moi*: an American scholar arisen from boll weevil rurality—both occasionally transnational, and after a fashion or two cosmopolitan (kind of); but for all that, local (kind of) as well. Our relationship—like anything politically fence-leaping—was enmeshed in official institutions of research and travel (requiring passports, visas, permits, licensing, etc.). But the poetics of seriocomic encounter do not reduce to official policies of border-patrolling or surreptitious palm-greasing. Nor have any attributes of power-knowledge separating "I Gde and I" ever worked only in one direction. Is it through mutual incongruities that irony—a two-way street—truly obtains, and cross-culturally as well?

If I had not been pre-persuaded of the volatility of that last question, it might have dawned on me during my return visit in 1992, or perhaps some future return. The proof, however, came not from I Gde himself, but from one of his descendants (*turunan*). I Gde had arrived at the customary hour of visitation (*sore*) to pay me (half-ironic, I have long felt) respect (*hormat*), fondly. Accompanying him (*yang ikut*) were his wife (call her Komang), plus their son (Putu) and daughter (Kadek, say); the children, an investigator of kinship might note, are siblings and third cousins too (see Boon 1977, 1982a: Chap. 5; 1982b; 1989, 1990a: Chaps. 4–6); and I have already remarked more generally on their very individual Balinese beauty. Komang remained shy enough (*malu*) of cosmopolitan settings to decline a restaurant meal I proposed; and Kadek was too young to voice her preferences for anything whatsoever. But Putu brightened at the prospect of partaking of the small hotel's snack service, when I jovially offered with winking, self-mocking insistence *quelque chose à boire*. (*Betul-betul?? Tidak mau minum?*)

"What would you like to drink," (*Mau minum apah?*) I asked in Indonesian, sugar-coated with my sprinkling of Balinese quips that tried comically to reverse status-markers while ludic-crudely (*kasar*) asserting the wherewithal to pay (something like: "*Ditiang ngelah pipis*"). (*Anything* to break the ice.) As for the serious-sounding response given by already-sparkling Putu—the first-born Balinese son of that first-born Balinese son, good old I Gde—all this anthropologist can affirm in conclusion is:

"It wasn't Pepsi."

Encores and Envoi

Burke, Cavell, etc., Unforgotten

What, when I name forgetfulness, and withal recognise what I name?
whence should I recognise it, did I not remember it? I speak not of the
sound of the name, but of the thing which it signifies: which if I had
forgotten, I could not recognise what that sound signifies. When then
I remember memory, memory is itself, through itself, present with
itself; but when I remember forgetfulness, there are present both
memory and forgetfulness; memory whereby I remember,
forgetfulness which I remember.
. . . And lo, the force of mine own memory is not understood by me;
though I cannot so much as name myself without it. For what shall I say,
when it is clear to me that I remember forgetfulness? Shall I say that that
is not in my memory, which I remember? or shall I say that forgetfulness
is for this purpose in my memory, that I might not forget? Both were most
absurd. What third way is there? . . . And yet, in whatever way,
although that way be past conceiving and explaining, yet certain am
I that I remember forgetfulness itself also, whereby what
we remember is effaced.
Great is the power of memory, a fearful thing, O my God, a deep and
boundless manifoldness; and this thing is the mind, and this am I
myself. . . .—over all these do I run, I fly; I dive on this side and on
that, as far as I can, and there is no end.
(*Augustine,* Confessions)[1]

LIKE AUGUSTINE—whom, like Freud, Kenneth Burke dutifully reread—
Burke himself seems unlikely to fall victim to critical fashion. He would be as
hard to declare obsolete as he was to proclaim *courant.* Burke-on-Augustine,
moreover, helps return this book's eccentric readers to key topics of manifold
rites, constitutive memory, everyday reflexivity (regardless of culture), and
ironies of first-person experience: "the force of mine own memory . . . not
understood by me." Consider,then, a few more extracts of Burke, who here
happens to be addressing neither Jimmy Durante nor Proust *per se* (see "Rehearsals"), but the rhetoric of Augustine's authority:

As one might expect, references to the "inwardness" of memory run throughout
the section. Memory is an "inner place not a place" where things are stored at

varying depths within. . . . He refers to the *sinus* of God's "deep secret," the place far from which he had been placed by the consequences of his transgressions. In the Latin dictionaries the range of the meanings for the word is given as: curve, fold, hollow, coil, bosom, lap, purse, money, bay, gulf, basin, valley; figuratively: love, affection, protection, intimacy, innermost part, heart, hiding-place. The Memory is also likened to a "vast *aula*," for which the range of meanings is: court, forecourt, inner court, yard, hall, palace, royal court, residence, courtiers, princely power, royalty.

There are many other references conveying connotations of great scope in connection with his ideas of the Memory. . . . He has a plenty (*copia*) of past experiences to draw on, when thinking of the future. Memory is a great power (*vis*). . . . It is a "profound and infinite multiplicity." It is also something vaguely dreadful (*nescio quid horrendum*).

. . . He is now ready for the reflexive stage, as with the thought that he remembers having remembered, puzzling as to how he can remember memory itself, how he truly remembers having heard things that were false, and how he even remembers forgetfulness, the "privation of memory." Without memory, he cannot even name his own name.

. . . Chapter XXV has a twist that one should consider, when trying to understand Augustine's psychology. Any contemporary psychologies that would use the words "mind" and "memory" would probably treat of "memory" as a *part* of the "mind." But in Augustine's usage "memory" is the more inclusive term, since the mind can remember itself. (Burke 1970: 125–26, 128, 134)[2]

Burke's annotations of Augustine may even clarify aromas of sacrifice—an Old Testamental (and also Brahmanical) issue briefly sensed in Chapter 2:

In the opening invocation of Book IV, when deriding Manichaean views on food and holiness, [Augustine] speaks of himself as sucking God's milk and eating of Him as a food that does not perish. Characteristically, when speaking of the Word made flesh . . ., he calls it a food whereby God's Wisdom (*sapientia*) might give milk (*lactesceret*) to our infancy. And when nearing conversion he likens the memory of God to the odor of an appetizing food that he smells but cannot eat. . . .

Augustine also indicates roundabout the strongly oral associations which words have for him when he finds it a matter of comment that Ambrose, besides his great gifts as a preacher, made it a habit to read solely with his eyes, "while voice and tongue were quiet" (*quiescebant*). Secondarily, we might recall here that it was Ambrose who most directly induced Augustine to abandon his earlier tendency to conceive of everything, perhaps after the fashion of the Stoics, as varying attenuations of the corporeal. (Burke 1970: 66, 67)[3]

Burke's comment on Stoic notions of everything as "attenuations of the corporeal" recalls an antique epistemology that conceivably folds over our (Foucauldian?) era's critical turn, or rather return, to subjects bodily.[4] Had Burke

experienced recent resurrections of a comfortably consolidated transdicipli-
nary theme ("You-Name-It-Of-The-Body"), he may well have countered—
virtually reflexively—by tacking on "and soul" or "spirit:" *de l'esprit*. Burke
was ever the rhetorical-dialectician, resisting attenuation.

Possibly for that very reason Kenneth Burke kept exploring intimations of
democratic perfectionism—a tradition whose Emersonian version Stanley
Cavell (for his part) "aversively" thinks through in wonderful "conversations"
worth interrupting as little as possible. Here, then, is some more Cavell (from
Conditions Handsome and Unhandsome, 1990)—solo insofar as this reader
can restrain himself:

[**1.**] Nietzsche is the pivot because of his early and late devotion to Emerson's
writing. . . . But no matter how often this connection of Nietzsche to Emerson is
stated, no matter how obvious to anyone who cares to verify it, it stays incredible,
it is always in a forgotten state. . . . (40)

[**2.**] I remarked that moral perfectionism has not found a secure home in modern
philosophy. There are various reasons for this homelessness, and, as I have said,
the title perfectionism covers more than a single view. Taking Emerson and
Nietzsche as my focal examples [as this book takes Thoreau and Burke], and
thinking of them, I surmise that the causes for the disapproval of perfectionism
will orbit around . . . a hatred of moralism—of what Emerson calls "conformity"—so passionate and ceaseless as to seem sometimes to amount to a hatred of morality altogether (Nietzsche calls himself the first antimoralist; Emerson
knows that he will seem antinomian, a refuser of any law, including the moral law
. . .). (46; my bracketed interruption)

[**3.**] We must become averse to this conformity, which means convert from it,
which means transform our conformity, as if we are to be born (again) [a theme
Cavell also detects in the screwball comedies that he justifiably adores].[5] (47; my
bracketed annotation)

[**4.**] Then how shall we understand Emerson's and Nietzsche's disdain for the
cultural institutions, or institutionalized culture, of the day? . . . The distribution
of nothing of high culture as it is now institutionalized is to be maximized in
Emersonian Perfectionism, which is in that sense *not a teleological theory at all*.
What Nietzsche calls "the pomp of culture" and "misemployed and appropriated
culture" is, on the contrary, to be scorned [or for the less arrogantly inclined,
perhaps, relativized]. (48; my emphasis)

Much like Burke (above), Cavell traces perfectionism to Plato and Aristotle,
and after them to Emerson and Nietzsche and Thoreau, who emphasized education and character and friendship (one thinks here also of Montaigne and
perhaps Erasmus); they tried to imagine how to overhaul the mediocrity, level-
ing, and vulgarity of equal existence. "There are undeniably aristocratic or

aesthetic perfectionisms," Cavell acknowledges; "but in Emerson it should, I would like to say, be taken as part of the training for democracy" (56). Cavell then broaches writing and reading—the place where democracy overcomes its characteristic or customary *banality* (my word):

[5.] . . . In answer to how Emerson's writing (re)presents the aspiration to the human, beginning from a famous early sentence of "Self-Reliance" I have already had occasion to cite: "In every work of genius we recognize our own rejected thoughts. They come back to us with a certain alienated majesty." The idea of a majesty alienated from us is a transcription of the idea of the sublime as Kant characterizes it. . . . Reading, as such, is taken by Emerson as of the sublime. (57)

[6.] This comes out in Emerson's (and Thoreau's) [Cavell's parentheses, welcome indeed to this reader] delirious denunciation of books, in the spectacle of writing their own books that dare us to read them and dare us not to; that ask us to conceive that they do not want us to read them, to see that they are teaching us how—how *not* to read, that they are creating the taste not to be read, the capacity to *leave* them. Think of it this way: If the thoughts of a text such as Emerson's . . . are yours, then you do not need them [cf. Burke on Freud in "Rehearsals" above; or Boon on Burke; or your reading now]. If its thoughts are *not* yours, they will not do you good. The problem is that the text's thoughts are neither exactly mine nor not mine. In their sublimity as my rejected—say repressed—thoughts, they represent my further, next, unattained but attainable, self. To think otherwise, to attribute the origin of my thoughts simply to the other, thoughts which are then, as it were, implanted in me—some would say caused—by let us say some Emerson, is idolatry. (What in "Politics of Interpretation" I call the theology of reading is pertinent here.) (57; my brackets, folding Cavell into the present book; and my emphasis on "leave.")

Cavell rounds off what "I call" ultraobjective writing on reading (really, ritual rereading—see Chap. 1) with a few more allusions to Freud and one more mention of Thoreau:

[7.] In becoming conscious of what in the text is (in Emerson's word) unconscious, the familiar is invaded by another familiar—the structure Freud calls the uncanny, and the reason he calls the psychoanalytic process itself uncanny. Emerson's process of transfiguring is such a structure, a necessity of his placing his work in the position of our rejected and further self, our "beyond." One of his ways of saying this is to say "I will stand here for humanity" as if he is waiting for us to catch up or catch on. (57–58)

[8.] If Emerson is . . . right, his aversion provides for the democratic aspiration the only internal measure of its truth to itself—a voice only this aspiration could have inspired, and, if it is lucky, must inspire. Since his aversion is a *continual turning away* from society, it is thereby a continual turning *toward* it. Toward and away; it is a motion of seduction . . . [compare Burke's "Vergings . . ."]. (59; my bracketed recommendation)

[**9.**] [a magic number] How is this domestication—call it finding a home for humanity; Emerson and Thoreau picture it as building a house, another edification—how is this a task for philosophy? (60; my bracketed interpolation)

I leave that last question to Stanley Cavell, philosopher-plus, noting only that while Emerson names his called-for "gradual domestication" of nonconformist culture "revolution" (60), Thoreau placed nonconformity under the sign of "extra-Vagance." That location helps avert matters—I parochially claim—toward interdisciplinary anthropology. But given a choice between Emerson and Thoreau; or between Cavell's essayist-epistemology and others' essayist-ethnography (or among anthropology, history, religion, literature, arts . . . showbiz), might we readers exercise a conspicuously democratic aspiration by voting: Aye! Regardless, rereading Cavell rereading Emerson (as did Nietzsche) and Thoreau (as did Gandhi) could even make one proud—if only in this one respect—of being an American, or rather of rereading American styles of perfectionism verging on—even as they emerged from—cross-cultural consequence.[6]

Not just Cavell but Kenneth Burke too (whom Cavell generously acknowledges) invoked Emerson. Indeed, Burke once observed that the "tiny 'transcendences'" in that sage's transcendentalism will be found "doing much the same as Whitman did with his infectious cult of the glad hand" (Burke 1966: 191, 195)![7]

Earlier in the essay on Emerson just cited, Burke drags in Walt Whitman—a move not unlike his conjoining Carlyle *and* Marx (see "Rehearsals") or the present study's coupling of Twain and Mauss (Chap. 6), or Bali and Manhattan (Chap. 4), or either of the latter and Venice (Chap. 5). Yes, Burke salutes Whitman winkily indeed; and it is very hard to keep up. Discussing catharsis, Burke finds its "purgation by the imitation of victimage" fundamental not just in the collective orgies of Dionysian rites (forerunners of tragedy—recall Chap. 1) but in apparently opposite kinds of "medicine," such as Emerson's brand of Transcendentalism. "There are traces of victimage even here," Burke asserts, as in Platonic dialogue, where some "speakers are sacrificed for the good of the dialogue as a whole (sacrificed in the sense of being proved wrong . . .)" (1966: 186–87). Who would presume to adjudicate whether Burke is winking at Emerson's essay on "Nature" or crediting it with winking, or crediting it with crediting Nature's winkings? Probably all three, and then some. In any case Emerson's transcendence turns out to be neither square nor wholesome; it's a lot trickier—more pervasively devious—than that:

> To be sure, the essay is a bit innocuous; but it is delightfully so. It has a kind of exaltation, thanks in large part to Emerson's profuse mixing of his ideas with ingratiating imagery. And we can readily understand why he was so enthusiastic about Whitman, before a more quizzical look at Whitman's poetic evangelism led him to see that it was beckoning "Come hither" to much more than a highly respectable vendor of uplift such as Emerson had bargained for. Both approached the conflicts of the century in terms that allowed for a joyous transcendental translation. To apply in a twisted way (and thereby twisting a twist) Rimbaud's demand for a poetry based on the "reasoned derangement of the senses," we might say that Emerson was as idealistically able as Whitman [materially?] to look upon traveling salesmen and see a band of angels. (Burke 1966: 189; my interjected question)

Even if his eyelid had by now fallen off, Burke managed to twist one turn further into true ironies of dialectical con/di-vergings—going so far as to import another author from the subsequent century (ours, in fact, for the time being):

> There can be transcendence upwards . . .; there can be transcendence downwards. . . . And there can be a fluctuating between the two. (Cf. in E. M. Forster's novel, *A Passage to India*, the wavering as to whether India is a "muddle" or a "mystery.") (Burke 1966: 189)

Emerson or Whitman? Or Thoreau, or Nietzsche, or Benedict, or Bateson . . .? Yep. Fluctuate. Elsewhere as well, Burke pours across boundaries and obstacles thrown up (like barricades) by overly dogmatic dialectics that are insufficiently seriocomic. Burke, for example, construed Wagner's *Ring* fecally—perhaps to out-Freud Freud, or in counterdistinction to Forster's own engaging construal of Wagner.[8] Burke arranges his interpretation as an intertextual "Thinking of the Body" oscillating across *Alice in Wonderland*, Flaubert's *Temptation of St. Anthony*, Aeschylus's *Prometheus Bound* (and elsewhere, the *Oresteia*, considered both in its own right and as a primary intertext of Wagner's tetralogy), plus Mallarmé's *sens plus pur aux mots de la tribu*.[9]

Through motivic panoplies ("chromatic" to this reader's ear), Burke particularly sets in abeyance one representative example of reductive polarity: Materialism/Mysticism ("both involve a narrowing of motivational circumference"—Burke 1962: 291). *I* "would like to say" (if one dared to echo Cavell's multiply modal prose) that this clumsy distinction—materialism/mysticism—is routinely regurgitated in methodical styles that advertise their "objectivity": *pour* the material, *contre* the mystical. I would like, moreover, to compare Burke's move to more Marxian (yet only partly so) attempts to "transcend" (down) both sides of any reductive mystic/materialist alternative. I have in mind Benjamin's fluctuations between Jewish-Gnostic concreteness on the "mystic" side and everyday material life of the public-masses—fluctuations that troubled critics inclined to ideological purism.[10] (Note too that the "Rehearsals" of this book already noted how Burke—quite independently of Benjamin—avoided Marx's perplexing avoidance of "popular culture"). But Burke was speaking of Whitman, so I'd better cite him; for he may be a welcome alternative for readers who "prefer not" Emerson (per Cavell), nor *mon Thoreau*, nor Burke.

Walt Whitman also invoked "extra-Vagance," but he looks to have divided its hyphen differently—judging from his passage incorporated, pragmatically, into the decorative railing along the upscale marina in New York's newly refurbished Battery Park, from which vantage Hoboken (across the Hudson) looms rather like Venice. There Whitman's usage of the magical *mot* splits like this:

TALL FACADES OF MARBLE AND IRON PROUD
AND PASSIONATE CITY
METTLESOME MAD EXTRAV AGANT CITY

Fieldworkers to the World Financial Center—not far from Bartleby's fictive digs, in fact—can read this dazzlingly rustproof epigraph for themselves (really); but I promise stay-at-home readers that Whitman's adjectival "extravagance" separates as just illustrated.

Whitman's wealth of voices continues today to attract diverse factions of hermeneuts—hoary, hip, and hovering—plus scads of critics, some inclined to diagnostics and/or identity politics. Casual visitors to Whitman's texts (like this reader) may want to bear in (embodied) mind how brainy *and* brawny his phrases could be. That goes for his lyrical fare but also his prose, such as an inviting "Preface to the Reader in the British Islands," devised for *Specimen Days*:

> If you will only take the following pages as you do some long and gossipy letter written for you by a relation or friend traveling through distant scenes and incidents and jotting them down lazily and informally . . . but ever veraciously (with occasional diversions of critical thought about somebody or something) it might remove all formal or literary impediments at once and bring you and me close together in the spirit in which the jottings were collated to be read.[11]

Rather like Mark Twain banishing moral-makers (or was it plot-mappers) from colonizing *Huck* (or was it *Tom*?), Whitman famously posted a no-trespassing sign over his song's unsoundable deeps:

> I too am not a bit tamed. . . . I too am untranslatable.[12]

So warned *Leaves of Grass*, a work published—like James George Frazer's *Golden Bough*, some forty years later—in ever-enlarging versions. Indeed,

Leaves kept budding, until Whitman's death in 1882—wasn't it?—exactly a century before preparation of this *Envoi* began six or seven years ago; I could as aptly now be invoking Frazer's proper-looking opus. They are both— Whitman's *Leaves* and Frazer's *Bough*—sufficiently extra-Vagant.[13] So, of course, is Gertrude Stein.

Still, what comparatist—lay or professional—could afford to forget Whitman, particularly if he or she is "American" (Poe preferred "Appala-chian"), or non-American, or anti-American (including anti-American Ameri-cans as well as non-Americans), or anti-anti-Americans (including anti-anti-American Americans . . .). And what critical critic, or critic thereof—whether anthropologist, historian, philosopher, *littérateur*, ethnographer of these, or again Gertrude Stein—could avoid the peculiar cosmopolitan-patriot who may have been earth's (and earthlings') most democratic visionary to date (count-ing even Carl Sagan). Even with the limited technologies available to Whitman—e.g., his merely figurative "Passage to India"—"our man in Man-hattan" (and Camden) established open-mouthed *dépense* rather than purse-lipped frugality at the heart of U.S. canonicity *and* countercanonicity (both customary) in their many guises—Imperialist, postmodernist, New Age, Old Guard, whatever.

The example of Whitman helps overthrow cozy critical superstitions that any nation's narrations or empire's canons—foremost those of the "sole remaining superpower"—simply assert an ideology (generally declared "patriarchal") that wholly deserves busting and burying. Some con/texts canonical are self-sufficiently self-upsetting. But by the same token, a canonically cosmopolitan discourse of *dépense* (such as Whitman's) deflects direct *utilization* for specific *causes*—including desirable liberations and worthy goals to put colonialism behind us once and for all. I hope that readers will recognize that I am arguing that anyone—regardless of discipline, nationality, hue, hybridity, stripe, state-regulated ethnic label, language (provided yours is willing to translate or be translated), puritanical or hedonistic proclivity, or customary style of contesta-tion—might find solace in Whitman's masterwork; but I salutarily doubt its use-value for legitimating particular "communities" of resistance.

Recent receptions of Whitman may help me reiterate this book's pleas to preserve interpretive between-the-lines alongside any analytic bottom-lines and decided agendas. Toward that *finale*, I would cite not America's immortal-virtual Poet Laureate himself, for that would hardly help anything conclude. Instead, I submit one scholarly page from Edwin Haviland Miller's *Walt Whitman's 'Song of Myself': A Mosaic of Interpretations* (1989), which "in-dexes" implicit themes in *Leaves of Grass*— forty-eight topics (two short of fifty), copied here complete and unabridged ("A, J, K, Q, U, and XYZ" entries are absent—wanting—in the original):

Bible (Eden; Jesus; New Testament;   Birth/death
   Old Testament)   Bisexuality

Catalogues
Childhood
Comedy

Democracy (slavery; socioeconomic,
    sociopolitical)

Eldest brother
Erethism

Fellatio
Food/feeding

Genre
Grass

Heterosexuality
Homosexuality
House/dwelling (carpentry)

The I and the reader (you)
Identity
Imagination
Incest
Incorporation/absorption

Language

Masturbation
Mother
Movement/motion

Music
Mysticism

Narcissism

Oedipal sexuality

Pantheism
Phallicism
Portrait of a hero/overman
Portrait of an artist
"Procreant urge"

Regressiveness
Religion
Respiration

Science
Self-portrait
Sexuality and creativity
Sodomy
Stream of Consciousness
Structure

Tactility
Tongue
Transcendentalism

Voyeurism

Water/sea

A list to reread, indeed; many comments crowd to spirit when perusing it;
I offer a selection. In Burke's terms, the array of topics culled from or projected onto Whitman seem "transcended down" from his actual lines; Burke
would doubtless argue that these *motives* could as accurately be "transcended
up;" I feel Burke was right. However "open" (to Freud, for example) the deviated index appears, it remains reductively "objective," rather than aspiringly
ultraobjective—as those concepts were developed in Chapter 1. For example,
no entry appears for "Opera,"—which Whitman emulated; readers may also
notice that entries seem manifestly gendered, although "genre" too is an entry.

Offered (or taken) as an adequate representation of Whitman's self-song,
this list (or any list, even longer) flubs. But taken (or offered) more as a self-
ironizing list-of-lists—a seriocomic catalogue of catalogues—its salience in-
creases. Ultraobjectively, any index of *Leaves* can do no more than catalogue
Whitman's own "American catalogue rhetoric"—as Robert Weisbuch, for
one, designates it. Weisbuch illustrates this U.S. *spécialité* with "Emerson's
strings of aphorisms, Whitman's Tallyings, the enumerations of Melville's

Ishmael"; the format implies a "sense of divine plenitudes in manifestation" (Weisbuch 1986: 212). Such listy discourse is prevalent in certain styles of critical *étude* (or whatever Emerson, Whitman, and Melville wrote); it impresses me as the other side of that absence of "ideology" in one nation's, or empire's, intellectual equipment. (Recall from our "Rehearsals" that Gayatri Spivak once chastised those she reproves stateside for this lack or want.)[14]

But if "catalogue rhetoric" is a kind of anti-ideology, how might catalogue rhetoric squared (e.g., the cited index to Whitman) enter essay-*études*? Lists-of-lists, I think, instantiate that wondrous hypotaxis and oozy metamorphosis encountered and enacted in Chapter 4. If obsessed over, any restrictive catalogue begins to acquire plausibility and persuasiveness, even a certain authority (that's what makes the catalogue "rhetoric"—see Geertz [1972]).[15] As repeatedly argued and intimated in this book, dangers lurk whenever a list's selectivities start exuding diagnostic undertones that seem foundational (or, some would say, "essential"). The peril and appeal of any catalogue (of catalogues) derives from a protean applicability to circumstances possibly foreign to its categories and terms. (Readers may want to compare in this regard psychoanalysis—see Chap. 3.)

This book has tried to coordinate critical tactics and interpretive moves regarding such matters. A list too confidently lofty deserves to be "transcended" down; a list too confidently edgy deserves to be "transcended" up. For example, any reading that uses the forty-eight entries from the Whitman "mosaic" to translate decisively ("objectively") the "untranslatable" of his *Leaves*—to tame the untamed—merits resisting. On the other hand, readings that help a catalogue transmogrify into something like a "second" faulty plenitude—one ironically assembling and alphabetizing shifting positions of Whitman's "I"—could augment reception of his passages. Whitman's gifts, like anything truly cultural, are worth experiencing ultraobjectively and, for lack of a better word, chromatically.

No Whitmanian myself, I have taught his work only once, indirectly, through an appealing chapter in Lewis Hyde's Maussian book, *The Gift*.[16] The above inventory (excavated from and/or Post-It-ed on the 1335 invigorated lines following Whitman's 1855 "I celebrate myself") was happened upon after earlier versions of Chapters 1–7 had been published. Yet—as with that Melville journal invoked at the close of Chapter 5—its topics can seem to echo (as in some uncanny scene) rites and writers and cultures and critiques commended or challenged here.

For example, the "M-N-O" words used to codify Whitman resonate with Chapter 3 (particularly if "Mysticism" be transmogrified into "Magic")—about accusations, inferences, and psychoanalysis of sexual preferences, versus musical tastes and artistic commemoration. Or the three "C" words indexing Whitman—"Catalogues, Childhood, Comedy," remember—could tie together Chapter 5 (on bygone musings plus showbiz humbug) and Chapter 7 (engaging Mark Twain's youthful Huckspeech and Marcel Mauss's inventories of techniques in his aphoristic writing on magic). Indeed, the chapters just recollected demonstrate that hypotactical (noncausal) lists are themselves, in generic terms, "magical": made of and for coincidence.

Whitmanian 'P' words (readers as amnesiac as this author will need to check back several paragraphs) echo ligaments of Chapter 1, although that *Portrait* is of an over*woman* (Ruth Benedict), and the "*Phallicism*" is projected by Jane Belo when annotating and interrupting Margaret Mead. There, then, both these "P's" become transformed and encompassed under the letter "M" for "menses." One need only peruse the latter letter (as it presumably pertains to Whitman's "world") to appreciate that this tally tied to Whitman's "voices" is no more innocent than Chapter 1 proved the index of Benedict's book to be, which omitted a major ritual (*chez* Kwakiutl) or its absence (*chez* Zuni) that truly pertained to the way she—Benedict—compared.

In brief, doubled "catalogue rhetoric" may take on an authority of its own, like anything else cultural or critical.[17] The error—or should one just say the peril—comes in imagining (even believing) that such rhetoric is constant, stable, unshifting, singular. Nowadays Whitman's "Phallicism" is apt to be narrowed, even as it has been enlarged, by creatively new-wave Gay Studies (e.g., M. Moon 1991); or that "P" may be boiled down to reassertions of a realpolitik behind his poetic in imposing researches by such scholars as Betsy Erkkila (1989). Citing just the latter:

> The image of the breast of the father is striking, suggesting the origin of the term *Paumanok* in what Whitman described as "the island with its breast drawn out, and laid against the sea." ... His impassioned supplication to the father has usually been read as a sign of Whitman's strained relationship with his authoritarian father. Within the context of the poem, however, the passage has a much broader cultural reference. The breast image and the affectionate language—hold, kiss, touch—also suggests the quest for a nurturant paternity that is founded in the revolutionary revolt against patriarchal authority. Experiencing a sense of ship-wreck—personal, political, and artistic—Whitman seeks not the authority of a patriarch but the assurance of historic order figured in the caress of a nurturant father(land).[18]

Without necessarily disputing such stances vis-à-vis Whitman, yet keeping interpretations chromatic here as well, I recall from Lewis Hyde that Whitman's eccentric work and life—whether or not pro-gay or anti-patriarchy—communicate a ruggedly maternal man, and a compassionate one:

> Whitman was a maternal man—a person, that is, who cares for and protects life—and the hospitals afforded him a chance to live out his maternalism, his "manly tenderness." Most of the soldiers were under twenty-five, and many were only fifteen or sixteen years old, almost literally "offspring taken soon out of their

mothers' laps," and now wounded or sick, weak and helpless. He mothered them. He entered into a life of active charity. If you look back at that wonderful catalog of the treats he dispensed in the wards you will see that its structure is simply "I give . . . I give . . . I give." (Hyde 1982: 206–207)

It is conceivable that Walt Whitman, that canonical font of U.S. "selfdom," imagined his (let's say) manhood as a breast, giving succour to those in dire need of nurture. His love for youths encompassed their "selves" (read beneath that keyword as you will), but also their sufferings inflicted in part by a wartime called "Civil" whose wounds they incurred. Whitman's involvements with these victims possibly preclude neither "paternalistic" undercurrents nor anal ones. Yet, analyses that seek to ascertain such dimensions—whether earlier styles ferreting out "strained relationships with patriarchal fathers" (the theme Erkkila challenges) or current accentuations of psycho-anality/orality— flirt with explaining-away alternative potentials of "lactating phalluses." Either critical disclosure—old Oedipal difficulties with father-figures, newly "queered" connections to heres and nows of politicized sexual preference— may misjudge how contrary to standardized "identity" (including standardized "counter-identity") orchestrated differences of gender and power and so forth can truly be.

If we experimentally expand simplified decipherings of Whitman with some cross-cultural reading, inscriptions of his motherly manhood find company that sets in constructive doubt (or interpretive contingency) rough and ready diagnoses alike. To token one vividly polyvalent example, Hindu cosmologies (in India, Bali, etc.) abound in transferals and reversals between semen and milk, via blood (of battle and bodily flows)—amply documented in the copious works of Wendy Doniger O'Flaherty:

> In the one Vedic model . . . the parallel to a man's seed was a woman's milk; the phallus corresponded to the breast, not to the womb. The late Vedas, on the other hand, suggested another model for the woman, attempting to account for her dual sites of sexuality: Blood in a man produced semen, while blood in a woman produced female seed *and* milk. Later still, this model was challenged by another: seed in a man corresponded with menstrual or uterine blood (*rajas* or *puspa*) in a woman. In true Indian fashion, the Vedic models were also retained, and a bastard compromise was sometimes attempted. . . . (1980: 33)

Some enthusiasts may desire to figure out for themselves what that "bastard compromise" (hybridity?) may have been, as Whitman apparently did for his "self." Other explorers may wish to keep tracking O'Flaherty's marvelous fence-leapings among the "happily contradictory" mythic possibilities that she pursues into assertively Tantric versions, whether figurative or literal:

> According to [one] text, milk is made, not from nonsexual blood, but from menstrual blood; the most polluting of substances is transmuted into the purest of

substances, rising from the genital site as semen rises in a man to become transmuted into Soma. . . . (42)

Milk in the woman comes to be explicitly equated with seed. . . . The magic wishing-cow is produced when the ocean is milked, and the ocean of milk flows from her udder . . .; thus the cow and the ocean are each other's mothers. (43)

In Tantric rituals, where female seed as well as male semen is procreative and magical, the adept drinks not only semen but menstrual blood. . . . This ceremony, in which the deity is said to enter into the ingested fluids, may be seen as a kind of *prasada*, or eucharist, albeit in an esoteric version . . . ; but in our context it functions as an instance of sexual power entering through ingested food. . . . The image of rice as seed [and] the image of the womb as a mouth is also a recurrent one. Through this imagery, every sexual act is an instance of the drinking of semen. (O'Flaherty 1980: 52–53)

Were it not time to conclude the present omnibus book, its pages might verge here on still other rites from Melanesia, where male-to-male nuturance through semen transmission is a crucial trope of politics and persons entangled among distinctive varieties of gendered rivalry, reproduction, and residence.[19]

I cite milk-sperm in India (which, of course, Whitman read about, in thoroughly "tamed" recensions) and I allude to sperm-milk in New Guinea (which Whitman ignored alogether, due to a dearth of ethnography in his day) to remember again how volatile comparison becomes. It can fling us from Brahmanic India to faraway New Guinea—in their exaggerated rites, a "Land of Milk" and a "Land of Semen," respectively—each incorporating its contrary, multiply signified. Translating such cultures—including Whitman's culture of alternative semen-milk (canonical to the U.S. of A.), and Burke-on-Augustine sucking God's milk (cited above)—implies more extra-Vagant transgressions than partisan agendas of critique may countenance. Indeed, engaging cultures (of here and there, now and then, here and now, there and then, or even here and here and now and now) isn't easy. However, normalization of identity/ differentiation, and that old (American) standby of "self-identity," may make it seem so.[20]

Qualms about normalization and standardization explain this book's playfully deficient allusions to patly Freudian themes (in Chaps. 3 and 4, and in the second "Boutade" to Chap. 2's survey of un/circumcisions). Similar qualms underpin my skepticism about advocating overall liberation from "repression," the only thing certain advocates can envision ritualized bodily alterations to be about. (Many critics today seem to prefer marketed "mutilations," "freely" chosen by consumers.)[21] Chapter 2 broached Buginese and Balinese differences in Indonesia, as insisted on and displayed to this author by a Bugis observer. I tried to reverberate the difference in question comparatively and historically, in order to suggest: (1) how ritual desires "transcend" (both up and down) power drives that universalists call "genital"; and (2) how discourses of desire complicate the politics of liberation/coercion. An *Envoi* might conclude by re-casting this comparative-interpretive resolve in an open couplet:

Other Cupidities, Other Hybridities.[22]

From many engaging candidates I have nominated Whitman as one "Etc." for these encores. My reservations regarding Whitman (or his reception) concern how his song's heavier-handed obliquities too comfortably merge with contemporary projects—many of them timely and important—of self-assertion (see Chap. 7). Thoreau's punning, in contrast—insofar as one translates unsettlingly back-towards it (or presumes to)—affords a style more radically deflective of partisan appropriations: antifoundational in a very down-to-earth way (ethnographically, one might almost say).[23] That at least is how I experience Thoreau's virtuoso prose. A reader who possibly anticipated me here was Marcel Proust, who in 1904 commended to the Comtesse de Noailles "les pages admirables de *Walden*":

> Il me semble qu'on les lise en soi-même tant elles sortent du fond de notre expérience intime.[24]

––––––––––

Stanley Cavell compellingly conveys how Thoreau cracks open off-the-rack conformity (in Emerson's sense), even without conspicuous extra-Vagance—e.g., reading Buddha and Brahma along with Moses. I thus cite "one more time"—the last one—Cavell-on-Thoreau to shift my multiply-aligned book's closing scene from either Phallicism à la Whitman or Menses à la Benedict (plus switches between either by both) to withdrawal—radical Thoreauvian withdrawal. And so, Cavell (*Themes Out of School*, 1984):

> [1.] Thoreau's withdrawal is more elaborately dramatized, its rebuke more continuous. In my book on *Walden*, I find that the writer who inhabits it asserts the priority in value of writing over speaking (at least for the present) in order to maintain silence, where this means first of all to withhold his voice, his consent, from his society. Hence the entire book is an act of civil disobedience, a confrontation which takes the form of a withdrawal. But his silence has many forces, as in such a sentence as this: "You only need sit still long enough in some attractive spot in the woods that all its inhabitants may exhibit themselves to you by turns." This is a fair summation of the point of the book as a whole. At the moment I focus on Thoreau's way of saying that reading his book is redemptive. I take it for granted that the scene is one of interpretation, of reading and being read . . . ; and

"by turns" also means by verses (that is, since this is not poetry, by portions) and also by conversions. . . . (50–51)

Antiphony: To Thoreauvian withdrawal readers might compare the desire of ascesis—following Deleuze.[25]

[**2.**] It ought to help to see that from the point of view of psychoanalytic therapy the situation of reading has typically been turned around, that it is not first of all the text that is subject to interpretation but we in the gaze or hearing of the text. I think good readers, or a certain kind of reader, have always known and acted on this, as in Thoreau's picture of reading by exposure to being read. But it is my impression that those who emphasize the psychoanalytic possibilities here tend to forget what a text is, the matter of its autonomy; while those who shun psychoanalysis tend not to offer a practice of reading that I can understand as having the consequence of therapy. (52)

Antiphony: Trying to balance this difference between a text's autonomy and the consequences of therapy was one task of several chapters in the present book—which?

[**3.**] The sentence I cited from *Walden* about sitting still long enough knows, for example, all about the seductions of this writing—its writer is sitting still, maintaining silence, in what he calls an "*attractive* spot in the woods" ("woods" being one of his words for "words," hence for his book, and [hence] for America). The text he is producing, for our conversion, is based, along with some other things, on an equation between morning (as dawning) and mourning (as grieving). The general idea is that we crave change (say therapy) but we are appalled by the prospect; that in our capacity for loss there is the chance of ecstasy. What bears here on the idea of a text as therapeutic is the structure of what I call in my book on *Walden* its "immense repetitiveness," something you might think of as a capacity for boredom, which I say Thoreau learned from the Old Testament prophets, together with his notation of endless detail. . . . (53–54)

Antiphony: Or did Thoreau learn it from Brahma or Buddha or that other "hybrid" source he read: Kabir, "an Indian mystic of the fifteenth century who tried to reconcile the religions of the Hindus and Moslems"?[26] (As readers of Chap. 2 may recall, any such reconciliation must cancel, bridge, disregard, or otherwise tolerate the absence versus presence of so-called [male] circumcision, among other ritual differences—e.g., cremation/burial.)

Finally in his *Themes* (54), Cavell clarifies—and intricately—what one might call Thoreau's cadential tonality:

[**4.**] For *Walden*'s writer I understand the morning of mourning, the dawning of grieving, to be the proposed alternative, the only alternative, to what he calls "our present constitution," which he says must end. He means our political constitution, with its slaves, but he means more than this; he means what permits this constitution in our souls. He means that mourning is the only alternative to our nostalgias, in which we will otherwise despair and die. He completes the building of his house by showing how to leave it.

Listen again to the book's parting line: "The sun is but a morning star."

AN EXTRA-VAGANT BOWS OUT: LEAVING IT

Wearied by the relatively relativist calling to engage manifold cultures, diverse disciplines, and rival critiques—identifying with none, friendly toward many, wary of some—this interpreter (his ear grown hoarse from ironies heard) now stills these notes of excess and loss with a musical rest. Still and again, other scenes beckon and further rereadings, lest translated truths be forgotten, even momentarily . . .

> But I don't know—I'm afraid I shall have to put *Walden* away and buy
> another book to travel with. Or possibly a link puzzle. One doesn't
> remember anything much from long association with a link puzzle.
> (*E. B. White, "The Retort Transcendental"*)[27]

Acknowledgments and Credits

PLENTIFUL PERSONS, generous in ways even Marcel Mauss neglected, have helped keep this book from foundering. Colleagues, students, and friends to thank in and around Princeton Anthropology include: A. Hammoudi, L. Rosen, K. Warren, R. Lederman, G. Obeyesekere, R. Obeyesekere, H. Geertz, V. Adams, E. Martin, I. Nabokov, C. Zanca, G. Vielbig, J. MacDougall, M. Huber, and once upon a time J. Kelly, J. Klor de Alva, A. Willis, K. Smyers, C. Krizancik, A. Dent, J. Marshall, L. Dubois, P. Bell, and many more. In and around Cornell Anthropology, let me thank R. Smith, K. Smith, D. Holmberg, K. March, T. Kirsch, Y. Kirsch, C. Greenhouse and F. Aman, S. Sangren, J. Rosenthal, and others earlier on. Princeton colleagues in European Cultural Studies and Cornell colleagues in the Southeast Asia Program, Western Societies Program, and Comparative Literature often were welcoming as well.

Many chapters benefited from conferences and from alert suggestions by individuals with ironies oblique to my own:

Chap. 1: J. Goldstein, R. Handler, K. Blu, E. Friedl; T. Schatzki, T. Hakansson, J. P. Jones, J. Pickles, J. Popkin, W. Natter, J. Engelberg, and others at Kentucky; R. Borofsky, J. Anderson, J. Borneman, B. J. Isbell, and friends at Cornell who came to hear an old colleague; D. Wolk and friends at Chicago who came to hear an old student.

Chap. 2: S. Schwartz, G. Dening, D. Dening, M. Penn, S. Gudeman, D. Merwick, R. Price, A. Reid, H. Liebersohn, D. Segal, N. Davis, J. Geller, J. Boyarin, D. Boyarin, S. Gilman, L. Engelstein, and L. Rosen.

Chap. 3: G. Stocking, R. Smith, S. Gilman, I. Hull, D. Schnieder; D. Lipsett and others in Anthropology at Minnesota who endured a version delivered as a lecture.

Chap. 4: D. Segal, H. Liebersohn, P. Strong, D. Prochaska, and others at the Claremont Colleges conference; G. Neville, J. Hunnicutt, A. Weiner, S. Ortner, M. Herzfeld, J. Peacock, T. W. Herbert, and others at Southwestern University; J. Ellison and J. Becker at Michigan, where S. Stewart also lectured and responded. T. Sebeok, S. Alpers, and others at a conference in Rochester.

Chap. 5: I. Karp, S. Lavine, C. Kreamer, J. Hahnhardt, M. Torgovnick, and more at the Whitney Museum in New York City.

Chap. 6: B. Engler, J. Blair, R. Waswo, N. Forsyth, J. Radway, F. La Saux, and others in Fribourg; R. Sharpe, N. Davis, R. Lederman, R. Connor, L. Hyde, M. Shell, and more at the Humanities Research Center; D. Pollock, B. Tedlock, D. Tedlock, and others at Buffalo; C. Lommitz, F. Myers, A. Weiner, L. Abu-Lughod, and others at New York University.

Chap. 7: K.-P. Koepping, G. Dening, and many colleagues and students at the University of Melbourne; G. Urban, B. Lee, and E. Mertz.

Chap. 8: B. Nolan, C. D. Benson, C. Zacher, K. Ashley, and others in the New Chaucer Society; D. Rutledge, H. Assand, and participants in Thomas Greene's Folger Library seminar.

Chap. 9: R. Oggins, R. Trexler, S. Kinser, and others "On the Margins" at the Center for Medieval and Early Renaissance Studies (Binghamton, N.Y.); J. Bowen, S. Ortner, N. Dirks, and participants in an American Anthropological Association panel on "Culture, History, Place."

Chap. 10: D. Brent.

Chap. 11: K. Woodward.

Chap. 12: R. Poirier and S. Hyman at *Raritan*; A. Becker, the late R. Murphy, C. Geertz, and other friendly readers. I. Ardika and many friends and acquaintances in Bali; C. and P. Ross in Atlanta.

Impossible to confine by chapter is the example set by many colleagues, near and distant: C. Geertz, D. Segal, J. Peacock, M. Manganaro, C. Greenhouse, J. Goldstein, S. Errington, J. Kuipers, I. Brady, I. Karp, J. Bowen, H. Liebersohn, A. Hammoudi, H. Varenne, C. Lévi-Strauss, F. Myers, R. DeMallie, R. Blair, A. Milner, A. Becker, S. Lindenbaum, M. Ebihara, G. Neville, the late D. Schneider, the late M. Singer, the late V. Turner, P. Friedrich, V. Daniel, B. Lee, J. Geller, W. Keane, H. Blau, E. Turner. P. Worsley, J. Sternberg.

Other scholars whose works make an interdisciplinary intruder feel, if not a social fact, slightly less aberrant include: C. Abbate, G. Dening, R. Connor, W. Doniger, M. Jennings, E. Traube, M. Lamont, L. Mitchell, C. Schorske, B. Faure, R. Darnton, A. Grafton, R. Paul, L. Englestein, N. Davis, R. Price, S. Price, R. Tyson, C. Emerson, D. LaCapra, P. Hohendahl, the late E. Blackall, S. Corngold, E. Showalter, M. Cadden, L. Gossmann, A. Nehamas, J. and J. Comroff, A. Appadurai, M. Wood, S. Teiser, S. Bermen, C. Rigolot, J. Culler, C. Chase, A. Gross, J. Clifford, G. Marcus, M. Silverstein, J. C. Rowe, and others in Critical Theory at Irvine. For this list to stop lengthening, one must arbitrarily halt.

I thank directly and profusely Mary Murrell at Princeton University Press and (once again) indirectly its director, Walter Lippincott.

Last and fervently: unending thanks be to Olivian, Tili, and Jess—three women whose being embodies rereading (Olivian even when proofreading: an art in its own right, generously bestowed and lovingly received).

Further tallies of professional debts appear in earlier versions of several chapters:

A few pages of the "Rehearsal" on opera, here revised, were included in *Recovering the Orient: Artists, Scholars, Appropriations*, eds. Andrew Gerstle and Anthony Milner (Harwood Academic Publishers, 1994).

Much of Chap. 1 was published in somewhat different form in *Objectivity and its Other*, eds. Wolfgang Natter, Theodore R. Schatzki, and John Paul Jones III (Guilford Publications, 1995).

Chap. 2 has been revised and expanded from my essay in *Implicit Understandings*, ed. Stuart B. Schwartz (Cambridge University Press, 1994).

Chap. 3 (minus the interlude) appeared with variations in *Malinowski, Rivers, Benedict, and Others (History of Anthropology, vol. 4)*, ed. George W. Stocking, Jr. (University of Wisconsin Press, 1986).

A version of Chap. 4 appeared in *Crossing Cultures*, ed. Daniel Segal (University of Arizona Press, 1992).

Chap. 5 has been reworked from an essay in *Exhibiting Cultures*, eds. Ivan Karp and Steven D. Lavine (Smithsonian Institution Press, 1991).

Chap. 7 derives from an essay in *Semiotics, Self, and Society*, eds. Greg Urban and Benjamin Lee (Mouton, 1989).

Chap. 11 contains two sections based on reviews in *Discourse*, 1991, and *The Journal of Asian Studies* 50(3), 1991.

Chap. 12 is revised from "America: Fringe Benefits" that appeared in *Raritan*, spring, 1983. A rehearsal for Chap. 6 was included in the Swiss journal *SPELL* (see Engler 1992).

The frontispiece illustration is from the McCaddon Collection. Theatre Collection. Visual Materials Division. Department of Rare Books and Special Collections. Princeton University Library.

Notes

Preface
AnThoreaupology: An Invitation

1. Thoreau (1985: 580–81); the allusion to Thoreau's anti-cat-counting is in Geertz (1973: 16). On Thoreau and anthropology, see also F. Turner (1986).

2. On Thoreau's extra-Vagance as an economy of excess to counter capitalist motives, see Grusin (1993); on *dépense* (Bataille 1985), see Chaps. 6, 12. From abundant secondary literature on Thoreau, I take cues from Poirier (1985, 1971); Cavell (1981b, 1988, 1990), Wagenknecht (1981), Donoghue (1987), and essays in Thoreau (1966).

3. Music enters verbalization extra-Vagantly; just as languages are mutually estranged, music seems estranged from the "lingual" generally. Music's storied resistance to paraphrase pertains to *höchste Lust*, the lowliest musical jingle, and the simulations thereof: Muzak. One serious source on Muzak and other brands of "easy listening" is Lanza (1994); on opera, see "Rehearsal" on that topic.

4. Burke (1962: 809); "verging" for Burke entails all its prefixings: converging, diverging, etc.

5. Kott (1987: 21); on hybrid Balinese studies, see Boon (1977, 1990); on postcolonialist hybridities, see Bhabha (1994) plus essays in Ashcroft et al. (1995); on "hybridizing" postcolonialist and Boasian hybridities, see Boon (1998).

6. For ethnographies of reading to overcome theory's obsession with writing, see J. Boyarin (1993); a previous call to describe comparative reading practices is Boon (1973).

7. I allude to Bourdieu (1984); for Bourdieu's value in analyzing European and American class, see Lamont (1992). My point about M. Douglas's collapsing distinctions between complex motives and singular "interests" (see Chap. 12) may also apply to Bourdieu; for another critique of Bourdieu, see M. Denning (1991).

8. L. Edel (1987: xii).

9. Contemporary scholars who take magic seriously—such as Taussig (1997), Luhrmann (1989), Favret-Saada (1981)—often accentuate the dark side, obviously important. But part of magic's reality is ambivalence, a fact that leads me to stress serio-comic dimensions. On magic's multiplicities see O'Keefe (1983), Sangren (1987, on magic and power in Taiwan), and Siegel (1991, with material on South Asian magic, including show business). Balinese studies have long been attentive to magical practices (e.g., Berthier and Sweeney 1976); see Boon (1990a: 159–66); see Chap. 1.

10. Lyotard (1993); on affinities of Novalis, Hoffmann, and Schlegel with modern (and surely postmodern) anthropology, see Boon (1982a: Chap. 7). A new novel on Novalis (P. Fitzgerald 1997) may reinforce this point; on Jean Paul and early Romantic novelists see Blackall (1983); see also Feldman and Richardson (1972).

11. On leaps and ironies see Kierkegaard (1989, 1980, 1983, 1987, etc.); Kierkegaard earlier leaped into anthropology via C. Geertz (1973: 120). On jolts see Benjamin (1969, 1978, etc.); Benjamin on Proust and Benjamin on translation is woven into cultural comparison in Boon (1982a: 213, 220, 153, 230). For religious sides of Ben-

jamin, see G. Smith (1989); on Benjamin and everyday popular life, see Charney and Schwartz (1995).

12. Yates and Foucault are hitched to comparative-historical reading in Boon (1982a: Chaps. 2 and 5); see Chaps. 2, 3.

13. Places to start on Serres are *The Parasite* (1982) and Serres and Latour (1995).

14. On so-called Tantrism and Bali, see Boon (1977: 235; 1982a: Chap. 6; 1990: *passim*); see Chap. 9.

15. "Esoterism" takes on many guises. The sympathy for epiphanal *conjunctio* evident in V. Turner, M. Eliade, and other fine scholars may be compared to its rough reversal in practices glorified in Foucault's name. On factions that have gathered see D. Eribon (1993), J. Miller (1992), Halperin (1997). For balanced representations of Foucault, see P. Rabinow (1984) and essays in D. Hoy (1986, particular M. Poster); apt tributes appear in de Certeau (1986).

My own skepticism about exercises in trancendence (whether symbolic or bodily) draws on Lévi-Strauss (1969: Chap. VII), resisting Jung's "archaic illusion" and archetypes; C. Geertz (1984b), abnegating all interpretive absolutes, including absolute relativism; and possibly Derrida's sliding-cancellation of any synthesis, origin, or climax, however achieved (see Chap. 10).

R. Noll's (1997) account of the "Jung cult," rightly critiques "vitalist" notions of identity, yet ignores how such notions could be transformed through linguistic turns; Merleau-Ponty (1964), for example, referred Bergsonian schemes (relatively vitalist, versus mechanist) to Saussurian linguistics, thus thwarting essentialism. Noll's book against Jung omits cross-cultural specifics of languages and translation, just as many Jungians do.

16. To bridge anthropology and musicology requires, I feel, displacing distinctions between upscale/right-on sonorous arts, rather than isolating ethnomusicology or popular music. One could cobble together, say, Kierkegaard, Schopenhauer (1970), Stendahl (1985), "Blind" Boone (see Monson 1994), Brunno Nettle, Nietzsche, Ethan Mordden (1990b), Suzanne Langer (1953), Wagner, Simmel (1991), Max Weber, Adorno, Charles Rosen (1972), Thomas Mann, Billy Taylor, Proust, Carolyn Abbate (1991), E.T.A. Hoffman, John Irwin (1980), Carl Dahlhaus (1989), Gershwin and Berlin and Porter and Kern (see Furia 1992; Bergreen 1990). See also Nattiez (1990), Frisch (1990), Attali (1985), W. Fitzgerald (1994), Feld (1990, 1997), and Roseman (1991); on music and irony see Rahn (1994, with thanks to Jamie Marshall).

17. See Steiner (1989); on Lévi-Strauss and music, see Boon (1972, 1989, 1992a, 1992b, 1995b); Lévi-Strauss (1993) reiterates music's priority. One might compare Steiner (1991) and Derrida (1989); see also S. Handelman (1983). On Benjamin, see G. Smith (1989); on Nietzsche, see R. Hayman (1990).

18. Burke (1957: 84).

Rehearsals

1. On Thoreau, see Cavell (1981b); see "Encores and Envoi." Screwball comedy is featured in Cavell (1981a; 1990: 102–104; 1984: 3–26, 169–72, etc.); Cavell philosophizes on "the facts of television" in (1984: 235ff); his studies of Alfred Hitchcock and of movie melodrama are also apposite.

2. Burke (1941: 221); it is tempting to compare Burke's desire of copying-out to Benjamin's mode of writing "arcades."

3. Heller in Mann (1970: 127). On Mann's irony, Schopenhauer's "double-bottomed philosophy," and Wittgenstein, see Safranski (1991: 338–44).

4. One overview of Foucault's corpus is O'Farrell (1989); see also Roth (1992).

5. Secondary sources on Burke include Rueckert (1982); Donoghue compares Thoreau's techniques to Burke's "perspectives by incongruity" (1987: 265–80) and counters both Lentricchia's (1983) appropriation of Burke and Jameson's scoldings of his work. For other thoughts on Jameson, see Boon (1982a; 1998). On Burke and "modernism," see Lorrigio (1990).

6. See Peacock (1975), Sills and Jensen (1992, vol. 1); see also Fernandez (1991).

7. R. Merton (1985).

8. Boon (1972: vii, 49); Boon (1977: 9, 213).

9. Boon (1982a: 144–47); Geertz (1987: Preface).

10. Burke (1962: 643); on coats, see Boon (1982a: 85–87); on cloth across cultures, see Weiner and Schnieder (1989). Lentricchia (1983) makes a "case for the work of Kenneth Burke as a native alternative to Marxism" (Simpson 1995: 164). To savor Burke's paradoxical embrace of Marx, consider these insights: "*Identity itself is a 'mystification.'* . . . Unless Marxists are ready to deny Marx by attacking his term 'alienation' itself, they must permit of research into the nature of alienation and into the nature of attempts, adequate and inadequate, to combat alienation" (Burke 1957: 265).

11. The cat-winks appear in the final paragraphs of Lévi-Strauss (1955). On Carlyle and Lévi-Strauss, see Morris (1979), reviewed in Boon (1982b).

12. Boon (1990a : 91).

13. On harmonic/melodic, see Burke (1970: 258). On Lévi-Strauss and Wagner, see Boon (1972, 1989), Backès-Clément (1970); Nattiez (1993); Zizek (1991, 1993).

14. Burke (1962: 113); Burke (1962: 566–68) seems compatible with Mauss (see Chap. 6). On Benedict's controversial evocation of Dobu and Kwakiutl econo-ritual practices, see Chap. 1.

15. Weber's reading of Simmel is mentioned in Gerth and Mills (1946: 4).

16. This passage is vintage Burkian conversationalese; on the Frankfurt School, see Jay (1973), Hohendahl (1982).

17. On Henry Adams, see Samuels (1989), Rowe (1976, 1996); on Benjamin and "popular culture," see Charney and Swartz (1995); see Chap. 5. For one anthropologist's sense of Benjamin, see Taussig (1992, 1993a); sensing Benjamin is a multitudinous task of translation (Boon 1982a: Chap. 6).

18. Webb (1995: 27–28). On William James, see Feinstein (1984), G. Allen (1967). Stressing habit and *Hamlet*, G. Cotkin forefronts James's deep dislikes—monism, determinism, and absolutism (1990: 115). On framing the anthropology of religion with James's sense of "polytheisms," see Boon (1987a).

19. On Boas and irony, see Krupat (1990). On Frazer as a (Romantic) ironist, see Boon (1982a: Chap. 1), Manganaro (1990), Ackerman (1987), and R. Fraser (1990). On Schlegel's *Lucinda*, see Blackall (1983, with thanks also to Jay Geller). Menippean satire across cultures is discussed in Boon (1982a: 264, 278–79; 1990a: 67–68, 88–91). On carnivalizing, see Babcock (1978); Bruner (1984); and accounts of Bakhtin— Holquist (1990), Emerson (1997); on its abject side, see Bernstein (1990).

20. How can one list sources on irony other than ironically? Some are Kierkegaard (1989), Booth (1974), de Man (1979), Chai (1987, on irony and comedy), Hutcheson (1994) . . .; it's hopeless. For an ironic shaking off of the fashionable attitude of irony, see Cavell (1984: 195ff.).

21. Boon (1990a: Chaps. 4, 3, 2; 1982a: 264, 278); see Chaps. 6, 8.

22. Lindenberger (1984: 23). Nothing is trickier than distinctions among parody, satire, and related forms of reflexivity; Menippean satire (more accurately "parody") is self-implicating rather than other-ridiculing. On Lucianic satire, see Casson (1962). On the Cynic Menippus (340–270 B.C.)—a Syrian slave who won his freedom, and "apparently the first non-dramatic writer of satire to make his work continuously funny," see Highet (1962: 36). On satire as "saturated with genres," see Lyotard (1993), and see Chaps. 4 and 6. On long-term parody, see Macdonald (1985). As for isolable "postmodern parody," I still don't believe in it (Boon 1990a: xiii–xvi).

23. A few of many sources consulted: on masques, Orgel (1981, 1996; see Boon 1982a: Chap. 5); on nineteenth-century musical institutions, Dahlhaus (1989); on Offenbach, Traubner (1983); on Bayreuth's stage, sights, and sounds, Di Gaetani (1978); on underscored movies, Eyman (1997), Barrios (1995). My allusion to castrati derives in part from a lecture delivered by Carolyn Abbate.

24. For potlatch, comparatively, see R. Benedict (1961), Mauss (1990), both drawing on Boas and Hunt's Kwakiutl researches. This classic institution figures in anthropological challenges to formalist economic theory (see Sahlins 1972, 1976; Jonaitis (1991); and Chap. 12.

25. For Mozart, one might consult Osborne (1978); for Wagner, Burbridge and Sutton (1979), D. Lodge and W. Weber (1984), and Di Gaetani (1978); for R. Strauss, Del Mar (1986). On institutionalizing *Gesamtkunst* enterprises, see the works of Michael Steinberg (1990).

26. On Hofmannsthal and Strauss, see Del Mar (1986), Hamburger (1972), Puffet (1989).

27. A key source on Mozart's *Magic Flute* as a Masonic opera is Chailley (1972); suggestive diversions in construing opera include P. Conrad (1977), Backès-Clément (1988), Kostenbaum (1993); diverse trends are covered in the magazine *Opera News*.

28. On *Die Sieger*, see C. Wagner (1978, 1980), discussed in Boon (1989); on Schopenhauer, see Safranski (1991).

29. Nietzsche's storied reaction against *Parsifal* occurs variously in Nietzsche (1967, 1959); I broach a bit of this endlessly thorny issue in Boon (1989).

30. On the contents of this paragraph, see Boon (1989, 1992a, 1995a).

31. The tradition (traced by Flaherty) of opera-cum-critical theory is being furthered by Gross and Parker (1988), Tomlinson (1993), Abbate (1991), and other transdisciplinary musicologists.

32. On such theories of "culture," see Boon (1973). On Herder—whose sense of *Volk* was devised to resist Napoleonic encroachments and universalizing legal codes— see Boon (1982a: Chap. 7), Sahlins (1996); Feldman and Richardson (1972). It is anachronistic to charge Herder with "racism" according to critical agendas in the aftermath of National Socialist *völkisch* movements; see Berman (1988).

33. On Strauss's operas, see Del Mar (1978).

34. Adorno (1981: 80); for more such thoughts, see Boon (1989).

35 Boon (1973; 1982a: Chap. 1; 1990a: Chap. 3; 1994). Arguments for, against, and ambivalent about "culture" overlap anthropology, cultural studies, critical theory, and kindred pursuits. For angles on Boasian moves and postcolonialist positions, see Boon (1998).

36. Poly- may imply apocalyptic as well; see, for example C. Patrides and

J. Wittreich (1984). Or saying so (and citing that source) may be "operatic"—exaggerated, like "cultures" (Boon 1982a: Chap. 1).

37. See the intertangled works listed under Melville in this book's bibliography.

38. Boon (1982a: 20, 149–51, 229, 273–74; 1990a: 194–97, 202–203). Melville's "vast allusiveness" is nicely earmarked by Poirier, who parallels Nabokov's design for Humbert Humbert, marked by "exuberances of imagination" and "extravagances of yearning" (1985: 251–52); see Chap. 4.

39. Rogin (1985: Chap. 5).

40. Melville is nudged toward Sedgwick (e.g., 1996) in some recent studies of *Pierre*; for more measured, historically sensitive readings, see Parker (1997), Blair (1996), Beaver (1973).

41. I first encountered Stanley Cavell when we both spoke at a *Daedalus* conference held at Emory University in 1979; too shy to converse, I listened willingly.

42. I allude to Spivak (1988, 1995); for an ironic response to Spivak, see Dirlik (1994); on this response and views of H. Bhabha, see Boon (1998). Tsing (1993: 13–17) astutely reopens issues of minority positions as waged by Spivak, Gates (1988), West (1993), Bhabha (1994), etc. Even when multiplying marginalities, Tsing notes, neighboring differences must be strategically ignored (1993: 313, fn. 4); see Chap. 9.

43. It is not only that genres blur, but blurrings blur, including the blurrings of "*genre*" (gender)—a funny word in the "English" language. (What is "*genre*" in German, in Indonesian, . . .? I intend the question rhetorically.)

44. On *Märchen* and anthropology see Boon (1982a). On early Romantic theories of myth, see Feldman and Richardson (1972); on Romantic novelists, see Blackall (1983); on folkloric studies and various philosophies, see Bendix (1997).

45. Intricacies of Hollywood screwball comedy are celebrated in Harvey (1987). On what makes eight such movies philosophically noteworthy, see Cavell (1981a); on Hollywood movies more generally "as they used to be," see Mordden (1988); on when they stopped being that, see Mordden (1990a). Pondering what Melville might have made of movies, were he not born too soon, could lead into murky depths and shimmering surfaces of institutionalized "show business" (Boon n.d.). A similar thought experiment might ponder what Montaigne would have made of Bali, had he been there (see Chap. 2).

46. Cavell (1984: 5) salutes Kern's *Swing Time*; for more on Kern, see Kreuger (1977); on a key interpreter of his songs, Irene Dunne, see Harvey (1987).

47. This "Birth of the Blues" annotation is from the entry under that title in S. Green (1981). On Nietzsche's *Birth*, see Nietzsche (1967), Sallis (1991), Hayman (1980); resonances between Proust and Nietzsche are offered in Nehamas (1985).

48. Two scholars I nominate to write it are Furia (1992) and Gabbard (1996, with thanks to David Brent).

49. On Madonna, see Paglia (1992); on Paglia-envy, see Paglia (1992); on Paglia (1990), see Paglia (1992). For paths through relatively recent showbiz that this study will not follow, see Goodwin (1992). Tracking the showbiz-info-mercial-mega-industry has become a core project of the new *New Yorker* that now reads a bit more like *Variety*. On "entertainment," spectacle, ritual, festival, etc., see Bauman (1992).

50. On Barnum, see Kunhardt (1995), Toll (1976); on Barnum and Thoreau, see Reynolds (1988: 497–98). Studies of "the show business" tend to polarize between "appreciations" and caustic critique. Often staked out are sexist, racist, classist, and

homophobic dimensions of showbiz (see, for example, Rogin (1994), Lott (1993), Feuer (1993). Subtler distinctions may also merit consideration; see, for example, R. Allen (1991) and especially W. Leach (1993); studies by Mordden nicely split the difference between 1) love of hybrid genres and 2) either frowning on or over-advocating virtually anything "showy." On "entertainment" (*hiburan*) in Indonesia, see G. Nugroho (1995, with thanks to John MacDougall).

51. Interest in tourist practices was kindled by D. MacCannell (1989, 1992); the anthropology and cultural studies of tourism has burgeoned; see Greenwood (1989), V. Adams (1996), Pratt (1992), Clifford (1997); see Chap. 5. On the reflowering of histories of tourist-going, see Liebersohn (1996). For earlier thoughts on tourism in Bali, see Boon (1977: Chap. 7); recent overviews of this topic include Bruner (1996), Picard (1992); on Southeast Asian tourism and literary travel-writing, see Hitchcock, King, and Parnwell (1993), Morgan (1996).

52. On Baudelaire, see Benjamin (1969, 1978, etc.); for Baudrillard, see Baudrillard (1988), discussed in Chap. 13.

53. On Irving Berlin, whose lyric refrain is being played on here, see Furia (1995, 1992). Horkheimer and Adorno's (1970) sense of the "culture industry" is revisited below, Chaps. 4, 12.

54. Alfred Hitchcock's *Spellbound* was his thirty-first feature film, which eventually numbered fifty-three by one way of reckoning (Spoto 1983). According to Sloan (1993), 895 annotatable books and articles (plus hundreds more merely listed) had been published on Hitchcock by 1990; I have read many of them and most everything since, a large number. Hitchcock never made a CinemaScope-shaped film (VistaVision was the nearest he came). On the emerging size of HDTV (that materialized sooner, I'm told, in Japan), see any business report on "communications media" of the last few years; see Chap. 13.

55. Indeed, as I sat writing this note in 1997, the late Carl Sagan's subsequent *Contact* (1985) was released in a blockbuster adaptation; promotions tried to launch the movie above a crowd of competitors by trumpeting the book's author along with the star, Jody Foster. For further misgivings about Sagan's own boosterism of science, see Lewontin (1997).

56. On revolution, see Karl Marx (1972); on conversion, see William James (1958); on abjection, see Bernstein (1990); on bureaucracy, see M. Weber (1946); on *Lust* (don't Anglicize), see Richard Wagner (1965); on Hong Kong, see the video archives of ABC coverage during the week leading up to July 1, 1997; on bio-power, see Rabinow (1996).

Chapter One
Re Menses

1. "Interpretive turns" in social sciences and *sciences humaines* can be sampled in Ricoeur (1981), Rabinow and Sullivan (1979), Skinner (1985), Todorov (1993); on interpretive anthropology, see C. Geertz (1973), Boon (1982a), Clifford and Marcus (1986), Brady (1991); the latter samples "harmony and argument" in various "Anthropological Poetics," drawing on linguistics, ethnographic narratology, and pragmatist, structuralist, dialogic, and postmodernist approaches. Recent collections bridging eth-

nographic, linguistic, literary, and philosophical interpretation include Daniel and Peck (1996) and Benson (1993); see also Crapanzano (1992), Jackson (1996).

2. On James's "radical empiricism," see Wild (1970), which compares James to Merleau-Ponty; see Boon (1982a: 281). On W. James and his families, see Feinstein (1984); on W. James and others (e.g., Henry Adams), see G. Allen (1967: 477).

3. For "interpretive conventions" accentuating reading and readers, see Mailloux (1982) on pragmatist, structuralist, post-Heideggerian, and deconstructive twists, plus reception theory and reader-response criticism. Issues of reading practice and historiographic rhetoric are broached by H. White (1978), de Certeau (1984, 1986), LaCapra (1985, 1987); on de Certeau himself, see Ahearne (1995).

4. See, for example, G. Dening (1996: 196–200). Since writing this essay, a new installment of the Freeman attack has flared up in a theatrical crossover; see Monaghan (1996); I allude to Freeman's *renommé* at the end of Boon (1994).

5. Nietzsche (1967); see particularly Sallis (1991). Lévi-Strauss wrote in the wake of French engagement with Wagner's work since Baudelaire; see Boon (1989). Some efforts (e.g., Prattis 1991) to explain Lévi-Strauss's concern with *Parsifal* neglect arts of corpus-making and relations between musical and textual description and evocation. Lévi-Strauss's attention to Wagner may appear on its surface a matter of parallel "synopses" of mythic plots; but its follow-through pertains to mythic and musical composition *as experienced*, or as read. The very technique of myth "synopsis" that Prattis forefronts (1991: 128–30; he compares it to Jung's!) is continually overturned in Lévi-Strauss's Wagnerian devices of sustained, motivic processes. What could be more different than Jung (see Noll 1997)?

6. See Boon (1982a: 106–8) and above "Rehearsal" on opera.

7. On Sapir's life, see Darnell (1990); on his relations with Benedict, see Caffrey (1989) and Mead (1959). On Sapir's work, see Handler (1986); on Benedict, see Handler (1990). Histories of styles of anthropology are offered in Stocking (1983, 1986, etc.), geared to diverse historicist, epistemological, interpretive, and political issues.

8. For biographical renderings of Benedict's "personal" life, see Modell (1983), Caffrey (1989); biography is itself oblique to "subjectivity"; see Boon (1990a: Postlude); see Chap. 3.

9. On the stylistic "eloquence" of such anthropologists as Frazer, Benedict, and Lowie, see Boon (1982a: Chap. 1, 97–111); on similar moments in Belo's style, see Chap. 3. On modernist anthropological textuality, see Manganera (1990).

10. On literary "closure" as it affects readers' memory, see Torgovnick (1981: 3–4); sources on this aspect of literatures include Rabinowitz (1987) and Eco (1979).

11. I have in mind Bloom (1973, 1975), although I lack both the expertise and the will to address implications of Bloomian "misprision"; Mailloux (1982) provides helpful bearings for journeys into inevitable misreading.

12. The classic source on Trobriand *kula* is Malinowski (1922); subsequent literature is abundant: from Mauss (1990), to Weiner (1976), and beyond.

13. See Jung (1971); a critique of Jungiana is Noll (1997).

14. Sapir noted Benedict's "mad love of psychic irregularities;" see Boon (1990a: 190).

15. A notion of *topos*, borrowed from literary history, is applied to Balinese anthropology in Boon (1977: 226). Topics of "topic" (*topos*) and rubrics of "ritual *cum* rheto-

ric" are pursued across comparative histories and discourse (from European rhetoric to Indic Tantrism) in Boon (1990a). On ritual topoi of (un)circumcision, see Chap. 2.

16. The so-called author repeatedly rereads "otherwise" his or her writing; metaphors of "text" (versus "work") in Roland Barthes's (1977) sense spring to mind (see Boon 1982a). Texts, then, are not static (as critics of "metaphors of the text" often charge); texts indeed have agency—in the reading of them; see Boon (1990a: Chap. 3); Dening (1996).

17. Diverse dialectics of power in gendered rituals are a theme of feminist readings; for relevant ethnographies of island Southeast Asia, see Atkinson and Errington (1990). Tsing (1993: 313–14) notes the "lack of marking of menstruation among the Rungus Dusun of northern Borneo"; one might compare Zuni and contrast Kwakiutl.

18. On this dimension of Lévi-Strauss, see Boon (1992a); Lévi-Strauss (1993) keeps rereading Boas; see Boon (1995b).

19. Yes, I was thirteen; *Patterns of Culture* was a gift from a friend (I forget what I gave "in return").

20. On "dialogic" approaches in ethnography, see D. Tedlock (1982) and Clifford and Marcus (1986). For radically more dialogic work on Zuni than Benedict's, see B. Tedlock (1992). On "dialogism" in novelistic arts and politics, see Bakhtin (1981); on Bakhtin and anthropology, see Bruner (1984), Boon (1990a: Chaps. 3–4). Bakhtin's "carnivalization" partly aligns with earlier anthropologies of ritual reversal, as in those "closing" movements (oscillating between Saturnalia and Balder) of Frazer's *Golden Bough* (1890 . . .), aptly redesignated in a French translation, *Le cycle de la rameau d'or*. "Cycle" nicely evokes Frazer's never-ending rereadability.

21. Mead (1959). For fascinating thoughts on Benedict-as-writer, see Babcock (1986)—reflexively intent on identifying. One Benedict biography is Caffrey (1989); on resisting reading "biography" as the "life behind" any text, including ethnographies, see Chap. 3.

22. Constructive reassessments of Benedict's *Chrysanthemum and the Sword* (1948) are being pursued by Ted Bestor in Anthropology and Asian Studies at Cornell University.

23. Jane Belo's life and work are the subject of research by Balinist Anne McCauley.

24. Readers of Mead's *Blackberry Winter* may suspect that related motives pervaded her "interpersonal" *recherches* as well; see Boon (1990a: Postlude). Pollmann's piece appeared in *Indonesia*; on fashions of abrasive critique, plus some admiring remarks about a part-parody of such exposé-style by Gita Mehta, see Chap. 7. A Balinese voice similar to Gita Mehta's, but possibly unparodic, is Ibu Gedong Bagus Oka, as cited by Pollmann. Of course, other Balinese-Balinist voices are as complex and non-transparent as Mead (or better, Benedict); an impressive list includes I Wayan Bhadra from the colonialist era, and since independence I Gusti Ngurah Bagus (e.g., 1991), I Made Bandem (Bandem and deBoer 1981), and hundreds more. All go-betweens (including Balinese translating Bali) have contradictory credentials as such. Similarly, a list of Samoans translating Samoa includes Albert Wendt among many more, all of whom (like Mead and Freeman) are contradictorily positioned (see Dening 1996). At risk of repeating myself: It is an objective fact that *any* translator blurs and shifts boundaries of "insider/outsider" (or Native/Stranger); taking representations of this fact into account yields ultraobjectivities, variously. Fuller acknowledgment of this paradox might help defuse entrenched academic disputes.

25. On Boas, see Stocking (1968, 1979, 1974, 1996), Krupat (1990).

26. See Bateson (1958, 1972) and Boon (1990a: Postlude).

27. On impasses of journalism, see J. Malcolm (1989); nor are political science or cultural studies devoid of such aporia.

28. Burke (1966); see Peacock (1975). I sometimes try to emulate rituals of writing-reading, whose analogies exist in many cultures and disciplines. "Processive writing" can be illustrated with Lévi-Strauss's corpus—saturated with ethnographic evidence, yet simultaneously devised to engage readers (musically) as such (see Boon 1972, 1982a, c, 1989, 1992a). That this Proustian dimension often falls on deaf anthropological (and deconstructive) ears recalls the professional history of refusing "processiveness" in Freud's writing; for more processive writing, see Chap. 4.

Chapter Two
Of Foreskins

1. Foster (1926); Layard (1942); both sources deserve rereading. On Freud, see below, "Boutade II."

2. The review is Moyer (1982).

3. C. Geertz (1960).

4. Schrieke (1921–22); on Balinese Muslims, see Barth (1993), reviewed in Boon (1995c).

5. "Symptomatological" is a keyword in Foucault (1970); see Chap. 3.

6. On "being there"—with apologies to Jerzy Kosinski—as a seriocomic metaphor of and for ethnography, see C. Geertz (1987); Boon (1982a: 5).

7. See Boon (1982a: 162–68; 1990a: 54–60; 1977: 212).

8. For more adequate summaries of Foucault's controversial approach, see Roth (1992), Rabinow (1984), O'Farrell (1989). On Foucault, Yates, and the history of anthropological ideas, see Boon (1982a: Chaps. 2, 5; 1990a: Chaps. 1–2, 4, 5–7; 1977: 237). On conjoining interestingly incongruous approaches to bodies (and souls) from cultures distantly past, see Peter Brown (1988).

9. Glimpses of Couliano's life, work, and death appear in Eco (1997).

10. Relevant works include Clifford (1988; 1997). My device of "beginnings" owes a bit to Said (1975) and more to Burke (1970). A burgeoning literature on travel-writing, ethnography, history, fiction, and cultural studies includes M. Campbell (1988), Pratt (1992), Leed (1991), Manganaro (1992), Brady (1991), Caesar (1992); see Chaps. 4, 5.

11. Pires (1944: 258); on other Southeast Asian historical sources see Reid (1981, 1994); on historiographic representations evading circumcision, see Boon (1977: 210ff.).

12. Lucianic aspects of anthropology appear in Boon (1982a: 264, 268, 279; 1990a: Chaps. 3–4). "Cross-cultural texts" derived from Menippean dialogue style include More's *Utopia* (1518), Multatuli's 1860 anticolonialist satire *Max Havelaar* (1982), and the contrasting *oeuvres* of Bakhtin and Northrop Frye; see Chap. 6.

13. Lévi-Strauss explores ambiguities of comparative knowing in tones of resignation, I feel, not nostalgia; on *figures* of his corpus, see Boon (1972, 1985a, 1989, 1982a: Chap. 7). A fine guide to ethnographic writing in *histoire* is de Certeau (1984, 1986, 1992).

14. A wide array of framing "Circumcision *and* or *versus* X" includes Brown et al. (1988), a survey of Southeast Asian penis inserts contrasted in part with circumcision (see below, Chap. 11). Australian subincision is a classic ethnographic topic; for other aboriginal topics, see Yengoyan (1989).

15. Readers interested in Derrida's approach to this matter are here "deferred" for several pages. Cynthia Chase, marvelously versed in deconstruction, has remarked of George Eliot's *Daniel Deronda*: "In the period in which Deronda's story takes place, male babies were not routinely circumcised. Circumcision was a ritual procedure practiced by Jews, so that evidence of circumcision amounted to evidence of Jewish origin. For Deronda not to have known he was Jewish until his mother told him means, in these terms, 'that he never looked down,' . . . an idea that exceeds, as much as does magical metamorphosis, the generous limits of realism. Deronda must have known, but he did not: otherwise, of course, there could be no story. The plot can function only if *la chose*, Deronda's circumcised penis, is disregarded . . . (Chase 1986: 169, citing S. Marcus). This reading may slight ritual "diacritics." Deronda could have looked down—quite obsessively, in fact—and never known he was different, unless he also looked over: across the difference, thus comparing *les choses*. Comparison can get sloughed off in deconstructive constructions (see Chap. 10).

16. The film is *Europa Europa* (see Rafferty 1991).

17. "Like all my other pals, I wanted one thing only: to be a good Muslim. . . . 'Above all don't move,'" advised one of those present. . . . I looked at my thick, blackish blood that flowed like a streamlet and mixed slowly with the plate of ashes. . . . All my hopes to become a true Muslim vanished . . ., for I realized that my parents were poor and that we did not possess what was required to make a pilgrimage" Toer (1968: 539, 545; my trans). See also D. Boyarin (1992).

18. Bowen's fine history of Gayo (Sumatra) reveals heirlooms and circumcision in social dialectics (1991: 232–33); other important conjunctions include circumcision and "warrior asceticism" (M. Weber 1967a: 92); circumcision and transvestism (Crawley 1927 I: 319); circumcision and initiation in Kenya (Kratz n.d.). Circumcision *and* writing (a style of incision) is an expansive figural and practical copula in several traditions.

19. The religious, ethnic, and sexual-preference politics of pro/anti-circumcision figure in too many partisan media to list; I thank L. Rosen and J. Geller for help with these sources. Extensive work on female excision and the medieval Near East is underway in Berkey (1995). A helpful review of the newsworthiness of "female circumcision," clitoridectomy, etc., is Walley (1997).

20. I learned this from an ABC TV "Good Morning America" segment on science, broadcast in early 1997, I think.

21. "The Muslim tradition relates that Abraham leads Ishmael and not Isaac to be sacrificed; however, there are differences among Islamic authors on this subject" (Hammoudi 1988:95); this ethnography is a subtle meditation on sacrifice in Islam and the masquerades in its lively margins.

22. Hocart (1954); Marett (1933); see Boon (1987a).

23. Vance (1978: 618–34). Luther, *Works* (3: 75–118, 133–35); see Edwards (1983: 5–6).

24. See also Hoffman (1996).

25. Dening (1980); see also Dening (1996, 1992, 1988).

26. Montaigne (1983); Schaefer (1989); for insights into Montaigne's contexts, see works by Quint (e.g., 1992).

27. Davenport (1983); for Waters's translation, see Montaigne (1903).

28. For a powerful evocation of both sixteenth- and twentieth-century censorships (of Rabelais), see Davis (1990); it would take such "stereoscopic" historical reading to begin fathoming possible allegiances in Montaigne's travels. Shell (1991) makes something of Montaigne's Morano mother.

29. Frame in Montaigne (1983: xx).

30. See Boon, "Birds, Words, and Orangutans" (1990a: Chap. 1).

31. On early modern carnival celebrations on the eve of Jewish circumcisons, see Horowitz (1989).

32. On meanings of "ultra-," recall Chap. 1. I am trying here to be unsymptomatological about an "ultradiagnostic" source; it isn't easy.

33. This paragraph (couched in a footnote in this essay's earlier version), which indeed implicates its author's condition, was overlooked by J. Boyarin (1996). Again, any effort to write unobliquely about circumcision or uncircumcision (whether own or other) may be problematic, I suspect.

34. Eliade (1978); see also Yates (1972).

35. A somewhat more historiographic rendering of this Foucauldian theme is Reiss (1982).

36. See Alpers (1983) and controversies she addresses and fuels.

37. The question is Kant's; cultural anthropology contributes to answering it, I think, by detouring through histories of rituals mediating cross-cultural encounters; see Boon (1982a: Chap. 2, "Comparative De-enlightenment"). For a more sanguine view of "Enlightenment" knowledge, see Darnton (1997), which may be recommending an anti-anti-Enlightenment position. Would such a stance adequately counter self-serving programs *for* rationality? My question implies a certain doubt. Foucault's own "What is Enlightenment?" phase is revisited in O'Farrell (1989), who also cites Merleau-Ponty's astute remarks on the "political mania" among newspaper-reading philosophers that produces neither good politics nor good philosophy (1989: viii, 3); see also Dreyfus and Rabinow (1986).

38. One difficult thing about nefarious regimes is that they can as well be *for* something (circumcision, say) as *against* it; the same is true of musics that tyrants (or petty officials, or programming directors) espouse. Neither ritual nor music is constantly indexible as a symptom of particular politics or prejudice. Everything would be much easier—but perhaps, too, even more evil—if they were.

39. For discussion of critical turns against "visual" practices of knowledge, see Jay (1986); see also Fabian (1982); for slight correctives to the latter's interesting critique, see Boon (1990a: 205).

40. It is paradoxical that some postmodern approaches nevertheless maintain rhetorics of transcendent liberation; I address this matter obliquely in Part Three's initial "polemics."

41. Freud (1955); for more on this essay's play of *unheimlich*, see Chap. 6.

42. L. Steinberg (1983); a subsequent edition has extended this second edition's already extensive excurses.

43. Melville (1970 [1891]).

44. For studies of obsessive-seeming ambivalence and "fetishism," see the essays in Apter and Pietz (1993).

45. L. Steinberg (1983); Schama (1987: 588).

46. My topic of "covering Islam" alludes to Said (1981); that work too, like his *Orientalism* (1979), proceeds too monolithically (albeit for a good cause).

47. For works that engage such subtleties of ceremonial practices, see Trexler (1993, 1995, 1997, etc.)

48. G. Dening (1994; 1996); Foucault (1970, 1972); Yates (1966, 1972).

49. The Shurreef source valuably falls between the cracks of theorized agendas in cultural critique; *gamme* is a musical metaphor important in approaches that mediate between so-called structuralism and so-called phenomenology (see, e.g., Jakobson 1990a, b). For another, unconnected "rereading" of Montaigne, see Lévi-Strauss (1983a); Merleau-Ponty, too, reread Montaigne.

50. For various ways to pose these questions, see Geller (1993), Gilman (1991, 1995).

51. Henry Adams (1961: 3); on Adams and Tahiti, see Boon (1990a: xv–xvi), and especially G. Dening (1996).

52. See sources by Gilman and Geller listed in the bibliography; see also Santner (1996), Malcolm (1984), Obeyesekere (1990), Paul (1996), Rieff (1954, 1979); I understand that H. Bhabha is pursuing Freudian hybridities.

53. Burke (1957, 1962, 1968); Mahony (1982, 1987); see above, "Rehearsals" and Chap. 1.

54. Vitz (1988); key to this study is Freud's Catholic nanny.

55. Gay (1988); making Freud a figure of "enlightenment" may be a crux of Gay's work; for gingerly critique, see Yerushalmi (1991: 116).

56. A similar fate has indeed befallen Foucault in Halperin (1997). Upon mentioning again Derrida, perhaps I should state only that no reference to Freud's circumcision enters Jones's biography's index (1953–57).

Chapter Three
About a Footnote

1. On interdisciplinary Balinese arts in the thirties and since, see H. Geertz (1995), de Zoete and Spies (1939), Bandem and deBoer (1981), Bakker (1985), Ramseyer (1977). On emergences of ethnography, philology, historiography, and performance studies in Bali, see Belo (1970), Boon (1977, 1990a), C. Geertz (1980), H. Geertz (1991), Agung (1991), Vickers (1989), Wiener (1995), Barth (1993); many other sources are continually itemized in F. deBoer, ed. *Bali Arts and Culture News*, published at Wesleyan University.

2. On Marcel Proust and memory—a rich strain of coinciding literature, philosophy, music, and related arts—see Chaps. 4 and 5. The topic of Proustian memory is endless; I sketch links between Proust and Lévi-Strauss's ethnology in Boon (1972: Chap. 5; 1982a: Chap. 7). By "charmed circle" I mean groups of impresarios and enthusiasts; see Mellow (1974).

3. "Space" is a new cliché woven through Foucauldian approaches. By "eventness"

I allude to *histoire événementelle* critiqued by historians of *mentalités*; see LaCapra and Kaplan (1982).

4. Lévi-Strauss's notion of "cold societies" never deserved notoriety for implying changeless peoples; see Boon (1995a: 48).

5. Benjamin (1978: 177); for more, see Chap. 4.

6. For more on this motive throughout Levi-Strauss, see Boon (1995a, b).

7. Clifford (1981), included in Clifford (1988).

8. Several transitions in this essay-*étude* are pastiches of phrases from writings in a commemorative mode—here Waugh's *Brideshead Revisited* (1945: 178), whose "subject was Julia."

9. Taylor (1983); see also Gabler (1988), Mordden (1988). Hollywood has been even more copiously covered than Bali. Shifting effects of the Depression on Hollywood—first it helped business, then it harmed—are evoked in Berg (1989).

10. Bateson and Mead (1942); see also H. Geertz (1995); for helpful background on Mead's techniques, see I. Jacknis (1988); Boasians varied dramatically in their practices of documenting rites and contexts.

11. Mead (1977); compare M. Mead (1959).

12. Richer approaches associated with "Culture and Personality" can be surveyed in the journal *Ethos*, edited by Robert Paul and later Thomas Csordas. On potentials of psychological anthropology, see Obeyesekere (1990), Csordas (1994), Shweder and LeVine (1984), Shore (1996), and Peacock (1975).

13. See Boon (1990a: Postlude).

14. Boon (1982a: 3–26, 54–111).

15. Much anthropology and cultural studies now experiment in this vein; for example, Taussig (1997); one tricky aspect of "transgression" is that it can become routine, contractual, indeed virtually bureaucratized (see Tanner 1979). One may be able to exit this "impasse" by leavening "shock" with a little propriety; that, I think, was Benjamin's way.

16. Discourses of sexual transgression were forefronted at a conference organized by Gilman and I. Hull at Cornell University; see Gilman (1989a).

17. I distinguish the old *New Yorker* from the new *New Yorker* edited by Tina Brown, who has diminished the magazine's leavening of propriety; for a bit of writing in the vein of the old *New Yorker*, see Chap. 4.

18. For the flavor of Dutch research, see Swellengrebel (1960, 1969); see also Boon (1977). On intricacies of Dutch work in Indonesia and the odd fish performing it, see Beekman (1988), reviewed in Boon (1990b).

19. On the Bali Beach Hotel, see Chap. 4. It burned down in the early-mid 1990s, a fact occasioning elaborate Balinese interpretations. Hedi Hinzler of Leiden University has mounted sensitive exhibitions featuring Spies and Dutch colleagues whose work in Bali, too, was more eccentric than stereotyped accounts against colonialist regimes tend to imply.

20. Intricacies of Forster's travels, jobs, return visit, and long-term correspondence with "India" are conveyed, however veiled, in his *Hill of Devi* (1953). Some studies of Foster stress his generosity—e.g., Santha Rama Rau (in Sonnenberg 1989: 259–79) on devising the theatrical play drawn from *A Passage*. Others (e.g., Suleri 1992) tend to reduce things to his sexuality—not just gay but anal, Suleri suggests, whereupon she rehashes the most conspicuous passages of *A Passage*.

21. See Boon (1990a).

22. Bateson (1984), Howard (1984), Caffrey (1989), etc.; an expanding literature rethinking the nature and genre of biography includes Sturrock (1996).

23. Indonesian for "etc."; indeed, Indonesian "translations" of and to these movements abound as well.

24. On Debussy, see Lockspeiser (1978), Howat (1994).

25. See Boon (1989, 1972, 1992a).

26. I found the old *Variety* (that "Bible" of America's showbiz industry) more entertaining than the new, which resembles a Web site for intercommunications-media-savvy simulated in hard copy. Everything is starting to read the same.

27. The sense of freedom bitingly ironized by Lévi-Strauss is one fulcrum of his legendary quarrel with Sartre; see L. Rosen (1971). On reading the "autobiography" of *Tristes tropiques* as profoundly ironic, see Boon (1972: Chap. 5; 1982a: 278–79; 1992a); see also Hardwick (1984: 253–57); C. Geertz (1987) expands his earlier reading (1973: Chap. 13) of *Tristes tropiques*, a work whose reception (which now includes conversion into an opera and a film) could fill a considerable bibliography.

28. One earlier example is Diamond (1975); see Boon (1982a: Appendix C).

29. Stocking (1984; 1986, 1995); these vital studies, too, can be too monolithic; see Boon (1987b); for an opposite (and equally understandable) flaw, see Lincoln (1989), reviewed in Boon (1991). It may be too obvious that I think alternatives between "lineal" and "dispersed" histories will remain agonistic.

30. Mellow (1974); also G. Dening (1980, 1996).

31. That fieldwork "happens" as memory is a fact partly appreciated in J. Boyarin (1994); for sensitive work on memory and time in anthropology, see Greenhouse (1996), Bahloul (1996).

32. Previous homages to that strange interlude called interwar Balinese studies portrayed it as a "musical," and an up-beat one at that; see Boon (1977: Chap. 7).

33. G. Bateson (1958, 1972). "Schismogenesis" may be inescapable (see Boon 1982a: dedication); but it cannot hurt to recognize that fact, "ultraobjectively."

34. Bresson (1986); for another use of "cinematographic notes" in historical ethnography, see G. Dening (1996: 168ff).

35. Ong (1983); one merit of Toulmin's study —its sharp focus on "Cartesian" simplifications—leads him to stress philosophical abstractions, rather than pedagogical habits of reading that instill universalistic modes of argument.

36. Panoff (1993: 168–70).

37. C. Geertz (1983).

38. G. Dening (1980, 1996).

Chapter Four
Cosmopolitan Moments

1. For glimpses of Indonesian cultures and the past five hundred years of history, see Peacock (1973). Recent ethnography and history in various Indonesian and Malaysian locales includes R. Barnes (1995), Bowen (1993), Milner (1994), Errington (1989), Tsing (1993), George (1996), Keane (1997), Atkinson and Errington (1990); McKinnon (1991), Steedly (1993). The long-term history of global commodification (including pilgrimages and tourisms that form part of regional and world trade) seem underesti-

mated in such works as Wolf (1982); helpful correctives are Mintz (1985), Segal (1988, 1992); see Chaps. 8, 9.

2. Boon (1977, 1982a: Chap. 5, 1990a); see also H. Geertz (1991); Djelantik (1986), Agung (1985, 1991), Bagus (1991), Vickers (1989), Zurbuchen (1987).

3. To clarify: The topos "Hindu Bali" names a counter-Muslim locale both "encrypted" and "displayed" within the world's most populous Islamic nation; a scene of and for translation, where meanings have collided among Austronesian linguistic variations (High/Middle/Low Balinese, Sanskritized Old Javanese or Kawi, modern Indonesian, etc.) across extra-Vagant intersections of Malayo-Polynesian cultures, European colonialisms, and diversely Indo-European expanses; also relevant are such facts that Singapore lies directly (by air) northwest and Australia south. All of this matters greatly today.

Bakhtin's notion of "chronotope" is applied to Bali in Boon (1984b), expanded in Boon (1990a). For another angle, see Hobart (1991). On European cornucopian rhetoric that proliferated in Renaissance texts, see Cave (1979).

4. On complex circumstances during Balinese-Dutch encounters, see Wiener (1995); this important book tips its narrative toward the paramount houses of Klungkung, neglecting alternative Balinese slants (see Boon 1977).

5. Unless readers wish to plot the "postmodern" through centuries, or millenia, as in Readings and Schaber (1993).

6. For fine insights into Stendahl's complex ironies, see Wood (1971), who mentions the dangers of "half-serious" attitudes, without quite suggesting how to avoid them.

7. E. Goffman (1959, 1974); for an encapsulation of Goffman's sense of "game," see C. Geertz (1983: Chap. 1).

8. Clifford and Marcus (1986), Lévi-Strauss (1955), G. Bateson (1938); or since Frazer's *Psyche's Task* (see Boon 1987a), or since R. Benedict's then-heterodox *Patterns of Culture* (1934). "Since" can keep receding.

9. Nabokov's *Lolita* (1970)—exponentially Menippean satirical—is devised to make a reader feel as if she or he has been reading it all of his or her "lives"; several relatively recent helpful readings of the annotated *Lolita* are Boyd (1991), Wood (1994), Nabokov (1983, 1990), and dozens more books on my shelves. I feel that I have been reading readings of annotated-*Lolita* all of my lives. Such is the heavenly seriocomic abyss that Nabokov opens before "innocent" readers.

10. For more tangents to Benjamin, see Chap. 6.

11. This moment in Percy joins my opening epigraph from Thoreau in rendering motivic certain moves, including my eventual emulation of old-*New Yorker* style. Percy's key novel remained, I suspect, *The Moviegoer* (1960), published the same year that Hitchcock released *Psycho*. (For other veerings "off the beaten track," see Buzard 1993.)

12. On Melville's *Moby Dick*, see Beaver (1973); on Melville's Melville, see Parker (1997).

13. "Garuda" (a Hindu mythical bird) is also Indonesia's official airline. I may be misremembering here; the carrier was possibly local, or interisland, instead of (trans)national. Regardless "(brandname: X)" echoes a moment in Proust (1981), when the narrator hears an airplane overhead: "(brandname: *Mystère*)."

14. On this series, see Kelleher and Merrill (1987), a source encountered long after these remarks were first published. For further dope on *Perry Mason*, contact Ted

Turner. The series' star (the late Raymond Burr) also played the murderer in Hitchcock's incomparable *Rear Window* (1954) and prior to that the district attorney (!) in William Wyler's *A Place in the Sun* (1952, based on Theodore Dreiser's *An American Tragedy*); this movie was broadcast over Indonesian television, subtitled in its national language, as received in Bali, in 1992, where and when I happened to tune in. Good *Garuda*.

15. Derrida probably pinched his slogan that prefaces are written last from Proust (1981, vol. 3: 154–59); I have deleted from this book a long extract of Proust that proves as much. For a Derridean-style always-already "preface" directed at Sartre, see LaCapra (1978).

16. *Breakfast at Tiffany's*, based (loosely, as a *Seinfeld* show insisted) on the novel by Truman Capote.

17. E. S. Gardner (n.d.; Herdian Suhardjono, translator); as usual, one desire in ironic responses would be to back-translate; *toko buku* means "book shop."

18. Coincidences—radically concrete and particular—have little if anything to do with "synchronicities" in a Jungian sense tied to resemblance rather than juxtaposition.

19. Poe may be as crucial to this essay as he was to Nabokov's *Lolita*, whose relevant allusions to Poe's heroines—and not just Annabel Lee—are documented by Apell (Nabokov 1970) on many pages. Poe, via Baudelaire's and Mallarmé's translations, came home (away from home) to roost in Proust (e.g., 1981, Vol. 1: 71). Similarly, this essay's conclusion could append from Poe the following: "It is a thousand pities that the puny witticisms of a few professional objectors should have power to prevent . . . the adoption of a name for our country. At present we have, clearly none. There should be no hesitation about 'Appalachia.' In the first place, it is distinctive. 'America' is not, and can never be made so. . . . In the second place 'Appalachia' is indigenous, springing from one of the most magnificent and distinctive features of the country itself. Thirdly, in employing this word we do honor to the Aborigines, whom, hitherto, we have at all points unmercifully despoiled, assassinated, and dishonored. . . . The last, and by far the most truly important consideration of all, however, is the music of 'Appalachia' itself; nothing could be more sonorous, more liquid, or of fuller volume, while its length is just sufficient for dignity. How the gutteral 'Alleghania' could ever have been preferred for a moment is difficult to conceive. I yet hope to find 'Appalachia' assumed" (Poe 1980: 46–47).

20. Lévi-Strauss's *Tristes tropiques* remains more invitingly accessible than his *Mythologiques* for eschewing "mythemes" when pursuing his distanced, compassionate *regard éloigné* (see Boon 1972, 1982, 1986, 1990).

21. Mehta (1979: 146); see Chap. 7.

22. On Busby Berkeley, see Barrios (1995), Berg (1989); or see *Footlight Parade* (1933).

23. The *Star Wars* trilogy derived from George Lucas's reading of Joseph Campbell; this chapter was written before its meta-(I mean mega-)spectacular comeback in 1996–97 (see Seabrook 1997).

24. On Proust translating Ruskin, see R. Macksey (1982); see Boon (1972) and Chap. 5. Proust's *madeleine* moments are a virtual "capital" of twentieth-century literature—at least locally (in France, or places translating to or from it).

25. Eco (1983: 73).

26. I thank true friends—May Ebihara and Marvin—for showing me the actual integrated pigeonstops in a walking tour of mid-Manhattan; for more on pigeonstops in NYC, see "The Rockdove" in E. B. White (1983: 24–25).

27. Harbison, *Eccentric Spaces* (1977); "space" and "sites" have become heavily theorized topics in recent critique; this fact enhances the appeal of Harbison's eccentricities as a countermeasure; the best map I know of Manhattan (rendering it rather peripheral) indicates trajectories of New Jersey PATH trains (on which see Chap. 11).

28. This circularity is what formalist economists (including Marxists, that include in turn Horkheimer and Adorno) miss. As indicated later in Chap. 12, and already alluded to in my "Rehearsal" on Burke, it is not just that emphasis on production and redistribution neglects consumption; it is that goods—produced-to-be-pillaged (see Chap. 5)—go crazy, or are already so "foundationally;" see Clifford (1988). Cycles of such extra-Vagance are, truly, all we have to go by, interpretively; see Chaps. 12, 13.

29. On Louis "Satchmo" Armstrong, see Gabbard (1996).

Chapter Five
Why Museums Make Me Sad

1. I have resisted, with only some success, the impulse to meta-comment upon these ruminations in a footnote apparatus; the conference proceedings in whose publication this piece originally appeared (Karp and Lavine 1991) was critiqued in print by Michael Fischer (1989), almost immediately after it occured. To meta- his meta- would only carry us further afield. My essay was devised to counter, gently, the conference's categorical distinctions among: (1) interpreting others' museums of others; (2) confessing favorite museum; or (3) dreaming ultimate museum. I tried weaving these together. A follow-up volume is Karp, Kreamer, and Lavine (1992); for recent responses to museums, see Kirshenblatt-Gimblet (1997), Clifford (1997).

2. See Hodgen (1964); Stocking (1985); Boon (1982a, 1990a); Joyce (1985), Mullaney (1988), Jenkins (1994)

3. See Stocking (1986).

4. P. T. Barnum (1886: 458–59); this book became one of the most successful publications of the nineteenth century, anywhere in this wonder-laden world.

5. This recognition reminds me of Thomas Mann; see for example, his correspondence (1975).

6. One helpful approach to Henry James, including his memoirs, is Agnew (1994); other approaches—from Trilling to Sedgewick, and before and since—are gathered in Yeazell (1994). See especially Rowe (1976, 1996). On James's *tristimania*, see Edel (1987), discussed at the close of Chap. 3. On the comic sense of Henry James, see Poirier (1967).

7. Stewart (1984); this is a haunting study.

8. Benjamin (1978: 152); on Benjamin and melancholia, see Pensky (1996).

9. *Guide Michelin: Benelux* (1974: 256); my commentary on this passage is juxtaposed with sundry other passages in R. Price and S. Price (1992).

10. Alpers (1983: 31–32): see Chap. 2.

11. Kolb in Proust (1983); when discussing Proust, I am forever indebted to J. Theodore Johnson.

12. Hewison (1978: 8); see also Sawyer (1985).

13. If scale is erased, even maps of Venice and of Bali look alike; regardless, histories of visually and textually representing them surely deserve comparison; in the case of Venice, see Tanner (1992).

14. On "accidence" and accidentals in prose, see Morris (1979), discussed in Boon (1982b). A reader might approach the James passages sampled as fragments of a serio-comic genre (call it "plangent humbug"). Implicitly acknowledging humbug as an ever-present possibility, that genre nevertheless refuses to reject plangency altogether. On Ruskin and the James family, see Feinstein (1984).

15. Twain, *Innocents Abroad* (1979: 896). Terms (in Burke's sense) from Twain that "motivate" the way my chapters are written include: "Venice mournes"; the gondolier with a "wooden peg" (illustrated in some editions) who can "flirt suddenly around a corner"; " 'scrooching', as the children say"; "a broadway confusion of busy craft"; the "little humbug trips"; "tears in these far-off foreign lands"; "digression" and appending "evidences, which I copied, verbatim"; plus scenes of tourists and barbers, with "no wild carnival" (all in Twain 1979: 896–911).

I have tried to blend "gondolizings" (Twain's term) with earlier glimpses by Melville, who also visited Venice, according to jottings in his *Journals* of 1857 (1989: 118–20); Melville likens "the charm" of St. Mark's Square to "Battery at N. York," and notes: flower girls, tumblers, and comic actors, Venetians "like pond lillies," "winds like a Susquehanna," sunset, gilt mosaics, "as if the Grand Turk had pitched his pavilion." Melville's guide Antonio is penciled in as a "good character for Con. Man." Might Twain and Melville together afford more adequate means of evoking borderlands anecdotally?

Chapter Six
Litterytoor 'n' Anthropolygee

1. Burke, *Attitudes toward History* (1937).

2. Twain, *Huckleberry Finn* (1977).

3. Imagine as well, an English-language gathering in Switzerland, sited precisely along the French-speaking/German-speaking border; see Engler (1992).

Other scholars (e.g., John Seelye) have mimicked Twain more thoroughly than do my efforts at partly proper-speaking mindful of non-native listeners, so to evoke diverse disciplinary pulls toward colloquial practice. (I thank Marc Manganaro for suggestions on this matter.)

4. These notions are neatly glossed in Bakhtin (1981).

5. Emerson (1997), Holquist (1990); Morson (1991); see also Boon (1990a; Chaps. 3–4).

6. On Saussure's *langue/parole* distinction as relational and possibly compatible with Peirce, see Boon (1982a, Chap. 4). On Saussurian reverberations in high structuralism, poststructuralism, and deconstruction, see Lodge (1988); on Peirce's semiotics and anthropology, see Singer (1984), Daniel (1984), Parmentier (1987), Mertz and Parmentier (1985), Keane (1997).

7. Sapir's "drift"—nonteleological change (e.g., toward isolated words and caseless nouns in English) is outlined in *Language* (1949); on pidgins and creoles, see Romaine (1988); on national language "building," see Wartburg (1946), Blackall (1978); synop-

ses of linguistic issues appear in Crystal (1987). On Sapir, postcolonial studies, and "countercanonicity," see Boon (1998).

8. Coward's *Private Lives* is featured in the initial pages of Steiner (1975).

9. Derrida's essay in both French and English formed the core of Graham (1985), a kind of writing-fest in translation-as-deconstruction, on which see Chap. 10.

10. Kristeva renders "gravidity" or pregnancy *tropique* in many studies; see Kristeva (1980, 1982, etc.).

11. "I am an American," opens "The Stranger's History" in Twain's *Connecticut Yankee* (1979: 791); see also and always and especially, Gertrude Stein (1965).

12. Already cited in "Rehearsals." Any salute to Dada (Dada) should be cited minimally twice, if only to show the difference a repetition makes a repetition makes; see again, Gertrude Stein (1965) (and did I mention Gertrude Stein?).

13. D. Tedlock (1982) remains a key encounter beween specifics of anthropological linguistic practice and high-flying theory (brought down to speaking-writing earth); for other artfully engaging linguistics, see Friedrich (1979, 1986), Becker (1989, 1995), Kuipers (1990), Lee and Urban (1989), Keeler (1987), and sources surveyed in Brady (1991); see also and always Jakobson (e.g., 1990a). Whorf's approaches are enjoying deserved rereading—by Silverstein (n.d.), Kelly, and others; for one approach to Whorf and Bakhtin, see Shutz (1990).

14. Richter (1992); on Rabelais, see Febvre (1982), Bakhtin (1968), Davis (1990).

15. One copious review of socially-embedded meanings of "magic" is O'Keefe (1983).

16. Benjamin's classic essay (1969: 69–82) devises figures of the translator's task and the "original's" between-the-line-ness. This piece was a preface to Benjamin's translations of Baudelaire (who translated Poe . . .). Alas, many commentaries lift Benjamin's essay out of its textual situation: fore-translation. Benjamin also translated (besides Proust) Bachofen, publishing his "between-the-lines" in French, not German. For serious readings of Bachofen and Basel, see Gossmann (1984, 1989, etc.). Bachofen is alluded to inadequately (and symptomatically) in Noll (1997), who sloshes him together with Jung. Bachofen (and his city) may be as tricky a task of translation as Burkhardt (also of Basel) or Nietzsche, who got his "professional" start there.

17. Twain, *Connecticut Yankee* (1979: 792–93).

18. On American "vernacular," see L. Marx (1988); Schmitz's work both clarifies and enacts "humor" *as theory*—pragmatically, you might say. On how Nietzsche read Mark Twain (aloud, by the way), whom he deemed "magnificent," see Gilman (1987: 52). On the key place of humor and carnivalization in "the American Renaissance," see Reynolds (1988: Chap. 15); and reread again and again and again Gertrude Stein (1965).

19. Kenner, *Stoic Comedians* (1974: 37); Ong sometimes reinforces a too-crisp orality/literacy dichotomy (e.g., Ong 1982) but as often refers the distinction to historical and comparative complexities (e.g., Ong 1983).

20. See Boon (1977, 1982a, 1990a); similarly, historians tend to avoid hard-to-standardize ritual differences, such as circumcision (Boon 1977: 210ff); see Chap. 2.

21. I do not enjoy offending linguists (or philologists, historians, or sibling-anthropologists); but ultraobjective readings of devious evidence sometimes produce this effect.

22. This essay, a favorite of Freud's literary rereaders, also appeals to this interdisciplinary anthropologist; it links interlingual dictionary-browsing to fragmentary topics that recur in Freud and his disciples and detractors alike. As suggested in my "Rehearsal" on Burke and Chap. 2, Freudiana proves endlessly de/reconstructable and interpretable-otherwise.

23. Malinowski (1935). On paradoxical aspects of world-wide "word lists" in the history of translation and circumnavigation, see Boon (1982a: Chap. 2; 1990a: Chap. 1); for more on Malinowski (who in his early years also read and wrote about Nietzsche) see essays by Roldán and by Skalník in Vermeulen and Roldán (1995); and see Malinowski (1993), edited by R. Thornton and P. Skalník.

24. All definitions are taken verbatim from *Webster's* (1963); other dictionaries could be substituted, although their definitions may differ.

25. On R. Bloch (1983), Indo-European expanses, and Balinese rites, see Boon (1990: Chaps. 5–7); see Bloch (1986).

26. This critical position spirits forth much of the present book, Chap. 10 in particular.

27. Faulkner (1946: 252); on Faulkner's Misssissippi 'n' Huck's Mississippi, see Schmitz (1983: 129).

28. My wavering transition into Mauss as *verna* is one *raison d'être* of this essay-*étude*.

29. On *L'Année sociologique*, the Collège de France, and scholars either or both rejected, see Lukes (1973), Richmann (1982, 1990); Belmont (1979), Cazeneuve (1972). A wave of responses to Mauss was stimulated by Lévi-Strauss (1950).

30. On sacrifice, see especially Herrenschmidt (1982).

31. For an alternative approach to "mimesis" see Taussig (1993a) and Jay (1973); my sense of mimesis stems from Auerbach (1957), as in Boon (1972: 147–48). For further arguments that ritual constitutes, rather than (per functionalism) reflects or reinforces, see Rosaldo (1989).

32. M. Weber (1946: 311); see also Boon (1982a: 175).

33. I received more than I was able to provide at a conference on "The Gift" organized by R. Sharpe, R. Lederman, and N. Davis at the National Humanities Center, generously hosted by Robert Connor.

34. Cunnison translation (Mauss 1967); the subsequent translation is by W. Halls (Mauss 1990). Like Louis Dumont (see Chap. 9), Pocock (1972) notes the key place of Sanskritic evidence in *The Gift*; see Boon (1990a: 167); on "the comic" in Sanskritic epics, see Langer (1953: Chap. 18).

35. Mauss's devices are echoed in Boon (1982a, Chap. 5; 1990a, Chap. 5); on Mauss's work overall, see Hollier (1990, with thanks to Judith Goldstein). Mauss's *figures* of "loss" remind this reader of Proust (see Goodkin: 60–61).

36. For theories of magic in social and historical studies, see O'Keefe (1983); on magic in India, see Siegel (1991); see also Malinowski's classic (1935) and Burke's "Rhetoric and Primitive Magic" (1962: 564–67) and his earlier rehearsal of that motive (1941: 5–8).

37. "Harum-scarum" stems, motivically, from the above-cited dictionary definition of *colloquial*.

38. Dismissive readers of Lévi-Strauss (1963: Chap. 5) assumed he meant that myths are easy to translate (because shared across cultures); that was wrong. Rather he

designated "myth" the operationally *traduisible* rather than, say, ineffable (see Boon 1972: Chaps. 3–6; 1982a: Chap. 7; 1984a; 1992a).

39. It is worth careful consideration that Mauss designates magic (like religion) a game of "value judgments" entailing *aphorisms*. Here we encounter Mauss at his most intricate—worthy of continual rereading. Given a chance, I would deem Mauss at times as artfully aphoristic as, say, Nietzsche.

40. Lévi-Strauss (1969: 493–97).

41. On Hocart, see Sahlins (1976), Needham (1970), Boon (1990a: Chap. 5); on Dumont, see Chap. 9; on Deleuze and desires for ascesis, see Part Three, "A Little Polemic. . . ."

42. Frye deserves more play in anthropology than he has received; his *religiosus* side put him *hors-jeu* in certain critical circles—an aspect of Frye readily relativized in less parochial worlds of comparative ritual and textual practices opened by ethnography; see Boon (1977: 3, 186, 225).

43. Stressing the "crudity" (versus *crudité*) of *cru*, could extend Lévi-Strauss's (winking) dichotomy of *cuit/cru* into poststructuralist (or surrealist) antipropriety.

44. For sources on relevant aspects of so-called Tantrism and on New Guinea's emphatically gendered rites, see Boon (1990: 159–70, 179–80); see "Encores and Envoi." See also Obeyesekere (1990).

45. Multatuli (1982 [1860]); *Max Havelaar* has had a profound impact on postcolonial Indonesian literature as well, including Pramoedya Ananta Toer (1990).

46. Burke (1968) addresses victimage, scapegoats, and related motives. For a complex sense of victims of violence in circumstances of political conflict, see Warren (1989, 1993), who notes pitfalls of patronizing subjects in duress—one troubling continuity of postcolonialism with the past.

47. James Scott (1985, 1990); Warren (1989; 1993).

48. When the most celebrated clone of our era (to date) was named "Dolly," the present *authour* (Twain's spelling) nearly died (for why, see Chap. 4). Said sheep, scientists explained, was named after Dolly Parton (a bad, sexist, and juvenile joke on their part). Comparatively, Parton has been graciously received in Japan. (See the newsclip included on p. 304, my final illustration.) I thank John Pemberton for ethnomusicological discussions of Parton's rendition of "Nine to Five" in the early 1980s, long before she became "Dorry" overseas; (I am still aping Nabokov—see Chap. 4).

A Little Polemic

1. Some scattered sources by and on this array and its attributes include: (1) Malinowski (1922, 1935, 1967); (2) Whorf (1964); (3) Panini: extracts in Freemantle (1974); (4) Augustine: extracts in Freemantle (1974), and Markus (1972); (5) Sapir (1949), and Boon (1998); (6) Freemantle (1974); (7) Wittgenstein (1958); on his erratic life, Monk (1990); on his philosophic contingencies, Rorty (1989) and Cavell (1990); on his Vienna, Janik and Toulmin (1973); otherwise on his Vienna, Schorske (1980); (8) Lévi-Strauss on Offenbach (Lévi-Strauss 1988); see Boon (1992b); (9) Lewis Carroll (1971, 1972); on his peculiar habits Morton Cohen (1995); (10) Saussure (1966); on his anagrams Starobinski (1971), Culler (1977); (11) Peirce (1955); (12) Jakobson (1990a, b); (13) Gates (1988, 1989); see Baker and Redmond (1989); (14) Kristeva (1980, 1982); (15) de Certeau (1984, 1986); on how he pertains to reading Mayan

PEOPLE IN THE NEWS

4|29|90   Associated Press

Japanese team says, 'Hello, Dolly'

Associated Press

PIGEON FORGE, Tenn. — Look out, Disney. Dolly has her sights set on a second Dollywood theme park — in Japan.

Dolly Parton, country music entertainer and part owner in the Pigeon Forge theme park that bears her name, announced Friday the Dollywood Co. is negotiating with Japanese developers to build a park near Tokyo.

Disney already has a theme park in Tokyo, which opened in 1983.

"It's going to be fun teaching them to say 'y'all' in Japan," said Ted Miller, vice president of development for Dollywood.

Parton

Dollywood is a regional park at the foot of the Great Smoky Mountains that capitalizes on the theme of Appalachian culture. The park, which attracts more than 1 million visitors a year, mixes country music with working

The proposed Japanese version, to be called Dollywood II, would be the same, only larger, Miller said. It would be the first of seven parks clustered together and linked by a common transportation system.

He stressed that further feasibility studies, planning and construction mean that the park is several years away from construction.

"I don't want anyone to panic, we are not selling Dollywood to the Japanese," Parton quipped as she opened the news conference.

Akio Hashimoto, president of the International Industry Development Inc. of Tokyo, the company developing the Japanese park, told reporters Parton's popularity in Japan "is just incredible."

The singer-actress is known for such hits as "Here You Come Again" and "My Tennessee Mountain Home" and for appearances in movies such as "9 to 5."

Fig. 16. A global show business extreme (see Chaps. 4, 6, 13). I call such formations "Coca-Colocalization" (a theory-slogan, trademark pending in Appalachia and beyond). Coincidental showbiz is not everything; but it is something; anthropology and sister pursuits can afford neither to become it nor to ignore it.

tourism Castañeda (1996); (16) Daniel (1996, 1989, 1984, with an exemplary reflexive note on his mother); (17) von Humboldt (1988, on *Kawisprache*) and Aarsleff (1988, 1982); (18) Nabokov (everything before *Ada* [1970] and after); (19) Bhabha (1994, 1990); personal impression; (20) Joanna Schopenhauer (see Safranski 1991).

2. A sad example of an ahistorical purge (in this case by historians) is the bogus polemic waged against Dumézil; see Eribon (1992). Such misrepresentation of Dumézil occurs when his *linguistic* work is forced back into a "vitalism" it was designed in part to contest. On how Dumézil's approach can help counter essentialized world "identities" by hyphenating alternatively, see Boon (1990a: 168–69). For exemplary work combining critical theory with careful history and philology (in this case of China and Japan), see Faure (1991, 1993).

3. On the endlessly debatable "paradox" (rather than "paradigm") of culture, see Boon (1972). Displacing reductive notions of culture is tantamount to opening it to what Deleuze (philosophically) calls desire. All the Deleuze passages about to be cited come from his *Reader* (Deleuze 1990).

4. Wilson (1972); I cite this study as an earlier recognition of Marx's motivic complexities; Eleanor Marx, by the way, translated *Madame Bovary*; that possibly made her a better *bourgeoisophobe* than her father (Karl). On Flaubert as a bourgeois bourgeoiso-

phobe, reread J. Barnes (1984); on the value of Barnes's novel in teaching, see Ray (1991), whose classroom experience in this respect parallels my own.

5. At Columbia in 1988, I chanced upon a flyer advertising a concert performance by Edward Said, but was regrettably unable to attend; some of his musical criticism appears in Said (1991).

6. For Dutch examples in Indonesia, see Beekman (1988); of particular note is the Bohemian hybridity plus linguistic virtuosity of H. Van der Tuuk; as much as Walter Spies (see Chap. 3), this odd philologist "authored" many contours of Balinese studies. Colonial history, seriously reread, reveals virtual rainbows of extra-Vagance on many sides; recognizing this fact neither ameliorates nor excuses such history; but it may preclude congratulating the present or the presumably "post" (see Boon 1990: Prelude, Chap. 2; 1982a: Chap. 5; 1977: Part 1). A few sources conveying complexities of discourse, institutionalizations, power, dialogue, idealizations, and racisms in different colonialisms are B. Cohn (1997), J. and J. Comaroff (1992), Crapanzano (1985), Dirks, Eley, and Ortner (1992), J. Fabian (1986), Mani (1987), Milner (1994), Prochaska (1990), Reid (1993; 1992), Sastrowardoyo (1990), Segal (1992), Schwartz (1994), Stocking (1993), Sullivan (1989), Thomas (1994), Trautman (1996). For representations of officially "postcolonialist" turns, see Ashcroft, Griffiths, and Tiffin (1995).

7. Trinh T. Minh–ha (1989, 1991).

8. Clifford (1988: Chap. 11); see also Clifford (1997).

9. Greenblatt (1983); more historically, see Greenblatt (1991a, 1993).

10. I am intentionally conflating two connected sources: Haraway (1989) and (1991); doubtless relevant too is Haraway's subsequent study, whose title winks (I presume) in computerese that interferes with this reader's remembering it (the publisher is Routledge, the date 1996, or so).

11. One important clearing house for related critical themes has been the journal *Cultural Anthropology*; edited successively by George Marcus, Fred Myers, and Dan Segal. Helpful collections on boundary-eroding anthropology are Fardon (1995), Gupta and Ferguson (1997), Olwig and Hastrup (1996), among many others; see also Boon (1997a, 1996, 1990a). For further critiques of critiques in cultural anthropology "proper," see Sangren (1988), D. Handelman (1994). For one history of modernist/postmodernist distinctions, see Calinescu (1987); for antidisciplinary postmodern twists, see Appiah (1991); for judicious assessment of postmodern turns, see Greenhouse (1996); on multicultural contexts for modernist/postmodernist worlds, see Hess (1995).

Chapter Seven
Against Coping Across Cultures

1. See Singer (1984); "Yankee City" refers to Newburyport Mass., scene of Lloyd Warner's (1963) famous studies of American culture, where Milton Singer often summered and researched.

2. I served as teaching intern for his "Comparison of Cultures" at the University of Chicago (in 1972, I think).

3. Van Gennep (1960); on his life and work, see Belmont (1979); on his marginal status among Durkheimians, see Lukes (1973). Sheehy (1976); Sheehy has since pur-

sued less fluffy passages of menopause (1995); invoking Mead as her mentor, she keeps crossing over between autobiography and public therapy.

4. Percy (1983); this was a rare lettristic challenge to the dominance of *Donahue*-style in U.S. media discourse.

5. "Free to be, you and me" was the lyric of an upbeat tune recorded for kids' consumption by Margo Thomas ("That Girl," whose husband Phil Donahue became) during the era being evoked.

6. See Chap. 1.; Mead's remarkable aptitude for, and agility in, shaping popular issues is evident in her study (1970a) of the "generation gap" that distinguishes "postfigurative, configurative, and prefigurative" cultures. On Mead and another wonderfully aberrant Boasian, Zora Neal Hurston, see Gordon (1990); on "contrarian" Hurston's controversiality in African-American literature, see Pierpont (1997). For a picture of Hurston from "the files of Jane Belo" (whom readers encountered in Chaps. 1 and 3), see Hurston (1990 [1935]).

7. The Weightmans' graceful handling of Lévi-Strauss's *je/nous* distinction that suddenly becomes "motivated" (in Burke's sense) occurs when they translate Lévi-Strauss (1971) in Lévi-Strauss (1981); see Boon (1982: Chap. 7; 1992a, 1995a).

8. I am alluding to Leach's review of Singer (1984), which is discussed in Singer (1989).

9. Boon (1982a: 7–8, 1990a: Postlude); see M. Mead (1970a).

10. For recent work by this talented novelist-*cum*-cultural-critic, see Mehta (1996).

11. See Boon (1982a: Chap. 1; 1977: Chaps. 1, 9).

12. Others, too, happily find her so; her novels and critiques are touted in the recent *New Yorker* (1997) devoted to virtuoso English prose from South Asian pens—most conspicuously, Salman Rushdie's.

13. V. S. Naipaul (1964, 1984) ; the late Shiva Naipaul (1984). "East Indian"—V. S. Naipaul's early, self-skewering comic essay (1984)—evokes complex ironies in his corpus. I tend to compare Naipaul's irony to E.M. Forster's, say; and I compare ironies of Salman Rushdie (1992, 1997) to those of Edward Dowes Dekker (Multatuli 1982 [1860])—also a Menippean satirist (see Chap. 6). For postcolonial writing against both Forster and Naipaul (and Rushdie), see Suleri (1992); her readings strike me as too "symptomatological" (fixated on Forster's anality, Naipaul's upper-crustiness, etc.)—a strange tendency, given the frequent invocation of Foucault in postcolonial critical circles.

14. Hose's works (1910, 1926, 1927) neatly encapsulate colonial official success stories; this does not make them transparent; *au contraire!* The illustrations alone (in Hose 1927) are worth the tome; they could keep keen readers "of photography" (e.g., Barthes 1977; Sontag 1977) very busy.

15. The history of "sports," organized athletics, and civilian styles of regimentation may be as important for *fin-de-siècle* colonialist history as for postcolonial, transnationalist times. The Olympics—"World's Fairs" of and for bodies—are one relevant area; see MacAloon (1984); E. Weber (1986).

16. Overgeneralized notions of "paternalistic order" are a weakness of much critical theory assailing "the bourgeoisie"—an "estate" no more monolithic, or less contradictory, than those positions countering "it."

17. The cited phrase rings the conclusion to Forster (1924, with thanks to Jorge Klor de Alva for once catching this drift).

18. Less marketable cross-cultural narrative is what the present book is partly about.

19. As I was preparing these notes, Charles Kurault passed away; his voice, too, will be missed by this anthropologist.

Chapter Eight
Errant Anthropology, with Apologies to Chaucer

1. On India, see W. Doniger O'Flaherty (1973, 1980, 1984, 1985); and peruse the journal *History of Religions*; see recently I. Nabokov (1997).

2. On Curtius's (1953) salience for anthropology and Balinese studies, see Boon (1977: 226; 1990a); Vance (1978).

For why "chivalry" may have been ironic from the start, see J. Huizinga: "Those who upheld the chivalric ideal were aware of its falsity, and it is for this reason that—almost from the very beginning—there was a tendency for the ideal to deny itself from time to time in irony and satire, parody and caricature. *Don Quixote* was merely the last, supreme expression of that irony . . ." (1984a [1959]: 89). Huizinga in 1959 had presumably not yet read *Lolita* (Nabokov 1970), first published in 1955, which if nothing else makes *Don Quixote* "next to last" in this respect; see Nabokov (1983); see also Davenport (1983a), and Chap. 4.

3. For example, V. Turner (1974, 1988), V. Turner and E. Turner (1978); for more anthropologies of pilgrimage, see Neville (1987), Peacock and Tyson (1989).

4. Geertz's remark is in (1983: Chap. 1); Lévi-Strauss (1971: 597; Boon 1982a: 142–43); Bynum (1991: Chap. 1). On ritual and political theater, see V. Turner (1974), Turner and Bruner (1986).

5. Geertz (1973: Chaps. 15, 12; 1980); his works on statecraft and ritual are closely linked. On *Annales*, the new historicisms, and swings toward ethnographies of the past, see Greenblatt (1988), Cavell (1984: 184–94), L. Hunt (1989); see also Boon (1977; 1982a: Chap. 5; 1990a: Chaps. 6–7).

6. Astell (1992); L. Johnson (1991).

7. Melville (1971 [1857]) is no more or less ironic (and extra-Vagant) than his other works, and not just *Mardi*.

8. Picture featured in F. Kermode (1973, vol. 1, plate 24, following p. 224). On medieval reading practices and the ethnography of "placing reading" (D. Boyarin's topos), see J. Boyarin (1993); essays by Noakes, Howe, Baker, and Fabian are particularly relevant; see also Boon (1972).

9. Frye (1957); see Chap. 6; see Manganaro (1992), Boon (1982a: 181, 297). One could compare Lyotard's (1988) distinctions among genre, style, reader, and mode to Frye's modes of mode.

10. I include diversely promising persuasions; but any *list* unwittingly excludes; see Chap. 9 and "Encores and Envoi."

11. On Tantrism—the "ism" part is a misleading Europeanism—as "internally alternative" to both Hindu and Buddhist persuasions—see Padoux (1990), Kakar (1982); O'Flaherty (1984); see Boon (1990a: 159–70); see Chap. 9.

12. On "Menippean satire," see Chap. 6; it remains paradoxical to seek to clarify Menippean turgidities.

13. Kermode (1973, vol. 1: 257), a wonderful anthology.

14. These same two examples from world ethnology are used to conclude Chap. 6 and "Encores and Envoi."

Chapter Nine
Margins and Hierarchies and Rhetorics that Subjugate

1. A note from Nietzsche's *Ecce Homo*: "I attack only causes which are victorious— and at times I wait until they are victorious. . . . I attack only causes against which I cannot expect to find allies, against which I shall stand alone—against which I shall compromise myself alone" (1959: 659).

2. Derrida (1982, etc.); see Chap. 10; Paglia (1990, 1992).

3. The admirable conference plans were announced in a flyer.

4. For a reverse view, see B. Lewis (1982); several of his subsequent works continue this theme.

5. To reference just one "othered" from this list: on "gypsies," see Fonseca (1995).

6. Many interdisciplinary historians—Brown (1988, etc.), Bynum (1991, 1995), L. Steinberg (1983), Trexler (1993, etc.), etc.—now give ritual specifics (often covered by the rubric "bodies") their due; see also Schwartz (1994).

7. For deft discussions of consciousness, see Peacock (1975); for recent ethnography of a literal "borderland," see Neville (1994).

8. One underestimated strength of Geertz's evocation of "thick description" (1973: Chap. 1) is its implication that no easy ethical way exists of *or* for ethnography. To "acknowledge" this fact one doesn't even have to read between the lines of Geertz's essay; one just has to (re)read it.

9. On this aspect of Frazer, see R. Fraser (1990); the *textual* complexity of Durkheim's evocations of set-apart effervescence are better conveyed in a new translation of *The Elementary Forms* by Karen Fields (Durkheim 1995); see Boon (1982a: 54–58).

10. On Mauss, see Chap. 6; on Douglas, Chap. 12; on Leach, see Boon (1982a: Appendix B).

11. For parallel or complementary approaches to ritual, see Manganara (1996); Rosaldo (1989); some aspects of Grimes (1990), C. Bell (1992); a thrust is that ritual practice is as complex as verbal and scriptive rhetorics (which, of course, ritual includes); see Boon (1987a).

12. Discussed in Chap. 6.

13. See, for example, Sedgwick (1996); Halperin (1997); for various overviews, see Herdt (1996); for voices from recent anthropological endeavors, see Segal (1997).

14. Boon (1982a 38, 165–68, 174). Trickier still are seriocomic representations with dire aspects addressed in Boon (1990a: 54–60); see Chap. 2. For a capsule account of Huguenot history, see F. and F. Manuel (1979).

15. Dumont's critical distinction between hierarchy and stratification gets washed out when scholars diametrically oppose any ranked sociality and "egalitarianism"; one example is Ladurie (1982), reviewed in Boon (1985b). Such cancellation of distinctions between hierarchy/stratification may stem from a critic's own uncritical "individualism" in Dumont's sense.

16. The most heated disputes were between Dumont and M. Marriott, or their followers (see sources in Boon 1982a: 276, n.3); later critics of Dumont's South Asian

studies include A. Appadurai (see Boon 1990a: 210, n.1), N. Dirks, and others; for one balanced assessment of Dumont, see Tambiah (1984).

17. The importance of Dumont (1982) cannot be overstated; the piece has provoked extensive commentary.

18. For critiques of "economism" (such as Dumont associates with individualism), see Sahlins (1976); aspects of ideological economism are summarized in C. Geertz (1984a), which revisits his *Agricultural Involution* (1963) and fills out infrastructural sides of his "Ideology as a Cultural System" (1973: Chap. 8).

19. M. Weber (1967b: 297); see Boon (1990a: Conclusions).

20. See Boon (1990a: Chaps. 5, 6, Conclusions).

21. "Renouncing renunciation" requires careful distinction from idealizing "redemption," lest one fall back into a "vitalist" thematics of substantive quest. Nietzsche is particularly tricky in this regard, because his radical sense of "renouncing renunciation" (with which I sympathize) can easily be mistaken as a call for re-vitalized redemption. Jung's popularity may stem from his converting "renouncing renunciation" to "redeeming redemption" (see Noll 1997). Nothing, I fear, is more dangerous when pursuing motives of rereading and repetition.

22. See Barkan (1986), Yates (1972, etc.), F. and F. Manuel (1979), Kott (1987), M. Abrams (1971), Foucault (1970). Neoplatonism is a key "murmur" in Western heterodoxy and/or heresy. For resonances between neoplatonist constructions and Balinese rites and institutions, see Boon (1977: 6; 1982a; 1990a).

23. On Tantric formations as neither corporate nor dogmatic, see Boon (1990a: xii–xiii, 159–70). To contrast standard approaches in the history of religions, see Boon (1987a); Eliade (1978) treats some aspects of alchemy in ways closer to what I am calling Tantric-style heterodoxies.

24. On the theoretical-*figure* of "rhizomes"—"the root book . . . , the radical system . . . that ceaselessly establishes connections between semiotic chains, organizations of power, and circumstances relative to the arts, sciences, and social struggles . . ."—see Deleuze (1993: 27–36); see Part Three, "A Little Polemic. . . ."

25. All my warnings about "racism" in this colonialist document are sincere, yet leery of designating as "racist" any and every prejudice; see Montagu (1964), West (1993), Shanklin (1995), Baker and Redmond (1989).

26. "Vituperation" is a topos of rhetoric in Burke's work (e.g., 1962, 1968); much politics coagulates along the thin membrane separating copious defamation from copious encomia. For praise of "Erasmian" sensitivities, see Boon (1990a: Chap. 3); for Erasmus, see Huizinga (1984a, 1984b), an Erasmian historian if ever there were one.

Chapter Ten
Evermore Derrida . . .

1. The sequel is Derrida (1995); for key variations in the receiving-Derrida industry—an important one, I feel—see Culler (1982), Abrams (1988), Attridge (1988), and so much more.

2. Mallarmé, particularly "Un coup de dès," is possibly for poststructuralism what Baudelaire (who, like Mallarmé, translated Poe) was for structuralism; see Boon (1972). On "Poetics" and "Poe tics" (i.e., the tics, or *idées fixes*, of Poe), see Burke (1968: 26); who else has gotten Burke's perfect pun?

3. Benveniste (1969); on Mauss, see above, Chap. 6.

4. One English translation of Baudelaire's prose-poem is by Louise Varèse (Baudelaire 1970); it is advisable to multiply such translations (in both directions).

5. Shell (1988, 1995, 1982); the structuralism in question is Lévi-Strauss (1969). Lévi-Strauss, of course, disputed Sartre; on Heidegger and Sartre, see Barthelme (1974: 164), and enjoy.

6. Burke (1968, 1957, 1962).

7. "Purloined Letter" alludes to Lacan's take on Poe's tale (and subsequent takings by Derrida, B. Johnson, etc.), which became a "central" text in structuralism-becoming-poststructuralist and post-Lacanian (if such a condition is imaginable). See Lacan (1988) or, better, the perfectly inspired taking up of all this (in the name of Poe and Borges) in Irwin (1994: 3–11, 442).

8. On Weber and Simmel, see Liebersohn (1988).

9. See Derrida (1967, 1976); to recapture this still-slippery historical moment, see Macksey and Donato (1972), revisited at the "solution" to Irwin (1994: 449).

10. Klein (1993).

11. Shell (1978, 1982); see Sawyer (1985).

12. For thoughts on Derrida's "effects" on philosophy, see Rorty (1989), who writes that reading Derrida reminds him of Proust; this reader feels differently: I am reminded of Proust, whose writing was circumstantial, when reading *Tristes tropiques* and its long aftermath in and as Lévi-Strauss's corpus. Other readers, other remindings.

13. Augustine's confessions, excerpted in Freemantle (1974) or reread in Burke (1970); see "Encores and Envoi." I espied a "resemblance" between Augustine and his fellow North African (J. D.) before the latter displaced himself thereupon or there-under (Bennington and Derrida 1993); see Chap. 2.

14. On everyday details of Nietzsche's life, see R. Hayman (1980); for an equally yet differently obsessive quotidien existence—Richard Wagner's—see C. Wagner (1978, 1980).

15. See Chaps. 4, 9.

16. Why I—nostalgically perhaps—find this implication uncalled for is sketched in Chap. 6.

17. De Man (1979); I first heard Paul de Man deliver lectures prefiguring his book at Duke University where I was teaching in 1975—a long, long time ago, history sighs.

18. To react *generally* against so-called deconstruction plays into its hand; deconstruction cannot be purged or routed, for it pertains to true nonreferentiality of any language. Still, *official* deconstruction's sometimes uppity tone seems designed to aggravate; sources that help counteract this effect are Attridge (1988), Lodge (1988), Culler (1982), Donougho (1992).

19. Again, an expansive critique of economism is Sahlins (1976); a succinct one is C. Geertz (1984a).

20. For ethnography on Buddhist alms, see Kirsch (1977), Keyes (1983), Tambiah (1984); for wonderful work on Chen (China) becoming Zen (Japan), see Faure (1991, 1993).

21. Derrida (1979, 1967, 1982, 1987, etc.); some readers find connections among these works, unless that seems constructive.

Chapter Eleven
Taking Torgovnick as She Takes Others

1. See, for example, Beekman (1988); reviewed in Boon (1990b); Stocking (1974, 1986); Aschroft et al. (1995).

2. "Baloma" is in Malinowski (1954); see also Skalník (1995); Boon (1996).

3. J. Conrad (1963); Mead (1935); Bourroughs (1963, 1964).

4. Key works by these speakers at the Whitney conference include Jonaitis (1991); Wollen (1991); A. Feldman (1991), and Preziosi (1979, 1989). On museums and resisting, reinventing, or ironizing them, see Karp and Lavine (1991); see also Clifford (1997), Kirshenblatt-Gimblett (1997); see Chap. 5.

5. Notes taken by this listener on Dr. Preziosi's lecture.

6. See Torgovnick (1994).

7. See Boon (1990a: 54–60; 8–12).

Chapter Twelve
Rerun (1980s)

1. Douglas (1966: 55): for comparisons with Leach, see Chap. 9; for comparisons with Lévi-Strauss, see Boon (1972: 56–57).

2. Douglas (1979: 63–64).

3. Douglas (1970: xv).

4. I allude to Ralph Nader (1966).

5. Douglas (1966: 168).

6. On Tönnies's distinction, see Liebersohn (1988).

7. Douglas (1978).

8. For a distinction between agonistic and "managed" knowledge and information, see Boon (1997a). For insights into the agonistic accents in Geertz's work, see Eidson (1996).

9. Weberian "ideal types" are more flexible—less empiricist—than Douglas's boxes; see Boon (1982a: 68–85; 1990a: 159ff); see Gerth and Mills's introduction in M. Weber (1946).

10. Mead (1959); Boon (1990a: Postlude); see Chaps. 1, 3.

11. Firth (1963); for thoughts on Firth's textual side, see C. Geertz (1987).

12. M. Weber (1958; 1948: Chap. 12); see also C. Campbell (1987), who complements Weber by viewing consumption as something other than "hedonist."

13. Wagenknecht (1981: 2–6); on the (extra-Vagant) contexts of intersecting ideas of Thoreau and such readers as Ghandi, see M. Green (1983). On debates about Thoreau, see S. Hyman in Thoreau (1966: 314–26). *Walden* is compared to Lévi-Strauss's *Tristes tropiques* as early as 1962; see R. Drinnon in Thoreau (1966: 420). On Thoreau and Romanticism, see P. Miller (1966).

14. Louis and Yazijian (1980); this volume appeared before the new, "improved," sweeter, transnationally-oriented Coke (whose early fizzle prompted the resurrection of "Classic Coke") complicated the picture. Journalistic coverage of these developments has since burgeoned no less than Coca-Cola's stock values.

15. Horkheimer and Adorno (1970).

16. My salute is to George Gershwin, but Ira's lyrics also deserve tooting; see Furia (1992, 1995) and Boon (n.d.); for those who believe in it, "pure" (versus commercial) jazz was/is greater still; on whether jazz can in fact be pure, see Gabbard (1996).

17. On paradoxes of belief's "foundation" being doubt, see Pouillon (1982), and Boon (1982c).

18. At this juncture readers might want to recall their own exposure to promotional coverage of Disney Land/World/etc. in California-Florida-France-Tokyo-Internet-Websites. Sources I have consulted include *Time* (July 29, 1991; "Disney's Amazing Architecture"); *Smithsonian Magazine* (July, 1992; "Eisner rivaling Renaissance Popes"); a twenty-two page insert into German magazines ("Euro Disney: Ein Traum ging in Erfüllung," 1992), with an add for Coca-Cola that "heisst das ... Resort willkommen"; articles in the *New York Times* (April 14, 1992) and *Times Literary Supplement* (September 18, 1992); articles in *Variety* (July 11–17, 1994; "Dwarfs Tell Disney: Draw" and " 'The Lion King's' Reign"); a *Newsweek* cover feature (September 5, 1994; "Disney's Dilemma: Can the Kingdom Keep its Magic?"); a section in *New Perspectives Quarterly* (Fall, 1995; "From Magic Kingdom to Media Empire"); articles and adds in *Variety* spotlighting Indonesia (July 17–23, 1995; "Seeking a Vid Boom," and "186 million people in the fourth most populated country in the world, Indonesia, says [*sic*] 'Rajawali Citra Televisi Indonesia OKAY!' "). The last item was not about Disney per se; but I forgot to mention another twenty-two page (American) magazine insert promoting Disney-MGM Studios from 1989—back when Chevrolet Luminas were driven by Goofy—which began with a "public service message" showing what in seamier surroundings would be called a synechdochic crotch-shot of (presumably) Mickey "buckling up: a sign of good character."

Chapter Thirteen
Up-date (1990s)

1. Baudrillard (1988).

2. The Chronical of Coca-Cola, last page (unnumbered).

3. On D. Selznick and M. Mitchell, see R. Haver (1980).

4. C. Anderson, "Hollywood in the Home," in Naremore and Brantlinger (1991: 99).

5. On "tolerance" as a never-pat, always-assertive activity that zealotry precludes, see Chap. 1 on R. Benedict.

6. I interject "hegemonic" ironically; on advantages and drawbacks to, along with misappropriations of, Gramsci's classic notion, see M. Denning, "The End of Mass Culture," (1991: 262); this piece is so sharp about limitations of Bourdieu and Gramsci, that it can almost be forgiven dismissing Burke (264)!

7. Coke's approach to neighboring Papua New Guinea and "beery" Melanesia, would presumably be different; on the impact of Pepsi and "Pepsico" there, see Gewertz and Errington (1996). (These matters were addressed in an *American Anthropological Association* panel organized by Rena Lederman in 1995.)

8. All quoted info-tainment happens at "The World of Coca-Cola."

9. This Japanese construal of Coke containers is reported in Fardon (1995); see Boon (1997a).

10. For a critique of Baudrillard on America as simulacra, see Watt (1991: Chap. 7).

11. On "Americans together," see Varenne (1977, 1986); see also Schneider (1980).

12. On Portman's edifices in Atlanta and in Singapore's Marina Square—*un complesso polifuncionale*—see Riani (1990).

13. Jameson follows up his critique of postmodern space in *Signatures of the Visible* (1990); see also Boon (1998).

14. For sources on missionaries and Bali, see Boon (1977); on recent dynamics of religions, conversion, and political change in Indonesia, see Kipp and Rogers (1987); for comparative studies, see Hefner (1993).

15. On naming, titles, etc. in Bali, see C. Geertz (1973: Chap. 14).

16. On "elective affinities" in Goethe, Weber, and elsewhere, see Boon (1990a: x); a place to begin again on this endless topic is S. Corngold's translation of Benjamin's essay on Goethe's *Wahlverwandshaften* in Bullock and Jennings's edition of his collected works (Benjamin 1996).

Encores and Envoi

1. Augustine in Freemantle (1974).

2. On arts of memory-place, see Yates (1966, 1971); see also Boon (1982a: Chap. 5). Much ethnography of memory has taken the form of research on ancestral commemoration; see, for example, R. Smith (1974), Feeley-Harnick (1989); Boon (1977: Chap. 4, 5), Bahloul (1996), Boyarin (1994).

3. To compare ritual and rhetorical sacrifice in Judaic and Brahmanical texts, see Herrenschmidt (1982); see Chap. 2.

4. Exemplary studies include Gallagher and Laqueur (1987), Martin (1992); the topic has indeed taken off.

5. Cavell (1981a, 1984, etc.)

6. Surely the "American Renaissance," the "Harlem Renaissance," etc., were as "trans-national" and profoundly translational as those shadowy achievements for which they were named. On the first-mentioned, see Reynolds (1988), Weisbuch (1986), Rogin (1985), Irwin (1980), and Chai (1987), helpful on Melvillian multiples in comedy and irony.

7. Burke is acknowledged, unless I am mistaken, in Cavell (1984).

8. Forster gives perhaps one cheer for Wagner and three cheers for Proust (whom he read when journeying back from his 1921 revisit to India, in time to revise accordingly *A Passage to India*) in *Two Cheers for Democracy* (1951: 125, 113). There too Forster observes that "Proust is what Walt Whitman is not—sophisticated, soigné, rusé, maladif. But he too listens to a septet and reacts to it visually, he is carried off his seat into a region which has nothing to do with the concert. It is the septet of Vinteuil . . . into which *la petite phrase* has entered" (1951: 111). On Lévi-Strauss's harnessing of Proust's *petite phrase* to New World sensoria and to Wagner, see Lévi-Strauss (1971: *Finale*) and commentaries in Boon (1989, 1995a).

Forster's "What I Believe" (in Forster 1951) reads Wagner *back against* fascist readings of Wagner ; and Forster offers a luminous critique of anti-Semitism as a puerile "survival" (1951: 12–13); no one attentively rereading Forster (or Kenneth Burke) can seriously imagine that irony avoids politics.

9. Burke enlists Wallace Fowlie's insights into Mallarmé to advance this parallel; see Boon (1972: Chap. 4).

10. I am thinking of Adorno as relatively "purist," troubled by such oscillations as Benjamin's; see essays in G. Smith (1989); see also Jay (1973).

11. I copied this wonderful passage from a display case in the New York Public Library; any errors in transcription are the fault of somebody else. On the centenary of Whitman's death, see Davenport (1992).

12. Whitman, *Leaves of Grass* (1855, line 1323) in E. H. Miller (1989: 43).

13. On Frazer's *Golden Bough* and his extra-Vagant corpus, see especially R. Fraser (1990) and Ackerman (1987), reviewed in Boon (1988).

14. See the mention of Spivak in "Rehearsals."

15. On rhetoric and/as cultural systems, see Geertz (1973, 1980, 1983); see also D. Battaglia (1995).

16. Hyde (1982: Chaps. 6, 10).

17. Schools of theory, critique, and comparison take on authority, as do cultures; see Boon (1972, 1982a), drawing in part on Geertz's (1973, 1983) sense of *activities* of interpretation.

18. Erkkila (1989: 167); commenting on Whitman, she draws parallels with Eliot's "fragments shored"; see Boon (1990a: xv).

19. From a vast literature on New Guinea, see Lindenbaum (1987), Herdt (1996); for other sources see Boon (1990a: 179–80).

20. Discourses of self-identity are, of course, common to American pragmatism and pragmaticism and to everyday life of consumption therapies (per Chap. 7); see Singer (1989).

21. On recent fashions in commodified bodily alterations, see Rosenblatt (1997); on recent politics of framing excision, female circumcision, etc. as "mutilation" see Walley (1997).

22. I capitalize "Cupidities" to tilt them toward Cupid, rather than narrowly literal "cupidity."

23. C. Geertz (1973, 1983, etc.) has long argued for down-to-earth antifoundationalism that is nevertheless (or rather therefore) highly philosophical; Cavell (1984: 187) expresses a sense of "striking affinities" with Geertz.

24. "It seems to me that one reads them in and of themselves insofar as they stem from the depths of our intimate experience." Proust, cited in Matthiessen (1966: 310); my trans. Poirier calls *Walden* a "fantasia of punning" in which "the phrase does not anxiously call attention to itself" (1985: 85, 86). This too seems exemplary. On Poirier in turn, see Posnock (1992).

25. Deleuze (1993); see Part Three, "A Little Polemic. . . ."

26. Kabir is tagged thusly by O. Thomas in Thoreau (1966: 215n); Thoreau read him in Garcin de Tassy's *History of Hindu Literature* (Paris, 1839).

27. E. B. White (1983: 65); for a tremendously different sensibility regarding link puzzles, see Perec (1987), a metamuseum of and from everyday life. In the sketch called "Calculating Machine," E. B. White cites part of the quotation from Thoreau on *extra-Vagance* that opens the present book (1983: 54–55).

References

Aarsleff, Hans. 1982. *From Locke to Saussure: Essays on the Study of Language and Intellectual History*. Minneapolis: University of Minnesota Press.

———. 1988. "Introduction." W. von Humboldt (1988: vii–lxv).

Abel, T. M. 1938. "Free Designs of Limited Scope as a Personality Index." In Belo (1970: 371–83).

Abbate, Carolyn. 1988. "Erik's Dream and Tannhäuser's Journey." In A. Gross and R. Parker (1988: 129–167).

———. 1991. *Unsung Voices: Opera and Musical Narrative in the Nineteenth Century*. Princeton: Princeton University Press.

Abrams, M. H. 1971. *Natural Supernaturalism: Tradition and Revolution in Romantic Literature*. New York: W. W. Norton.

———. 1988. "The Deconstructive Angel." In D. Lodge (1988: 265–76).

Abrahams, Roger. 1986. "Ordinary and Extraordinary Experience." In V. Turner and E. Bruner (1986: 45–72).

Ackerman, Robert. 1987. *J. G. Frazer: His Life and Work*. New York: Cambridge University Press.

Adams, Henry. 1959 [1904]. *Mont-Saint-Michel and Chartres*. New York: Doubleday.

———. 1961 [1918]. *The Education of Henry Adams*. Boston: Houghton Mifflin.

Adams, Robert M. 1983. "The Dance of Language" (Review of Rueckert 1982). *Times Literary Supplement*, July 8, 1983.

Adams, Vincanne. *Tigers of the Snow and Other Virtual Sherpas: An Ethnography of Himalayan Encounters*. Princeton: Princeton University Press.

Adorno, Theodor. 1981. *In Search of Wagner*. R. Livingstone, trans. New York: Schocken Books.

Agnew, Jean-Christophe. 1994. "The Consuming Vision." In Yeazell (1994: 190–206).

Agung, Ide Anak Agung Gde. 1985. "Voorwoord" to Bakker (1985).

———. 1991. *Bali in the 19th Century*. Jakarta: Yayasan Obor Indonesia.

Ahearne, Jeremy. 1995. *Michel de Certeau: Interpretation and its Other*. Stanford: Stanford University Press.

Ahlstrom, Sydney. 1972. *A Religious History of the American People*. New Haven: Yale University Press.

Allen, Gay Wilson. 1967. *William James*. New York: Viking Press.

Allen, Robert C. 1991. *Horrible Prettiness: Burlesque and American Culture*. Chapel Hill: University of North Carolina Press.

Alpers, Svetlana. 1983. *The Art of Describing: Dutch Art in the Seventeenth Century*. Chicago: University of Chicago Press.

Appadurai, Arjun. 1995. "The Production of Locality." In R. Fardon, ed. (1995: 204–25).

Appadurai, Arjun, ed. 1986. *The Social Life of Things: Commodities in Cultural Perspective*. Cambridge: Cambridge University Press.

Appiah, Kwame Anthony. 1991. "Is the Post- in Postmodernism the Post- in Postcolonial?" *Critical Inquiry* 17(2): 336–57.

Apter, Emily, and William Pietz, ed. 1993. *Fetishism as Cultural Discourse*. Ithaca: Cornell University Press.

Asad, Talal. 1993. *Genealogies of Religion: Discipline and Reasons of Power in Christianity and Islam*. Baltimore: Johns Hopkins University Press.

Asad, Talal, ed. 1973. *Anthropology and the Colonial Encounter*. New York: Humanities Press.

Ashcroft, Bill, G. Griffiths, and H. Tiffin, eds. 1995. *The Post-colonial Studies Reader*. New York: Routledge.

Associated Press. 1990. "Japanese Team Says, 'Hello, Dolly.'" Dateline: Pigeon Forge, Tenn. (April 29, 1990).

Astell, Ann W. 1992. "Chaucer's 'Literature Group' and the Medieval Causes of Books." *ELH* 59(2): 269–89.

Atkinson, Jane, and Shelly Errington, eds. 1990. *Power and Difference: Gender in Island Southeast Asia*. Stanford: Stanford University Press.

Attali, Jacques. 1985. *Noise: The Political Economy of Music*. B. Massumi, trans. Minneapolis: University of Minnesota Press.

Attridge, Derek. 1988. *Peculiar Language: Literature as Difference from the Renaissance to James Joyce*. Ithaca: Cornell University Press.

Auerbach, Erich. 1957. *Mimesis: The Representation of Reality in Western Literature*. W. Trask, trans. New York: Doubleday.

Augustine. 1974. "From *Confessions* of Augustine." In Freemantle (1974: 88–96).

Auster, Paul, ed. 1984. *The Random House Book of Twentieth–Century French Poetry*. New York: Vintage.

Babcock, Barbara. 1978. *The Reversible World: Essays in Symbolic Inversion*. Ithaca: Cornell University Press.

———. 1986. "Not in the Absolute Singular: Re-reading Ruth Benedict." Paper distributed for Wenner-Gren Conference, "Daughters of the Desert."

Backès-Clément, C. 1970. *Lévi-Strauss*. Paris: Seghers.

———. 1988. *Opera, or, The Undoing of Women*. Betsy Wing, trans. Minneapolis: University of Minnesota Press.

Bagus, I Gusti Ngurah. 1991. "Bali in the 1950s: The Role of the Pemuda Pejuang in Balinese Political Processes." In H. Geertz, ed. (1991: 199–212).

Bahloul, Joëlle. 1996. *The Architecture of Memory: A Jewish-Muslim Household in Colonial Algeria, 1937–1962*. Cambridge: Cambridge University Press.

Baker, Houston, and Patricia Redmond, eds. 1989. *Afro-American Literary Study in the 1990s*. Chicago: University of Chicago Press.

Bakhtin, M. 1968. *Rabelais and His World*. H. Iswolsky, trans. Cambridge: M.I.T. Press.

———. 1981. *The Dialogic Imagination*. M. Holquist and C. Emerson, trans. Austin: University of Texas Press.

Bakker, Wim. 1985. *Bali Verbeeld*. Delft: Volkendundig Museum Nusantara.

Bandem, I Made, and F. deBoer. 1981. *Kaja and Kelod: Balinese Dance in Transition*. Kuala Lumpur: Oxford University Press.

Barber, Lynn. 1980. *The Heyday of Natural History, 1820–1870*. Garden City: Doubleday.

Barkan, Leonard. 1986. *The Gods Made Flesh: Metamorphosis and the Pursuit of Paganism*. New Haven: Yale University Press.

Barnes, Julian. 1984. *Flaubert's Parrot*. New York: McGraw Hill.

Barnes, R. H. 1995. "Lamakera, Solor: Ethnohistory of a Muslim Whaling Village of Eastern Indonesia." *Anthropos* 90: 497–509.

Barnum, P. T. 1886. *The Story of My Life*. Cincinnati: Forshee and McMakin.

Barrios, Richard. 1995. *A Song in the Dark: The Birth of the Musical Film*. New York: Oxford University Press.

Barth, Fredrik. 1993. *Balinese Worlds*. Chicago: University of Chicago Press.

Barthelme, Donald. 1974. *Guilty Pleasures*. New York: Delta Books.

Barthes, Roland. 1976. *Sade/Fourier/Loyala*. R. Miller, trans. New York: Farrar Straus and Giroux.

———. 1977. *Image, Music, Text*. S. Heath, trans. New York: Hill and Wang.

———. 1988. "Textual Analysis: Poe's 'Valdemar.'" In D. Lodge, ed. (1988: 172–95).

Bataille, Georges. 1985. *Visions of Excess: Selected Writings, 1927–1939*. A. Stoekl, trans. Minneapolis: University of Minnesota Press.

———. 1989. *Theory of Religion*. R. Hurley, trans. New York: Zone Books.

Bateson, Gregory. 1937. "An Old Temple and a New Myth." In Belo (1970: 111–36).

———. 1958. *Naven: A Survey of the Problems Suggested by a Composite Picture of the Culture of a New Guinea Tribe Drawn from Three Points of View*. Stanford: Stanford University Press.

———. 1972. *Steps to an Ecology of Mind*. New York: Ballantine Books.

Bateson, Gregory, and Margaret Mead. 1942. *Balinese Character: A Photographic Analysis*. New York: Academy of Sciences.

Bateson, Mary Catharine. 1984. *With a Daughter's Eye: A Memoir of Margaret Mead and Gregory Bateson*. New York: Harper.

Battaglia, Debbora, ed. 1995. *Rhetorics of Self-Making*. Berkeley: University of California Press.

Baudelaire, Charles. 1970. *Paris Spleen, 1869*. Louise Varèse, trans. New York: New Directions.

Baudrillard, Jean. 1988. *Selected Writings*. Mark Poster, ed. Stanford: Stanford University Press.

Bauman, Richard, ed. 1992. *Folklore, Cultural Performances, and Popular Entertainments*. New York: Oxford University Press.

Baxandall, Michael. 1973. *Painting and Experience in Fifteenth-Century Florence*. London: Oxford University Press.

Beaver, Harold. 1973. "Introduction and Notes." In Melville (1973).

Becker, A. L. 1989. "Aridharma: Framing an Old Javanese Tale." In A. Becker, ed. (1989: 281–317).

———. 1995. *Beyond Translation: Essays toward a Modern Philology*. Ann Arbor: University of Michigan Press.

Becker, A. L., ed. 1989. *Writing on the Tongue*. Ann Arbor: University of Michigan Press.

Becker, A. L., and A. Yengoyan, eds. 1979. *The Imagination of Reality*. Norwood, N.J.: Ablex.

Beekman, E. M., ed. 1988. *Fugitive Dreams: An Anthology of Dutch Colonial Literature*. Amherst: University of Massachusetts Press.

Beidelman, Thomas. 1987. "Circumcision." *Encyclopedia of Religion*. M. Eliade, ed. New York: Macmillan.

Being There. 1979. Lorimar Productions. Hal Ashby, dir., Peter Sellers, star. (Based on the novel by Jerzy Kosinski).

Bell, Catherine. 1992. *Ritual Theory, Ritual Practice*. New York: Oxford University Press.

Bellour, Raymond, and C. Clément, eds. 1979. *Claude Lévi-Strauss*. Paris: Gallimard.

Belmont, Nicole. 1979. *Arnold Van Gennep: The Creator of French Ethnography*. D. Coltman, trans. Chicago: University of Chicago Press.

Belo, Jane. 1935. "A Study of Customs Pertaining to Twins in Bali." In Belo 1970: 3–56.

———. 1949. *Bali: Rangda and Barong*. Monographs of the American Ethnological Society. Seattle: University of Washington Press.

———. 1953. *Bali: Temple Festival*. Seattle: University of Washington Press.

———. 1960. *Trance in Bali*. New York: Columbia University Press.

Belo, Jane, ed. 1970. *Traditional Balinese Culture*. New York: Columbia University Press.

Bendix, Regina. 1997. *In Search of Authenticity: The Formation of Folklore*. Madison: University of Wisconsin Press.

Benedek, Emily. 1996. "How Circumcision Came Full Circle." *New York Times*.

Benedict, B. 1983. *The Anthropology of World's Fairs*. London: Scholar Press.

Benedict, Ruth. 1948. *The Chrysanthemum and the Sword*. Boston: Houghton Mifflin.

———. 1961 [1934]. *Patterns of Culture*. New York: Houghton Mifflin.

Benjamin, Walter. 1969. *Illuminations*. H. Zohn., trans. New York: Schocken.

———. 1978. *Reflections*. P. Demetz, ed.; E. Jephcott, trans. New York: Harcourt Brace Jovanovich.

———. 1996. *Selected Writings. Vol. 1, 1913–1926*. M. Bullock and M. W. Jennings, eds. Cambridge: Harvard University Press.

Bennington, Geoffrey, and Jacques Derrida. 1993. *Jacques Derrida*. Chicago: University of Chicago Press.

Benson, Paul, ed. 1993. *Anthropology and Literature*. Urbana: University of Illinois Press.

Benveniste, Emile. 1969. *Le Vocabulaire des institutions européennes*. Paris: Minuit.

Berg, A. Scott. 1989. *Goldwyn: A Biography*. New York: Ballantine Books.

Bergreen, Laurence. 1990. *As Thousands Cheer: The Life of Irving Berlin*. New York: Penguin Books.

Berkey, Jonathan P. 1995. "Gender and Alterity in Near Eastern Societies. (Circumcision Circumscribed: Female Excision and Cultural Accommodation in the Medieval Near East)." Mellon Seminar, Spring, 1995. Princeton University.

Berman, R. 1988. "Literary Criticism from Empire to Dictatorship." In Hohendahl (1988: 277–358).

Bernstein, Michael André. 1990. *Bitter Carnival: Ressentiment and the Abject Hero*. Princeton: Princeton University Press.

Bertelsen, Lance. 1992. "Journalism, Carnival, and *Jubilate Agno*." *ELH* 59(2): 357–84.

Berthier, M.-T., and J.-T. Sweeney. 1976. *Bali: L'Art de la magie*. Paris: Librairie Armand Colin.

Bhabha, Homi. 1994. *The Location of Culture*. London: Routledge.

Bhabha, Homi, ed. 1990. *Nation and Narration*. London: Routledge.

Blackall, Eric A. 1978. *The Emergence of German as a Literary Language, 1700–1775*. 2nd ed. Ithaca: Cornell University Press.

———. 1983. *The Novels of the German Romantics*. Ithaca: Cornell University Press.

Blair, Ruth. 1996. "Introduction" in Melville (1996).

Bloch, Maurice. 1987. *From Blessing to Violence*. Cambridge: Cambridge University Press.

Bloch, R. Howard. 1983. *Etymologies and Genealogies: A Literary Anthropology of the French Middle Ages*. Chicago: University of Chicago Press.

———. 1986. *The Scandal of the Fabliaux*. Chicago: University of Chicago Press.

Bloom, Harold. 1973. *The Anxiety of Influence*. New York: Oxford University Press.

———. 1975. *A Map of Misreading*. New York: Oxford University Press.

Boas, Franz. 1940. *Race, Language, and Culture*. Chicago: University of Chicago Press.

———. 1963. *Introduction of the Handbook of American Indian Languages*. Washington: Georgetown University Press.

———. 1965 [1911]. *The Mind of Primitive Man*. New York: Free Press.

———. 1974. See Stocking (1974).

Boon, James A. 1972. *From Symbolism to Structuralism: Lévi-Strauss in a Literary Tradition*. New York: Harper and Row.

———. 1973. "Further Operations of 'Culture' in Anthropology: A Synthesis of and for Debate." In *The Idea of Culture in the Social Sciences*. L. Schneider and C. Bonjean, eds. New York: Cambridge University Press.

———. 1977. *The Anthropological Romance of Bali, 1597–1972: Dynamic Perspectives in Marriage and Caste, Politics and Religion*. New York: Cambridge University Press.

———. 1982a. *Other Tribes, Other Scribes: Symbolic Anthropology in the Comparative Study of Cultures, Histories, Religions, and Texts*. New York: Cambridge University Press.

———. 1982b. Review of W. Morris (1981). *Novel* 15(3): 260–62.

———. 1982c. "Introduction" in M. Izard and P. Smith (1982).

———. 1984a. "Structuralism Routinized, Structuralism Fractured." *American Ethnologist* 11(4): 807–12.

———. 1984b. "Folly, Bali and Anthropology, or Satire Across Cultures." In E. Bruner (1984).

———. 1985a. "Claude Lévi-Strauss." In Skinner (1985: 159–76).

———. 1985b. Review of Ladurie (1982). *The Journal of Modern History* 57(1).

———. 1987a. "Anthropology, Ethnology, and Religion." In *Encyclopedia of Religion*. M. Eliade, ed. New York: Macmillan.

———. 1987b. Review of Stocking (1986). *Science* 237(4821): 1516–17.

———. 1988. "Among the Golden Boughs." Review of Ackerman (1987). *New York Times*, Sunday Book Review. March 6, 1988, 16–17.

———. 1989. "Lévi-Strauss, Wagner, Romanticism: A Reading Back." In G. Stocking, ed. (1989: 124–68).

———. 1990a. *Affinities and Extremes: Crisscrossing the Bittersweet Ethnology of East Indies History, Hindu-Balinese Culture, and Indo-European Allure*. Chicago: University of Chicago Press.

Boon, James A. 1990b. Review of Beekman (1988). *Journal of Asian Studies* 49(1): 198–99.

———. 1991. Review of B. Lincoln (1989). *American Anthropologist* 93(1): 220–21.

———. 1992a. "The Reticulated Corpus of Claude Lévi-Strauss." In C. Sills and Jensen (1992, vol. 2: 21–43).

———. 1992b. Review of Lévi-Strauss (1991). *Man* 27(3): 625.

———. 1994. "'Extravagant Art' and Balinese Ritual." In D. Gerstle and A. Milner, ed. (1994: 339–56).

———. 1995a. "Panofsky and Lévi-Strauss (and Iconographers and *Mythologiques*) . . . Re-regarded." In I. Lavin (1995): 33–48.

———. 1995b. Review of Lévi-Strauss (1993). *American Anthropologist* 97(4): 814–15.

———. 1995c. Review of F. Barth (1993). *Current Anthropology* 36(5): 884–86.

———. 1996. Review of H. Vermeulen and A. Roldan, eds. (1995). *ISIS: Journal of the History of Science Society* 87(3): 524–26.

———. 1997a. Review of R. Fardon (1995). *American Anthropologist* 99(3): 20–22.

———. 1997b. "The Cross-Cultural Kiss: Edwardian and Earlier, Postmodern and Since." David Skomp Lecture. Department of Anthropology. Indiana University.

———. 1998. "Accenting Hybridity: Postcolonial Cultural Theory, a Boasian Anthropologist, and I." In John Carlos Rowe, ed. *Culture and the Problems of the Disciplines.* New York: Columbia University Press.

———.n.d. "Show Business as a Cross-cultural System (I): Circuses, Geertz, and Song." Files of the Author.

Booth, Wayne C. 1974. *A Rhetoric of Irony.* Chicago: University of Chicago Press.

Bourdieu, Pierre. 1984. *Distinction: A Social Critique of the Judgement of Taste.* Richard Nice, trans. Cambridge: Harvard University Press.

Bourroughs, Edgar Rice. 1963 [1912]. *Tarzan of the Apes.* New York: Ballantine.

———. 1964 [1931]. *Tarzan Triumphant.* New York: Ballantine.

Bowen, John R. 1991. *Sumatran Politics and Poetics: Gayo History, 1900–89.* Yale: Yale University Press.

———. 1993. *Muslims Through Discourse.* Princeton: Princeton University Press.

Bowlby, Rachel. 1985. *Just Looking: Consumer Culture in Dreiser, Gissing, and Zola.* New York: Methuen.

Boyarin, Daniel. 1990. *Intertextuality and the Reading of Midrash.* Bloomington: Indiana University Press.

———. 1992. "'This We Know to be the Carnal Israel': Circumcision and the Erotic Life of God and Israel." *Critical Inquiry* 18.

Boyarin, Jonathan. 1992. *Storm from Paradise: The Politics of Jewish Memory.* Minneapolis: University of Minnesota Press.

———. 1996. *Thinking in Jewish.* Chicago: University of Chicago Press.

Boyarin, Jonathan, ed. 1993. *The Ethnography of Reading.* Berkeley: University of California Press.

———. 1994. *Remapping Memory: The Politics of TimeSpace.* Minneapolis: University of Minnesota Press.

Boyd, Brian. 1990. *Vladimir Nabokov: The Russian Years.* Princeton: Princeton University Press.

———. 1991. *Vladimir Nabokov: The American Years*. Princeton: Princeton University Press.

Brady, Ivan, ed. 1991. *Anthropological Poetics*. Savage, Md.: Rowman and Littlefield.

———. 1993. "Tribal Fire and Scribal Ice." In P. Benson (1993: 249–78).

Breakfast at Tiffany's. 1961. Paramount. Henry Mancini, music. (Freely based on novel by Truman Capote).

Bresson, Robert. 1986. *Notes on the Cinematographer*. J. Griffin, trans. London: Quartet Books.

Brown, Donald, J. Edwards, and R. Moore. 1988. *The Penis Inserts of Southeast Asia*, Occasional Paper No. 15, Center for South and Southeast Asian Studies. Berkeley.

Brown, Gary. 1990. "Introduction" to "Richard Wagner in Bayreuth." In Nietzsche (1990: 229–52).

Brown, Peter. 1988. *The Body and Society: Men, Women and Sexual Renunciation in Early Christianity*. New York: Columbia University Press.

Bruner, Edward M. 1996. "Tourism in the Balinese Borderzone." In *Displacement, Diaspora, and Geographies of Identity*. S. Lavie and T. Swedenburg, eds. Durham: Duke University Press.

Bruner, Edward M., ed. 1984. *Text, Play and Story: The Construction and Reconstruction of Self and Society*. Prospect Heights: Waveland Press.

Burbridge, Peter, and Richard Sutton. 1979. T*he Wagner Companion*. New York: Cambridge University Press.

Burke, Kenneth. 1957 [1941]. *The Philosophy of Literary Form: Studies in Symbolic Action*. New York: Vintage Books.

———. 1962. *A Grammar of Motives* [1945] *and a Rhetoric of Motives* [1950]. Cleveland: Meridian Books.

———. 1966. *Language as Symbolic Action*. Berkeley: University of California Press.

———. 1968. "Interaction: Dramatism." *International Encyclopedia of the Social Sciences*. New York: Macmillan.

———. 1970. *Rhetoric of Religion*. Berkeley: University of California Press.

———. 1984. *Attitudes Toward History*. 3rd ed. Berkeley: University of California Press.

Burton, Robert. 1977 [1621]. *The Anatomy of Melancholy: What It Is, with All the Kinds, Causes, Symptomes, Prognostickes, and severall Cures of It*. New York: Random House.

Buzard, James. 1993. *The Beaten Track: European Tourism, Literature, and the Ways to Culture, 1800–1918*. New York: Oxford University Press.

Bynum, Carolyn. 1991. *Fragmentation and Redemption: Essays on Gender and the Human Body in Medieval Religion*. New York: Zone Books.

———. 1995. *The Resurrection of the Body in Western Christianity*. New York: Columbia University Press.

Caesar, Terry. 1992. "Traveling Through Ethnography." *Criticism* 34: 411–34.

Caffrey, Margaret M. 1989. *Stranger in this Land*. Austin: University of Texas Press.

Calinescu, Matei. 1987. *Five Faces of Modernity*. Durham: Duke University Press.

Calvino, Italo. 1986. *The Uses of Literature*. P. Creagh, trans. New York: Harcourt Brace Jovanovitch.

Campbell, Colin. 1987. *The Romantic Ethic and the Spirit of Modern Consumerism*. Oxford: Blackwell.

Campbell, Mary. 1988. *The Witness and the Other World: Exotic European Travel Writing, 400–1600*. Ithaca: Cornell University Press.

Cannel, Ward, and June Macklin. 1973. *The Human Nature Industry: How Human Nature is Manufactured, Distributed, Advertised, and Consumed in the United States and parts of Canada*. Garden City: Anchor Press.

Cantor, Norman F. 1991. *Inventing the Middle Ages*. New York: William Morrow.

Carlyle, Thomas. 1908. *Sartor Resartus* [1831]. *On Heroes and Hero Worship* [1841]. New York: Everyman's Library.

Carroll, Lewis. 1971. *Alice in Wonderland*. D. J. Gray, ed. New York: Norton Critical Editions.

———. 1972. *Aventures d'Alice au pays des merveilles*. Henri Bué, trans. New York: Dover Publications.

Casson, Lionel, ed. 1962. *Selected Satires of Lucian*. New York: Norton.

Castañeda, Quetzil E. 1996. *In the Museum of Maya Culture*. Minneapolis: University of Minnesota Press.

Caton, H., ed. *The Samoa Reader: Anthropologists Take Stock*. Lanham, Md.: University Press of America.

Cave, T. C. 1979. *The Cornucopian Text: Problems of Writing in the French Renaissance*. Oxford: Clarendon Press.

Cavell, Stanley. 1981a. *Pursuits of Happiness: The Hollywood Comedy of Remarriage*. Cambridge: Harvard University Press.

———. 1981b. *The Senses of Walden*. San Francisco: North Point Press.

———. 1984. *Themes Out of School: Effects and Causes*. Chicago: University of Chicago Press.

———. 1990. *Conditions Handsome and Unhandsome: The Constitutions of Emersonian Perfectionism*. Chicago: University of Chicago Press.

Cazeneuve, Jean. 1972. *Lucien Lévy-Bruhl*. New York: Harper and Row.

Chai, Leon. 1987. *The Romantic Foundations of the American Renaissance*. Ithaca: Cornell University Press.

Chailley, Jacques. 1972. *"The Magic Flute," Masonic Opera*. Gollancz.

Charney, Leo, and Vanessa Schwartz, eds. 1995. *Cinema and the Invention of Modern Life*. Berkeley: University of California Press.

Chase, Cynthia. 1986. *Decomposing Figures: Rhetorical Readings in the Romantic Tradition*. Baltimore: Johns Hopkins University Press.

Chaucer, Geoffrey. 1948. *Canterbury Tales: An Interlinear Translation*. Vincent F. Hopper, trans. Woodbury: Barron's.

Clifford, James. 1981. "On Ethnographic Surrealism." *Comparative Studies in Society and History* 23(4): 539–64.

———. 1982. *Person and Myth: Maurice Leenhardt in the Melanesian World*. Berkeley: University of California Press.

———. 1988 *The Predicament of Culture*. Cambridge: Harvard University Press.

———. 1997. *Routes: Travel and Translation*. Cambridge: Harvard University Press.

Clifford, James, and George Marcus, eds. 1986. *Writing Culture*. Berkeley: University of California Press.

Coca-Cola. n.d. *The Chronicle of Coca-Cola Since 1886*. Official Guidebook to "The World of Coca-Cola." Atlanta.

Cohen, Mark R., ed. 1988. *The Autobiography of a Seventeenth-Century Venetian Rabbi. Leon Modena's Life of Judah*. Princeton: Princeton University Press.

Cohen, Morton. 1995. *Lewis Carroll: A Biography*. New York: Knopf.

Cohen, Roger. 1991. "For Coke, World is Its Oyster." *New York Times*, November 21, 1991, sec. D, 17.

Cohn, Bernard S. 1997. *Colonialism and its Forms of Knowledge: The British in India*. Princeton: Princeton University Press.

Comaroff, Jean, and John Comaroff. 1991. *Of Revelation and Revolution: Christianity, Colonialism, and Consciousness in South Africa*. Chicago: University of Chicago Press.

Comaroff, John, and Jean Comaroff. 1992. *Ethnography and the Historical Imagination*. Boulder: Westview.

Conrad, Joseph. 1963 [1899]. *Heart of Darkness*. Robert Kimbrough, ed. New York: Norton Critical Editions.

Conrad, Peter. 1977. *Romantic Opera and Literary Form*. Berkeley: University of California Press.

Cotkin, George. 1990. *William James: Public Philosopher*. Baltimore: Johns Hopkins University Press.

Couliano, I. P. 1987. *Eros and Magic in the Renaissance*. Chicago: University of Chicago Press.

Covarrubias, Miguel. 1937. *Island of Bali*. New York: Knopf.

Crapanzano, Vincent. 1985. *Waiting: The Whites of South Africa*. New York: Random House.

———. 1992. *Hermes' Dilemma and Hamlet's Desire: On the Epistemology of Interpretation*. Cambridge: Harvard University Press.

Crawley, Ernest. 1927. *The Mystic Rose*. T. Besterman, ed. New York: Meridian Books.

Critchley, Simon. 1996. "Angels in Disguise: Michel Serres's Attempt to Re-Enchant the World." *Times Literary Supplement*, January 19, 1996.

Crystal, David. 1987. *The Cambridge Encyclopedia of Language*. Cambridge: Cambridge University Press.

Csordas, Thomas J. 1994. *The Sacred Self: Cultural Phenomenology of Charismatic Healing*. Berkeley: University of California Press.

———. 1997. *Language, Charisma, and Creativity: The Ritual Life of a Religious Movement*. Berkeley: University of California Press.

Culler, Jonathan. 1977. *Ferdinand de Saussure*. Ithaca: Cornell University Press.

———. 1982. *On Deconstruction: Theory and Criticism after Structuralism*. Ithaca: Cornell University Press.

Curtius, E. R. 1953. *European Literature and the Latin Middle Ages*. Princeton: Princeton University Press.

Dahlhaus, Carl. 1989. *Nineteenth-Century Music*. J. B. Robinson, trans. Berkeley: University of California Press.

DaMatta, Roberto: 1984. "On Carnival, Informality, and Magic: A Point of View from Brazil." In E. Bruner, ed. (1984: 230–46).

Daniel, E. Valentine. 1984. *Fluid Signs: Being a Person the Tamil Way*. Berkeley: University of California Press.

Daniel, E. Valentine. 1989. "The Semeiosis of Suicide in Sri Lanka." In Lee and Urban (1989: 69–100).

———. 1996. *Charred Lullabies: Chapters in an Anthropology of Violence*. Princeton: Princeton University Press.

Daniel, E. Valentine, and J. M. Peck. 1996. *Culture/Contexture: Explorations in Anthropology and Literary Studies*. Berkeley: University of California Press.

Darnell, Regna. 1990. *Edward Sapir: Linguist, Anthropologist, Humanist*. Berkeley: University of California Press.

Darnton, Robert. 1995. *The Forbidden Best Sellers of Pre-Revolutionary France*. New York: Norton.

———. 1997. "George Washington's False Teeth." *New York Review of Books* 44 (5): 34–38.

Davenport, Guy. 1981. *The Geography of the Imagination: Forty Essays*. San Francisco: North Point Press.

———. 1983a. "Foreword" to Nabokov (1983: xiii–xix).

———. 1983b. "Foreword" to Montaigne (1983).

———. 1987. *Every Force Evolves a Form: Twenty Essays*. San Francisco: North Point Press.

———. 1992. "Whitman a Century after His Death." *The Yale Review* 80(4): 1–12.

Davis, Natalie Zemon. 1988. "Fame and Secrecy: Leon Modena's *Life* as an Early Modern Autobiography." In Cohen 1988: 50–72.

———. 1990. "Rabelais Among the Censors (1940s, 1540s)." *Representations* 32: 1–32.

deBoer, Fredrik E., ed. 1993. *Bali Arts and Culture News* (31) (April 1993).

De Certeau, Michel. 1984. *The Practice of Everyday Life*. S.F. Rendall, trans. Berkeley: University of California Press.

———. 1986. *Heterologies: Discourse on the Other*. B. Massumi, trans. Minneapolis: University of Minneapolis Press.

———. 1992. *The Mystic Fable: The Sixteenth and Seventeenth Centuries*. M. Smith, trans. Chicago: University of Chicago Press.

Deleuze, Gilles. 1993. *The Deleuze Reader*. Constantin Boundas, ed. New York: Columbia University Press.

Del Mar, Norman. 1986. 3 vols. *Richard Strauss: A Critical Commentary on his Life and Work*. Ithaca: Cornell University Press.

De Man, Paul. 1971. *Blindness and Insight: Essays in the Rhetoric of Contemporary Criticism*. New York: Oxford University Press.

———. 1979. *Allegories of Reading: Figural Language in Rousseau, Nietzsche, Rilke, and Proust*. New Haven: Yale University Press.

Dening, Greg. 1980. *Islands and Beaches: Discourse on a Silent Land; Marquesas, 1774–1880*. Honolulu: University Press of Hawaii.

———. 1986. "Possessing Tahiti." *Archaeology in Oceania* 21: 103–18.

———. 1988. *History's Anthropology: The Death of William Gooch*. Washington: University Press of America.

———. 1992. *Mr. Bligh's Bad Language: Passion, Power and Theater on the Bounty*. New York: Cambridge University Press.

———. 1994. "The Theatricality of Observing and Being Observed: 'Eighteenth-century Europe' 'discovers' the ? century 'Pacific.'" In Schwartz (1994: 451–58).

————. 1996. *Performances*. Chicago: University of Chicago Press.

Denning, Michael. 1991. "The End of Mass Culture." In Naremore and Brantlinger (1991: 253–68).

Derrida, Jacques. 1967. *Writing and Difference*. Alan Bass, trans. Chicago: University of Chicago Press.

————. 1976. *Of Grammatology*. Gayatri C. Spivak, trans. Baltimore: Johns Hopkins University Press.

————. 1979. *Spurs: Nietzsche's Styles*. Barbara Harlow, trans. Chicago: University of Chicago Press.

————. 1982. *Margins of Philosophy*. Alan Bass, trans. Chicago: University of Chicago Press.

————. 1985. "Des tours de Babel." In Graham (1985: 165–248).

————. 1987. *The Postcard: From Socrates to Freud and Beyond*. Alan Bass, trans. Chicago: University of Chicago Press.

————. 1989. *Of Spirit: Heidegger and the Question*. G. Bennington and R. Bowlby, trans. Chicago: University of Chicago Press.

————. 1991. *Donner le temps*. Paris: Editions Galilée.

————. 1992. *Given Time: I. Counterfeit Money*. Peggy Kamuf, trans. Chicago: University of Chicago Press.

————. 1995. *The Gift of Death*. D. Wills, trans. Chicago: University of Chicago Press.

Derrida, Jacques, and J. Bennington. See Bennington and Derrida.

Diamond, Stanley. 1975. *In Search of the Primitive: A Critique of Civilization*. New Brunswick: Transaction Books.

Di Gaetani, John L. 1978. *Penetrating Wagner's Ring*. New York: Da Capo.

Dirks, Nicholas, Geoff Eley, and Sherry Ortner, eds. 1993. *Culture/Power/History: A Reader in Contemporary Social Theory*. Princeton: Princeton University Press.

Dirlik, Arif. 1994. "The Postcolonial Aura: Third World Criticism in the Age of Global Capitalism." *Critical Inquiry* 20(2): 328–56.

Dixon, R. B. 1907. *The Shasta*. New York: Bulletin of the American Museum of Natural History 17: 381–498.

Djelantik, A.A.M. 1986. *Balinese Paintings*. Singapore: Oxford University Press.

Donoghue, Denis. 1987. *Reading America: Essays on American Literature*. Berkeley: University of California Press.

Donougho, Martin. 1992. "The Derridean Turn." In Sills and Jensen (1992: 66–101).

Douglas, Mary. 1966. *Purity and Danger*. New York: Praeger.

————. 1970. *Natural Symbols*. New York: Random House. (2nd ed. New York: Routledge, 1996).

————. 1975. *Implicit Meanings*. London: Routledge & Kegan Paul.

————. 1978. *Cultural Bias*. London: Royal Anthropological Institute, Occasional Paper no. 35.

————. 1979. *The World of Goods* (with Baron Isherwood). Boston: Basic Books. (2nd ed. New York: Routledge, 1996).

————. 1982. "The Effects of Modernization on Religious Change." *Daedalus* 111(1): 1–19.

Douglas, Mary, and Aaron Wildavsky. 1982. *Risk and Culture: An Essay on the Selection of Technological and Environmental Dangers*. Berkeley: University of California Press.

Dreyfus, Herbert, and Paul Rabinow. 1986. "What is Maturity: Habermas and Foucault on 'What is Enlightenment.'" In Hoy (1986: 109–22).

Duby, Georges. 1983. *The Knight, the Lady, and the Priest.* B. Bray, trans. New York: Pantheon.

———. 1984. *The Three Orders: Feudal Society Imagined.* A. Goldhammer, trans. Chicago: University of Chicago Press.

Dumézil, Georges. *Mythe et épopée.* 3 vols. Paris: Gallimard.

Dumont, Louis.1977. *From Mandeville to Marx.* Chicago: University of Chicago Press.

———. 1980 [1966]. *Homo Hierarchicus: The Caste System and Its Implications.* Rev. ed. Chicago: University of Chicago Press.

———. 1982. "A Modified View of Our Origins: The Christian Beginnings of Modern Individualism." *Religion* (12): 1–27.

———. 1986. *Essays on Individualism: Modern Ideology in Anthropological Perspective.* Chicago: University of Chicago Press.

Dupee, F. W. 1983. "Introduction" in H. James (1983: vii–xiv).

Durkheim, Emile. 1995 [1912]. *The Elementary Forms of Religious Life.* Karen E. Fields, trans. New York: The Free Press.

Durkheim, Emile, and Marcel Mauss. 1963 [1903]. *Primitive Classification.* R. Needham, trans. Chicago: University of Chicago Press.

Eco, Umberto. 1979. *The Role of the Reader.* Bloomington: University of Indiana Press.

———. 1983. *The Name of the Rose.* W. Weaver, trans. New York: Harcourt Brace Jovanovich.

———. 1986. *Travels in Hyperreality.* London: Picador.

———. 1997. "Murder in Chicago," review of Anton (1996). *New York Review of Books* 44 (6): 4–7.

Edel, Leon. 1987. "Introduction: Colloquies with His Good Angel." In H. James (1987: ix–xvii).

Edinburgh Review. 1803. Commentary on *An Account of the Island of Ceylon.* Robert Percival (London: C. & R. Baldwin).

Edwards, Mark U., Jr. 1983. *Luther's Last Battles: Politics and Polemics, 1531–43.* Ithaca: Cornell University Press.

Eidson, John R. 1996. "*Homo symbolans agonisticus*: Geertz's 'agonistic' vision and its implications for historical anthropology." *Focaal* 26/27: 109–23.

Eilberg-Schwartz, Howard. 1990. *The Savage in Judaism: An Anthropology of Israelite Religion and Ancient Judaism.* Bloomington: Indiana University Press.

Eliade, Mircea. 1978. *The Forge and the Crucible.* 2nd ed. Chicago: University of Chicago Press.

Ellmann, Richard. 1990. *A Long the Riverrun: Selected Essays.* New York: Vintage.

———. 1988. *Oscar Wilde.* New York: Knopf.

Emerson, Caryl. 1997. *The First Hundred Years of Mikhail Bakhtin.* Princeton: Princeton University Press.

Encyclopedia of Islam, IV. 1957. "*Khafd*" (female excision). "*Khitan*" (circumcision). Leiden: E. J. Brill.

Engler, Balz, ed. 1992. *Writing & Culture.* Swiss Papers in English Language and Literature (*SPELL*), vol. 6. Tübingen: Narr.

Eribon, Didier. 1992. *Faut-il brûler Dumézil?* Paris: Flammarion.

———. 1993. *Michel Foucault.* Betsy Wing, trans. Cambridge: Harvard University Press.

Eribon, Didier, and C. Lévi-Strauss. See Lévi-Strauss (1991).

Erkkila, Betsy. 1989. *Whitman: The Political Poet.* New York: Oxford University Press.

Errington, Shelly. 1989. *Meaning and Power in a Southeast Asian Realm.* Princeton: Princeton University Press.

———. 1995. "Myth and Structure at Disney World" In I. Lavin (1995: 85–105).

Eyman, Scott. 1997. *The Speed of Sound: Hollywood and the Talkie Revolution, 1926–1930.* New York: Simon and Schuster.

Fabian, Johannes. 1982. *Time and the Other.* New York: Columbia University Press.

———. 1986. *Language and Colonial Power.* Cambridge: Cambridge University Press.

Fardon, Richard, ed. 1995. *Counterworks: Managing the Diversity of Knowledge.* New York: Routledge.

Faulkner, William. 1946. *The Sound and the Fury.* New York: Random House.

Faure, Bernard. 1991. *The Rhetoric of Immediacy: A Cultural Critique of Chan/Zen Buddhism.* Princeton: Princeton University Press.

———. 1993. *Chan Insights and Oversights: An Epistemological Critique of the Chan Tradition.* Princeton: Princeton University Press.

Favret-Saada, J. 1981. *Deadly Words.* Cambridge: Cambridge University Press.

Febvre, L. 1982 [1942]. *The Problem of Unbelief in the Sixteenth Century: The Religion of Rabelais.* B. Gottlieb, trans. Cambridge: Harvard University Press.

Feeley-Harnick, Gillian. 1989. "Cloth and the Creation of Ancestors." In Weiner and Schneider (1989: 73–116).

Feinstein, Howard M. 1984. *Becoming William James.* Ithaca: Cornell University Press.

Feld, Steven. 1990. *Sound and Sentiment: Birds, Weeping, Poetics, and Song in Kaluli Expression.* Philadelphia: University of Pennsylvania Press.

———. 1997. "From Schizophonia to Schismogenesis: The Discourses and Practices of World Music and World Beat." In G. Marcus and F. Myers (1997).

Feldman, Allen. 1991. *Formations of Violence.* Chicago: University of Chicago Press.

Feldman, Burton, and Robert D. Richardson. 1972. *The Rise of Modern Mythology, 1680–1860.* Bloomington: Indiana University Press.

Fernandez, James, ed. 1991. *Beyond Metaphor: The Theory of Tropes in Anthropology.* Stanford: Stanford University Press.

Feuer, Jane. 1993. *The Hollywood Musical.* 2nd ed. Bloomington: Indiana University Press.

Firth, Raymond. 1963. *We, the Tikopia.* Boston: Beacon Press.

Fischer, Michael M. J. 1989. "Museums and Festivals: Note on the Poetics and Politics of Representation Conference, Smithsonian." *Cultural Anthropology* 4: 204–21.

Fitzgerald, Penelope. 1997. *The Blue Flower.* New York: Houghton Mifflin.

Fitzgerald, William. 1994. "The Questionability of Music." *Representations* 46: 121–47.

Fjellman, Stephen. 1992. *Vinyl Leaves: Walt Disney World and America.* Boulder: Westview Press.

Flaherty, Gloria. 1978. *Opera in the Development of German Critical Thought*. Princeton: Princeton University Press.

Fonseca, Isabel. 1995. *Bury Me Standing: The Gypsies and their Journey*. New York: Knopf.

Footlight Parade. 1933. Hal B. Wallis, prod. Busby Berkeley, choreog. Warner Brothers.

Forster, E. M. 1924. *A Passage to India*. New York: Harcourt Brace and World.

———. 1951. *Two Cheers for Democracy*. New York: Harcourt Brace and World.

———. 1953. *The Hill of Devi*. Harcourt Brace Jovanovich.

Foster, Frances A. 1926. *A Stanzaic Life of Christ*. Compiled from Higden's *Polychronicon* and the *Legenda Aurea*, edited from Ms. Harley 3909. London: The Early English Text Society; Oxford University Press.

Foucault, Michel. 1970. *The Order of Things*. New York: Vintage.

———. 1972. *The Archaeology of Knowledge*. A. Sheridan, trans. New York: Harper and Row.

———. 1977. *Discipline and Punish: The Birth of the Prison*. A. Sheridan, trans. New York: Vintage.

———. 1982. *This is Not a Pipe*. J. Harkness, trans. Berkeley: University of California Press.

———. 1984. *The Foucault Reader*. Paul Rabinow, ed. New York: Pantheon.

Fraser, Robert. 1990. *The Making of The Golden Bough: The Origins and Growth of an Argument*. New York: St. Martin's Press.

Frazer, James George. 1911–15. *The Golden Bough*. 12 vols. London: Macmillan.

———. 1909. *Psyche's Task*. (Reprinted in *The Devil's Advocate*). London: Macmillan.

Freeman, Derek. 1983. *Margaret Mead and Samoa: The Making and Unmaking of an Anthropological Myth*. Cambridge: Harvard University Press. [Revised ed., *Franz Boas and the Flower of Heaven: "Coming of Age in Samoa" and the Fateful Hoaxing of Margaret Mead*, 1996].

Freeman, John. 1992. "Discourse in More's *Utopia*: Alibi/Pretext/Postscript." *ELH* 59(2): 289–311.

Freemantle, Anne. 1974. *A Primer of Linguistics*. New York: St. Martin's Press.

Freud, Sigmund. 1955 [1919]. "The 'Uncanny.'" In *The Standard Edition of the Complete Psychological Works*, vol. 17: 217–56. London: Hogarth Press.

———. 1964 [1938]. *Moses and Monotheism*. In *The Standard Edition of the Complete Psychological Works*, vol. 23: 3–137. London: Hogarth Press.

Friedrich, Paul. 1979. *Language, Context, and the Imagination*. Stanford: Stanford University Press.

———. 1986. *The Language Parallex*. Austin: University of Texas Press.

Frisch, Walter. 1990. "Music and Jugendstil." *Critical Inquiry* 17(1): 138–61.

Frye, Northrop. 1957. *Anatomy of Criticism: Four Essays*. Princeton: Princeton University Press.

Furia, Philip. 1992. *The Poets of Tin Pan Alley*. New York: Oxford University Press.

———. 1995. *Ira Gershwin: The Art of the Lyricist*. New York: Oxford University Press.

———. 1997. "Something to Sing About." *The American Scholar* 66(3): 379–94.

Gabbard, Krin. 1996. *Jammin' at the Margins: Jazz and the American Cinema*. Chicago: University of Chicago Press.

Gabler, Neil. 1988. *An Empire of their Own: How the Jews Invented Hollywood*. New York: Crown.

Gallagher, Catherine, and Thomas Laqueur. 1987. *The Making of the Modern Body: Sexuality and Society in the Nineteenth Century*. Berkeley: University of California Press.

Gardner, Erle Stanley. n.d. *Simanis dan Harta Warisan*. Herdian Suhardjono, trans. Jakarta: Saka Widya.

Gates, Henry Louis, Jr. 1988. *The Signifying Monkey: A Theory of Afro-American Literary Criticism*. New York: Oxford University Press.

————. 1989. "Canon-Formation, Literary History, and the Afro-American Tradition: From the Seen to the Told." In H. Baker and P. Redmond, ed. (1989: 14–39).

Gay, Peter. 1988. *Freud: A Life for Our Time*. New York: W.W. Norton.

Geertz, Clifford. 1960. *The Religion of Java*. New York: The Free Press.

————. 1963. *Agricultural Involution*. Berkeley: University of California Press.

————. 1968. *Islam Observed*. New Haven: Yale University Press.

————. 1973. *The Interpretation of Cultures*. New York: Basic Books.

————. 1980. *Negara: The Theater State in Nineteenth-Century Bali*. Princeton: Princeton University Press.

————. 1983. *Local Knowledge*. New York: Basic Books.

————. 1984a. "Culture and Social Change: The Indonesian Case." *Man* 19: 511–32.

————. 1984b. "Anti Anti-Relativism." *American Anthropologist* 86(2): 263–78.

————. 1985. "The Uses of Diversity." The Tanner Lectures on Human Values. Ann Arbor: University of Michigan.

————. 1987 *Works and Lives: The Anthropologist as Author*. Stanford: Stanford University Press.

————. 1995. *After the Fact: Two Countries, Four Decades, One Anthropologist*. Cambridge: Harvard University Press.

Geertz, Hildred. 1963. "Indonesian Cultures and Communities." In *Indonesia*. R. T. McVey, ed. New Haven: HRAF Press.

————. 1995. *Images of Power: Balinese Paintings Made for Gregory Bateson and Margaret Mead*. Honolulu: University of Hawaii Press.

Geertz, Hildred, ed. 1991. *State and Society in Bali*. Leiden: KITLV Press.

Geller, Jay. 1992. "The Unmanning of the Wandering Jew." *American Imago*, 49(2): 227–62.

————. 1993. "A Paleontological View of Freud's Study of Religion: Unearthing the *Leitfossil* Circumcision." *Modern Judaism* 13: 49–70.

————. 1997. "Idols, Fetishes and Foreskins: The Other of Religion." *Religion* 27: 117–22.

George, Kenneth M. 1996. *Showing Signs of Violence: The Cultural Politics of a Twentieth-Century Headhunting Ritual*. Berkeley: University of California Press.

Gerstle, Andrew, and Anthony Milner, eds. 1994. *Recovering the Orient: Artists, Scholars, Appropriations*. Reading: Harwood Academic Publishers.

Gerth, H. H., and C. Wright Mills. 1946. "Introduction: The Man and His Work." In M. Weber (1946: 1–74).

Gewertz, Deborah, and Frederick Errington. 1996. "On PepsiCo and Piety in a Papua New Guinea 'modernity.'" *American Ethnologist* 23(3): 476–93.

Gilman, Sander. 1985. *Difference and Pathology: Stereotypes of Sexuality, Race, and Madness*. Ithaca: Cornell University Press.

———. 1986. *Jewish Self-Hatred: Anti-Semitism and the Hidden Language of the Jews*. Baltimore: Johns Hopkins University Press.

———. 1989a. *Sexuality: An Illustrated History*. New York: John Wiley and Sons.

———. 1989b. "Introduction" to Nietzsche (1989).

———. 1991. "The Indelibility of Circumcision." *Koroth* 9(11–12): 806–17.

———. 1995. *Freud, Race, and Gender*. Princeton: Princeton University Press.

Gilman, Sander, ed.1987. *Conversations with Nietzsche: A Life in the Words of His Contemporaries*. David Parent, trans. New York: Oxford University Press.

Girouard, Mark. 1978. *Life in the English Country House*. New York: Penguin.

Glenn, Jules. 1966. "Opposite Sex twins." *Journal of the American Psychoanalytical Association* 16: 736–59.

Goffman, Erving. 1959. *The Presentation of Self in Everyday Life*. Garden City: Doubleday.

———. 1974. *Frame Analysis*. New York: Harper.

Goldberg, Jonathan. 1983. *James I and the Politics of Literature*. Stanford: Stanford University Press.

———. 1990. *Writing Matter: From the Hands of the English Renaissance*. Stanford: Stanford University Press.

———. 1992. *Sodometries: Renaissance Texts, Modern Sexualities*. Stanford: Stanford University Press.

Goldstein, Judith. 1987. "Lifestyles of the Rich and Tyrannical." *The American Scholar* 56(2): 235–47.

———. 1997. "The Female Aesthetic Community." In G. Marcus and F. Myers (1997).

Goodkin, Richard E. 1991. *Around Proust*. Princeton: Princeton University Press.

Goodwin, Andrew. 1992. *Dancing in the Distraction Factory: Music, Television, and Popular Culture*. Minneapolis: University of Minnesota Press.

Gordon, Deborah. 1990. "The Politics of Ethnographic Authority: Race and Writing in the Ethnography of Margaret Mead and Zora Neale Hurston." In Manganaro (1990: 183–214).

Gossman, Lionel. 1984. "Basle and Bachofen." *Journal of the Warburg and Courtauld Institute* 47: 136–85.

———. 1989. "Antimodernism in Nineteenth-Century Basle: Franz Overbeck's Antitheology and J. J. Bachofen's Antiphilology." *Interpretation* 16(3): 359–89.

Graham, Joseph F., ed. 1985. *Difference in Translation*. Ithaca: Cornell University Press.

Green, Martin. 1972. *Cities of Light, Sons of the Morning*. Boston: Little, Brown.

———. 1983. *Tolstoy and Gandhi: Men of Peace*. New York: Basic Books.

———. 1988. *The Van Richtofen Sisters*. University of New Mexico Press.

Green, Stanley. 1981. *Encyclopaedia of the Musical Film*. New York: Oxford University Press.

Greenblatt, Stephen. 1983. "China: Visiting Rites." *Raritan* (spring 1983).

———. 1991a. "Resonance and Wonder." In I. Karp and Lavine, eds. (1991: 42–56).

———. 1991b. *Marvelous Possessions: The Wonders of the New World*. Chicago: University of Chicago Press.

Greenblatt, Stephen, ed. 1988. *Representing the English Renaissance*. Berkeley: University of California Press.

———. 1993. *New World Encounters*. Berkeley: University of California Press.

Greenhouse, Carol J. 1996. *A Moment's Notice: Time Politics Across Cultures*. Ithaca: Cornell University Press.

Greenwood, Davydd. 1989. "Culture by the Pound: An Anthropological Perspective on Tourism as Cultural Commoditization." In V. Smith (1989).

Grimes, Ronald L. 1990. *Ritual Criticism*. Columbia: University of South Carolina Press.

Gross, Arthur, and Roger Parker. 1988. *Reading Opera*. Princeton: Princeton University Press.

Grusin, Richard. 1993. "Thoreau, Extravagance, and the Economy of Nature." *American Literary History* 5(1): 31–50.

Gupta, Akhil, and James Ferguson, eds. 1997. *Anthropological Locations: Boundaries and Grounds of a Field Science*. Berkeley: University of California Press.

Halperin, David M. 1997. *Saint Foucault: Towards a Gay Hagiography*. New York: Oxford University Press.

Hamburger, Michael. 1972. *Hofmannsthal: Three Essays*. Princeton: Princeton University Press.

Hammoudi, Abdellah. 1988. *La Victime et ses masques*. Paris: Seuil.

———. 1993. *The Victim and Its Masks: An Essay on Sacrifice and Masquerade in the Maghreb*. P. Wissing, trans. Chicago: University of Chicago Press.

Handelman, Don. 1994. "Critiques of Anthropology: Literary Turns, Slippery Bends." *Poetics Today* 15(3): 341–81.

Handelman, Susan. 1983. "Jacques Derrida and the Heretic Hermeneutic." In Krupnick (1983: 98–129).

Handler, Richard. 1986. "Vigorous Male and Aspiring Female: Poetry, Personality, and Culture in Edward Sapir and Ruth Benedict." In Stocking (1986: 127–55).

———. 1990. "Ruth Benedict and the Modernist sensibility." In Manganaro (1990: 163–180).

Handler, Richard, and Daniel Segal. 1990. *Jane Austin and the Fiction of Culture*. Tucson: University of Arizona Press.

Haraway, Donna. 1989. *Primate Visions: Gender, Race and Nature in the World of Modern Science*. New York: Routledge.

———. 1991. "A Cyborg Manifesto." In *Simians, Cyborgs, and Women: The Reinvention of Nature*. New York Routledge (149–81).

Harbison, Robert. 1977. *Eccentric Spaces*. London: Andrew Deutsch.

Hardwick, Elizabeth. 1984. *Bartleby in Manhattan and Other Essays*. New York: Vintage.

Harvey, James. 1987. *Romantic Comedy*. New York: Knopf.

Harwood, Britton J. 1981. "The 'Nether Ye' and its Antitheses: A Structuralist Reading of 'The Miller's Tale'." *Annuale Mediaevale* (21): 5–30.

Hastrup, Kirsten. 1990. "The Ethnographic Present: A Reinvention." *Cultural Anthropology* 5(1): 45–61.

Hastrup and Olwig. See Olwig.

Haver, Ronald. 1980. *David O. Selznick's Hollywood*. New York: Bonanza Books.

Hayman, Ronald. 1980. *Nietzsche: A Critical Life*. New York: Penguin Books.

Heald, Suzette. 1982. "The Making of Men: The Relevance of Vernacular Psychology to the Interpretation of a Gisu Ritual." *Africa* 52(1): 15–35.

Hefner, Robert. 1987. *Hindu Javanese*. Princeton: Princeton University Press.

Hefner, Robert, ed. 1993. *Conversion to Christianity: Historical and Anthropological Perspectives on a Great Transformation*. Berkeley: University of California Press.

Heidegger, Martin. 1962. *Being and Time*. J. Macquarrie and E. Robinson, trans. New York: Harper and Row.

Heller, Erich. 1970. "Autobiography and Literature." In Mann (1970: 101–27).

Hello Dolly! 1969. Gene Kelly, dir. Jerry Herman, music and lyrics (based on his Broadway musical). Twentieth-Century Fox.

Herdt, Gilbert, ed. 1996. *Third Sex, Third Gender: Beyond Sexual Dimorphism in Culture and History*. New York: Zone Books.

Herrenschmidt, O. 1982. "Sacrifice, Symbolic or Effective?" In M. Izard and P. Smith (1982).

Herzfeld, Michael. 1987. *Anthropology Through the Looking Glass: Critical Ethnography in the Margins of Europe*. Cambridge: Cambridge University Press.

———. 1997. *Cultural Intimacy: Social Poetics in the Nation State*. New York: Routledge.

Hess, David J. 1995. *Science and Technology in a Multicultural World: The Cultural Politics of Facts and Artifacts*. New York: Columbia University Press.

Hewison, Robert. 1978. *Ruskin and Venice*. London: Thames and Hudson.

Highet, Gilbert. 1962. *The Anatomy of Satire*. Princeton: Princeton University Press.

Hinsley, Curtis M. 1991. "The World as Marketplace: Commodification of the Exotic at the World's Columbian Exposition, Chicago, 1893." In Karp and Lavine, eds. (1991: 344–65).

Hitchcock, Michael, V. King, and M. Parnwell, eds. 1993. *Tourism in South-East Asia*. New York: Routledge.

Hobart, Mark. 1991. "Criticizing Genres: Bakhtin and Bali," in P. Baxter and R. Fardon, eds. *Voice, Genre, Text: Anthropological Essays in Africa and Beyond*. Bulletin of the John Rylands University Library of Manchester 73(3): 195–216.

———. 1995. "As I Lay Laughing: Encountering Global Knowledge in Bali." In R. Fardon (1995: 49–72).

Hobsbawm, Eric, and T. Ranger, eds. 1985. *The Invention of Tradition*. Cambridge: Cambridge University Press.

Hocart, A. M. 1954. *Social Origins*. London: Watts.

———. 1970. *Kings and Councillors*. Chicago: University of Chicago Press.

Hodgen, Margaret. 1964. *Early Anthropology in the Sixteenth and Seventeenth Centuries*. Philadelphia: University of Pennsylvania Press.

Hoffman, Lawrence A. 1996. *Covenant of Blood: Circumcision and Gender in Rabbinic Judaism*. Chicago: University of Chicago Press.

Hohendahl, Peter Uwe. 1982. *The Institution of Criticism*. Ithaca: Cornell University Press.

———. 1989. *Building a National Literature: The Case of Germany, 1830–1870*. R. B. Franciscono, trans. Ithaca: Cornell University Press.

Hohendahl, Peter Uwe, ed. 1988. *A History of German Literary Criticism*. Lincoln: University of Nebraska Press.

Holbrook, Jackson. 1977. "Introduction" in R. Burton (1977).

Hollier, Denis, ed. 1990. *Marcel Mauss*. L'Arc: Librairie Duponchelle.

Holmberg, David. 1989. *Order in Paradox: Myth, Ritual, and Exchange among Nepal's Tamang*. Ithaca: Cornell University Press.

Holquist, Michael. 1990. *Dialogism: Bakhtin and his World*. New York: Routledge.

Holt, Claire. 1936. "'Bandit Island': A Short Exploration Trip to Nusa Penida." In Belo 1970: 67–84.

Horkheimer, Max, and T. Adorno. 1972. *Dialectic of Enlightenment*. J. Cumming, trans. New York: Seabury.

Horowitz, Elliott. 1989. "The Eve of the Circumcision: A Chapter in the History of Jewish Nightlife." *Journal of Social History* 23(1): 45–69.

Hose, Charles. 1910. *Pagan Tribes of Borneo: A Description of Their Physical, Moral, and Intellectual Condition, with Some Discussion of the Ethnic Relations*. London: Macmillan.

———. 1926. *Natural Man: A Record from Borneo*. London: Macmillan and Co.

———. 1927. *Fifty Years of Romance and Research, or, A Jungle Wallah at Large*. London: Hutchinson and Co.

Howard, Jane. 1984. *Margaret Mead: A Life*. New York: Simon and Schuster.

Howat, Roy. 1994. "Debussy and the Orient." In Gerstle and Milner (1994: 45–82).

Hoy, David Couzens, ed. 1986. *Foucault: A Critical Reader*. Oxford: Basil Blackwell.

Hubert, Robert, and Marcel Mauss. 1964. *Sacrifice: Its Nature and Function*. W. Hall, trans. Chicago: University of Chicago Press.

Huizinga, Johan. 1984a [1959]. *Men and Ideas: History, the Middle Ages, the Renaissance*. J. S. Holmes and H. van Marle, trans. Princeton: Princeton University Press.

———. 1984b. *Erasmus and the Age of Reformation*. Princeton: Princeton University Press.

Humboldt, Wilhelm von. 1988 [1836–40]. *On Language*. P. Heath, trans. Cambridge: Cambridge University Press.

Hunt, John Dixon, and F. M. Holland, eds. 1982. *The Ruskin Polygon: Essays on the Imagination of John Ruskin*. Manchester: Manchester University Press.

Hunt, Lynn, ed. 1989. *The New Cultural History*. Berkeley: University of California Press.

Hurston, Zora Neale. 1990 [1935]. *Mules and Men*. F. Boas, pref.; A. Rampersad, fore.; M. Covarrubias, illus.; H. Gates, series ed. New York: Harper and Row.

Hutcheson, Linda. 1994. *Irony's Edge: The Theory and Politics of Irony*. New York: Routledge.

Hyde, Lewis. 1982. *The Gift: Imagination and the Erotic Life of Property*. New York: Vintage.

Hyman, Stanley Edgar. 1966. "Henry Thoreau in Our Time." In Thoreau (1966: 314–27).

Hymes, Dell, ed. 1964. *Language in Culture and Society*. New York: Harper and Row.

———. 1973. *Reinventing Anthropology*. New York: Random House.

Irwin, John T. 1980. *American Hieroglyphics: The Symbol of the Egyptian Hieroglyphics in the American Renaissance*. New Haven: Yale University Press.

Irwin, John T. 1994. *The Mystery to a Solution: Poe, Borges, and the Analytic Detective Story*. Baltimore: Johns Hopkins University Press.

Izard, Michel, and Pierre Smith, eds. 1982. *Between Belief and Transgression*. J. Leavitt, trans. Chicago: University of Chicago Press.

Jacknis, Ira. 1988. "Margaret Mead and Gregory Bateson in Bali: Their Use of Photography and Film." *Cultural Anthropology* 3(2): 160–78.

Jackson, Holbrook. "Introduction to Burton (1977: v–vii).

Jackson, Michael, ed. 1996. *Things As They Are: New Directions in Phenomenological Anthropology*. Bloomington: Indiana University Press.

Jakobson, Roman. 1990a. *Language in Literature*. K. Pomorska and S. Rudy, eds. Cambridge: Harvard University Press.

———. 1990b. *On Language*. L. Waugh and M. Monville-Burston, eds. Cambridge: Harvard University Press.

James, Henry. 1976 [1888]. *The Aspern Papers and Other Stories*. New York: Penguin.

———. 1983 [1913–17]. *Autobiography (A Small Boy and Others; Notes of a Son and Brother; The Middle years)*. F. W. Dupee, ed. Princeton: Princeton University Press.

———. 1987. *The Complete Notebooks of Henry James*. L. Edel and L. Powers, eds. New York: Oxford University Press.

———. 1988. [1892 . . .] *Henry James on Italy* [Selections from *Italian Hours*]. New York: Weidenfeld and Nicolson.

James, William. 1958 [1901–02]. *The Varieties of Religious Experience*. New York: New American Library.

Jameson, Frederick. 1990. *Signatures of the Visible*. New York: Routledge.

Janik, Allan, and Stephen Toulmin. 1973. *Wittgenstein's Vienna*. 1973. New York: Simon and Schuster.

Jankowiak, William, ed. 1995. *Romantic Passion: A Universal Experience?* New York: Columbia University Press.

Jasen, David A., and Trebor Jay Tichenor. 1989. *Rags and Ragtime: A Musical History*. New York: Dover Books.

Jay, Martin. 1973. *The Dialectical Imagination: A History of the Frankfurt School and the Institute of Social Research, 1923–1950*. Boston: Little Brown.

———. 1986. "The Empire of the Gaze: Foucault and the Denigration of Vision in Twentieth Century French Thought." In Hoy (1986: 175–204).

Jenkins, David. 1994. "Object Lessons and Ethnographic Displays." In *Comparative Studies in Society and History* 36(2): 242–55.

Johnson, Galen A., ed. 1993. *The Merleau-Ponty Aesthetics Reader: Philosophy and Painting*. M. Smith, trans. ed. Evanston: Northwestern University Press.

Johnson, Lynn Staley. 1991. "The Trope of the Scribe and the Question of Literary Authority in the Works of Julian of Norwich and Margery Kempe." *Speculum* (66): 820–40.

Johnston, John. 1992. "Lyotard: From Libidinal Aesthetics to Language Games." In Sills and Jensen (1992: 125–54).

Jonaitis, Aldona, ed. 1991. *Chiefly Feasts: The Enduring Kwakiutl Potlatch*. Seattle: University of Washington Press.

Jones, Ernest. 1953–57. *The Life and Work of Sigmund Freud*. New York: Basic Books.

Joyce, James. 1985. "Museum Tour" (from *Finnegans Wake*). In Macdonald (1985: 440–42).

Jung, Carl. 1971. *The Portable Jung*. J. Campbell, ed., R. Hull, trans. New York: Penguin Books.

———. 1973. *Synchronicity*. R.F.C. Hull, trans. Princeton: Princeton University Press.

Kakar, Sudhir. 1982. *Shamans, Mystics, and Doctors: A Psychological Inquiry into India and its Healing Traditions*. Boston: Beacon Press.

Kallmann, F.J.A. 1952. "A Comparative Twin Study on the Genetic Aspects of Male Homosexuals (85 Homosexual Male Twin Index Cases)." *Journal of Nervous and Mental Disease* 95: 283–98.

Karp, Ivan, and Steven D. Lavine. 1991. *Exhibiting Cultures: The Poetics and Politics of Museum Display*. Washington: Smithsonian Institution Press.

Karp, Ivan, C. M. Kreamer, and S. D. Lavine. 1992. *Museums and Communities: The Politics of Public Culture*. Washington: Smithsonian Institution Press.

Keane, Webb. 1997. *Signs of Recognition: Powers and Hazards of Representation in an Indonesian Society*. Berkeley: University of California Press.

Keeler, Ward. 1987. *Javanese Shadow Plays, Javanese Selves*. Princeton: Princeton University Press.

Keil, Charles, and Steven Feld, eds. 1994. *Music Grooves*. Chicago: University of Chicago Press.

Kelleher, Brian, and Diana Merrill. 1987. *The Perry Mason TV Show Book*. New York: St. Martin's Press.

Kelly, John D., and Martha Kaplan. 1990. "History, Structure, and Ritual." *Annual Reviews in Anthropology* 19: 119–50.

Kenner, Hugh. 1974. *The Stoic Comedians: Flaubert, Joyce, and Beckett*. Berkeley: University of California Press.

———. 1971. *The Pound Era*. Berkeley: University of California Press.

Kermode, Frank. 1967. *The Sense of an Ending: Studies in the Theory of Fiction*. Oxford: Oxford University Press.

Kermode, Frank, John Hollander, *et al.* 1973. *The Oxford Anthology of English Literature*. Vol. I. Oxford: Oxford University Press.

Kessler, E. J. 1996. "Activists Declare War on Circumcision." *Forward*, October 11, 1996.

Keyes, Charles F. 1983. "Merit-Transference in the Kammic Theory of Popular Theravada Buddhism." In *Karma: An Anthropological Inquiry*. C. F. Keyes and E. V. Daniel, eds. Berkeley: University of California Press.

Kierkegaard, Søren. 1980 [1844]. *The Concept of Anxiety*. R. Thomte and A. Anderson, eds. and trans. Princeton: Princeton University Press.

———. 1983 [1843]. *Fear and Trembling. Repetition*. H. V. and E. H. Hong, eds. and trans. Princeton: Princeton University Press.

———. 1987 [1843]. *Either/Or*. Part I. H. V. and E. H. Hong, eds. and trans. Princeton: Princeton University Press.

———. 1989. *The Concept of Irony*. H. V. and E. H. Hong, trans. Princeton: Princeton University Press.

Kipp, Rita Smith, and Susan Rodgers, eds. 1987. *Indonesian Religions in Transition*. Tucson: University of Arizona Press.

Kirsch, A. Thomas. 1977. "Complexity in the Thai Religious System." *Journal of Asian Studies* 36(2): 241–66.

Kirshenblatt-Gimblett, Barbara. 1991. "Objects of Ethnography." In Karp and Lavine, eds. (1991: 386–443).

———. 1997. *Destination Culture*. Berkeley: University of California Press.

Klein, Richard. 1993. *Cigarettes are Sublime*. Durham: Duke University Press.

Kostenbaum, Wayne. 1993. *The Queen's Throat*. New York: Vintage Books.

Kott, Jan. 1987. *The Bottom Translation: Marlowe and Shakespeare and the Carnival Tradition*. D. Miedzyrzecka and L. Vallee, trans. Evanston: Northwestern University Press.

Kratz, Corinne A. n.d. "Affecting Performance: Meaning, Movement and Experience in Okiek Women's Initiation." (Appendix A: Initiation and Circumcision). Files of the Author.

Kreuger, Miles. 1977. *Show Boat: The Story of a Classic American Musical*. New York: Da Capo.

Kristeva, Julia. 1980. *Desire in Language*. L. S. Roudiez, ed. New York: Columbia University Press.

———. 1982. *Powers of Horror: An Essay on Abjection*. L. S. Roudiez, trans. New York: Columbia University Press.

———. 1989. *Language: the Unknown*. A. Menke, trans. New York: Columbia University Press.

Krupat, Arnold. 1979. *Woodsmen, or, Thoreau and the Indians*. New York: The Letter Press.

———. 1990. "Irony in Anthropology: The Work of Franz Boas." In Manganaro (1990: 133–45).

Krupnick, Mark, ed. 1983. *Displacement: Derrida and After*. Bloomington: Indiana University Press.

Kuipers, Joel C. 1990. *Power in Performance: The Creation of Textual Authority in Weyewa Ritual Speech*. Philadelphia: University of Pennsylvania Press.

Kunhardt, P. B. 1995. *P. T. Barnum: America's Greatest Showman*. New York: Knopf.

Lacan, Jacques. 1988. "The Insistence of the Letter in the Unconscious." In D. Lodge, ed. (1988: 80–106).

LaCapra, Dominick, 1978. *A Preface to Sartre*. Ithaca: Cornell University Press.

———. 1985. *History and Criticism*. Ithaca: Cornell University Press.

———. 1987. *History, Politics, and the Novel*. Ithaca: Cornell University Press.

———. 1989. *Soundings in Critical Theory*. Ithaca: Cornell University Press.

LaCapra, Dominick, and Steven L. Kaplan, eds. 1982. *Modern European Intellectual History: Reappraisals and New Perspectives*. Ithaca: Cornell University Press.

Ladurie, Le Roy. 1982. *Love, Death, and Money in the Pays d'Oc*. Alan Sheridan, trans. New York: George Braziller.

Lamont, Michelle. 1992. *Money, Morals, and Manners: The Culture of the French and American Upper-middle Class*. Chicago: University of Chicago Press.

Langer, Susanne. 1953. *Feeling and Form: A Theory of Art Developed from Philosophy in a New Key*. New York: Scribner's.

Lanza, Joseph. 1994. *Elevator Music: A Surreal History of Muzak, Easy-Listening, and Other Moodsong*. New York: St. Martin's Press.

Large, David C., and William Weber, eds. 1984. *Wagnerism in European Culture and Politics*. Ithaca: Cornell University Press.

Lavin, Irving, ed. 1995. *Meaning in the Visual Arts: Views from the Outside*. Princeton: Princeton University Press.

Layard, John. 1942. *Stone Men of Malekula (Vao)*. London: Chatto and Windus.

———. 1944. *The Lady of the Hare*. London: Faber and Faber.

Leach, Edmund. 1968. *A Runaway World?* New York: Oxford University Press.

———. 1976. *Culture and Communication*. Cambridge: Cambridge University Press.

———. 1984. "Intolerance." *London Review of Books*, May 16, 1984: 22–23.

Leach, William. 1993. *Land of Desire: Merchants, Power, and the Rise of a New American Culture*. New York: Pantheon.

Lederman, Rena. 1986. *What Gifts Engender: Social Relations and Politics in Mendi, Highland Papua New Guinea*. Cambridge: Cambridge University Press.

Lee, Benjamin. 1989. "Semiotic Origins of the Mind-Body Dualism." In Lee and Urban (1989: 193–228).

Lee, Benjamin, and Greg Urban. 1989. *Semiotics, Self, and Society*. New York: Mouton de Gruyter.

Leed, Eric J. 1991. *The Mind of the Traveler: From Gilgamesh to Global Tourism*. New York: Basic Books.

Lentricchia, Frank. 1983. *Criticism and Social Change*. Chicago: University of Chicago Press.

Levin, Harry. 1987. *Playboys and Killjoys: An Essay on the Theory and Practice of Comedy*. New York: Oxford University Press.

Lévi-Strauss, Claude. 1950. "Introduction à l'oeuvre de M. Mauss." In Mauss (1983).

———. 1955. *Tristes tropiques*. Paris: Plon.

———. 1963. *Structural Anthropology*. C. Jacobson and B. Grundfest Schoepf, trans. New York: Doubleday.

———. 1964–71. *Mythologiques*. 4 vols. Paris: Plon.

———. 1966. *Du Miel aux cendres*. Paris: Plon.

———. 1969 [1948]. *The Elementary Structures of Kinship*. R. Needham, ed. and trans. Boston: Beacon Press.

———. 1971. *L'Homme nu*. Paris: Plon.

———. 1974 [1955]. *Tristes tropiques*. J. and D. Weightman, trans. New York: Atheneum.

———. 1978. *The Origin of Table Manners*. J. and D. Weightman, trans. Chicago: University of Chicago Press.

———. 1981. *The Naked Man*. J. and D. Weightman, trans. Chicago: University of Chicago Press.

———. 1983a. *Le Regard éloigné*. Paris: Plon.

———. 1983b. *The Way of the Masks*. 2nd ed. S. Modelski, trans. London: Jonathan Cape.

———. 1988. *De Près et de loin*. (With D. Eribon). Paris: Odile Jacob.

———. 1991. *Conversations with Claude Lévi-Strauss*. D. Eribon, ed. Paula Wissing, trans. Chicago: University of Chicago Press.

———. 1993. *Regarder Ecouter Lire*. Paris: Plon.

Lévy-Bruhl, Lucien. 1985 [1926]. *How Natives Think*. L. Clare, trans. Princeton: Princeton University Press.

Lewis, Bernard. 1982. *The Muslim Discovery of Europe*. New York: Norton.

Lewis, Joseph. 1967. *In the Name of Humanity*. New York: Freethought Press.

Lewontin, Richard. 1997. "Billions and Billions of Demons." *New York Review of Books*. 44 (1): 28–32.

Liebersohn, Harry. 1988. *Fate and Utopia in German Sociology, 1870–1923*. Cambridge: M.I.T. Press.

———. 1996. "Recent Works on Travel Writing." *The Journal of Modern History* 68: 617–28.

Lincoln, Bruce. 1989. *Discourse and the Constructions of Society: Comparative Studies of Myth, Ritual, and Classification*. New York: Oxford University Press.

Lindenbaum, Shirley. 1987. "The Mystification of Female Labors." In *Gender and Kinship*. J. Collier and S. Yanigisako, eds. Stanford: Stanford University Press.

Lindenberger, Herbert. 1984. *Opera: The Extravagant Art*. Ithaca: Cornell University Press.

Littleton, C. Scott. 1985. "Introduction" to Lévy-Bruhl (1985: v–xlviii).

Lockspeiser, Edward. 1978. *Debussy: His Life and Mind*. 2 vols. New York: Cambridge University Press.

Lodge, David, ed. 1988. *Modern Criticism and Theory: A Reader*. New York: Longman.

Lodge, David C., and William Weber. 1984. *Wagnerism in European Culture and Politics*. Ithaca: Cornell University Press.

Lorrigio, Francesco. 1990. "Anthropology, Literary Theory, and the Traditions of Modernism." In Manganaro (1990: 215–42).

Lott, Eric. 1993. *Love and Theft: Blackface, Minstrelsy and the American Working Class*. New York: Oxford University Press.

Louis, J. C. and H. Z. Yazijian. 1980. *The Cola Wars*. New York: Everest House.

Lovejoy, Arthur O. 1964. *The Great Chain of Being*. Cambridge: Harvard University Press.

Lucian. 1962. *Selected Satires of Lucian*. Lionel Casson, ed. and trans. New York: Norton.

Luhrman, T. M. 1989. *Persuasion of the Witch's Craft*. Harvard: Harvard University Press.

Lukes, Steven. 1973. *Emile Durkheim: His Life and Work*. Stanford: Stanford University Press.

Luther, Martin. 1955–86. *Works*. 55 vols. J. Pelikan, ed. Saint Louis: Concordia.

Lyotard, Jean-François. 1988. *The Differend: Phrases in Dispute*. Minnesota: University of Minnesota Press.

———. 1993. "Excerpts from *Discours, figure*" and "Philosophy and Painting in the Age of Their Experimentation: Contribution to a Theory of Postmodernity." In G. Johnson, ed. (1993: 309–35, 407–10).

MacAloon, John, ed. 1984. *Rite, Drama, Festival, Spectacle: Rehearsals Towards a Theory of Cultural Performance*. Philadelphia: Institute for the Study of Human Issues.

MacCannell, Dean. 1989. *The Tourist: A New Theory of the Leisure Class*. New York: Schocken.

———. 1992. *Empty Meeting Grounds: The Tourist Papers*. London: Routledge.

Macdonald, Dwight. 1985. "Appendix: Some Notes on Parody." In Macdonald, ed. (1985: 557–68).

Macdonald, Dwight, ed. 1985 [1960]. *Parodies: An Anthology from Chaucer to Beer-bohm—and After*. New York: Da Capo.

Macksey, Richard. "Proust in the Margins of Ruskin." In J. Hunt and F. Holland (1982).

Macksey, Richard, and E. Donato, eds. 1972. *The Structuralist Controversy*. Baltimore: Johns Hopkins University Press.

Mahony, Patrick J. 1982. *Freud as a Writer*. New York: International Universities Press.

———. 1987. *Freud as a Writer*. Expanded ed. New Haven: Yale University Press.

Mailloux, Steven. 1982. *Interpretive Conventions: The Reader in the Study of American Fiction*. Ithaca: Cornell University Press.

Malcolm, Janet. 1984. *In the Freud Archives*. New York: Knopf.

———. 1989. "Reflections (Journalism)," Parts 1 and 2. *The New Yorker*, March 13, March 20, 1989.

Malinowski, Bronislau. 1922. *Argonauts of the Western Pacific: An Account of Native Enterprise and Adventure in the Archipelagoes of Melanesian New Guinea*. London: Routledge.

———. 1935. *Coral Gardens and Their Magic*. New York: American Books.

———. 1954. *Magic, Science, and Religion and Other Essays*. New York: Anchor Books.

———. 1967. *A Diary in the Strict Sense of the Term*. London: Routledge and Kegan Paul.

———. 1993. *The Early Writings of B. Malinowski*. R. Thornton and P. Skalník, eds. Cambridge: Cambridge University Press.

Mallarmé, Stéphane. 1965. The Penguin Poets. Anthony Hartley, ed. Baltimore: Penguin Books.

Manganaro, Marc, ed. 1990. *Modernist Anthropology: From Fieldwork to Text*. Princeton: Princeton University Press.

———. 1992. *Myth, Rhetoric, and the Voice of Authority: A Critique of Frazer, Eliot, Frye, and Campbell*. New Haven: Yale University Press.

———. 1996. "A Funeral in North Lebanon: On Narratives of Other Cultural Encounters." *Public Culture* 8: 567–85.

Mani, Lata. 1987. "Contentious Traditions: The Debate on SATI in Colonial India." *Cultural Critique* 7(Fall): 119–56.

Mann, Thomas. 1970 [1912]. *Death in Venice*. Kenneth Burke, trans. [1924]. New York: Random House.

———. 1975. *Letters of Thomas Mann, 1889–1955*. R. and C. Winston, trans. New York: Vintage.

Manuel, Frank E., and Fritzie P. Manuel. 1979. *Utopian Thought in the Western World*. Cambridge: Harvard University Press.

Marcus, George E., and Fred R. Myers. 1997. *The Traffic in Culture: Refiguring Art and Anthropology*. Berkeley: University of California Press.

Marett, R. R. 1933. *Sacraments of Simple Folk*. Oxford: The Clarendon Press.

Markus, R. A. 1972. *Augustine: A Collection of Critical Theory*. New York: Anchor Books.

Martin, Emily. 1992. *The Woman in the Body: A Cultural Analysis of Reproduction*. Boston: Beacon Press.

———. 1996. *Flexible Bodies: Tracking Immunity in America from the Days of Polio to the Age of AIDS*. Boston: Beacon Press.

Marx, Karl. 1972. *The Marx-Engels Reader*. Robert C. Tucker, ed. New York: Norton.

Marx, Leo. 1988. "The Vernacular Tradition in American Writing." In *The Pilot and the Passenger*. New York: Oxford University Press.

Matthiessen, F. O. 1966. "*Walden*: Craftsmanship vs. Technique." In Thoreau (1966: 305–13).

Mauss, Marcel. 1967. *The Gift*. Ian Cunnison, trans. New York: Norton.

———. 1972. *A General Theory of Magic*. Robert Brain, trans. New York: Norton.

———. 1983 [1950]. *Sociologie et anthropologie*. 8th ed. (Includes "Essai sur le don," 143–279). Paris: Presses Universitaires de France.

———. 1990. *The Gift: The Form and Reason for Exchange in Archaic Societies*. W. D. Halls, trans. New York: Norton.

Mauss, Marcel, and Robert Hubert. See Hubert.

Maybury-Lewis, David, and Uri Almagor, eds. 1989. *The Attraction of Opposites: Thought and Society in the Dualistic Mode*. Ann Arbor: University of Michigan Press.

McKinnon, Susan. 1991. *From a Shattered Sun: Hierarchy, Gender, and Alliance in the Tanimbar Islands*. Madison: University of Wisconsin Press.

Mead, Margaret. 1935. *Sex and Temperament in Three Primitive Societies*. New York: Morrow.

———. 1959. *An Anthropologist at Work: Writings of Ruth Benedict*. Boston: Houghton Mifflin.

———. 1970a. *Culture and Commitment: A Study of the Generation Gap*. New York: Doubleday.

———. 1970b. "Foreword." In Belo (1970: v).

———. 1975 [1972]. *Blackberry Winter: My Earlier Years*. New York: Morrow, Pocketbook ed.

———. 1977. *Letters from the Field, 1925–75*. New York: Harper and Row.

Mehta, Gita. 1979. *Karma Cola: Marketing the Mystic East*. New York: Schocken Books.

———. 1996. *Snakes and Ladders*. New York: Doubleday.

Mellow, J. R. 1974. *Charmed Circle: Gertrude Stein and Company*. New York: Avon Books.

Melville, Herman. 1964 [1852]. *Pierre, or, The Ambiguities*. Lawrence Thompson, foreword. New York: Signet.

———. 1970 [1891]. *Billy Budd, Sailor*. H. Hayford and M. Sealts, eds. Chicago: University of Chicago Press.

———. 1970 [1849]. *Mardi, and A Voyage Thither*. Evanston and Chicago: Northwestern University Press and the Newberry Library.

———. 1971 [1857]. *The Confidence Man*. H. Parker, ed. New York: Norton Critical Edition.

———. 1973 [1851]. *Moby Dick*. Harold Beaver, ed. London: Penguin Books.

———. 1982 [1847]. *Omoo*. In *Typee, Omoo, Mardi*. New York: Library of America.

———. 1989. [1849–60]. *Journals*. H. Horsford and L. Horth, eds. Evanston and Chicago: Northwestern University Press and the Newberry Library.

———. 1996 [1846]. *Typee*. Ruth Blair, ed. Oxford: Oxford University Press.

Merleau-Ponty, Maurice. 1964. *Signs*. R. McCleary, trans. Evanston: Northwestern University Press.

————. 1993. *Aesthetic Writings*. See G. Johnson (1993).

Merton, Robert K. 1985. *On the Shoulders of Giants: A Shandean Postscript*. 2nd ed. New York: Harcourt Brace Jovanovich.

Mertz, Elizabeth, and R. Parmentier, eds. 1985. *Semiotic Mediations*. New York: Academic Press.

Michelin. 1974. *Guide Michelin: Benelux*. Paris: Pneu Michelin, Services de tourisme.

Miller, Edwin Haviland. 1989. *Walt Whitman's "Song of Myself": A Mosaic of Interpretations*. Iowa City: University of Iowa Press.

Miller, James. 1992. *The Passion of Michel Foucault*. New York: Simon and Schuster.

Miller, Perry. 1966. "Thoreau in the Context of International Romanticism." In Thoreau (1966: 390–400).

Milner, Anthony. 1994. *The Invention of Politics in Colonial Malaya: Contesting Nationalism and the Expansion of the Public Sphere*. Cambridge: Cambridge University Press.

Milner, A., and D. Gerstle. See Gerstle and Milner.

Mintz, Sidney. 1985. *Sweetness and Power. The Place of Sugar in Modern History*, 31(2): New York: Viking Penguin.

Mitchell, Timothy. 1989. "The World as Exhibition." *Comparative Studies of Society and History* 31(2): pp. 217–36.

Modell, Judith. 1983. *Ruth Benedict: Patterns of a Life*. Philadelphia: University of Pennsylvania Press.

Monaghan, Peter. 1996. "Fantasy Island." *Lingua Franca* (July/August 1996).

Monk, Ray. 1990. *Ludwig Wittgenstein: The Duty of Genius*. New York: The Free Press.

Monson, Ingrid. 1994. "Doubleness and Jazz Improvisation: Irony, Parody, and Ethnomusicology." *Critical Inquiry* 20(2): 283–313.

Montagu, Ashley. 1964. *Man's Most Dangerous Myth: The Fallacy of Race*. New York: Meridian.

Montaigne, Michel de. 1903. *The Journal of Montaigne's Travels in 1580 and 1581*. W. G. Waters, trans. London: John Murray.

————. 1965. *The Complete Essays*. Donald Frame, trans. Stanford: Stanford University Press.

————. 1983. *Travel Journal*. Donald Frame, trans. San Francisco: Northpoint Press.

Moon, Michael. 1991. *Disseminating Whitman: Revision and Corporality in "Leaves of Grass."* Cambridge: Cambridge University Press.

Mordden, Ethan. 1988. *The Hollywood Studios: Their Unique Styles during the Golden Age of Movies*. New York: Simon and Schuster.

————. 1990a. *Medium Cool: The Movies of the 1960s*. New York: Knopf.

————. 1990b. "A Critic At Large: I Got a Song." *The New Yorker*, Oct. 22, 1990, 110–42.

More, Thomas. 1975 [1518]. *Utopia*. Robert M. Adams, trans. and ed. New York: Norton Critical Editions.

Morgan, Susan. 1996. *Place Matters: Gendered Geography in Victorian Women's Travel Books about Southeast Asia*. New Brunswick: Rutgers University Press.

Morris, Wesley. 1979. *Friday's Footprint: Structuralism and the Articulated Text*. Columbus: Ohio State University Press.

Morson, Gary Saul. 1991. "Bakhtin and the Present Moment." *The American Scholar* (spring): 201–22.

Moyer, David. 1982. Review of J. Boon (1977). *American Anthropologist* 84(1): 220–21.

Mullaney, Steven. 1988. "Strange Things, Gross Terms, Curious Customs: The Rehearsal of Cultures in the Late Renaissance." In Greenblatt, ed. (1988: 65–92).

Multatuli (Eduard Douwes Dekker). 1982 [1860]. *Max Havelaar*. R. Edwards, trans.; D. H. Lawrence, intro.; E. Beekman, ed. Amherst: University of Massachusetts Press.

Nabokov, Isabella. 1997. "Expel the Lover, Recover the Wife: Symbolic Analysis of a South Indian Exorcism." *The Journal of the Royal Anthropological Institute* (N.S.) 3: 297–316.

Nabokov, Vladimir. 1970 [1955]. *The Annotated Lolita*. Alfred Appel, Jr., ed. New York: McGraw-Hill.

———. 1983. *Lectures on Don Quixote*. Fredson Bowers, ed. New York: Harcourt Brace Jovanovich.

———. 1990 [1973]. *Strong Opinions*. New York: Vintage.

Nader, Ralph. 1966. *Unsafe at Any Speed*. New York: Pocketbooks.

Naipaul, Shiva. 1984. *Beyond the Dragon's Mouth: Stories and Pieces*. New York: Penguin Books.

Naipaul, V.S. 1964. *An Area of Darkness*. New York: Vintage.

———. 1984. *The Overcrowded Barracoon*. New York: Vintage.

Naremore, James, and Patrick Brantlinger, eds. 1991. *Modernity and Mass Culture*. Bloomington: Indiana University Press.

Natter, Wolfgang, T. Schatski, and J. P. Jones, eds. 1995. *Objectivity and its Other*. Lexington: University of Kentucky Press.

Nattiez, Jean-Jacques. 1990. *Music and Discourse: Toward a Semiology of Music*. C. Abbate, trans. Princeton: Princeton University Press.

———. 1993. *Wagner Androgyne*. Princeton: Princeton University Press.

Needham, Rodney. "Introduction" to Hocart (1970).

Nehamas, Alexander. 1985. *Nietzsche: Life as Literature*. Cambridge: Harvard University Press.

Neiman, C. 1980. "Art and Anthropology: The Crossroads." *October* 14: 3–46.

Neville, Gwen Kennedy. 1987. *Kinship and Pilgrimage: Rituals of Reunion in American Protestant Culture*. New York: Oxford University Press.

———. 1994. *The Mother Town: Civic Ritual, Symbol, and Experience in the Borders of Scotland*. New York: Oxford University Press.

The New English Bible, with the Apocrypha. 1970. New York: Oxford and Cambridge University Presses.

The New Yorker. June 23 and 30, 1997. (Double Issue on Literature: South Asian authors in English).

Newman, Ernest. 1937. *The Life of Richard Wagner*. 4 vols. New York: Cambridge University Press.

Nietzsche, Friedrich. 1959. "From *Ecce Homo*." In *The Portable Nietzsche*. Walter Kaufmann, ed. and trans. London: Penguin.

———. 1967 [1872, 1886]. *The Birth of Tragedy and The Case of Wagner*. W. Kaufmann, trans. New York: Vintage.

———. 1983. *Untimely Meditations*. R. J. Hollingdale, trans. Cambridge: Cambridge University Press.

————. 1989. *Friedrich Nietzsche on Rhetoric and Language*. S. Gilman, C. Blair, and D. Parnet, eds. and trans. New York: Oxford University Press.

————. 1990. *Unmodern Observations*. William Arrowsmith, ed. and trans. New Haven: Yale University Press.

Noll, Richard. 1997. *The Jung Cult: Origins of a Charismatic Movement*. New York: The Free Press.

Norwich, John Julius. 1982. *A History of Venice*. New York: Knopf.

Nugroho, Garin. 1995. *Kekuasaan dan Hiburan*. Yogyakarta: Yayasan Bentang Budaya.

Obeyesekere, Gannanath. 1990. *The Work of Culture*. Chicago: University of Chicago Press.

O'Farrell, Clare. 1989. *Foucault: Historian or Philosopher?* New York: St. Martin's Press.

O'Flaherty, Wendy Doniger. 1973. *Asceticism and Eroticism in the Mythology of Siva*. Oxford: Oxford University Press.

————. 1980. *Women, Androgynes, and Other Mythical Beasts*. Chicago University of Chicago Press.

————. 1984. *Dreams, Illusions, and Other Realities*. Chicago: University of Chicago Press.

————. 1985. *Tales of Sex and Violence: Folklore, Sacrifice, and Danger in the Jaiminiya Brahmana*. Chicago: University of Chicago Press.

O'Keefe, Daniel. 1983. *Stolen Lightning: The Social Theory of Magic*. New York: Vintage.

Olson, Glending. 1982. *Literature as Recreation in the Later Middle Ages*. Ithaca: Cornell University Press.

Olwig, Karen Fog, and Kirsten Hastrup. 1996. *Siting Culture: The Shifting Anthropological Object*. New York: Routledge.

On The Town. 1949. Arthur Freed, prod. Betty Comden and Adolph Green, lyrics. Metro Goldwyn Mayer.

Ong, Walter J. 1982. *Orality and Literacy*. London: Methuen, 1982.

————. 1983. *Ramus: Method and the Decay of Dialogue*. Cambridge: Harvard University Press.

Orgel, Stephen. 1981. *The Jonsonian Masque*. New York: Columbia University Press.

————. 1996. *Impersonations: The Performance of Gender in Shakespeare's England*. New York: Cambridge University Press.

Ortner, Sherry. 1989. *High Religion*. Princeton: Princeton University Press.

Osborne, Charles. 1978. *The Complete Operas of Mozart: A Critical Guide*. New York: Atheneum.

Oxford English Dictionary, Compact Edition. 1971. Complete Text Reproduced Micrographically. New York.

Padoux, André. 1990. *Vac: The Concept of the Word in Selected Hindu Tantras*. Jacques Gondier, trans. Albany: State University of New York Press.

Paglia, Camille. 1990. *Sexual Personae: Art and Decadence from Nefertiti to Emily Dickinson*. New Haven: Yale University Press.

————. 1992. *Sex, Art, and American Culture*. New York: Vintage.

Paige, Karen Ericksen. 1978. "The Ritual of Circumcision." *Human Nature* (May 1978): 40–48.

Panoff, Michel. 1993. Review of Stocking (1986). *L'Homme* 125, 33(1): 168–70.

Parker, Hershel. 1997. *Herman Melville: A Biography.* Vol. 1, *1819–1851.* Baltimore: Johns Hopkins University Press.

Parkes, Graham, ed. 1991. *Nietzsche and Asian Thought.* Chicago: University of Chicago Press.

Parmentier, Richard J. 1987. *The Sacred Remains: Myth, History, and Polity in Belau.* Chicago: University of Chicago Press.

Patrides, C. A., and J. Wittreich, eds. 1984. *The Apocalypse in English Renaissance Thought and Literature.* Ithaca: Cornell University Press.

Paul, Robert A. 1996. *Moses and Civilization: The Meaning Behind Freud's Myth.* New Haven: Yale University Press.

Payne, F. A. 1981. *Chaucer and Menippean Satire.* Madison: University of Wisconsin Press.

Peacock, James L., 1968. *Rites of Modernization.* Chicago: University of Chicago Press.

———. 1973. *Indonesia: An Anthropological Perspective.* Pacific Palisades: Goodyear.

———. 1975. *Consciousness and Change.* New York: John Wiley.

———. 1978. *Muslim Puritans: Reformist Psychology in Southeast Asian Islam.* Berkeley: University of California Press.

Peacock, James L., and Ruel W. Tyson, Jr. 1989. *Pilgrims of Paradox: Calvinism and Experience among the Primitive Baptists of the Blue Ridge.* Washington: Smithsonian Institution Press.

Peirce, Charles Sanders. 1931–38. *The Collected Papers of C. S. Peirce.* C. H. Shorne and P. Weiss, eds. Cambridge: Harvard University Press.

———. 1955 [1893–1910]. *Philosophical Writings.* J. Buchler, ed. New York: Dover.

Pensky, Max. 1996. *Melancholy Dialectics: Walter Benjamin and the Play of Mourning.* Amherst: University of Massachusetts Press.

Percival, Robert. See *Edinburgh Review.*

Percy, Walker. 1960. *The Moviegoer.* New York: Avon Books.

———. 1975. *The Message in the Bottle.* New York: Farrar, Straus and Giroux.

———. 1983. *Lost in the Cosmos: The Last Self-help Book.* New York: Farrar, Straus and Giroux.

Perec, Georges. 1967. *Les Choses.* Paris: Julliard.

———. 1987. *Life: A User's Manual.* D. Bellos, trans. Boston: Godine.

Picard, Michel. 1992. *Bali: Tourisme culturel et culture touristique.* Paris: Edition L'harmattan.

Pierpont, Claudia Roth. 1997. "A Society of One: Zora Neale Hurston, American Contrarian." *The New Yorker,* February 17, 1997, 80–91.

Pigafetta, A. 1906. *Magellan's Voyage Around the World.* The Original Text of the Ambrosian MS. 2 vols. J. A. Robertson, trans. Cleveland: A. H. Clerk.

Pires, Tomé. 1944. *The Summa Oriental.* Armando Cortesao, trans. London: Hakluyt Society, Series 2, Vol. 15.

Pocock, David. "Foreword" to Mauss (1972: 1–6).

Poe, Edgar Allan. 1980. *The Unknown Poe: An Anthology of Fugitive Writings by Edgar Allan Poe; with appreciations by Charles Baudelaire, Stéphane Mallarmé,*

Paul Valéry, J. K. Huysmans, & André Breton. Raymond Foye, ed. San Francisco: City Lights Books.

Poirier, Richard. 1967. *The Comic Sense of Henry James*. New York: Oxford University Press.

———. 1971. *The Performing Self: Compositions and Decompositions in the Languages of Contemporary Life*. New York: Oxford University Press.

———. 1985 [1966]. *A World Elsewhere: The Place of Style in American Literature*. Madison: University of Wisconsin Press.

———. 1992. "Pragmatism and the Sentence of Death." *The Yale Review* 80(3): 74–100.

Pollmann, Tessel. 1990. "Margaret Mead's Balinese: The Fitting Symbols of the American Dream." *Indonesia* 49: 1–35.

Posnock, Ross. 1992. "Reading Poirier Pragmatically." *The Yale Review* 80(3): 156–70.

Poster, Mark. 1986. "Foucault and the Tyranny of Greece." In Hoy (1986: 205–20).

———. 1988. "Introduction" In Baudrillard (1988).

Pouillon, Jean. 1982. "Some Thoughts on the Verb 'to Believe.'" In M. Izard and P. Smith (1982).

Pratt, Mary. 1992. *Imperial Eyes: Travel Writing and Transculturation*. New York: Routledge.

Prattis, J. Iain. 1991. "'Parsifal' and Semiotic Structuralism." In Brady (1991: 111–31).

Preziosi, Donald. 1979. *The Semiotics of the Built Environment*. Bloomington: University of Indiana Press.

———. 1989. *Rethinking Art History: Meditations on a Coy Science*. New Haven: Yale University Press.

Price, Richard. 1990. *Alabi's World*. Baltimore: Johns Hopkins University Press.

Price, Richard, and Sally Price. 1992. *Equatoria*. New York: Routledge.

Price, Sally. 1989. *Primitive Art in Civilized Places*. Chicago: University of Chicago Press.

Prochaska, David. 1990. *Making Algeria French: Colonialism in Bône, 1870–1920*. Cambridge: Cambridge University Press.

———. 1992. "Tales of the City: Between *Algérie Française* and *Algérie Algérienne*." In D. Segal (1992: 182–225).

Proust, Marcel. 1954 [1913–]. *A la recherche du temps perdu*. 3 vols. Paris: Gallimard.

———. 1981 [1913–]. *Remembrance of Things Past*. C. K. Scott Moncrieff and T. Kilmartin, trans. 3 vols. New York: Random House.

———. 1983. *Selected Letters, 1880–1903*. Philip Kolb, ed.; R. Manheim, trans. Garden City: Doubleday.

Puffett, Derrick. 1989. *Richard Strauss "Salome."* Cambridge: Cambridge University Press.

Quint, David, ed. 1992. *Creative Imitation: New Essays in Renaissance Literature in Honor of Thomas Greene*. Binghamton, New York.

Rabinow, Paul. 1996. *Essays on the Anthropology of Reason*. Princeton: Princeton University Press.

Rabinow, Paul, ed. 1984. *A Foucault Reader*. New York: Pantheon.

Rabinow, Paul, and W. Sullivan, eds. 1979. *Interpretive Social Science*. Berkeley: University of California Press.

Rabinowitz, Peter J. 1987. *Before Reading: Narrative Conventions and the Politics of Interpretation*. Ithaca: Cornell University Press.

Rafferty, Terence. "Divided Self." *The New Yorker*, July 1, 1991, 81–83 [Review of "Europa Europa," Agnieszka Holland, dir., based on a novel by Salomon Perel].

Rahn, John, ed. 1994. *Perspectives on Musical Aesthetics*. New York: Norton.

Ramseyer, Urs. 1977. *The Art and Culture of Bali*. Oxford: Oxford University Press.

Rau, Santha Rama. 1989. "Remembering E. M. Forster." In Sonnenberg (1989: 259–79).

Ravid, Benjamin C. I. 1988. "The Venetian Ghetto in Historical Perspective." In M. Cohen (1988: 279–83).

Ray, Robert B. 1991. "The Avant-Garde Finds Andy Hardy." In Naremore and Brantlinger (1991: 224–52).

Readings, Bill, and B. Schaber. 1993. *Postmodernism Across the Ages*. Syracuse: Syracuse University Press.

Reid, Anthony. 1981. "A Great Seventeenth Century Indonesian Family: Matoaya and Patinggaloang of Makassar." *Masyarakat Indonesia* 7: 1–28.

———. 1988. *Asia in the Age of Commerce I: The Lands Below the Winds*. New Haven: Yale University Press.

———. 1994. "Early Southeast Asian Categorizations of Europeans." In Schwartz (1994: 268–94).

Reid, Anthony, ed. 1993. *Southeast Asia in the Early Modern Era: Trade, Power, and Belief*. Ithaca: Cornell University Press.

Reiss, Timothy. 1982. *The Discourse of Modernism*. Ithaca: Cornell University Press.

Remondino, P. C. 1891. *History of Circumcision, From the Earliest Times to the Present*. Philadelphia: F. A. Davis.

Resink, G. J. 1984. "La musique de Debussy dans la vie de Walter Spies." *Archipel* 27: 45–49.

Reynolds, David S. 1988. *Beneath the American Renaissance: The Subversive Imagination in the Age of Emerson and Melville*. Cambridge: Harvard University Press.

Rhodius, H. ed. 1965. *Schönheit und Reichtum des Lebens: Walter Spies (Maler und Musiker auf Bali, 1895–1942)*. The Hague: L. Boucher.

Rhodius, H., and J. Darling. 1980. *Walter Spies and Balinese Art*. J. Stowell, ed. Amsterdam: Terra Zutphen.

Riani, Paolo. 1990. *John Portman*. (Interview with Portman by P. Goldberger; M. Portman and T. Hursley, photogs.) Washington: American Institute of Architects Press; Milan: l'Arcaedizioni.

Richman, Michèle H. 1982. *Reading Georges Bataille: Beyond the Gift*. Baltimore: Johns Hopkins University Press.

———. 1990. "Anthropology and Modernism in France: From Durkheim to the *Collège de sociologie*." In Manganaro (1990: 183–214).

Richter, Jean Paul. 1992. *Jean Paul: A Reader*. T. J. Casey, ed.; E. Casey, trans. Baltimore: Johns Hopkins University Press.

Ricoeur, Paul. 1981. *Hermeneutics and the Human Sciences*. J. B. Thompson, trans. Cambridge: Cambridge University Press.

Rieff, Philip. 1954. "The Authority of the Past: Sickness and Society in Freud's Thought." *Social Research* 21 (4).

————. 1979. *Freud: the Mind of the Moralist*, 3rd ed. Chicago: University of Chicago Press.

Rivers, W.H.R. 1926. *Psychology and Ethnology*. New York: Harcourt Brace.

Robbins, Bruce. 1993. *Secular Vocations*. New York: Verso.

Robinson, Geoffrey. 1995. *The Dark Side of Paradise: Political Violence in Bali*. Ithaca: Cornell University Press.

Rogin, Michael Paul. 1985. *Subversive Genealogy: The Politics and Art of Herman Melville*. Berkeley: University of California Press.

————. 1994. " 'Democracy and Burnt Cork': The End of Blackface, the Beginning of Civil Rights." *Representations* 46: 1–34.

Romaine, Suzanne. 1988. *Pidgin and Creole Languages*. London: Longman.

Rorty, Richard. 1979. *Philosophy and the Mirror of Nature*. Princeton: Princeton University Press.

————. 1989. *Contingency, Irony, and Solidarity*. New York: Cambridge University Press.

Rosaldo, Renato. 1989. *Culture and Truth: The Remaking of Social Analysis*. Boston: Beacon Press.

Roseman, Marina. 1991. *Healing Sounds from the Malaysian Rainforest: Temiar Music and Medicine*. Berkeley: University of California Press.

Rosen, Charles. 1972. *The Classical Style: Haydn, Mozart, Beethoven*. New York: Norton.

————. 1995. *The Romantic Generation*. Cambridge: Harvard University Press.

Rosen, Lawrence. 1971. "Language, History, and the Logic of Inquiry in Lévi-Strauss and Sartre." *History and Theory* 10: 269–94.

————. 1984. *Bargaining for Reality: The Construction of Social Relations in a Muslim Community*. Chicago: University of Chicago Press.

Rosenblatt, Daniel. 1997. "The Antisocial Skin: Structure, Resistance, and 'Modern Primitive' Adornment in the United States." *Cultural Anthropology* 12(3): 287–334.

Ross, Andrew. 1989. *No Respect: Intellectuals and Popular Culture*. New York: Routledge.

Roth, Michael S. 1992. "Foucault on Discourse and History: A Style of Delegitimation." In C. Sills and Jensen (1992: 102–21).

Rowe, John Carlos. 1976. *Henry James and Henry Adams*. Ithaca: Cornell University Press.

————. 1997. *At Emerson's Tomb: The Politics of Classic American Literature*. New York: Columbia University Press.

Rowe, John Carlos, ed. 1996. *New Essays on the Education of Henry Adams*. New York: Cambridge University Press.

Rueckert, William H. 1982. *Kenneth Burke and the Drama of Human Relations*. Berkeley: University of California Press.

Rushdie, Salman. 1992. *The Wizard of Oz*. London: British Film Institute Film Classics.

————. 1997. "Damme, This is the Oriental Scene for You!" *The New Yorker*. June 23 & 30, 1997, 50–61.

Ruskin, John. 1871–84. *Fors Clavigera*. n.p.: Library Edition.

Safranski, Rüdiger. 1991. *Schopenhauer and the Wild Years of Philosophy*. E. Osers, trans. Cambridge: Harvard University Press.

Sagan, Carl. 1977. *The Dragons of Eden: Speculations on the Evolution of Human Intelligence*. New York: Ballantine Books.

———. 1985. *Contact: A Novel*. New York: Simon and Schuster.

Sahlins, Marshall. 1972. *Stone Age Economics*. Chicago: Aldine.

———. 1976. *Culture and Practical Reason*. Chicago: University of Chicago Press.

———. 1996. "The Sadness of Sweetness: The Native Anthropology of Western Cosmology." *Current Anthropology* 37(3): 395–428.

Said, Edward. 1975. *Beginnings*. Baltimore: Johns Hopkins University Press.

———. 1978. *Orientalism*. New York: Pantheon Books.

———. 1981. *Covering Islam: How the Media and the Experts Determine How We See the Rest of the World*. New York: Pantheon.

———. 1991. *Musical Elaborations*. New York: Columbia University Press.

———. 1992. *Culture and Imperialism*. London: Chatto and Windus.

Sallis, John. 1991. *Crossings: Nietzsche and the Space of Tragedy*. Chicago: University of Chicago Press.

Samuels, Ernest. 1989. *Henry Adams*. Cambridge: Harvard University Press.

Sangren, P. Steven. 1987. *History and Magical Power in a Chinese Community*. Stanford: Stanford University Press.

———. 1988. "Rhetoric and the Authority of Ethnography." *Current Anthropology* 29: 405–35.

Santner, Eric. 1996. *My Own Private Germany.: Daniel Paul Schreber's Secret History of Modernity*. Princeton: Princeton University Press.

Sapir, Edward. 1949 [1921]. *Language*. New York: Harcourt Brace.

Sartre, Jean-Paul. 1977. *Life/Situations: Essays Written and Spoken*. P. Auster and L. Davis, eds. New York: Pantheon.

Sastrowardoyo, Subagio. 1990. *Sastra Hindia Belanda dan Kita*. Jakarta: Balai Pustaka.

Saussure, Ferdinand. 1966 [1911]. *Course in General Linguistics*. W. Baskin, trans. New York: McGraw-Hill.

Sawyer, Paul L. 1985. *Ruskin's Poetic Argument: The Design of the Major Works*. Ithaca: Cornell University Press.

Schaefer, David L. 1989. *The Political Philosophy of Montaigne*. Ithaca: Cornell University Press.

Schama, Simon. 1987. *The Embarrassment of Riches*. New York: Knopf.

Schechner, Richard. 1986. *Between Theater and Anthropology*. Philadelphia: University of Pennsylvania Press.

Schlegel, Friedrich von. 1991. *Philosophical Fragments*. P. Firchow, trans. Minneapolis: University of Minnesota Press.

Schmidgall, Gary. 1977. *Literature as Opera*. New York: Oxford University Press.

Schmitz, Neil. 1983. *Of Huck and Alice: Humorous Writing in American Literature*. Minneapolis: University of Minnesota Press.

Schneider, David. 1980 [1968]. *American Kinship: A Cultural Account*. 2nd ed. Chicago: University of Chicago Press.

Schopenhauer, Arthur. 1970. *Essays and Aphorisms*. R. J. Hollingdale, trans. New York: Penguin Classics.

Schorske, Carl. 1980. *Fin-de-siècle Vienna: Politics and Culture*. New York: Knopf.

Schrieke, B.J.O. 1921–22. "Allerlei over de besnijdenis." *Tijdschrift voor Indische Taal-, Land- en Volkenkunde* 60: 373–578; 61: 1–94.

Schulte Nordholt, Henk. 1991. "Temple and Authority in South Bali, 1900–1980." In H. Geertz, ed. (1991: 137–64).

Schutz, Emily A. 1990. *A Dialogue at the Margins: Whorf, Bakhtin, and Linguistic Relativity*. Madison: University of Wisconsin Press.

Schwartz, Stuart B., ed. 1994. *Implicit Understandings: Observing, Reporting, and Reflecting on the Encounters between Europeans and Other Peoples in the Early Modern Era*. New York: Cambridge University Press.

Scott, James. 1985. *Weapons of the Weak*. New Haven: Yale University Press.

———. 1990. *Domination and the Arts of Resistance: Hidden Transcripts*. New Haven: Yale University Press.

Seabrook, John. 1997. "Why is the Force Still With Us?" *The New Yorker*, January 6, 1997, 40–53.

Sedgwick, Eve Kosofsky. 1994. "The Beast in the Closet." In Yeazell (1994: 154–70).

———. 1996. *Tendencies*. Durham: Duke University Press.

Segal, Daniel. 1988. "Nationalism, Comparatively Speaking." *Journal of Historical Sociology* 1(3): 300–21.

———. 1994. "Living Ancestors: Nationalism and the Past in Postcolonial Trinidad and Tobago." In J. Boyarin (1994: 221–40).

Segal, Daniel, ed. 1992. *Crossing Cultures: Essays in the Displacement of Western Civilization*. Tucson: University of Arizona Press.

———. 1997. "An Exchange with David M. Schneider on Gay and Lesbian Kinship" (R. Herrell, R. Gutiérrez, M. Strathern). *Cultural Anthropology* 12(2): 269–81.

Serres, Michel, 1982. *The Parasite*. L. Schehr, trans. Baltimore: Johns Hopkins University Press.

Serres, Michel, and Bruno Latour. 1995. *Conversations on Science, Culture, and Time*. R. Lapidus, trans. Ann Arbor: University of Michigan Press.

Shanklin, Eugenia. 1995. *Anthropology and Race*. Belmont, CA.: Wadsworth.

Shapiro, Susan E. 1983. "Introduction: Negative Theology, Heretic Hermeneutics." In Krupnick (1983: 95–97).

Sheehy, Gail. 1976. *Passages: Predictable Crises of Adult Life*. New York: Dutton.

———. 1995. *New Passages: Mapping Your Life Across Time*. New York: Ballantine.

Shell, Marc. 1978. *The Economy of Literature*. Baltimore: Johns Hopkins University Press.

———. 1982. *Money, Language, and Thought: Literary and Philosophic Economies from the Medieval to the Modern Era*. Berkeley: University of California Press.

———. 1988. *The End of Kinship: "Measure for Measure," Incest, and the Ideal of Universal Siblinghood*. Stanford: Stanford University Press.

———. 1991. "Marranos (Pigs), or, From Coexistence to Toleration." *Critical Inquiry*: 17(2): 306–35.

———. 1995. "The Want of Incest in the Human Family: Or, Kin and Kind in Christian Thought." *Journal of the American Academy of Religion* 62(3): 625–50.

Shore, Brad. 1982. *Salailua: A Samoan Mystery*. New York: Columbia University Press.

———. 1996. *Culture in Mind: Cognition, Culture, and the Problem of Meaning*. New York: Oxford.

Shurreef, Jaffur. 1832. *Qanoon-e-Islam, or, The Customs of the Moosulmans of India*. G. A. Herklots, trans. London: Parbury, Allen.

Shweder, Richard A., and Robert A. LeVine. 1984. *Culture Theory: Essays on Mind, Self, and Emotion*. Cambridge: Cambridge University Press.

Siegel, Lee. 1991. *Net of Magic: Wonders and Deceptions in India*. Chicago: University of Chicago Press.

Sills, Chip, and George H. Jensen, eds. 1992. *The Philosophy of Discourse: The Rhetorical Turn in Twentieth-Century Thought*. 2 vols. Portsmouth: Heinemann.

Silverstein, Michael. n.d. "Whorfianism and the Linguistic Imagination of Nationality." Revised Paper presented at the School of American Research, Advanced Seminar on "Language Ideologies." Santa Fe, April 1994.

Simmel, Georg. 1978 [1900]. *The Philosophy of Money*. T. Bottomore and D. Frisby, trans. London: Routledge & Kegan Paul.

———. 1991. *Schopenhauer and Nietzsche*. H. Loiskandl, trans. Urbana: University of Illinois Press.

Simpson, David. 1995. *The Academic Postmodern and the Rule of Literature: A Report on Half-Knowledge*. Chicago: University of Chicago Press.

Singer, Milton. 1984. *Man's Glassy Essence: Explorations in Semiotic Anthropology*. Bloomington: Indiana University Press.

———. 1989. "Pronouns, Persons, and the Semiotic Self." In B. Lee and G. Urban (1989: 229–96).

Skalník, Peter. 1995. "Bronislaw Kasper Malinowski and Stanislaw Ignacy Witkiewicz: Science versus Art in the Conceptualization of Culture." In Vermeulen and Roldán (1995: 129–42).

Skinner, Quentin, ed. 1985. *The Return of Grand Theory in the Social Sciences*. Cambridge: Cambridge University Press.

Sloan, Jane E. 1993. *Alfred Hitchcock: A Guide to References and Resources*. New York: G. K. Hall.

Smith, Gary, ed. 1989. *Benjamin: Philosophy, Aesthetics, History*. Chicago: University of Chicago Press.

Smith, Robert J. 1974. *Ancestor Worship in Contemporary Japan*. Stanford: Stanford University Press.

Smith, Valene, ed. 1989. *Hosts and Guests: The Anthropology of Tourism*, 2nd ed. Philadelphia: University of Pennsylvania Press.

Sonnenberg, Ben, ed. 1989. *Performance and Reality: Essays from "Grand Street."* New Brunswick: Rutgers University Press.

Sontag, Susan. 1977. *On Photography*. New York: Delta Books.

Spellbound. 1945. David O. Selznick, prod. Alfred Hitchcock, dir. Ingrid Bergman and Gregory Peck, stars.

Spencer, Herbert. 1896. *The Principles of Sociology*. Vol. 1. New York: Appleton.

Spivak, Gayatri Chakravorty. 1988. *In Other Worlds: Essays in Cultural Politics*. New York: Methuen.

———. 1995. "Can the Subaltern Speak?" In Ashcroft, Griffiths, and Tiffin, eds. (1995: 24–28).

Spoto, Donald. 1987. *The Dark Side of Genius: The Life of Alfred Hitchcock*. New York: Ballantine.

Stallybrass, Peter, and A. White. 1986. *The Politics and Poetics of Transgression*. Ithaca: Cornell University Press.

Stanley, Henry M. 1988 [1899]. *Through the Dark Continent*. Mineola: Dover Publications.

Starobinski, Jean. 1971. *Les Mots sous les mots: Les anagrammes de F. de Saussure*. Paris: Gallimard.

———. 1988. *Jean-Jacques Rousseau: Transparency and Obstruction*. A. Goldhammer, trans. Chicago: University of Chicago Press.

Steedly, Mary Margaret. 1993. *Hanging without a Rope: Narrative Experience in Colonial and Postcolonial Karoland*. Princeton: Princeton University Press.

Stein, Gertrude. 1965 [1933–47]. *Gertrude Stein's America: Your Native Land is Your Native Land It Certainly is . . . .* G. A. Harrison, ed. New York: Liveright.

Steinberg, Leo. 1983. *The Sexuality of Christ in Renaissance Art and in Modern Oblivion*. New York: Pantheon/October.

Steinberg, Michael. 1990. *The Meaning of the Salzburg Festival: Austria as Theater and Ideology, 1890–1938*. Ithaca: Cornell University Press.

Steiner, George. 1975. *After Babel: Aspects of Language and Translation*. New York: Oxford University Press.

———. 1989. *Real Presences*. Chicago: University of Chicago Press.

———. 1991. *Martin Heidegger, with a New Introduction*. Chicago: University of Chicago Press.

Stendhal (Marie-Henri, Beyle). 1975. *Love*. G. and S. Sale, trans. New York: Penguin Books.

———. 1985. *The Life of Rossini*. R. Coe, trans. New York: Riverrun Press.

Stern, J. P. 1983. "Introduction" to Nietzsche (1983: vii–xxxii).

Stewart, Susan. 1984. *On Longing: Narratives of the Miniature, the Gigantic, the Souvenir, the Collection*. Baltimore: Johns Hopkins University Press.

Stocking, George. 1968. *Race, Culture and Evolution*. Chicago: University of Chicago Press.

———. 1979. "Anthropology as *Kulturkampf*: Science and Politics in the Career of Franz Boas." In *The Uses of Anthropology*. Special Publications ll. Washington, D.C.: American Anthropological Association.

———. 1984. "Radcliffe-Brown and British Social Anthropology." *Functionalism Historicized*. History of Anthropology, vol. 2: 131–91. G. Stocking, ed. Madison: University of Wisconsin Press.

———. 1986. *Victorian Anthropology*. New York: The Free Press.

———. 1995. *After Tylor: British Social Anthropology, 1888–1951*. Madison: University of Wisconsin Press.

Stocking, George, ed. 1974. *The Shaping of American Anthropology: A Franz Boas Reader*. New York: Basic Books.

———. 1983. *Observers Observed*. History of Anthropology, vol. l. Madison: University of Wisconsin Press.

———. 1985. *Objects and Others*. History of Anthropology, vol. 3. Madison: University of Wisconsin Press.

———. 1986. *Malinowski, Rivers, Benedict, and Others*. History of Anthropology, vol. 4. Madison: University of Wisconsin Press.

———. 1989. *Romantic Motives. History of Anthropology*, vol. 6. Madison: University of Wisconsin Press.

Stocking, George. 1993. *Colonial Situations*. History of Anthropology, vol. 7. Madison: University of Wisconsin Press.

———. 1996. *Volksgeist as Method and Ethic: Essays on Boasian Anthropology and the German Anthropological Tradition*. History of Anthropology, vol. 8. Madison: University of Wisconsin Press.

Strathern, Marilyn. 1990. "Out of Context." In Manganaro (1990: 80–132).

———. 1991. *Partial Connections*. Association for Social Anthropology in Oceania. Savage, Md.: Rowman and Littlefield.

Sturrock, John. 1996. *The Language of Autobiography*. Cambridge: Cambridge University Press.

Suleri, Sara. 1992. *The Rhetoric of English India*. Chicago: University of Chicago Press.

Sullivan, Paul. 1989. *Unfinished Conversations: Mayas and Foreigners Between Two Wars*. New York: Knopf.

Swellengrebel, J. L. 1960. "Bali, Some General Information." In *Bali: Studies in Life, Thought and Ritual* (3–76). The Hague: W. van Hoeve.

———. 1969. *Bali: Further Studies in Life, Thought, and Ritual*. The Hague: W. van Hoeve.

Tambiah, Stanley. 1984. *The Buddhist Saints of the Forest and the Cult of Amulets*. Cambridge: Cambridge University Press.

———. 1990. *Magic, Science, Religion, and the Scope of Rationality*. Cambridge: Cambridge University Press.

Tanner, Tony. 1979. *Adultery in the Novel: Contract and Transgression*. Baltimore: Johns Hopkins University Press.

———. 1992. *Venice Desired*. Oxford: Blackwell.

Taussig, Michael. 1992. *The Nervous System*. New York: Routledge.

———. 1993a. *Mimesis and Alterity: A Particular History of the Senses*. New York: Routledge.

———. 1993b. "Maleficium: State Fetishism." In Apter and Pietz (1993: 217–50).

———. 1997. *The Magic of the State*. New York: Routledge.

Taylor, J. R. 1983. *Strangers in Paradise: The Hollywood Émigrés, 1933–1950*. New York: Holt, Rinehart and Winston.

Tedlock, Barbara. 1992. *The Beautiful and the Dangerous: Encounters with Zuni Indians*. New York: Viking.

Tedlock, Dennis. 1982. *The Spoken Word and the Work of Interpretation*. Philadelphia: University of Pennsylvania Press.

Thiébaux, Marcelle. 1974. *The Stag of Love: The Chase in Medieval Literature*. Ithaca: Cornell University Press.

Thomas, Nicholas. 1994. *Colonialism's Culture: Anthropology, Travel, and Government*. Princeton: Princeton University Press.

Thoreau, Henry David. 1966. *Walden and Civil Disobedience*. Owen Thomas, ed. New York: Norton Critical Editions.

———. 1985 [1849, 1852]. *A Week on the Concord and Merrimack Rivers. Walden; or, Life in the Woods. The Maine Woods. Cape Cod*. Robert F. Sayre, ed. New York: The Library of America.

Todorov, Tzvetan. 1993. *On Human Diversity: Nationalism, Racism, and Exoticism in French Thought*. C. Porter, trans. Cambridge: Harvard University Press.

Toer, Pramoedya Ananta. 1968. "La Circoncision" (*Sunat*), In *Histoires courtes d'Indonésie*. Denys Lombard, trans. Publications de l'École Française d'Extrême-Orient.

———. 1990 [1975]. *Awakenings (This Earth of Mankind; A Child of All Nations)*. M. Lane, trans. London: Penguin Books.

Toll, Robert. 1976. *On with the Show: The First Century of Show Business in America*. New York: Oxford University Press.

Tomlinson, Gary. 1993. *Music in Renaissance Magic: Toward a Historiography of Others*. Chicago: University of Chicago Press.

Tönnies, Ferdinand. 1963. *Community and Society*. C. P. Loomis, trans. New York: Harper and Row.

———. 1974. *On Social Ideas and Ideologies*. D. G. Jacoby, ed. and trans. New York: Harper and Row.

Torgovnick, Marianna. 1981. *Closure in the Novel*. Princeton: Princeton University Press.

———. 1990. *Gone Primitive: Savage Intellects, Modern Lives*. Chicago: University of Chicago Press.

———. 1994. *Crossing Ocean Parkway: Readings by an Italian-American Daughter*. Chicago: University of Chicago Press.

———. 1997. *Primitive Passions: Men, Women, and the Quest for Ecstasy*. New York: Knopf.

Toulmin, Stephen. 1990. *Cosmopolis: The Hidden Agenda of Modernity*. University of Chicago Press.

Traubner, Richard. 1983. *Operetta: A Theatrical History*. New York: Oxford University Press.

Trautmann, Thomas R. 1996. *Aryans and British India*. Berkeley: University of California Press.

Trexler, Richard C. 1993. *Power and Dependence in Renaissance Florence*. Binghamton, N.Y.: Center for Medieval and Renaissance Studies.

———. 1995. *Sex and Conquest: Gendered Violence, Political Order, and the European Conquest of the Americas*. Cambridge, UK: Polity Press.

———. 1997. *The Journey of the Magi: Meanings in History of a Christian Story*. Princeton: Princeton University Press.

Trinh T. Minh-ha. 1991. *When the Moon Waxes Red: Representation, Gender and Cultural Politics*. New York: Routledge.

Trinh T. Minh-ha, ed. 1989 "Introduction" to "(Un)naming Cultures." *Discourse* 11(2): 5–17.

Tsing, Anna. 1993. *In the Realm of the Diamond Queen*. Princeton: Princeton University Press.

Turnbull, Colin M. 1961. *The Forest People*. New York: Simon and Schuster.

———. 1972. *The Mountain People*. New York: Simon and Schuster.

———. 1983. *The Human Cycle*. New York: Simon and Schuster.

Turner, Frederick. 1986. "Reflexivity as Evolution in Thoreau's *Walden*." In Turner and Bruner (1986: 73–96).

Turner, Victor. 1974. *Dramas, Fields, and Metaphors*. Ithaca: Cornell University Press.

———. 1988. *The Anthropology of Performance*. New York: Performing Arts Journal Publications.

Turner, Victor, and Edward Bruner, eds. 1986. *The Anthropology of Experience*. Urbana: University of Illinois Press.

Turner, Victor, and Edith Turner. 1978. *Image and Pilgrimage in Christian Culture*. New York: Columbia University Press.

Twain, Mark (Samuel Clemens). 1977. *Adventures of Huckleberry Finn*. S. Bradley, R. Beatty, E. Long, and T. Cooley, eds. New York: Norton Critical Editions.

———. 1979. *Illustrated Works of Mark Twain*. M. P. Hearn, ed. New York: Avenel Books.

———. 1991. *Letters from the Earth: Uncensored Writings by Mark Twain*. Bernard De Voto, ed. New York: Harper Perennial.

Updike, John. 1983 *Hugging the Shore*. New York: Knopf.

Vance, Eugene. 1978. "Augustine's Confessions and the Poetics of the Law." *Modern Language Notes* 93: 618–34.

Van Gennep, Arnold. 1960. *The Rites of Passage*. M. B. Vizedom and G. L. Caffee, trans. Chicago: University of Chicago Press.

Varenne, Hervé. 1977. *Americans Together: Structured Diversity in a Midwestern Town*. New York: Teachers College Press.

———. 1986. *Symbolizing America*. Lincoln: The University of Nebraska Press.

———. 1989. "A Confusion of Signs: The Semiosis of Anthropological Ireland." In Lee and Urban (1989: 121–52).

Vermeulen, Han F., and Arturo Alvarez Roldán, eds. 1995. *Fieldwork and Footnotes: Studies in the History of European Anthropology*. New York: Routledge.

Vickers, Adrian. 1989. *Bali: A Paradise Created*. Victoria, Australia: Penguin Books.

Vitz, Paul C. 1988. *Sigmund Freud's Christian Unconscious*. New York: The Guilford Press.

Wagenknecht, Edward. 1981. *Henry David Thoreau: What Manner of Man?* Amherst: University of Massachusetts Press.

Wagner, Cosima. 1978, 1980. *Cosima Wagner's Diaries, 1869–1877, 1878–1883*. 2 vols. M. Gregor-Dellin and D. Mack, eds.; G. Skelton, trans. New York: Harcourt Brace Jovanovich.

Wagner, Richard. 1965 [1865]. *Tristan and Isolde*. Stewart Robb, trans. New York: E. P. Dutton.

Wagner, Roy. 1975. *The Invention of Culture*. Englewood Cliffs, N.J.: Prentice-Hall.

Walley, Christine J. 1997. "Searching for 'Voices': Feminism, Anthropology, and the Global Debate over Female Genital Operations." *Cultural Anthropology* 12(3): 405–38.

Warner, W. Lloyd 1963. *Yankee City*. New Haven: Yale University Press.

Warren, Kay. 1989. *The Symbolism of Subordination*. Austin: University of Texas Press.

Warren, Kay, ed. 1993. *The Violence Within: Cultural and Political Opposition in Divided Nations*. Boulder: Westview Press.

Wartburg, W. v. 1946. *Évolution et structure de la langue française*. Berne: Éditions Francke.

Watt, Stephen. 1991. "Baudrillard's America (and Ours?)." In Naremore and Brantlinger (1991: 135–57).

Waugh, Evelyn. 1945. *Brideshead Revisited*. Boston: Little, Brown.

Webb, Stephen. 1995. "The Rhetoric of and about Excess in William James's *The Varieties of Religious Experience*." *Religion and Literature* 27(2): 27–45.

———. 1996. *The Gifting God: A Trinitarian Ethics of Excess.* New York: Oxford University Press.

Weber, Eugen. 1986. *France: Fin de Siècle.* Cambridge: Harvard University Press.

Weber, Max. 1946. *From Max Weber.* H. Gerth and C. Wright Mills, eds. New York: Oxford.

———. 1958 [1904–05]. *The Protestant Ethic and the Spirit of Capitalism.* T. Parsons, trans. New York: Scribner.

———. 1967a. *Ancient Judaism.* H. Gerth, trans. New York: The Free Press.

———. 1967b. *The Religion of India.* H. Gerth and C. Wright Mills, eds. New York: The Free Press.

———. 1969 [1911, 1921]. *The Rational and Social Foundations of Music.* D. Martindale, trans. Carbondale: Southern Illinois University Press.

Webster, Steven. 1990. "The Historical Materialist Critique of Surrealism and Postmodernist Ethnography." In Manganaro (1990: 266–300).

Webster's New Collegiate Dictionary. 1963. Springfield, Mass.: G. & C. Merriam.

Weiner, Annette B., 1976. *Women of Value, Men of Renown: New Perspectives in Trobriand Exchange.* Austin: University of Texas Press.

Weiner, Annette B., and Jane Schneider, eds. 1989. *Cloth and Human Experience.* Washington: Smithsonian Institution Press.

Weisbuch, Robert. 1986. *Atlantic Double-Cross: American Literature and British Influence in the Age of Emerson.* Chicago: University of Chicago Press.

West, Cornel. 1993. *Race Matters.* Boston: Beacon Press.

White, E. B. 1983. *Poems and Sketches.* New York: Harper and Row.

White, Hayden. 1978. *Tropics of Discourse.* Baltimore: Johns Hopkins University Press.

Whitman, Walt. n.d. [1855]. *Leaves of Grass (An Exact Copy of the First Edition 1855 as issued by Whitman and Received by Emerson).* New York: The Eakins Press.

Whorf, Benjamin. 1964. *Language, Thought, and Reality.* John B. Carroll, ed. Cambridge: M.I.T. Press.

Widstrand, Carl Gosta, 1964. "Female Infibulation." *Studia Ethnographica Upsaliensia* 20: 95–122.

Wiener, Margaret. 1995. *Visible and Invisible Realms: Power, Magic, and Colonial Conquest in Bali.* Chicago: University of Chicago Press.

Wikan, Unni. 1990. *Managing Turbulent Hearts: A Balinese Formula for Living.* Chicago: University of Chicago Press.

Wild, John. 1970. *The Radical Empiricism of William James.* Garden City: Doubleday Anchor.

Wilson, Edmund. 1972 [1940]. *To the Finland Station: A Study in the Writing and Acting of History.* New York: Noonday.

Wittgenstein, Ludwig. 1958. *Philosophical Investigations.* 3rd ed. G. Anscombe, trans. New York: Macmillan.

Wolf, Eric. 1982. *Europe and the People without History.* Berkeley: University of California Press.

Wolfson, Eliott. 1988. "Circumcision, Vision of God, and Textual Interpretation: From Midrashic Trope to Mystical Symbol." *History of Religions* 27(2): 189–215.

Wollen, Peter. 1991. "Cinema/Americanism/The Robot." In Naremore and Brantlinger (1991: 42–69).

Wood, Michael. 1971. *Stendhal.* Ithaca: Cornell University Press.

Wood, Michael. 1994. *The Magician's Doubt: Nabokov and the Risks of Fiction*. Princeton: Princeton University Press.

Yates, Frances A. 1966. *The Art of Memory*. Chicago: University of Chicago Press.

———. 1971. *Theater of the World*. Chicago: University of Chicago Press.

———. 1972. *The Rosicrucian Enlightenment*. London: Routledge and Kegan Paul.

Yeazell, Ruth B., ed. 1994. *Henry James: A Collection of Critical Essays*. Englewood Cliffs, N.J.: Prentice-Hall.

Yengoyan, Aram. 1989. "Language and Conceptual Dualism: Sacred and Secular Concepts in Australian Aboriginal Cosmology and Myth." In D. Maybury-Lewis and U. Almagor (1989: 171–90).

Yerushalmi, Yosef Hayim. 1991. *Freud's Moses: Judaism Terminable and Interminable*. New Haven: Yale University Press.

Zizek, Slavoj. 1991. *Looking Awry: An Introduction to Jacques Lacan through Popular Culture*. Cambridge: M.I.T. Press.

———. 1993. *Tarrying with the Negative: Kant, Hegel, and the Critique of Ideology*. Durham: Duke University Press.

Zoete, Beryl de, and Walter Spies. 1939. *Dance and Drama in Bali*. New York: Harper's Magazine Press.

Zurbuchen, Mary. 1987. *The Language of Balinese Shadow Theater*. Princeton: Princeton University Press.

Index

Abel, T., 77–78
Abrams, M., xx, 13, 16
Adams, H., 7, 21, 70
Adorno, T., 13, 18, 172, 247, 299n.28
alchemy, xx, 197, 309n.23
Alpers, S., 64, 135
American culture, discourse, and ideology, 15–16, 117, 146–47, 182–83, 227, 230–48, 256
amusement industry, 6–7, 18, 248. *See also* show business
anti-Jewish policies and antisemitism, 39, 52, 62–63, 201
aphorism, 126, 161–62, 271
Apollonian and Dionysian values, 25, 31, 36, 267
Appalachia, 106, 123, 298n.19
Armstrong, L., 122–23
ascesis and asceticism, 162, 171–72, 205, 207, 217, 238, 242, 277, 309n.21
asparagus, 115, 258
Atlanta, 18, 249, 252, 258, 313n.12
Augustine, 51, 52, 167, 169, 215, 263, 275, 310n.13
Auster, P., 15–16, 146–47

Bakhtin, M., 9, 144–45, 163, 194
Bali (Indonesia), xi, 5, 18, 22, 29, 36–41, 44–46, 72–94, 103–04, 108–15, 122, 125–26, 136, 144–45, 228, 239, 250, 258–62, 290n.24, 294n.1, 297nn.3,4
Barber, L., 128, 129
Barnum, P. T., 17, 117, 129, 131–32, 299n.4
Bataille, G., 75, 155, 216, 226
Bateson, G., 25, 37, 73, 77–79, 81, 106, 174, 268
Baudelaire, C., 17, 107, 212–14, 309n.2
Baudrillard, J., 17, 105, 249, 254–56
Belo, J., 24, 29, 36–42, 73, 76–85, 97, 98, 273
Benedict, R., 6, 17, 24–37, 39–42, 97, 161, 239, 268, 273, 276
Benjamin, W., 7, 10, 75, 107, 134, 146, 147, 268, 284n.2, 285n.17, 295n.15, 301n.16, 313n.16
births, actual and metaphorical, 17, 18, 97, 146
Bloch, H., 152–53, 192

Boas, F., 24, 27, 31, 39, 77, 226
borderlands. *See* margins and marginality
Borges, J., 118
Borneo, 184–88
Bourdieu, P., xvii, 283n.7, 312n.6
boyhoods, girlhoods, and childhoods, 29, 37–38, 45, 81, 127, 130-31, 187
bricolage, 16, 18
Britain, 62, 135, 177, 185–87, 190, 209, 235
Brown, P., 53
Buddhist practices, 310n.20. *See also* Indic rites and practices
Buginese, 45, 259, 275
Burke, K., xiv, xxi, 3–7, 41, 71, 75, 116, 148, 161, 164, 167, 168, 173, 207, 210, 211, 214, 259, 261, 263–69, 275, 284n.2, 285nn.5,10, 303n.46, 309n.26, 309n.2
Burton, R., 126, 127, 196

Calvin and Calvinism, 116, 206
Cantor, N., 199
Carlyle, T., 5, 194
carnivalization, 8, 9, 144, 198, 202, 207, 290n.20, 301n.18
catalogues and catalogue rhetoric, 141–42, 270–73. *See also* lists and copiousness
Cavell, S., 3, 15, 16, 263, 265–68, 276–78, 284n.1, 287n.41
Chase, C., 292n.15
Chaucer, 191–97, 201
Chicago, 11, 120, 130
Christian rites and contexts, 52–56, 63, 68–70, 120, 133, 203–8
chromatic nuance, xxi, 90–92, 96, 99, 135, 174, 257–58, 268, 270, 273–74
chronotopes. *See* Bakhtin; carnivalization
circumcisions, 30, 43–71, 144, 200, 227, 259, 277, 292nn.15,18,19
Clifford, J., 48, 75, 106, 154–55, 172, 221–22
Coca-Cola, 182, 246–47, 249–59, 304, 311n.14. *See also* Pepsi
coincidence and experience, xvii, 14, 101, 105, 107, 110, 123, 221, 225, 298n.18
colonialisms, 14, 39–40, 84, 86–87, 103, 125, 187, 189, 196, 200, 206, 208–10, 224, 270, 295nn.18,19, 305n.6, 306nn.14,15